THE CONSTITUTIONAL

JURISPRUDENCE OF THE FEDERAL

REPUBLIC OF GERMANY

THE CONSTITUTIONAL

JURISPRUDENCE OF THE FEDERAL

REPUBLIC OF GERMANY

SECOND EDITION

———————

Donald P. Kommers

———

Duke University Press   Durham and London   1997

© 1997 Duke University Press
All rights reserved
Printed in the United States of America on acid-free paper ∞
Typeset in Galliard by Keystone Typesetting, Inc.
Permissions for reprinting previously published materials
appear at the end of this book.
Library of Congress Cataloging-in-Publication Data appear
on the last printed page of this book.

For Nancy

CONTENTS

FOREWORD TO THE SECOND EDITION

David P. Currie

The German Basic Law is one of the great constitutions of the world. Adopted to govern the western part of a divided nation in 1949, it became the constitution of all Germany upon unification in 1990. It deserves study both for its own sake and for the insights into our own Constitution that comparative study can provide.

The Basic Law establishes a democratic state governed by the rule of law. Like the United States, Germany has a parliamentary system in which the executive is chosen and removable by the legislature; yet more care has been taken in Germany than in this country to ensure that legislative policy is determined by the legislature, that judicial business is handled by independent judges, and that administration of the laws is subject to unified executive control. There is judicial review of both legislative action and executive action, but much of it takes place before a special Constitutional Court, which has jurisdiction not only over traditional constitutional complaints but also over an interesting array of intergovernmental abstract proceedings unknown in the courts of the United States. There is an extensive catalogue of fundamental rights, which has been held to include a general freedom to do whatever one pleases. Many of these rights are expressly made subject to restriction, but only in accordance with a stringent proportionality test that has been found implicit in the rule of law. Moreover, partly under the influence of a novel provision declaring the Federal Republic to be a "social state," a number of fundamental rights have been held to have a positive dimension: in addition to protecting the individual from state intrusions on liberty, they impose affirmative protective duties on the state.

There is much food for thought here for any student of government or law. In this invaluable book Donald Kommers has made it accessible for the first time to the English-speaking reader.

With an expert hand shaped by many years of careful study, Professor Kommers has painstakingly selected, edited, and translated a wide panoply of decisions

David P. Currie is Edward H. Levi Distinguished Service Professor of Law at the University of Chicago.

from the more than ninety volumes of cases decided by the Constitutional Court, which are essential to an understanding of the Basic Law. But this is more than a mere casebook; Professor Kommers has also provided extensive and authoritative textual material that places the decisions in context, furnishes a running commentary on them, and supplies a wealth of additional information.

The present edition not only incorporates the lessons of six years of successful classroom use but brings the book right up to the moment, including the crucial decisions that grew out of the unprecedented unification process. It remains the indispensable basis of any serious course for the student of German constitutional law.

December 1995

FOREWORD TO THE FIRST EDITION

Roman Herzog

My colleagues and I welcome the publication in the United States of this long-awaited book on the jurisprudence of the Federal Constitutional Court. It is not just our feelings of friendship for the author which occasion this sentiment; rather, the reason for our satisfaction lies deeper.

Constitutional law informs us not only about a state's organization and procedure, but also about the ideas which dominate that state and determine its politics. If in such a state there is no recourse to a constitutional court, a chasm may gradually develop between the ideas contained in the text of the constitution and the fundamental political beliefs prevailing at a given time. By contrast, if a court of review is responsible primarily for the interpretation and continued development of the constitution, then no such chasm should occur — that is, if the system functions properly. At the same time the decisions of this court — the Federal Constitutional Court — should underscore more or less clearly not only the ideas which remain constant with changing times, but also those ideas which move a particular generation. All persons working together to achieve the common goals of a nation should be familiar with these ideas. The alliance to which the United States of America and the Federal Republic of Germany belong is only secondarily military. It is primarily a community linked together by common values and concerned with ensuring that these values continue to flourish. Every member nation of this community should have the opportunity to become conversant with the issues and fundamental concepts that move other nations of the alliance, and the mutual knowledge of each other's constitutional jurisprudence is not the worst way to accomplish this purpose.

The sensitive reader, incidentally, is likely to notice that many fundamental ideas of German constitutional law trace their origin to American constitutionalism. For example, the German federal state and its interpretation through federal law would be unthinkable without the *Federalist Papers*. The concept that a law can be

At the time he wrote this foreword, Professor Dr. Roman Herzog was president of the Federal Constitutional Court. He was elected president of the Federal Republic of Germany in 1994.

null and void because it contravenes the Constitution developed earlier and with more precision in America than in Europe. Another basic tenet of constitutional review, particularly in its German variant, was also first conceptualized in America; namely, that judges need not enforce a constitutionally invalid law. In the absence of the influence of the renowned Chief Justice John Marshall, there would probably have been no judicial review of the constitutionality of laws in Germany.

This book reminds its readers that many ideas rooted in the American experience have left their mark on European constitutional law; in Germany, as in other European countries, some of these ideas will certainly have been transformed, adapted to local circumstances, and, of course, enriched by traditions distinctive to Europe. My hope is that the response to this book will be as sympathetic as my respect for its author.

PREFACE TO THE SECOND EDITION

When the first edition of this book appeared in 1989 I had not the slightest intention of preparing a second. After all, there were other frontiers to explore in German jurisprudence and in the developing field of comparative constitutional law. But three years later, to my pleasant surprise, the Duke University Press informed me that its stock of paperback and hardback editions had dwindled to a few dozen copies. When they disappeared, the press planned to run a second printing, but at that moment, encouraged by colleagues across the country to update the book, I agreed to prepare a second edition, and confidently asserted that I could have it ready in six months to a year. Rather than do another printing, the press decided to wait for the new edition. That was three years ago.

I soon learned that a book of this size and complexity would take far more time to prepare than I had originally expected, particularly if I were to do justice to the constitutional issues arising out of Germany's reunification. In addition, owing to important developments in German constitutional law over the past six years, I felt compelled to substantially revise several sections of this book and to add sections conspicuous for their absence from the first edition. Finally, the second edition includes nine new cases, making a total of seventy-six, including the highly controversial religious liberty and free speech cases handed down in 1995, as well as notes on numerous other cases decided since 1989.

The purposes of this book are described in the preface to the first edition. I would add only the following: Considering the book's favorable reception in the United States and abroad, it seems to have its intended effect of enhancing interest in Germany's constitutional law, particularly since that country's reunification, and of stimulating the further growth of the study of comparative constitutional law. American legal scholars exposed to Germany's constitutional case law have found it appealing for comparative purposes; first, because Germany's forty-five-year-old Constitution rivals our own in the jurisprudence of personal liberty and political democracy it has produced and, second, because this jurisprudence invites Americans and others to rethink aspects of their own constitutional traditions and policies.

Plainly, this book is far from an exhaustive account of German constitutional law. Coverage is limited to judicial policy areas that I thought would be most interesting and relevant for comparative purposes, and even so the cases discussed in the notes and other commentary were carefully selected to underscore themes related to the edited cases reprinted in the text. (The second edition cites about 500 of the 2,300 or so Federal Constitutional Court decisions appearing in the ninety-two volumes of official reports published between 1951 and 1996.) In the preface to the first edition I noted that my original plan had been to include chapters on equal protection and the military and foreign affairs powers. Although time and space dictated adherence to the plan of the first edition, substantial subsections in both subject areas have been included in chapters 6 (Economic Liberties) and 4 (Separation of Powers), respectively. The subsection on equality deals mainly with gender discrimination, the other with the treaty-making power and the constitutional conflict surrounding the deployment of German military forces outside the area of the North Atlantic Treaty Organization.

Finally, in the first edition I remarked: "Like the United States Supreme Court, the Federal Constitutional Court has been in the eye of many a political storm, but has survived these storms with its reputation intact and its influence unimpaired." This statement needs to be qualified in the light of the passions triggered by recent constitutional rulings in the *Tucholsky* and *Classroom Crucifix* cases, both of which are reprinted and discussed in this edition. Both cases were greeted by angry denunciations. Prominent political and religious leaders even counseled noncompliance with the *Classroom Crucifix* ruling against displaying the cross in public school classrooms. This and other highly controversial decisions, such as the *Hashish Drug* case, have tarnished the court's reputation in the eyes of many Germans and raised questions, even among well-known legal scholars and other respected commentators, about the legitimacy of judicial review over the subject areas in dispute. Negative reactions of this intensity, not uncommon in the United States, have been a rare occurrence in Germany, and in the minds of many, including the German Judges' Association, have become disturbingly frequent in the last few years. Nevertheless, the Constitutional Court remains one of Germany's most resilient and durable institutions and, like the U.S. Supreme Court, the chief symbol of the rule of law and constitutional government.

The first edition of this book introduced American and other English-speaking audiences to the jurisprudence of West Germany's Federal Constitutional Court. The creation of this tribunal in 1951, two years after the Basic Law (Grundgesetz) entered into force, marked the beginning of a German experiment in constitutional democracy. Few people realized at the time that the Constitutional Court would play a vital role in shaping the politics and public philosophy of postwar Germany. Fewer anticipated its evolution into one of the world's most powerful and influential courts, serving as a model, in competition with the United States Supreme

Court, for other liberal democracies attracted by the prospect of placing fundamental law under the protection of independent courts of justice.

As *the* authoritative interpreter of the Basic Law, the Federal Constitutional Court has handed down a vast number of cases and opinions that invite comparison with the constitutional jurisprudence of other advanced liberal democracies. Currently imbedded in ninety-two volumes of *Entscheidungen des Bundesverfassungsgerichts* (Decisions of the Federal Constitutional Court), German constitutional case law easily rivals the intellectual work product of the United States Supreme Court. These volumes contain a literature of freedom bristling with ideas familiar to the Anglo-American experience. But they also contain rich insights and challenging strands of thought rooted in Germany's own constitutional tradition.

My purpose in preparing the first edition was not only to welcome Anglo-American readers into the fascinating world of German constitutional law, but also to contribute to the further development of comparative constitutional law as a discipline of valid current applicability. Because of the rapid spread of judicial review around the world since 1945, a development that traces its influence at least in part to the American experience, judicially created constitutional doctrine was ripe for comparative study and analysis in 1989. The comparative perspective promised to enrich our understanding of constitutionalism generally and thus to provide the basis for a rethinking of our own constitutional values and practices.

At the level of theory, the comparative approach to constitutional law can be a search for principles of justice and political obligation that transcend the culture-bound opinions and conventions of a particular legal community. Equally important at a more practical level, judges and litigators entrusted with the resolution of difficult problems of governance, particularly in drawing the boundary between private rights and public power, are very likely to benefit from the opinions of constitutional tribunals operating in other countries with different political and legal traditions but with an equally strong commitment to constitutionalism and democracy.

ACKNOWLEDGMENTS

Preparing the second edition of this book was hard work, and it could not have been completed without the generous assistance and encouragement of many persons. For their helpful comments on the first edition I thank Winfried Brugger (Heidelberg University), David P. Currie (University of Chicago), David Danelski (Stanford University), Mary Ann Glendon (Harvard University), Walter F. Murphy (Princeton University), Gerald L. Neuman (Columbia University), and Peter E. Quint (University of Maryland). In the course of preparing the second edition I benefited from the help of David M. Beatty (University of Toronto), Ernst Benda (Freiburg University), Michael Bothe (Frankfurt University), Erhard Denninger

(Frankfurt University), Georg Ress (Saarbrücken University), Eberhard Schmidt-Assmann (Heidelberg University), Torsten Stein (Saarbrücken University), Klaus Stern (Cologne University), and Dieter Umbach (Potsdam University). Justices of the Federal Constitutional Court to whom I owe thanks are Dieter Grimm, Paul Kirchhof, and Helga Seibert. I am particularly grateful to Karl-Georg Zierlein, administrative director of the Federal Constitutional Court, for giving me access to the court's archives and supplying me with needed statistical and decisional materials.

Part of the work on this edition was carried out in Heidelberg's Max Planck Institute for Comparative and International Public Law under a generous grant from Germany's Max Planck Society. I have been a frequent guest of the Max Planck Institute over the years, and the institute has always been most generous in providing me with office space and ready access to its splendid library and unsurpassed bibliographical resources. The camaraderie, kindness, and hospitality that I continue to experience in this enviable research setting are a scholar's delight and a stimulus to thinking and writing. Again my thanks to Rudolf Bernhardt and Jochen Frowein, the institute's codirectors, for welcoming me aboard for still another tour of pleasant duty. Helmut Steinberger, the institute's third codirector and a former justice of the Federal Constitutional Court, merits a special word of thanks. He was particularly supportive of my work, shared his time and expertise with me, and manifested his friendship in many other ways. I am also indebted to the institute's professional research staff, particularly Michael Hahn, Georg Nolte, Stephan Oeter, Thomas Giegerich, and Werner Morvay.

Finally, and closer to home, I am deeply grateful to Dean David Link and Associate Dean Patricia Leonard of the Notre Dame Law School for generous — and indispensable — research support in the summer of 1995, when the manuscript was in its final stages of completion. My thanks also to my research assistants Brian Burchett, Bradley Lewis, Edward Wingenbach, Peter Meilander, Frank Colucci, and Melissa Brown for the labor they performed on various parts of the manuscript; to Albert Wimmer (University of Notre Dame) and Jo Ann Franchowski (a Canadian lawyer) for their invaluable assistance in translating several German cases into English; to Valerie Millholland and Pam Morrison of the Duke University Press for their patience in waiting — far too long — for the submission of this manuscript; and to Mindy Conner, whose sharp skills remain unparalleled in the world of copyediting. Last, I thank David P. Currie, a friendly critic of my work and one of this country's foremost authorities on German and American constitutional law, for agreeing to write the foreword to this edition.

January 1996

NOTE ON TRANSLATION AND

JUDICIAL OPINIONS

Edmund Wilson once remarked that "the best translations — the *Rubaiyat*, for example — are those that depart most widely from the originals — that is, if the translator himself is a poet." However sound such advice might be with respect to the translation of literary works such as novels and poems, it is most certainly bad advice when one is rendering foreign legal documents into English. The decisions and opinions presented here are controversial, complex, and philosophically profound. In dealing with documents of this character, the translator must exercise scrupulous care to achieve English equivalents absolutely faithful to the original German and yet fully comprehensible to the Anglo-American reader. Intellectual honesty demands no less of the translator who would wish to advance the study of comparative law.

The translations were the most arduous task of this enterprise. As initially rendered, they were largely transliterations. Successive drafts converted them into idiomatic English, but in the interest of understanding my assistants and I often preferred accuracy to elegance. Walter Murphy and Peter Quint, literary stylists in their own right as well as close students of German constitutional law, were kind enough to read the translations, suggest alterations, and point out scores of ambiguous or unclear passages. At this stage most of the translations were checked once again against the original German. The final result, I trust, is translations that are both readable and faithful presentations of German constitutional thought.

The original translations were far longer than they needed to be, attributable in part to the convoluted and repetitious prose characteristic of German cases. As a consequence, I cut out passages considered superfluous, used ellipses freely, and inserted interpolations where an English summary would do as well and at the same time conserve space. Anglo-American readers will find nevertheless that the translations are substantial enough to give them a real appreciation of the style and depth of argumentation on the Federal Constitutional Court. Some repetition, however, is unavoidable and indeed even desirable in order to underscore important doctrinal themes as well as the court's approach to constitutional interpretation.

Each reported decision of the Constitutional Court follows a common plan of organization. The typical opinion begins with a brief statement of the result and the reasons therefore; proceeds to describe the factual background of the case; continues with a detailed presentation of the arguments on both sides, first on behalf of the complainant or petitioner, then on behalf of the respondent; and concludes with the court's own reasoning on the merits. The translations in this book are confined largely to selected passages from the court's reasoning, preceded by my bracketed summary of the background facts. The original opinions are lavish with citations to existing constitutional case law and secondary literature, including well-known commentaries on the Basic Law. With rare exceptions I omitted these notes from the translations. German judicial cases do not bear titles, just as the names of private plaintiffs and defendants remain undisclosed. The latter are usually designated by a letter of the alphabet (e.g., John H.). For purposes of identification, however, I have arbitrarily assigned a title to each case, including the cases cited in my commentary and notes. Unless the identity of the complainant is publicly known, the case titles generally describe the issue, institution, or location of the conflict rather than the individuals involved.

I have translated the terms *Beschwerdeführer* and *Antragssteller* variously as "complainant," "plaintiff," and "petitioner." Complainant refers to an entity (juristic person or association) or ordinary person who files a constitutional complaint (*Verfassungsbeschwerde*) with the Federal Constitutional Court. All other proceedings before the Constitutional Court involve petitions or referrals by officials and agencies of government. A petitioner is an agency or official who initiates one of these proceedings. I often refer to the plaintiff as the litigant before a lower court where the lower court refers a constitutional issue in the pending case to the Federal Constitutional Court in an action known as a concrete judicial-review proceeding.

Several translations that appear in this book first appeared in other published works, although in each instance I found it necessary to edit them, on occasion heavily, to conform to the style and terminology used in this book and to add passages that some of the original translations omitted. The authors and publishers of these translations kindly consented to their reproduction here (see list of copyright permissions). In addition, I thank the following persons for allowing me to use their previously unpublished translations of particular decisions: David Currie for the *Financial Subsidies* case (no. 3.6), the *Aircraft Noise Control* case (no. 4.3), and the *Nocturnal Employment* case (no. 6.10); Günter Frankenburg for the *Civil Servant Loyalty* case (no. 5.14); Edmund Jahn for the *Schleyer Kidnapping* case (no. 7.11); and Gerhard Casper for the *Spiegel* case (no. 8.7). Unless otherwise indicated, all other translations are those of myself and my assistants.

Finally, in preparing the translations we used the following sources: Carl Creifelds and Lutz Meyer-Gossner, eds., *Rechtswörterbuch,* 9th rev. ed. (Munich: C. H. Beck'sche Verlagsbuchhandlung, 1988); Alfred Romain, *Wörterbuch der Rechts- und Wirtschaftssprache,* vol. 1: *Englisch-Deutsch,* 3d rev. ed. (Munich: C. H. Beck'sche Verlagsbuchhandlung, 1983); Alfred Romain, *Wörterbuch der Rechts- und Wirt-*

schaftssprache, vol. 2: *Deutsch-Englisch,* 2d rev. ed. (Munich: C. H. Beck'sche Verlags-buchhandlung, 1985); Peter Terrell et al., *Collins German-English, English-German Dictionary* (Stuttgart: Klett, 1981); Gerhard Wahrig, *Deutsches Wörterbuch* (Munich: Mosaik Verlag GmbH, 1980); and *Law Dictionary, German-English/Deutsch-Englisch,* 4th ed. (Berlin: Walter de Gruyter, 1991).

ABBREVIATIONS

BGBl	*Bundesgesetzblatt* (Federal Law Gazette [statutes at large])
BVerfGE	*Entscheidungen des Bundesverfassungsgerichts* (Decisions of the Federal Constitutional Court)
CDU	Christian Democratic Union (Christlich-Demokratische Union)
CSU	Christian Social Union (Christlich-Soziale Union)
DKP	German Communist Party (Deutsche Kommunistische Partei)
DP	German Party (Deutsche Partei)
FCCA	Federal Constitutional Court Act (Bundesverfassungsgerichtsgesetz)
FDP	Free Democratic Party (Freie Demokratische Partei)
GJA	German Judges' Act (Deutsches Richtergesetz)
GOB	Rules of Procedure of the Federal Constitutional Court (Geschäftsordnung des Bundesverfassungsgerichts)
JSC	Judicial Selection Committee
KPD	Communist Party of Germany (Kommunistische Partei Deutschland)
NATO	North Atlantic Treaty Organization
NPD	National Democratic Party (Nationaldemokratische Partei Deutschlands)
RGZ	Decision of the (Reich) Supreme Court in civil matters (Entscheidungen des Reichsgerichts in Zivilsachen)
SPD	Social Democratic Party (Sozialdemokratische Partei Deutschlands)
SRP	Socialist Reich Party (Sozialistische Reichspartei)
StGB	Strafgesetzbuch (German Penal Code)
EuGRZ	*Europäische Grundrechte-Zeitschrift*

PART I

WEST GERMAN CONSTITUTIONALISM

The Federal Constitutional Court, with its sweeping powers of judicial review, is only as old as the Basic Law. To the surprise of many observers this tribunal has developed into an institution of major policy-making importance in the Federal Republic. Judicial review is a relatively new departure in German constitutional history. Postwar German leaders believed that the traditional parliamentary and judicial institutions that had failed to protect the Weimar Constitution were insufficient to safeguard the new liberal democratic order. They created a national constitutional tribunal to serve as a guardian of political democracy, to enforce a consistent reading of the Constitution on all branches and levels of government, and to protect the basic liberties of German citizens. With this decision, German constitution makers gave up the old positivist idea that law and morality are separate domains. Constitutional morality would now govern both law and politics.

Part 1 furnishes the backdrop to this treatment of German constitutional law and policy. It seems useful at the outset to introduce the reader to the powers and organization of the Federal Constitutional Court and to set forth, in one place, a systematic account of the Basic Law and the principles governing its interpretation. Accordingly, chapter 1 describes the Federal Constitutional Court's origin, structure, powers, and decisional procedures. It also includes an account of important organizational and staff changes that have taken place over the course of the court's forty-five years of operation.

Chapter 2 focuses on the main features of the Basic Law and the principles on which they are grounded. Unlike previous German constitutions, the Basic Law creates a binding order of values having the force of law and enforceable by judicial decision. It also creates a "free democratic basic order" based on individual liberties, equality, majority rule, responsible party government, separation of powers, the rule of law, and the observance by citizens of certain principles of political obligation. The Constitutional Court's function in Germany's judicial democracy is to define, protect, and reconcile these various and often conflicting constitutional values. In performing this task, the court has been a crucial player in German constitutional politics. In some areas of constitutional adjudication, its role has been no less than transformative. Gravitating between the poles of judicial activism and restraint, the court has also developed a number of decision-making tools designed at least in part to resolve the ongoing tension between democracy and constitutionalism.

1

THE FEDERAL CONSTITUTIONAL

COURT

The jurisdiction of the United States Supreme Court extends to cases and controversies arising under the Constitution and federal law. Its authority extends even to private law when the parties in dispute are citizens of different states. By contrast, Germany's Federal Constitutional Court, as guardian of the constitutional order, is a specialized tribunal empowered to decide only constitutional questions and a limited set of public-law controversies. Thus Germany ranks among those civil-law countries with a centralized system of judicial review.[1] The deeply ingrained Continental belief that judicial review is a political act, following the assumption that "constitutional law — like international law — is genuine political law, in contrast, for example, to civil and criminal law,"[2] prompted Germans to vest the power to declare laws unconstitutional in a special tribunal staffed with judges elected by parliament and widely representative of the political community rather than in a multijurisdictional high court of justice dominated by appointed legal technicians.

Another factor that encouraged the framers of the Basic Law to assign the function of constitutional judicial review to a single court was the traditional structure of the German judiciary and the unfamiliarity of its judges with constitutional adjudication. The German judiciary includes separate hierarchies of administrative, labor, fiscal, and social courts, while ordinary civil and criminal jurisdiction is vested in another, much larger, system of regular courts.[3] All trial and intermediate courts of appeal are *Land* (state) tribunals; federal courts serve as courts of last resort. The Federal Administrative Court (Bundesverwaltungsgericht), Federal Labor Court (Bundesarbeitsgericht), Federal Finance Court (Bundesfinanzgericht), Federal Social Court (Bundessozialgericht), and Federal Court of Justice (Bundesgerichtshof) are at the respective apexes of these judicial hierarchies. Like the appellate courts generally, these tribunals are staffed by a host of judges (125 on the Federal Court of Justice alone) who sit in panels of five. The complexity of this structure and the lack of any tradition of *stare decisis* would have rendered an American-style decentralized system of judicial review, in which all courts may declare laws unconstitutional, unworkable in Germany.

Judicial attitudes toward constitutional review also militated against a decentralized system. The background and professional training of the 20,672 career judges (as of January 1, 1993) who staff the German judiciary are unlikely to produce the independence of mind typical of judges in the Anglo-American tradition. The typical German judge enters the judiciary at the conclusion of his or her legal training, and success is denoted by promotion within the ranks of the judicial bureaucracy. In contrast, the typical American judge is appointed at a later stage of his career, usually after achieving success in public office or as a private lawyer. German judges have been characterized as persons seeking to clothe themselves in anonymity and to insist that it is the court and not the judge who decides; moreover, the judicial task is to apply the law as written and with exacting objectivity.[4] Although this portrayal of the typical German judge is less true today than it was forty-five years ago, the conservative reputation and public distrust of the regular judiciary at the time the Basic Law was created were sufficient to ensure that the power of judicial review would be concentrated in a single and independent tribunal.

ORIGIN

Historical Antecedents

German legal scholars have traditionally distinguished between constitutional review (*Verfassungsstreitigkeit*) and judicial review (*richterliches Prüfungsrecht*). Judicial review, the more inclusive term, signifies the authority of judges to rule on the constitutionality of law. Constitutional review, which in Germany antedates judicial review, is associated with Germany's tradition of monarchical constitutionalism, stretching from the German Confederation of 1815 through the Constitution of 1867 (establishing the North German Confederation) and up to and including the Imperial Constitution of 1871. During this period (1815–1918), when German constitutional thought pivoted on the concepts of state and sovereignty,[5] constitutional review provided the mechanism for defining the rights of sovereign states and their relationship to the larger union incorporating them. Judicial review, on the other hand — a device for protecting individual rights — is associated with Germany's republican tradition, beginning roughly with the abortive Frankfurt Constitution of 1849, continuing with the Weimar Constitution of 1918, and ending with the Basic Law of 1949.

CONSTITUTIONAL REVIEW. Constitutional review appeared in embryonic form during the Holy Roman Empire. The need for unity among the principalities of the empire and peace among their warring princes prompted Maximilian I in 1495 to create the Reichskammergericht (Court of the Imperial Chamber), before which the monarchs resolved their differences. By the seventeenth century the Imperial Court and some local courts occasionally enforced the "constitutional" rights of estates against crown princes. Compacts or treaties governed their mutual rights and obligations. Constitutional review commenced when these tribunals enforced — to the extent that their rulings could be enforced — the corporate rights of estates under these documents.[6]

Constitutional review in its modern form emerged in the nineteenth century.[7] Again, it served as a principal tool for the resolution of constitutional disputes among and within the individual states of the German Empire and often between the states and the national government.[8] Under Germany's monarchical constitutions, the forum for the resolution of such disputes was usually the parliamentary chamber in which the states were corporately represented. Under Germany's republican constitutions, on the other hand, the forum was usually a specialized constitutional tribunal, the most notable of which, prior to the creation of the Federal Constitutional Court, was the Weimar Republic's Staatsgerichtshof. As major agencies of public law commissioned to decide sensitive political issues, these courts were independent of the regular judiciary and were staffed with judges selected by legislators.

Like most constitutional courts at the state level before and after the Nazi period, the Staatsgerichtshof was a part-time tribunal whose members convened periodically to decide constitutional disputes. Its jurisdiction included (1) the trial of impeachments brought by parliament (the Reichstag) against the president, chancellor, or federal ministers for any willful violation of the constitution; (2) the resolution of differences of opinion concerning a state's administration of national law; and (3) the settlement of constitutional conflicts within and among the separate states as well as between states and the Reich. The court's membership varied according to the nature of the dispute before it; the more "political" the dispute the more insistent was parliament on electing its members.[9]

These structures and powers, which influenced the shape of the Federal Constitutional Court, highlight three salient features of constitutional review in German history. First, as just noted, an institution independent of the regular judiciary exercises such review. Second, it takes cases on original jurisdiction, deciding them in response to a simple complaint or petition, unfettered by the technicalities of an ordinary lawsuit. Finally, it settles constitutional disputes between and within governments. Constitutional review is thus a means of protecting the government from itself and also from the excesses of administrative power, "but [it] would not have judges intervening on behalf of citizens against the executive branch of government."[10] The German legal order has always distinguished sharply between administrative and constitutional law. The juridical basis of the distinction, according to Franz Jerusalem, is that the former concerns the execution of the state's will once it is made, whereas the latter concerns those organs of government constitutionally obligated to form the state's will.[11] These organs — the constitutionally prescribed units of the political system — and these alone are the subjects of constitutional review.

JUDICIAL REVIEW. The doctrine of judicial review, unlike constitutional review, was alien to the theory of judicial decision in Germany.[12] A judge's only duty under the traditional German doctrine of separation of powers was to enforce the law as written. About the mid-nineteenth century, however, some German legal scholars and judges sought to cultivate ground in which judicial review might blossom. In 1860, Robert von Mohl, who was acquainted with the *Federalist Papers* and the work of the United States Supreme Court, published a major legal treatise in defense of judicial review.[13] Two years later, an association of German jurists, with Rudolf von Ihering emerging as its chief spokesman, went on record in favor of judicial review.[14] Jurists attending the meeting recalled provisions of the Frankfurt Constitution (1849) authorizing the Federal Supreme Court (Reichsgericht) to hear complaints by a state against national laws allegedly in violation of the Constitution and even by ordinary citizens claiming a governmental invasion of their fundamental rights, foreshadowing by a century similar authority conferred on the Federal Constitutional Court. Their views, however, like the provisions of the 1849 Constitution, failed to take root in the legal soil of monarchical Germany (1871–1918).[15]

The Weimar Republic provided a climate more sympathetic to judicial review. Inspired by the work of the Frankfurt Assembly, the 1919 Constitution established a constitutional democracy undergirded by a bill of rights. The Weimar period also witnessed the continuing influence of the "free law" school (*Freirechtsschule*) of judicial interpretation,[16] marking a significant challenge to the dominant tradition of legal positivism. And although the Constitution remained silent with respect to the power of the courts to review the constitutionality of law,[17] judicial review as a principle of limited government enjoyed strong support in the Weimar National Assembly.

But, as Hugo Preuss predicted — and warned — the Weimar Constitution's failure expressly to ban judicial review prompted courts to arrogate this power to themselves.[18] In the early 1920s, several federal high courts, including the Reichsgericht, suggested in dicta that they possessed the power to examine the constitutionality of laws.[19] On January 15, 1924, deeply disturbed by the swelling controversy over the revaluation of debts, the Association of German Judges confidently announced that courts of law were indeed empowered to protect the right of contract and, if necessary, to strike down national laws and other state actions — or inactions that failed to safeguard property rights — on substantive constitutional grounds.[20] Several months later, the Reichsgericht announced that "in principle courts of law are authorized to examine the formal and material validity of laws and ordinances."[21]

State courts during the Weimar period held firm to the German tradition that judges are subject to law and have the duty to apply it even in the face of conflicting constitutional norms. Yet even here, differing postures toward judicial review were beginning to emerge. Although most state constitutions said nothing about judicial review, some courts followed the lead of the Reichsgericht by accepting judicial review in principle; however, they seldom invoked it to nullify legislation. Only the Bavarian Constitution expressly authorized courts to review laws in light of both state and national constitutions. The Schaumburg-Lippe Constitution, echoing the still-dominant German view, expressly denied this power to the courts.[22]

When the German states (now known as *Länder*) reemerged as viable political units after World War II, judicial review appeared once more, this time as an articulate principle of several state (*Land*) constitutions. Perhaps because of the Weimar experience, however, these documents did not authorize the regular courts to review the constitutionality of laws. Once again, consistent with an older tradition of constitutional review, this authority was vested in specialized courts staffed with judges chosen by parliament from a variety of courts or constituencies. In any event, as this survey of German constitutional review demonstrates, the framers of the Basic Law had plenty of precedents on which to draw in constructing their own version of constitutional democracy.

The Herrenchiemsee Conference

It should now be clear that judicial review in Germany did not spring full-blown out of the Basic Law of 1949. It was not adopted, as is often supposed, in response to American pressure during the occupation. The Allied powers did, of course, concern themselves with the reorganization of the judicial system.[23] For one thing, they insisted that any future government of Germany must be federal, democratic, and constitutional. Later, when the military governors commissioned the Germans to draft a constitution for the Western zones of occupation, they made it clear that judicial review was implicit in their understanding of an independent judiciary.[24] Yet the military governors did not impose judicial review on a reluctant nation. The Germans decided on their own to establish a constitutional court, to vest it with authority to nullify laws contrary to the Constitution, and to elevate this authority into an express principle of constitutional governance.[25] While they were familiar with the American system of judicial review and were guided by the American experience in shaping their constitutional democracy, Germans relied mainly on their own tradition of constitutional review.

The groundwork for the Basic Law was prepared in a resplendent nineteenth-century castle on an island in Lake Chiemsee during August 1948. On the initiative of Bavaria's state governor, Minister-President Hans Ehard, the *Länder* in the Allied zones of occupation called on a group of constitutional law experts to produce a first draft of a constitution to expedite the work of the ensuing constitutional convention known as the Parliamentary Council.[26] The Herrenchiemsee proposals, which included provisions for a national constitutional tribunal,[27] followed the recommendations of Professor Hans Nawiasky, commonly regarded as the father of the postwar Bavarian Constitution, which, like many other state constitutions drafted in 1946 and 1947, provided for a state constitutional court. In cooperation with Hans

Kelsen, Nawiasky had prepared a working paper proposing the establishment of a constitutional tribunal modeled after the Weimar Republic's Staatsgerichtshof. Nawiasky was a strong advocate of judicial review during the Weimar period, and Kelsen had been one of the creators of the Austrian Constitutional Court.[28] Claus Leusser, an Ehard associate and later a justice of the Federal Constitutional Court, also helped to draft the Herrenchiemsee judicial proposals.[29]

The Herrenchiemsee drafters looked mainly to the experience of Weimar's Staatsgerichtshof for guidance in defining the powers of the proposed constitutional court.[30] The draft plan envisioned a tribunal vested with both the competence of the Staatsgerichtshof (i.e., its constitutional review jurisdiction) and the authority to hear the complaint of any person alleging that any public agency had violated his or her constitutional rights. Aware of the potential power of the proposed court, the conferees recommended a plan of judicial recruitment that would broaden the court's political support. The plan included proposals for (1) the election of justices in equal numbers by the Bundestag (the federal parliament) and the Bundesrat (the council of state governments), (2) the participation of both houses in selecting the court's presiding officer (the president), and (3) the selection of one-half of the justices from the high federal courts of appeal and the highest state courts.[31] But the drafters were at odds over how the new court should be structured; the discord centered on whether it should be organized as a tribunal separate from and independent of all other courts or carved out of one of the federal high courts of appeal.[32]

The Parliamentary Council

The debate over the new court's structure continued in the constitutional convention (i.e., the Parliamentary Council).[33] It all boiled down to a dispute over the nature of the new tribunal. Should it be like Weimar's Staatsgerichtshof and serve mainly as an organ for resolving conflicts between branches and levels of government (i.e., a court of constitutional review)? Or should it combine such jurisdiction with the general power to review the constitutionality of legislation (i.e., judicial review)? In line with the Herrenchiemsee plan, the framers finally agreed to create a constitutional tribunal independent of other public-law courts, but they disagreed over how much of the constitutional jurisdiction listed in the proposed constitution should be conferred on it as opposed to other high federal courts.

The controversy centered on the distinction between what some delegates regarded as the "political" role of a constitutional court and the more "objective" law-interpreting role of the regular judiciary. Some delegates preferred two separate courts — one to review the constitutionality of laws (i.e., judicial review), the other to decide essentially political disputes among branches and levels of government (i.e., constitutional review). Others favored one grand multipurpose tribunal divided into several panels, each specializing in a particular area of public or constitutional law. This proposal was strenuously opposed by many German judges, who were alarmed by any such mixing of law and politics in a single institution.[34] The upshot was a compromise resulting in a separate constitutional tribunal with exclusive jurisdiction over all constitutional disputes, including the authority to review the constitutionality of laws.

The final version of the Basic Law extended the court's jurisdiction to twelve categories of disputes and "such other cases as are assigned to it by federal legislation" (Article 93 [2]). This jurisdiction, however, could be invoked only by federal and state governments (i.e., the chancellor or minister-president and his cabinet), parliamentary political parties, and, in certain circumstances, courts of law. The framers rejected the Herrenchiemsee proposal to confer on private parties the constitutional right to petition the court, a decision in line with the general practice of constitutional review in Weimar Germany and Austria. (As noted below, however, the individual right to petition the constitutional court was restored by legislation in 1951 and incorporated into the Basic Law in 1969.) In any event, the two main parties in the Parliamentary Council favored these limited rules of access, the Social Democrats because they would protect political minorities in and out of parliament, and the Christian Democrats because they saw the rules as equally useful in preserving German federalism.[35]

The interests of both political parties were also reflected in judicial selection clauses specifying that the Federal Constitutional Court shall consist of "federal judges and other members," half "to be elected by the Bundestag and half by the Bundesrat" (Article 94). Christian Democrats were thus assured of a strong "federal" presence on the court, just as Social Democrats could take comfort in knowing that the court would not be dominated by professional judges drawn wholly from a conservative judiciary. Impatient to get on with their work of producing a constitution, the framers stopped there, leaving other details of the Constitutional Court's organization and procedure to later legislation.

The Legislative Phase

Almost two additional years of debate were necessary to produce the enabling statute creating the Federal Constitutional Court. The shape of the new tribunal represented a compromise between the conflicting perspectives of the federal government, the Social Democrats, and the Bundesrat on such matters as judicial selection and tenure, the ratio of career judges to "other members," the qualifications of judicial nominees, the court's size and structure, and the degree of control over the court to be exercised by the Federal Ministry of Justice.[36] All participants in the debate recognized that the court's political acceptance would depend on broad agreement on these matters across party and institutional lines. Finally, after months of intensive negotiation within and between the Bundestag and the Bundesrat, a bill emerged with the overwhelming support of the major parliamentary parties and all branches of government. The result was the Federal Constitutional Court Act (Bundesverfassungsgerichtsgesetz, hereafter cited as FCCA) of March 12, 1951.[37]

In its current version the FCCA includes 105 sections that codify and flesh out the Basic Law's provisions relating to the court's organization, powers, and procedures, important features of which are discussed below. Representing numerous political compromises, the FCCA (1) lays down the qualifications and tenure of the court's members, (2) specifies the procedures of judicial selection, (3) provides for a two-senate tribunal, (4) enumerates the jurisdiction of each senate, (5) prescribes the rules of access under each jurisdictional category, (6) defines the authority of the Plenum (both senates sitting together), and (7) establishes the conditions for the removal or retirement of the court's members.

JURISDICTION

The United States Constitution contains no express reference to any judicial power to pass upon the validity of legislative or executive decisions. Chief Justice John Marshall laid down the doctrine of judicial review by inference from the constitutional text in the seminal case *Marbury* v. *Madison*.[38] The Basic Law, by contrast, leaves nothing to inference, as it enumerates all of the Constitutional Court's jurisdiction. The court is authorized to hear cases involving the following actions:

Forfeiture of basic rights (Article 1)
Constitutionality of political parties (Article 21 [2])
Review of election results (Article 41 [2])
Impeachment of the federal president (Article 61)
Disputes between high state organs (Article 93 [1] 1)
Abstract judicial review (Article 93 [1] 2)
Federal-state conflicts (Articles 93 [1] 3 and 84 [4])
Concrete judicial review (Article 100 [1])
Removal of judges (Article 98)
Intrastate constitutional disputes (Article 99)
Public international law actions (Article 100 [2])
State constitutional court references (Article 100 [3])
Applicability of federal law (Article 126)
Other disputes specified by law (Article 93 [2])
Constitutional complaints (Article 93 [1] 4a and 4b)

The court thus has the authority not only to settle conventional constitutional controversies but also to try impeachments of the federal president, to review decisions of the Bundestag relating to the validity of an election, and to decide questions critical to the definition and administration of federal law. International law is particularly important here, for Article 25 of the Basic Law makes "the general rules of public international law . . . an integral part of federal law." Whether such rules are an integral part of federal law and whether they create rights and duties for persons living in Germany are questions only the Constitutional Court can decide.

Table 1.1. Federal Constitutional Cases, 1951–1994

Proceeding	Docketed	Decided
Unconstitutional parties	5	5
Disputes between federal organs	107	51
Federal-state conflicts	26	14
Abstract judicial review	124	68
Concrete judicial review	2,901	959
Constitutional complaints	97,007	80,767*
Other proceedings	1,097	652
Total	101,268	82,516

Source: Statistical summary prepared by the administrative offices of the two senates (1951 to December 31, 1994; typescript).

* Of these, 3,750 were decided by the full senates, most prior to the establishment of the chambers within each senate.

Each of the jurisdictional categories listed above is assigned to either the First Senate or the Second Senate.[39] For our purposes, the most important of these categories involve the constitutionality of political parties, federal-state conflicts, disputes between high organs of the national government, constitutional complaints brought by ordinary citizens, abstract judicial review, and concrete judicial review — importance here being measured by the number of cases filed in each category or by their political significance. As table 1.1 shows, constitutional complaints make up about 95 percent of the court's caseload. As we shall see, however, some of the court's most politically important work arises in other jurisdictional areas.

Prohibiting Political Parties

The Federal Constitutional Court's function as guardian of the constitutional order finds its most vivid expression in Article 21 (2) of the Basic Law. Under this provision, political parties seeking "to impair or abolish the free democratic basic order or to endanger the existence of the Federal Republic of Germany shall be unconstitutional." The article goes on to declare that only the Federal Constitutional Court may declare parties unconstitutional. To minimize any abuse of this provision, the FCCA authorizes only the Bundestag, the Bundesrat, and the federal government (i.e., the federal chancellor and his cabinet) to initiate an Article 21 action. A *Land* government may apply to have a party declared unconstitutional if that party's organization is confined to its territory. Like most other proceedings before the court, this jurisdiction is compulsory; unless the moving party withdraws its petition, the court is obligated to decide the case, although it may take its time in doing so.

Up to now, as table 1.1 indicates, the court has ruled on five such petitions. In two of the cases, decided early on, the court sustained the petitions: in 1952 when it banned the neo-Nazi Socialist Reich party, and in 1956 when it ruled the Communist party unconstitutional.[40] In 1994, however, the court rejected the petitions of the Bundesrat and the federal government to have the Free German Workers party (FGWP) declared unconstitutional as well as Hamburg's petition to ban the National List (NL) operating on its territory. The court ruled that although the FGWP and the NL advanced views hostile to political democracy, neither group qualified as a political party within the meaning of the law or the Constitution.[41]

Disputes between High Federal Organs

Conflicts known as *Organstreit* proceedings involve constitutional disputes between the highest "organs," or branches, of the German Federal Republic. The court's function here is to supervise the operation and internal procedures of these executive and legislative organs and to maintain the proper institutional balance between them.[42] The governmental organs qualified to bring cases under this jurisdiction are the federal president, Bundesrat, federal government, Bundestag, and units of these organs vested with independent rights by their rules of procedure or the Basic Law.[43] Included among these units are individual members of parliament, any one of whom may initiate an *Organstreit* proceeding to vindicate his or her status as a parliamentary representative.[44] These units also include the parliamentary political parties.[45] Early on, the Plenum ruled that even nonparliamentary political parties may invoke this jurisdiction.[46] They may do so in their capacity as vote-getting agencies or organizers of the electoral process because, in fulfilling this task, political parties function as "constitutional" or federal organs within the meaning of the Basic Law (Article 93 (1) [1]).[47] If a political party is denied a place on the ballot, or if its right to mount electoral activity is infringed by one of the high organs of the Federal Republic, it can initiate an *Organstreit* proceeding against the federal organ in question. An *Organstreit* proceeding is not available, however, to administrative agencies, governmental corporations, churches, or other corporate bodies with quasi-public status.[48]

Federal-State Conflicts

Constitutional disputes between a state and the national government ordinarily arise out of conflicts involving a state's administration of federal law or the federal government's supervision of state administration. Proceedings may be brought only by a state government or by the federal government acting in the name of its cabinet. In addition, the court may hear "other public law disputes" between the federation and the states, between different states, or within a state if no other legal recourse is provided. Here again, only the respective governments in question are authorized to bring such suits. As in *Organstreit* proceedings, the complaining party must assert that the act or omission complained of has resulted in a direct infringement of a right or duty assigned by the Basic Law. For its part, the Constitutional Court is obligated by law to declare whether the act or omission infringes the Basic Law and to specify the provision violated. In the process of deciding such a case, the court "may also decide a point of law relevant to the interpretation of the [applicable] provision of the Basic Law."[49]

Concrete Judicial Review

Concrete, or collateral, judicial review arises from an ordinary lawsuit. If a German court is convinced that a relevant federal or state law under which a case has arisen violates the Basic Law, it must refer the constitutional question to the Federal Constitutional Court before the case can be decided. Judicial referrals do not depend on the issue of constitutionality having been raised by one of the parties. A lower court is obliged to make such a referral when it is convinced that a law under which a case has arisen is in conflict with the Constitution. If a collegial court is involved, a majority of its members must vote to refer the question. The petition must be signed by the judges who vote in favor of referral and accompanied by a statement of the legal provision at issue, the provision of the Basic Law allegedly violated, and the extent to which a constitutional ruling is necessary to decide the dispute.[50] The Federal Constitutional Court will dismiss the case if the judges below it manifest less than a genuine conviction that a law or provision of law is unconstitutional or if the case can be decided without settling the constitutional question.[51] As a procedural matter, the court must permit the highest federal organs or a state government to enter the case and must also afford the parties involved in the earlier proceeding an opportunity to be heard. The parties make their representations through written briefs.

Abstract Judicial Review

Whereas the United States Supreme Court requires a real controversy and adverse parties before it can decide a constitutional question, the Federal Constitutional Court may decide differences of opinion or doubts about the compatibility of a federal or state law with the Basic Law on the mere request of the federal or a state government or of one-third of the members of the Bundestag.[52] The relevant parties in these cases are required to submit written briefs. Oral argument before the court, a rarity in most cases, is always permitted in abstract review proceedings. The question of the law's validity is squarely before the court in these proceedings, and a decision against validity renders the law null and void.[53]

   When deciding cases on abstract review, the court is said to be engaged in the "objective" determination of the validity or invalidity of a legal norm or statute.[54] The proceeding is described as objective because it is intended to vindicate neither an individual's subjective right nor the claim of the official entity petitioning for review; its sole purpose is to declare what the Constitution means. In so doing, the court is free to consider any and every argument and any and every fact bearing on any and every aspect of a statute or legal norm under examination. Indeed, once the federal government, a *Land* government, or one-third of the Bundestag's members lays a statute or legal norm before the court on abstract review, the case cannot be withdrawn without the court's permission, a condition that reinforces the principle of judicial independence that allows the court to speak in the public interest when necessity demands it.

Constitutional Complaints

In the proceedings discussed so far, access to the Federal Constitutional Court is limited to governmental units, certain parliamentary groups, and judicial tribunals. A constitutional complaint, by contrast, may be brought by individuals and entities vested with particular rights under the Constitution. After exhausting all other available means to find relief in the ordinary courts,[55] any person who claims that the state has violated one or more of his or her rights under the Basic Law may file a constitutional complaint in the Federal Constitutional Court. Constitutional complaints must be lodged within a certain time, identify the offending action or omission and the agency responsible, and specify the constitutional right that has been violated.[56] The FCCA requires the court to accept any complaint if it is constitutionally significant or if the failure to accept it would work a grave hardship on the complainant.[57]

The right of an individual to file a constitutional complaint was originally a gift bestowed by legislation, and German citizens took advantage of their statutory right in increasing numbers over the years. By the mid-1960s the court was awash in such complaints, and Germans had come to regard the constitutional complaint as an important prerogative — almost a vested right — of citizenship. From the beginning, these complaints constituted the court's major source of business. In response, and with the court's backing, federal legislators anchored the right to file constitutional complaints in the Basic Law itself (Article 93 (1) [4a]). A companion amendment ratified in the same year (1969) vested municipalities with the right to file a constitutional complaint if a law violates their right to self-government under Article 28.[58] The popularity of the constitutional complaint was such that no responsible public official opposed these amendments.[59] Years later, the president of the Federal Constitutional Court was moved to say that the "administration of justice in the Federal Republic of Germany would be unthinkable without the complaint of unconstitutionality."[60]

According to Article 93 (1) [4a] of the Basic Law, any person may enter a complaint of unconstitutionality if one of his or her fundamental substantive or procedural rights under the Constitution has been violated by "public authority." "Any person" within the meaning of this provision includes natural persons with the legal capacity to sue as well as corporate bodies and other "legal persons" possessing rights under the Basic Law.[61] As a general rule, only domestic legal persons are permitted to file constitutional complaints, although the Second Senate has ruled that foreign corporations are entitled to file procedural complaints involving the right to a fair trial.[62] The public authority clause of Article 93 (1) [4a] permits constitutional complaints to be brought against any governmental action, including judicial decisions, administrative decrees, and legislative acts. No ordinary judicial remedy is available against legislative acts. If, however, such an act is likely to cause a person serious and irreversible harm, he or she may file the complaint against the act without exhausting other remedies. Finally, over and above these basic threshold requirements, a complaint must be "clearly founded" (*offensichlich begründet*) if it is to be accepted and decided on its merits.[63]

The procedure for filing complaints in the Constitutional Court is relatively easy and inexpensive. No filing fees or formal papers are required. Most complaints are handwritten and prepared without the aid of a lawyer (about a third are prepared by counsel). No legal assistance is required at any stage of the complaint proceeding. As a consequence of these rather permissive "standing" rules, the court has been flooded with complaints, which have swelled in number from well under 1,000 per year in the 1950s, to around 3,500 per year in the mid-1980s, to more than 5,000 per year in the mid-1990s, when constitutional complaints began to rival the numbers on the appellate docket of the United States Supreme Court.[64] The court grants full dress review to barely more than 1 percent of all constitutional complaints, but such complaints result in some of its most significant decisions and make up about 55 percent of its published opinions.

INSTITUTION

Status

When the Constitutional Court opened its doors for business in Karlsruhe on September 28, 1951, its status within the governmental framework of separated powers, and even its relationship to the other high federal courts, remained an unsettled issue. The Basic Law itself was ambivalent on the matter of the court's status. On the one hand, the wide-ranging powers of the court laid down in the constitutional charter pointed to a tribunal commensurate in status with the other independent constitutional organs (i.e., the Bundesrat, Bundestag, president, and federal government [chancellor and cabinet]) created by the Constitution. On the other hand, the Basic Law authorized parliament to regulate the court's organization and procedure. Initially, the new tribunal was placed under the authority of the Federal Ministry of Justice, a situation that irritated several justices, including the court's first president, Hermann Höpker-Aschoff. As a consequence, the justices boldly set out, in their first year of operation, to defend the court's autonomy, foreshadowing the fierce independence they would later exercise in adjudicating constitutional disputes.[65]

On June 27, 1951, after months of planning, the court released a memorandum originally drafted by Justice Gerhard Leibholz, one of its most prestigious members, that called for an end to any supervisory authority by the Justice Ministry, complete budgetary autonomy, and the court's full control over its internal administration, including the power to appoint its own officials and law clerks. The memorandum added that the Federal Constitutional Court is a supreme constitutional organ coordinate in rank with the Bundestag, Bundesrat, federal chancellor, and federal president. Its members, then, are in no sense civil servants or ordinary federal judges but rather supreme guardians of the Basic Law entrusted with the execution of its grand purposes, no less than other high constitutional organs of the Federal Republic of Germany. Indeed, the memorandum continued, the court has an even greater duty: to ensure that other constitutional organs observe the limits of the Basic Law.[66]

The memorandum from Karlsruhe generated a strong tremor in Bonn; it startled the government, angered the Ministry of Justice, and set off several years of skirmishing that yielded alignments almost identical to those that had formed in the early stages of the parliamentary debate on the structure of the proposed tribunal. Social Democrats and the Bundesrat generally supported the justices' demands, while the coalition parties in the Bundestag generally opposed them. The real tangle, however, was between the Ministry of Justice and the Constitutional Court, and it featured an occasional unseemly public exchange between two Free Democrats who as members of the Parliamentary Council had played major roles in drafting the Basic Law, namely, Thomas Dehler, minister of justice, and President Hermann Höpker-Aschoff, the stately and highly respected "chief justice."[67]

In 1953, the Bundestag severed the court's ties to the Ministry of Justice, and by 1960, with the gradual growth of the court's prestige and influence, all of the "demands" articulated in the Leibholz memorandum had been met.[68] In Bonn's official ranking order, the court's president now enjoyed the fifth highest position in the Federal Republic, following the federal president, the federal chancellor, and the presidents of the two "houses" of parliament. As "supreme guardians of the constitution," the remaining justices followed behind. Eventually they were even exempted from the disciplinary code regulating all other German judges.[69] The court's hard-won constitutional status was best symbolized by a 1968 amendment to the Basic Law providing that the "function of the Federal Constitutional Court and its justices must not be impaired" even in a state of emergency. During such a time, the special body responsible for acting on behalf of the Bundestag and the Bundesrat is even barred from amending the FCCA unless such an amendment is required, "in the opinion of the Federal Constitutional Court, to maintain the capability of the court to function."[70]

The Two-Senate Structure

The most important structural feature of the Constitutional Court is its division into two senates with mutually exclusive jurisdiction and personnel.[71] The Plenum—the two senates sitting together—meets periodically to resolve jurisdic-

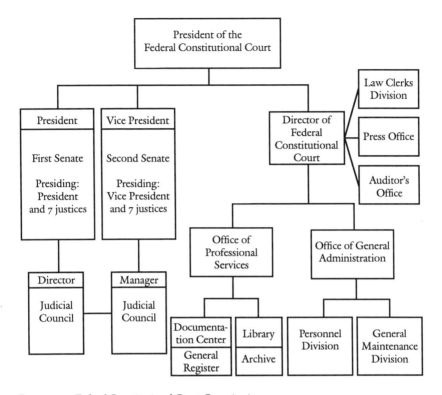

Figure 1.1.   Federal Constitutional Court Organization

tional conflicts between the senates and to issue rules on judicial administration. Justices are elected to either the First Senate or the Second Senate. The president ordinarily presides over the First Senate and the vice president over the Second Senate. Both "chief justices" are wholly independent with respect to judicial matters before their respective senates. Finally, each senate is equipped with its own administrative office for the organization and distribution of its workload (see figure 1.1).[72]

The twin-senate idea was a compromise between legislators who preferred a fluid system of twenty-four justices rotating on smaller panels and those who preferred a fixed body like that of the United States Supreme Court. More important, the bifurcation was the institutional expression of the old debate between those who viewed the court in conventional legal terms and those who saw it in political terms. The original division of jurisdiction showed that the senates were intended to fulfill very different functions. The Second Senate was designed to function much like Weimar's Staatsgerichtshof; it would decide political disputes between branches and levels of government, settle contested elections, rule on the constitutionality of political parties,[73] preside over impeachment proceedings, and decide abstract questions of constitutional law. The First Senate was vested with the authority to review the constitutionality of laws and to resolve constitutional doubts arising out of ordinary litigation. More concerned with the "nonpolitical" side of the court's docket and the "objective" process of constitutional interpretation, the First Senate would hear the constitutional complaints of ordinary citizens as well as referrals from other courts. As already noted, a lower tribunal that seriously doubts the constitutionality of a statute under which an actual case arises is obliged, before deciding the case, to certify the constitutional issue to the Constitutional Court for its decision.[74]

This division of labor resulted initially in a huge imbalance between the workloads of the two panels. The Second Senate decided only a handful of political cases, while the First Senate found itself flooded with constitutional complaints and concrete review cases. As a consequence, the federal parliament amended the FCCA in 1956 to distribute the caseload more evenly between the senates. Much of the First Senate's work was transferred to the Second Senate, thus eroding the original rationale of the two-senate system. The Second Senate, while retaining its "political" docket, would henceforth decide all constitutional complaints and concrete judicial review cases dealing with issues of civil and criminal procedure. The First Senate would continue to decide all such cases involving issues of substantive law. In addition, the Plenum was authorized by law to reallocate jurisdiction in a manner that would maintain relatively equal caseloads between the senates.[75]

The number of justices serving on the two senates has also changed over the years. The FCCA originally provided for twelve members per senate. In 1956 the number was reduced to ten; in 1962 it was further reduced to eight, fixing the court's total membership at sixteen (see Appendix B).[76] Considerations of efficiency, coupled with the politics of judicial recruitment,[77] prompted these reductions. For all practical purposes, then, the Constitutional Court comprises two independent tribunals, although each functions in the name of the court as a whole. In 1983, however, parliament modified the ironclad rule against any interchange among justices. The FCCA now provides that if one senate is unable to convene because of the incapacity or unavailability of one or more of its justices—a quorum consists of six justices—one justice from the other senate may be chosen by lot to serve temporarily in the understaffed senate. The presiding officers of the two senates are excluded from serving as substitute justices.[78]

Intrasenate Chamber System

To speed up the court's decision-making process, the FCCA changed the internal structure of the two senates in 1956 by authorizing each senate to set up three or more preliminary examining committees, each consisting of three justices, to filter out frivolous constitutional complaints.[79] At the beginning of each business year, each senate appoints its respective committees, subject to the rule that no three justices may serve together on the same committee for more than three years.[80] The president and vice president serve as chairs of their respective committees, as does the senior justice on each of the remaining committees. A committee may dismiss a complaint if all three of its members consider it to be "inadmissible or to offer no prospect of success for other reasons."[81] Under current procedure, if one of the three justices votes to accept a complaint — that is, if he or she thinks it has some chance of success — it is forwarded to the full senate.[82] At this stage, the "rule of three" controls; if at least three justices in the full senate are convinced that the complaint raises a question of constitutional law likely to be clarified by a judicial decision, or that the complainant will suffer serious harm in the absence of a decision, the complaint will be held acceptable.[83] Thereafter, and on the basis of more detailed examination, a senate majority could still reject the complaint as inadmissible or trivial.[84]

In 1986, on the Constitutional Court's own recommendation, the federal parliament enhanced the power of the three-judge committees, henceforth called chambers (*Kammer*). In addition to their normal screening function, the chambers are now empowered to rule on the merits of a constitutional complaint if all three justices agree with the result and the decision clearly lies within standards already laid down in a case decided by the full senate.[85] The authority to declare a statute unconstitutional or in conflict with federal law is reserved to the full senate.[86] Under current procedures, a chamber is not required to file a formal opinion justifying its refusal to accept a complaint for a decision on the merits.[87] As a matter of practice, however, whether deciding a complaint on the merits or on the question of admissibility (*Zulässigkeit*), a chamber often accompanies its decision with an opinion one to several pages long.[88] Most of these decisions remain unpublished, and they are cataloged in the court's own files for internal use and reference.[89] Occasionally, however, and in consultation with the full senate, chamber decisions are published in the court's official reports.[90] Other chamber opinions that serve to clarify points of law already laid down in previous cases or likely to command public attention may be released for publication in major legal periodicals such as *Neue Juristische Wochenschrift* and *Deutsche Juristenzeitung*.[91]

By separating the wheat from the chaff, the chambers dispose of 95 percent of all complaints, relieving the full senates of what would otherwise be an impossible task. Chambers are no longer required to offer reasons for the dismissal of a complaint if the complainant is notified at the outset that there is little hope for the success of his or her petition, a practice that helps the court to clear its docket.[92] To discourage the filing of trivial complaints, the FCCA authorizes the court to fine petitioners who "abuse" the constitutional complaint procedure. Currently, the court may level a fine of up to DM 5,000 ($3,600) on abusers.[93] As of 1986, the chambers were given the additional authority to impose a fee of up to DM 1,000 ($720) on any petitioner whose complaint it refuses to accept because it is either clearly inadmissible or wholly unlikely to succeed.[94] This practice, however, failed to decrease the number of complaints arriving at the court, and it was recently abandoned.

The chamber system has been the subject of several constitutional challenges, the complainant having argued in each case that a chamber's dismissal of his complaint denied him the right to "the jurisdiction of his lawful judge" under Article 101 of the Basic Law. Since the Basic Law provides for *one* constitutional court, argued the complainants, the full senate is constitutionally required to decide every case. In the three *Three-Justice Committee* cases,[95] involving decisions by both senates, the court ruled against the complainant on the basis of its original statutory authority to establish internal committees. In one instance, seemingly piqued by the audacity of the complainant who challenged its decision-making procedures, the Second Senate slapped a nominal fine on the complainant for "abusing the constitutional complaint procedure."[96] These decisions, all rendered before the right to file a constitutional complaint was entrenched in the Basic Law, underscored the finality of committee decisions unanimously rejecting complaints. In short, if a complaint is unanimously rejected, no "appeal" lay to the full senate, its sister senate, or the Plenum.

The constitutionalization of the complaint procedure in 1969 appeared to erode the foundation of the *Three-Justice Committee* cases. In recent years, however, no challenge has been hurled against the chamber system on constitutional grounds, "and in any event it is rather hard to imagine the court undermining its own protective ramparts."[97] Clearly, some form of gatekeeping procedure involving less than full senate membership is necessary as a practical matter if the court is to cope with a system that "entitles [anyone] to complain to it about virtually anything."[98] On the other hand, the system could permit hidden criteria to influence the summary disposition process and thus perhaps to "resolve" matters rightfully within the full senate's competence.[99] There is also the chance that different standards may exist from chamber to chamber, possibly invading the Plenum's right to ensure uniform judgments across senates, although the three-year rolling membership requirement would seem to mitigate this problem.

Qualifications and Tenure

To qualify for a seat on the Constitutional Court, persons must be forty years of age, eligible for election to the Bundestag, and possess the qualifications for judicial office specified in the German Judges Act (Deutsches Richtergesetz).[100] This means that prospective justices must have successfully passed the first and second major state bar examinations. Additionally, justices may not simultaneously hold office in the legislative or executive branch of the federal or a state government. Finally, the FCCA provides that the "functions of a justice shall preclude any other professional occupation save that of a professor of law at a German institution of higher education," and that the justice's judicial functions must take precedence over any and all professorial duties.[101]

The FCCA originally provided lifetime terms for the federal judges on each senate (i.e., those chosen from the high federal courts). The other members — justices not required to be chosen from the federal courts — were limited to renewable eight-year terms of office. The recruitment of a certain number of judges from the federal courts for the duration of their terms on those courts was expected to bring judicial experience and continuity to the Constitutional Court's work. Parliament amended the FCCA in 1970, however, to provide for single twelve-year terms for all justices, with no possibility of reelection.[102] Three of the current eight justices per senate must, as before, be elected from the federal judiciary. All justices — federal judges and other members — must retire at age sixty-eight, even though they may not have served for twelve years.

The debate on judicial tenure prior to the 1970 change in the law was entangled with the question of whether justices should be authorized to publish dissenting opinions.[103] As early as 1968, lawmakers, supported by a majority of the justices, seemed prepared to sanction signed dissenting opinions. But the feeling was widespread that the justices could not be expected to speak their minds if their tenure depended on the continuing pleasure of parliament. The justices themselves favored lifetime appointments. The government in turn responded with a bill that provided for both dissenting opinions and a twelve-year term with the possibility of reelection for a single second term of twelve years. Social Democrats, however, insisted on a single fixed term of twelve years, conditioning their support of the dissenting opinion largely on the acceptance of this proposal. But the question was not hotly contested among the political parties. A single twelve-year term, combined with the dissenting opinion, was generally thought to be an adequate solution to both the problem of judicial independence and the need for a greater measure of judicial openness on the Constitutional Court.[104]

Machinery for Judicial Selection

The Basic Law provides that half the court's members be elected by the Bundestag and half by the Bundesrat. Under the FCCA, however, the Bundestag elects its eight justices indirectly through a twelve-person Judicial Selection Committee (JSC) known as the Wahlmännerausschuss. Party representation on the JSC is proportionate to each party's strength in the Bundestag; eight votes are required to elect.[105] The Bundesrat, on the other hand, votes as a whole for its eight justices, a two-thirds vote also being required to elect.[106] Although each house elects four members of each senate, the FCCA stipulates that of the three justices in each senate "selected from among the judges of the highest federal courts, one shall be elected by one [house] and two by the other, and of the remaining five judges, three shall be elected by one [house] and two by the other."[107] Which house elects each combination is a matter of informal agreement between the two chambers, although the Bundestag and Bundesrat alternate in selecting the court's president and vice president (the Bundestag was authorized to elect the first president and the Bundesrat the first vice president).[108]

Prior to the selection process the minister of justice is required to compile a list of all the federal judges who meet the qualifications for appointment, as well as a list of the candidates submitted by the parliamentary parties, the federal government, or a state government. The minister delivers these lists to the electoral organs at least one week before they convene. If either house fails to elect a new justice within two months of the expiration of a sitting justice's term, the chairman of the JSC — the oldest member of the committee — or the president of the Bundesrat (depending on the house doing the electing) must request the Constitutional Court itself to propose a list of three candidates; if several justices are to be elected simultaneously, the court is required to "propose twice as many candidates as the number of justices to be elected."[109] The Plenum selects the list by a simple majority vote. But parliament is not obligated to choose the appointee from this or any other list.

In reality, the actual process of judicial selection is highly politicized. The JSC, which consists of senior party officials and the top legal experts of each parliamentary party, conducts its proceedings behind closed doors and after extended consultation with the Bundesrat.[110] Although the parliamentary parties may not legally instruct their representatives on the JSC how to vote, committee members do in fact speak for the leaders of their respective parties. The two-thirds majority required to elect a justice endows opposition parties in the JSC with considerable leverage over appointments to the Constitutional Court. Social and Christian Democrats are in a position to veto each other's judicial nominees, and the Free Democratic party, when in coalition with one of the larger parties, occasionally wins a seat for itself through intracoalition bargaining. Compromise is thus a practical necessity.

Compromise among contending interests and candidacies is equally necessary in the Bundesrat, where the interests of the various states, often independent of party affiliation, play a paramount role in the selection of the justices. An advisory commission consisting of the state justice ministers prepares a short list of potentially electable nominees. The justice ministers on the commission, like certain state governors (i.e., ministers-president) and members of the Bundestag's JSC, are often themselves leading candidates for seats on the Constitutional Court. Informal agreements emerge from the commission's proceedings, specifying which states shall choose prospective justices and in what order. Throughout this process the commission coordinates its work with that of the JSC. It is important to avoid duplicate judicial selections, and the two chambers need to agree on the particular senate seats each is going to fill and which of these seats are to be filled with justices recruited from the federal high courts (three justices of each senate must be recruited from these courts).[111]

PROCESS

Internal Administration

The Federal Constitutional Court achieved a major victory when it won the authority early on to administer its own internal affairs. Administrative autonomy had two notable consequences for the court's institutional development. First, armed with the power to prepare its own budget in direct consultation with parliament and the Ministry of Finance, the court was able to plan its own future. In 1964 it even won approval for an ultramodern building designed by its own architects and engineers. Second, the president's administrative authority was substantially enlarged. While only *primus inter pares* in the judicial conference room, he or she is *primus* on all other matters of internal administration, a situation that once aggravated relations between the president and several associate justices.

In 1975, after years of discord between the president and individual justices over their respective duties and powers, parliament enacted a set of standing rules of procedure governing the court's internal operations.[112] The new rules charge the Plenum, over which the president presides, with preparing the budget, deciding all questions pertaining to the justices' duties, and formulating general principles of judicial administration. They authorize the Plenum to establish several standing committees for the purpose of recommending policies dealing with matters such as record keeping, budgetary policy, personnel administration, and library administration. The rules require the president to carry out these policies and to represent the court in its official relations with other government agencies and on ceremonial occasions. In addition, the rules entitle each senate to an administrative director, who is responsible to its presiding justice. Overall judicial administration is the responsibility of the Constitutional Court's director, the highest administrative official in the court, who answers only to the president.[113] The director, like the justices themselves, must be a lawyer qualified for judicial office. (Indeed, one previous director, Walter Rudi Wand, was elected to the Second Senate in 1970.) Finally, each justice is entitled to three research assistants or clerks of his or her own choosing. Law clerks are not recent law school graduates as in the United States. They are usually in their thirties or early forties and already embarked on legal careers as judges, civil servants, or professors of law. Most serve for two or three years, although some clerks have stayed on for longer periods.

Decision-Making Procedures

The FCCA, along with the Constitutional Court's General Rules of Procedure, sets forth each senate's internal practices and procedures. For its part, the FCCA includes general and special provisions governing each category of jurisdiction (e.g., party prohibition cases, federal-state conflicts, collateral judicial-review references, etc.). The General Rules of Procedure deal with (1) conditions under which a justice may be excluded from a case; (2) procedures to be followed in various types of cases; (3) rights of the parties involved in litigation before the court, including the qualifications of those legally entitled to represent them; (4) obligations of public officials and judges to cooperate with the court in disposing of certain cases; (5) special rules accompanying the issuance of temporary orders; and (6) the manner in which decisions are made and announced.[114]

The procedures on judicial removal require a justice to recuse himself from a case if he is related to one of the parties or has a personal interest in its outcome.[115] Recusation, however, is beyond a justice's own discretion. Whether he or she initiates the recusal or resists a formal challenge of bias by one of the parties, the full senate decides the matter in his or her absence. A decision denying or upholding a voluntary recusal or a challenge to a justice refusing to withdraw from a case must be supported in writing and included among the court's published opinions.[116]

A justice who refuses to recuse himself in the face of motions against his participation must provide his colleagues with a formal statement in defense of his involvement. The statement is included in the senate's formal opinion on the recusal. The critical issue in such cases is not whether the justice in question is in fact biased, but whether a party to the case has a sufficient reason for believing that he or she may be incapable of making an impartial judgment. So far, two justices have been excluded under these procedures: Justice Gerhard Leibholz in the third *Party Finance III* case (1966),[117] and Justice Joachim Rottmann in the *East-West Basic Treaty* case (1973).[118] Both produced moments of high tension on the court. In each instance petitioners complained that the justice compromised his impartiality by making off-the-bench — and admittedly indiscreet — public comments on the merits of pending litigation.[119]

The Constitutional Court's deliberations are secret, and the justices render their decisions on the basis of the official record. The rules require that each senate decision be justified by official opinions signed by all participating justices (six justices constitute a quorum).[120] Oral arguments are the exception; they are limited to cases of major political importance. Of fifty reported cases handed down in 1991, only eight were decided subsequent to oral argument. A decision handed down on the basis of an oral proceeding is known as a judgment (*Urteil*); a decision handed down in the absence of oral argument is labeled an order, or ruling (*Beschluss*). The distinction is formal, however; whether an *Urteil* or a *Beschluss*, the judgment binds all state authorities, and decisions having the force of general law — for example, most abstract and concrete judicial review cases — must be published in the *Federal Law Gazette*,[121] along with all parliamentary resolutions and laws.

ASSIGNMENT. Specialization is a major feature of the judicial process within the Federal Constitutional Court. As noted earlier, each senate has a specified jurisdiction. Once incoming cases have been processed in the Office of the Director, they are channeled to the appropriate senate and then passed on to the various justices according to their areas of expertise.[122] Before the start of the business year, each senate establishes the ground rules for the assignment of cases. By mutual agreement, and in consultation with his or her senate's presiding officer, each justice agrees to serve as the rapporteur (*Berichterstatter*) in cases related to his or her particular interest or specialty. At least one justice of the Second Senate, for example, typically has a background in international law and serves as the rapporteur in cases involving international legal issues such as asylum, extradition, and deportation.

Another justice might take charge of cases involving tax and social security law, while still another might be assigned cases dealing with issues arising from laws relating to marriage and the family.

The rapporteur's job is to prepare a written document, or brief (votum) whose preparation is a crucial stage in the decisional process. Assisted by his or her law clerks, the rapporteur prepares what amounts to a major research report. He describes the background and facts of the dispute, surveys the court's own precedents and the legal literature, presents fully documented arguments advanced on both sides of the question, and concludes with the personal view of how the case should be decided. A votum, which may be well over a hundred pages long, may take weeks, even months, to prepare, and often it forms the basis of the first draft of the court's final opinion.[123] In any one calendar year each justice prepares several major votums, studies thirty to forty additional ones authored by his or her colleagues, drafts shorter reports (minivotums) — about two hundred per year — for his two colleagues on the three-judge chambers, writes the opinion in cases assigned to him as rapporteur, and readies himself for the weekly conference.

ORAL ARGUMENT. As already noted, formal hearings before the court are rare. Each senate hears oral argument in three or four cases annually, usually in *Organstreit* and abstract judicial-review cases, in which oral argument is mandatory unless waived by the major organs or units of government bringing these cases. The rapporteur, who by this time has neared the completion of his or her votum, usually dominates the questioning. The main function of the oral argument is less to refine legal issues than to uncover, if possible, additional facts bearing on them. The public hearing also adds legitimacy to the decision-making process in cases of major political importance, particularly when minority political parties allege that the established parties have treated them unconstitutionally.[124] The generous time allotted to oral presentations — a full day or more — and the court's readiness to hear the full gamut of argumentation on both sides of a disputed question are intended to generate goodwill and convey a sense of fairness and openness to winners and losers alike.

CONFERENCE. The presiding officer of each senate schedules weekly — occasionally semiweekly — meetings to decide cases and dispose of other judicial business. Except for August and September, when the court is not in session, meetings are normally held every Tuesday, frequently spilling over into Wednesday and Thursday. Votums and draft opinions of cases already decided dominate the agenda. In considering a votum, the presiding justice calls on the rapporteur to summarize the case and state the reasons for his recommendation. The rapporteur's role is crucial here, for a carefully drafted and well-organized votum usually carries the day in conference. In addition, the pressure of time often prompts justices to defer to the rapporteur's expertise and judgment.[125]

Still, the rapporteur has to win the consent of his colleagues. It is his responsibility, along with that of the "chief justice," to marshal a majority or find a broad basis of agreement. In this process, skill and personality are important. The rapporteur who does his homework, solicits the views of colleagues, and negotiates artfully is likely to prevail in conference. Justices who lack these gifts or the full confidence of their colleagues are unlikely to prevail. If, on the other hand, the rapporteur is in the minority — and even the most influential justices occasionally find themselves in this position — he does not necessarily lose his influence over the case, for he still has the task of writing the court's opinion. If he combines political sagacity with a deft literary hand, he may leave his imprint on the finished product. A rapporteur with strong dissenting views may request that the writing of the opinion be assigned to another justice, but this rarely happens. If he knows the requisites of judicial statesmanship, he will draft an opinion broadly reflective of a wide common denominator of agreement, often representing a compromise among conflicting constitutional arguments.[126]

The production of such opinions — that is, opinions which reduce discord on the bench and preserve the court's moral authority in the public mind — is likely to be a function of the presiding officer's capacity for leadership. His task is to guide discussion, frame the questions to be voted on, and marshal the largest majority possible behind judicial decisions. His leadership is particularly important in the sessions in which opinions undergo final and often meticulous editing. Despite the introduction of signed dissenting opinions in 1971, the court continues unanimously to decide more than 90 percent of its reported cases. Although these reports disclose the identities of the justices participating in a case, majority opinions remain unsigned. It is common knowledge among informed observers, however, that the rapporteur in a unanimous decision is the principal author of the final opinion. The institutional bias against personalized judicial opinions has tended to minimize published dissents. Dissenting justices — even if they have circulated written dissents inside the court — more often than not choose not to publish their dissents or even to be identified as dissenters partly out of a sense of institutional loyalty. The prevailing norm seems to be that personalized dissenting opinions are proper only when prompted by deep personal convictions.

Caseload and Impact

Table 1.1 presents an overview of the court's workload during its first forty-three years of operation. These statistics, however, do not tell the full story of the business before the court or its function in the German polity. In a given calendar year the court receives eight to ten thousand letters, notes, or communications from citizens throughout the Federal Republic. Inadmissible under the court's regular procedures, these "cases" are consigned to the custody of the General Register's Office (see figure 1.1).[127] The General Register responds to these petitioner's, in most instances advising them that their inquiries are misdirected. If, however, the petitioner

Table 1.2. The Federal Constitutional Court's Caseload in 1991, 1992, and 1993

Jurisdictional category	1991	1992	1993
Election disputes	19	—	—
Disputes between federal organs	5	4	8
Abstract judicial review	2	8	2
Concrete judicial review	99	137	90
Other public law disputes	9	7	2
Requests for temporary injunctions	36	57	88
Constitutional complaints	3,904	4,214	5,246

Source: Statistical summary prepared by senate administrative offices (1993; typescript).

writes back demanding to be heard, his or her file is forwarded to one of the senates.[128] In 1993, 1,441 such claims were screened by the respective chambers of the two senates; all were rejected.[129] The General Register thus serves as an important checkpoint. Through it pass only the most insistent of complainants. At the same time the court bestows the courtesy of a response on every person who appeals to it.

As table 1.2 shows, constitutional complaints and concrete judicial review references make up the bulk of the Constitutional Court's load. Still, the number of concrete review references is extremely low in light of a judiciary consisting of twenty thousand judges. In 1994, German judges referred only fifty-five cases to the Constitutional Court. The apparent reluctance of judges to refer constitutional questions may be attributed to the strong tradition of legal positivism that continues to hold sway in the regular judiciary. Jealous of their own limited power of judicial review, judges usually resolve doubts about the constitutional validity of laws at issue in pending cases by upholding them or interpreting them so as to avoid questions of constitutionality, thus obviating the necessity of appeal to Karlsruhe.

The constitutional complaint procedure, on the other hand, has served as an escape hatch for litigants upset with the performance of the judiciary. Seventy-five percent of all constitutional complaints are brought against judicial decisions (table 1.3). Nearly all complaints against court decisions alleged to have violated the procedural guarantees of the Basic Law are disposed of by the Second Senate. The First Senate has jurisdiction over most complaints involving claims to substantive constitutional rights such as equal protection (Article 3); life, liberty, or personality (Article 2); human dignity (Article 1); property (Article 14); and the freedom to choose a trade or profession (Article 12).[130] Even though the full senates decide a mere handful of such cases — 22 of 5,194 complaints filed in 1994 — the constitutional complaint procedure is now deeply rooted in Germany's legal culture. The right of any citizen to take his or her complaint to Karlsruhe is an important factor in

Table 1.3. Sources of Constitutional Complaints, 1993

Filed against	Heard by		Total
	First Senate	Second Senate	
Ordinary courts			
Civil	1,394	443	1,837
Criminal	14	1,026	1,040
Administrative courts	319	1,264*	1,583
Social courts	166	—	166
Finance courts	6	132	138
Labor courts	117	1	118

Source: Statistical summary prepared by senate administrative offices (1993; typescript).

*Of these, 1,021 cases involved asylum proceedings.

the court's high rating in public opinion pools and perhaps the chief reason for the development of a rising constitutional consciousness among Germans generally.[131]

Most of the court's manifest political jurisprudence falls into other jurisdictional categories, particularly conflicts between branches of government, disputed elections, federal-state controversies, and abstract judicial-review proceedings. Although few in number (see table 1.1), the political impact of these cases is substantial.[132] The most politically sensitive cases in recent years have involved constitutional challenges to policies growing out of German reunification, particularly issues relating to property rights, abortion, and the dismissal of public employees. The ongoing unification process continues to preoccupy German courts, and many pending cases, such as the criminal prosecutions brought against former GDR citizens accused of elementary human rights abuses, will make their way to the Federal Constitutional Court.[133] The more important of these cases are taken up briefly, where appropriate, in the following chapters.

In general, however, the Constitutional Court is most politically exposed when deciding cases on abstract judicial review. These cases are almost always initiated by a political party on the short end of a legislative vote in the federal parliament or by the national or a state government challenging an action of another level of government controlled by an opposing political party or coalition of parties. The apparent manipulation of the judicial process for political purposes in these cases has led some observers to favor the abolition of abstract judicial review.[134] But those who decry the judicialization of politics — or, alternatively, the politicization of justice — have not gained much parliamentary support for the constitutional amendment that would be necessary to abolish abstract review. Equally disconcerting for those who would eliminate the thin line between law and politics trod by the court in these cases is the failure of the justices themselves to mount any opposition to abstract judicial review. Indeed, the elimination of abstract review would run counter to the view of constitutionalism currently prevalent in the Federal Republic: the view that the court, as guardian of the constitutional order, is to construe and enforce the Constitution whenever statutes or other governmental actions raise major disputes over its interpretation. This observation clears the way for a more extensive treatment of the Basic Law, its interpretation, and the Constitutional Court's role in the German polity.

2

THE BASIC LAW AND ITS

INTERPRETATION

STRUCTURE AND PRINCIPLES

The Basic Law of the Federal Republic of Germany (FRG) entered into force on May 23, 1949. It was called a "basic law" (*Grundgesetz*) because the Parliamentary Council did not want to bestow the dignified term "constitution" (*Verfassung*) on a document drafted to govern a part of Germany for a transitional period that would only last until national reunification. On that faraway day — or so it seemed at the time — the Basic Law would cease to exist with the adoption of a German constitution "by a free decision of [all] the German people."[1] When that day finally did arrive, on October 3, 1990, following a remarkable series of events, German unity was achieved within the framework of the Basic Law. The decision to retain the Basic Law as an all-German constitution, and to continue its designation as the *Grundgesetz,* was not unanticipated. Over the course of the preceding forty years, particularly in the light of the huge body of decisional law created by the Federal Constitutional Court, the Basic Law had come to assume the character of a document framed to last in perpetuity.

The treaty under which the German Democratic Republic (GDR) became a part of the FRG, however, instructed the soon-to-be-chosen all-German parliament to consider amendments to the Basic Law in light of questions raised by unification. Whether the Basic Law should be ratified in a popular referendum was one of these questions. The Basic Law had never been submitted to a popular vote. State legislatures had chosen the original delegates to the Parliamentary Council, and those same bodies ratified it. But now that Germany was unified, thus changing the composition of the German people, a referendum on the Basic Law would ostensibly infuse it with the popular legitimacy it arguably lacked. A parliamentary commission on constitutional revision established in 1991 nevertheless rejected the idea of holding a popular referendum. The commission appeared to accept the prevailing view among Germany's constitutional lawyers that twelve national elections in forty years expressed overwhelming popular support for the existing constitutional order and established the Basic Law's fundamental legitimacy. The GDR's voluntary accession to the Federal Republic under the Basic Law—a decision unmistakably affirmed in East Germany' first free election on March 18, 1990—was also regarded as evidence of the document's broad acceptance among East Germans.[2]

The parliamentary commission also considered a long list of proposed amendments to the Basic Law calculated to reflect Germany's new social and political identity. Many of these proposals responded to the socialist aspirations of reform-minded democrats in the old GDR. These reform democrats also supported initiatives on the part of certain West German groups for the adoption of plebiscitary institutions at the national level, a constitutional change that would radically alter Germany's governmental system. The commission rejected nearly all of these proposals, including the suggested referenda and recommendations for the incorporation of social welfare goals in the Basic Law. A short list of proposals, however, did win the commission's approval, and a few of them received the necessary two-thirds vote—in both Bundestag and Bundesrat—required to amend the Constitution. Where appropriate, these amendments and those incorporated into the Unity Treaty are discussed in the following pages and chapters.[3] It suffices to note here that none of these amendments modified the Basic Law's essential features or affected the fundamental structure of the political system as originally constituted.

The New Constitutionalism

In content and style the Basic Law follows a pattern typical of constitutions adopted by other liberal democracies (see Appendix A). It guarantees individual rights independent of the state, creates a political system of separated and divided powers, provides for an independent judiciary crowned by a high court of constitutional review, and establishes the Constitution as the supreme law of the land. Moreover, in a major reformulation of German constitutionalism, the Basic Law freezes certain structures and principles in perpetuity. Article 79 (3)—the so-called eternity clause—prohibits any amendment to the Basic Law that would change the *federal* character of the political system or impinge on the basic principles laid down in Articles 1 and 20.

Article 1 proclaims that the "dignity of man is inviolable," and Article 20 sets up a "democratic, social, and federal state" based on the rules of "law and justice." As the Constitutional Court has said on numerous occasions, these core principles manifest themselves in the list of human rights enumerated in the Basic Law. These principles and rights may also be said to be rooted in three major legal traditions that have shaped contemporary German constitutionalism, namely, classical-liberal, socialist, and Christian–natural law thought. Each of these traditions played a formative role in German legal history; each was powerfully represented at the Constitutional Convention of 1949; each finds many of its central values represented in the text of the Basic Law; and each continues its representation in German political life today. The Free Democratic party (FDP) represents the classical-liberal tradition; the Social Democratic party (SPD) the socialist tradition; and the Christian Democratic Union (CDU), together with its Bavarian affiliate, the Christian Social Union (CSU), the Christian–natural law tradition. In drafting the Basic Law, the representatives of these parties shed their historical antagonisms and, in a remarkable display of concord, drew willingly from the humanistic content of each tradition to create a constitution that combines the main values of each in a workable, if not always easy, alliance.[4]

At the risk of oversimplifying, one could say that the classical liberal tradition was responsible for many of the *individual* freedoms listed in several articles of the bill of rights (e.g., the rights to life and physical integrity [Article 2], equality [Article 3], religious exercise [Article 4], freedom of expression [Article 5], assembly [Article 8], association [Article 9], privacy [Article 10], movement [Article 11], and property [Article 14]); the socialist tradition contributed certain *social welfare* clauses, including provisions concerning the duties of property and the socialization of economic resources; and the Christian tradition added *communal* guarantees dealing with the protection of marriage and the family, the right of parents to educate their children, and the institutional prerogatives of the established churches. Philosophically, these traditions might be said to represent conflicting visions of the common good, yet they converge on a common core of belief about the nature of constitutionalism and the dignity of the human person.

The substantive values represented by these traditions are enormously important in the jurisprudence of the Federal Constitutional Court, although in the aftermath of reunification the political and social tradition of the old GDR may affect the interpretation of these values. There is no debate in Germany, however, as there is in the United States, over whether the Constitution is primarily procedural or value oriented. Germans no longer understand their constitution as the simple expression of an existential order of power. They commonly agree that the Basic Law is fundamentally a normative constitution embracing values, rights, and duties. That the Basic Law is a value-oriented document — indeed, one that establishes a hierarchical value order — is a familiar refrain, as we shall see, in German constitutional case law.

HUMAN RIGHTS AND DIGNITY. Article 1, appropriately, is the cornerstone of the Basic Law. Paragraph 1 declares: "The dignity of man is inviolable. To respect and protect it is the duty of all state authority." The principle of human dignity, as the Constitutional Court has repeatedly emphasized, is the highest value of the Basic Law, the ultimate basis of the constitutional order, and the foundation of all guaranteed rights.[5] The second paragraph continues: "The German people therefore acknowledge inviolable and inalienable rights as the basis of every community, of peace and of justice in the world." Paragraph 3, finally, declares that the basic rights enumerated in the Constitution (Articles 1–19) "shall bind the legislature, the executive, and the judiciary as directly enforceable law." Article 19 (2) underscores the preeminence of these rights by prohibiting, in the fashion of the perpetuity clause of Article 79, any encroachment on "the essential content of a basic right" under the Constitution. Finally, Article 19 (4) secures these rights by making courts of law accessible to any person whose rights are violated by state authority.

Many of the fundamental guarantees of the Bonn Constitution are word-for-word reproductions of corresponding articles in the Weimar Constitution. The difference is that the Weimar Constitution recognized basic rights as goals, but they were not judicially enforceable. The notion of "inviolable and inalienable" rights is also sharply at variance with the spirit of earlier German constitutions, for the Basic Law is Germany's first national constitution to recognize the preconstitutional existence of guaranteed rights. Contrary to the legal positivism underlying the Weimar Constitution,[6] fundamental rights are not the creations of law, nor are they distinctive to the German people. By some interpretations they are vested in persons by nature; by others the Basic Law simply acknowledges preexisting rights rooted in the universal concept of human dignity. General law (i.e., positive law) may limit rights, but for the first time those laws are themselves to be measured by the higher-law norms of the Constitution.

STATE AND MORALITY. The constitutional system of the Federal Republic also differs from past regimes in its refusal to treat individual freedom as a reflection of the state itself. The traditional theory of rights in Germany drew no clear distinction between state and society. The citizen was an organic part of the state, and the state itself was an agent of human liberation.[7] The German "*Staat*" and the English "state" are not equivalent terms. *Der Staat* is more than the body politic. It represents, in Kant,[8] the perfect synthesis between individual freedom and the objective authority of law, and, in Hegel, a moral organism in which individual liberty finds perfect realization in the unified will of the people: not arbitrary will, but rather "the power of reason actualizing itself in will."[9] In brief, the *Staat* is considered to be a superior form of human association, a uniting of individuals and society in a higher synthesis, a reality "in which the individual has and enjoys his freedom, [albeit] on condition of his recognizing, believing in, and willing that which is common to the whole."[10] Some features of the Basic Law, particularly its communitarian values, lend themselves to greater understanding in the light of these traditional German notions of liberty and state, notions suggestive of aspects of the Aristotelian *polis* and the early American tradition of civic republicanism.[11] Nevertheless, as Leonard Krieger has pointed out, the founders of the Basic Law, in the light of the Nazi experience, discovered the "bankruptcy of the state as a liberalizing institution." "Dominant now," he concluded in a monumental study of the German idea of freedom, "is an attitude which views the state as a morally neutral, purely utilitarian organization of public power."[12]

Krieger's assessment, while generally correct, needs to be qualified. The Basic Law as a modern twentieth-century constitution is interesting precisely because it subjects positive law to a higher moral order. To be sure, the Basic Law's list of fundamental rights protects the ideological pluralism and moral diversity of the German people. But some rights, such as that to the free development of personality, are limited by the "moral code," as that term is used within the meaning of Article 2 (2), as well as by certain conceptions of man and society found by the Federal Constitutional Court to be implicit in the constitutional concept of human dignity. The Constitutional Court itself rejects the notion of a value-neutral state. Instead, as noted later in this chapter, it speaks of a constitutional polity deeply committed to an "objective order of values."[13]

The Nature of the Polity

Article 20, as already noted, sets forth the fundamental principles of the new republic. In addition to describing the new polity as a "democratic and social federal state," paragraph 1 decrees that "all state authority emanates from the people." Under paragraph 2 the people are to exercise their authority "by means of elections and voting and by specific legislative, executive, and judicial organs." The Basic Law thus creates a representative democracy undergirded by the doctrine of separation of powers. Paragraph 3 subjects legislation "to the constitutional order," just as "the executive and judiciary are bound by law *and justice*" (emphasis added). Finally, to ensure the realization of these values at all levels of government, Article 28 — the so-called homogeneity clause — decrees that state and local governments "must conform to the principles of republican, democratic, and social government based on the rule of law."[14]

The Basic Law builds on and strengthens older doctrines and practices in the German constitutional tradition: Popular sovereignty, affirmed once again, now manifests itself in representative institutions rather than plebiscites; political parties, fortified by a new electoral system combining single-member districts with proportional representation, organize these institutions in the public interest; a strong chancellor, unremovable save by a constructive vote of no-confidence,[15] stabilizes the government; the basic structure of federalism, now beyond the power of the people to amend, is established in perpetuity; separation of powers includes judicial control of constitutionality; and, finally, majority rule is overlaid with a complex system of checks and balances, not to mention the indirect election of the federal president.

Four conceptions of the state that have achieved authoritative status in German constitutional law capture most of these institutional features and principles of government. These are the concepts of *Parteienstaat* (political party state), *Sozialstaat* (social welfare state), *Rechtsstaat* (state based on the rule of law), and *streitbare Demokratie* (militant democracy). The new polity is, of course, also a *Bundesstaat* (federal state), but this aspect of the polity is discussed in chapter 3. Several provisions of the Basic Law identify the new polity as a "free liberal democratic order," a phrase that fairly well encapsulates the nature of the modern German state.

PARTEIENSTAAT. Under the Basic Law, popular sovereignty is to be achieved through political parties competing in free and equal elections. In a departure from tradition as radical as judicial review itself, Article 21 of the Basic Law permits the free establishment of political parties, virtually certifying them as the chief agencies of political representation in the new polity. Yet, in an effort to secure genuine majority rule, the Constitution requires parties to organize themselves democratically and to account publicly for the sources of their funds. Additionally, and in language recalling an older German theory of the state, Article 21 declares that "political parties shall participate in forming the political will of the people."[16]

Article 38, which provides for the "general, direct, free, equal, and secret" election of parliamentary delegates, pulls in the opposite direction, toward an older, representative theory of democracy. Members of parliament, Article 38 declares, "shall be representatives of the whole people, not bound by orders and instructions, and shall be subject only to their conscience." Here a natural-law principle — conscience — intrudes to limit the party loyalty implied, perhaps even mandated, by Article 21. The federal structure, like the theory of party responsibility, also tempers majority rule, for the states enjoy a corporate right to participate in the national legislative process and often exercise that right to delay or refuse their consent to bills passed by the Bundestag. In the end, the Constitution seems ordained not only to achieve, under the rubric of majority rule, some semblance of correspondence between public policy and popular will, but also, as a consequence of its federal structure, to serve as an instrument of political conciliation, consensus, and cohesion.[17]

SOZIALSTAAT. The Basic Law, however, is more than a framework for the process of government. It incorporates a number of substantive values. As chapter 6 (on economic rights) shows, the *Sozialstaat* stands for social justice and obligates the government to provide for the basic needs of all Germans. This commitment, however, does not mean that every social benefit conferred by law is mandated by the principle of social justice. Whether particular policies such as family allowances or educational benefits are constitutionally required by the principle of the social welfare state is a matter of dispute among constitutional scholars,[18] a dispute that has reached a new level of intensity in reunified Germany. In any event, the concept of the social state, like that of the *Rechtsstaat,* has a good pedigree in German constitutional thought.[19] Its roots lie deep in the old Lutheran notion that while the people owe allegiance to the prince, the prince in turn is bound to see to the welfare of his subjects, an idea that finds its most prominent modern expression in the social security and protective labor legislation of the Bismarckian era. Backed by strong socialist influences, the social state as a concept of political order gradually worked its way into the Weimar Constitution, and today even neoliberal, market-oriented spokesmen, not to mention Christian Democrats schooled in Catholic social thought, regard the *Sozialstaat* as an important ingredient of Germany's constitutional tradition.[20]

Nevertheless, a lively academic debate over the relationship between the *Sozial-*

staat and the *Rechtsstaat* continues to engage German constitutional theorists. The *Rechtsstaat,* formally conceived, emphasizes the crucial importance of individual liberty, the right to choose one's trade, and the right to acquire and dispose of one's property. At what point do the demands and arrangements of the *Sozialstaat* begin to undermine the *Rechtsstaat*'s liberty-securing values and structures? German views range from the conservative perspective of Ernst Forsthoff, who has argued that the Basic Law constitutionalizes an individualistically based, market-oriented, free enterprise economy, all the way over to the extreme left-wing perspective — one shared today by many East Germans — that the *Sozialstaat* constitutionally requires major redistributive socioeconomic and tax policies.[21] As we shall see in chapter 6, the Federal Constitutional Court, like the majority of constitutional scholars, has taken a far less dogmatic view of the *Sozialstaat.*

RECHTSSTAAT. There is no equivalent term in English for the German *Rechtsstaat.* It is often loosely translated as "law state," "rule of law," or "a state governed by law," but the concept, in both its older and newer incarnations, embodies more than the idea of a government of laws.[22] As developed originally in the nineteenth century, the *Rechtsstaat* was a "state governed by the law of reason," one that insisted on the freedom, equality, and autonomy of each individual within the framework of a unified legal order defined by legislation and administered by independent courts of law. The traditional liberal *Rechtsstaat,* while emphasizing the importance of formal liberty, was indifferent to whether the government of the day, as opposed to the timeless *Staat,* was monarchical, aristocratic, or democratic in form. It was not until later, toward the end of the nineteenth century, under the influence of constitutional theorists such as Otto von Gierke and Rudolf von Gneist, that the *Rechtsstaat* began to integrate state and society and to proclaim the unity of law and the state. Although bound by laws administered by independent courts, the state took on a life of its own, undermining the individualistic rationale of the earlier *Rechtsstaat.* Finally, in the early twentieth century and during the Weimar Republic, the concept of the *Rechtsstaat* was increasingly associated with legal positivism. Statute law was supreme law, supreme because it reflected the popular will, the ultimate basis of the *Rechtsstaat*'s traditional legitimacy. In this system, the courts had the duty to uphold the law as defined by statute and to ensure that all state activity was conducted according to the supreme legislative will. There was no place for judicial review.

The Bonn Constitution did not completely abandon the principles of the old *Rechtsstaat;* it remains a crowning principle of German constitutionalism. But the Basic Law now uses the term "law" (*lex*) in the sense of both *Gesetz* (statutory law) and *Recht* (right or justice).[23] As put forth in Article 20 (3), "the executive and the judiciary are bound by law and justice" just as "legislation is subject to the constitutional order."[24] According to the Federal Constitutional Court, this "constitutional order" is a value-oriented legal order. In short, the Basic Law not only subjects law to the concept of justice; it also creates a fundamental system of values in terms of

which all legislation or other official acts must be assessed. Ernst-Wolfgang Böckenförde, a justice of the Federal Constitutional Court, put it this way:

> The logic of thinking about values and justice demands that the constitution
> conceived along the lines of the material *Rechtsstaat* should lay claim to an
> absolute validity extending to all spheres of social life. It thus sanctions certain
> basic politico-ethnic convictions, giving them general legal validity, and dis-
> criminates against others that run counter to them. It no longer guarantees
> liberty unconditionally by way of formal legal demarcation; it does so only
> *within* the fundamental system of values [*Wertgrundlage*] embodied in the
> constitution.[25]

These values and the concept of justice, as Böckenförde suggests, may trump liberty
when they come into conflict. Under the United States Constitution, on the other
hand, liberty would win over what the Germans have come to understand as values
as well as over the unwritten constitutional principles that the term "justice" implies. In short, the social *Rechtsstaat* is not only governed by law; it is also perceived
as a substantive charter of justice. All positive law must conform to the Basic Law's
order of values — as distinguished from guaranteed individual rights — informing
the Constitution as a whole.

In contemporary German constitutional theory, the Basic Law is supreme and
the Federal Constitutional Court has the authority to enforce it. Judicial review
is therefore a key element of the *Rechtsstaat* under the Basic Law. Of course, all
branches of government are responsible for the implementation of the Constitution, but as the highest institutional expression of the rule of law, the court has a
special role in this regard, a role explicitly sanctioned by the constitutional text.
Thus any branch or level of government that violates the Constitution or refuses to
carry out a constitutional duty can be called to account in a proper proceeding
before the court. In addition, the Basic Law authorizes the court to review the
constitutionality of laws and to hear complaints from ordinary citizens claiming a
violation of their fundamental freedoms by any agency or branch of government.
These powers, together with the ability of all other judges to refer constitutional
questions to the court for resolution, impart additional normative force to the
Constitution.

STREITBARE DEMOKRATIE (*MILITANT DEMOCRACY*). The term "militant democracy" appeared originally in the *Communist Party* case (1956), the decision which
declared the Communist Party of Germany unconstitutional because of its ideological opposition to the "free democratic basic order."[26] The concept finds its ground-
ing in the text of the Basic Law itself. The Nazi experience and the emergence of a
communist dictatorship in East Germany "fostered a strongly antitotalitarian mind-
set in the framers of the *Grundgesetz.*"[27] Article 21 (2) declares that political parties
which "by reason of their aims or the behavior of their adherents seek to impair or

abolish the free democratic order or to endanger the existence of the Federal Re-public of Germany shall be unconstitutional." Indeed, the principle of democracy in the Basic Law offers no refuge to the enemies of democracy. Article 18 is yet another expression of the constitutional principle that democracy is entitled to defend itself against internal enemies. According to this provision, any person who abuses the basic freedoms of speech, press, teaching, assembly, association, or property "in order to combat the free democratic basic order" forfeits these rights.[28] Indeed, under Article 20 (4), even ordinary "Germans have the right to resist any person attempting to do away with this constitutional order, should no other remedy be possible."

These constitutional perspectives differ from the Weimar Constitution in their requirement of absolute adherence to the value order of the existing political system. To minimize any abuse of power conferred by Articles 18 and 21, the Basic Law authorizes only the Federal Constitutional Court to order the forfeiture of rights or to declare parties unconstitutional. During the Weimar period the president of the Republic could ban parties and curtail rights on his own authority under the emer-gency provisions of Article 48. Under the Basic Law, by contrast, the Constitutional Court retains its authority during a state of emergency, including the authority to determine the forfeiture of basic rights under Article 18. In short, the Basic Law joins the protection of the *Rechtsstaat* to the principle that the democracy is not helpless in defending itself against parties or political movements bent on using the Constitution to undermine or destroy it.

Enforceable Charter

In view of the previous discussion, Germany might be said to have three constitu-tions. The first is the unamendable constitution, the one that Article 79 (3) of the Basic Law establishes in perpetuity. Indeed, as declared by the Federal Constitu-tional Court, any amendment to the Basic Law that would undermine or corrode any one of its core values would be an unconstitutional constitutional amendment. The second is the amendable constitution, namely, those parts of the written text that can be altered without affecting the Basic Law's core values. Finally, there are the unwritten, or suprapositive, principles implicit in such terms as "justice," "dig-nity," and "moral code." These governing principles, like the hierarchical value order that the Constitutional Court has extracted from the text of the Basic Law, are an important part of Germany's constitutional order. Germany's real constitution, then, includes more than the written text of the Basic Law itself.

Each of the three constitutions is judicially enforceable, a practice that departs radically from the traditional judicial role in Germany. Germany's variant of judicial review, however, differs from the American. The difference is at once subtle and profound, and it may be summarized as follows: Whereas American constitutional-ism has historically entailed a creative interaction between the constitutional text and evolving political practice, German constitutionalism tends to place greater emphasis on the capacity of the formal text to influence political practice. One manifestation of this tendency is abstract judicial review. This procedure under-scores the sovereignty and universality of constitutional norms and affirms the es-sential unity of the Constitution, a concept of constitutionalism seemingly related to the old notion of the *Rechtsstaat,* which envisioned the state or polity as a purely juristic construction.[29] In short, while judicial review under the Basic Law repre-sents a major break with the German legal tradition of the *Rechtsstaat,* it nevertheless continues to manifest elements of that tradition.

Perhaps the following remarks will clarify this point. The American Constitu-tion has historically served as a framework for the process of government. While the constitutional text and the polity have influenced one another, the bond between them is far from perfect.[30] American pragmatism leaves a lot to chance and circum-stance, is comfortable with constitutional ambiguity, and does not insist on the application of constitutional morality in all of its particulars. The Supreme Court has developed a battery of techniques to avoid constitutional decisions in certain cases and even to permit — for example, under the aegis of the "political question" doctrine, the "case or controversy" requirement, and other devices for avoiding decision — contraconstitutional developments within the polity. The American pub-lic mind is comfortable with the uncertainty that often prevails when for prudential reasons the Supreme Court declines to consider constitutional issues. Thus, the written Constitution is far from coextensive with the American polity.

In Germany, on the other hand, the Basic Law was designed not only to create a system of governance but also to foster a secure and preferred way of life.[31] German constitutional scholars often speak of the steering, integrating, and legit-imizing functions of the Constitution, as if to suggest a perfect bonding between text and polity.[32] They insist on the strict enforcement of the Basic Law in all of its particulars, for to do otherwise would be to sanction a lawless society. In brief, there is less tolerance of uncertainty or ambiguity in constitutional matters. Conflicts between text and polity cause crises in the German public mind and commotion among legal scholars and others concerned with the proper relationship between the "normativity" of the Constitution and the "existentiality" of political reality.[33]

This complex of attitudes has implications for judicial review. Abstract ques-tions of constitutional law matter in Germany, in contrast to the Holmesian view — a predominantly American perspective — that general propositions do not decide con-crete cases. Questions of constitutionality that arise in the course of enacting legisla-tion must be confronted, not avoided; there is thus a tendency to have the constitu-tional correctness of every important and controversial statute scrutinized by the Constitutional Court in Karlsruhe. The feeling exists that if legislation, however triv-ial or noncontroversial, is unconstitutional, it is contrary to the *Rechtsstaat* and there-fore bad for the body politic. In this spirit, as Karl Heinrich Friauf has written, con-stitutional interpretation in Germany "forms a part of what we might call the eternal struggle for the self-realization of constitutional law in the life of the community."[34]

CONSTITUTIONAL INTERPRETATION

Background

The German approach to constitutional interpretation needs to be understood within the wider context of Germany's legal culture. The nature of German constitutionalism is perhaps best explained by describing the general legal context in which the Constitutional Court functions and showing how this context differs from the American system. But a cautionary word is necessary. I deliberately focus on contrasts between German and American law rather than on their similarities so as to impart a sharp sense of the mind-set engaged in the process of constitutional interpretation in Germany. The similarities should be clear enough in this discussion of the methods and principles of constitutional interpretation. The vocabulary of constitutional debate, however, differs in the two countries, and these differences match the countries' respective conceptions of law and the judicial process.

The German public mind, schooled in the tradition of *Begriffsjurisprudenz* (conceptual jurisprudence), or legal positivism, has tended to envision law as a self-contained, rational, deductive system of rules and norms. Positing a sharp separation between law and morals — between the "is" and the "ought" — *Begriffsjurisprudenz* has sought to create a science of law marked by its own internal standards of validity. Its object is to keep law entirely separate from the domains of politics, psychology, and sociology.[35] Law, in short, rests on an independent foundation of reason and logic. The concept of judicial decision generated by this mode of legal thought is the idea of a court — an autonomous legal institution — entrusted with the systematic if not the mechanical application of fixed rules of law. Its major theme is fidelity to law. Similarly, the process of judging exemplifies the unity, clarity, and simplicity typical of the structure of the German civil code.[36]

The American conception of law, by contrast, derives its spirit from the common law, the essence of which is captured in Oliver Wendell Holmes's endlessly quoted aphorism, "The life of the law has not been logic, it has been experience."[37] Like Holmes, Americans generally have understood law as a pragmatic enterprise. Correspondingly, they understand the concept of judicial decision as a context-sensitive, inductive process open to extralegal influences, responsive to social reality, and sharply aware of the limits of formal law in the management of human affairs. Judging, therefore, while guided by established rules and principles, is largely a creative process to be exercised in the light of social need and enlightened public policy.[38] Finally, and fundamentally, common law, and therefore the bulk of constitutional law, is not something created by the state as supreme legislator. It is made primarily by judges and is calculated at once to limit the state and to promote the release of individual and group energy.[39]

Even if it be noted that these observations relate chiefly to private law, code-law reasoning in Germany, like common-law reasoning in the United States, has exerted a powerful influence on the development of public law, including constitutional law.

If the spirit of American public law is symbolized by figures like Holmes, Pound, Llewellyn, Cardozo, Frank, and Hand,[40] the spirit of German public law is symbolized by legal theorists such as Jellinek, Anschütz, Laband, Puchta, Radbruch, and Bergbohm.[41] Similarly, if American constitutional jurisprudence locates its indigenous spiritual roots in the commonsense realism of Madison, Hamilton, and Wilson,[42] German constitutional jurisprudence finds its guiding light in the idealistic rationalism of Hegel, Kant, and Fichte.[43] This may blur important distinctions among German schools of legal thought, yet the one notion that emerges relatively intact, in contrast to the American theory, is the reality and ubiquity of the state. German legal theorists have commonly assumed that law and justice would thrive solely within the bosom of that perfect society known as the state.

The Basic Law represents a major break from this tradition. It does not regard the state as the source of fundamental rights. The core of individual freedom, like human dignity itself, is anterior to the state. Thus, law and justice, as we have seen, now measure the validity of governmental actions, including judicial decisions. Inalienable rights, justice, values, and other such notions arguably present in the Basic Law militate against the methodology of legal positivism. And yet, for all that, and of immediate interest to us, the approach to judicial reasoning in *Begriffs-jurisprudenz* has outlasted positivism and has had a lasting influence throughout Europe, including Germany.[44] As we shall see, German constitutional scholars no less than the justices of the Federal Constitutional Court have made significant attempts to build a theory of judicial decision based on reason and logic.

In discussing these contrasts between legal cultures, we should observe that in both Germany and the United States, countervailing theories of law have always challenged the dominant mode of legal thought. In Germany, for example, the extent to which judges were free to depart from the will of the legislator was a central issue in legal argument during much of the nineteenth century. *Begriffs-jurisprudenz,* while it predominated during this period, had to defend itself against the historical school of jurisprudence.[45] By the same token, in the early years of the twentieth century the "free law" school of judicial interpretation and the *Interessen-jurisprudenz* of Philipp Heck and Rudolf von Ihering assailed the prevailing school of legal positivism.[46] Then too, during the Weimar Republic — against the backdrop of the continuing revolt against legal positivism — neo-Hegelian, neo-Kantian, and phenomenological schools of legal thought were developing new theories of law and judicial interpretation in an effort to overcome the dualism of "is" and "ought" at the basis of positivist dogma.[47] Finally, after World War II, natural-law theory, breaking out afresh from both Catholic and Protestant sources, tried to depose legal positivism.[48] In the United States, pragmatic jurisprudence had to face similar challenges, ranging from those of David Dudley Field, Christopher Langdell, and Owen Roberts, all of whom tried to build a true science of law or judging, to those of the value-oriented natural-law "moralists" and fundamental rights "objectivists" of our own time.[49]

Approaches to Interpretation

Constitutional interpretation as practiced today by the Federal Constitutional Court draws on several of West Germany's competing traditions of law and judicial decision. Thus we observe styles of argument ranging from reliance on linguistic analysis to the invocation of "suprapositivist" norms reputedly underlying the Basic Law.[50] Like the United States Supreme Court, the Constitutional Court employs a variety of interpretive modes, including arguments based on history, structure, teleology, text, interest balancing, and natural law. The one technique that is not formally followed in German constitutional analysis is that of *stare decisis* — which is unknown in the judiciaries of code-law countries — although as a matter of practice the court's opinions brim with citations to previous cases. The techniques and modes of analysis that are used have generated a critical literature in Germany as abundant as it is controversial. Like its equivalent in the United States, this literature is concerned largely with the legitimacy and justification of judicial decision making.[51]

THE DOMINANT TRADITION. Any discussion of constitutional interpretation in Germany, on or off the Constitutional Court, begins with the usual reference to the grammatical, systematic, teleological, and historical methods of analysis.[52] In resorting to one or more of these forms of argument, the Constitutional Court is drawing on the conventional approach to judicial decision in German statutory law that originated in the extreme conceptualism of the nineteenth-century school of jurisprudence known as pandectology.[53] Grammatical, or textual, analysis, often the starting point of judicial interpretation, focuses on the ordinary or technical meaning of the words and phrases in a given constitutional provision. Systematic, or structural, analysis seeks to interpret particular provisions of the Basic Law as part of a constitutional totality. Teleological, or purposive, analysis — a favored form of judicial reasoning in Germany — represents a search for the goals or aspirations behind the language of the Constitution. Finally, historical analysis involves the elucidation of the text by reference to the original intent of the framers or to the values they constitutionalized. The grammatical, historical, and systematic methods focus on textual interpretation. The teleological method, on the other hand, is a more open-ended approach to judicial decision making.

It is difficult, however, to rank these methods in any fixed order of priority. Like the American Supreme Court, the Constitutional Court uses whatever method or combination of methods seems suitable in a given situation. An exception is that in Germany, original history — that is, the intentions of the framers — is seldom dispositive in resolving the meaning of the Basic Law.[54] The court has declared that "the original history of a particular provision of the Basic Law has no decisive importance" in constitutional interpretation.[55] Original history performs, at best, the auxiliary function of lending support to a result already arrived at by other interpretive methods. When there is conflict, however, arguments based on text, structure, or teleology will prevail over those based on history.[56]

These canons of interpretation, German commentators note, are ways of discovering the "objective will" of the Constitution's framers. Even the teleological method assumes that there is, here and now, a "right" meaning of the constitutional text, although the standards used in discovering the *telos* of the Basic Law are unclear. One standard, of course, is original history, but as just noted, the "subjective will" of the framers is merely an auxiliary aid to interpretation. In truth, the teleological approach is itself susceptible to the subjectivism that the dominant tradition wishes to avoid. Karl Heinrich Friauf has observed that the teleological approach is a "gateway through which consideration of social policy and even the political philosophy of the judges flow into the interpretation of the Constitution."[57] Judges and scholars do not always so readily acknowledge the creative character of constitutional interpretation.

However, most commentators are aware of the limits of these customary methods of interpretation. As Konrad Hesse, a former justice of the Constitutional Court, has pointed out, the "objective will" thesis, so assiduously applied in statutory construction, is unsuited to constitutional interpretation.[58] For one thing, no order of priority among these methods exists when their application leads to different results. For another, as Friauf has suggested, there is no mechanical way of applying these methods to the open-ended words and phrases of the Basic Law. When these methods fail and the court is faced with a dispute involving competing constitutional values, it often resorts to ad hoc balancing. Indeed, the rhetoric of conceptual jurisprudence belies the "pragmatic, flexible and undogmatic" approach to constitutional interpretation that often characterizes the court's work.[59]

JUDICIAL FUNCTION: COMPETING VISIONS. The tension between objectivity and creativity that commentators have noticed in the court's work reflects a larger conflict between competing visions of the judicial function. Two general approaches to judicial decision making emerge from the materials in this book. The first approach, which distinguishes sharply between the functions of judge and legislator, is as familiar to Americans as it is to Germans. In this view, making law is not a part of judicial interpretation. The judge is bound to the prescribed norms of the Constitution; his task is to discover the content of these norms and then to apply them uncompromisingly, a process known as *Normgebundenheitstheorie* (theory of binding norms).[60] German no less than American justices have sought to perpetuate this traditional view of the judicial function. "The Court can only unfold what already is contained . . . in the Constitution," wrote Professor Ernst Friesenhahn, a former Constitutional Court justice.[61] "As an independent, neutral body, which renders decisions solely in terms of law, it determines the law with binding effect when it is disputed, doubted or under attack. In doing so, it bears no political responsibility, though its decisions may have great political significance."[62]

Justice Gerhard Leibholz, an influential member of the Second Senate for twenty years, also drew a bright line between "politics" and the "political law" of the Constitution.[63] He distinguished between "disputes of [a] legal-political character which can be placed under legal constitutional control" and disputes of a "purely political nature . . . which cannot be decided according to the rules of Law."[64] Consistent with the conventional German approach to constitutional review, the Constitutional Court, in Leibholz's view, is under a duty to explore every relevant fact and aspect of law in a case so as "to find the truth objectively."[65] In a similar vein, Justice Helmut Simon, a former member of the First Senate, has said that the Federal Constitutional Court "neither creates norms nor belongs to those political institutions responsible for the active structure of our common life or the future of the community. As an organ of the judiciary, its function, like that of other courts, is limited within the framework of a judicial proceeding, to the application and interpretation of laws originating in some other forum. . . . [It has no other power] except that of declaring acts of public authority constitutional or unconstitutional."[66]

Nevertheless, a number of justices and constitutional scholars have acknowledged the inherent limits of *Normgebundenheitstheorie*. Professor Konrad Hesse, appointed to the First Senate in 1975 (see Appendix B) and the author of a leading treatise in constitutional law, is openly critical of the judicial function conceived as a simple act of cognition or an objective process of discovery upon the application of a given methodology.[67] For him, constitutional interpretation is an art flowing from the interplay between text and interpreter: The judge perceives the meaning of a constitutional text as he reflects on the present in the light of constitutional language drafted within a given historical context. In the view of Justice Ernst-Wolfgang Böckenförde, a member of the Second Senate since 1983, constitutional interpretation requires a delicate balancing of competing values as well as competing theories of the polity expressed in such concepts as the liberal state, the social state, and the democratic state.[68] Justice Dieter Grimm, appointed to the First Senate in 1987, is even more candid: "There is no preestablished difference between courts and legislatures which a particular constitution has to adopt and which an interpreter has to enforce regardless of what the constitution says. In addition, constitutional courts inevitably cross the line between law and politics," because "the constitution does not offer an unambiguous and complete standard for [reviewing the validity of legislation]."[69] In Grimm's view, this reality argues for less rather than more judicial intervention by the Constitutional Court in the political and legislative arenas.

After eleven years on the court, even Justice Leibholz wrote that it would be "an illusion and . . . inadmissible formalistic positivism, to suppose that it would be possible or permissible to apply . . . general constitutional principles . . . without at the same time attempting to put them into a reasonable relationship with the given political order." "The constitutional judge cannot do anything except relate the rules [of the Basic Law] to political reality."[70] In 1971, as he was about to leave the court, Leibholz remarked that "the existing conflict between constitution and constitutional reality does not admit either of a purely legalistic solution in favor of the Constitution, or of an exclusively sociological solution in favor of constitutional reality. Rather, this conflict must be viewed as [a dialectical one] between normativity and existentiality."[71]

An even deeper political understanding of constitutional decision making emerged in a series of interviews with the justices, most of whom readily acknowledge the importance of statesmanship — a keen sense of the political — on the bench. Most consider the political consequences of their decisions and at the same time remark that such consequences can never be dispositive of a constitutional issue.[72] Justice Leibholz concedes that the constitutional judge, "more than the 'ordinary judge,' [must] understand something of the essence of politics and of those social forces which determine political life."[73] Some of the justices equate judicial statesmanship with the court's capacity to achieve consensus. President Wolfgang Zeidler, the "chief justice" of the Second Senate from 1983 to November 1987, even ventured to observe that "objectivity" in constitutional interpretation manifests itself most clearly when the justices of a given senate, who collectively represent diverse career backgrounds, ideologies, and political attachments, manage to surmount their differences and reach unanimous agreement.[74] Other justices see a dialectical process at work: The "right" answer in a given case is the product of collective decision making; a "right" or "good" decision is one that has banished disagreement in the solvent of group discussion and dialogue.[75]

The Structural Unity of the Basic Law

In its first major decision — the *Southwest State* case (1951; no. 3.1) — the Federal Constitutional Court underscored the internal coherence and structural unity of the Basic Law as a whole.[76] "No single constitutional provision may be taken out of its context and interpreted by itself," declared the court. "Every constitutional provision must always be interpreted in such a way as to render it compatible with the fundamental principles of the Constitution and the intentions of its authors."[77] Justice Gerhard Leibholz, commenting on *Southwest*, elaborated: "The Court holds that each constitutional clause is in a definite relationship with all other clauses, and that together they form an entity. It considers certain constitutional principles and basic concepts to have emerged from the whole of the Basic Law to which other constitutional regulations are subordinate."[78] In one important case the court alluded to the "unity of the Constitution as a logical-teleological entity," a concept traceable to Rudolf Smend's "integration" theory of the Constitution.[79] Smend regarded the Constitution as a living reality founded on and unified by the communal values embodied in the German nation. In Smend's theory, the Constitution not only represents a unity of values, it also functions to further integrate and unify the nation around these values.[80]

Closely related to the concept of the Constitution as a structural unity is the principle of practical concordance (*praktische Konkordanz*), according to which constitutionally protected legal values must be harmonized with one another when such values conflict. One constitutional value may not be realized at the expense of a competing constitutional value. In short, constitutional interpretation is not a zero-sum game. The value of free speech, for example, rarely attains total victory over a competing constitutional value such as the right to the development of one's personality. Both values must be preserved in creative unity. Professor Konrad Hesse wrote: "The principle of the Constitution's unity requires the optimization of [values in conflict]: Both legal values need to be limited so that each can attain its optimal effect. In each concrete case, therefore, the limitations must satisfy the principle of proportionality; that is, they may not go any further than necessary to produce a concordance of both legal values."[81]

PROPORTIONALITY. The principle of proportionality, like the concept of an objective value order discussed in the next section, is crucial to any understanding of German constitutional law. Proportionality plays a role similar to the American doctrine of due process of law. The Basic Law contains no explicit reference to proportionality, but the Constitutional Court regards it as an indispensable element of a state based on the rule of law. The court consistently invokes the principle of proportionality in determining whether legislation and other governmental acts conform to the values and principles of the Basic Law. In much of its work, the court seems less concerned with *interpreting* the Constitution—that is, defining the meaning of the documentary text—than in applying an ends-means test for determining whether a particular right has been overburdened in the light of a given set of facts. In fact, the German approach is not so different from the methodology often employed by the United States Supreme Court in fundamental rights cases.

In its German version, proportionality reasoning is a three-step process. First, whenever parliament enacts a law impinging on a basic right, the means used must be appropriate (*Eignung*) to the achievement of a legitimate end. Because rights in the Basic Law are circumscribed by duties and are often limited by objectives and values specified in the constitutional text, the Constitutional Court receives considerable guidance in determining the legitimacy of a state purpose. The sparse language of the United States Constitution, by contrast, often encourages the Supreme Court to rely on nontextual philosophical arguments to determine the validity of a state purpose that impinges on a constitutional right. Second, the means used to achieve a valid purpose must have the least restrictive effect (*Erforderlichkeit*) on a constitutional value. This test is applied flexibly and must meet the standard of rationality. As applied by the Constitutional Court, it is less than the "strict scrutiny" and more than the "minimum rationality" test of American constitutional law. Finally, the means used must be proportionate to the end. The burden on the right must not be excessive relative to the benefits secured by the state's objective (*Zumutbarkeit*).[82] This three-pronged test of proportionality seems fully compatible with, if not required by, the principle of practical concordance.

AN OBJECTIVE ORDER OF VALUES. In its search for constitutional first principles, the Constitutional Court has seen fit to interpret the Basic Law in terms of its overall structural unity. Perhaps "ideological unity" would be the more accurate term, for the Constitutional Court envisions the Basic Law as a unified structure of *substantive* values.[83] The centerpiece of this interpretive strategy is the concept of an objective order of values, a concept that derives from the gloss the Federal Constitutional Court has put on the text of the Basic Law. According to this concept, the Constitution incorporates the basic value decisions of the founders, the most basic of which is their choice of a free democratic basic order—a liberal, representative, federal, parliamentary democracy—buttressed and reinforced by basic rights and liberties. These basic values are objective because they are said to have an independent reality under the Constitution, imposing on all organs of government an affirmative duty to see that they are realized in practice.

The notion of an objective value order may be stated in another way. Every basic right in the Constitution—for example, freedom of speech, press, religion, association, and the right to property or the right to choose one's profession or occupation—has a corresponding value. A basic right is a negative right against the state, but this right also represents a value, and as a value it imposes a positive obligation on the state to ensure that it becomes an integral part of the general legal order.[84] One example may suffice: The *right* to freedom of the press protects a newspaper against any action of the state that would encroach on its independence, but as an objective *value* applicable to society as a whole, the state is duty bound to create the conditions that make freedom of the press both possible and effective. In practice, this means that the state may have to regulate the press to promote the value of democracy; for example, by enacting legislation to prevent the press from becoming the captive of any dominant group or interest.

This view of the Constitution as a hierarchical value system commands the general support of German constitutional theorists, notwithstanding intense controversy on and off the bench over the application of the theory to specific situations.[85] From some jurisprudential perspectives this theory allows the court to engage in open-ended decision making while appearing to be text-bound. It is an ingenious—some critics would say disingenuous—judicial methodology. As Clarence Mann has written, "It harbors the illusions of determinate norms in the fact [*sic*] of inarticulated value premises and of judicial neutrality aloof from the creative search for normative content," yet, in contrast to *Begriffsjurisprudenz*, it does "not necessarily exclude considerations of political reality in the construction and application of the constitution."[86] In short, it satisfies the traditional German yearning for objectivity in the sense of separating law from politics yet tolerates the search for purpose in constitutional law.

Indeed, the Constitutional Court has occasionally spoken of certain suprapositivist norms that presumably govern the entire constitutional order. In an early case decided in 1953, the court, recalling the Nazi experience, rejected "value-free legal positivism."[87] The First Senate, at that time presided over by President Josef Wintrich, an influential Catholic jurist with roots in the Thomistic tradition, appeared to accept natural law as an independent standard of review.[88] Since then, particularly when interpreting the Basic Law's equality clauses, the court has tended to speak more of "justice" or the "fundamental principles of justice."[89] Some constitutional cases, however, appear to defend such principles on a theory of legal positivism where the reference is to positive constitutional norms of lower and higher rank. In this reckoning the value order of the Basic Law is an essential part of the positive legal order. Still, it is not altogether clear from the court's jurisprudence whether the suprapositivist norms underlying the Constitution exist outside the text, reflect the express values of the text, or account for the hierarchical order that the court has discerned among the values constitutionalized by the framers. Whatever the answer, the hierarchical system of values found to inhere in the Basic Law is itself largely a product of constitutional interpretation.

UNCONSTITUTIONAL CONSTITUTIONAL AMENDMENT. One doctrine that has emerged from viewing the Constitution as a structural unity and a hierarchical system of values is the concept of the unconstitutional constitutional amendment.[90] The doctrine holds that even a constitutional amendment would be unconstitutional were it to conflict with the core values or spirit of the Basic Law as a whole. Some see this as a contradiction in terms; others find a textual basis for such a construction in those unamendable provisions of the Basic Law harboring the highest values of the constitutional polity. The Constitutional Court accepted the concept of the unconstitutional constitutional amendment as valid doctrine in the *Article 117* case (1953).[91] It has figured more recently in the *Klass* case (1970), in which dissenting justices were prepared to invalidate an amendment to Article 10 of the Basic Law limiting the "inviolable" right of "privacy of posts and telecommunications."[92]

The doctrine of the unconstitutional constitutional amendment is one of several unwritten constitutional principles the court has deduced from the overall structure of the Basic Law. Other examples are the principles of federal comity, the party state, and militant democracy. Comity has been inferred from the Basic Law's general structure of federal-state relationships (see chapter 3), the party state from the language of Article 21 (see chapter 5), and militant democracy from the oft-repeated words "free liberal democratic order" (see chapter 5). These are also among the highest values of the German polity, and they have taken their place along with other fundamental norms found within the objective value order of the Basic Law.

THEORY OF BASIC RIGHTS. In the seminal *Lüth* case (1958; no. 8.1), the Constitutional Court remarked that the Basic Law's objective system of values "expresses and reinforces the validity of the [enumerated] basic rights."[93] Given the importance of this system, declared the court, these objective values "must apply as a constitutional axiom throughout the whole legal system," influencing private as well as public law. The court ruled that while basic rights apply *directly* to state action, they apply *indirectly* to substantive private law. Accordingly, in deciding conflicts between private parties, judges are obligated to consider the "radiating effect" of basic rights on third parties (*Drittwirkung*). In private-law disputes, then, the interpretation of private law must be consistent with the objective values underlying guaranteed basic rights.

A collateral search for a coherent theory of basic rights (*Grundsrechtstheorie*) has also evolved out of the concept of an objective system of values. The attempt to construct a coherent theory of rights, however, confronts an interpretive difficulty. For one thing, open-ended words and phrases like "democracy," "constitutional order" and, above all, "free democratic basic order," are indeterminate concepts. Additionally, under the Basic Law, persons have duties as well as rights, but rights and duties are not easily reconciled. Developing a philosophically coherent jurisprudence of rights under any circumstance is a difficult task. To do so in the light of the text of the Basic Law is even more difficult.

In truth, German constitutional theorists have advanced five normative theories of basic rights: liberal, institutional, value oriented, democratic, and social.[94] Each finds some support in the literature of constitutional theory; each draws some support from particular decisions of the Federal Constitutional Court.[95] Liberal theory, based on postulates of economic liberty and enlightened self-determination, emphasizes the negative rights of the individual against the state. Institutional theory focuses on guaranteed rights associated with organizations or communities such as religious groups, the media, universities (research and teaching), and marriage and the family. Value-oriented theory places its emphasis on human dignity as it relates to rights flowing from the nature of the human personality. Democratic theory is concerned with certain political functions incident to the rights of speech and association and the role of elections and political parties. Social theory, finally, highlights the importance of social justice, cultural rights, and economic security. Not surprisingly, scholars and judges have linked each of these theories to one or another of the conceptions of state discussed earlier.

It is possible through interpretation to regard one of these five theories as dominant. Yet each, like each conception of the state, has some basis in the text of the Basic Law. Like their counterparts in the United States, many constitutional theorists expend considerable energy debating whether or not there is an "objectively" correct interpretation of the Basic Law's fundamental rights provisions. For its part, the Constitutional Court seems content to decide human rights disputes on a case-by-case basis, using what it regards as the most convincing argument or theory available in a given situation. The justices can easily draw on the logic of any of the five theories, for they are not wholly inconsistent with one another. Tensions between them do exist, and much of the work product of the Federal Constitutional Court described in this book is best understood as a playing out of these tensions.

JUDICIAL REVIEW IN OPERATION

A major function of constitutional theory in Germany, as in the United States, is to resolve "the tension between representative democracy and constitutional review in a way that both justifie[s] and regulate[s] their coexistence."[96] Numerous commentators have sought to mark the boundary between legislation and constitutional adjudication and to comprehend the fine line that the Federal Constitutional Court has drawn between law and politics.[97] The following discussion summarizes the strategies devised to temper judicial activism with restraint and thus to preserve the creative coexistence between democracy and constitutionalism.

The Scope of Review

The Constitutional Court renders its decisions largely in declaratory form. In cases of major importance it may issue a temporary injunction against a political department of the government, pending the clarification of a constitutional question. The court normally confines itself, however, to declaring laws null and void or simply incompatible with some particular provision of the Basic Law. As noted earlier, the court is unbound by any case or controversy requirement. By remaining on the high road of broad-ranging, principled declarations, the court in a sense elevates the status of the parties, assuming their moral autonomy in the face of decision. As Justice Hans G. Rupp explained: "The only marshal there is to enforce the court's ruling is its moral authority, the conscience of the parties concerned, and in the last resort, the people's respect for law and good government. It is mainly this limitation which renders it less objectionable to let a court settle legal issues which are closely connected with domestic or international politics."[98]

Apart from this limitation, the Constitutional Court follows a number of guidelines analogous to certain maxims of judicial self-restraint advanced by Justice Brandeis in *Ashwander* v. *Tennessee Valley Authority*.[99] For example, the rule that the United States Supreme Court will not pass upon the constitutionality of legislation in a nonadversary proceeding has its equivalent in the Constitutional Court's refusal to decide moot questions. We have seen that concrete judicial-review references must arise within the framework of actual litigation. The justiciability of a constitutional complaint likewise depends on certain attributes of concreteness and particularity. Even cases coming before the court on abstract judicial review require real conflicts of opinion within or among governing institutions.

By the same token, the court will not anticipate a question of constitutional law in advance of the necessity for deciding it. In short, while every case properly before the court involves a constitutional question, the court usually refrains from deciding ancillary constitutional issues not yet ripe for decision. For example, the court may strike down a particular federal regulation interfering with a state's administration of federal law but decline to set forth the general conditions under which federal administrative control would prevail.[100] The court also is reluctant to issue tempo-

rary injunctions against government agencies about to engage in allegedly unconstitutional behavior, preferring as a matter of strategy to allow the challenged activity to proceed until the court has had time to consider the matter on its merits.[101]
Yet here, as with much of its authority, the court's sense of self-restraint is the only
check on the exercise of its power.

American legal scholars will recognize other *Ashwander* maxims in the court's
general approach to constitutional disputes. A leading principle of judicial review in
Germany obliges the court to interpret statutes, when possible, in conformity with
the Basic Law (*Pflicht zur verfassungskonformen Auslegung*).[102] If a statute lends itself
to alternative constructions for and against its constitutionality, the court follows
the reading that saves the statute, unless the saving construction distorts the meaning of its provisions. The court also has stated on numerous occasions that it will not
substitute its judgment of sound or wise public policy for that of the legislature,[103] a
rule particularly relevant in equal protection analysis. Nor will statutes be overturned simply because the legislature may have inaccurately predicted the consequences of social or economic policy. As the *Codetermination* (1978; no. 6.6)
and *Kalkar I* (1978; no. 4.6) cases make plain,[104] the court grants a generous mar-
gin of error to the legislature. It will uphold an ordinary statute unless the statute
clearly violates the principle of proportionality (*Verhältnismässigkeit*), the rule of law
(*Rechtsstaatlichkeit*), or some related principle of justice such as legal security, clarity,
or predictability.[105]

The court applies these same principles with respect to laws examined in the
course of ordinary civil and criminal proceedings. In addition, the justices have
developed several rules for limiting the number of referrals (*Vorlageverfahren*) from
courts of law.[106] One such rule requires lower courts to certify statutes for review
when they are convinced that the law under which a dispute arises is unconstitutional,[107] but only when a ruling of unconstitutionality would change the outcome
of the case. Another is that only statutes passed since the ratification of the Basic
Law qualify as subjects of concrete judicial review to be decided by the Constitutional Court. Any court may review and nullify on constitutional grounds pre-1949
legislation as well as administrative regulations and local ordinances. These so-called
preconstitutional laws rank lower than laws passed since May 23, 1949.[108] The
Constitutional Court has ruled, however, that such laws are within the scope of its
concrete review procedure when they have been reenacted or substantially amended
under the Basic Law. The appropriate parties may nevertheless challenge an un-
touched preconstitutional law in an *abstract* judicial-review proceeding.[109]

Finally, while the court does not enjoy discretion akin to the *certiorari* power of
the Supreme Court, it does have limited control over its docket through the three-
judge chambers. Since 1993, the chambers have been empowered to decide concrete
review cases, provided the decision conforms to rules already laid down in previous
decisions by the senates. (In 1994, the chambers heard twenty of the twenty-eight
judicial references decided by the senates.) In addition, as we saw in chapter 1, these

chambers may reject trivial constitutional complaints as well as those unlikely to result in any clarification of an important constitutional question. Most constitutional complaints stem from judicial decisions. In reviewing such decisions, the court has steadfastly maintained that it will not act as a general court of review (*Revisionsgericht*).[110] Ordinary errors of fact and law are not reviewable by the Federal Constitutional Court. On the other hand, an arbitrary finding of facts or a wholly unreasonable application of the law in a given case would not survive constitutional analysis. But where a complainant raises a constitutional issue under another court's reasonable interpretation of an ordinary law, the Constitutional Court usually confines itself to a determination of whether the lower court adequately considered the values of the Basic Law. The court will usually sustain the lower court's judgment if that court assessed the statute in the full light of the relevant constitutional values.[111]

Form and Effect of Decisions

The court applies most principles of constitutional interpretation with considerable flexibility and prudence. On first impression, however, and contrary to the canons of judicial restraint mentioned in the previous section, the court's decision-making record might suggest a tribunal embarked on a path of relentless activism. By January 1, 1992, the court had invalidated 423 laws and administrative regulations (or particular provisions thereof) under the Basic Law (see table 2.1). Of these negative rulings, the First Senate decided 243 and the Second Senate 180, nearly 70 percent of which involved provisions of federal law, a figure explained by the predominant lawmaking role of the federal government in nearly every major area of public policy. The large majority of these rulings admittedly involved minor legal provisions, but a fair number featured important public policies in fields such as education, taxation, employment, social insurance, and labor law.[112]

As table 2.1 indicates, the Constitutional Court may hold laws or regulations

Table 2.1. Invalidated Legal Provisions, 1951–1989

| | Federal law | | State law | | |
	Void	Incompatible	Void	Incompatible	Total
Senate					
First	108	81	37	17	243
Second	65	39	54	22	180
Total	173	119	91	39	423

Source: Compiled from statistical summaries provided by administrative offices of the Federal Constitutional Court (1992; typescript).

Note: The figures include laws (*Gesetz*) and administrative regulations (*Verordnungen*).

that it considers unconstitutional either null and void (*nichtig*) or incompatible (*unvereinbar*) with the Basic Law. When held to be *nichtig,* the statute immediately ceases to operate; when declared *unvereinbar,* the statute or legal norm is held to be unconstitutional but not void, and it remains in force during a transition period pending its correction by the legislature, a decisional mode that now has the sanction of law and, as the table shows, is an option the court frequently exercises.[113]

These overrulings, however, are dwarfed by the number of laws or statutory norms that the court has sustained over the years. With respect to laws that are upheld, the court distinguishes between so-called unobjectionable (*unbeanstandeten*) norms and those held to be in conformity with the Basic Law. Unobjectional norms are those the court sustains in the normal course of deciding constitutional complaints. The other category includes statutory provisions questioned in concrete review cases but sustained in accordance with the principle that requires the court to interpret a norm consistent with the Basic Law. Between 1951 and 1993 these unobjectionable and *verfassungskonforme* statutory provisions numbered 1,367.[114]

The practice of declaring a legal provision unconstitutional but not void is one of two strategies used by the court to soften the political impact of its decisions. This first strategy uses admonitory decisions (*Appellentscheidung*) to tender advice to parliament with respect to statutes or legislative omissions that run afoul of the Basic Law or are likely to do so.[115] This strategy of declaring a law or practice unconstitutional but not void is designed to prevent the greater hardship or inconvenience that would flow from the complete voidance of a statute. How long and under what conditions an unconstitutional but unvoided law can remain in force is a matter the court reserves to itself to decide. The court usually sets a deadline for corrective legislative action and occasionally directs parliament to adopt a specific solution. More often the court lays down the general guidelines within which parliament is required to legislate.[116]

Under the second strategy, the court actually sustains a challenged statute but warns the legislature that it will void it in the future unless the legislature acts to amend or repeal the law. Cases employing this decisional mode often involve equal protection claims arising out of statutes that deny benefits or privileges to some persons while conferring them on others.[117] Such decisions are prudential judgments designed to give the legislature time to adjust to changing conditions or to avoid the political or economic chaos that might result from a declaration of unconstitutionality. By resorting to this procedure, the court keeps the constitutional dialogue going and furnishes parliament with the flexibility it needs to work out creative solutions to the problem under scrutiny.

In some situations, however, when the court declares a statute unconstitutional and void, rather than keeping parliament in a quandary as to what alternative policy or program would survive constitutional analysis, it tenders "advice" that leaves little discretion to lawmakers.[118] In the important *Party Finance* case (1966) it went so far as to tell parliament that federal funding would have to be provided to minor political parties securing 0.5 percent of all votes cast in a federal election instead of the 1.5 percent limit previously established by law.[119] In the well-known first *Abortion* case (1975; no. 7.10), which invalidated a permissive abortion statute, the court effectively rewrote the law, which parliament subsequently felt obliged to pass. This practice, as noted in the next section, has come under increasing criticism in Germany.

These rulings, like all of the court's decisions, including those that declare a statute or other legal provision compatible with the Basic Law, have the force of law, and as a consequence bind all branches and levels of government.[120] In the *Southwest State* case (1951; no. 3.1) the court made it clear that the binding effect of its decisions also bars the legislature from reenacting a law after it has been declared unconstitutional. The binding effect principle applies to the actual ruling of a case and to the "essential" reasoning or rationale on which it is based. What constitutes "essential reasoning," however, is not always clear. It does not embrace all arguments marshaled in support of a given result, although it seems to include those basic standards of review in terms of which a law is sustained or nullified, for these standards bind courts of law in their own interpretation of ordinary law.[121] The one exception to the binding effect rule is the Federal Constitutional Court itself. (The rule of *stare decisis* does not bind the German judiciary.) While reluctant to depart from principles laid down in its case law, the court will readily do so if convinced that it erred in an earlier ruling. Indeed, as the *Census Act* case (1983; no. 7.6) underscores, constitutional provisions may themselves take on new significance in the light of changing social conditions.

Whenever the Constitutional Court strikes down a law in whole or in part, the effect is prospective (*ex tunc*). This rule is qualified, however, by a provision of the FCCA that permits new trials in criminal cases in which a court convicts a defendant under a subsequently voided statute.[122] Statutes declared incompatible with the Basic Law but not void may continue to be enforced, but only under conditions laid down by the Constitutional Court. The effect of such decisions on other courts is substantial; they may not proceed with pending cases arising under such statutes until the legislature has amended or corrected the statute in conformity with the guidelines set by the Constitutional Court.[123]

It is important to remember that the Constitutional Court's rulings are exclusively declaratory. The FCCA includes a provision that actually bars any direct enforcement of the court's rulings.[124] Its decisions are "enforceable" through ordinary legislation and judicial proceedings. It is well to remember also that the court's jurisdiction is compulsory. It lacks a storehouse of "passive virtues" by which it might for prudential reasons avoid a ruling on a constitutional issue.[125] Moreover, the court's declaratory authority is sweeping, for it is at liberty to range beyond the immediate issue before it and review the constitutionality of any part of a statute challenged in an abstract or concrete judicial-review proceeding. To link judicial power of this character with direct executive implementation would pose an enormous threat to representative democracy in Germany. The court's ultimate legitimacy in the German system, as noted earlier, rests on its moral authority and the willingness of the political arms of the government to follow its mandates.

The court's own sense of self-restraint is another key to its acceptance and durability. But the court is faced with a dilemma. If it is to perform its steering and integrative role in the German system, objectify the values of the Basic Law, and bring constitutional normativity into conformity with constitutional reality, it must rule, according to the modern German version of the *Rechtsstaat,* on a properly presented constitutional issue, even though such a ruling may thrust it headlong into a politically exposed position. The court has learned to cope with this politically exposed position. For example, in cases involving disputes between high constitutional organs (i.e., separation of powers, or *Organstreit,* proceedings) or those brought by political minorities on abstract judicial review, the court occasionally makes an ally of time, delaying decision until the controversy loses its urgency or is settled by political means, prompting the initiating party ultimately to withdraw the case. Largely because of this tactic, the court has decided, up to 1995, only 51 of the 107 *Organstreit* proceedings and 68 of the 124 abstract review proceedings submitted to it.

JUDICIAL REVIEW AND THE POLITY

As this summary of constitutional review suggests, and as subsequent chapters show, the Constitutional Court is at the epicenter of Germany's constitutional democracy. "The Basic Law is now virtually identical with its interpretation by the Federal Constitutional Court," remarked Professor Rudolf Smend on the court's tenth anniversary.[126] Already by the 1990s Smend's view was conventional wisdom among German public lawyers and constitutional scholars. Most scholars and legal professionals accept the court as a legitimate participant in the larger community decision-making process, a remarkable achievement of postwar institution building in the Federal Republic. Professor Christian Starck, one of the Basic Law's leading commentators, described this consensus when he referred to the court as the "crowning completion of the constitutional state" and applauded its "decisive influence upon the development of our constitutional law."[127]

We may hazard some guesses as to why West Germany's legal community accepts the court as the final, authoritative interpreter of the Basic Law. First, and most obvious, the court functions as a specialized constitutional tribunal, with clear authority derived from the constitutional charter itself. Second, a democratic legislature chooses the members of the court just as it controls the court's organization and procedures. Constitutionally prescribed recruitment procedures all but guarantee that the court will consist of members acceptable to the established political parties and be broadly representative of established political interests, including the interests of the states as corporate entities within the German system. Third, after years of experimentation with various terms of office, including life tenure for justices elected from the federal courts, Germans settled for a simple, nonrenewable term of twelve years for each justice, the effect of which is to secure both the court's independence and a continuing membership profile not too unlike that of parliament itself. Finally, parliament permitted the introduction of dissenting opinions in 1971 — a practice barred in all other German courts — one sign of the growing maturity of German constitutional jurisprudence.

At the same time, the Constitutional Court, like the United States Supreme Court, often finds itself in the eye of a political storm. Despite its democratic legitimacy, or perhaps because of it, the Constitutional Court has developed into a fiercely independent institution and has struck down large numbers of statutory provisions and administrative regulations. A veritable *Blitzkrieg* of public lectures, newspaper and television commentaries, articles in legal periodicals — some authored by former justices — and legal monographs have criticized the court, although for the most part respectfully, for "judicializing politics" or "politicizing justice."[128] Some of these publications take the court to task for many of its admonitory decisions, which in the view of some critics have turned the court into a quasi-legislative institution. The *Abortion I, Party Finance IV, Census Act, East-West Basic Treaty,* and *Higher Education Admission* cases are examples of decisions faulted for improperly exceeding the limits of judicial power.[129] Even more devastating, other critics have charged, is the court's dampening effect on legislative confidence and mobility. Some argue that parliament legislates too much in the shadow of the court, fearful that its laws may run afoul of some judicial order, standard, or admonition.[130] These critics point to the tendency of legislators to tailor their work to anticipated court decisions and to scrutinize constitutional cases for hints on how to shape public policy. If this tendency does prevail, the court's role in the polity is not exhausted by an analysis simply of its formal powers or its case law. The mere presence of the court would seem to inhibit certain kinds of legislative activity.

This criticism, harsh as it is, is nevertheless predicated on a shared commitment to the court as an institution. There is another stream of commentary, however, identified mainly but not exclusively with neo-Marxist critics, that manifests far less sympathy for the court's institutional roles in German politics. In the eyes of these critics, the court serves as a brake on social change and is the main force responsible for the imposition of a constitutional ideology that sanctifies consolidation and stability, defends the status quo, and promotes consensus politics. There may be some grounds for this criticism, for the court has often used its power — with prominent exceptions duly noted in the following chapters — to invalidate reforms regarded as progressive and liberalizing by large segments of German society.[131]

Still, the court's prestige appears to be very high. A series of public opinion polls taken in recent years shows that it enjoys substantially more public trust than any other major political or social institution, including parliament, the military establishment, the regular judiciary, the television industry, and even churches and universities.[132] This public trust is also evident in the former East German regime. East Germans are making appeals to the Constitutional Court in increasing numbers, just as the court, on a number of occasions mentioned in later chapters, has vindicated constitutional claims originating in the new eastern states. The absence of any major political effort to curtail the court's powers despite its location at the center of many political storms is perhaps another manifestation of its general support throughout Germany. Even proposals by respected academic figures to abolish the court's controversial abstract judicial-review jurisdiction,[133] which the court could well do without in light of the political manipulation that often accompanies the invocation of this procedure, has fallen on deaf ears.

The Constitutional Court's durability is traceable to more than general public support. The court owes much to West Germany's community of scholars, despite the acerbic pens of some writers. The literature on the court, ranging from doctrinal controversy in professional journals to informed media accounts of particular cases, is comparable to the volume and sophistication of commentary on the United States Supreme Court. German commentators form an ever-widening interpretive community organized around a deepening interest in the court's work. According to Professor Peter Häberle, among the most learned of Germany's judicial scholars, the commentators see themselves engaged in a common enterprise with the Federal Constitutional Court.[134] Their constructive criticism and increasing assertiveness have been stimulated in part by the use and popularity of the court's own dissenting opinions.[135]

The high-spirited give-and-take between the justices and the commentators has become an important element in the growing maturity of German constitutional law and consciousness. That both court and commentators see themselves engaged in actualizing the Constitution in the public life of the nation undoubtedly reflects the authoritative role of constitutional commentary in argumentation before the court and in the general influence of the professorate on and off the bench. The court's twenty-fifth anniversary celebration was an important symbol of this cooperation between bench and academy: Professor Christian Starck, a former law clerk to Justice Herbert Scholtissek and himself a leading commentator on the Basic Law, delivered a brief address before the assembled justices in the name of all German constitutional scholars,[136] while Chief Justice Ernst Benda in response acknowledged the "critical importance" of their "partnership" with the justices in contributing to the court's total work product.[137]

PART II

CONSTITUTIONAL STRUCTURES AND

RELATIONSHIPS

Chapters 3, 4, and 5 focus on what may be regarded as the structural provisions of the Basic Law. These provisions include the framers' most significant innovations, among them the general scheme of separated and divided powers, the constructive vote of no-confidence, the limits on presidential authority, the creation of the Federal Constitutional Court, and the ban on unconstitutional political parties. Later, in the form of constituent legislation, German political leaders also introduced a new electoral system combining elements of majoritarian and proportional representation. This careful attention to institutional structures and relationships is not surprising. After the Third Reich, Germans were primarily interested in creating a constitution that would bring about stability, democracy, and limited government.

They sought to achieve stability by strengthening the position of the chancellor, by doing away with plebiscitary institutions such as national referenda and the direct election of the president, and by establishing mechanisms designed to avoid the excessive fragmentation of the electorate and to keep splinter parties out of parliament. They endeavored to bring about a more responsible democracy through representative institutions, free and equal elections, and a chancellor responsible to parliament. Finally, they hoped to create a *constitutional* democracy by installing an entrenched bill of rights, limiting the power to amend the Basic Law, and establishing a supreme constitutional tribunal whose decisions would have the force of law.

Federalism and separation of powers are the controlling principles of German constitutionalism. Both principles are deeply anchored in Germany's constitutional tradition. What is new about their reincarnation in the Basic Law is their linkage, in Article 20, to the ideas of democracy and justice as well as to the more traditional principle of the rule of law. The adoption of federalism as a mainstay of the new polity reflected postwar Germany's determination to avoid the extremes of particularism and authoritarianism. Too little power at the center would inhibit, as it did throughout most of German history, the full flowering of parliamentary democracy, whereas too much power at the center would retard the growth of constitutionalism. Separation of powers in turn was expected to moderate the exercise of power at all levels of government and thus prevent the reemergence of political absolutism. Fused with democracy and bound by justice, the two principles were calculated to lock liberty and the rule of law in a firm mutual embrace.

Chapters 3 and 4 deal, respectively, with federalism and separation of powers. Particular subjects taken up in chapter 3 are the organization of the federal territory and admission of new states (including the GDR's accession to the FRG), the distribution of power between national and state governments, the doctrine of federal comity, Germany's distinctive brand of administrative federalism, and the role of the Bundesrat. Chapter 5 takes up the subject of representative democracy. The materials presented deal mainly with the interpretation of the constitutional provisions related to elections and representation, the ban on unconstitutional political parties, election campaign spending, and the corporate rights of political parties within state and federal legislatures. Inasmuch as this chapter deals with the rights of voters and political parties, it constitutes a transition that links the structural concerns of part 2 with the materials on civil liberties in part 3.

3

FEDERALISM

Federalism in Germany is not a new creation of the Basic Law. Modern German history can be traced through successive stages of economic and political unity, beginning with the Confederation of 1815 and ending with the highly unified federation represented by the Weimar Republic.[1] The desire for economic integration provided the driving force behind the development of German federalism. Customs unions, uniform economic legislation, and laws designed to protect industry against parochial pressures helped to create a common market and a common identity among a people historically fractured by a multiplicity of sovereign kingdoms and principalities.[2] Much of this integration, however — as well as the political unity that accompanied it — was achieved under the dominance of Prussia, a German state known for its militaristic and authoritarian tradition as well as its efficient bureaucracy. After World War II the Allies decided to break up Prussia in the hope of establishing greater equality among the states.

TERRITORIAL ORGANIZATION

NOTE: FEDERALISM IN PERPETUITY. The principle of federalism, like that of democracy, is permanently incorporated into the Basic Law. Article 79 (3) prohibits any amendment to the Basic Law that would affect the division of the federal territory into states (*Länder*). Germany now comprises sixteen constituent states. Prior to reunification, West Germany included the states of Baden-Württemberg, Bavaria, Berlin, Bremen, Hamburg, Hesse, Lower Saxony, North Rhine–Westphalia, Rhineland-Palatinate, Saarland, and Schleswig-Holstein. Bavaria and the city-states of Hamburg and Bremen — and now Berlin — correspond to their historical borders. Schleswig-Holstein also contains much of its former territory, as do the new states of Brandenburg, Mecklenburg–Western Pomerania, Saxony, Saxony-Anhalt, and Thuringia. The remaining states were carved artificially out of postwar zones of occupation assigned to the United States, Great Britain, and France, yet these boundaries have proven remarkably durable. The reorganization of the southwestern states in 1952, the subject of the *Southwest State* case (no. 3.1), has been the only major change in the original borders. Several proposals have been advanced over the years to consolidate the existing states into larger and more integrated political and economic units, but none of these master plans for federal reorganization has succeeded.[3] With regard to the western *Länder,* Philip Blair noted that they "have taken root so firmly that [such plans] can scarcely be regarded as still a practical possibility."[4] A possibility in the near future, however, is the merger of the eastern *Länder* of Brandenburg and Berlin, a measure already approved by the legislatures of the two states.

Article 29 of the Basic Law provides that "the federal territory may be reorganized to ensure that the states by their size and capacity are able effectively to fill the functions incumbent upon them." Any proposal for redrawing state boundary lines needs the sanction of federal law and the approval of the majority of the voters in the affected states. Under the terms of Article 29 (3), however, two-thirds of the voters in the particular area affected by such a proposal may by their approval overcome a majority vote against it in any one of the affected states "unless in the entire territory of the affected *Land* a majority of two-thirds rejects the modification."

The *Southwest State* case arose out of the decision of the Allied powers to divide the former states of Württemberg and Baden into three southwestern states: Württemberg-Baden, Baden, and Württemberg-Hohenzollern. Germans bridled over this arrangement because it split up two historic states, sundering a relatively integrated political community. Article 118 of the Basic Law sought to cope with this situation. A *lex specialis,* it modified the general policy of Article 29 by authorizing the southwestern states to reorganize themselves by mutual agreement.[5] The most likely possibilities were the restoration of the former states of Baden and Württemberg and the consolidation of the three existing states into a single state. Unable to agree on a plan of reorganization, the states effectively turned the matter over to the federal government. Article 118 empowered the federal government to reorganize these states by law in the absence of a tri-state agreement.[6]

Southwest arose under an earlier version of Article 29. In its original form it required the reorganization of the federal territory as a whole by federal law. A majority of voters in an area affected by a proposed boundary change had to approve the proposal in a referendum. In addition, Article 29 (4) required the Bundestag to reintroduce the law if it should be rejected by the voters; if it was reenacted, a majority of voters would have to approve the measure in a national referendum. Article 118, as noted, circumvented these procedures with respect to the reorganization of the southwestern states.

3.1 Southwest State Case (1951)
1 BVerfGE 14

[When tri-state negotiations collapsed in November 1950, the federal government enacted two reorganization statutes. The first extended the terms of the Württemberg-Hohenzollern and Baden legislatures, a measure designed to avoid new state elections in April 1951 because reorganization was likely to be approved; the second specified the procedures by which the proposed referendum would be carried out. The proposal provided for merging the three states into the single state of Baden-Württemberg, subject to the approval of a majority of voters in three of four electoral districts established for purposes of the referendum. The small and cohesive 150-year-old state of Baden challenged the constitutionality of these statutes on the ground that they violated the principles of democracy and federalism: democracy because the electoral districts were created in such a way as to dilute the votes of persons casting ballots in Baden; federalism because the federal government is powerless to tamper with the legislature of an independent state.]

Judgment of the Second Senate. . . .

D. [First Reorganization Law]. . . .

2. . . . An individual constitutional provision cannot be considered as an isolated clause and interpreted alone. A constitution has an inner unity, and the meaning of any one part is linked to that of other provisions. Taken as a unit, a constitution reflects certain overarching principles and fundamental decisions to which individual provisions are subordinate. Article 79 (3) makes it clear that the Basic Law makes this assumption. Thus this court agrees with the statement of the Bavarian Constitutional Court: "That a constitutional provision itself may be null and void is not conceptually impossible just because it is a part of the Constitution. There are constitutional principles that are so fundamental and so much an expression of a law that has precedence even over the Constitution that they also bind the framers of the Constitution, and other constitutional provisions that do not rank so high may be null and void because they contravene these principles." From this rule of interpretation, it follows that any constitutional provision must be interpreted in such a way that it is compatible with those elementary principles and with the basic decisions of the framers of the Constitution. This rule applies also to Article 118.

3. The Basic Law has chosen democracy as the basis for the governmental system (Articles 20, 28): The Federal Republic is a democratic, federal state. The constitutional order in the states must conform to the principles of a democratic state based on the rule of law within the meaning of the Basic Law. The federation guarantees that the constitutional order of the states will conform to this political order.

As prescribed by the Basic Law, democracy requires not only that parliament control the government but also that the right to vote of eligible voters is not removed or impaired by unconstitutional means. . . . It is true that the democratic principle does not imply that the term of a state legislature must not exceed four years or that it cannot be extended for important reasons. But this principle does require that the term of a state legislature, whose length was set by the people in accepting their constitution, can be extended only through procedures prescribed in that constitution, i.e., only with the consent of the people.

If the federation prevents an election scheduled by the state constitution without the consent of the people of the state, then it violates the fundamental right of a citizen in a democratic state, the right to vote, as protected by Article 28 (3) of the Basic Law.

4. Another fundamental principle of the Basic Law is that of federalism (Articles 20, 18, 30). As members of the federation, *Länder* are states with their own sovereign power. This power, even if limited in subject matter, is not derived from the federation but recognized by it. As long as it remains within the framework of Article 28 (1), a state's constitutional order falls within the state's jurisdiction. In particular, it is exclusively incumbent upon the state to determine the rules that govern the formation of the state's constitutional organs and their functions. Th[e] state's competency also includes setting regulations which determine how often and on what occasions citizens may vote as well as when and under what conditions the term of a state legislature expires. . . .

This rule also applies equally to legislation [enacted] pursuant to Article 118. It is true that, in order to effect reorganization, the federal legislature has power to "retrench" the states of Baden, Württemberg-Baden, and Württemberg-Hohenzollern. But it cannot disturb the constitutional structures of these states as long as they exist in their entirety.

One may not argue that, by eliminating the three state legislatures in the process of reorganization, the federation shortens their terms of office and consequently can also extend them for a transitional period.

. . . Elimination of the state legislatures is a necessary consequence of the elimination of these states; thus [this act] does not constitute a curtailment of [the legislatures'] terms of office. By contrast, extension of the legislative terms may occur with respect to existing state legislatures. This extension requires a special legislative act which the federation cannot pass for the aforementioned reasons. A state cannot dispose of its legislative authority. And the federation cannot by virtue of a state's consent obtain legislative authority which the Basic Law does not grant. Therefore, the fact that Württemberg-Hohenzollern consented to the measure taken by the federation is without legal significance.

5. Article 118 [2] authorizes the federal legislature only to regulate "reorganization" and thus draws constitutional limits. . . . The federal legislature could extend the electoral terms of the state legislatures only if . . . the "matter cannot be effectively regulated by legislation of individual states" [Article 72 (2) of the Basic Law]. This limitation precludes extending the terms of state legislatures. . . . Such authority remains primarily a matter for the states. . . .

6. In view of these legal restraints, reasons neither of practicality, political necessity, nor similar considerations can confer unfettered discretion on the federal

legislature to enact any regulations that seem reasonable and proper under the guise of reorganizing states. . . .

7. . . . The Federal Constitutional Court must hold a legal provision null and void if it is inconsistent with the Basic Law. Hence we declare that the First Reorganization Law . . . is null and void. . . . This declaration has legal force and is to be published in the *Federal Law Gazette*. This declaration, along with the main reasons for the decision, bind[s] all constitutional organs of the federation . . . in such a way that legislative bodies may not again deliberate upon and enact a federal law with the same content, nor can the federal president promulgate such a law.

E. [Second Reorganization Law]. . . .

8. (a) It has been asserted that a federation cannot eliminate a member state against its population's will. As a rule, a federal constitution guarantees the existence and territory of member states. But the Basic Law expressly deviates from this rule. Article 79 (3) guarantees as an inviolable principle only that the federation must be divided "into states." The Basic Law does not contain any guarantee for presently existing states and their borders. On the contrary, it provides—as follows from Articles 29 and 118—for changes in territorial conditions of individual states as well as for a reorganization of federal territory which may entail the elimination of one or more existing states. This reorganization may even be effected against the will of the population of the state concerned. . . . The Basic Law thus espouses a "changeable federal state." . . .

(b) It follows from Article 29 (4), however, that an ordinary federal law cannot supersede the will of a member state's population—only a new vote of the federal legislature and a referendum of the entire federal population can do so. Thus only the will of the population of the higher unit suffices, and not merely the will of the population of one or several neighboring states.

The question [necessarily] arises, whether this principle also applies to regulations pursuant to Article 118 [2]. The provision that protects a state's existence is an outgrowth of the Basic Law's principle of federalism. . . . This determination impeding interference with a state's existence flows from the federalistic principle set forth in the Constitution and is thus an important basic constitutional decision. This— the legislative history of Article 118 which emerged from Article 29 only at the end of deliberations in the Parliamentary Council in the fourth reading of the law—as well as the generally accepted view that the principles contained in Article 29 (1) are also to be applied to regulations pursuant to Article 118, could speak for the [proposition] that the principle contained in Article 29 (4) also applies to Article 118. On the other hand, the framers of the Basic Law . . . expressly declared in Article 118 that reorganization may "deviat[e] from the provisions of Article 29." . . . But, in particular, the deliberations in the Parliamentary Council [which framed the Basic Law], the public discussion in the past few years, and consultations among the three state governments produced a general consensus that present public law conditions in the southwest area were especially unsatisfactory and therefore ripe for immediate reorganization. Consequently, [the consensus of the people] was to endorse a fast and simple reorganization. The opposition of one state's population must not frustrate this [reorganization]. . . .

(c) Baden claims that, aside from the principle contained in Article 29 (4), other clauses of the Basic Law recognize the democratic principle (Articles 20, 28). . . . Democracy means self-determination of the people. [The Second Reorganization Law, Baden argues,] deprives the people of Baden of this right because it forces them to become part of a southwest state against their will.

That, in principle, a people must themselves determine their basic order . . . certainly follows from the notion of democracy. . . . The state of Baden, as a member of the federation, is a state to which necessarily belongs a body politic. This body politic . . . possesses the right of self-determination. It is decisive, however, that Baden as a member state of a federation is not autonomous and independent but is part of a federal order which restricts its sovereign power in various respects. . . . To a certain extent a tension exists between the principles of democracy and federalism concerning the position of a member state in the federation. There can be a compromise between the two only if both suffer certain restrictions. In the case of reorganization of federal territory consigned to the federation, it is the nature of things that the people's right to self-determination in a state be restricted in the interest of the more comprehensive unit. Within the scope of what is possible in a federal state, the Basic Law's provisions in Article 29 and in Article 118 safeguard the democratic principle by setting forth that the bodies politic, respectively, of the federation and of the area to be reorganized will ultimately decide. . . .

NOTE: *SOUTHWEST*— GERMANY'S *MARBURY V. MADISON*. *Southwest* was the Federal Constitutional Court's first major decision and the first time it set aside a federal law as unconstitutional. Because of its significance in German constitutional law, the case has been compared with *Marbury* v. *Madison*.[7] *Marbury* made it clear that the Supreme Court could refuse to enforce an unconstitutional law, and it put forth an elaborate rationale in support of judicial review. No such rationale was necessary in *Southwest*, for the Basic Law explicitly confers this power on the Constitutional Court. *Southwest*'s foundational character is rooted in the general principles of constitutional interpretation stated therein and in the clarity — and forthrightness — with which the Constitutional Court defines the scope of its authority under the Basic Law. The court boldly asserted that its judgment and the opinion on which it rests are binding on all constitutional organs, even to the extent of foreclosing parliament from debating and passing another law of the same content.

For the first time, too, the Federal Constitutional Court laid down a fundamental tenet of interpretation. Because the Basic Law represents a logical unity, said the court, no clause or provision may be interpreted independently; it must be seen in relationship to all other clauses and to the Constitution as a whole. *Southwest* was also the first case in which the court endorsed the novel notion of an unconstitutional constitutional amendment. "A constitution," said the court, "has an inner unity, and the meaning of any one part is linked to that of other provisions. Taken as a unit, a constitution reflects certain overarching principles and fundamental decisions to which individual provisions are subordinate."[8] Thus even a particular constitutional provision or constitutional amendment may be unconstitutional if it conflicts with these "overarching principles and fundamental decisions." Democracy and federalism, said the court, are among these overarching principles. The justices also acknowledged the existence of a higher law, transcending positive law, that binds constitution makers and legislators. In the end the court made it very clear that any constitutional provision or amendment in conflict with higher law or the fundamental principles of the Basic Law would be judged unconstitutional.

Baden had argued, on the basis of the Constitution's inner unity, that Article 118 of the Basic Law is invalid because it contradicts the general policy of Article 29. Recall that Article 118 permits the reorganization of the federal territory "in derogation of the provisions of Article 29." Article 118 authorizes the federal government to consolidate the southwestern states over the objection of Baden and without resorting to the national referendum required by Article 29. (With respect to the *Länder* of Berlin and Brandenburg, a 1994 amendment to the Basic Law—Article 118a—provides a similar exception to the policy of Article 29. The two *Länder* may now be combined into a single state "by agreement between the two states and with the participation of their electorates.") The Constitutional Court, however, sustained the procedural aspects of the referendum proposal, noting that the Basic Law, while requiring the division of the federal territory into states, does not guarantee their status quo. An otherwise valid reorganization proposal may abolish a particular state, even against the will of its population.

NOTE: AFTERMATH OF *SOUTHWEST.* In 1952, pursuant to a legitimate referendum and in accordance with the court's instructions, the new state of Baden-Württemberg, which took the place of the three former states, came into being. Unlike the hostile Jeffersonian response to *Marbury* v. *Madison,*[9] the general political reaction to *Southwest* was deferential and compliant. Justice Gerhard Leibholz wrote:

> It may be said that the raging political controversies which ensued from the disputes in southwestern Germany, especially between Württemberg and Baden, subsided visibly as a result of the judgment of the Federal Constitutional Court, which was readily accepted by all parties concerned. Even at this early date there can be no doubt that the judgment of the court had a pacifying influence on the political life of all states involved in the controversy, and that it cleared the political atmosphere considerably. Beyond that, it had a politically unifying effect which proved beneficial to the new German state as a whole.[10]

Except for the reintegration of the Saarland into the Federal Republic in 1959, there were no further changes in state boundaries prior to reunification. With German unity, however, East and West Berlin combined to form a single state, and plans are now under way to combine Berlin and Brandenburg into a single state. The most significant effort to overhaul the entire federal structure was Hesse's endeavor to compel the federal government to change the boundaries of the states under the compulsory reorganization provision of Article 29. The Constitutional Court turned back this attempt in the *Territorial Reorganization* case (1961).[11] Hesse had claimed that it could not adequately plan its own future as an autonomous state in the face of uncertainty with regard to federal reorganization. The court answered that the time and character of territorial changes were for the federal government to decide in the interest of the federation as a whole.[12] By this time public sentiment for major territorial change had well nigh disappeared, and in 1969 Article 29 was amended to make any such change optional rather than obligatory.[13]

The *Oldenburg State* case (1978) is the most recent effort to force federal action under Article 29. A majority of the residents of the former Weimar state of Oldenburg, which was absorbed into Lower Saxony in 1946, voted in favor of reestablishing Oldenburg as an independent state. In addition to denying standing to those invoking the rights of the former state, the Constitutional Court held that the federal government's authority to reorganize the federal territory was a power conferred "neither in the interest of the existing states nor for the preservation of the interests of former states." In adhering to the basic teaching of the *Territorial Reorganization* case, the court declared that the Basic Law permits territorial change only at the discretion of the federal government and for the well-being of the entire nation.[14]

NOTE: THE NATURE OF GERMAN FEDERALISM. Constitutional theorists have long disputed the nature of the *Bundesstaat* (federal state) created by the Basic Law. What elements of the *Zentralstaat* (unitary state) does it contain? What elements of the *Staatenbund* (confederation)? Both forms of government have figured prominently in German constitutional history. Is the *Bundesstaat* a two-tier (*zweigliedrig*) or a three-tier (*dreigliedrig*) structure? *Zweigliedrigkeit* suggests that the parts (states) are subordinate to the whole (federation); *Dreigliedrigkeit,* that national and state governments — both equal and coordinate — combine to form a third "state," namely the state as a whole (*Gesamtstaat*). Konrad Hesse, a leading commentator on the Basic Law and a Federal Constitutional Court justice from 1975 to 1987, defines the Bonn Republic as a "unitary federal state," suggesting a strong tilt toward centralism.[15] Others, such as Ulrich Scheuner, accentuate the Basic Law's federalistic underpinnings.[16] Still others emphasize the solidarity contained in the idea of a strong federal union. Theodore Maunz's view is representative: "The *Bundesstaat* is not a battle of member states against the whole, but rather a joint effort for achieving the ends assigned to each level [of government] under the Basic Law."[17]

The argument over the nature of the *Bundesstaat* assumed considerable importance in 1957 when the Federal Constitutional Court decided the *Concordat* case (no. 3.4), which involved an area of public policy over which both state and federal governments could claim jurisdiction. *Concordat* appeared to embrace the three-tier concept by sustaining the legal validity of an international agreement negotiated by a previous national government but denying to the present central government, in the presumed interest of the Federal Republic as a whole, any control over the educational policy of the individual states. Several years later, however, in the *Territorial Reorganization* case, the court appeared to accept the two-tier theory. "The *Bundesstaat* as the state of the whole [*Gesamtstaat*]," said the court, "does not consist of an independent central state [*Zentralstaat*] but only of a central organization which, together with the organizations of the member states, carries out, within the sphere of operation prescribed by the Basic Law, all those governmental functions that in a unified state devolve upon a unified state organization. The Basic Law divides authority only between the organs of the federation and those of the states, whereby the state as a whole [*Gesamtstaat*] arises out of an alliance among the states in the form of a federation [*Bund*]."[18]

DOCTRINE OF FEDERAL COMITY

The Constitutional Court oscillated early on between the two-tier and three-tier concepts of federalism.[19] Eventually, however, it settled for a more pragmatic approach to the federal-state relationship in an effort to weigh and balance the vital interests of both state and national governments. This concern for balance and practicality induced the court to proclaim the principle of federal comity (*Bundestreue*), which obligates federal and state governments to consider each other's interests in exercising their authority. The doctrine of comity, which the court invoked for the first time in the *Housing Funding* case (1952),[20] does not appear in the text of the Basic Law. It is, rather, an unwritten principle inferred by the court from the various structures and relationships created by the Constitution. German federalism, said the court, is essentially a relationship of trust between state and national governments. Each government has a constitutional duty to keep "faith" (*Treue*) with the other and to respect the rightful prerogatives of the other. The doctrine received special emphasis in the *Television I* case.

3.2 Television I Case (1961)
12 BVerfGE 205

[The television controversy grew out of Chancellor Konrad Adenauer's effort to create a federally operated television station. One major television channel controlled by the states was already operating in the Federal Republic. The chancellor, who was also the leader of the Christian Democratic Union, was at the time strongly opposed by states under the control of the Social Democratic party. Finally, and notwithstanding opposition from both Social Democratic and Christian Democratic states, the federal chancellor established a second television station by decree. Several states immediately challenged the validity of the decree before the Constitutional Court. They relied on Articles 30 and 70 (1) of the Basic Law, claiming that these provisions confer no such power on the federation. In response, the federation relied on Articles 87 (1) and 73 (7), which confer exclusive authority on the federation to regulate "postal and telecommunication services."]

Judgment of the Second Senate. . . .

D. II. 3. (b) The Basic Law regulates the legislative authority of federation and states on the basis of a principle that favors the jurisdiction of the states. . . . The federation has legislative authority only insofar as the Basic Law confers it (Article 70 [1]). Thus, as a rule, federal legislative powers can be derived only from an express statement to that effect in the Basic Law. In cases of doubt there is no presumption in favor of the federation's jurisdiction. Rather, the systematic order of the Basic Law demands a strict interpretation of Article 73 [and other provisions which confer power on the federation].   *

In addition, broadcasting is a cultural matter. To the extent that cultural affairs are subject to governmental regulation at all, the Basic Law has made a fundamental decision (Articles 30, 70 *et seq.*, and 83 *et seq.*) *that they come within* the jurisdiction of the states. . . . Exceptions occur only when special provisions of the Basic Law provide that the federation has authority. This fundamental decision of the Constitution, a decision in favor of the federal structure of the nation in the interest of an effective division of powers, specifically prohibits the assumption that the federation has jurisdiction over cultural matters. The federation has authority only when there is a clear exception spelled out in the Basic Law. This sort of provision is lacking here.

(c) Article 87 (1) provides that the federal postal service shall be conducted as a matter of direct federal administration. [We] can draw no conclusions as to the extent of the federation's legislative authority from this.

[States usually administer federal laws "as matters of their own concern" (Article 83). Under Article 87 (1), however, the federal government administers selected subjects such as federal railroads and the federal postal service. The court suggests here that the primacy of federal administration in these areas does not define the full extent of the national government's *legislative* authority.]

. . . Moreover, "postal and telecommunication services" in Article 73 (7), and "federal postal administration" in Article 87 (1), refer to the same subject. The scope of "federal postal administration" follows from what is to be understood by "postal and telecommunication services."

4. The public interest demands the regulation of radio communications— something only the federation can do effectively. This is also true of broadcasting. To prevent chaos, the allocation and delimitation of frequency ranges of stations, determination of their locations and transmitting powers . . . control of radio communication, protection from widespread and local disturbances, and implementation of international agreements must be subject to uniform regulations.

Article 73 (7) makes it possible to enact uniform regulations that are indispensable to these and similar matters. But implementation of this objective does not require that, in addition to technical questions of radio communication, federal law also [should] regulate the production of broadcasts. . . .

5. A historical interpretation of the term "telecommunication services" does not produce any different results. . . .

6. (a) The federation is not entitled to any further legislative authority over broadcasting on the basis of *Sachzusammenhang*. Neither the regulation of studio technology nor of program production . . . is an indispensable requirement for regulating technical matters relating to broadcasting.

[The notion of *Sachzusammenhang* (loosely translated, "connected to the thing itself") suggests an implied power. As used here, it means that the federal government may regulate a subject matter not within its express powers if it cannot avoid such regulation when making law in an area where it has express constitutional authority. One example would be the federal regulation of court fees. This subject is so closely related to the federal government's authority in the fields of civil law and court procedure that any regulation of the latter necessarily involves a regulation of the former.]

Transmission and production of programs are areas which [legislators] can treat separately. In this respect "broadcasting" is not an entire area which must be treated uniformly and which consequently the federation can regulate. . . .

(c) The federation has no authority to regulate broadcasting beyond the technical aspects of transmission. . . .

7. (b) The federation must . . . observe the principle of profederal behavior. . . . This principle would be violated if the federation today used its authority to regulate the telecommunication system so as to deprive existing broadcasting companies of the right to dispose of transmitting facilities which they own and operate. The same would be true if the federation took away from these companies their frequency ranges, and in distributing frequencies to be used now or in the future, did not duly consider the companies in light of state regulations concerning producers of programs. . . .

E. II. In the German federal state the unwritten constitutional principle of the reciprocal obligation of the federation and the states to behave in a profederal manner governs all constitutional relationships between the nation as a whole and its members and the constitutional relationships among members. . . . From this principle the federal Constitution has developed a number of concrete legal obligations. In considering the constitutionality of the so-called horizontal financial adjustment, this court said: "The federal principle by its nature creates not only rights but also obligations. One of these obligations consists in financially strong states having to give assistance within certain limits to financially weaker states . . ." [citing Finance Equalization Case I, 1 BVerfGE 117, 131 (1952)]. Furthermore, in cases where a law demands that the federation and the states come to an understanding, this constitutional principle can create an increased obligation of cooperation on all parties concerned. . . . In the decision which concerned granting Christmas bonuses to public employees, this court held that states must maintain *Bundestreue* [loyalty to the union] and therefore show consideration for the overall financial structure of federation and states. . . . This legal restraint, derived from the concept of loyalty to the union, becomes even more evident in the exercise of legislative powers: "If the effects of a law are not limited to the territory of a state, the state legislature must show consideration for the interests of the federation and other states . . ." [citing North Rhine–Westphalia Salaries Case, 4 BVerfGE 115, 140 (1954)]. The constitutional principle of the obligation to act in a profederal manner can further imply the duty of states to observe international treaties concluded by the federation. . . . Finally, under certain circumstances, loyalty to the union can obligate a state to use its supervisory authority over local governments to intervene against communities that encroach upon an exclusive federal competency. . . . In the execution of federal jurisdiction over the field of broadcasting, the principle of profederal behavior is also of fundamental importance. . . .

Previous decisions show that additional concrete obligations of the states can be developed from this principle — obligations that surpass constitutional obligations explicitly laid down in the Basic Law. . . .

The case at hand offers an occasion to develop further the constitutional principle of the obligation to act profederally in a different direction: The rule of profederal behavior also governs the procedure and style of the negotiations required in constitutional life between the federation and its members as well as between the states. In the Federal Republic of Germany all states have the same constitutional status; they are states entitled to equal treatment when dealing with the federation. Whenever the federation tries to achieve a constitutionally relevant agreement in a matter in which all states are interested and participating, the obligation to act in a profederal manner prohibits the federation from trying to "divide and conquer"; that is, from attempting to divide the states, to seek an agreement with only some of them and then force the others to join. In negotiations that concern all states, that principle also prohibits the federal government from treating state governments differently because of their party orientation and, in particular, from inviting to politically decisive discussions only representatives from those state governments politically close to the federal government and ex-cluding state governments which are close to opposition parties in the federal parliament. . . .

The year-long efforts to reorganize the broadcasting system entered a new phase in early 1958 when the federal government considered drafting a federal law. After the draft of a federal law had been discussed several times during 1959 with state representatives, the states in January 1960 agreed to set up a commission, consisting of two Christian Democratic and two Social Democratic members of state governments, to represent the state governments in negotiations with the federation. The federal government, however, never let this commission partici-pate in negotiations. Only one of its members, the Christian Democratic minister-president of the Rhineland-Palatinate, participated—not in this role, but as a mem-ber of his party—in a number of debates between politicians and deputies of the Christian Democratic Union and the Christian Social Union. . . . The fact that the minister-president of the Rhineland-Palatinate informed the state govern-ments led by Social Democratic ministers-president of these plans in a letter dated July 16, 1960, and at the same time invited them, together with the other ministers-president, to a discussion of these plans on July 22, 1960, did not release the federal government from its obligation to confer directly with all state governments con-cerning the plan it had drafted. That it neglected to do so violated the obligation to act profederally.

The federal government's behavior toward the states in the last few days before the foundation of the company also was incompatible with this obligation. The federal government knew that the ministers-president of the states . . . had their first opportunity on July 22, 1960, to discuss the plan for the federation and states to set up a limited partnership to establish a second television network. The ministers-president, including those of the Christian Democratic Union and the Christian Social Union, did not fully accept the federal government's proposal, but made counterproposals by a letter of July 22, 1960—thus fully informing the federal government of the result of these discussions. Nevertheless, the federal government insisted that the corporate contract that it alone had drafted be signed on July 25, 1960. The federal government's letter dated July 23, 1960, was mailed in Bonn on July 24, 1960, 5:00 P.M., and reached the addressee, the minister-president of Rhineland-Palatinate, on July 25, 1960, 4:15 P.M. That is, [it reached him] at a time when the corporate contract had already been notarized. . . . Such a proceeding is blatantly incompatible with the obligation to act profederally, even if the federal government had reason to be displeased with the delaying opposition of the states or some state governments. At issue here is not whether the federal government could consider negotiations with the states as having failed and follow a course it considered constitutionally admissible, . . . [but] the fact that each state government as the constitutional body of a member state of the Federal Republic of Germany could expect the federal government not to answer the counterproposals of the states concerning a new plan with a fait accompli — not to mention that it was with inappropriately short notice. . . .

NOTE: THE JURISPRUDENCE OF COMITY. The Federal Constitutional Court did not invent the concept of comity. It was well known in the thought of constitutional theorists concerned with federal-state relations under the Reich Constitution of 1871. The first *Finance Equalization* case (1952),[21] which sustained a federal statute providing for the transfer of tax revenues from the richer to the poorer states, alluded to this history in assigning comity a major place in the Federal Republic's constitutional jurisprudence. In several subsequent cases the court seized on the concept of comity to vindicate the financial interests of the various states, even when the letter of the Constitution might have suggested a contrary result.[22] Still later, in *Atomic Weapons Referenda I* and *Concordat* (nos. 3.3 and 3.4),[23] the court invoked the doctrine to admonish the *Länder* and the federal government each to respect the primacy of the other in their assigned fields of endeavor. As Philip M. Blair suggested, these decisions "establish for the states in their relations with each other and with the 'greater whole,' and for the federation in its relations with the states, a duty in constitutional law to keep 'faith' (*Treue*) and reach a common understanding" with respect to certain matters of public policy.[24]

After the *Television I* case, the Constitutional Court was less inclined to decide federal-state conflicts on the basis of an express appeal to comity. Theoretical and practical reasons prompted this result: theoretical because inferences from the structure of federalism proved to be extremely indeterminate; practical because the sharp conflicts of the 1950s paled before the advance of "cooperative federalism" (i.e., levels of government working together voluntarily to achieve certain tasks).[25] References to comity continued to appear in constitutional cases, but the court seemed to regard it as a principle of decreasing vitality. But in the 1990s, comity has rushed back into prominence. In *Kalkar II* (1990; no. 3.5), which involved a conflict between federal and state authorities over the construction of a nuclear power plant, the court reaffirmed the "unwritten principle of a duty of reciprocal loyalty [requiring] the federal government and the *Länder* . . . to consider the interests of [each other]."[26] In the *Finance Equalization III* case (1992) the federal government was found to have offended this principle in its distribution of "equalization" grants to the financially weak *Länder* of Bremen and Saarland.[27]

Comity also assumed considerable importance in light of the developing European Union. This became clear in the spring of 1995 when the court was asked to rule on the constitutionality of the federal cabinet's decision to approve European Community guidelines on television programming. Recall that under Article 70 governmental power resides with the *Länder* unless otherwise provided for in the Basic Law. Moreover, regulation of television programming, being a cultural matter, is reserved to the states. Bavaria, supported by eight other states, brought the action against the federal government.[28] The court approved the guidelines but found that the federal government, by ignoring the opposing view of the states, had violated the principle of comity. When the federal government approves a community regulation affecting a power reserved to the *Länder*, said the court, state governments are entitled to be consulted before the regulation is approved.[29] The term "consult," however, does not imply a state veto power over the adoption of such a regulation.

DIVISION OF POWERS

NOTE: ADMINISTRATIVE FEDERALISM. The German states are autonomous governments with their own legislative, executive, and judicial institutions. Like the American states, they share power with the federal government within the same territory and over the same people. But the comparison between the two federal systems ends there. In Germany the bulk of legislative power is vested in the federal government, and the administration of federal law is the main responsibility of the states. This system of "legislative-executive" or "administrative" federalism, as it is sometimes called, encourages flexibility in adjusting general policy to local conditions.[30] But the system is also complex. At least forty-three articles of the Constitution deal with relations between state and national governments, and many, such as those on fiscal administration (Articles 104a and 109) and the execution of federal law (Articles 82–86), contain exceedingly detailed provisions. The specificity of these provisions has invited numerous constitutional amendments over the years, in many instances shifting power from the state to the federal level, usually to meet needs not contemplated by the framers and occasionally in response to Federal Constitutional Court decisions.[31]

NOTE: NATIONAL POWERS. The national government's legislative power extends to subjects falling within parliament's "exclusive" or "concurrent" authority. The catalog of exclusive powers is short, covering such areas as foreign affairs and defense, customs and international trade, citizenship and immigration, and postal and telecommunication services (Article 73). Aviation and railways remain, as before, among these exclusive powers, but amendments to the Basic Law in 1992 and 1993 authorize parliament to privatize these institutions.[32] These exclusive powers have been narrowly interpreted. In the *Television* case, for example, the court excluded broadcasting from the area of services in the field of telecommunication over which the federal government has exclusive control. As for the *Länder*, they may legislate in matters of exclusive federal legislation, but "only where and to the extent that they are explicitly empowered [to do so] by federal law" (Article 71).

Article 74, on the other hand, embraces a list of twenty-eight general subject areas over which the federal government enjoys concurrent jurisdiction with the states. This jurisdiction includes ordinary civil and criminal law, weapons and explosives, inland waterways, public welfare, measures to prevent the abuse of economic power, the production and utilization of nuclear energy for peaceful purposes, and other general areas which, taken together, nearly cover the whole range of public policy. Article 72 (1) permits the states to legislate on these topics "as long as, and to the extent that, the federation does not exercise its right to legislate." If the federal government chooses to exercise its concurrent powers—and for the most part it has—then federal law preempts state law altogether.

Article 72 (2), however, declares that the federal government's concurrent authority may be exercised only when there is a *need* for federal regulation because state legislation (1) cannot effectively regulate the matter, (2) might prejudice the interests of other states, or (3) would threaten "the maintenance of legal or economic unity, especially the maintenance of uniformity of living conditions beyond the territory of any one state." Whether a need does in fact exist when the federal government exercises its concurrent jurisdiction is a question the Constitutional Court has left to parliament,[33] although it has reserved for itself the right independently to review any *abuse* of this discretion.[34]

As for the federal government's concurrent powers, they too have been narrowly construed in light of the Basic Law's proclamation that the "*Länder* have the right to legislate insofar as this Basic Law does not confer legislative power on the federation." The Basic Law's theory of federalism leaves little room for a jurisprudence of implied national power. For example, in 1962 the court struck down a federal law regulating the use of explosives because it could not be justified under the concurrent power over "economic affairs." The law, said the court, had more to do with maintaining order and security than with furthering economic objectives.[35] Ten years later, parliament circumvented this decision by amending Article 74 to include "weapons and explosives" among the federal government's concurrent powers (Article 74 [4a]).

3.3 Atomic Weapons Referenda Case I (1958)
8 BVerfGE 104

[In the mid-1950s, equipping the German army with tactical nuclear weapons was at the top of the Adenauer government's military agenda. In the lengthy debate over this issue, Social Democrats bitterly opposed the plan for nuclear armaments. In an effort to show that public opinion opposed nuclear weapons on German soil, several Social Democratic–controlled cities and states planned to hold referenda on the issue. The Adenauer government challenged the constitutionality of these referenda as an invasion of the federation's exclusive power over military affairs. This case, brought in the form of an abstract review proceeding, challenged the validity of referenda in Hamburg and Bremen.]

Judgment of the Second Senate. . . .

B. III. . . . In a federal state, the constitution of the national state limits the authority of states — and therefore the jurisdiction within which the state organ of the state's body politic can generally become active. The referendum laws of Hamburg and Bremen transgress constitutional limits drawn by the Basic Law.

1. Matters of defense fall within the exclusive jurisdiction of the federation; Article 73 (1) of the Basic Law sets out the domain of the legislature, and Articles 65a, 87a, and 87b confirm the domain of the executive (including the government). . . . Thus the federation has sole and unlimited authority over the task of "defense" as far as it concerns the federal army and its equipment. . . .

Neither the two laws nor the participation of the people of Hamburg and Bremen in the referenda interfere with the federation's exclusive authority so as to determine or technically regulate a matter of defense — for example, equipping the federal army. However, that is not the decisive point. What is decisive is the clearly recognizable purpose of the laws and referenda of Hamburg and Bremen. In the area of defense, especially with respect to equipping the army, the federal government has chosen a particular policy with the Bundestag's approval. The opposition in the Bundestag considers this policy wrong and has fought it passionately. The opposition has not been able to win in the Bundestag but believes that a majority of the people shares its view. It hopes that political pressure resulting from successful referenda will force the federal government to reverse its policy. Speeches of Social Democrats in the Bundestag have clearly expressed this belief. . . .

The clear goal of these two referenda — to force the competent constitutional organs of the federation to change a decision about a matter of defense that these organs consider right — represents an attempted infringement upon the exclusive jurisdiction of the federation. States infringe on the exclusive, autonomous authority of federal organs not only when they try to regulate a matter themselves, but also when they schedule a referendum in an effort to pressure federal organs into changing their decisions. The infringement occurs when a state attempts to form a "will of the state" to oppose the constitutionally formed "will of the federation."

2. [One] reaches the same result if one examines legislative authority to order referenda. . . . [I]n a merely consultative referendum the people take part in the exercise of state authority just as they do in elections and plebiscites. The general catalog of authority in the Basic Law (Articles 73–75) does not contain any provision relating to the authority of the federation or states to enact electoral laws. Nevertheless, until now it has never been seriously doubted that the federation cannot pass electoral laws for a state parliamentary election or that a state cannot

pass electoral laws for the Bundestag election. A state cannot permit either a referendum or a plebiscite on a question belonging exclusively to the competence of the federation or a state referendum on a matter of exclusive federal jurisdiction. . . .

NOTE: COMITY REVISITED. In *Atomic Weapons Referenda II* (1958), the Federal Constitutional Court rebuked Hesse for permitting local referenda within its borders.[36] Hesse's failure to ban the referenda, said the court, violated the principle of federal comity. In its defense the state advanced two arguments: first, the federal government had itself offended the Constitution by manipulating public opinion in such a way as to undermine the principle of majority rule implicit in the concept of democracy;[37] second, federal comity was not impaired, because the state acted out of goodwill and in the best interest of the Federal Republic. Both arguments, said the court, were incapable of judicial resolution. It concluded its opinion by saying that a decision based on comity did not imply a spirit of ill will on the part of the state or a reproach (*Vorwurf*) of the state. Comity, said the court, "is exclusively an objective idea of constitutional law, and it assumes that the participants, with respect to a given subject matter, are convinced [subjectively] of the constitutionality of their mutual dealings."[38] As noted earlier, the principle of comity emerged again in *Kalkar II,* a case involving federal supervision of local administration.

NOTE: STATE GOVERNMENT AND THE PRINCIPLE OF HOMOGENEITY. An important issue of German federalism is the extent to which state and local governments must follow the constitutional order of the federation. Article 28 declares: "The constitutional order in the states must conform to the principles of republican, democratic, and social government based on the rule of law." This provision, although labeled the "homogeneity clause," is not a prescription for uniformity in governmental organization. Article 28 (1) has been generally understood to require states and localities to adhere to the *basic* principles of the "democratic, social-welfare state bound by the rule of law."[39] This has been interpreted to mean representative political institutions and governmental structures indispensable to the operation of a *federal* state. It also incorporates the principle of subsidiarity. What is important here is the local autonomy, not a particular structural form. In addition, the formalities of the governmental process must be organized in such a way as to make the *sozialer Rechtsstaat* possible. But how much flexibility do state and local governments have in establishing institutional procedures for the adoption of public policies? This was a central issue in the *Startbahn West* case (1982),[40] the result of a controversy arising out of Hesse's rejection of a popular initiative to hold a referendum on the state government's decision to expand Frankfurt's international airport. The Hessian state government and constitutional court rejected the popular-initiative proposal on state constitutional grounds and refused to consider related issues of federal law deemed to conflict with the airport expansion proposal, including the threat to the constitutional right of personality (Article 2 [1]) allegedly posed by the further destruction of the environment. In their appeal to the Federal Constitutional Court, complainants argued that the case could not be decided by reference to the state constitution alone, and that the issues in controversy would have to be settled by the Federal Constitutional Court in accordance with federal law and federal constitutional principles.

In a significant victory for the states, the court ruled that Hesse's refusal to proceed with the referendum did not violate a fundamental right under the Basic Law. After remarking that state and federal constitutional law are "separate domains," the court said:

> As members of the federation, the *Länder* are states vested with their own sovereign powers—even though limited as to subject matter—derived not from but rather recognized by the federation (*Bund*). . . . The Basic Law requires only a certain degree of identity between federal and state constitutions. To the extent that the Basic Law [does not provide otherwise] the states are free to construct their own constitutional orders. Their discretion [in this respect] most certainly extends to determining whether the legislature should reserve to itself the passage of a law or provide for [its approval] in a popular referendum.[41]

Recall from our earlier discussion that Article 29 allows referenda on the federal level only in the limited instance of territorial reorganization. The court said that this does not prevent the states from employing the referendum in other situations. In short, no conflict with federal prerogatives could arise in this case, because the decision to hold a referendum was a matter of the state's own choice.

The court went on to say that its power of review is restricted to examining the constitutionality of state law. Because Hesse rejected a proposed referendum measure, the Federal Constitutional Court had no authority to become involved. Thus the court confirmed the authority of a state constitutional court to review a state law under its own constitution, even when a case before it implicates a fundamental right under the Basic Law. To suggest, as the complainants did here, that only the Federal Constitutional Court could hear such cases "would seriously undermine [the integrity] of state constitutional law."[42]

NOTE: RESERVED POWERS. As already noted, the Basic Law omits an implied-powers provision comparable to the "necessary and proper" clause found in the Constitution of the United States. Accordingly, as the *Television I* case underscored, the states possess those powers and responsibilities not expressly conferred on the federation. These fully reserved—and unlisted—powers include cultural matters, education, hospitals, and various social services. The list is short. And as the *Concordat* case shows, the court has tended to guard these powers closely, probably because they are so few.[43] The state's victory in *Concordat* is remarkable in that a local interest prevailed over the national government's treaty-making authority, producing a result directly opposed to the outcome in the American case of *Missouri v. Holland*.[44]

3.4 Concordat Case (1957)
6 BVerfGE 309

[In 1933 Hitler's regime concluded a concordat with the Holy See. The concordat recognized the right of the Catholic church to freedom of religion and control over church properties. It also included guarantees of religious education in the public schools and state-supported confessional schools for the children of Catholic parents. In 1954 Lower Saxony, a predominantly Protestant state, provided for nondenominational schools for all children. The federal government, at the urging of the Holy See, contested the validity of the state's new policy, claiming that the state had usurped federal authority to conduct foreign relations. The court sustained the validity of the concordat under the general principles of international law, but then proceeded to rule that Article 23 of the concordat, guaranteeing confessional schools, is not enforceable in states with conflicting school legislation. This case needs to be understood in light of the vigilance with which the court tends to guard the narrow domain of authority the states have managed to reserve to themselves.]

Judgment of the Second Senate. . . .

E. II. We need not here examine the extent of the state's obligation toward the federation to honor treaties internationally binding upon the Federal Republic of Germany. In no case could the states' obligation toward the federation to honor the concordat's educational provisions . . . be derived from the constitutional order created by the Basic Law. Articles 7, 30, and 70 *et seq.* of the Basic Law have made certain fundamental choices that shape the relationship between federation and states. . . . These choices reflect no such obligation. In contrast to the Weimar Constitution, these provisions establish the states as the exclusive custodians of cultural leadership. In the area of denominational organization of the school system, only the provisions of Articles 7 and 141 limit this exclusive authority. This allocation is an important element of the federal structure of the Federal Republic of Germany.

   1. We must proceed from the view that the states alone are entitled to make law where they possess exclusive legislative authority. In Articles 30 and 70 *et seq.* the Basic Law very clearly expresses this principle. Only obligations arising from federal constitutional law limit the legislative freedom of the states in this area, because the federal legislature cannot pass a law in an area where states have exclusive legislative authority.

We must therefore consider as an important principle of federal constitutional law that states are subject to no limitation upon their legislative authority other than that imposed by the Basic Law. This principle also applies to state legislation pursuant to [preconstitutional] law having continued validity under Articles 123 (1) and (2). . . .

To bind the states constitutionally to the educational provisions of the concordat would flatly contradict their authority to make educational law freely within the limits of the Constitution.

2. With respect to the organization of the school system along denominational lines, the Basic Law made a specific choice that rejected constitutionally binding the states to the educational provisions of the concordat. Based upon the states' freedom of action, Articles 7 and 141 of the Basic Law establish the limits within which the state legislature should be confined in this particular area. . . . This choice is not reconcilable with the educational provisions of the concordat. . . .

3. [One] can correctly understand the meaning of Article 7 . . . only by considering the background of the entire situation surrounding the [framing of the] Basic Law for the area of educational law.

From 1933 to 1945 [the Hitler regime] did not enforce the educational provisions of the concordat and in many cases allowed them to be violated.

After the collapse of the Reich in 1945, the states helped to accomplish the civil reconstruction of Germany. They reconstructed civil life during a period when the entire German state was not yet capable of action. As a result, the states could alter previous laws of the Reich during this time. Thus the Basic Law also expressly recognized the changes the states had made in earlier laws of the Reich during this period (Article 125 [2]).

In the governmental structure of the states, the issue of education had particular importance and was the subject of lively dispute; the states often deviated from the educational provisions of the concordat. . . .

The Constitution's framers thus had to proceed from the fact that the new educational law of a large part of the territory enacted under the Basic Law contradicted the educational provisions of the concordat. How these events are to be evaluated from the standpoint of international law cannot concern us here. . . . This legal situation . . . made it imperative for the Basic Law to state expressly any intention to constitutionally obligate the states to fulfill the educational provisions of the concordat. In view of the diversified legal situation in education among the states and the Basic Law's own choices in this area (Articles 7 and 141), the Constitution could not have been silent on educational matters if it wished to oblige the states to observe the educational provisions of the concordat. Moreover, the Basic Law could not have been content generally to ordain the constitutional validity of domestic law corresponding to international treaties of the German Reich. This order neither removed contradictory state laws nor bound the state legislature to the continued validity of the law.

5. To understand correctly the constitutional order of the Federal Republic of Germany, one must realize that the Basic Law's division of authority between federation and states was not a matter of apportioning the power of a totalitarian state. . . . The events from 1945 to 1949 meant more than a change in the form of government. . . . Rather, a fundamental reconstruction gave German state power an entirely new structure and form in the federation and states, in place of the state organization which completely collapsed in 1945 and was entirely removed. The fact that this reconstruction took place during a lag time between the development of governmental power in the states and the reorganization of the entire German state confronted the framers of the Basic Law with two faits accomp4s. On the one hand, state law had largely developed independently and to such a degree . . . that the Basic Law could not ignore it. . . . On the other hand, [the Basic Law] could not arbitrarily curb the authority of the states, if only because of their political influence. The parliaments of two-thirds of the states had to accept the Basic Law for it to become effective. . . . In this constitutional and political situation, the federal Constitution could not guarantee the states' acceptance of obligations contracted by the Reich government to the same extent it might perhaps have been able to . . . had it had as its task the distribution between federation and states of the unlimited power of a totalitarian state.

In interpreting the Basic Law, one must proceed from the inner harmony of the constitutional structure which gave the German state a new federal and democratic order in place of a totalitarian dictatorship. The supposition that states are obligated vis-à-vis the federation to observe the concordat's educational provisions is irreconcilable with the basic decisions of the constitutional structure, including [the decision to confer] upon the states supremacy over education as policy.

> [In the next section of its opinion the court invoked once again the doctrine of federal comity. It seemed necessary to speak of comity here as a way of bridging the gap between the right of a state to legislate in areas within its authority and the right of the federation to have the states respect its international treaty obligations. "*Bundestreue* demands," said the court, "that each state consider the interest . . . of the federation, particularly . . . in the area of foreign relations, where the federation alone is competent." The court wished to emphasize the states' duty of fidelity to the federation in foreign affairs even while vindicating the state in this instance.]

NOTE: THE IMPLEMENTATION OF FEDERAL LAW. An equally important linchpin in the structure of German federalism is the right of the states "to execute federal law as matters of their own concern" (i.e., in their own right) unless the Constitution specifies otherwise (Article 83). State governments in turn delegate the actual implementation of most laws (federal and state) to still lower levels of administration.[45] Thus state and local governments predominate in the field of public administration, for they establish and operate nearly all of the country's administrative agencies. As a consequence, the states are primarily responsible for putting into force most rules and regulations pertaining to the training and employment of civil servants. Federal law, however, controls the general legal status of civil servants, including their classification and educational qualifications, a legal status that the states must respect in enacting laws to fill gaps in federal policy.

Federal administrative substructures, on the other hand, exist only in those limited areas of the federation's exclusive legislative competence (Article 73) and in matters in which the Basic Law expressly provides for *direct* federal administration. Under constitutional amendments adopted in 1993, these matters include foreign affairs, federal financial administration, waterways and shipping, and the armed services (Article 86). In addition, autonomous and self-governing federal agencies administer certain insurance programs (e.g., health plans, accident insurance, and pension funds). Under Article 87 (2), these programs are administered as federal corporate bodies if their "sphere of competence extends beyond the territory of one state." Federal-state conflicts occasionally arise under this and related provisions of the Basic Law when these federal agencies receive mandates under federal law that are alleged to interfere with the day-to-day operations of analogous state agencies.[46] The prevailing view among constitutional commentators, cited approvingly in the *Chimney Sweep* case (1983), is that the spheres of federal and state administration are to remain organizationally separate and independent.[47]

The federal government, however, is authorized to supervise the administration of federal law and, with the Bundesrat's consent, even to issue directives to state agencies. *Kalkar II* is a landmark case involving a clash between federal and state administrative orders; understanding it requires close attention to the Basic Law's distinction between two forms of *Land* administration. Under Article 84 the *Länder* are empowered to implement federal laws as a matter of their own concern, in accord with their own procedures, and through their own agencies unless otherwise provided with the Bundesrat's consent. Here the line between federal legislation and *Land* administration is clear. Under Article 85, however, the *Länder* are empowered to administer federal law as *agents* of the federal government. They act as the federation's agents when with respect to a given subject matter the Basic Law so declares or when the regulated matter is subject to more immediate federal control. In this situation, Article 85 (3) authorizes the highest federal official in charge of the regulated matter to issue directives to the highest corresponding *Land* official.

Kalkar II dealt with the extent of the federation's authority under Article 85 (3). The issue of comity also surfaced once more in *Kalkar*. The court resolved the dispute in favor of the federal minister but admonished the federation to observe the principle of comity in laying down procedures to be carried out at the local level.

3.5 Kalkar II Case (1990)
81 BVerfGE 310

[Pursuant to its concurrent authority over the production of nuclear energy, parliament enacted the Federal Nuclear Energy Act, which, among other things, regulates licensing procedures for the construction of fast breeder reactors. (Article 87c declares that nuclear energy laws may be administered by the *Länder* for the federation with the Bundesrat's consent.) Such a reactor had been under construction in Kalkar since the early 1970s. (A related decision, reprinted as case no. 4.6 — *Kalkar I* — involved an earlier controversy arising from the decision to build the reactor.) Prompted by the nuclear disaster at the Soviet Union's fast breeder reactor in Chernobyl in 1986, North Rhine–Westphalia's minister in charge of technology ordered a reassessment of the plans for the reactor's safety system before permitting the installation of the reactor core. The federal minister in charge of environmental matters, Klaus Toepfer, issued a contrary directive based on an earlier report that all safety measures had been met. The *Land* government, appealing to the Constitutional Court, charged that the federal directive was beyond the competence of the national government.]

Judgment of the Second Senate. . . .

C. The application is unfounded.

The [federal] directive is legally valid under Article 85 (3) of the Basic Law. It relates to the licensing procedure under section 7 of the Nuclear Energy Act . . . and implicates the authority of the *Länder* to execute federal laws as agents of the federation. As a procedural order, the federal directive is permissible under Article 85 (3). . . . Objectively . . . the federal order complies with the conditions of and restrictions on federal competence under Article 85 (3). The order did not violate the principle of reciprocal loyalty between the *Länder* and the federation.

I. Article 83 empowers the *Länder* to enforce federal laws unless otherwise specified in the Basic Law. In principle, the *Länder* administer federal laws as matters of their own concern (Articles 83 and 84). The *Länder* are also empowered to act as "agents of the federation" in certain designated matters (Article 85 [1]).

1. The administrative agency in question here is a form of *Land* administration. The *Länder* exercise their own authority as such, and their administrative agencies act as their organs, and not as organs of the federation. This view is supported by the language of Article 85 (1), as well as the distribution of powers in Part VIII of the Basic Law, which distinguishes two forms of *Land* administration; namely, when the *Länder* execute federal laws in their own right and when they serve as agents of the federation, [i.e., when they derive their authority] from the federal govern-

ment's own administrative power (Article 86). The debates in the Parliamentary Council also proceeded on the assumption that *Land* and federal governments would serve as equals in administrative matters and that *Land* and federal agencies would be kept separate.

Admittedly the autonomy of the *Länder* in administrative matters is substantially restricted. Where the *Länder* execute federal laws in their own right the federal government exercises a supervisory power to ensure legal conformity [with federal law] and reserves the right to issue individual instructions in particular cases where it is permitted by federal statute (Article 84 [5]). The federal government has broad powers to intervene in the functioning of administrative agencies. Its supervisory power extends to ensuring the lawfulness and appropriateness of administration, for which purpose the federal government may require the *Länder* to submit documents [for its inspection] and dispatch representatives to the [*Land*] administrative agency. Most important, the directives of a *Land* agency are subordinate to those of the federal authority; accordingly, the latter must be executed by the highest state authority . . . (Article 85 [3]).

It follows that the administrative competence of the *Länder* is limited by the original distribution of competences [to each level of government]. The *Länder* retain exclusive authority in the administration of their functions as against third parties; Article 85 of the Basic Law does not contemplate a federal right to interfere with this power. But this is not the case with respect to substantive decision making. Although this power resides primarily in the *Länder,* the federal government can vest this power in itself by exercising its power to issue orders. This exercise is not limited to exceptional cases and does not require justification. Article 85 (3) of the Basic Law contemplates this as a normal means of settling differences, such that the federal vision of the common good may prevail. The power of the *Länder* to make substantive decisions is limited only by the reservation of rights at the federal level.

The legislative history of Article 85 (3) supports this view. According to the reporting committee of the Parliamentary Council, state administrative agencies were to be subordinate to the will of the highest responsible federal agency. . . . Accordingly, a federal directive to a *Land* agency discharging functions within its competence is invalid only when the directive . . . is unconstitutionally issued. . . .

II. . . . 2. Article 85 (3) of the Basic Law places additional legal restrictions on the [federal] power to issue directives. These restrictions relate to the nature of the directives and the substantive decision-making authority on which they are based. The order must precisely define the respective spheres of [*Land* and federal] competence. The subordinate agency must be able to recognize that it is the recipient of an order, and that certain standards will apply to certain administrative processes. The order must be drafted such that the recipient is able to make objective sense of it, using all the potential sources of technical and legal knowledge available to him in a fully equipped *Land* agency. In this context, previous communication with the superior federal authority may be of significance. The requirement of precision does not prohibit the use of concepts whose realization requires a judgment call. This is not contrary to a directional order.

3. When issuing orders, the federal government is bound by the duty of reciprocal loyalty. Certain conditions and restrictions for the execution of competences can be derived from this. In the German federal state the entire constitutional relationship between the federal government and its member *Länder* is guided by the unwritten constitutional principle of a duty of reciprocal loyalty; that is, the federal government and the *Länder* must act in a manner that promotes the [interests of the] federation [as a whole]. This duty requires that in exercising their functions, the federal government and the *Länder* reasonably consider the overall interests of the federation and the concerns of the *Länder.* The federal government does not violate its duty solely by executing a constitutionally assigned competence. Rather, it can be deduced from the principle that the exercise must be abusive or in violation of procedural requirements. Which further conclusions can be drawn from this principle can be determined only in individual cases. . . .

III. 1. According to this interpretation of Article 85 (3) of the Basic Law, the petitioning *Land* cannot proceed with its submission that the [federal] directive was incompatible with section 7 (2) or with the licensing procedures of the Nuclear Energy Act; or that it incorrectly assessed the effect of the concatenation of individual permits; or that it misconstrued the content of the prior positive assessments of the whole project. The *Land* cannot argue that the order restricts its execution of the constitutional duty to protect the life and health of its citizens under Article 2 (2) of the Basic Law. The execution and fulfillment of this duty lie solely with the federal government, insofar as it issues an order within its competence. . . .

2. The order complies with the constitutional conditions and restrictions placed on the competence to issue orders under Article 85 (3) as described under II.1. The content is procedural, as it draws the state minister's attention to legal opinions about the protection of property for which permits were already issued and about the collective effect of prior positive assessments. Taking the events at Chernobyl into consideration, the order annuls the previous standards of evaluation and the previous plans for the safety system of the reactor by raising the possibility of another expert report, thereby deviating from the position of the Reactor Safety Committee on April 15, 1987.

3. (a) Contrary to the perspective of the petitioning *Land*, the fulfillment of *Land* duties in the area of disaster prevention is not affected by this order. The order does not forbid the *Land* to commission a report addressing the issue of disaster prevention (e.g., emergency shelters).

(b) Further, the order satisfies the requirement of precision. . . .

4. In issuing this order, the federal government has also met its duty of reciprocal loyalty. The Constitutional Court must assess not only the order, but the actions

which preceded it. It is not a question of whether the federal government did everything required by the duty of reciprocal loyalty to avoid any misunderstanding on the part of the *Land* after issuing the order, or whether the *Land* for its part did everything reasonably required to understand the content of the order. . . .

NOTE: ARBITRATING THE FEDERAL-STATE RELATIONSHIP UNDER EXCLUSIVE AND CONCURRENT POWERS. The legalism inherent in German federalism contains the seeds of perpetual constitutional conflict. As a council of states, the Bundesrat itself would be capable of mounting challenge after challenge to the centralizing tendencies of the federation. In truth, however, most federal-state conflicts never reach the Constitutional Court. They are usually resolved politically through the mechanisms of cooperative federalism and various forms of coordinated activity among the states. Even when governed by different political parties, the federal government and states prefer bargaining over litigation as the usual method of settling their differences. Still, the Constitutional Court's federalism jurisprudence is substantial. "Despite the tendency, in a climate of cooperative federalism, for major developments in the federal system to pass the Court by," remarked Blair, "rulings of the *Bundesverfassungsgericht* have been sought and given over a wide range of federal issues and have affected in detail the relations between the *Bund* and *Länder.*"[48]

Many federal-state conflicts that come before the Constitutional Court involve the interpretation of specific provisions conferring exclusive or concurrent authority on the federal government. A large number of these cases arise under the financial provisions of the Basic Law. The cumulative impact of these cases on federal-state relations has been substantial. The *Engineer's* case (1969), like the *Television I* and *Concordat* cases, resulted in a victory for the states. The court's reasoning in *Engineer* reflects a tendency not to read any implied powers into Article 74. Indeed, as already suggested, the vast scope of federal legislation has prompted the Constitutional Court to guard with special vigilance the little authority that remains with the states under the Basic Law. In this sense the residual powers clause of Article 30 is a greater limitation on federal power than the reserved powers clause of the United States Constitution's Tenth Amendment.

3.6 Engineer's Case (1969)
26 BVerfGE 246

[Article 74 (1) of the Basic Law grants the federation concurrent authority over "economic matters (mining, industry, supply of power, crafts, trades, commerce, banking, stock exchanges, and private insurance)." In 1965 the federal government, presumably acting under this authority, adopted a statute designed to protect the professional title "engineer." The statute set forth educational and occupational standards for the use of the title; it did not regulate the practice of engineering. Three persons whose prior training failed to satisfy the new requirements lodged constitutional complaints against the statute, claiming a violation of the right to the free development of personality. The Constitutional Court sustained the complaints after ruling that the federal law exceeded the federal government's authority under Article 74.]

Judgment of the Second Senate. . . .

C. II. 1. . . . The restriction of the [federal] regulation to "persons gainfully employed in the economy, particularly in manufacturing or other commercial enterprises," reflects the concern originally raised against the legislative competence of the federation when the matter was being considered in the Bundesrat. By confining the regulation to this group, lawmakers thought that they were legitimately exercising their authority under the concurrent jurisdiction conferred on the federation by Article 74 (11).

2. The subject regulated by the Engineer Act does not involve a law relating to "economic matters" within the meaning of Article 74 (11). In contrast to the Reich Constitution of 1871 and the Weimar Constitution, the Basic Law forbids a broad interpretation of provisions conferring authority on the federal government. Article 30 underscores the jurisdictional primacy of the states. Article 70 (1) makes this clear by providing that the states enjoy the right to legislate to the extent that the Basic Law does not confer legislative power on the federation. The federation is limited to the enumerated powers specified in Articles 73 through 75.

"Economic matters" within the meaning of Article 74 (11) extend to regulations of economic life and to commercial activities as such, particularly to the processes of production, manufacturing, and distribution of goods. Regulations pertaining to economic competition and consumer protection are also "economic matters" within the meaning of the Basic Law. Thus the Ministry of Economics defends the Engineer Act as a measure designed to promote clarity and truth in the conduct of business. A person should be able to transact business in the knowledge that a business partner labeling himself an engineer possesses certain qualifications.

The Engineer Act, however, does not accomplish these purposes: It neither prevents unqualified persons from offering engineering services nor guarantees that business partners who identify themselves as engineers do in fact have certain credentials. . . . If such persons have engaged in engineering services prior to the law and have registered within a two-year period following its effective date of enforcement, they may continue to use the title. . . . Moreover, the Engineer Act does not pretend to define the professional activity of engineering. . . . Under Article 74 (11), the federal government may indeed regulate jobs "in commerce and industry," define the substance of such positions, and specify the qualifications needed to fill them. . . .

3. The federal government lacks authority to pass the Engineer Act, however, because the law is not connected to a subject matter within its express authority under the Basic Law [reference here is to the principle of *Sachzusammenhang,* a connection to a subject matter within the federal government's authority]. Federal authority would obtain here only if a subject within the express jurisdiction of the federal government could not be regulated without simultaneously regulating a subject not specifically within the competence of the federation. In short, encroaching upon a subject matter not within the federation's jurisdiction must be a necessary condition for regulating a subject expressly within its power. [The federation] may regulate the former only when also regulating the latter. That condition, however, does not exist here.

4. Federal jurisdiction also fails in this case because of the nature of the subject matter [*Natur der Sache*].

[*Natur der Sache* is a guideline for interpreting the Constitution that entails deducing federal legislative authority from the subject matter to be regulated which, according to its nature, would normally not fall within federal jurisdiction but that only the federation can effectively regulate. The argumentation must be based on an express authorization of federal legislative power and not on an authorization that has no basis at all in the Constitution. Examples are the authority to determine the seat of the federal government and to create national symbols (see Plenum Building Law Case I, 3 BVerfGE 407, 422 [1954]).]

The argument that a national uniform policy on the use of the title "engineer" is feasible does not sufficiently warrant an [expanded interpretation] of federal power. The Federal Constitutional Court . . . has recognized federal jurisdiction based upon the nature of the subject matter only if the federation, and only the federation, can regulate certain fields because they constitute by their very nature a most individual matter removed *a priori* from the legislative authority of the federation. Protection of the professional title "engineer," to the extent that such protection is needed, does not require one uniform plan of regulation [by the federation]. Uniformity can easily be achieved in this instance by congruent state laws. . . .

III. Because federal lawmakers lack jurisdiction, the applicable provision of the Engineer Act is incompatible with the Basic Law. It violates complainants' basic right under Article 2 (1) and is therefore void. . . .

NOTE: THE *STATE LIABILITY* CASE. The *State Liability* case (1982) is another dramatic instance of the federal government's failure to convince the court that it had legislated properly within its concurrent powers.[49] In 1981 the Bundestag enacted a comprehensive and uniform law regulating the extent and basis of the state's liability for injuries to third parties caused by the negligent conduct of public officials in the exercise of their official duties. The statute shifted liability under the Civil Code from public servants themselves to the state and from a fault to a no-fault basis. In strictly construing the federation's concurrent jurisdiction — a mode of interpretation "required by the structure of the Basic Law" — the court ruled that the Bundestag was not legislating in the area of civil law as understood within the meaning of Article 74 (1). Laws dealing with the relationship of civil servants to the state, said the court, were within the domain of public law as well as a matter over which historically the states had exercised jurisdiction. And once again the court reminded both federal and state governments of their obligation to be considerate of one another under the doctrine of federal comity.

According to Article 72 (2), the federation may exercise its concurrent legislative authority when there is a "need for [such] legislation" because (1) the separate states cannot adequately regulate the matter, (2) state regulation may interfere with the interests of other states, or (3) legal or economic unity beyond the borders of a single state requires national legislation. Whether such a need exists is a question that the Federal Constitutional Court has left mainly to the political discretion of parliament unless federal legislation (as the court seemed to suggest in *State Liability*) invades an area of traditional state concern. In fact, the federation has enacted comprehensive codes in most areas of its concurrent authority, thus preempting parallel or contrary state legislation under the doctrine of federal supremacy. The existence of such codes, however, does not exclude all state legislation in these areas. States may enact supplementary legislation if the nature of the subject matter regulated does not interfere with the federal plan or directly contradict a provision of federal law.

COOPERATIVE FEDERALISM

In addition to forms of cooperation between the states and federation dictated by practical necessity, the Basic Law itself sets up an intricate web of intergovernmental relations, particularly in the area of fiscal policy. Articles 104a to 115 fix the distribution of revenue to be shared between federal, state, and local governments.[50] Carrying out the terms of these provisions requires extensive coordination between levels of government. Article 107 (2), in turn, obligates the federal government to ensure reasonable equality between financially strong and financially weak states, a situation that may require federal grants to weaker states (vertical financial adjustments) as well as transfer payments from rich to poor *Länder* (horizontal financial adjustments). The formula for these transfers is regulated by federal law for which the Bundesrat's consent is necessary.

This system has caused several constitutional conflicts between federal and state governments. Three major financial equalization cases — *Finance Equalization I*

(1952), *II* (1986), and *III* (1992) — may be noted briefly. In *Finance Equalization I,* the court sustained a horizontal equalization measure that required two well-to-do *Länder* to subsidize several poor *Länder* up to specified amounts. The more wealthy *Länder* argued that the dictated amounts violated the central principle of fiscal federalism, including Article 109, which declares that the federation and the states are "autonomous and independent of each other with regard to their respective budgets." In sustaining the statute, the First Senate conceded that there are constitutional limits on the federation's power to enforce "horizontal financial adjustments." "The equalization statute would offend the federal principle," said the First Senate, "if it would weaken the [financial] capacity of the contributing states or lead to a financial leveling of the states." But such was not the case, and in any event, said the Senate, "the states have duties as well as rights." Where the stronger states are concerned, one of these duties is "to assist, within limits, the financially poorer states."[51]

In *Finance Equalization II* (1986), however, the Second Senate invalidated an "equalization" statute for its failure to ensure, in accordance with Article 107 (2), reasonable financial equalization between rich and poor states; whereupon, in a classic example of an admonitory decision, the senate instructed parliament to change the basis for allocating tax revenues among the states by fiscal year 1988.[52] *Finance Equalization III,* decided on May 27, 1992, involved the city-states of Bremen and Hamburg and the state of Saarland. Bremen and Hamburg argued that their transfer payments to other states were too large in view of their own outlays for the maintenance and improvement of harbor facilities that are also used by other states. The court rejected this claim, but found that Bremen had been the victim of constitutional discrimination because the city had received no transfer payments for several years and later received less financial aid than Saarland even though Bremen had substantially higher debts than Saarland. Finally, the court ruled that the federal government's vertical payments to Bremen and Saarland had been too low in view of the serious budgetary problems of both states. Accordingly, the federal government and other states would be required to assist both states with appropriate measures.[53] (On financial equalization at the local level, see the section below on local self-government.)

The *Vocational Training Act* case (1980) is another illustration of cooperative federalism collapsing into litigation.[54] In 1976, without obtaining the Bundesrat's approval, the SPD-FDP coalition government secured the passage of major reforms in vocational training. (Federal laws affecting the vital interests of the states require the Bundesrat's consent.) The statute called for the federal government to administer the program and provided grants, financed by a special tax on certain employers, to the unemployed. Six states challenged the validity of the statute in an abstract norm-control proceeding before the Federal Constitutional Court: Bavaria on the ground that any tax levied under Article 105 (3) requires the consent of the Bundesrat; the remaining states on the ground that the administration of the program by the federal government also requires the Bundesrat's consent under Article 84 (1).

The court rejected Bavaria's argument by ruling that the tax imposed on employers was not a "tax" within the meaning of Article 105 but rather a "special levy" that the Bundestag could impose under its Article 74 (11) power to regulate economic matters. It was necessary, said the Second Senate, to distinguish between special levies aimed at regulating particular trades and general tax receipts for the support of government if federal financial equalization among the states were to be achieved under the fiscal provisions (Articles 104a–115) of the Constitution.[55] But then the court nullified the act because the Bundesrat had not consented to its federal administration under the terms of Article 84 (1).

NOTE: FRAMEWORK LAWS. Article 75 of the Basic Law authorizes the federal government to enact general, or "framework," statutes (*Rahmengesetze*) regarding matters traditionally within the states' domain but of a nature requiring federal participation in the interest of more uniform national policy. The assigned topical areas include regional planning and water management, the legal status of the press and the film industry, and, following constitutional amendments adopted in 1969 and 1971, the legal status of persons in the public service of the *Länder* and the general principles governing higher education. The states would continue to dominate these fields, but within preestablished federal guidelines.

More recent examples of framework legislation are the Civil Service Framework Act and the Higher Education Framework Act.[56] The Civil Service Act defines the status and nature of the civil service, specifies the general qualifications of public servants, prescribes the conditions of termination and retirement, and lays down general norms of professional behavior and comportment. The Higher Education Act sets forth general guidelines for the governance of universities and authorizes the creation of reform commissions to coordinate and support changes in research and teaching programs.

Litigation under these and similar framework statutes takes the form either of a challenge to a federal statute alleged to regulate the relevant subject matter in excessive detail or, more commonly, a challenge to a state statute alleged to interfere with the federation's authority to lay down the broader legislative framework. An example of the latter is a judicial reference questioning Schleswig-Holstein's Higher Education Act, which provided that elections to university governing bodies be held by majority vote. The Constitutional Court struck down the state's election system because it conflicted with the general principle of proportional representation set forth in the Higher Education Act.[57]

The extent to which the federal government may control the details of a matter regulated within its framework jurisdiction is a difficult issue requiring delicate judicial balancing. In the *North Rhine–Westphalia Salaries* case, the court argued that "the state legislation must fit into the federal framework but must be left free to take account of the particular conditions of the state concerned; that the federal framework provisions need not be restricted to fundamental principles yet must not exceed their declared purpose of forming a boundary for discretionary regulation by the states nor confine the latter to a choice between predetermined legal alternatives."[58] If, on the other hand, the matter regulated is one in which there is a strong and legitimate interest in national uniformity, federal legislation may provide the details with respect to that matter, assuming, of course, that the matter falls within the federation's framework authority.[59]

NOTE: JOINT TASKS. Articles 91a and 91b — 1969 amendments to the Basic Law — define areas of public policy for which the federation and states shall be jointly responsible. Article 91a authorizes the federation to help the *Länder* carry out certain duties in the fields of higher education, regional economic planning, and coastal preservation. The federation participates in these tasks, provided the Bundesrat consents, so long as the community as a whole is implicated and the federal role is "necessary to improve living conditions." Article 91b, adopted like its twin at the height of West Germany's education crisis,[60] permits joint cooperation, "pursuant to agreements," in educational planning, the promotion of research institutions, and projects of supraregional importance. These amendments constitutionalized forms of cooperation between levels of government that had long begun to supersede the older system of divided powers.[61]

3.7 Financial Subsidies Case (1975)
39 BVerfGE 96

[The Urban Renewal Act of 1971 helped the states to restore their inner cities and to develop new neighborhoods. Article 104a (4) of the Basic Law authorizes the federation to assist the states with grants-in-aid for the purpose of "averting a disturbance of the overall economic equilibrium or to equalize differences of economic capacities within the federal territory." On the other hand, urban planning is one of the many subjects the states are entitled to administer, under Articles 83 and 84, "as a matter of their own concern." Bavaria challenged the constitutionality of section 72 (3) of the statute because it placed the planning, coordination with related projects, and disbursement of funds under the complete control of the federal minister of housing. The state claimed in an abstract judicial-review proceeding that the statute conflicted with Article 104a (4) in conjunction with Articles 30, 83, 20 (1), and 79 (3).]

Judgment of the Second Senate. . . .

C. I. 1. The constitution of a federal state requires a stable division of public funds, particularly of tax revenues, between federal and state governments. This is so because monetary resources going from the federal budget to the states for purely state matters make the states dependent on the federal government and thus interfere with the autonomy of the states. Thus a federal order must first ensure that financial grants to the states from the federal budget remain the exception. [It must also make sure] that the law regulates such grants so that they do not become ways to exert influence over the freedom of decision of member states in carrying out those duties they are bound to carry out. This danger is greatest whenever the federal state alone decides whether and how to provide financial assistance. [In this case] the states are dependent on federal resources, while at the same time [the federal government] decides who will get the assistance, largely by reference to the budgetary resources of the states because the grant of federal assistance depends on their financial participation. Accordingly, the conflict over the interpretation of Article 104a (4) of the Basic Law concerns a central problem of the federal order. . . .

If the Constitution does not entrust any further powers to the federal government, as is the case with Article 104a (4), then under the presumptions set out above, the federal state will have exhausted its jurisdiction in granting financial aid. The administrative jurisdiction and responsibility of the states will remain intact, binding the states [even] in the case of federal subsidies. Any incursion on the freedom of the states to carry out their governmental duties independently and free of outside direction contradicts the federal structure of the Federal Republic and the closely connected right of the states to organize for themselves the scope of their duties. Even the jurisdiction of the federal government under Article 104a (4) can have no greater scope than any other federal powers that coincide with powers of the states. . . .

3. The power in Article 104a (4) [1] of the Basic Law to place at the disposal of the states financial assistance for state investments . . . is not an instrument of direct or indirect regulation of investments aimed at carrying out general federal economic, monetary, zoning, or structural-political goals in the states. Apart from the goals of Article 104a (4) [1] of the Basic Law, these federal subsidies do not allow the federal point of view to influence the execution of their duties by the states. . . .

In accordance with its position in Part X of the Basic Law, under "Finance," and in the constitutional rules governing public finances of the Federal Republic, Article 104a (4) of the Basic Law has only one function: to supplement the carefully balanced distribution of the tax revenues achieved through vertical and horizontal financial adjustments, according to the operational financial needs of the federal government and the states. Such supplementation results only if a proportional financial distribution is not achieved and the states cannot fulfill the important governmental tasks entrusted to them despite adequate efforts to do so. In view of its character as an exception in the financial system of the federal state, federal financial aid is restricted to those governmental areas in which the federal government itself has a particular interest by reason of its responsibility for the total economic development of the [nation] and its duty of interregional coordination. . . .

5. The federal laws enacted pursuant to Article 104a (4) [2] of the Basic Law

not only set out the types of investments to be furthered; they also regulate as a body the details of the federal financial assistance. That has particular significance here, for federal law requires the concurrence of the Bundesrat. The reason is obvious: as mentioned above, the ways and means of granting financial aid affect in a fundamental fashion the positions of the states as well as their interests. Thus they should definitely be able to shape the contents of the regulations that affect them. In particular, they should be able to make sure that federal financing does not restrict or impair their freedom in carrying out their own governmental tasks. . . .

II. The relevant provisions of the City Planning Law permit an interpretation that is consistent with the constitutional basis for public finances and the limits set forth by the federal system of the Basic Law for federal benefits under Article 104a (4).

1. Localities plan and carry out urban construction, development, and urban renewal projects. Sections 71 (1), 72 (3) [4], and 72 (4) of the City Planning Law make clear that the federal government can grant subsidies to the states only under Article 104a (4) [1] of the Basic Law. The responsibility for distribution of funds to local investors lies in the hands of the states. The federal government and the states are always the federal partners in federal financial assistance to municipal investments, never the federal government and the municipalities, even when the municipalities actually carry out the investment project being aided.

2. Section 71 (3) of the City Planning Law mandates the use of financial assistance to promote the development of urban construction and urban renewal projects according to spatial or factual considerations as well as in accordance with the importance of the investments for the economic development and urban building development to the entire federal nation. But in the absence of administrative authorization this mandate cannot confer upon the federal government the power to become a coplanner or share any other powers when choosing which projects are to be subsidized under the aspect of federal unity. When implementing the statute, states must independently put this provision of substantive law into effect. . . . Thus this mandate is directed to the states; they must observe this statutory provision in drawing up their state programs "[for] urban renewal and construction projects . . . [for] federal financial assistance under section 71 . . ." (section 72 (2) [1] City Planning Law). The states have the obligation — and as bearers of this duty vis-à-vis the federal government they alone are competent — to develop areas of emphasis within which federal goals of the federal financial aid can be achieved concerning the specific project. The federal government remains restricted to rejecting individual investment plans which are inconsistent with the requirements and objectives of the financial aid of which for other reasons cannot advance the constitutional aims of Article 104a (4) [1] of the Basic Law. . . .

3. . . . Section 71 (3) of the City Planning Law requires a consensus between the federal government and the states. In particular, the federal minister for zoning, building, and city planning, who makes the grants of federal financial aid, must

work for a consensus at least until this effort proves unavailing in that either the federal government or the states adhere to their position in violation of the principle of federal comity. . . . The subject matter of consultation consists only of the state programs drawn up and maintained under section 72 (1) [2]. The federal minister cannot make city planning projects not contained in that state's programs the subject of negotiations without approval of the states. . . .

5. The fact that to some extent the City Planning Law does not itself contain the rules discussed above does not partially nullify that statute, because these rules can be inferred from the Constitution. . . .

6. The Bavarian state government's complaint is also directed against section 72 (3) [4] of the City Planning Law. It is true the states do not have free access to the financial assistance allotted to them under the terms of the federal program. But in making the allocation, the federal government has made a legally binding promise to the states of its financial support in a certain amount and for a certain purpose. . . . It is no longer possible for the federal government to intervene in the management of the federal program or to control the distribution of funds through the states. The competent state officials have the responsibility of overseeing the administration of the federal aid. In so doing, they are subject to [state] parliamentary control and to the control of the state accounting office, while the parliamentary control of the Bundestag and that of the federal accounting office reaches only up to the time when the financial aid is disbursed to the states. Nonetheless, each state has a duty — in this case resulting from the cooperation between the federal government and the states — to keep the federal government informed of the proper use of the federal aid. No federal authority to investigate the planning, execution, and impact of individual projects follows from this, however.

D. Under this interpretation, sections 71 and 72 of the City Planning Law are consistent with the Basic Law. This decision is issued by unanimous vote.

POWERS OF THE BUNDESRAT

The Council of State Governments (Bundesrat), the mainstay of German federalism, was designed to safeguard the interests of the *Länder*. Unlike the United States Senate, the Bundesrat represents the *Länder* in their corporate capacities. Thus each *Land* delegation, or the person appointed to represent the state, votes as a unit in accordance with instructions of the *Land* government. To accommodate the interests of the new eastern *Länder*, the Unity Treaty amended Article 51 of the Basic Law, changing the allocation of votes in the Bundesrat. As before, each state is entitled to at least three voting members, but now states with more than two million people are entitled to four votes, those with more than six million receive five votes, and those with more than seven million receive six votes. (In the past, the largest states had five votes.)

The Basic Law does not place the Bundesrat on an equal footing with the Bundestag. As the popularly elected house, the Bundestag is the nation's highest parliamentary body. By contrast, the Bundesrat enjoys the right to *participate* in the national legislative process. Yet it has a suspensive veto over legislation generally and an absolute veto over all legislation affecting the vital interests of the *Länder*. A suspensive veto can be overridden by an equivalent vote in the Bundestag. If the legislation affects the interests of the *Länder,* the Bundesrat's consent is required. Actions constitutionally requiring the Bundesrat's consent include proposed constitutional amendments, all laws affecting state tax revenues, and all laws and directives impinging on the administration of federal law by a state.

There is, however, a twilight zone in which the Bundesrat encounters opposition from the Bundestag over the scope of its consent power. Conflicts over the range and extent of the Bundesrat's consent power are most likely to reach the Constitutional Court when the Bundestag and Bundesrat are controlled by different political parties, as they were in the early 1990s when a CDU-FDP-dominated Bundestag confronted an SPD-dominated Bundesrat. The same situation occurred in the mid-1970s when the Bundesrat, dominated by Christian Democrats, wielded its authority against an SPD-controlled parliamentary majority in a manner that virtually asserted the Bundesrat's equality with the Bundestag in the national legislative process. The theory of coresponsibility, as several state governments called it, was a central issue in the well-known *Bundesrat* case (1975; no. 3.8).

NOTE: BUNDESRAT'S AUTHORITY UNDER FIRE. The *Abortion I* (1975; no. 7.10) and *Conscientious Objector II* (1978) cases are examples of challenges to the Bundesrat's authority.[62] When the Bundesrat objected to an abortion bill passed by the Bundestag, the latter in turn voted to override the objection, holding that the Bundesrat's consent was unnecessary. The dispute resolved itself into a disagreement over the nature of the statute. Was it a substantive change in public policy, for which the Bundesrat's consent would not be required, or was it a matter affecting the administration of federal law, in which case consent would be required? The Bundesrat argued that its consent was necessary because the substantive legal change vitally affected the meaning and scope of the states' administrative procedures. The court rejected this claim on the authority of the rule set forth in the *Bundesrat* case, holding that the states enjoyed even wider latitude than previously to structure the administration of the statute.

The outcome of the *Conscientious Objector II* case (1978), however, favored the Bundesrat. In 1977 the Bundestag modified the procedure for determining whether a prospective draftee is entitled to conscientious objector status. Instead of appearing before a board to establish the sincerity of his claim — a process administered in different ways in the various states — an applicant now could automatically receive the exemption by simply notifying the board in writing that he was conscientiously opposed to military service. The statute did not receive, nor did the Bundestag seek, the consent of the Bundesrat. Pursuant to Article 87b (2) the conscription statute had authorized the states to implement the legislation on behalf of the federation.[63] The court held that since the statute expanded the administrative responsibility of the *Länder*—a responsibility transferred to the states with the Bundesrat's consent—the Bundesrat's consent was once again required. The newly liberalized rule on conscientious objection "fundamentally transformed civilian alternative service into a second form of community service,"[64] thus imposing on the states a much greater responsibility than previously for finding community service jobs for conscientious objectors. Such a large shift of responsibility, said the court, is permissible only with the consent of the Bundesrat.

The upshot of these and related cases is that any law containing provisions extending or prolonging the administrative procedures of state agencies requires the consent of the Bundesrat even though the law as originally enacted had already received its required consent.[65] Even if a subject matter is clearly within the federation's exclusive legislative authority, and even if the law in question is silent with respect to local administrative procedures, the Bundesrat's consent may nevertheless be necessary if the law substantially affects those procedures or effectively requires the *Länder* to change them in order to effectively administer the federal law.[66]

3.8 Pension Insurance Amendment Case (1975) ("Bundesrat Case")
37 BVerfGE 363

[The question in this case is whether a later amendment of a law requiring the original consent of the Bundesrat is also subject to an absolute veto, even if the amendment itself does not affect a matter requiring the Bundesrat's assent. In 1972 the Bundestag passed the Pension Reform Act. Because the act regulated the procedures of state administration, it required and received the Bundesrat's approval. The Bundestag amended the act one year later, but the amendment did not change its essential content. Thus the Bundestag maintained that the amendment did not require the Bundesrat's consent. Rhineland-Palatinate and Bavaria petitioned the Constitutional Court to vindicate the Bundesrat's claims to its veto right and to a position of coresponsibility with the Bundestag in West Germany's parliamentary system.]

———————

Judgment of the Second Senate. . . .

C. II. 1. . . . [The fact] that the Pension Reform Act required the consent of the Bundesrat . . . does not establish that the . . . amending act also requires such consent. Not every statute amending a law requiring consent is for this reason alone subject to the consent requirement. The Basic Law contains no provisions from which to deduce such a principle. . . .

(a) The distribution of authority between the federation and the states, as provided by the Basic Law, demands protective measures against the danger that ordinary legislation may produce distortions of the system that are not within the purview of the Basic Law. The provisions in the Basic Law requiring consent of the Bundesrat—including Article 84 (1)—serve this purpose in the interest of the states. Consequently, this article requires that a law containing provisions which regulate the state administrative process obtain the consent of the Bundesrat—as the federal body through which the states participate in the making of federal laws. By approving the Pension Reform Act in its entirety, the Bundesrat also gave its approval to [those parts of the act] regulating the administrative procedure of the states. The Bundesrat has by its consent to the [original] Reform Bill approved this "penetration" into the sphere of administrative execution of federal laws which Article 83 guarantees to the states. If, in a later amending act, no new "penetration" into the sphere reserved to the states occurs and no renewed distortion of the system results, then this amending act does not require the consent of the Bundesrat. . . .

(b) . . . The Bundestag adopts federal laws pursuant to Article 77 (1). The Bundesrat merely participates in the legislative process (Article 50). . . . In this connection it is important [to realize] that the requirement of consent to a statute under the Basic Law represents an exception to the rule. Only in certain explicitly enumerated cases in which the states' field of interest will be affected in a particularly intensive way does the Basic Law require consent. . . . The Bundesrat has no general right of control which may be derived from this principle. . . .

(c) It is true that the Bundesrat examines the entire content of every law requiring its consent, not only those provisions which bring the consent requirement into play. It therefore may refuse its consent to a law containing substantive norms as well as provisions respecting states' administrative procedures because it disagrees with the substantive provisions. . . .

(d) But it does not follow from the fact that the consent of the Bundesrat applies to the entire statute as a legislative unit that every amendment itself requires the Bundesrat's consent. Rather, the view that a law requiring consent is a legislative unit speaks against a consent requirement for amending statutes. . . .

The amending statute is also a technical legislative unit. The court must independently and continually examine all prerequisites for its legislative adoption just as in the case of any other law: It must determine whether the federal legislature had the authority to enact a law of this content and whether the law requires consent by virtue of its content. If the law does not itself contain provisions requiring consent, and if it also amends no such provisions, then it does not require consent. . . .

(e) A further consideration supports this result: Nothing precludes the Bundestag, in exercising its legislative discretion, from using several laws to regulate a subject. It can, for example, put the substantive provisions in one law, as to which the Bundesrat has only a suspensive veto [see Article 77], and can enact provisions respecting administrative procedures of the states in another law requiring Bundesrat consent—as not infrequently happens in practice. If one accepted the argument of the Bundesrat [that every amendment of a law requiring its consent in turn requires consent], then a later amendment of the original statute containing only substantive law would not require consent; but if substantive and procedural provisions were in one statute (requiring consent), then every later amendment of this law would similarly require consent. But it would be absurd to decide these two cases differently. . . .

2. Nonetheless, there are a number of cases in which the Bundesrat's consent is necessary for the amendment of a law that itself requires such consent. This is apparent when the amending law contains new provisions which in their own right require consent. The same is true when the amendment affects those provisions of the amended statute that caused that statute to require Bundesrat consent. Also included is the case in which a statute amends another statute requiring consent and containing substantive norms as well as provisions respecting states' administration. To be sure, [the amending statute may be] confined to substantive matters but nevertheless make such changes in this realm as to give an essentially different meaning and scope to the administrative provisions it does not expressly amend. . . .

[The court went on to find that the amending law in this case did not regulate state procedure and thus held that the Bundesrat's consent was not required.]

Justices von Schlabrendorff, Geiger, and Rinck, dissenting . . .

Everyone agrees that the Basic Law contains no express provision requiring the Bundesrat's consent for the amendment of every statute that itself requires such consent. It cannot in the least be deduced from this that an amendment would require consent only when it falls within the rule of Article 84 (1) or another express provision of the Basic Law—especially since, according to our decision of February 24, 1970 [citing the *Telephone Charges* case 28 BVerfGE 70], the Basic Law does not exhaustively list the cases in which a law requires consent.

3. (a) . . . The assumption that requiring Bundesrat consent for *every* law amending a statute which itself requires consent would lead to an imbalance between federal legislative bodies to the detriment of the Bundestag assumes what is to be proved. . . . The argument . . . that the exception would become the rule and the rule the exception is just as unconvincing. . . .

(b) For the instant case . . . it is quite irrelevant how [we should] generally determine the relationship between Bundestag and Bundesrat in the legislative process. . . . When a statute requires consent, the position of the Bundesrat is no weaker than that of the Bundestag. . . . Everyone agrees that consent to a statute means consent to the entire statute as a legislative unit. . . .

. . . The amending law is, to be sure, a new legislative unit, . . . [but] not an . . .

independent, enforceable regulation in itself; [it] derives its meaning only in connection with the law it amends. . . . The essential content of the amending statute necessarily becomes a part of a statute that undoubtedly required consent because of its content and continues to require consent so long as it exists. . . .

Finally, the consent requirement . . . follows from the further consideration that legislation is a political process that demands compromise. . . . The addition of new material by an amending law . . . alters the content of that compromise, and one cannot preclude the possibility — indeed it is quite likely — that the Bundesrat would not have agreed to this new compromise. . . .

4. In addition, this conclusion is consistent with what the Federal Constitutional Court has already decided . . . [citing *inter alia* the *Legalization of Documents* case, 24 BVerfGE 184 (1968), which held that the Bundesrat must approve all regulations issued under a statute requiring consent pursuant to Article 80 (2)]. It would hardly be comprehensible to assume that regulations implementing such a law . . . required Bundesrat consent, whereas amendments did not.

NOTE: EXPANSION OF THE BUNDESRAT'S POWER. Although the *Bundesrat* case rejected the theory of coresponsibility, the Bundesrat has developed into a virtually equal player on the field of national legislation. David Conradt noted that

> originally, the framers of the Basic Law anticipated that only about 10 percent of all federal legislation would require Bundesrat approval and hence be subject to Bundesrat veto. In practice, however, through bargaining in the legal committees in each house, and judicial interpretation, the scope of the Bundesrat's absolute veto power has been enlarged to the point where it can now veto roughly 60 percent of all federal legislation. This unforeseen development occurred largely because many federal laws which refer to matters not subject to veto nonetheless contain provisions that set forth how the states are to administer and implement the legislation. Citing Article 84 of the Basic Law, the states have argued that, since they are instructed as to how the federal legislation is to be administered, the legislation, in both its substantive and procedural aspects, requires Bundesrat approval.[67]

By jealously guarding and in some instances broadly interpreting the Bundesrat's consent power, as Conradt noted, the Constitutional Court has helped to transform the Bundesrat from the mere checking institution that it was in the 1950s and 1960s into one of the most powerful institutions in the Federal Republic.[68] Moreover, in giving its consent to numerous constitutional amendments over the years, at least half of which resulted in the expansion of the federation's power, the Bundesrat, through skillful maneuvering, has ensured that its consent would be constitutionally required in the exercise of these new powers. Since the adoption of a constitutional amendment in 1992 (Article 23), the Bundesrat's power extends more deeply than ever before into the realm of European and foreign policy (see concluding note in this chapter).

LOCAL SELF-GOVERNMENT

Local government is a prominent feature of Germany's constitutional structure. The German states, Arthur Gunlicks has written, "are responsible for executing as matters of their own concern most national laws, a large majority of which in turn are given to the local governments which serve also as field agencies. Local governments also execute most state (*Land*) laws, in addition to the ordinances and regulations passed by the local councils in their roles as instruments of local self-government. Thus the local level is the primary focus for the administration of the laws and regulations of all levels in Germany."[69]

Local government has a long and checkered history in Germany. Baron von Stein laid its foundation in the Prussian City Charter Act of 1809, and it came to full realization in the free Hanseatic cities later in the century.[70] The autonomy of local government in most parts of Germany, however, was severely limited under the Bismarck Reich and altogether crushed during the Nazi era. After World War II, in accordance with their policy of decentralization, the Allied powers rebuilt the German political structure from the bottom up, restoring local government responsibility before authorizing the rebuilding of the states.

Later, when the states were reestablished, each state constitution contained provisions guaranteeing local self-government, reflecting not only the policy of the occupying powers but also the precedents set by similar provisions laid down in the Frankfurt Constitution (Article 184), the Prussian Constitution of 1850 (Article 105), and the Weimar Constitution (Article 127). Article 28 of the Basic Law carries on the tradition. Paragraph 2 declares: "The communes [towns, counties, and municipalities] must be guaranteed the right to regulate on their own responsibility all the affairs of the local community within the limits set by law." What constitutes an "affair of the local community" is a matter that occasionally works its way into the Federal Constitutional Court, as the *Hoheneggelsen* case (1982) demonstrates. Later, in 1985, the Second Senate declared that financial autonomy is part of the municipal autonomy secured by the Basic Law.[71]

Article 93 (1) [1] [4b] of the Basic Law authorizes local governments to lodge constitutional complaints against laws impinging on their right to self-government. This guarantee of local self-government, however, is an institutional guarantee. The Constitutional Court has thus declined to hear the complaints of individual municipalities whose existence is threatened by otherwise valid boundary changes or annexations.[72] As Gunlicks noted, "The institutional guarantee enjoyed by local governments protects the essential content (*Wesensgehalt*) of local self-government. The concept of essential content refers to activities that cannot be removed without changing the status and structure of the institution."[73] The *Hoheneggelsen* case illustrates a recent application of the "core function" doctrine.

3.9. Hoheneggelsen Case (1982)
59 BVerfGE 216

[In 1974 the SPD-controlled legislature of Lower Saxony passed a law consolidating several communities into one united municipality. The communities in which two-thirds of the population lived wanted to call the new municipality "Söhlde," while the others preferred "Hoheneggelsen." The legislature designated the new municipality "Söhlde," in keeping with the practice of naming a new entity after the largest city in the group of consolidated municipalities. After the CDU defeated the SPD in Lower Saxony's 1976 election, the legislature passed a new law renaming Söhlde "Hoheneggelsen." The legislators explained that the choice of "Söhlde" had not reflected prevailing local conditions. By renaming the municipality, they wished to correct the prior mistake as well as to encourage investment in the more centrally located Hoheneggelsen. The city of Söhlde filed a constitutional complaint on the ground that the new statute interfered with its right of local self-government in violation of Article 28 (2).]

Judgment of the Second Senate. . . .

A. The constitutional complaint concerns the issue of whether and under what conditions state legislators may once again change the name of a municipality after [they have passed a law] to newly form and name the municipality only a few years prior in the course of a comprehensive territorial reorganization of local government.

B. II. The constitutional complaint is justified. The provision under attack violates the complainant's right of self-government (Article 28).

 1. Article 28 (2) [1] guarantees local units of government jurisdiction over virtually all matters concerning the local community as well as the authority to transact business autonomously in this area. [State legislatures] may impose legal restrictions on local self-government if and insofar as these restrictions leave the core functions of [this right] intact. In determining what constitutes these core functions, [one] may take historical developments as well as various historical manifestations of self-government into account.

[The court went on to say that part of the historical tradition of local government sovereignty is its right to use the name it has chosen. The locality's name conveys its legal identity and manifests its individuality. This right consequently falls within the essence of Article 28 (2) [1]. However, communities have not historically been immune from state-imposed name changes. Accordingly, most municipal codes provide that either the state legislature or the secretary of the interior can change a municipality's name under certain conditions. The historical findings indicate that this right was one of those consigned to the sovereignty of the state. To this extent Article 28 (2) [1] contains an institutional but not an individual guarantee of municipal sovereign rights.]

3. However, part of the constitutionally protected essence of communal autonomy, as it has developed historically, is that such name changes will be made only after the municipality has been granted a hearing. This applies not only to name changes necessary within the context of reorganization procedures but also to all other cases where a municipality is to be renamed against its will. Even section 10 (2) of the German Municipal Code provided for an obligatory prior hearing of the municipality. The municipal codes of all states now contain this obligation, insofar as they do not already make a name change dependent upon an express petition of the municipality in question.

A municipality's right to use its properly determined name as a manifestation of its individuality and as part of the historical tradition of local sovereignty is not the only consideration which justifies its right to a prior hearing. The principle of the rule of law, which states that a municipality may not be made into the object of state action during a name change, also demands this [result].

The complainant received a proper hearing during the legislative proceedings. The bill of June 19, 1980, contained the following explanation of complainant's redesignation: The original naming was an erroneous decision because the district of Hoheneggelsen is geographically the more central district of complainant; [the drafters of the bill] expected that the complainant would consider its central location and meaning differently in the future than it has in the past when making investments, if the municipality's continued unchanged existence is to be assured. With this [list, the drafters] briefly but completely set forth the fundamental reasons for the redesignation.

[The court explained that the legislature may infringe on the guarantee of Article 28 (2) [1] only in the public interest and that this guideline stems from the principle of the rule of law. Although the redesignation of a municipality requires that its effect on the common good be considered, ultimately the legislators determine whether a given norm is in the public interest. Consequently, the court gives lawmakers great leeway in this evaluative judgment.]

When regulating for the first time an area which consolidates several local communities, [the legislature] cannot, as a rule, maintain the former names of the communities being consolidated but rather must find a common name. For this reason legislators have relatively broad discretion when restructuring an area — especially if the communities in question disagree about the name of the newly consolidated municipality. However, once the consolidation has taken place and a new municipality with its own name has been formed, the guarantee of local self-government resumes its full weight. [The legislature] must cite overriding considerations of the public good which plausibly explain a redesignation against the municipality's will. These are lacking in the instant case.

When [the legislature] restructured the complainant in 1974, it chose the name of the largest community participating in the consolidation in view of the existing dispute between the former communities over the name which the new municipality would use, just as it had in other comparable cases. The fundamental reason for the name change by the corrective, reformatory law of February 1981 was the legislature's aim of taking the "central location and meaning of the district of Hoheneggelsen" into account. Further, it wanted to change prospectively the complainant's past investment behavior, which it considered wrong. This aim cannot justify the violation of complainant's right to use its name. Moreover, it deviates from the generally applicable aims and procedures for state regional planning in Lower Saxony, according to which the municipality itself may determine the location of the center of its administrative area. No apparent reason justifies why the complainant alone should be deprived of its acknowledged right to determine its own internal development and be compelled under threat of legal sanctions to move its center to Hoheneggelsen because of its prior investments. And this, despite [the fact] that the state of Lower Saxony already approved and encouraged [the municipality's] investments [only] a few years earlier by incorporating the locality of Söhlde into the regional planning program.

Further, the law's professed aim is based upon a misunderstanding of the meaning and scope of the right to local self-government. [This right] vests local government with authority over developmental planning and the resulting investment decisions of individual communities to the extent that regional interests meriting protection do not make restrictions necessary. Special statutory treatment which is burdensome [only] to a few municipalities is inconsistent with this [right]; that is, treatment which has as its aim to teach local representatives to behave the way the state legislative majority wishes in the realm of local self-government as well as treatment aimed particularly at teaching them to heed certain local special interests when deciding upon plans and investments. [Legislators] also cannot justify this treatment by combining [these reasons] with the speculative hope of reducing tensions and facilitating integration.

We need not reach the issue of whether the redesignation of the complainant would have been an appropriate and reasonable means for attaining the goal pursued by the legislators, since [the legislators] cite no constitutionally recognized grounds for the name change which are in the public interest.

NOTE: THE CORE FUNCTIONS OF LOCAL GOVERNMENT. When the Constitutional Court speaks of the essence of communal autonomy, it is referring to certain core functions (*Kernbereich*) of local government that must be protected against federal or state encroachment. Not all local affairs, however, are core functions. The transfer of certain powers to the national government, the expansion of cooperative federalism, and the consequent reduction in the number of policy areas deemed exclusively municipal complicate efforts to distinguish between local and nonlocal affairs. On the other hand, the court's historical approach to determining the essence of local government "could also be used to protect newly acquired local functions."[74] German commentators are unable to agree on a complete list of functions protected by the *Kernbereich* theory — some reject the theory of core functions altogether — but they, like the court, do include local rule making, internal governmental organization, and certain aspects of land-use planning as well as personnel and finance administration.

The *Kernbereich* theory echoes the federalism controversy in the United States triggered by *National League of Cities* v. *Usery* (1976).[75] *Usery* held that the commerce clause did not permit Congress to impair the states' "ability to function effectively in a federal system" or to displace their "integral governmental functions." In 1985, however, the Supreme Court overruled *Usery*, claiming, contrary to the approach of the Federal Constitutional Court, that any "reliance on history as an organizing principle [for determining the 'core functions' of state governments — thus rendering them immune to federal regulation] — results in linedrawing of the most arbitrary sort."[76] But as Gunlicks noted, "it is much easier for the German Court to take a position in favor of local governments, since Article 28 (2) of the Basic Law grants local governments explicit protection, while there is sharp disagreement whether the Tenth Amendment is relevant to protecting American local governments from federal incursions."[77]

NOTE: THE *WASTE DISPOSAL* CASE. The Federal Waste Disposal Act of 1972, enacted within the federation's concurrent powers, laid down regulations for the collection, treatment, storage, and disposal of waste. Lower Saxony, in implementing the statute, placed the responsibility for waste disposal in the hands of county (*Kreis*) authorities, in effect taking this function away from lower levels of government. Rastrede, a municipality of seventeen thousand inhabitants with its own garbage pickup and disposal system, filed a constitutional complaint under Article 93 (1.4b) of the Basic Law, alleging a violation of its constitutional right to self-government. The court's decision reaffirmed the principle of local self-government, holding, as it had in the *Hoheneggelsen* case, that "the essential content of communal self-government cannot be undermined."[78]

In *Waste Disposal* (1988) the court remarked that "the essence of communal self-government cannot be compiled into an objectively determinable catalog of functions based on fixed features, but is merely the communal power to assume control over all affairs of a local nature that are not subsumed under powers assigned to other levels of government."[79] The court held that pursuant to federal law, a *Land* government could legitimately assign the task of waste disposal to public corporations other than local cities. Also, in the light of developing technologies and the administrative efficiency associated with more centralized jurisdiction, waste disposal could no longer be regarded as exclusively an affair of the local community.

Waste Disposal embodied a cautious judgment, however. Economic considerations alone, said the court, may not be allowed to defeat the principle of local self-government, and in weighing economic efficiency against the value of local control, a heavy thumb must be placed on the side of the latter to ensure that the principle of self-government is given its proper place in the Basic Law's overall governmental scheme. Just as other decisions considered in this chapter underscore the active role of the Constitutional Court in adjudicating conflicts between federal and state governments, *Waste Disposal* signals the court's intention to continue serving as a balance fulcrum between state and local governments.

GERMAN FEDERALISM AND THE EUROPEAN UNION

The Treaty on European Union (TEU), signed at Maastricht, Holland, on February 7, 1992, was designed to bring about "an ever closer union among the peoples of Europe." Under the Maastricht Treaty, the European Economic Community (EEC) would weld itself into a tighter political, social, and economic union. Economic union would proceed in three stages, culminating in a single European currency superintended by a Central European Bank. Social union would come about by Europe-wide advances in the fields of education, culture, and public health. Political union would be achieved through common foreign and security policies along with a common European citizenship. In addition, freedom of movement and residence within the union would be guaranteed, a common visa policy enforced, and citizens of member states entitled to vote and stand for public office in local elections.

By December 18, 1992, both German parliamentary chambers had ratified the Maastricht Treaty.[80] Simultaneously, however, in order to remove all constitutional doubts about the TEU, they also amended several articles of the Basic Law. The centerpiece of these amendments is the new Article 23, the so-called European Article,[81] which supports the goal of European union, authorizes the national government to transfer its sovereign powers to the union, and enhances parliament's right to participate in the decision-making process on Europe-related matters. Beyond this, the federation must consider the Bundesrat's opinion on such matters when they affect the vital interests of the *Länder*. Finally, any transfer of national authority to the European Union that would result in any change in the Basic Law must conform to paragraphs 2 and 3 of Article 79, respectively requiring a formal amendment to the Basic Law and barring any infringement of its unalterable principles.

Article 24 (1) was likewise amended to authorize the *Länder* to transfer, with the federal government's consent, their power to "transnational institutions in neighboring regions." (As originally drafted, Article 24 constitutionalized the principle of internationalism to which the German people committed themselves after the Second World War. It empowered the federation generally to transfer sovereign authority to transnational [i.e., intergovernmental] institutions and, in the interest of "a peaceful and lasting order in Europe," to enter systems of collective security. See chapter 4, pp. 157–63, for further discussion of this article.) Other TEU-related amendments to the Basic Law include provisions granting nationals of member states the right to vote in local elections (Article 28 [1]), authorizing both houses of parliament to establish committees on European union capable of making decisions in the name of their parent bodies (Articles 45 and 52 [3a]), and empowering Germany's Federal Bank to transfer its duties and functions to a European central bank (Article 88).

Notwithstanding these amendments, the TEU invited an immediate legal challenge in the form of constitutional complaints brought by a German former member of the European Commission and German "Green" party members of the European Parliament suing as private citizens. They claimed that the surrender of national authority to the European Union would deprive them of certain guaranteed freedoms in tandem with important democratic rights secured by Articles 21 (1) (the right of political parties to form public opinion) and 38 (1) (the right to vote in parliamentary elections).[82] They also alleged that the transfer of sovereign national powers to the European Union infringed the unamendable principles of federalism, democracy, and popular sovereignty in contravention of Article 79 (3).

As for national sovereignty, the complainants argued that Article 24 permits the transfer of powers to *intergovernmental* organizations, not to a superstate-like entity such as the European Union. Provisions in the Maastricht Treaty for a single currency, a common citizenship, and uniform social policies, they maintained — not to mention the Union's alleged capacity to determine its own competence in certain fields (competence-competence) — virtually transform the European Union into a supranational federal state capable of eroding Germany's constitutional order. On the matter of democracy, they argued that the transfer of decision-making powers to Union executive officials in the face of the limited authority of the European Parliament failed to meet the minimum requirements of democratic legitimacy. Federalism also, they maintained, was a victim of the TEU because it threatened to diminish the rights and status of the *Länder* in the German governmental system.

In the *Maastricht* case (1993), reprinted in part below, the court dismissed all complaints except the one based on democracy and the right to vote. Although this complaint was found to be admissible (*zulässig*), the court rejected it after considering the merits of the case, but not before admonishing the federal government that any transfer of sovereign rights to the European Union must satisfy the minimal requirements of democratic legitimation. To the alarm of some pro-European commentators, the court also appeared to charge the federal government with the responsibility of developing the European Union into an entity that would meet German constitutional standards pertaining to basic rights as well as democracy. In the end, however, noting that the Basic Law commits Germany to European integration and that as presently constituted the EU leaves plenty of room for development along democratic lines, the court sustained the constitutionality of the treaty.

3.10 Maastricht Case (1993)
89 BVerfGE 155

[In this landmark case, the Federal Constitutional Court addressed critical issues related to the meaning of democracy, separation of powers, federalism, and national sovereignty. As noted above, the court upheld the constitutionality of the Maastricht Treaty but placed the development of the European Union under the judgment of the Basic Law and its principles. In the extracts below, the court considers the nature of the European Union and its implications for German federalism. For extracts on other issues arising out of the Maastricht Treaty, see case 5.5.]

Judgment of the Second Senate. . . .

C. II. . . . As already noted, the Maastricht Treaty establishes an inter-governmental community for the creation of an ever closer union among the peoples of Europe. These peoples are organized at the level of the state and not as a state based on the people of one European nation (Article A). In view of this fact, the question raised by the first complainant as to whether the Basic Law allows or excludes German membership in a European state does not arise. Only the act of accession to German membership in a federation of states need be examined here.

    1. (a) The member states have established the European Union in order to perform some of their duties and to exercise some of their sovereignty jointly. In the resolution that they passed at Edinburgh on December 11 and 12, 1992, the heads of state who are united in the European Council resolved — in the context of the Maastricht Treaty — of their own free will and in accordance with existing treaties, to exercise some of their powers jointly. Accordingly, the Maastricht Treaty takes account of the independence and sovereignty of the member-states, in that it imposes an obligation upon the European Union to respect the national identities of its member states, and grants the European Union and the European Communities specific powers and responsibilities but only on the basis of the principle of limited individual powers. By so doing, it has elevated the principle of subsidiarity to

the level of a binding legal principle for the European Union (Article B (2) of the Maastricht Treaty) and the European Community (Article 3 b (2) of the EC Treaty).

The term "European Union" may indeed suggest that the direction ultimately to be taken by the process of European integration after further amendments to the Treaty is one which will lead toward further integration, but in fact the actual intention expressed does not confirm this. In any case, there is no intention at the moment to establish a "United States of Europe" comparable in structure to the United States of America. . . .

Therefore, even after the Maastricht Treaty has entered into force, the Federal Republic of Germany remains a member of an inter-governmental community, the authority of which is derived from the member states; this authority has binding effects within Germany's sovereign sphere only when a German decree governing application of the law [*Rechtsanwendungsbefehl*] is issued in respect to it. Germany is one of the "high contracting parties" which have given as the reason for their commitment to the Maastricht Treaty — a treaty concluded "for an unlimited period" (Article Q) — their desire to be members of the European Union for a lengthy period; such membership may, however, be terminated by means of appropriate legislation. . . . Germany thus retains the quality of a sovereign state in its own right as well as the status of sovereign equality with other states within the meaning of Article 2 (1) of the United Nations Charter of June 26, 1945.

(b) The required influence of the Bundestag is guaranteed in the first instance by the fact that Article 23 (1) of the Basic Law makes it necessary for an act to be passed before Germany may become a member of the European Union, or before such membership may develop further by an amendment to the basic treaty instruments or an extension of the European Union's powers; if the conditions shown in sentence three are fulfilled, an act of this nature requires the affirmative vote for which Article 79 (2) of the Basic Law provides. Under the terms of Article 23 (2) and (3) of the Basic Law and the terms of the law of March 12, 1993, dealing with the cooperation of the Bundestag and the federal government in matters pertaining to European Union — adopted for the purpose of its implementation — the Bundestag contributes to the process of forming the federal government's political will in such matters. These interrelated powers are to be exercised by the federal government and the Bundestag in a spirit of institutional loyalty [*Organtreue*].

Finally, the Bundestag also influences the federal government's European policy, because the federal government is responsible to parliament under Articles 63 and 67 of the Basic Law (citing 68 BVerfGE 1, 109). This function of control and creation, which the Bundestag as a matter of course performs in public sessions, brings the public and the political parties into contact with the federal government's European policy, and therefore becomes a factor in the decision which citizens have to make on how to cast their votes. . . .

By signing the Maastricht Treaty, the governments of the member states have also emphasized the substantial importance attached to national parliaments within the European Union. Their statement on the role of national parliaments in the European Union emphasizes the need for the increased involvement of the parliaments of the member states in the activities of the European Union, and imposes an obligation upon these governments to inform their respective parliaments in due time of proposals made by the Commission, so that the parliaments may examine such proposals.

C. II. 2. (a) . . . The first paragraph of the new principle contained in Article 3b of the EC Treaty also states that the Community shall act only within the limit of the powers conferred upon it by the Treaty and the objectives assigned to it. The regulations on the principle of subsidiarity (Article 3b (2) of the EC Treaty) and on the principle of proportionality (Article 3b (3) of the EC Treaty) which follow thereafter are intended to define the limits of the Community's powers. The European Council which met in Edinburgh on December 11 and 12, 1992, stressed, in its overall concept for the application of the principle of subsidiarity, that Article 3 (4) of the EC Treaty imposes strict limits upon the activities of the Community. It said that the requirement for powers to be assigned by means of treaties has always been a fundamental element of Community law, and that while the allocation of powers to the individual states is the general rule, the allocation of powers to the Community is the exception. . . .

(c) . . . The subsidiarity principle, therefore, does not establish any powers for the European Community; in fact it limits the implementation of powers which have already been granted elsewhere. Under Article B (2) of the Union Treaty the objectives of the Union can be achieved only as provided by the treaty and in accordance with the conditions and timetable set out in it; at the same time regard is to be had to the subsidiarity principle. Accordingly, Article 3b (1) of the EC Treaty specifies as a primary condition for action by the Community that a power has been conferred upon it by the treaty, and its exercise is then subject to the subsidiarity principle by virtue of Article 3b (2).

That means that if there is a power under the treaty to take action, the subsidiarity principle determines whether and how the Community may act. If the Community legislature wishes to exercise a power conferred upon it to pass a law, it must first make sure (and also, by virtue of Article 190 of the EC Treaty, show plausibly) that the objectives of the measure in question could not be sufficiently achieved by the member states at the national level. This finding must then justify the further conclusion that, in view of the scale and effects of the measure, the objectives can be better achieved at the Community level.

Through this principle of subsidiarity, adherence to which is a matter for the European Court to scrutinize, the national identities of the member states are to be preserved and their powers to be retained. How far the subsidiarity principle will counteract an erosion of the jurisdictions of the member states, and therefore an exhaustion of the functions and powers of the Bundestag, depends to an important extent (apart from the case law of the European Court relating to the subsidiarity principle) on the practice of the council as the Community's real legislative body. It is there that the federal government has to assert its influence in favor of a strict treatment of Article 3b (2) of the EC Treaty and so fulfill the constitutional duty imposed on it by Article 23 (1) of the Basic Law. The Bundestag for its part has the opportunity, by using its right of cooperation in the formation of Germany's internal political intentions established by Article 23 (3) of the Basic Law, to have an effect on the council's practices and to exercise an influence on them within the terms of the subsidiarity principle. In so doing the Bundestag will also be performing a constitutional duty incumbent upon it under Article 23 (1). In addition, it is to be expected that the Bundesrat, too, will pay particular attention to the subsidiarity principle.

D. . . . Any further development of the European Union must conform to the conceptual framework set out above. In amending the Basic Law, the Bundestag took this into account. The new Article 23 inserted into the Basic Law expressly mentions the [future] development of the European Union and subjects it to the principles of democracy and the rule of law, the principles of the social and federal state, and the principle of subsidiarity. What is decisive, therefore, from the vantage point of both the treaties and the Basic Law, is that the democratic foundation of the Union will progress in tandem with the process of integration. By the same token, it is expected that a living democracy will be maintained in the member states as integration proceeds.

NOTE: THE PRINCIPLE OF SUBSIDIARITY. The first sentence of the Basic Law's "European Article" defines the European Union as committed to the "principle of subsidiarity." Except for this provision (Article 23 [1]) there is no express reference to subsidiarity in the Basic Law. Constitutional commentators, however, have distilled this principle from the Basic Law's general structure, particularly its provisions on federalism and democracy, and from various fundamental rights, among the most important of which is Article 6 (1) and (2), which, respectively, confer the state's "special protection" on marriage and the family and recognize the "natural rights of parents" to care for and educate their children.[83]

Article 6 (2) provided the Constitutional Court with one of its rare opportunities, prior to the *Maastricht* case, to invoke the principle of subsidiarity. In sustaining a statute broadening the discretion of a guardianship court in resolving a dispute between parents over their children, the First Senate alluded to "the principle of 'subsidiarity' in the sense of allowing the state to intervene only when the task of caring for children cannot be performed by the smaller community" (i.e., the family).[84] So defined, the principle traces its origin to Catholic social thought, which "affirms that there is nothing done by a higher or larger organization that cannot be done as well by a lower or smaller one."[85]

Although subsidiarity had played an important role in German social and economic law,[86] until *Maastricht* it was not accepted as a binding constitutional norm. Undoubtedly there were good reasons for this. Apart from the division of authority laid down in the Basic Law, the limits of state intervention in fields such as education, health, labor, and welfare are difficult to discern. In addition, the jurisprudence of the human dignity (Article 1 [1]) and personality (Article 2 [1]) clauses of the Basic Law, which has marked off wide boundaries for the free play of individual liberty, obviates the need for an authoritative definition of subsidiarity as a constitutional principle.

Subsidiarity, however, has come to play a defining role in determining the relationship between individual nation-states and supranational organizations such as the European Union. Germany, along with Great Britain, insisted on incorporating the principle into Article 3b of the Maastricht Treaty.[87] Moreover, the treaty permits a member state to petition the European Court of Justice for a decision on whether the Union has transgressed the principle of subsidiarity. What is more notable about the *Maastricht* case is that the Federal Constitutional Court appears to have decided that Article 23 is not only a valid constitutional amendment — thus rejecting the argument based on its unconstitutionality — but also that its power extends to the review of any transfer of power by the Bundestag to the European Union in violation of the principle of subsidiarity.[88]

CONCLUSION

The issues and cases discussed in this chapter underscore the shape and form of federal-state conflicts adjudicated by the Federal Constitutional Court. The Basic Law's complex system of federal-state relations, including its detailed provisions on *Land* administration of federal law and the apportionment of tax revenue between levels of government, measures the extent to which the process of government is subject to constitutional legality. And as we shall see in the next chapter, a similar framework of legality engirds the principle of separated powers.

The cases featured in this chapter provided the Constitutional Court with opportunities to perpetuate its vision of the political order created by the Basic Law. Although firmly upholding the principle of federal supremacy in those areas of public policy expressly committed to the federal government, this vision also includes a critical and autonomous role for the individual *Länder*. For one thing, the court has tended to construe strictly the long list of concurrent powers granted to the federal government under Article 74, probably because a broad construction of these powers would virtually obliterate the *Länder* as effective units of the federal system. For another, the court has invoked the principle of comity to impose a variety of obligations on both federal and *Land* governments in their relations with each other. With the *Maastricht* decision, finally, the court appears ready to reassess the federal-state relationship in terms of the principle of subsidiarity.

4

SEPARATION OF POWERS

The principle of separation of powers finds its clearest expression in Article 20 (2) of the Basic Law, which declares that "all state authority [*Staatsgewalt*] . . . shall be exercised . . . by specific legislative, executive, and judicial organs."[1] The Federal Constitutional Court, however, recognizes that this principle cannot be realized in pure form. Separation of powers is, rather, a "system of reciprocal controls" marked by numerous checks and balances.[2] German constitution makers believed that they could secure liberty and avoid oppressive government by setting up a system of shared powers similar to constitutional arrangements in the United States. In their view, the dispersion of political power was implicit in the Constitution's version of the *Rechtsstaat*.[3]

Separation of powers in the Federal Republic is unlike the division of authority among the branches of the United States government. For one thing, the German variant of separated powers is linked with issues of federalism, a linkage born of the federation's preeminence in the field of legislation and the states' preeminence in the field of public administration. As a result, executive-legislative conflicts often resolve themselves into disputes between federal lawmakers and state bureaucracies. Federal-state conflicts, therefore, also implicate the principle of separation of powers.

At the federal level, the Basic Law disperses authority within and among several institutions, or "branches" of government, that are distinctive to West Germany's parliamentary system. While dividing executive authority between the federal president and the federal government (i.e., between the chancellor and his or her cabinet), it vests legislative authority in the Bundestag—authority shared with the Bundesrat—and at the same time confers independent rights on certain units thereof.[4] These four institutions—government (chancellor and cabinet), president, Bundestag, and Bundesrat—together with the Federal Constitutional Court constitute the highest constitutional organs of the Federal Republic. The Constitutional Court is *primus inter pares* among these federal organs because it has the authority to define their institutional rights and duties when resolving conflicts between them. Such disputes arrive at the court in the form of *Organstreit* proceedings,[5] the German equivalent of a conflict based on separation of powers in the United States.

But when German constitutional scholars speak and write about separation of powers, they have more in mind than the technical formalities of an *Organstreit* proceeding. They often see separation of powers in terms of a creative tension between parliament and government, a view anchored in the Basic Law itself. Parliament elects the chancellor (Article 63), but the chancellor is responsible for setting the "general policy guidelines" of the federal government (Article 65). In addition, as noted in the next section, the constructive vote of no-confidence (Article 67) reinforces the chancellor's independence as a political leader. Indeed, Konrad Adenauer's strong leadership during the first decade of the Federal Republic's existence led many commentators to describe the new German polity as a "chancellor democracy."[6]

Ideally, under this system a legislature made up of "representatives of the whole people, not bound by orders and instructions" (Article 38), constitutes the check necessary to control and discipline the chancellor. The unamendable principle of separated powers (*Gewaltenteilung*) combines with the equally entrenched principles of popular sovereignty (*Volks-souveränität*) and executive responsibility (*Verantwortlichkeit der Regierung*) to produce an accountable government marked by democratic legitimacy. "In practice," however, as one leading commentator recently noted, "this required separation of power between the government and parliament no longer exists in the face of the [development] of our party democracy."[7] The increasing importance of political parties in the creation and election of a particular government or governing coalition prompted constitutional theorists to highlight the importance of the opposition *in* parliament rather than the opposition *of* parliament as the most effective check on the "executive branch."[8] Perhaps this is why the Federal Constitutional Court ranks the principles of multipartyism (*Mehrparteienprinzip*), equality of parties (*Chancengleichheit der Parteien*), and the right of opposition (*Recht auf Opposition*) as equal to those of popular government, executive responsibility, and separation of powers.

EXECUTIVE-LEGISLATIVE RELATIONS

NOTE: THE BASIC STRUCTURE OF SEPARATED POWERS. As in other parliamentary systems, the German legislature (Bundestag) chooses the head of the government (Article 63), who in turn is responsible to the legislature. Federal ministers, however, owe their primary allegiance to the chancellor. He effectively appoints — and dismisses — them (Article 64) and establishes the general policies within which they are constitutionally obligated to operate their respective ministries. Within these limits cabinet officials conduct their departmental affairs "autonomously and on [their] own responsibility" (Article 65). The cabinet as a whole resolves policy disagreements between federal ministers (Article 65). The Basic Law, finally, does not insist on separating legislative and executive personnel. Constitutional practice in Germany allows the chancellor and members of his cabinet, not to mention administrative officials of lesser rank, to hold seats in parliament. By the same token, certain members of parliament, in their capacity as parliamentary state secretaries, serve as officials within the federal ministries.[9]

Lawmaking

The large majority of legislative proposals in West Germany are bills proposed by the federal government. The government must submit such bills to the Bundesrat before transmitting them to the Bundestag. Bills originating in the Bundesrat, on the other hand, make their way to the Bundestag by way of the federal government, whose own views must first be solicited. Legislation is therefore generally the product of a broad consensus reached by the three institutions.[10] Constitutional conflicts among these institutions, as exemplified by the *"Bundesrat"* case (no. 3.8), seldom arise in the Federal Republic. After the Bundestag passes legislation, either the chancellor or the appropriate federal minister must countersign it (Article 82). A president could, according to some authorities, refuse to promulgate a statute he regards as unconstitutional; however, such an action could trigger impeachment proceedings against him. The validity of those proceedings would in turn have to be resolved by the Federal Constitutional Court.[11]

NOTE: VOTE OF NO-CONFIDENCE AND THE POWER OF DISSOLUTION. The Basic Law's scheme of separated powers involves a system of checks and balances rare among parliamentary democracies and considerably at variance with the Constitution of the Weimar Republic. In contrast to Weimar, the chancellor holds a strong position in Bonn's governing system. A vote of no-confidence is insufficient to drive him out of office. Parliament may remove him only when a majority of its members simultaneously elects his successor, a procedure commonly known as a constructive vote of no-confidence. But parliament is also better protected from dissolution by the executive. The Weimar Constitution (Article 25) permitted the president to dissolve parliament at any time and for any reason. Under the Basic Law the president may dissolve parliament in only two situations: after a chancellor's own motion for a vote of confidence fails, and then only pursuant to the chancellor's request (Article 68); and when the Bundestag fails initially to elect a chancellor after several ballots (Article 63). As the *Parliamentary Dissolution* case (1984; no. 4.1) shows, parliamentary representatives may challenge the federal president's power to dissolve the Bundestag in an *Organstreit* proceeding before the Federal Constitutional Court.

The Basic Law provides for a vote of confidence in two situations: when the Bundestag itself initiates the procedure under Article 67, and, as just noted, when the chancellor himself asks for a vote of confidence under Article 68. The Bundestag has initiated a confidence vote under Article 67 on only two occasions: on April 27, 1972, Chancellor Willy Brandt survived a Christian Democratic challenge to his leadership; and on October 1, 1982, Free Democrats abandoned Helmut Schmidt's coalition government to elect Helmut Kohl, a Christian Democrat, as chancellor. The chancellor himself has asked for a vote of confidence under Article 68 on three occasions: on September 22, 1972, Willy Brandt "lost" the vote in a deliberate ploy to call new elections; on February 3, 1982, Helmut Schmidt sought and won the confidence of the Bundestag; and on December 17, 1982, Helmut Kohl "lost" his vote of confidence. The *Parliamentary Dissolution* case arose out of circumstances surrounding the last of these three votes.

4.1 Parliamentary Dissolution Case (1984)
62 BVerfGE 1

[Chancellor Kohl, like Willy Brandt in 1972, contrived to lose the vote of confidence held on December 17, 1982. Only then could he request the federal president, as planned, to dissolve the Bundestag so that new elections could take place in March, a full year and a half before the regularly scheduled election. Shortly thereafter, on January 7, 1983, the federal president dissolved the Bundestag, on the chancellor's request. Despite an all-party agreement to hold new elections, certain members of the Bundestag argued that the dissolution order infringed their electoral mandates, whereupon they challenged the validity of the president's decree in an *Organstreit* proceeding before the Federal Constitutional Court.

The fundamental legal issues were whether the chancellor may call for a vote of no-confidence when he commands the support of a parliamentary majority, and, if he loses in a contrived vote, whether pursuant to his request the president may dissolve the Bundestag. Under the Basic Law the president's power of dissolution is closely constrained by Articles 63 and 68. When considered in tandem with Article 38, which provides for parliamentary terms of four years, these provisions appear to limit dissolution to two situations: (1) when the Bundestag fails to elect a chancellor after a federal election, and (2) when the chancellor genuinely loses a vote of confidence (and then only pursuant to the chancellor's request). The clear intent of these constitutional provisions is to prevent governments from being brought down unnecessarily, and thus to stabilize the political system. In this case, however, the chancellor and the president were accused of manipulating the Constitution for political purposes.

The Federal Constitutional Court's Second Senate was wholly preoccupied with this case in the first six weeks of 1983. It handed down its opinion on February 16, 1983, barely three weeks before the newly scheduled federal election. In a 116-page opinion, and with two justices dissenting, the senate upheld the dissolution order, contending, essentially, that the president had reasonably exercised his discretion in light of the complex political circumstances surrounding the chancellor's call for a confidence vote and his subsequent request for an order of dissolution. The numbered paragraphs below are the headnotes (*Leitsätze*) of the decision. They consist of the Second Senate's own summary of the principles underlying this case.]

---

1. In litigation between federal governmental bodies, a parliamentary representative has standing to assert the violation of any right constitutionally related to his status as a parliamentarian. Part of this status includes the guarantee set forth in Article 39 (1) of the Basic Law, which relates to the duration of his term in office.

2. An order to dissolve the federal parliament or the refusal to do so pursuant to Article 68 of the Basic Law is a political decision within the lawful discretion of the federal president. The president may exercise his discretionary authority under Article 68 (1) only when the constitutional prerequisites are fulfilled at the time of his decision.

3. Article 68 of the Basic Law . . . prescribes a particular sequence of events [when the dissolution of parliament is being considered]. Constitutional violations occurring at any one of these stages must be taken into consideration by the federal president when the federal chancellor proposes that he dissolve parliament.

4. (a) Article 68 (1) is an open-ended constitutional provision in need of concretization.

(b) Concretizing Article 68 (1) is a function not only of the Federal Constitutional Court; this duty is also vested in other supreme constitutional organs [e.g., the federal president and the Bundestag].

(c) When [concretizing Article 68 (1)], the highest constitutional organs must adhere to prior constitutional rulings and to the basic political judgments [laid down in the Basic Law]. In giving specific meaning to the Constitution as a basic legal order, they must implement [their decisions] consistently and with a view to their long-term impact. This is especially true because a high degree of consensus among the supreme constitutional organs of the Federal Republic is necessary when they are called upon to assess all the constitutional and political aspects of the situation. A politically contested parliamentary decision of the ruling majority that becomes the subject of a legal dispute does not meet this [high] standard [of evaluation].

5. In the tradition of German constitutional history, the term "confidence" within the meaning of Article 68 refers to parliament's official approval — manifested in the act of voting — of the chancellor's programs with respect to personnel and substantive issues.

6. Under Article 68, the chancellor may try to dissolve the Bundestag only when he finds that it is no longer politically possible to govern with the prevailing

configuration of parliamentary votes. This configuration must so severely cripple or impair the capacity to govern that the chancellor can no longer expect to advance his political program in a meaningful way and [at the same time] secure the continuing support of the parliamentary majority. This principle is part of the unwritten [text] of Article 68 (1).

7. Article 68 (1) cannot be construed to allow a chancellor who is certain of receiving a parliamentary majority in support of his program to request a no confidence vote merely because he thinks it would be convenient [to hold new elections].

8. (a) Before the chancellor asks for a vote of no confidence for the purpose of requesting the president to dissolve parliament, he must determine whether there is still a good chance that a majority will endorse his policy and do so with continuing confidence.

(b) When deciding whether the chancellor's petition [for a confidence vote] and proposal [to dissolve parliament] are constitutional under Article 68, the president must . . . respect the chancellor's authority to judge and evaluate the [political situation] unless some other [valid] assessment of the situation would clearly forbid parliament's dissolution.

(c) The unanimous decision of the [political] parties represented in parliament to bring about new elections should not serve as a limit on the president's discretion; he may construe such unanimity as an additional indication that the dissolution of parliament would produce a result closer to the intent of Article 68 than a decision against dissolution.

9. The three highest constitutional organs [i.e., president, chancellor, and Bundestag] enjoy [considerable] latitude in judging, evaluating, and making political decisions [under Article 68 (1)]. Thus, in interpreting Article 68, the standard of [judicial] review is narrower than would be the case in assessing the validity of [ordinary] legislation and its implementation. Here the Basic Law relies mainly on the internal system of checks and balances between the highest constitutional organs mentioned in Article 68. The Federal Constitutional Court may find a constitutional violation here only when standards expressly laid down in the Basic Law have been ignored.

[In setting forth these guidelines the Constitutional Court examined not only the language and structure of Article 68, but also the relationship of the latter to other constitutional provisions dealing with the status and dissolution of parliament. The court treated the infrequency of no-confidence votes in the political history of the Bonn Republic as gloss on the meaning of these constitutional relationships. As the Second Senate noted, the Basic Law has created a "representative democracy" marked by general elections at regular intervals. Thus Article 68 may not be used to "legitimate" any political decision reached in a constitutional manner or to get out of some political difficulty that emerges in the course of a legislative term. The Basic Law does not prescribe an unlimited right of dissolution. Yet the court was unwilling to hold that a chancellor is constitutionally barred from calling for a vote of confidence simply and only because he has the support of a parliamentary majority. The standard for invoking Article 68 is more complicated than this; it requires the assessment that "an extraordinary situation" exists in which "the federal chancellor [has] reason . . . to believe that a lasting, stable parliamentary majority could no longer be brought into existence." In any event, as the court emphasized, each participant in this process must independently assess the propriety of resorting to the procedure under Article 68: the chancellor when he calls for a vote of confidence, members of the Bundestag when they vote on it, and the president when he is asked by the chancellor to dissolve the Bundestag.

Two justices dissented and one concurred in the court's opinion. Justice Rottmann agreed with the legal criteria set forth by the majority for dissolving parliament, but felt that they were incorrectly applied in this case. Justice Rinck, on the other hand, taking a literalist approach, held that dissolution is always impermissible when a parliamentary majority, however slim, supports the person and program of the chancellor. Justice Zeidler, on the other hand, pointed out that a crisis of legitimacy had emerged in the light of the FDP's behavior. Free Democrats had originally pledged in the 1979 election campaign to continue their coalition with the SPD. They broke this pledge when they formed a coalition with Christian Democrats in 1982 to elect Helmut Kohl as chancellor in a constructive vote of no-confidence under Article 67. In Zeidler's view, the new coalition had to return to the electorate for the sake of its own legitimacy.]

NOTE: IMPACT OF THE *DISSOLUTION* CASE. The *Dissolution* case remains an extremely controversial decision. As former federal president Karl Carstens himself acknowledged — it was Carstens who dissolved the parliament — most German constitutional scholars questioned the constitutionality of the dissolution order.[12] Yet, as others have pointed out, the case was one of unusual political delicacy. A decision against the dissolution order, one commentator wrote, might have "tarnished the credibility of the highest governmental organs," including that of the president himself, and thus "damage[d] public confidence in the entire constitutional system."[13] Others found this argument unconvincing because it was tantamount to saying that the Constitution should be violated to avoid tarnishing the government. The drama ended with the election of March 6, 1983, when the new coalition received the resounding support of the electorate, thus seeming to vindicate the federal president as well as the court's own judicious statesmanship.[14]

It is worth emphasizing that the *Dissolution* case took the form of a declaratory judgment. In conflicts between the highest organs of the Federal Republic —

Organstreit proceedings — the court is authorized only to "interpret" the Basic Law (Article 93 [1]), not to invalidate governmental action. The framers were themselves conscious of the political sensitivity of such disputes and accordingly allocated limited authority to the Constitutional Court to intervene. Thus a decision against the validity of the dissolution order would not necessarily have caused the cancellation of the March election. Yet the federal president clearly took the measure of the Federal Constitutional Court's influence by informing the German nation in a televised address that he would rescind his dissolution order in the event of a judicial interpretation incompatible with his own view of his constitutional duty under the Basic Law.

NOTE: EXECUTIVE PRIVILEGE AND THE *FLICK* CASE. Major constitutional clashes between the highest organs of the Federal Republic occur infrequently; the *Parliamentary Dissolution* case is an exception. Some commentators have seen separation of powers more directly implicated in certain decisions of the Federal Constitutional Court itself. The court's invalidation of major social policies, together with the instructions and warnings it has frequently hurled at the legislature, have led to charges that the court has overstepped its proper bounds by encroaching on the powers of parliament.[15] But these are not classic separation-of-powers cases in the mold of the *American Steel Seizure* case, or even the *Legislative Veto* case.[16]

One issue that has produced a significant comparable case in Germany is the claim of executive privilege. In *United States* v. *Nixon,*[17] the Supreme Court ruled that a federal court could direct the president to produce certain recordings and documents over his objection that such executive communications enjoyed an unqualified privilege of immunity. Similarly, in the *Flick* case (1984),[18] the Federal Constitutional Court ruled that the Federal Finance and Economics Ministry must deliver certain corporate records to a parliamentary committee investigating an exemption of DM 1.5 million in capital gains earned by the Flick corporation from its sale of Daimler-Benz stock. The committee was looking into charges that influential persons in Flick's managerial hierarchy had "transferred" large sums of money to high civil servants and politicians in exchange for the tax exemption. The ministry refused to produce certain documents on the ground that they contained trade and tax secrets whose confidentiality was required by the tax code, whereupon Green and Social Democratic committee members petitioned the Constitutional Court to order the full disclosure of the missing records.

The court declared that in investigating the activities of the federal cabinet, a parliamentary committee's right to take evidence under the terms of Article 44 (1) of the Basic Law includes the right to demand documentary evidence. Even as the Second Senate acknowledged the existence of a "core sphere of executive autonomy" in which "a range of initiatives, consultations, and activities is immune to parliamentary oversight," it held that in the circumstances of this case the Ministry of

Finance and Economics had violated Article 44 by failing to comply with the committee's request. "Where the cabinet is accountable to parliament," said the senate, "documentary disclosure is an integral part of parliamentary control." The senate emphasized that parliament's right to documentary evidence of the kind sought here is an essential aspect of the principle of separated powers. In its unanimous view, the senate went on to note that if circumstances permit, the legitimate concerns of the executive for confidentiality can be satisfied by the committee's examination of the relevant records in closed session.

NOTE: LEGISLATIVE-EXECUTIVE RELATIONS AND THE BUDGET. The budgetary provisions of the Basic Law embody numerous checks and balances within and between various constitutional organs. The federal government must submit all tax and appropriation bills simultaneously to the Bundesrat and the Bundestag (Article 110 [3]), where legislative delay, pending further negotiation, is always possible. Expenditures in excess of budgetary appropriations require the consent of the federal minister of finance, who in turn may grant his consent only "in case of an unforeseen and compelling necessity" (Article 112). By the same token, any law that exceeds the budgetary limit proposed by the executive requires the federal government's consent (Article 113 [1]); the federal government may even "require the Bundestag to postpone its vote on such bills" (Article 113 [1]). Should the legislature fail to approve a new budget, the federal government may, according to Article 111, continue to make the payments necessary to meet its contractual responsibilities, execute the laws, and maintain institutions established by law.

In the *Budget Control* case (1977),[19] the Constitutional Court clarified the meaning of some of these provisions. After affirming the paramount and exclusive authority of the legislature to establish budgetary policy, the Second Senate emphasized the duty of all constitutional organs to cooperate in the timely enactment of a budget bill. In passages that recall the principle of comity in the federal-state field, the senate announced that constitutional organs are obliged to consider each other's interests in the exercise of their constitutional responsibilities. In the exercise of his authority under Article 112, the federal minister of finance must, if time permits, communicate and consult with the legislature for the purpose of securing its consent to an expenditure in excess of what has been authorized. An "unforeseen and compelling necessity" within the meaning of this article exists "only if additional expenditures have become so urgent that the drafting and introduction of a supplementary budget or budget amendment or a postponement until the next fiscal year can no longer be viewed as a reasonable alternative after a judicious assessment of the situation."[20] The duty to communicate in these special situations also extends to the relationship between the federal finance minister and the federal government. According to the court, the government infringes on the authority of the legislature if, in the exercise of its special powers under Article 111, it has not received adequate information on the basis of which a decision regarding the ability of the legislature to meet the crisis might have been made.

JUDICIAL VERSUS LEGISLATIVE AUTHORITY

The German legal system, unlike the Anglo-American, does not regard judicial decisions as sources of law. Separation of powers as understood by Montesquieu and followed in the Continental legal tradition implies a regime of positive law in which legislatures are the supreme lawmakers. The following propositions fairly well summarize the German and largely Continental theory of lawmaking and judicial authority: the focus of all lawmaking authority within the state is the sovereign legislature; law is a closed system of logically arranged and internally coherent rules; all legal disputes must be resolved by reference to such rules; courts of law, independent of the legislature, are the proper agencies for interpreting law; courts should interpret laws literally and in strict accordance with the legislator's will; their function, therefore, is to administer the law as written. This model of the judicial role obviously exaggerates the difference between the function of courts in civil- and common-law systems. Nevertheless, the model broadly identifies a state of mind that helps to explain traditional German attitudes toward law and the judicial role. The *Princess Soraya* case provided the court with an opportunity to reflect anew on the role of courts in a constitutional democracy.

4.2 Princess Soraya Case (1973)
34 BVerfGE 269

[This dispute arose out of a civil damage suit for defamation brought by the ex-wife of the Shah of Iran against *Die Welt* and a freelance journalist. The defendants had published a fictitious interview with Princess Soraya in which intimate details of her private life were revealed. The German Civil Code, however, contains no provision for a civil damage award for an invasion of privacy. Such an invasion constitutes a criminal offense in German law. Tort recovery is possible under section 823 of the Civil Code if the plaintiff can show injury to "life, body, health, freedom, property, or some other right." The Federal High Court of Justice eventually interpreted "some other right" to include the "right to personality." But section 253 of the Civil Code bars monetary relief for nonpecuniary injuries. Recovery for such injuries is possible only "in cases provided by [written] law." No law allows recovery for the injury sustained by the plaintiff. The Federal High Court of Justice nevertheless authorized such recovery in the light of changing social conditions and the fundamental values of the Basic Law, one of these values being the right to protect one's personality. The affirmation of a money damage award in the present case was contested in part on the ground that the courts had exceeded their proper authority under the Constitution. The following extract deals with this particular issue.]

Judgment of the Second Senate. . . .

C. IV. 1. The judge is traditionally bound by the law. This is an inherent element of the principle of separation of powers, and thus of the rule of law. Article 20 of our Constitution, however, has somewhat changed the traditional formulation by providing that the judge is bound by "law and justice." The generally prevailing view implies the rejection of a narrow reliance upon [formally] enacted laws. The formulation chosen in Article 20 keeps us aware of the fact that although "law and justice" are generally coextensive, they may not always be so. Justice is not identical with the aggregate of the written laws. Under certain circumstances law can exist beyond the positive norms which the state enacts — law which has its source in the constitutional legal order as a meaningful, all-embracing system, and which functions as a corrective of the written norms. The courts have the task of finding this law and making it a reality in binding cases. The Constitution does not restrict the judge to applying the language of legislative mandates to the particular case before him. This concept [of the judicial function] presupposes that no gaps in the written legal order exist — a condition which may be desirable in the interest of legal certainty but which in practice is unattainable. The judge's task is not confined to ascertaining and implementing legislative decisions. He may have to make a value judgment (an act which necessarily has volitional elements); that is, bring to light and implement in his decisions those value concepts which are inherent in the constitutional legal order, but which are not, or not adequately, expressed in the language of the written laws. In performing this task, the judge must guard against arbitrariness; his decision must be based upon rational arguments. He must make it clear that the written law fails to perform its function of providing a just solution for the legal problem at hand. Where th[e written law fails], the judge's decision fills the existing gap by using common sense and "general concepts of justice established by the community."

In principle, [no one] has questioned the judge's power and duty to hand down "creative decisions" since the adoption of our present Constitution. The highest courts have claimed this power from the beginning, [and t]he Federal Constitutional Court has always recognized it. The legislature has expressly bestowed upon the highest federal courts sitting *en banc* [i.e., when all the senates of the federal high court in question convene to decide a case together] the task of "further development of the law." In some areas of the law, such as labor law, this task has become particularly important because legislation has not kept up with the rapid pace of social development.

The only remaining question is what limits to impose upon such creative [judicial] decision making. We must keep in mind that the judge is bound by written law, a principle which [we] cannot abandon if the rule of law is to be maintained. We cannot reduce these limits to a formula equally applicable to all areas of the law and to all legal relationships.

2. For purposes of the present decision, [we] confine the formulation of the issue to the area of private law. In this area, the judge is confronted with a great codification, the Civil Code, which has been in force for over seventy years. This [fact] has dual significance: first, the judge's freedom to creatively develop the law necessarily grows with the "aging of codifications," with the increased distance in time between the enactment of the legislative mandate and the judge's decision in an individual case. The interpretation of a written norm cannot always or for an unlimited period remain tied to the meaning the norm had at the time of its enactment. One must explore what reasonable function the [norm] initially served. The norm always remains in the context of the social conditions and sociopolitical views it affects. As these conditions and views change, the thrust of the norm can, and under certain circumstances must, be adjusted to such change. This is especially true when, between the time of enacting and implementing a law, conditions of life and popular views on legal matters have changed as radically as they have in the present century. The judge cannot, by simply pointing to the unchanged language of the written law, avoid the conflict that has arisen between the norm [as written] and a changed society's substantive notions of justice. If he is not to be derelict in his duty to pronounce "justice," he must implement legal norms more freely. Second, as experience dictates, legislative reforms encounter particularly great difficulties and obstacles when they are intended to revise great bodies of legislation which shape the system and character of the entire legal order as does the codification of private law contained in the Civil Code.

3. The decisions presently being challenged concern an issue [i.e., the question of recoverability of money damages for injury to an intangible interest] which was already controversial when the preparatory work on the draft of the Civil Code was in progress. Criticism of the solution chosen by the legislature was immediate and has never ceased, although it did not at that time involve constitutional arguments. Critics referred to legal development in other countries of the Western world which have taken a more liberal approach toward the possibility of recovering money damages for injuries to intangible interests. [The court here cited several comparative studies.] Consequently, [critics] could point out that nowhere in the West did an unlawful act so frequently remain without civil sanctions as in Germany—and for the sole reason that the act had "only" caused nonphysical damages. [Opponents] characterized the rule as a "legislative failure" because it limited the recovery of money damages for injury to intangible interests to a few enumerated special cases—cases, moreover, selected with a certain lack of underlying concept. Criticism became even sharper after the courts, under the influence of "the Constitution's

power to shape private law," took the step of recognizing the general right of personality. The gap that existed in the available remedies for a violation of that right thus became apparent. This problem, the importance of which [the framers] could not anticipate when drafting the Civil Code, now urgently demanded a solution responsive to a changed consciousness of legal rights and values which a new constitution influenced. [One] could not deduce this solution from the enumerative provision of section 253.

The courts faced the question of whether to close this gap by the methods at their disposal or wait for legislative intervention. When the courts chose the first alternative, they found support from the writings of influential legal authors who had advocated the former course. For this reason, legal scholars widely approved the relevant decisions of the Federal High Court of Justice and of other courts from the very beginning. This [fact] illustrates that these decisions were consistent with generally recognized concepts of justice and were not regarded as intolerable restrictions upon freedom of opinion or freedom of the press. . . . To the extent that these decisions were criticized, the [opponents] directed their criticism less against the result the Federal High Court of Justice reached than against the methodological and doctrinal considerations with which the courts justified the new approach. Insofar as this involves a question of methodology in private law, it is not within the Federal Constitutional Court's province to determine the validity of the critics' objections. But one should not overlook [the fact] that the majority of authors specializing in private law apparently regard the reasoning of the courts as dogmatically unobjectionable. . . .

The other alternative, to wait for legislative regulation, cannot be regarded as constitutionally mandated under the circumstances. It is true that the federal government has tried twice to bring about a legislative solution to the problem of protecting an individual's personality right in the area of private law. But the bills drafted in 1959 and 1967 died early in the legislative process, even though there was no indication of any legislative intention to perpetuate the status quo. One cannot blame the judge if, compelled to decide every case submitted to him and convinced that he cannot rely upon the uncertain future intervention of the legislature, he does not adhere to the literal meaning of the existing written law in a case where adherence would largely sacrifice justice in a particular case.

The method by which the Federal High Court of Justice reached the decisions in question is constitutionally unobjectionable for a further reason: This method deviated from the written law only to the extent absolutely necessary to resolve the legal problem presented by the instant case. The Federal High Court of Justice has not regarded section 253 in its entirety as no longer binding. Nor has it treated that provision as unconstitutional. . . . The court has left the enumerative principle expressed in section 253 intact, and has merely added one situation to the legislature's own enumeration of situations in which money damages can be recovered for injury to intangible interests. The Federal High Court of Justice found this addition to be compellingly justified by the evolution of social conditions as well as by a new law of higher rank; to wit, Articles 1 and 2 of the Constitution. Thus, the Federal High Court of Justice and other courts following its holdings have neither abandoned the system of the legal order nor have they exhibited an intention to go their own way in making policy. They have merely taken a further step in developing and concretizing basic ideas inherent in the legal order molded by the Constitution, and they have done so by means which remain within this system. Therefore, the legal rule found [by creative judicial decision] is a legitimate part of the legal order, constituting a limitation upon the freedom of the press as a "general statute" within the meaning of Article 5 of the Constitution. The rule's purpose is to guarantee effective protection of the individual's personality and dignity — i.e., of interests at the center of the constitutional ordering of values — and thus, within a particular area of the law, to strengthen the effect of constitutionally protected fundamental rights. For these reasons, complainants' constitutional arguments must fail. . . .

NOTE: THE *KLASS* CASE. In a politically charged case decided three years before *Soraya,* the Constitutional Court had also considered the relationship between legislature and judiciary. The *Klass* case (1970) involved an amendment to the Basic Law that would permit wiretaps and other interferences with private letters and telephone conversations when necessary to combat foreign and domestic enemies. The amendment (Article 10 [2]) further stipulated "that recourse to the courts shall be replaced by a review of the case by bodies and auxiliary agencies appointed by parliament." Separation of powers was one of the grounds on which the amendment's validity was questioned. The court answered as follows:

> Nor does substitution of recourse to the law by some other judicial control as provided for in Article 10 (2) [2] violate the principle of separation of powers. . . . For this principle does not demand a strict separation of powers, but in exceptional cases permits legislative functions to be exercised by governmental and administrative bodies, or government and administration to be exercised by legislative bodies. In exceptional cases, the principle of separation of powers also permits legal protection against acts of the executive to be furnished not by courts, but by independent institutions, appointed or established by parliament and operating within the framework of the executive department. The essential point is that the rationale for separation of powers, namely reciprocal restriction and control of state power, is still fulfilled.[21]

4.3 Aircraft Noise Control Case (1981)
56 BVerfGE 54

[*Soraya* underscores the inevitability of judicial lawmaking when gaps appear in written law or when a literal interpretation of written law would lead to unacceptable consequences in the light of governing constitutional values. In the *Aircraft Noise Control* case, by contrast, the court declined to fill an alleged omission in the law. In this case, property owners living near the Düsseldorf-Lohausen airport lodged constitutional complaints against administrative authorities and existing statutory law for failing to protect the complainants, pursuant to the Anti–Aircraft Noise Act of 1971, against noise emanating from the airport. The Constitutional Court rejected complaints against the administrative authorities because the complainants had not yet exhausted all of their administrative remedies. The court also rejected the complaints against the statute because the complainants had failed to file their complaints within one year of the statute's enactment, as required by the FCCA. However, the complaints were accepted to the extent that they alleged an unconstitutional omission on the part of the legislature. The complaints argued that in enacting the antinoise statute, the legislature failed to adequately consider the requirements of Article 2 (2) of the Basic Law, which guarantees the rights to life and the inviolability of one's person.]

Judgment of the First Senate. . . .

B. II. . . . Until now, we have admitted complaints of this type [i.e., complaints against the legislature's failure to consider constitutional requirements] only exceptionally and only when the complainant could invoke an explicit commitment in the Basic Law that essentially defines the content and extent of the legislature's duty. Obviously this requirement is not fulfilled here. . . . After the [filing date] for challenging the implementation of specific legislation has expired, a constitutional complaint arising out of an omission [of the legislature] may be considered only under the special aspect elaborated upon in more recent opinions; namely, that the legislature by its inaction might have violated a constitutional duty to amend a statute originally regarded as constitutional.

Because of the great importance of noise abatement the Federal Constitutional Court has put aside these problems of justiciability so that it may clarify the issue of substantive law in this case. . . .

C. I. 1. The constitutional standard under consideration is the right of physical integrity protected by Article 2 (2). Our accepted jurisprudence does not merely protect the individual rights of the citizens against governmental intrusion. Rather, governmental bodies have the duty based upon the objective legal content of Article 2 (2) to shield and promote the legal interests therein enumerated. In particular, [they must] protect these interests from unlawful infringement by others. . . .

2. . . . In its recent opinions the Federal Constitutional Court has repeatedly explained that the legislature may be constitutionally required to amend a statute even though it was regarded as constitutional when originally enacted [citing sev-

eral cases]. [In *Kalkar I* (no. 4.6) the court declared]: "If the legislature has made a decision the basis of which has become questionable due to new, originally unanticipated developments, then it might be obliged by the Constitution to examine whether or not the original decision is to be upheld under the changed circumstances. The duty to remedy this defect may be considered primarily in areas relating to basic rights if the government, by creating licensing requirements and granting licenses, has accepted responsibility for the possible impairment of basic rights. . . ."

It is possible to argue that the legislature has a duty to amend the original antinoise statute because the frequency of flights has rapidly increased since the early 1960s and [in the meantime] the transition to jet-powered aircraft has seriously aggravated the noise situation. In addition, we agree with the complainant's view that, in the light of these developments, the legislature may not confine itself to limiting the acceptable noise level to that which the current technical state of the art makes unavoidable. . . . In a legal order oriented toward the individual, the governing principle must be an assessment of what harm or danger the individual can be expected to bear after weighing competing interests. . . .

II. 1. Contrary to the opinion of the complainant, the legislature has not violated any protective duty resulting from Article 2 (2) by failing to amend the statute. . . . This result is based on the fact that the Federal Constitutional Court, within the framework of a constitutional complaint of the type presented here, may intervene only if the legislature has manifestly violated its duty.

In the *Abortion I* case [no. 7.10] and then again in the *Schleyer* case [no. 7.12] the Federal Constitutional Court emphasized that governmental bodies (legislative and executive branches) are themselves responsible for the form and manner in which they fulfill the [government's] duty under Article 2 (2). They must decide what measures are necessary and proper for carrying out this duty. . . . This limit on constitutional review seems necessary because deciding how the state is to implement its affirmative duty to act and protect [objective values of the Constitution] through active legislative measures is a highly complex issue. [We] derive this duty on the part of the government to act and to protect [the citizen] from the fundamental decisions embodied in the basic rights [put forth in the Constitution]." Various solutions are possible depending on the assessment of the facts, the concrete legislative aims, and the suitability of the imaginable ways and means. A policy decision in this area, which often demands compromise, is subject to the principles of separation of powers and parliamentary democracy. . . . Normally, the Federal Constitutional Court may review such a decision only up to a certain point, unless legal interests of the highest importance are at stake. These considerations are of even greater weight if the issue concerns not just whether the legislature has violated its affirmative duty to protect [objective values] but whether it did so by not amending an existing law. The Federal Constitutional Court can declare this [failure to amend] unconstitutional only if it is evident that an originally valid statute is now defective because of changing circumstances and, if notwithstanding this, the legislature has either done nothing or has taken obviously erroneous measures to remedy [the situation]. In the realm of aircraft noise abatement one may not disregard the fact that no reliable scientific findings are available concerning the limits of reasonable aircraft noise burdens. Additionally, because international air traffic is so complex, the legislature must have sufficient flexibility . . . to pass legislation on this matter.

2. Considering this standard of review, we cannot conclude that the legislature has manifestly neglected its duty to protect citizens against noxious aircraft noise by its failure to amend existing legislation. The measures taken since the early 1970s to carry out [the statute] defy such a conclusion.

GOVERNMENTAL PROCESSES AND PERSONNEL

NOTE: JUDICIAL INDEPENDENCE. The Basic Law vests judicial power in judges who "shall be independent and subject only to law" (Article 97).[22] Another provision bans extraordinary courts, and as a corollary provides that no person "may be removed from the jurisdiction of his lawful judge" (Article 101). In addition, Article 19 completely breaks an older link in German history between administrative courts and the administrative process. The separation created by Article 19 is reinforced by a federal law barring judges from simultaneously exercising legislative and executive powers and — in contrast to the situation in the Weimar Republic — by the creation of a judiciary apart from and wholly independent of the executive and the bureaucracy.[23]

The principle of judicial independence, particularly the requirement that every person has a right to a hearing before an independent and impartial judge, appeared to have been breached by a 1968 amendment to the Basic Law. Article 10 (2), as noted, allows "recourse to the courts [to] be replaced by a review of the case by bodies and auxiliary bodies appointed by parliament" in situations in which the government feels that it must tap telephone lines and interfere with other private communications in the interest of national security. This scheme received the court's blessing in the *Klass* case. The *Kramer* case (1981) posed a related issue.[24] Could the executive branch determine the manner of submitting evidence in a criminal proceeding? *Kramer* involved a member of Bavaria's state legislature convicted of passing information to a foreign intelligence service. The conviction was based on the testimony of a defector from the same service. So as not to reveal the identity of the defector, whose life was threatened by agents of the hostile power, German security officials introduced sworn statements of the former agent and testified to the authenticity of his signature. The defendant challenged his conviction as a denial of due process and separation of powers. Although upholding the conviction and dismissing the complaint, the Constitutional Court laid down several requirements that the courts must observe in sustaining a conviction based on such an exceptional procedure. These requirements include cabinet-level certification that the witness in question is not available for a court appearance, a statement of reasons sufficient to enable the courts to independently assess the plausibility of the government's action, and evidence confirming the out-of-court testimony.

Apart from such exceptions the Constitutional Court has always insisted on the separation of administrative and judicial personnel. In the *Josef-Franziska* case (1959), for example, the court invalidated Baden-Württemberg's creation of special justice-of-the-peace courts staffed in part by local civil servants. The participation of civil servants in the resolution of petty criminal and civil suits, said the court, however convenient and economically feasible such tribunals may be, violated the principle of judicial independence and the defendant's right under Article 101 to be tried by "his lawful judge."[25] This principle of judicial neutrality applies also to the disciplinary courts of professional associations regulated by public law. Accordingly, the court held that it is unconstitutional for a doctor to be disciplined by a professional tribunal staffed in part by members of the medical association's chamber of deputies.[26]

NOTE: CIVIL SERVANTS AND LEGISLATIVE INDEPENDENCE. Ministerial autonomy within the meaning of Article 65 (each federal minister conducts "the affairs of his department autonomously and on his own responsibility") is buttressed by the elevated and permanent status accorded to the professional civil service under Article 33. It is nevertheless a common practice in Germany for civil servants and other public employees to run for public office. Under the terms of Article 137, however, this right may be restricted by legislation. The issue raised in this section is the extent to which the Federal Constitutional Court may review parliamentary regulations affecting the salaries of civil servants sitting in the legislature. Article 48 (3) stipulates that legislators "shall be entitled to remuneration adequate to ensure their independence," and Article 38 (1) requires that they "be representatives of the whole people." In the *Saarland Compensation* case (1975),[27] the court had sustained the constitutionality of a regulation requiring a member of a state legislature to resign his position as an executive in a private company because the state itself owned more than 30 percent of the company's stock. (The legislator's forced resignation from the company resulted in legislative compensation substantially lower than his former salary.)

Financial Status of Parliamentary Representatives

The *Saarland Compensation* case set the stage for a full-dress review of the entire system of parliamentary remuneration. Even though Article 48 (3) of the Basic Law declares that members of parliament "shall be entitled to a remuneration adequate to ensure their independence," legislative compensation was, until recently, relatively low. Instead of regular salaries, representatives received tax-free allowances for travel, office space, and secretarial assistance as well as reimbursement for expenses incurred in the course of their parliamentary duties. This system of compensation was a throwback to the Weimar period and before, when membership in parliament was regarded as an honorary position.[28] This unsalaried system is one reason civil servants have been — and still are — so heavily represented in German parliaments, for they could serve as legislators while still holding their administrative positions or drawing their pensions.

Although many Germans continued to defend the unsalaried parliament and the related proposition that the position of a representative is not a professional calling, the nature of legislative remuneration had changed over the decades. When in 1958 the Bundestag pegged legislative subsistence allowances to a percentage of ministerial salaries and later introduced a pension plan keyed to length of parliamentary service, legislative "compensation" (*Entschädigung*), as it was called, took on the character of a "salary" (*Gehalt*), a development that the Constitutional Court took judicial notice of in the *Parliamentary Pension* case (1971).[29] Yet, legislative allowances remained tax free, a practice that many commentators regarded as unconstitutional. Constitutional assaults on this practice increased in the early 1970s when several state legislatures adopted pension plans of their own and raised the basic annual compensation of their members. The *Legislative Pay* case provided the court with its first major opportunity to consider the validity of tax-free emoluments and other practices related to legislative compensation as well as the special status and pay of civil servants in the legislature.

4.4 Legislative Pay Case (1975)
40 BVerfGE 296

[A former member of Saarland's Landtag who declined to run for another parliamentary term pending the resolution of his complaint against regulations governing the financial status of parliamentary representatives filed this constitutional complaint. Because the provisions of the Saarland State Parliament Act in question here were almost identical with those governing many other German parliaments, including the Bundestag, the traditional pay structure for members of parliament was challenged in this case. Parliamentary delegates had been accustomed to receiving a tax-exempt expense allowance rather than a regular salary, a practice encouraged by the large number of representatives who enjoyed incomes from their regular occupations. The tax-exempt status of these legislative allowances, along with the cancellation of pensions granted to parliamentary deputies previously in the civil service, were at issue in *Legislative Pay*. The question posed was their compatibility with Article 48 (3), which guarantees to all legislators "remuneration adequate to ensure their independence." The headnotes (*Leitsätze*) to the opinion are reprinted immediately below. These are followed by brief passages from the court's opinion.]

---

1. The compensation required by Article 48 (3), once considered reimbursement for special expenditures incurred in connection with [one's legislative] mandate, has taken on the character of [general] support payments for representatives and their dependents from government funds. [These payments] were made [in recognition] of the fact that [carrying out] the legislative mandate had become a full-time occupation.

The [Bundestag] representative who as a result did not become a "civil servant" but remained a holder of public office with the support of his constituents — [i.e.,] a holder of a "free mandate" and a "representative of the whole people" — is no longer merely entitled to reimbursement for his expenses but to a [genuine] salary paid out of state funds.

2. (a) The formal principle of equality requires that every representative receive equal compensation regardless of the amount of time he devotes to his parliamentary duties, the amount of his expenditures, or the amount of his [outside] professional income.

(b) Support payments are to be calculated in such a way that representatives who, for whatever reason, have no independent income, as well as those who suffer a total or partial loss of income because of their [legislative] mandate, will be able to maintain a standard of living commensurate with their office.

3. Support payments for representatives that have the character of income must be taxed according to principles that apply equally to all [persons]. The only payments that are tax free are those made to reimburse a representative for expenses actually and justifiably incurred in the course of his legislative duties.

4. (a) [The special] regulations that [have always] applied to civil servants among the representatives are substantively a part of their status rights as representatives, regardless of whether they are contained in statutes relating to their legal position, daily allowances, or the civil service.

(b) A civil servant elected to parliament retains his salary or, if he retires, receives his retirement benefits. This practice has been a mandate-related privilege from the very beginning and continues to be sanctioned by current regulations.

(c) This privilege, however, loses its legal basis within the law regulating the status of representatives the moment legislators begin to receive adequate support payments. Moreover, this privilege contradicts the formal principle of equality.

5. Article 48 (3) in conjunction with Article 38 (1) of the Basic Law requires [the enactment of] legal provisions that prevent representatives from receiving pay as salaried employees of a company or as so-called consultants or the like not because they provide [actual] contractual services but because they are expected to represent the interests of the paying employer, entrepreneur, or other large organi-

zation in parliament and to try to procure benefits for [their client]. Such income is incompatible with the independent status of representatives and their right to equal financial compensation for as long as their mandate shall last.

6. The principles of democracy and the rule of law (Article 20) demand that the formation of the parliamentary will which determines the amount of compensation and detailed financial regulations with respect to a representative's status be comprehensible to all citizens and that the results be decided in public.

[Extracts from the Judgment of the Second Senate follow.]

C. I. . . . Although the status of [legislative] delegates has remained the same, the [conditions under which they function] have changed considerably. Recognizing this, the Federal Constitutional Court has noted:

> . . . The activity of the representative, given the full range of his duties, has grown into a demanding vocation; thus today, the representative is able legitimately to claim compensation sufficient for the support of himself and his family. . . . Already an "expense allowance" allocated on the basis of a certain percentage of the salary of a federal minister shows clearly the extent to which mere "reimbursement allowances" have become in reality "payment" for parliamentary service. The changed character of [these so-called] reimbursement expenses is especially clear from the introduction of retirement benefits [for legislators]. One may label [such benefits] a supplement designed to protect the independence [of the legislator] up to the time of his retirement, but the pension benefit today is in reality payment for services rendered as a parliamentary delegate [citing 32 BVerfGE 157, 164].

II. 1. In the light of this clear, necessary, logical, and hardly reversible development, Article 48 (3) of the Basic Law takes on new meaning. Representatives are entitled [as a matter of constitutional law] to a "suitable and assured income, for the sake of their independence," for the duration of their membership in parliament. Moreover, this [income] must be keyed to the significance of the office, the burden and responsibility connected with it, and the proper rank of the office within the constitutional structure. The income must be at a level that will ensure the representative's freedom of action as well as his ability to dedicate himself to his parliamentary duties even at the expense of losing in whole or in part his [regular] occupational income. . . .

IV. 5. According to Section 16 (1) [2] of the Saarland State Parliament Act, the compensation accorded to the representative under sections 11 and 14 is tax free. This provision violates the constitutional principle of equal treatment for all before the law (Article 3 [1]). . . .

(b) Up to now the tax exemption for per diem allowances has been based on the customary notion of legislative reimbursement as compensation for additional expenditures and loss of income stemming from the exercise of [one's legislative] mandate. Afterward, these payments took on the character of support payments from government funds for the purpose of securing [legislators'] independence as well as economic security for themselves and their families during their terms of office. [For all practical purposes] these payments had assumed the character of income. The principle of equality requires that this income be subject to taxation. An arbitrary tax privilege according to specific income is incompatible with Article 3 (1) of the Basic Law. Nothing more can be deduced from the purpose of Article 48 (3) [1] considered in conjunction with Article 38 (1) [2] of the Basic Law.

> [Justice Seuffert, presiding judge of the Second Senate, dissented. His dissent was based on the court's failure to lay down specific criteria to guide the legislature in determining the amount of a proper salary and allowances within the meaning of Article 48. In support of this view he appealed to section 95 (1) of the Federal Constitutional Court Act, which declares: "If a complaint of unconstitutionality is upheld, the decision shall state which provision of the Basic Law has been infringed upon and by what act or omission." Justice Seuffert argued that this provision required the court to define the precise boundaries within which the legislature would be obligated to enact a new pay schedule.]

NOTE: IMPACT OF *LEGISLATIVE PAY*. In *Legislative Pay* the court held that the principle of legislative independence under Article 48 (3) requires that former civil servants not receive pensions in addition to their regular compensation as members of the legislature. Nor may parliamentary salaries be linked to civil servant pay scales. The allure of periodic increases for public employees, said the court, places elected civil servants in a compromising position, jeopardizing their independence and undermining their ability to serve the interests of the "whole people." The court went on to hold that the salaries of parliamentary representatives in Bonn must be equal and subject to the general income tax. At the same time the court decreed that legislators must receive a salary that "allows them to enjoy a lifestyle suited to the dignity of their office."

Legislative Pay caused an uproar in the Bundestag and a flood of public commentary, much of it severely critical.[30] Many commentators feared that the decision would lead to a legislature made up of career politicians and to the professionalization of politics. At the time of the decision, representatives received a nontaxable monthly allowance of about $2,500; this would now be taxed. The decision created a dilemma for most legislators. They could scarcely afford to lose a sizable chunk of their current income to the tax collector, but they were also reluctant in the face of an upcoming national election campaign to raise their salaries to the amount necessary to maintain a net income equivalent to their nontaxable allowances. Eventually, however, and on the advice of an independent commission previously organized to study the problem of legislative salaries, the Bundestag adopted a politically accept-able plan based on a percentage of the salaries of other high federal and state of-ficials. By 1979 the critics' worst fears had come to pass: representatives were receiv-ing a basic salary of $69,000, more than United States representatives were getting and more than double the salaries of Italian, French, and Canadian legislators.[31]

The most recent chapter in the legislative pay imbroglio occurred in 1995. Over the combined opposition of the FDP, PDS, and the Greens, the CDU/CSU and the SPD joined forces to pass a bill that linked legislative salaries to those of top federal judges. The measure was designed to double legislative salaries immediately and, after the year 2000, automatically to result in pay equal to that of the judges of Germany's highest courts. Constitutional issues loomed large in the legislative arena as well as in the general public debate. Opponents of the automatic linkage to judicial salaries argued that any and every legislative pay increase must be debated openly and voted upon in the Bundestag. The chapter ended when the Bundesrat refused its consent to the bill. Shortly thereafter, the Bundestag established a com-mission to study parliament's salary structure and report back to the Bundestag with its recommendations.

DELEGATION OF LEGISLATIVE POWER

The Basic Law establishes the primacy of the legislature in the making of law. Legislative authority may be delegated, but the principle of "legality of administra-tion" (*Gesetzmässigkeit der Verwaltung*) puts sharp limits on such delegations. Article 80 (1), the Basic Law's main delegation clause, authorizes national and state officials to issue regulations (*Rechtsverordnungen*) having the force of law, but "the content, purpose, and scope of the authorization so conferred must be set forth in such law." In addition, the legal basis of any such authorization must appear in the regulation, and "if a law provides that such authorization may be delegated, such delegation shall [in turn] require another ordinance having the force of law." As one commen-tary on the Basic Law notes, Article 80 represents a "conscious departure" from the Weimar practice of conferring virtually unlimited discretion on executive officials to carry out the will of the lawmaker.[32] Bonn's Constitution thus imposes a high standard of rationality and accountability on the administrative process.[33]

4.5 Emergency Price Control Case (1958)
8 BVerfGE 274

[Sections 1 and 2 of the Price Control Act authorize the federal director of economic administration as well as the directors of the highest state admin-istrative agencies to set prices, rents, and fees when market conditions in a given area are in a deplorable state. To implement these price controls section

2 empowers the director of the competent administrative agency to issue administrative orders. Five citizens filed objections to orders that forced them to use statutory prices as the basis for the rents and fees they charged to their customers. Besides challenging the orders themselves, these citizens also questioned the constitutionality of section 2. They contended that the provision was incompatible with Article 80 of the Basic Law because it failed adequately to define the delegation of authority according to content, subject matter, purpose, and scope. Confronted with an issue of constitutional magnitude, the courts involved set aside judicial proceedings and submitted the question to the Federal Constitutional Court pursuant to Article 100 (1) of the Basic Law. In holding section 2 of the Price Act constitutional, the court reaffirmed the constitutional principles embodied in Article 80.]

Judgment of the Second Senate. . . .

C. VI. 2. The basic tenets of the rule of law require that an empowering statute adequately limit and define executive authorization to issue burdensome administrative orders according to content, subject matter, purpose, and scope . . . so that official action [will] be comprehensible and to a certain extent predictable for the citizen.

This result follows specifically from the principle that an administrative agency must function lawfully, which requires . . . a limited and narrowly defined executive authorization for the issuance of burdensome administrative orders. Its purpose is to make encroachments by the state as predictable as possible. The statute must regulate the agency's activity and may not confine itself to articulating general principles. Limiting the encroaching agency through solely procedural principles also will not suffice. A "vague blanket provision" that would permit the executive [branch] to determine in detail the limits of [the individual's] freedom conflicts with the principle that an administrative agency must function according to law.

Further, the principle of separation of powers dictates this result. If [a statute] does not adequately define executive powers, then the executive branch will no longer implement the law and act within legislative guidelines but will substitute its own decisions for those of the legislature. This violates the principle of the separation of powers.

Finally, the principle of the rule of law supports this holding. This principle requires the most comprehensive judicial protection possible from state encroachments upon the legal sphere of the individual, as guaranteed today by Article 19 (4) of the Basic Law. The judiciary's mandate to protect [the citizen] legally [from encroachment by the state] can be carried out only if the courts can review the implementation of the norm by the executive [agency] encroaching upon the citizen's legal sphere. For this reason as well [the statute] must adequately define the authorization for encroachment.

NOTE: LIMITS OF ADMINISTRATIVE LAWMAKING. Persons harmed by any governmental authority may challenge the legality of the act in question before an administrative tribunal unless federal legislation has assigned a given sphere of public law to another set of specialized (e.g., social, labor, or finance) courts. Administrative courts also hear disputes between governmental agencies over their respective obligations under public law. A typical administrative law case involves a complaint against a licensing agency for failing, canceling, or refusing to grant an individual or legal entity a permit to carry on some trade or activity regulated by public law. If the agency has exceeded the limits of its discretion or otherwise acted illegally, the courts may annul such action. Ordinarily such cases do not raise constitutional questions.

The impact of the Basic Law on administrative law is nevertheless substantial.[34] First, courts may nullify administrative regulations and executive decrees if officials abuse their discretion or their acts violate fundamental law. Second, and particularly within the sphere of licensing, the Federal Constitutional Court has recently tended "to extrapolate standards for the shaping of procedural law from the constitutional rights of individuals."[35] For example, in the well-known *Mülheim-Kärlich* case (1979),[36] the court found the peaceful use of nuclear energy constitutional in the face of an objection that nuclear power threatens constitutional rights to life and bodily inviolability (Article 2 [2]). The court, however, cautioned that certain kinds of formalities, such as public participation in nuclear power licensing procedures, may be necessary to protect basic rights and liberties. Finally, Article 100 (1) of the Basic Law requires courts to submit their doubts about the validity of a statutory delegation to the Federal Constitutional Court for resolution. The first *Kalkar* case (1978) arose when the Administrative Court of Appeals of North Rhine–Westphalia referred the Atomic Energy Act to the Constitutional Court for a decision on the validity of its provisions delegating authority to administrative officials. Much of the opinion quoted below deals with whether the statute adequately specified the technical and scientific standards used in licensing nuclear power plants.

4.6 Kalkar Case I (1978)
49 BVerfGE 89

[Section 7 (1) of the Atomic Energy Act provides that any person who constructs or operates an installation for the production or fission of nuclear fuel requires a license. Authorities may grant such a license under section 7 (2) only if the licensee "takes every necessary precaution in the light of existing scientific knowledge and technology to prevent damage resulting from the construction and operation of the installation." On December 18, 1972, licensing authorities granted a first partial construction permit for the SNR-300 fast breeder nuclear power station in Kalkar.

The owner of a farm within a mile of the station sued to have the reactor's license revoked because the plant failed to follow certain administrative procedures under section 7 (2). A local administrative court denied his claim and rejected the argument that these acts of omission invaded his rights to life and personality. In view of the awesome implications for public safety and the rights of citizens involved in the production and recycling of plutonium, however, the North Rhine–Westphalia Administrative Court felt that parliament had a duty to establish more concrete criteria for the construction of fast breeder reactors than those provided in the Atomic Energy Act. The court of appeals referred this question to the Constitutional Court.]

Judgment of the Second Senate. . . .

B. II. Section 7, paragraphs 1 and 2, of the Atomic Energy Act are compatible with the Basic Law.

1. (a) The Basic Law does not confer on parliament total priority in fundamental decision making. By insisting upon separation of powers it imposes limits on parliament's authority. The Basic Law relegates far-reaching decisions, particularly those of a political nature, to other supreme constitutional organs. Examples include the chancellor's power to determine general policy guidelines (Article 65 [1]) and the president's authority to dissolve the Bundestag (Article 68) and declare a state of legislative emergency (Article 81). . . . The Bundestag may check the exercise of such powers by electing a new chancellor and bringing down the federal government. . . . A monistic theory of power, incorrectly deduced from the principle of democracy, which would confer a monopoly of decision-making power on parliament must not undermine the concrete distribution and balance of political power guaranteed by the Basic Law. Other institutions and organs of political authority do not lack democratic legitimacy [merely] because parliamentary delegates are the only officials elected by direct popular vote. Legislative, executive, and judicial organs derive their institutional and functional democratic legitimacy from Article 20 (2) of the Basic Law. . . . Nevertheless, we are able to deduce from the principle of parliamentary democracy that parliament and its decisions do have priority vis-à-vis other branches [of government]. We hold this to be a principle of interpretation transcending all concrete allocations of authority. . . .

(b) The case at bar deals with legislation, an area where the Basic Law specifically allocates authority to the Bundestag. It follows from the principle of legality that executive acts which significantly affect the freedom and equality of citizens must be based on law.

2. Section 7, paragraphs 1 and 2, of the Atomic Energy Act do not violate this principle. . . .

(a) Separation of powers is not specifically mentioned in the Constitution. Its validity, however, follows from the terms of Article 20 (3). The interpretation of this principle has undergone change in recent years, especially in the light of its democratic component. Today our established case law makes clear that the legislature is obligated . . . to make all crucial decisions in fundamental normative areas, especially in those cases where basic rights become subject to governmental regulation. . . . To determine those areas in which governmental acts require a basis in law, [one must] consider the subject matter and "intensity" of the planned or enacted regulation, particularly taking into account the fundamental rights granted by the Basic Law.

[One] must also use similar criteria to judge whether the legislature has established the essential legal standards for the matter to be regulated as the constitutional requirement of a specific enactment mandates and has not left this for the administration to determine. [The principle of constitutional requirement of specific enactment (*Gesetzesvorbehalt*) means that only the legislature may enact statutory restraints upon fundamental rights contained in the Constitution where the language of the Constitution expressly provides for such restraints.]

(b) The normative decision whether to permit the peaceful uses of nuclear energy in the Federal Republic of Germany is a fundamental and essential decision in the sense that a specific enactment is constitutionally required. This is so because of [the decision's] far-reaching effects on citizens, in particular on their sphere of freedom and equality, as well as on their general living conditions; and because of the kind and intensity of regulation necessarily connected with it. Only the legislature has the authority to make such a decision. The same applies to regulations fixing the licensing of nuclear installations within the meaning of section 7 (1) of the Atomic Energy Act. . . .

The legislature has decided to promote the peaceful use of nuclear energy by means of a formally enacted law — the Atomic Energy Act. This decision includes fast breeder reactors. . . .

Contrary to the opinion of the court below, the legislature was not bound to include in the act a provision declaring that it was ready to accept the risks possibly resulting from such a reactor. The legislature bears the political responsibility for the consequences of its decision. . . .

. . . In direct relation to [whether this norm is unconstitutional because it is too vague and thus fails to meet the substantive constitutional requirement of specific enactment] is whether section 7 of the Atomic Energy Act contains essentials precise enough to permit the licensing of the fast breeder. We must answer in the affirmative. Sections 7 (1) and 7 (2) regulate all essential and fundamental questions of the licensing procedure and fix with sufficient precision the requirements for the construction, operation, and modification of nuclear installations, including fast breeder reactors.

(c) . . . If the legislature enacts a policy on the basis of which new, unanticipated developments have been called into question, the Constitution may oblige the legislature to reexamine whether the original policy is to be upheld in the light of changed circumstances. . . .

It is constitutionally unobjectionable that the legislature has not yet examined the fast breeder technology and its possible consequences — for instance, the issue of atomic waste disposal. As the federal government has always emphasized, the reactor to be built in Kalkar is only a prototype. The construction and operation of this reactor do not mean a decision to use it on a large industrial scale. [The reactor's] purpose is rather to help to prepare for the decision which [the legislature] will make in the 1990s at the earliest. [We] cannot now foresee whether the court below is correct in assuming that the industrial use of the fast breeder may lead to dangerous constraints and consequences. Suitable means may be available [in the future] to counter the dangers to individual freedoms which the lower court fears. . . . Taking evidence on these questions would serve little purpose since these issues are mainly related to possible political developments of the most general nature.

Only the future will show whether this decision to implement breeder technology will be useful or harmful. In this necessarily uncertain situation the legislature and the government primarily have the political responsibility for making what they consider pragmatic decisions within the confines of their respective authority. Under these circumstances, it is not the function of the courts to substitute their judgment for that of the political branches when assessing the situation, because legal criteria for such decisions do not exist.

Where reasonable doubts are possible — whether or not the dangers feared by the court below materialize — all organs of the state, and thus the legislature as well, have the constitutional duty to make every effort to recognize possible dangers in time and to counter them by constitutional means. If, in the future, some probability of these dangers exists — in the judgment of the . . . responsible political organs — the legislature would again have a duty to act. . . .

3. Sections 7 (1) and 7 (2) of the Atomic Energy Act do not violate the constitutional requirement that laws be drafted with sufficient precision. . . .

(b) . . . The provisions of the statute in question make use of undefined legal terms such as "reliability" and "necessary knowledge" [*unbestimmte Rechtsbegriffe*] — terms which are not precisely defined. [The analysis centers on whether such terms should be void on account of their vagueness.] The use of these terms is constitutionally permissible. The degree of precision required depends on the nature of the matter to be regulated and the intensity of the regulation. . . . [In any case, such terminology] has been traditionally subject to interpretation by the legislature, executive, and judiciary. . . .

Section 7 (2), no. 3, is also sufficiently precise. This provision relates to the field of technical safety. Any legislative regulation of this field . . . must confront the particular difficulties which reside in the nature of the matter to be regulated.

When fixing norms which keep abreast of scientific and technological developments, the legislature has a number of options available for making these developments legally binding. These norms have one common feature: by using undefined legal terms [the legislature] shifts the difficulties involved in giving these terms specific, binding content and adjusting them to scientific and technological developments to the administrative and — should litigation arise — the judicial levels. Thus, administrative authorities and courts have to make up the "regulatory deficit" incurred by the legislature.

The law may, for example, refer to "generally recognized technical rules." In this case, agencies and courts may limit themselves to ascertaining the majority opinion among practicing technicians when deciding whether or not the technical work materials may be brought into the stream of commerce. This criterion has the disadvantage of lagging behind developing technology.

[One way to] avoid this drawback [is] to refer [instead] to the "state of the art," which does not require general recognition and practical confirmation but makes it more difficult for courts and agencies to establish and assess relevant facts.

Section 7 (2), no. 3, of the Atomic Energy Act goes a step further by referring to "existing scientific knowledge," which requires the legislature to make even stronger efforts to keep regulations abreast of scientific and technological developments.

It is within the legislature's discretion to use either undefined legal terms or precise terminology. Good reasons support the use of undefined legal terms in section 7 (2), no. 3. The wording of section 7 (2), no. 3, of the Atomic Energy Act, which is open to future developments, serves as a dynamic protection of fundamental rights. It furthers the protective purpose of section 1, no. 2, of the Atomic Energy Act in the best possible way currently available. To fix a safety standard by establishing rigid rules, if that is even possible, would impede rather than promote technical development and adequate safeguards for fundamental rights. Setting up rigid rules would be regression at the expense of safety. [We must] tolerate some uncertainty of the law, at least where the legislature would otherwise be forced to adopt impractical regulations or to refrain from any regulation at all. Both [alternatives] would eventually impair the protection of fundamental rights. . . .

These considerations apply equally to the so-called residual risk which [one] must consider in the context of section 7 (2), no. 3. While this provision does not allow for residual damage resulting from the construction or operation of a nuclear installation, it permits licensing even if the probability of future damage cannot be precluded with absolute certainty. The law leaves it to the executive to determine . . . the kind and extent of the risk which may or may not be accepted. With regard to the vagueness doctrine, which has the primary constitutional function of defining when the executive is to act vis-à-vis the legislature, section 7 (2) does not violate the Constitution — especially in the light of the subject matter to be regulated.

It follows from the protective purpose of section 1, nos. 2 and 3, as well as section 7 (2) and other provisions of the Atomic Energy Act, that the legislature wants all damage, danger, and risks specific to the installation and operation [of the reactor] to be considered and that the probability of an accident, which may be accepted when licensing an installation, must be as low as possible. Indeed, this probability must be lower as the type and consequences of harm become more serious. By referring to existing scientific knowledge and technology, the law forces the executive [agency] to observe the principle of the best possible protection against dangers and risks. The legislature was not bound, however, to define with precision the possible kinds and factors of risk. . . . The assessment of risks resulting from a nuclear installation depends upon a multitude of circumstances, many of which are constantly evolving. . . . In the interest of flexible protection of life and property the executive must assess and constantly adjust safety measures — a task it is better equipped to perform than the legislature. The unavoidable degree of uncertainty in assessing such risks resides in the nature of human knowledge.

NOTE: DYNAMIC INTERPRETATION AND LEGISLATIVE FACTS. *Kalkar I*, which represents a new development in German constitutional law, stands for what might be called a dynamic interpretation of basic rights. Nuclear technology, the court suggested, is a fast-developing field with life-threatening implications; the legislature has a duty, therefore, to keep abreast of such developments so that it may take whatever mandatory measures are necessary to avoid the threat to a basic right. *Kalkar* grants to the legislature a certain amount of "prognostic leeway" (*Prognosespielraum*) in situations in which it cannot accurately predict the results of a particular legal regulation. But the legislature must continue to monitor the situation to ensure that the regulation does not threaten vested rights under the Basic Law.

The court's approach in *Kalkar* is one way of reconciling tensions between judicial review and majority rule. While recognizing the political character of legislative fact finding and the primacy of the legislature's competence in given subject areas, *Kalkar* holds out the strong possibility of judicial intervention if in the court's independent judgment newly accumulated facts should seriously challenge the original prognosis. The degree of judicial scrutiny in such cases depends on the particularity with which parliament examines the factual basis of a regulatory plan of action.[37] If this process is exacting, and if parliament identifies the facts on the basis of which it enacts law, taking care to protect constitutional interests, the court will not invalidate the regulatory scheme merely because the legislature did not accurately predict the result of its action. In this situation, however, in which regulation threatens constitutional interests, the rule of law requires continuing parliamentary vigilance.

The seeds of the prognosis doctrine took root in some early equal protection cases. For example, in the *Widower's Social Security Benefits* case (1963),[38] the Constitutional Court sustained a provision of the Social Security Act conferring benefits on a widower only if his wife had been primarily responsible for the family's support, a limitation that did not apply to a widow. Years later, however, married women constituted a significant portion of the labor force, just as they had obtained greater equality under law within the marital relationship. By 1975, when the widower's provision was once again challenged, the court instructed the legislature to amend the statute in the light of these changing social conditions.[39]

Returning to *Kalkar,* we see that this decision, like that in the *Mülheim-Kärlich* case,[40] is the product of a major political controversy in West Germany over the use of nuclear energy. Licensing procedures in this field are complex, requiring a whole series of permits in the course of a plant's construction and installation.[41] Governmental officials concerned about the slowness as well as the legitimacy of the nuclear licensing process have advanced proposals ranging from increased legislative participation in the process — even to the point of specifying the details of site planning — to narrowing the scope of judicial review over administrative decisions.[42] Both proposals raise separation-of-powers questions of their own, particularly the latter, since any limitation of judicial review over administrative discretion may conflict with the right of "any person" under Article 19 (4) to repair to a court of law when his rights have been violated by public authority.

Kalkar, though it sustained the delegation in question, appears to require a high threshold of specificity with respect to legislative delegations. And yet, as the Constitutional Court reminded us in the *Judicial Qualification* case (1972), which dealt with the delegation of authority at the state level, the doctrine of separated powers requires some elasticity in its application when the three branches of government are spliced together in a system of reciprocal and mutual restraint. What is important, according to the court, is that the core of each power be preserved from invasion by a coordinate branch.

4.7 Judicial Qualification Case (1972)
34 BVerfGE 52

[The facts are set forth in the opinion.]

Judgment of the Second Senate. . . .

A. I. An applicant for judicial office must pass two state examinations. The state of Hesse requires an examination fee. The fee for the second judicial examination amounts to DM 200, the legal basis for which is found in section 42 (1) [3] of the Judicial Training Regulation (JTR) of September 10, 1965. The Hesse state government issued the JTR in the form of a legal regulation, declaring as [the regulation's] legal basis section 93 (2) [1] of the Hessian Judges Act (HJA) of October 19, 1962. With regard to the issuance of legal regulations, section 93 states:

> 1. The state government is authorized to issue legal regulations required for the implementation of this law.

2. The state government is authorized to issue a judicial training regulation. This provision shall regulate the establishment of examination centers, the composition of the board of examiners, examination procedures, and the duration and division of the preparatory service within the framework of section 5 (6) of the German Judges Act [a federal statute] as well as . . . [matters relating to the] repeated failure of [applicants to pass the] second examination. . . .

II. 1. The plaintiff in the original proceeding passed the second judicial examination in Hesse in 1966. He had paid the required examination fee prior to taking the examination. Later he brought suit before the administrative court in Frankfurt (Main), claiming that the examination fee had been demanded without a legal basis. He stated further that section 93 (2) [1] of the Hessian Judges Act did not authorize section 42 (1) of the Judicial Training Regulation. . . .

B. II. 2. As was determined by the decision of the Hesse State Constitutional Court in a decision dated December 4, 1968, section 93 (2) of the HJA is consistent with Articles 107 and 118 of the Hesse Constitution. [The Hesse State Constitutional Court (Hessischer Staatsgerichtshof) is the highest court in Hesse; it is responsible only for state constitutional issues.] Therefore, section 93 (2) [1] of the HJA does not violate the principle of separation of powers, just as these Hessian constitutional provisions do not violate the principle of the separation of powers which the states must observe under Article 28 (1) [1] of the Basic Law. [A state legislature] can give this constitutional principle, which binds the states, concrete expression in its constitution in various ways. Article 80 (1) [2] represents only one of these possibilities; it applies only to the domain of federal legislation. Articles 107 and 118 of the constitution of the state of Hesse (HC) contain a different way of concretizing this [mandate] which, at least as interpreted by the Hesse State Constitutional Court, also satisfies this constitutional principle.

(a) The separation of powers is a fundamental constitutional principle for the organization and function [of the state]. The Basic Law provides for a distribution of political power, the harmonious cooperation of the three branches, and the moderation of political rule which will result from it. The principle of separation of powers is not, however, realized in pure form in the federal arena. Numerous interconnections and balances of power exist. It is not an absolute separation of powers which we must glean from the constitutional design of the Basic Law but [rather] mutual control, restraint, and moderation.

[Even] if the separation of powers cannot be understood as meaning a clear-cut separation of the functions of political power, [we] must retain the distribution of weight among the three powers as outlined by the Constitution. No branch may obtain a predominance not intended by the Constitution over another power. Nor may [one branch] deprive another of the authority needed to fulfill its constitutional tasks. The core functions of the different governmental branches cannot be altered. This precludes one of the powers from relinquishing tasks which — according to the Constitution — are typically within its purview.

The following considerations apply to the relationship between the legislature and the executive. In a free democratic and constitutional system, parliament has the constitutional task of enacting laws. Only parliament possesses the democratic legitimacy to make fundamental political decisions. To be sure, the Basic Law approves — as illustrated by Article 80 — of a "delegated" legislation by the executive. However, the executive can legislate only within limits which the legislature prescribes. Parliament cannot neglect its responsibility as a legislative body by delegating part of its legislative authority to the executive without beforehand reflecting upon and determining the limitations of these delegated powers. If the legislature does not satisfy this requirement, then [it] will shift unfavorably the balance of powers presupposed by the Basic Law in the area of legislation. A total delegation of legislative power to the executive branch violates the principle of the separation of powers.

(b) [We] also derive this [conclusion] from the principle of the rule of law insofar as it requires that citizens be sufficiently able to evaluate the content of a regulation based on statutory authority.

To the extent that [a statute] delegates the authority to issue regulations to the executive, the legislative intent must provide . . . a guide for the content of the regulation. The statute must give expression to the legislative intent. It must be clear whether or not the executive confined itself to the express limits [of the delegating statute] in issuing the regulation. If the content [of the regulation] goes beyond the legislative intent, then the issuer of the regulation overstepped the boundaries of its delegated power. The regulation is then invalid because it has insufficient legal basis. It is not within the Federal Constitutional Court's authority to decide this case, which falls within the procedur[al] [provisions] of Article 100 (1). But it is within this court's authority to decide if the statutory delegation is compatible with the aforementioned principles.

(c) Section 93 (2) [1] of the HJA does not transgress the boundaries established by the principles of separation of powers and the rule of law for delegating the authority to issue regulations. The legislature did not relinquish its inalienable duty and responsibility. [Section 93 (2) [1]] preserves the fundamental priority of the legislative intent. This intent, which should serve as a guiding principle for the issue of a regulation, is clearly recognizable. Section 93 (2) [1] of the HJA only grants the issuer of the regulation supplementary authority to set norms. This section does not contain a delegation of authority which is devoid of all content. The subject of the legal regulation to be issued by the state government is "judicial training." The German Judges Act and the Hessian Judges Act provide an initial framework for the issuer of a regulation. The Hessian legislature particularly emphasizes examination procedures. Moreover, it is not regulating this subject matter for the first time. The legal basis for the regulatory authority over judicial training is itself tied to the existing norms concerning training regulations [enacted on] November 27, 1957. If an authorization refers to an area governed by prior regulations, then the legislature is clearly stating that the existing principles are to guide the regulating entity in issuing its rules. The legislature does not preclude any change; however, it does expect the issuer of the regulation not to depart from concepts established by the earlier regulations for no reason at all. Section 93 (2) [1] of the HJA is therefore not written in such general terms that it would be impossible for the executive meaningfully to comprehend the legislature's concept [for this statute]. Charging fees for special administrative services has long been a part of government activity. The principles of defraying expenses and proportionality are corrective guides for the issuer of the regulation. The legislature may assume that the regulating body will observe these principles. Thus the fact that section 93 (2) [1] of the HJA does not expressly provide exact figures for a fee schedule does not jeopardize the fundamental separation of powers and legislative independence vis-à-vis the regulating executive. The fee stated in the regulation is clearly within the general limitations discussed above.

NOTE: THE *CARTEL ADMINISTRATIVE FEE* CASE. The delegation doctrine, as the foregoing cases indicate, is a vital principle of German constitutional law. *Cartel* nullified the imposition of administrative costs on firms appearing before various tribunals in cartel proceedings. According to the court:

> Because fees constitute public levies, their imposition requires a specific regulation [authorized by statute]. Fee schedules imposed by authorities exercising sovereign powers can work drastic consequences on citizens by making it difficult for them to assert their rights. This is the reason the legislator has regulated by formal law the fees to be charged for taking advantage of administrative services in almost all areas [of public law]. If, however, the legislator delegates this power, he must himself specify the range and extent of the regulation so that its content is fairly predictable. He must establish for the regulator the boundaries within which he should function. Thus he must himself have addressed the subject to be regulated.[43]

Cartel is one more illustration of the vitality of the delegation doctrine in German constitutional law.

EXECUTIVE-LEGISLATIVE TENSIONS IN FOREIGN AND MILITARY AFFAIRS

Just as the United States Constitution allocates power over foreign affairs to both president and Congress, so too does the Basic Law apportion shares of this power to parliament and the executive. The Basic Law, however, incorporates a more complex system of checks and balances in the field of foreign relations as well as more detailed provisions on foreign and military affairs than the U.S. Constitution. The main point to be noted about Germany's foreign affairs power is its concentration at the federal level. Article 73 (1) confers on the federation (i.e., the national government) *exclusive* legislative authority over "foreign affairs." In addition, Article 87 (1) empowers the federation to establish foreign and consular offices, just as Article 32 (1) authorizes it to conduct "relations with other states." Article 32 (3), however, qualifies this exclusivity; it permits the *Länder,* with the federal government's consent, to conclude treaties with foreign states in policy areas over which the *Länder* have exclusive jurisdiction. As the Constitutional Court noted in the *Concordat* case, the federal government's treaty-making power may be limited to the extent that it invades these reserved powers. The federation nevertheless has primary responsibility over the broad field of foreign affairs.

NOTE: DISTRIBUTION OF THE FOREIGN AFFAIRS POWERS. The foreign relations power falls mainly into the domain of executive responsibility. Executive authority, however, is divided between the chancellor and the federal president. Under Article 59 (1), the president concludes treaties, receives envoys, and represents the federation in its international relations. But these roles are largely ceremonial. Effective power resides in the hands of the chancellor. According to Article 63, he determines general policy guidelines, although in Germany's parliamentary system he shares this power with the cabinet. Indeed, the procedural rules promulgated under Article 65 require the chancellor to submit foreign policy matters of general importance to the cabinet for debate and decision, but any decision taken in this field must fall within the chancellor's general policy guidelines.

Yet parliament is deeply implicated in the foreign policy–making process. For one thing, executive and legislature are far less separate than in the United States. The chancellor is Germany's chief executive, but like the cabinet ministers he appoints, he is also a member of parliament. Unlike the members of his cabinet, however, he also answers to and can be removed by parliament.[44] In addition, parliament has extensive supervisory authority in the foreign relations field. The Basic Law itself provides for the establishment of parliamentary committees on foreign affairs and defense (Article 45a) before which federal ministers may be compelled to appear. As noted in Chapter 3, the Basic Law was also amended recently to provide for a Bundestag Committee on European Union (Article 45). Finally, under Article 44, the Bundestag is obligated to form committees of inquiry into any policy matter — domestic or foreign — at the request of one-quarter of its members. As this brief summary might suggest, the Basic Law incorporates a degree of executive accountability as high as any likely to be found among the world's constitutional democracies.

NOTE: EXECUTIVE DISCRETION, PARLIAMENTARY CONSENT, AND THE TREATY-MAKING POWER. Article 59 (2) of the Basic Law provides that "treaties which regulate the political relations of the federation or relate to matters of federal legislation shall require the approval or participation of the appropriate legislative body in the form of a federal law." The *Petersberg* and *Commercial Treaty* cases (1952) were the first to challenge the executive's refusal to seek parliamentary approval of a treaty. *Petersberg* involved an executive agreement between the Adenauer government and the high commissioners of the three Allied powers. The treaty provided the new West German government more freedom to manage its own affairs and to explore ways to bring Germany into a European economic community. Social Democratic members of the Bundestag petitioned the Constitutional Court, claiming that the agreement was a treaty within the meaning of Article 59 (2) and thus invalid without parliament's approval.

The *Petersberg* decision was significant, first, because the court granted a minority parliamentary party standing to assert its right as a constituent unit of the Bundestag, and, second, because it defined a treaty within the meaning of Article 59 (2) as one concluded with a foreign state or an international agency of equal rank. The Allied High Commission was regarded as less than that. The commission did not represent the three Allied governments as such but rather constituted an independent organ of governance on German territory. Moreover, declared the court, the Basic Law is "the constitution of a sovereign state" and points toward Germany's "equal standing in the community of nations." The Petersberg Agreement was the product of unequals because Germany was clearly in a position subordinate to the occupying powers.[45]

As the text of Article 59 (2) makes clear, parliament plays a crucial role in the treaty-making process, but that role is confined to two kinds of treaties: those that regulate the FRG's "political" relations and those whose implementation requires the enactment of a federal statute. Treaties or agreements not falling into one of these two categories may presumably be carried out at the discretion of the executive. But what constitutes a treaty that regulates the nation's "political relations" or touches on federal legislation? These issues arose early on, in the *Commercial Treaty* case (1952).

4.8 Commercial Treaty Case (1952)
1 BVerfGE 372

[The Paris Trade Agreement of 1950 between Germany and France removed trade restrictions on goods produced in the two countries, established currency exchange regulations, imposed quotas on certain products, and laid down conditions for the issuance of import and export licenses. Once again the SPD, led by Kurt Schumacher, objected to the government's failure to seek the consent of the Bundestag. The main constitutional issue before the court

was whether a commercial treaty altering the basic trade and payment relations between the Federal Republic and another state is a "political" treaty
within the meaning of Article 59 (2).]

———————

Judgment of the Second Senate. . . .

C. I. 1. A treaty does not become a political treaty within the meaning of Article 59
(2) of the Constitution merely because it deals quite generally with public affairs,
the good of the community, or affairs of state. If this were so, every treaty would be a
political treaty, and the limitation contained in Article 59 (2) would be devoid of
meaning. In addition to the conditions just mentioned, a treaty must also directly
affect the existence of the state, its territorial integrity, its independence, and its
position or relative weight within the community of states. Political treaties in this
sense are those directed at asserting, securing, or expanding one state's position of
strength vis-à-vis other states. [They] include treaties relating to alliances and guarantees; agreements on political cooperation; nonaggression pacts; treaties on peace,
neutrality, disarmament, and arbitration; and similar international agreements.

The history of Article 59 (2) permits an interpretation that does justice to
constantly changing conditions. In contrast to the Weimar Constitution (Article
45), the Basic Law has adopted broader language so as to enlarge the category of
treaties beyond alliances requiring the approval of parliament. . . .

Article 59 (2) of the Basic Law requires the participation of the legislative
bodies only for those treaties that regulate the political relations of the federation.
"Political relations" must substantially and directly affect the existence of the state,
its position and weight within the community of states, or the order of the community of states. The content or purpose of a treaty within the meaning of Article 59
(2) of the Basic Law must be directed at the regulation of the political relations with
foreign states. The treaty itself must regulate or purport to regulate the political
relations with foreign states; it is insufficient when the treaty has merely a secondary,
perhaps even unintentional or unexpected effect on such relations. Even though a
treaty may be of political significance for the Federal Republic — for example, it may
have an important bearing on the internal political, economic, or social circumstances of the country — [that] does not make it a "political treaty" within the
meaning of Article 59 (2) of the Basic Law.

The traditional teachings of public international law generally did not regard
commercial treaties as political treaties. This theory, however, does not in its gener-
ality correspond to the reality of present-day international relations. In special circumstances a commercial treaty may have a political character like that of a treaty of
alliance; for example, where the contracting parties, by concluding a commercial
treaty, intend to strengthen their economic position in competition with other
states generally. In such a case, nonpolitical market relations may become power

relations. Today the conclusion of a commercial treaty may possibly have more influence on a state's position of strength within the community of states than the conclusion of a treaty of neutrality, a nonaggression pact, or a treaty of guarantee. In referring to power in this context, we do not confine ourselves to the position of states in the struggle for political hegemony; we refer generally to their relative weight within the community of states.

Whether a treaty is political in the above-mentioned sense can be determined only in the individual case by reference to the special circumstances and the actual political situation of the Federal Republic and the other contracting parties.

[The court then embarked on a detailed examination of the treaty's provisions, finding that they were short-term measures for liberalizing trade and were not designed to fix the FRG's political position relative to other states. The court added that in any event the Federal Republic of Germany, still subject to the occupying powers with regard to certain foreign policy matters, was not at that time in a position to make political decisions. It stressed more particularly that the treaty did not contain any provision indicating a desire on the part of the Federal Republic to support European integration or to acknowledge that the Saarland Territory was no longer part of Germany. The court thus denied the political character of the treaty.]

3. In a parliamentary democracy, legislation is basically reserved for parliament, with government and administration being assigned to the executive branch. To the latter belongs also the conduct of foreign policy and trade policy. According to Article 65 of the Basic Law, the federal chancellor determines, and is responsible for, the general policy guidelines. Within the limits set by these guidelines, each federal minister conducts the affairs of his department autonomously and on his own responsibility. There is a legal presumption in favor of the exclusivity of these expressly constituted competencies of government. The Bundestag may not assume these functions unless expressly permitted to do so. The legislature's sharing of this exceptional authority of the executive has been established by Article 59 (2) of the Basic Law within highly specified limits. . . . Above and beyond [the two instances in which parliament participates in the treaty-making process] Article 59 (2) has not given the Bundestag a right to intervene in the government's zone of responsibility. It[s role] remains limited to the general constitutional powers of supervision. Rather than governing and administering in this field, [the Bundestag] controls the government. Should it disapprove of the latter's policies, it is empowered to express its lack of confidence in the federal chancellor (Article 67) and bring down the government. But it is not able to conduct policy making of its own accord.

[When does a treaty relate to federal legislation, thus requiring parliamentary approval in the form of a law? In answering this query the court noted that the Basic Law's list of enumerated powers conferred on the federal government is not controlling. For example, merely because money, coinage, and customs fall within the scope of federal legislation does not mean that a treaty related to these matters requires legislative approval. Rather, said the court, parliamentary participation is necessary "when the federation assumes obligations that can be fulfilled only through the enactment of a federal law." In such a case parliamentary approval is necessary to give democratic legitimacy to a policy requiring domestic application. In the instant case, however, the executive was able to implement the commercial treaty without legislative participation. Moreover, parliament was disempowered from acting in this instance because the powers reserved by the Occupation Authority precluded any internal legislation on the trade and foreign exchange provisions of the treaty. In the conclusion of its opinion the court underscored the federal government's primacy in the field of foreign relations.]

NOTE: JUDICIAL RESTRAINT IN FOREIGN AFFAIRS. All questions arising under the Basic Law are amenable to judicial resolution if properly initiated under one of various procedures authorized for the adjudication of constitutional issues. These issues include the highly politicized field of foreign affairs. The court cannot avoid a decision by taking cover under an American-style political question doctrine.[46] If no jurisdictional issue disqualifies the court from hearing a case on its merits, it must decide. In doing so, however, the court often defers to the federation's political judgment so long as that judgment remains within the boundaries of legitimate discretion. Occasionally, the court will sustain a foreign policy decision of the political branches but at the same time lay down rather stringent rules for carrying it out.

A particularly dramatic example of this last situation — where judicial activism and restraint combine in an interesting mix — involved the Basic Treaty between East Germany and West Germany. In the early 1970s the West German government, now controlled by the SPD in coalition with the FDP, sought to "normalize" the relationship between the two German states and between Germany, the Soviet Union, and other Eastern European nations. The Basic Treaty was the capstone of Brandt's eastern policy (*Ostpolitik*). Under the treaty, the FRG and the GDR agreed to respect each other's right to self-determination, "to refrain from the threat or use of force," to improve trade relations, to cooperate in various cultural and technological fields, and to desist from any claim to represent the other in the international arena. By any standard the treaty qualified as the most crucial step taken by the two German states in the postwar era.

Parliament had barely consented to the treaty when Bavaria petitioned for its nullification in an abstract judicial-review proceeding. Bavaria argued that the treaty rejected the Basic Law's commitment to the principle of national unity. In response, the court sustained the constitutionality of the treaty, declaring that in meeting constitutional goals, particularly in the area of foreign policy, flexibility and discretion were essential. Yet, to the chagrin of the ruling coalition, the court used this case to make wide-ranging pronouncements on the scope of judicial review, the nature of the West German state, and the principle of reunification, leaving no doubt in any person's mind that the court's word would be the last even in the sensitive area of international diplomacy.

In fact, the court rebuked the federal government for trying to "outmaneuver" the First Senate, in which the case was pending, by attempting to ratify the treaty before the senate had rendered its decision. With respect to national unity, the court declared that the goal of reunification, stated in the Preamble to the Basic Law, is legally binding on "all constitutional organs," each of which is "required to keep the claim of reunification alive domestically, to vigorously push it in foreign relations, and to refrain from any activity that would undermine the goal of reunification." The *East-West Basic Treaty* case (1973), then, has something of the flavor of *Marbury* v. *Madison* (1803). It handed the government a crucial victory, but qualified that victory with a lecture on the rule of law and warnings about exceeding the limits of executive discretion.

The *Rudolf Hess* case (1980) is an equally prominent example of judicial restraint.[47] Hess's son filed a constitutional complaint in 1980 charging the federal government with failure to take the steps necessary for securing the release of his father from the Berlin-Spandau Military Prison, in which he had been incarcerated, alone, since 1967. (Hess had been sentenced to life imprisonment in 1945 by the Nuremberg War Crimes Tribunal.) The complaint charged that the federal government's reluctance to undertake negotiations with the Allied governments for the purpose of liberating Hess from his isolated imprisonment violated several provisions of the Basic Law, including the right to human dignity and the European Convention on Human Rights. The court accepted the complaint, implying that it was justiciable, but then wrote an opinion in which some scholars found the seeds of a political question doctrine.[48]

Hess underscores the broad discretion enjoyed by governmental organs in dealing with political matters: "The breadth of this discretion in foreign affairs has its basis in the nature of foreign relations," said the Second Senate. "Such events are not governed solely by the will of the federation," the senate continued, "but rather are dependent on many circumstances over which it has little control. In order to facilitate the realization of the federation's political goals within the framework of what is constitutionally permissible . . . the Constitution confers considerable discretion on foreign affairs agencies in assessing the practicality and feasibility of certain policies or actions."[49] The First Senate reached a similar conclusion in the *Schleyer Kidnapping* case (1977). Whether the federation should negotiate for the release of a hostage out of respect for the right to life secured by Article 2 (2) of the Basic Law or resort to other actions in dealing with terrorists, held the senate, is wholly within the discretion of the politically responsible organs of government.[50]

4.9 Pershing 2 and Cruise Missile Case I (1983)
66 BVerfGE 39

[In 1983 several persons filed constitutional complaints against the Federal Republic's forthcoming deployment of weapons equipped with nuclear warheads on West German territory. This deployment was to be undertaken in accordance with a decision of the foreign and defense ministers of member states of the North Atlantic Treaty Organization (NATO). On November 22, 1983, the Bundestag passed a resolution supporting the federal government's decision. The gravamen of the complaint was that the missiles would endanger the life and health of the complainants, in violation of Article 2 (2). Complainants' argument was also based on separation of powers. Article 2 (2) provides that the right to life and personal inviolability "may be encroached upon only pursuant to a law." The legislature's failure to support deployment in the form of a statute, they argued, violated this provision.]

Judgment of the Second Senate. . . .

A. II. 5. . . . The complainants base their constitutional complaints on the following arguments: The quality of the new weapons and their deployment on European territory near the Soviet Union change the political-strategic constellation of chances and risks in favor of the United States of America. There are several possible Soviet reactions to this, each of which brings with it the risk of a destructive strike by the Soviet Union against Pershing II and Cruise missile sites. Deploying these weapons, therefore, endangers the lives of the population of the Federal Republic. In addition, the Soviet Union has announced the installation of a computer-controlled responsive-strike system which may give rise to the use of nuclear weapons in the case of even limited military operations by the member states of NATO. [The possibility] also cannot be precluded that an atomic attack may be brought about by a technical failure in this system. Deploying Pershing 2 and Cruise missiles is therefore incompatible with the state's duty to protect life pursuant to Article 2 (2) [1] of the Basic Law. The Constitution's decision to provide for a national defense does not authorize the impending destruction of the entire population of the Federal Republic or significant portions of it. It is true that the competent government authorities have the basic responsibility to decide how to fulfill their duty to protect life, arising under Article 2 (2) [1] of the Basic Law. However, [they] cannot justify the installation of new weapons as a measure to protect life. [The deployment of new weapons] is also an inappropriate defensive measure because it neither averts a Soviet attack with ss-20 missiles nor permits a first strike aimed at disarmament. The new weapons have no defensive value for the Federal Republic because the Federal Republic has no control over their use. If the federal government believes it must modernize its weapons, it can choose the less dangerous alternative of deploying new weapons at sea.

> [Complainants argued that (1) the Basic Law permits defensive weapons only, (2) the Pershing and Cruise missiles are not necessary for the defense of the Federal Republic, (3) the missiles are more dangerous than alternative means of defense (e.g., sea-based missiles), (4) American control of the weapons violates German sovereignty, and (5) deployment violates the Federal Republic's duties under international law.]

C. . . . The constitutional complaints are inadmissible.

1. To the extent that the complainants can be interpreted as assailing the conduct of non-German public power in connection with the deployment of Pershing 2 and Cruise missiles, their constitutional complaint is inadmissible. It is true that the protected sphere of human rights, including the basic rights and freedoms recognized in the Basic Law, applies against every from of sovereign power. However, under Article 93 (1) [4a] of the Basic Law and section 90 of the FCCA, the remedy of a constitutional complaint can be brought only against actions of the German state.

2. To the extent that they attack conduct attributable to German sovereign power, it follows neither from the complainants' allegations nor from other circumstances that German state action caused the asserted threat and therefore would fall within the realm of protected basic rights claimed to have been injured by an act of the German state. . . .

Even accepting the complainants' premise that deploying Pershing 2 and Cruise missiles increases the danger of a Soviet nuclear attack against targets in the Federal Republic, and therefore the risk to legal rights protected by Article 2 (2) of the Basic Law, it is still questionable whether the asserted violation of complainants' life and limb by German sovereign power rises to the level of a real danger under the Basic Law. In those cases where the Federal Constitutional Court has issued an opinion on the degree of intervention necessary to endanger basic rights, [it was possible] to make certain not entirely indefinite statements about the probability that the asserted dangers would actually occur. In those cases the essential sources of risk were susceptible to investigation by scientific methods, even if such methods were naturally conditioned upon and limited by the state and type of knowledge at the time. In the present case, on the contrary, no suitable, reliable process exists by which the [judge] might ascertain the increased degree of danger to complainants' life and limb. For, in dealing with the ultimate source of this danger, we are dealing with the decisions of a foreign sovereign state in the context of the general world political situation and changing political and military relations. Under the prevailing circumstances [we cannot make] judicially verifiable findings concerning such decisions in advance. Moreover, the possible violation of basic rights asserted in this case does not fall within the protective purview of these rights, since [basic rights] are aimed at German state action; this, however, is the action complainants have attacked.

(b) . . . Because [we] lack legally manageable criteria [for deciding this case], the Federal Constitutional Court cannot determine whether or not the German state action challenged by complainants has any influence on decisions of the Soviet Union which may or may not trigger the military measures (a preventive or responsive nuclear strike) complainants fear. The federal organs responsible for the foreign and defense policy of the Federal Republic must make such evaluations. Within the intended goals of the Basic Law, especially as they have been expressed in the present context in Article 1 (2) and Article 24 (2), and within the scope of what is permissible under international law, the constitutional authority of these organs for foreign and defense policy includes the authority to defend the Federal Republic effectively. It is within their political decision-making power and responsibility to decide what measures promise success. To the extent that unpredictable areas of risk remain, as will often be the case, the political body constitutionally responsible for the decision must include these [considerations] in their deliberations and assume political responsibility. It is not the function of the Federal Constitutional Court to substitute its opinions for the opinions and deliberations of the competent political branch of the federation over and above standard legal handicaps in this area. This applies equally for the question of how the state should fulfill its affirmative legal duty to protect basic rights in the sphere of foreign policy and defense matters vis-à-vis foreign states. In the light of the fact that the dangerous situation which complainants presume to exist depends significantly on the political decision of a foreign sovereign state in the context of the global political situation, the Federal Constitutional Court has no legally manageable criteria for judging whether the German state action being challenged is the decisive [factor] in the creation of this situation, or whether it is at least contributory and therefore causal. It is quite possible that the danger of a Soviet nuclear attack, as the complainants fear, already existed before the federal government agreed to deploy the missiles, or will come into being independent of the deployment. Nor do we have legally manageable standards to judge whether one may correctly say, based on empirical knowledge, that the creation of the danger of a Soviet nuclear attack represents a change of existing circumstances "legally" connected to the conduct that complainants censure. . . .

D. This decision is issued unanimously as to the result, with one vote dissenting as to the grounds of the judgment.

NOTE: GERMAN CONSTITUTIONALISM AND INTERNATIONAL LAW. In addition to the already cited constitutional provisions affecting the foreign relations power, the Basic Law commits the Federal Republic to internationalism and peace. Regarding internationalism, Article 24 (1) of the Basic Law authorizes the federation "to transfer sovereign power to international organizations [in the form of a law]," the first time in history that a German constitution has permitted any surrender of Germany's national prerogatives. Moreover, in the interest of securing "a peaceful and lasting order in Europe and among the nations of the world," paragraph 2 of Article 24 permits Germany to further limit its sovereign powers by "becoming a party to a system of collective security." (As we shall see below, these provisions were crucial in the Constitutional Court's disposition of the *Military Deployment* case.) In addition, Article 25 makes the "general rules of international law . . . an integral part of federal law," with the latter taking precedence over domestic law. Any court doubting in the course of litigation whether such a rule is in fact an integral part of federal law, the answer to which is relevant to a decision in the case, must certify the question to the Constitutional Court (Article 100 [2]).[51]

Article 26 (1), finally, echoes the Preamble's "resolve to serve world peace." It goes so far as to hold unconstitutional any "preparation for military aggression" as well as any acts "intended to disturb the peaceful relations between nations." The last sentence of this provision even requires Germany to criminalize all such acts. When the two German states and the four Allied powers signed the Final Peace Treaty (the Two Plus Four Settlement) on September 12, 1990, marking the last step to Germany's unification, the clauses of Article 26 (1) were recalled and re-affirmed, subjecting Germany to added limits on its sovereignty even with its full recovery under the Final Peace Treaty.[52]

NOTE: THE *PERSHING* AND *CRUISE MISSILE* II CASE. In *Cruise Missile I,* the Consti-tutional Court declined the invitation to intervene in the political decision to install nuclear missiles on German soil. Petitioners in the case also argued that the installa-tion of the missiles violated a general principle of international law within the meaning of Article 25. Rejecting this argument forthwith, the court said that "gen-eral principles of international law . . . must be based on the general and established practice of states, and must be practiced legally in the conviction that such conduct is lawful."[53] The Second Senate could find no general or established practice in inter-national law that would prevent certain nations from deterring a possible nuclear attack from the Soviet Union.

The principle of separated powers was more directly implicated in *Cruise Missile II.* Unlike the constitutional complaint at issue in *Cruise Missile I,* the present pro-ceeding was an *Organstreit* action initiated by the Green parliamentary party to vindicate the presumed rights of the Bundestag against the executive. The Greens maintained that by agreeing to install nuclear-equipped American intermediate mis-siles on German soil in the absence of statutory authority to do so, the federal government "indirectly infringed the rights of the Bundestag."[54] In response, the Constitutional Court noted that an act of executive assent taken within the frame-work of an existing treaty—here the NATO treaty—requires no new legislation under Article 59 (2).

The challenged action would have survived constitutional analysis even if it had been taken independently of the treaty, for the assent granted here would have been classified neither as a "political treaty" nor as a "matter of federal legislation" under Article 59 (2). The court sought to clarify its understanding of Article 59 (2) as it relates to the principle of separated powers:

> Article 59 (2) . . . allows the Bundestag some powers of participation in the making of foreign policy. . . . Yet Article 59 (2) confines this participation to the [two situations already mentioned]. . . . Thus, with respect to Article 59 (2), the Bundestag can neither compel the federal government to refrain from, embark upon, or break off treaty negotiations or produce treaty drafts of a particular content, nor prevent it from doing so; nor can it force the executive to conclude a treaty that requires parliamentary consent under Article 59 (2) or force [the executive] to terminate a treaty in international law. . . . The Basic Law does not confer on the legislature any power to initiate foreign policy or to control its administration. Nor can the provision be taken to mean that whenever an act of the federal government in international transactions regulates the political relationships of the Federal Republic of Germany or affects objects of federal legislation that the form of a treaty requiring legislative assent must be chosen, as the petitioner thinks.
>
> This strict demarcation of the powers allowed the legislative bodies under Article 59 (2) is an element in the separation of powers set up by the Basic Law. . . . But the concentration of political power which would lie in assigning the Bundestag central decision-making powers of an executive nature in foreign affairs beyond those assigned to it in the Basic Law would run counter to that structure of apportioning power, responsibility, and control laid down at present by the Basic Law. This is in no way changed by the fact that, at the federal level, only Bundestag members are directly elected by the people. The specific order of the apportionment and balancing of state power which the Basic Law wishes to see guaranteed must not be undermined by a monism of powers falsely derived from the democracy principle in the form of an all-embracing reservation on behalf of parliament. Again, the principle of parliamentary responsibility of the government necessarily presupposes a core area of the executive's own responsibility. The democracy constituted by the Basic Law is a democracy *under the rule of law,* and this means, in relation to the mutual relations of the organs of state, above all a democracy *with separation of powers.*[55]

Finally, over the dissenting opinion of Justice Ernst-Wolfgang Mahrenholz, the court also rejected Green party arguments based on Article 24 (1) of the Basic Law. This article, as indicated in the discussion of internationalism above, permits the federation to transfer "by legislation" its sovereign powers to intergovernmental institutions. The Greens argued that under existing treaties the Bundestag did not consent to the installation of nuclear weapons on German soil or transfer to the U.S.

president the power to grant final clearance for the use of such weapons. To authorize such vast power to the head of a single nation and to accept the risk of atomic war by the installation of nuclear weapons on German soil — a condition not set forth in the original treaty — requires, argued the Greens, explicit statutory authority under Article 24 (1).

Disagreeing, the court ruled that the federal government's declaration of assent constituted a "transfer of sovereign rights within the meaning of Article 24 (1)."[56] Consenting to the installation of nuclear weapons on German soil, with the proviso that only the president of the United States could give final approval of their use, was fully permissible under legislation confirming the Brussels and North Atlantic treaties (1954) as well as the Convention of 1955 dealing with the presence of foreign forces in the Federal Republic. These treaties transferred sovereign rights not to the United States, which would have been impermissible, but to an intergovernmental institution. The treaties created an international military command structure governed by a detailed and elaborate system of consultation within whose context the United States, in its capacity as an Alliance partner and within the framework of the Alliance system's legal commitments, would have to give its clearance for any military use of NATO's weapons. "The appropriate organization of joint defense and the measures necessary cannot be fully specified beforehand,"[57] said the court.

The court continued: "Detailed treaty provisions on strategic conceptions and plans; on the organization, nature, size, and stationing of forces and their equipment; and on command structures could very soon prove outdated in present circumstances given the objective of the treaty, namely, guaranteeing security and peace for the treaty parties. If the object of the Alliance is to be achieved, speedy, flexible measures must be possible, the content and legal forms of which cannot be fully determined in advance."[58] The power in question, said the court, had already been transferred. The treaty's silence with respect to the installation of nuclear weapons on German soil did not negate a command decision by the supranational agency on the placement of weapons within the Alliance system. This was particularly true, because in passing the required legislation under Article 24 (1), the Bundestag had failed to make an explicit or tacit reservation regarding NATO's power to deploy particular types of weapons on German territory. Sovereign power once surrendered in accordance with the Basic Law cannot be reclaimed in the fashion suggested.[59]

NOTE: MILITARY AFFAIRS POWER. As originally drafted, the Basic Law conferred no power to establish an armed military force, to appoint a commander in chief, or to declare war. On these issues the Constitution was silent. Moreover, by the terms of the Preamble and Article 1 (2) of the Basic Law, the German people committed themselves to peace and justice in a united Europe and the world. To stress the point further, Article 26 banned as "unconstitutional" any activity intended to disturb peaceful international relations or any preparation for military aggression. Social

Democratic members of the Bundestag invoked these provisions in 1952 when they petitioned the Federal Constitutional Court to stop the Adenauer government's decision to rearm Germany within the framework of the proposed European Defense Community (EDC).[60] The Basic Law, they claimed, was a "peace constitution," and remilitarization could not validly be undertaken in the absence of a constitutional amendment explicitly permitting rearmament.

Adenauer and his governing coalition, however, appealed to other provisions of the Basic Law to justify West Germany's entry into the EDC. They argued that the federation's power over "foreign affairs" under Article 73 (1) implies the authority to legislate in the field of military affairs. They drew the same conclusion from Article 4 (3), which raises conscientious objection to military service to a constitutional right. Articles 24 and 25 were also invoked to establish the presence of a military affairs power. Among the rules of public international law that Article 25 (1) incorporates into domestic law, they argued, is the right of every nation to engage in defensive warfare. Finally, as noted earlier, Article 24 (1) allows Germany to transfer its sovereign powers to intergovernmental organizations. Arguably, under paragraph 2, such an organization would include the EDC, for Article 24 (2) allows the federation to become a party to a "system of collective security" in the interest of "bringing about and securing a peaceful and lasting order in Europe and among the nations of the world."

The French parliament's failure to ratify the EDC terminated the heated political clash over German rearmament. In the light of West Germany's prospective membership in the proposed North Atlantic Treaty Organization (NATO), however, the constitutional debate continued. It ended after the 1953 election when Adenauer and his coalition partners won enough seats to amend the Basic Law. Four amendments ratified by the necessary two-thirds vote in 1954 paved the way for West Germany's entry into NATO. Article 73 (1) was amended to confer on the federation exclusive power over "defense" as well as foreign affairs. Article 142a makes clear that the "provisions of the Basic Law do not prevent the conclusion and entering into force of any peace treaty or treaty for the defense of the Federal Republic." Finally, Article 59a empowers the Bundestag "to declare a state of defense" just as Article 87a provides for the establishment of the "armed forces for defense purposes."

In 1968, after prolonged and heated debate punctuated by student demonstrations throughout West Germany, the Basic Law was amended once again to include a new section on the "state of defense," the provisions of which lay down multiple rules and regulations for the use of the armed forces in the event of an armed attack on the Federal Republic. The provisions were also designed to ensure a role for parliament in declaring a state of defense. In addition, Article 87a was amended to include a new paragraph 2: "Apart from defense, the Armed Forces may be used only to the extent explicitly permitted by this Basic Law." Article 87a (2), like Articles 24 (2) and 59 (2) would figure prominently in the *Military Deployment* case (1993).

NOTE: THE *MILITARY DEPLOYMENT* CASE. By the late 1980s, against the backdrop of international pressures to involve German military units in efforts to establish peace in the Persian Gulf, German political leaders were virtually unanimous in maintaining that the Basic Law ruled out any use of the armed forces except for the purpose of self-defense and within the framework of the alliances covered by the NATO and WEU (Western European Union) treaties. Foreign Minister Hans-Dieter Genscher, for example, held insistently to the view that the Basic Law barred the use of German troops outside the NATO-WEU area, even for peace-keeping purposes. It is worth remarking that this restricted view of the military affairs power was not the prevailing view among German constitutional scholars.

In 1990, however, supported by cogent scholarly commentary and in the face of unified Germany's increased international influence, the consensus among political leaders against the use of military units outside the NATO area began to break down. A major conflict erupted in the early 1990s when Chancellor Helmut Kohl's government decided to deploy military forces outside the NATO countries. The conflict developed into an important chapter in German constitutional politics, featuring legal warfare between executive and parliament reminiscent of recent clashes in the United States between the president and Congress over the extent of their authority in the field of military affairs.[61] The major difference between the German and American experiences was the willingness of the Constitutional Court to intervene in such conflicts.[62]

The *Military Deployment* case involved constitutional challenges to cabinet decisions approving the participation of German military units in NATO's monitoring of compliance with the UN embargo against Serbia, in enforcing a UN resolution establishing a "no-fly zone" over Bosnia and Herzegovina, and in the UN humanitarian mission in Somalia.[63] Minority parties in parliament challenged each of these out-of-area deployments of German military units as violative of the Basic Law. It is worth recalling in full the text of the relevant articles:

> Article 87a (2): Other than for defense purposes the Armed Forces may be employed only to the extent explicitly permitted by this Basic Law.
>
> Article 59 (2): Treaties that regulate the political relations of the Federation . . . shall require the approval or participation of the appropriate legislative body in the form of a federal law.
>
> Article 24 (2): With a view to maintaining peace the federation may become a party to a system of collective security; in doing so it shall consent to such limitations upon its sovereign powers as will bring about and secure a peaceful and lasting order in Europe and among the nations of the world.

The centerpiece of the argument against these out-of-area deployments of German military units was Article 87a (2). Numerous arguments, many of them originating in the legal academy, parsed every word of Article 87a (2), focusing heavily on the historical and literal meaning behind the words "employed" and "defense." Those parties and groups challenging the validity of these military deployments read this language literally, claiming that there could be *no* use of the armed forces inside or outside Germany without explicit constitutional authorization. The government and its defenders, on the other hand, argued that Article 87a (2) was intended to apply to the use of the armed forces inside, not outside, Germany.[64]

The formal constitutional battle began when FDP members of parliament asked the Constitutional Court to issue a preliminary injunction against NATO's use of German aircraft in the AWACS (Airborne Warning and Control System) action over Bosnia-Herzegovina. This was a highly unusual political move because the FDP was a junior partner in the governmental coalition against whom the action was brought. In a 5 to 3 vote, the Second Senate denied the injunction pending a full review of the constitutional issues presented.[65] A few weeks later, the senate unanimously rejected the SPD's application for a preliminary injunction against the operation in Somalia.[66] These two cases, along with the action against Germany's participation in the UN embargo against Serbia, were consolidated for decision in the *Military Deployment* case.

In upholding the executive's actions in all three instances, the court gave surprisingly little consideration to Article 87a (2), the provision of the Basic Law on which legal scholars and other commentators had exhausted most of their attention. Instead, the court focused on Article 24 (2) and the meaning of a "system of collective security." It ruled that both the UN and NATO treaties constituted systems of collective security within the meaning of Article 24 (2), and that the Bundestag's approval of these treaties under Article 59 (2) embraced the implied authority to fulfill the terms of these agreements, including, if necessary, the deployment of German military forces.[67]

In a complex and divided opinion exceeding one hundred pages, the Second Senate handed down several rulings. First, the senate sustained the validity of the UN Somalia action, although three justices dissented from the majority's view that the Bundestag's original assent to the UN treaty included an agreement to place German troops under an international command. Second, although the senate ruled unanimously that the deployment of German military units within the framework of NATO and the WEU (Western European Union) pursuant to UN resolutions was compatible with Article 24, the justices divided 4 to 4 over whether these treaties covered military actions outside NATO and the WEU. (An even split on the court sustained the challenged governmental action or policy.)

The dissenting justices (Limbach, Böckenförde, Kruis, and Sommer) argued that the NATO-AWACS operation fell outside the original purpose of NATO. To validate the operation, therefore, the government would need to amend the treaty accordingly and secure renewed parliamentary approval under Article 59 (2); anything less than this, said the dissenters, would violate the rights of parliament. The justices in the "majority" (Kirchhof, Grasshof, Klein, and Winter) insisted on a more "dynamic" approach to Article 59 (2) so that treaties could be adapted and applied to changing circumstances without going through the laborious process of being formally amended.[68]

Finally, although handing the government a victory, the court went on to hold that under the Basic Law, the chancellor and his cabinet would be required to seek the Bundestag's explicit approval prior to any deployment of the armed services outside the NATO area and pursuant to a valid international agreement. In so holding, the court ultimately vindicated parliament's right to participate in cabinet decisions to deploy military units abroad. This right of participation the court found in Germany's constitutional history. The court referred particularly to Article 45 of the Weimar Constitution, which required the Reichstag's approval for a "declaration of war and the conclusion of peace." This history, together with the original debates surrounding Article 59 (2) of the Basic Law, was invoked to justify the important constitutional role that *Military Deployment* assigns to the legislative branch of the German government.[69]

CONCLUSION

Former justice Konrad Hesse, the author of a major text on the basic principles of the German Constitution, wrote that

> the allocation of various powers under the Constitution permits formation of a differentiated political structure geared to uniform cooperation and embodying the state's capacity to act through the formal activities of its [major] organs. Thus separation of powers reveals the details of the political structure, confers specified responsibilities, and has a rationalizing effect. Similarly, the separation of powers specifies and coordinates the more active elements of political leadership and decision making as well as the more static elements of technical and administrative rule making, and in addition safeguards the rule of law in the political arena. [This combination of structures and relationships] not only incorporates an optimal measure of self-government but also facilitates adjustment to historical change and is therefore capable of assuring relative continuity over time. In rationalizing, stabilizing, and limiting political power, separation of powers constitutes the basic organizational principle of the Constitution.[70]

In the light of these remarks and of the materials contained in this chapter we can begin to perceive an essential difference between separation of powers as understood in Germany and separation of powers as known in the United States. In American constitutional theory, as Madison wrote, "each department should have a will of its own,"[71] pitting ambition against ambition, as the veto power of the president might suggest. "To what purpose separate the executive and the judiciary from the legislative," wrote Hamilton in the same vein, "if both the executive and the judiciary are so constituted as to be at the absolute devotion of the legislative"?[72] In this model of separated powers — rooted as it is in Lockean and Hobbesian concepts of society and human nature — the three departments are independent and coordinate with one another.

In the Basic Law's model of separated powers, on the other hand — rooted as it is in traditional German theories of the state — state authority, or *Staatsgewalt,* represents the unified will of the commonwealth as expressed in public policy formulated by parties, elections, and political representation. Unless laws adopted by parliament offend some provision of the Constitution, they represent binding decisions requiring implementation by both the executive and the judiciary. Unlike the "inevitable friction incident to the distribution of governmental power among [the] three departments" found implicit by Justice Brandeis in the American doctrine of separation of powers, the German doctrine assumes that all the branches will operate under a condition of harmonious interdependence.

5

POLITICAL REPRESENTATION AND

DEMOCRACY

Democracy, like federalism, separation of powers, and the rule of law (*Rechtsstaat-lichkeit*), is a fundamental principle of the German polity.[1] The Basic Law does not, however, define the term "democracy"; it rather is defined through its association with various structures and procedures of self-government specified in the Constitution or established by law. These include regular elections, the secret ballot, proportional representation, the two-ballot and multiparty systems, parliamentary representation, and the legitimacy of political opposition. But the system also contains mechanisms designed to promote stable government, discourage antidemocratic movements, and prevent excessive splintering of political parties. This chapter organizes the constitutional cases dealing with these structures and procedures under four headings: parliamentary democracy, elections and voting, political parties and the party state, and militant democracy.

PARLIAMENTARY DEMOCRACY

Article 20 (1) of the Basic Law defines the Federal Republic as a "democratic state." Paragraph 2 of the same article reinforces this provision by declaring that "all state authority emanates from the people." The next sentence, however, emphasizes the representative character of the political system, for the authority emanating from the people "shall be exercised by . . . means of elections and voting and by specific legislative, executive, and judicial organs."[2] The Basic Law thus establishes a parliamentary democracy, but not, of course, in the British sense of parliamentary supremacy. As this and all the chapters of this book make clear, the Basic Law as interpreted by the Federal Constitutional Court controls parliament as well as every other branch of government.

The meaning of democracy has been the subject of considerable commentary in German legal literature.[3] Like the Federal Constitutional Court, most commentators have tended to associate Germany's brand of democracy with the following institutions and principles of the Basic Law: regular elections and the secret ballot (Articles 20 [2], 38 [1], and 39 [1]), indirect representation (Articles 38 [1] and 28 [1]), majority rule (Articles 42 [2], 52 [3], 54 [6], 61 [1], 63 [2–4], 67 [1], 68 [1], and 121), equality in voting for legislative representatives and equal access to public office (Articles 3 [1], 38 [1], and 33 [1 and 2]), free speech and press (Article 5 [1]), and a multiparty system (Article 21 [1]).[4] Partnership, compromise, political pluralism, and competition among political elites are related values inferred from and promoted by these institutions and practices.[5] Competition among political elites is particularly important, as the *Schleswig-Holstein Investigative Committee* case underscores.

5.1 Schleswig-Holstein Investigative Committee Case (1978)
49 BVerfGE 70

[Article 15 (1) of Schleswig-Holstein's constitution confers a duty on the state's parliament to appoint, on the application of one-fourth of its members, an investigating committee to take evidence on any matter related to the public interest. On April 19, 1977, twenty-five Social Democratic legislators — more than the required one-fourth — secured the formation of such a committee to look into charges linking various state officials, including prominent Christian Democratic legislators, to conflicts of interests and influence peddling in connection with various state building projects. The committee agreed to confront witnesses with thirteen specific queries. Christian Democrats, who were in the majority, later voted to add two more questions to the committee's list, one of them designed to investigate a similar charge brought against the leader of the opposition. Social Democratic party legislators objected, charging the majority with obstructing the investigation, and sought to vindicate their right as a parliamentary minority in a special proceeding before the Federal Constitutional Court.]

Judgment of the Second Senate. . . .

C. III. 1. The original history of Article 5, when considered together with comparable regulations and decisions, demonstrates that the right of [a legislative] minority to move for an investigating committee and to specify the objects of its investigation at the same time limits the right of the majority to expand [the committee's agenda] by adding questions against the minority's will.

2. Only this interpretation of the state's charter satisfies the [principle] of justice at issue here. Investigative committees play an important role in a parliamentary democracy. They enable parliament to examine the facts for itself independently of the government, its officials, and the courts [while] using power otherwise

granted only to courts and special agencies. [These committees] are thus able to examine facts the clarification of which they deem necessary to fulfill their constitutional duty as institutions of popular government. The task of [investigative] committees is to support the work of parliament and to lay the groundwork for [parliamentary] decisions. The focus of an investigation is naturally centered on parliament's control of the government and administration. [The investigation] is designed to clarify governmental events that suggest abuses. Such control has great importance as an aspect of separation of powers. It can be guaranteed only when a relationship of political tension exists between parliament and the executive. . . . The constitutional meaning of the rights of the minority lies in the safeguarding of this control. The original tension between parliament and government — as it existed during the constitutional monarchy — has changed. In a parliamentary democracy the majority [party] normally dominates the government. Today, this relationship is characterized by the political tension between the government and the parliamentary fractions supporting it, on the one hand, and the opposition [party or parties], on the other hand. In a parliamentary system of government [therefore] the majority does not primarily watch over the government. This is rather the task of the opposition, and thus, as a rule, of the minority [party]. If parliamentary control is to fulfill its purpose, the constitutionally guaranteed right of the minority to establish an investigating committee must not be impaired.

But the right to demand an investigating committee does not alone suffice to secure the minority's right of control. Additional guarantees are necessary. Above all, the minority must be left free to define the nature of the investigation. As a matter of principle, the subject matter of the investigation may not be changed or expanded against the minority's will.

This interpretation of the minority's right is supported by the fact that any expansion of the investigation [to reach issues not part of the committee's original mandate] would necessarily require additional explanation and thus increase the committee's work. This could easily lead to a deadlock in the investigation, or at least to a significant delay, . . . and [could thus] significantly jeopardize the effectiveness of parliamentary control. It is important to note that a committee ceases to exist at the end of a given electoral term. It must therefore dispatch its work as quickly as possible — especially at the conclusion of the legislative term. Any additional "investigative task" can prove to be an impediment which will completely nullify the investigation. Such an obstruction is constitutionally indefensible. The minority party which petitioned for the committee need not tolerate such action. To this extent, it is immaterial whether the majority agrees that the committee [should] investigate only the issues framed by the minority and make a partial report on these [matters]. For whether the committee will adhere to this procedure in later investigations depends upon the will of the majority of the committee — in turn selected by the majority of the parliament. If the right of the minority — and thus the parliamentary right to control — is not to be weakened unduly, then the minority must not be left at the mercy of the majority. This could prevent [the minority] from unqualifiedly investigating circumstances embarrassing to the existing majority. Thus, the parliamentary opposition would be deprived of an instrument with which it was entrusted not just in its own interest but rather in the interest of the democratic state; that is, to exercise control over the majority-supported government and its executive organs. [Such a deprivation] is not consistent with the Constitution. Of course, the majority still has the right independently to investigate facts it thinks should be clarified with respect to an investigation initiated by the minority.

3. . . . In principle, then, the majority may not force the investigating committee to look into additional issues against the will of the petitioners. This could lead to an unjustifiable delay in the work of the committee and obscure the goal and the result of the investigation. However, there are exceptions to this rule. Committee procedures lose their meaningfulness if, from the outset, the committee examines issues [under investigation] only from a narrow point of view, thus conveying at best a distorted picture of the facts to parliament and the public. Additional queries are therefore constitutionally permissible, even if they lead to a delay in the committee's work, provided they are necessary to convey a more complete and realistic picture of the alleged abuses. [But such additional queries must not change the nature of the investigation]. . . .

IV. . . . The additional questions voted upon by the majority constituted an impermissible expansion of the investigation. These resolutions are incompatible with Article 15 (1) of the state constitution.

The petitioners were concerned with uncovering abuses allegedly stemming from the business interests of representative G and corporation X. Whether the leader of the opposition, representative M, was guilty of similar behavior is a different issue. . . . Admittedly, the latter question is loosely connected to the subject matter of the investigation. [The latter investigation] was meant to reveal how the opposition obtained the information which prompted its attacks on representative G and corporation X. Nevertheless, the question addresses a different issue because the abuse to be uncovered concerned the field of information acquisition and irregularities attendant to this acquisition. This question does not address whether representative G and corporation X's business interests influenced state politics in Schleswig-Holstein.

NOTE: THE RIGHTS OF MINORITY PARTIES. *Schleswig-Holstein* is one of many cases in which the Constitutional Court has been asked to vindicate the participatory rights of minority parties, particularly *parliamentary* parties opposing the dominant coalition.[6] As the opinion points out, an effective parliamentary opposition is an important aspect of the principle of separation of powers in a political system in which the same coalition controls both legislature and executive. For this reason, as several of the cases reprinted in this chapter show, the Constitutional Court has vigilantly defended the rights of opposition parties unless such parties are found to reject the central core of the constitutional order.

The Green party, which burst on the West German political scene in the federal election campaign of 1983,[7] tested parliament's capacity for tolerating a party that opposed the established parliamentary parties on almost every significant issue before the public and whose unconventional political style antagonized most of their members. In 1983 several ecological, antinuclear, feminist, and peace groups organized themselves into a loose alliance known as the Greens, a grass-roots countercultural movement disillusioned with politics as usual and the "corruption" of the established parties. They opposed the installation of nuclear missiles in Germany, the Federal Republic's participation in military alliances, the multiparty political consensus that had been achieved in many areas of domestic policy—including the agreement to push forward with the development of nuclear energy—and even the German system of parliamentary representation.

Running on this platform, the Greens won 5.6 percent of the votes in the 1983 federal election, entitling them to twenty-seven seats in the Bundestag. Older representatives viewed the new delegation with amusement and scoffed at its "outlandish" proposals and behavior. Uncooperative and rancorous, the Greens seemed more effective as a burr under the saddle of the established parties than as a unit offering concrete proposals for reordering society. The older parties also distrusted the Greens, especially in matters of national security, and as a consequence denied them a seat on a special committee responsible for the budget of the intelligence services. The *Green Party Exclusion* case (1986) is one of several suits initiated by the Greens over the years to vindicate their institutional or representational rights.[8]

5.2 Green Party Exclusion Case (1986)
70 BVerfGE 324

[In 1984 and 1985 the Bundestag excluded Green party representatives from the list of delegates elected to the special five-member Parliamentary Committee for the Control of the Secret Service. This committee, whose members are elected by a majority of the whole parliament and whose membership normally includes at least one representative of each parliamentary party, has jurisdiction over the budgets of the intelligence agencies. The Greens challenged their exclusion in an *Organstreit* proceeding on several constitutional grounds. Most importantly, they argued that the Bundestag's actions violated Article 38 (1), which in their view gave the Greens a right, as "representatives of the whole people," to be represented on all parliamentary committees. They also claimed that the secrecy of the committee's deliberations offended Article 110 (1) of the Basic Law, which requires "all revenues and expenditures to be included in the budget."]

Judgment of the Second Senate. . . .

[The Second Senate upheld the Bundestag's procedures in this case. The court affirmed the basic right of an "individual representative under Article 38 (1) of the Basic Law to information that would allow him or her competently to assess the [soundness] of the budget." Article 110 (1), however, does not "absolutely require publicity" in all circumstances. Parliament is entitled, said the court, to "adopt a certain mode of deliberation that serves classified interests so long as it observes at the same time the principles of parliamentary democracy." These principles were observed here inasmuch as parliament (1) is autonomous in matters pertaining to its own procedures, (2) provided by law for a special committee to deal with budgetary proposals related to the secret service, and (3) had overwhelmingly compelling reasons for proceeding in this matter. In the following extract, the court underscored the parliamentary need for committee members who personally enjoy the confidence of the majority.]

C. II. 3. (a) The importance of secrecy in meetings concerning the budget [of the intelligence services] requires a high measure of precaution. It is not the Constitutional Court's function to weigh the particulars of how far such precautions should extend. The decision to leave this area of concern to a very small parliamentary committee is constitutionally permissible. In previous budgetary years it was also customary to confine deliberation over the budget of the secret service to a very small committee, a subcommittee of the Budgetary Committee. The reasons advanced by the respondents [the federal government and president of the Bundestag] for the small size of the committee under the terms of section 4 (9) of the 1984 Budget Act are plausible. The most sensitive issues of national security are discussed in this committee. Bundestag representative Kühbacher, in hearings before [this court] noted that on the basis of the information received by the committee one could assemble a coherent picture of the concrete operations of the secret services in a way that would endanger [the lives] of particular individuals. [Under these circumstances], to minimize the risk of disclosure, there are valid reasons for keeping the committee as small as possible.

(b) A majority of the Bundestag's members chose the members of the committee. . . . This procedure was designed to ensure that only those delegates would be chosen who personally enjoy the confidence of a parliamentary majority. The purpose of the procedure is to make sure that the majority is convinced that the persons selected are both competent and discreet. This procedure is unusual and for that reason approaches the borderline of constitutionality because it is possible that the majority may not observe the proper criteria in making such decisions, but rather . . . ignore the [rights] of the minority and from purely political [motives] stack a committee with persons [of their own political persuasion].

That has not happened here. The five members of the committee, under the terms of the budgetary law for 1984, were selected on the recommendations of the CDU/CSU, SPD, and FDP. The committee consisted of three representatives from the [coalition] parties and two from the opposition. The majority has not, therefore, abused the right of the minority. . . .

[Justices Mahrenholz and Böckenförde dissented. The following extract is from Justice Böckenförde's opinion.]

I am unable to agree with the decision of the court. The exclusion of the Green party from participation in the budgetary deliberations concerning the secret service violates principles protected by Articles 38 (1) and 20 (1) and (2). . . .

I. 1. As the direct representatives of the German people, all the delegates [elected to the] Bundestag have the right to participate in its deliberations. The representatives *as a whole* make up the parliament (Article 38 (1) [1]). Each individual delegate is a representative of all the people (Article 38 (1) [2]); jointly they make up the "representation of the people" and they are empowered by the people, in their capacity as an active citizenry, to represent the people as a whole.

As a consequence, every individual representative is called upon to represent the people and to participate in the parliament's negotiations and decisions. Each has a specific and equal right to such participation. Only in this way can a representative responsibly carry out the official function for which he has been elected. Representatives are not to be divided into classes depending upon their identification with a political group or on whether they are affiliated with the majority or the minority [parties].

2. What is basic to parliamentary democracy is the participation of all the representatives in negotiations conducted by the people's representatives; this is the basis of majority rule among the representatives of the people, ensuring that all [legislative] decisions will be [truly] representative in nature and reflect the totality of the people's [will]. It is precisely this general participation in the formation of the political will of parliament — a process emanating from general intellectual and political discussion and argumentation — which legitimates the inherent right of a parliamentary majority to decide [issues of public policy.] One [process] cannot be separated from the other.

This [principle] applies especially to those core functions of the parliament, particularly the right of members to participate in the process of legislation and to pass laws dealing with the budget. Even deliberations within the type of committee established by section 4 (6) of the 1984 and 1985 budget laws are subject to this principle. Parliament may not [surrender] its right to deliberate by transferring certain aspects of budgetary planning to a small committee operating in secret. . . .

4. The principle of complete participation of all — by the individual as well as by the parliamentary party — is not merely an axiom but is also an inalienable principle

of a representative parliamentary democracy. A parliamentary majority thus cannot do away with this principle, not even within the framework of its admitted authority over matters of procedure. . . .

5. . . . To be sure, the majority [of the court] underscores the [importance] of the equal participatory rights of all parliamentary parties; however, the majority treats [this] idea as a notion or a rule, and not as an inalienable principle essential for the structuring of the representation of the people. This is the reason the court . . . permits exceptions [to the principle] based on factual considerations set forth in the majority decision. Admittedly, the court tries to limit these exceptions so as to be able to restrict them to "narrowly limited exceptions." However, . . . these limitations are so general and open-ended . . . as to permit . . . a parliamentary party to be excluded from participating in parliamentary deliberation merely on the basis of unsubstantiated conjectures.

The [situation here] clearly illustrates [the arbitrariness of the Bundestag's action]. The Bundestag has never charged the representative or the parliamentary party requesting participation [in its committee deliberations] with failing to maintain secrecy in similar cases; nor did the Bundestag declare with certainty that [the representatives from the Green party] would not maintain secrecy in the deliberations at hand. According to the oral arguments, neither the representative nor the parliamentary party was specifically asked if they were ready to maintain secrecy concerning the economic matters [in question] and the agreements already made in connection with these matters. The majority's general distrust of the Green party and the utterance of one of its members immediately following the March 6, 1983, federal elections that she felt no obligation to maintain confidentiality about information to which she had access — an utterance contradicted within the Green party — apparently was enough. Without any further explanation and without any procedural measures, a path was chosen for deliberating on these economic plans which was . . . calculated to effectively exclude the parliamentary party from participating in the deliberations.

By proclaiming this procedure constitutional, the court indicates [both] its recognition of the authority of a given parliamentary majority to dispose of the principle of universal participation and how little validity it attributes to this principle. Ultimately, the maxims of trust and suspicion suffice to determine when and how one will depart from it. In my opinion this is not right.

NOTE: MINORITY PARTY ADJUDICATION. Although the Greens lost the *Exclusion* case, they could take some comfort in the strong dissenting opinions of Justices Mahrenholz and Böckenförde. These opinions laid the basis for other constitutional challenges against practices the Greens considered equally discriminatory. In fact, the Greens won a victory six months later when the Constitutional Court struck down a major provision of a tax statute affecting the financial status of political parties.[9] Dissenting once again, Justice Böckenförde would have gone even further to protect small parties like the Greens. In his view, legislation that bolsters the "oligarchical" and "careerist" elements of the established parties erodes parliament's representative character.[10]

Before proceeding to the *Wüppesahl* case (1989), which concerns the rights of a non-party-affiliated representative in the Bundestag, it might be noted that the Greens are today very much a part of the political establishment. In the early 1990s the Greens transformed themselves from an "antiparty" party concerned mainly with ecological issues into a responsible party of the left pragmatic enough to enter coalitions with the SPD in several *Land* governments and broad enough to threaten the position of the FDP as the major third force in German politics. In 1993 the western Greens merged with eastern Germany's Alliance 90—a federation of several reform groups in the old GDR—and became the Alliance 90/Greens, a party that stood to the right of the Party of Democratic Socialism (PDS), the GDR's old Socialist Unity party (SED).[11] In 1990 these parties—the PDS and the Alliance 90/Greens, along with the radical right Republicans—brought—and won—one of the most important cases involving the rights of minority parties in postunification Germany (see *National Unity Election* case, no. 5.6).

5.3 Wüppesahl Case (1989)
80 BVerfGE 188

[Thomas Wüppesahl was elected to the Bundestag in 1987 as a member of the Green party. He represented the party on several legislative committees. When he resigned from the party in January 1988, the Green party stripped him of his committee positions and appointed another member of the party to take his place. As an independent deputy, Wüppesahl challenged a number of parliamentary rules which, he alleged, unconstitutionally limited the rights of independent deputies. Specifically, he questioned the validity of the rules prescribing the proportional representation of parties on committees and granting the parties the authority to name their committee members. In addition, he claimed in his petition to the Constitutional Court that the rule revoking a deputy's committee membership on resigning from his party infringed his rights as a parliamentary representative.]

Judgment of the Second Senate. . . .

C. With respect to the first allegation, the application is well-founded. The remaining allegations are admissible but dismissed as unfounded.

I. 1. Parliament is the direct representative organ of the people, composed of elected representatives who represent the whole people. The basis for parliament's position as the "specific organ" (Article 20 [2] of the Basic Law) of the people lies in the constitutionally guaranteed status of members of parliament as representatives of the whole people (Article 38 [1] of the Basic Law); representatives exercise state authority that emanates from the people. . . . The tasks and powers constitutionally assigned to parliament cannot be asserted independently of its members. Thus each member is entitled to participate in all of parliament's activities. Parliament must organize its work in a manner consistent with the constitutional framework and based on the principle of universal participation. The rights of representatives include, above all, the right to speak, the right to vote, the right to ask questions and obtain information, the right to participate in parliamentary voting, and the right to unite with other representatives to form a political party. By exercising these rights, representatives perform the tasks of legislating, shaping the budget, obtaining information, supervising the executive, and otherwise carrying out the duties of their offices.

All representatives have equal rights and duties because parliament as a whole, not individuals or groups of legislators, represents the people. This assumes that each member participates equally in the legislative process.

2. The rules of parliamentary procedure (RPP) assist representatives in carrying out their parliamentary duties. The power to pass [rules] independently and to shape their content is constitutionally granted to Parliament (Article 40 [1] of the Basic Law). Parliament's sphere of authority has traditionally included matters of procedure and discipline; it also embraces the [general] power to fulfill its assigned tasks. For instance, parliament must be able to shape the legislative process and to specify all its concomitant rights and duties (e.g., defining committee functions, composition, and procedure; initiating laws; collecting information; specifying the rights of parliamentary parties; and laying down the rights of speaking in Parliament), to the extent that these matters are not regulated by the Constitution itself. The rights of representatives are derived from their constitutional status, not from parliament's rules of procedure; the rules [only] set out the basic condition for the exercise of these [constitutionally guaranteed] rights. These rights exist as, and can only be realized as, membership rights; they can be granted and reconciled only in relation to each other. Only in this way can parliament properly fulfill its tasks. [But] at the same time, the rights of individual legislators must be limited, for these rights are exercised within the framework of the collective exercise of parliamentary rights. In any case, the right of each individual representative to contribute knowledge and experience to the initiatives and decision-making process of parliament cannot be challenged precisely for reasons of representational capacity and functional efficiency. The rights of each representative may be limited but in principle they cannot be revoked. The proper standard against which parliamentary organization and procedure must be measured is the principle of universal participation.

The political structure in which parliament must fulfill its tasks is one of party democracy. Political parties are institutions necessary to the constitutional life of the nation and thus crucial to shaping the people's political will. Party formation depends on the free and conscientious decisions of parliamentary representatives. When drafting rules of parliamentary procedure, parliament must consider the individual rights of representatives when defining the powers of the parties.

3. When testing the constitutionality of such rules, it must be assumed (under Article 40 [1] of the Basic Law) that parliament has the power to decide how deputies and parties will participate [in the legislative process]. The definition and limitation of this regulatory power—e.g., the right to speak, to engage in party deliberations, and to receive information, etc.—will be determined in individual cases.

Generally, parliament has broad discretion in making rules pertaining to its organization and procedure. The principle of universal participation in parliamentary functions, however, acts as a constitutional check on this power.

4. . . . (a) The constitutional protection of parliamentary minorities—a right following from the principle of democracy—also applies to independent representatives, but that does not give the independent representative any rights over and above those secured by Article 38 (1) of the Basic Law.

(b) The principle of formal equality, which has been developed by the Constitutional Court in its jurisprudence dealing with the right to vote, cannot be interpreted to grant additional rights. In the present context it requires only that all representatives be placed in a position of formal equality with respect to one another; their constitutional status under Article 38 (1) of the Basic Law guarantees them equal rights. It follows that the Rules of Parliamentary Procedure cannot [adversely] affect the equal right of representatives to express their views during the process of parliamentary consensus building, even though each representative's influence on the process and content of parliamentary decision-making will differ not only in terms of personal capacity, work assignments, and parliamentary offices held, but according to party membership and nonmembership.

(c) The principle of representative democracy does not extend the parliamentary rights of representatives beyond those secured under Article 38 (1) of the Basic Law. Rather, it has been exhausted in this context. . . .

[The court went on to hold that as a matter of principle a representative's rights under Article 38 (1) would be infringed if he were denied membership on a legislative committee. The petitioner's other claims, however, were rejected. Although the court found no constitutional flaw in legislative rules empowering the parliamentary parties to nominate representatives for committee membership, it ruled that an alternate procedure would be required to ensure that independent legislators would receive committee assignments. The court also sustained the denial of an independent's right to vote in committee, claiming that this would disrupt the work of the committee. In addition, the court approved regulations limiting an independent's speaking time in the Bundestag and rejecting his or her claim to financial support proportionate to that received by the parliamentary parties. Germany, said the court, is a party democracy, and only political parties are capable of "completing the work of the state." Finally, the Greens were permitted to remove the petitioner from several committees since he was no longer in a position to represent the views of the party that nominated him in the first place. Justice Ernst Gottfried Mahrenholz, presiding justice — and vice president — of the Second Senate, dissented, claiming that membership and participation on a committee would be meaningless in the absence of the rights to vote and initiate legislation.]

NOTE: PARLIAMENTARY COMMITTEES, POLITICAL PARTIES, AND THE BUNDESTAG. Legislative committees are the workhorses of the Bundestag. Organized by subject matter, they are empowered to hold hearings on matters referred to them and to prepare bills for parliamentary consideration. The Basic Law itself requires several permanent committees, including the Committees on Election Scrutiny (Article 41), Foreign Affairs and Defense (Article 45a), Petitions (Article 45c), Judicial Selection (Article 95), and European Union (Article 45). The Bundestag's Rules of Procedure govern the membership and the conduct of these and all other committees. Under Rule 12 the parliamentary parties appoint committee chairs and members proportionate to their numbers in the house as a whole. Thus, the parties play a crucial role in determining who gets appointed to what committees. In the aftermath of *Wüppesahl,* every member of the Bundestag is entitled to serve on at least one committee, and if he or she is independent, the Bundestag's president is authorized to make the committee assignment, although under Rule 57 (2) the member in question is not entitled to vote.[12]

5.4 Official Propaganda Case (1977)
44 BVerfGE 125

[During the federal election campaign of 1976, the German Press and Information Office and the publications divisions of several federal ministries distributed millions of leaflets, pamphlets, and brochures disclosing the records of and benefits conferred by various governmental agencies. Although some of these publications were informational (e.g., service publications and the text of laws and treaties), many advanced the cause of the SPD-FDP coalition government. In addition, funds allocated to the publications divisions of various agencies were used to take out advertisements in prominent magazines and newspapers, listing the accomplishments of the incumbent government. For example, between May 24 and July 26, 1976, *Der Spiegel* carried a government-sponsored advertisement, three to five pages in length, under the caption, "All in all, this government has brought you more freedom." Of the six million copies of these advertisements issued between January and July 1976, 59 percent were allotted to the Social and Free Democratic parties and only 0.26 percent to Christian Democrats. The general secretary and Executive Council of the Christian Democratic Union challenged the validity of these expenditures in an *Organstreit* proceeding before the Federal Constitutional Court. The CDU claimed that the use of public funds to further the cause of the government parties in an election campaign violates the principle of parliamentary democracy under Article 20, the equality of political parties under Article 21, and free and equal elections under Article 38. The following extract focuses on the court's discussion of parliamentary democracy.]

Judgment of the Second Senate. . . .

C. I. [Our consideration] of Article 20 (1) and (2) together with Article 2 (2) [guaranteeing rights of liberty] leads to [these conclusions]:

1. In the kind of free democracy designed by the Basic Law for the Federal Republic of Germany, all public authority emanates from the people by means of elections and voting and [is exercised] by specific organs of legislation as well as by executive and judicial authorities (Article 20 [1–2]). . . .

2. Elections can confer democratic legitimation in the sense of Article 20 (2) only if they are free. Not only must the actual act of casting the ballot remain free of coercion and undue pressure as stipulated by Article 38 (1) of the Basic Law, but the voters must be able to form and utter their opinions freely and openly (citing 20 BVerfGE 56). The democratic basic order established by the Basic Law lays down the constitutional conditions for a free and open process of forming the popular will. [This is accomplished] especially through numerous constitutional guarantees of freedom and equality as well as through institutional and procedural mechanisms such as the fundamentally public nature of Bundestag and Bundesrat meetings (Articles 42 (1) and 52 (3) of the Basic Law) or the promulgation of enacted laws (Articles 76, 77, and 82 [2]). . . .

4. The integrity of the fundamental act of democratic legitimation — that is, the election of parliamentary representatives — must be ensured. Through the act of voting in the sense intended by Article 20 (2) the formation of the popular will takes place, rising from the people to the constitutional organs, and not the other way around. Admittedly, the conduct of these constitutional organs has a rather strong effect on the formation of the will and opinion of the voters — conduct that is itself instrumental in the voters' decision. Yet the constitutional organs may not in their official capacity [try to] influence the formation of the popular will by employing additional special measures during elections in order to gain control over these organs. They are constitutionally barred from identifying themselves, as constitutional organs, with political parties during election campaigns and from supporting or opposing political parties with public funds. They are particularly forbidden from influencing the decision of voters through advertising.

In addition, the constitutional principle that limits the tenure of the Bundestag and the federal government does not permit the current federal government in its capacity as a constitutional organ to seek reelection, as it were, and to promote itself as the "future government." Of course, this does not prevent a member of the federal government from entering the election campaign on behalf of a political party in a nonofficial capacity.

5. The Basic Law as a democratic [governmental] structure provides that basic political decisions be reached by majority rule (citing Articles 42 (2), 63 (2–4), 67 (1), 52 (3), and 54 (6)).

. . . Only if the majority emerges in the free and open process of forming the [popular] will and [public] opinion — a process that requires constant renewal and in which all citizens of voting age share equally — only then does the decision of the majority . . . constitute the will of all. [Only then does the decision] generate a binding commitment for all in accordance with the idea of free self-determination for all citizens. [The majority] must keep the common good in mind during the decision-making process, particularly the rights and interests of the minority, whose chances of becoming a majority must neither be taken away nor curtailed. . . .

Basically, all citizens, regardless of their political convictions or affiliations, bear the burden of financially supporting the state. These [financial] resources are also entrusted to the state for use on behalf of the common good. As a state based on the rule of law and on social justice [the Federal Republic] serves this purpose in many different ways, especially by supporting parts and groups in the population of a pluralistic society and its most diverse interests. . . . However, this commitment [to serve diverse groups] does not extend to a politically vital situation such as a parliamentary election if the financial funding and potential supplied and generated by the general public are used to favor or disfavor one political party or candidate over others. The Basic Law tolerates extralegal inequalities of citizens and their political groups in the process of forming popular political opinion and the people's will which culminates in the act of voting. However, it bars the state from taking sides during an election campaign in order to influence the competitive relations among the political powers. Organs of the state must serve everyone and remain neutral during an election campaign.

> [The court proceeded to invalidate the public relations measures taken by the government during the 1976 federal election campaign. The expenditures were invalidated on three principal grounds: (1) they offended the idea of democracy within the meaning of Article 20, (2) they violated the principle of equality among political parties under Article 21, and (3) they offended the principle of free and equal elections under Article 38.]

Justice Rottmann, dissenting,

I dissent from the limitations imposed on federal government activities during the parliamentary election campaign which the majority derives from the principle of democracy and the constitutional principle of equal opportunity for political parties. . . .

I. The senate bases its ruling on an ideal of parliamentary democracy which fails to do justice to the structure of the political party system in the Federal Republic. Furthermore, it does not sufficiently take into consideration constitutional reality since the founding of the Federal Republic.

Democracy as outlined by the Basic Law is a party democracy. Political parties enjoy a legally privileged position under Article 21 (1) of the Basic Law. [Article 21 (1)] raises them to the level of constitutional institutions and recognizes them as active political units which our modern democracy needs to unite voters in politically active and operational groups, thus giving citizens the possibility of influencing political events. Consequently, [political parties] constitute a factual monopoly in the constitutive creation of constitutional organs at the federal and state levels. Without them . . . the "creative organs" [of the Federal Republic] cannot function, and political offices in a modern mass democracy cannot be filled.

[Justice Rottmann went on to describe the party state under the Basic Law as having the following characteristics: (1) Political parties nominate candidates to parliament and effectively elect the chancellor. (2) The chancellor and his cabinet are, respectively, the party chairman and either top party functionaries or members of parliament. According to Justice Rottmann, the consequence of these two attributes of the party state is that the federal government functions as the executive committee of the ruling coalition of parties. (3) While the government has an obligation to the entire state, Rottmann argued, it actually seeks to implement its party platform. In so doing, the majority party or coalition uses its platform as one of several concepts of the common good which the people have already approved through national elections. Thus the will of the people authorizes the ruling coalition to implement and defend its platform against the contrary efforts of the minority parties.

The second prong of the dissent focuses on the federal government's past practice of using official resources during election campaigns. Rottmann traced the history of election campaigns since the founding of the Federal Republic. He then noted that the chancellor and most cabinet ministers have campaigned not only as party members but also in their official capacities, using resources of their office to do so. Hence, the idea that the federal government remains neutral during a campaign is a novel idea. Rottmann viewed the practice of using government resources to achieve reelection as an essential and characteristic part of political life as it has developed under the Basic Law.]

(i) . . . The Federal Constitutional Court cannot simply change [past practice] without prior announcement of guidelines. [It cannot make changes] by deriving standards from the Basic Law [and calling them] constitutional principles which have supposedly always restricted the actions of the federal government. Constitutional reality contradicts this. For, in truth, in the almost thirty-year history of the Federal Republic, politically active persons have not gleaned these constitutional restrictions on the federal government from the Basic Law. In the final analysis, nobody had any knowledge of [these restrictions], with the result that no federal chancellor, no federal government, no Bundestag, no political party could be familiar with these limitations which are supposedly required by the Constitution.

———————————

NOTE: PARLIAMENTARY GRIDLOCK. In recent years, the parliamentary system of the Federal Republic has been the subject of increasing criticism, on and off the bench. Recall Justice Böckenförde's reference to the "oligarchical" tendency that he observed in the established parties,[13] a tendency that a former president of the Federal Constitutional Court believed the Second Senate had reinforced in the *Legislative Pay* case (1975; no. 4.4).[14] More recently, in 1992, federal president Richard von Weizäcker mounted a slashing attack on Germany's established parties, faulting them for their ossification and lack of creativity.[15] Another leading public official spoke of the "representational deficit" afflicting the German Bundestag today and advocated more participatory democracy including institutional reforms such as the initiative and referendum.[16] Indeed, the Greens owe much of their success, particularly among the young, to the grass-roots character of their movement as well as to their support of such reforms and other citizen's initiatives (*Bürgerinitiativen*). As interpreted by the Federal Constitutional Court, however, the principle of representative, or indirect, democracy embodied in Article 20 (2) would seem to exclude any institutional reform at the national level that would interfere with parliament's exclusive control over legislation.[17]

Article 20 (2) provides for the exercise of state authority "by the people by means of elections and voting and by specific legislative, executive, and judicial organs." Some constitutional scholars are beginning to suggest that a liberal interpretation of the term "voting" would permit some forms of direct democracy.[18] They believe that referenda on fundamental political issues and even the popular ratification of constitutional amendments would be good political therapy for a body politic not altogether satisfied with a sometimes stumbling and indecisive parliament.[19] The prevailing view, however, is that the adoption of plebiscitary devices at the national level would require an amendment to the Basic Law. The Joint Commission of the Bundestag and Bundesrat formed in the aftermath of reunification seriously considered such an amendment but was unable to acquire the two-thirds vote required to amend the Basic Law.

ELECTIONS AND VOTING

The major principles governing the German electoral process are set forth in the Basic Law. Article 20 (2) provides that "the people [shall exercise all state authority] by means of elections and voting." Article 38 (1), the provision at issue in this section, states that parliamentary representatives "shall be elected in general, direct, free, equal, and secret elections," principles that also bind the states under the terms of Article 28. Article 38 (1) declares further that legislators "shall be representatives of the whole people, not bound by orders and instructions, and shall be subject only to their conscience"; whereas paragraph 2 confers the right to vote on all citizens who have attained the age of eighteen years. Article 39 (1), finally, provides for legislative terms of four years.

The *Maastricht* case (1993) bridges nearly all the concerns of this chapter. It constitutes the most recent and comprehensive declaration of the meaning of German parliamentary democracy. As noted in Chapter 3 (see case no. 3.10), the Maastricht Treaty creates a European Union to which the sovereign rights of member states may be assigned. The assignment of such rights to the Union, however, implicates certain inviolable principles of democracy secured by the Basic Law. According to the *Maastricht* court, the principles of democracy and free elections do not bar German membership in a supranational interstate community so long as the transfer of such powers remains rooted in the right of German citizens to vote and thus to participate in the national lawmaking process.

5.5 Maastricht Case (1993)
89 BVerfGE 155

[The essential argument, based on Article 38 of the Basic Law, proceeds as follows: The Basic Law confers on German citizens an equal right to vote for their parliamentary representatives. Consistent with the core principle of democracy, citizen-voters participate in the exercise of state authority through their parliamentary deputies (Article 20 [2]). To the extent that this authority has been transferred to a supranational institution beyond the control of German legislators, citizen-voters have lost their right to participate in the national legislative process. In short, they are disabled from influencing the determination of national policy through the act of voting. Additionally, the European Union itself suffers from a democratic deficit, for the European Parliament lacks authentic lawmaking power and Germany's deputies play no significant role in lawmaking at the European Community level. For additional details, see case no. 3.10.]

Judgment of the Second Senate. . . .

III. B. 1. The first complainant has shown that the Act of Accession may violate his equal right to vote as guaranteed by Article 38 (1) of the Constitution.

(a) Article 38 (1) and (2) guarantee to all Germans entitled to vote the subjective right to participate in electing Bundestag representatives. The power of the State emanates from the people through the voting process. The Bundestag then exercises that power as a legislative body, choosing the federal chancellor and controlling the government. Article 38 does more than ensure that citizens have the right to elect the Bundestag and that constitutional principles will be protected in the election process. It also extends this safeguard to the fundamental democratic content of that right: the fact that any German citizen who is entitled to vote has the right to participate in the election of representatives to the Bundestag also means that he has the right to participate in the legitimation of State power and to influence its exercise. . . .

If the Bundestag relinquishes its duties and responsibilities, especially as to legislation or the election and control of others who exercise state power, then this affects matters within the scope of Article 38 and its democratic content. Article 23 (1) of the Constitution enables the federal legislature (under specified conditions) to grant the European Union the right to independent exercise of sovereign powers, up to the limits imposed by Article 79 (3) (see Article 23 [1], third sentence). The legislature created this constitutional provision by amendment to the Constitution specifically for the purposes of European integration and its progress. In doing so, it also defined the substance of the right guaranteed by Article 38. Where Article 23 applies, Article 38 forbids the weakening of the legitimate State power gained through an election; it also forbids [any weakening] of the voters' influence on the exercise of such power by a transfer of power so extensive that it breaches the democratic principle declared inviolable by Article 79 (3) in conjunction with Article 20 (1) and (2).

The complainant's right arising from Article 38 . . . , therefore, can be infringed if the exercise of the responsibilities of the Bundestag is transferred to an institution of the European Union or European Communities so extensively that the minimum requirement of Article 20 (1) and (2) (in conjunction with Article 79 [3]) are violated, and the requirements of legitimation of the sovereign power are not met. . . .

C. To the extent that the constitutional complaint filed by the first complainant is admissible, it is unfounded. In this case, when examining the granting of sovereign powers to the European Community and the communities within it, the Federal Constitutional Court can apply only the criterion of the guarantees within Article 38 of the Constitution. Those guarantees are not violated by the Act of Accession, as the content of the treaty shows. . . . The functions of the European Union and the powers granted to implement these functions are regulated in a sufficiently foreseeable manner; because [the treaty] reflects the principle of limited individual powers, the European Union does not have the power to extend its own authority, and the claiming of additional functions and powers depends on supplementing or amending the treaty; thus it is subject to the consent of the national parliaments. . . .

I. 1. The right granted [to eligible voters] by Article 38 of the Constitution to participate in the legitimation of State power and to influence its exercise by voting precludes the possibility, within the scope of Article 23, of the right being weakened through transferring functions and powers of the Bundestag in such a way as to violate the democratic principle. . . .

2. Part of the inviolable content of the democratic principle under Article 79 (3) of the Constitution is that the exercise of state functions and powers is derived from the people, and those who [exercise state power] are fundamentally responsible to the people. This relationship of responsibility is established in varied ways, not just one form. The decisive factor is that a sufficiently effective proportion or level of legitimation be achieved.

(a) If the Federal Republic of Germany becomes a member of a community of states entitled to act on its own in sovereign matters, and if that community is given the right to exercise independent, sovereign powers (both of which are expressly allowed by the Constitution, for the purpose of creating a unified Europe), then democratic legitimation for these purposes cannot be produced the same way it is for a national order, governed uniformly and conclusively by a state constitution. If sovereign rights are granted to international institutions, then the representative body elected by the people (the Bundestag) and the voting populace necessarily lose some influence over the process of forming the political will and making political decisions. Any entry into an international community results in the members of the community being bound to adhere to community decisions.

[In the following and related passages, the court examined the Maastricht Treaty in the light of the Basic Law's new Article 23. The court found that the Bundestag has not been frozen out of the Union's process of making policy. It held that since the European Union is an organization of states rather than a superfederal state, the Bundestag retained sufficient control over its functions and powers to satisfy the principle of democracy. In the end, the court suggested that the legitimacy of Union policy will depend on maintaining a link between German voters, the Bundestag, and the European Parliament.]

(b) Thus, the democratic principle does not prevent the Federal Republic of Germany from becoming a member of a community of states organized on a supranational basis. However, it is a precondition for membership that the legitimation derived from the people be preserved within the alliance of states.

(b) (1) According to its self-definition as a union of the peoples of Europe, the European Union is a federation of states seeking dynamic development. If it is to carry out sovereign tasks and exercise sovereign powers toward that aim, the national peoples of the member states must first, through their own national parliaments, provide the democratic legitimation for such action.

At the same time, as the functions and powers of the European Community grow, it is increasingly necessary for the people of individual states to be represented within a European Parliament that supplements the democratic legitimation and influence gained through the national parliaments; this will form the basis of democratic support for the policies of the European Union. The establishment of union citizenship by the Maastricht Treaty has formed a legal bond between the nationals of the individual member states; this bond is intended to be lasting, and, though it does not have the strength of common nationality that unites a single state, it does provide the legally binding expression of an existing, de facto community. The influence flowing from the citizens of the Union can eventually provide the democratic legitimation of European institutions to the extent that the following conditions are met on the part of the peoples of the European Union:

If democracy is to be more than merely a formal principle of accountability, it depends on the presence of certain prelegal conditions, such as continuous free debate between opposing social forces, interests, and ideas; in the course of such debate political goals are clarified and changed, and public opinion emerges as a precursor to the forming of the political will. For this to happen, it is essential that the institutions which exercise sovereign power and implement political objectives engage in a decision-making process which is clear and comprehensible, and that citizens entitled to vote can communicate in their own language with the sovereign authority to which they are subject. . . .

(b) (2) Within the federation of states which is the European Union, democratic legitimation necessarily emerges as information about the activities of the European institution flows back through the parliaments of the individual member states. Democratic legitimation within the structure of the Union is also provided through the election of a European Parliament, chosen by the citizens of the member states, increasing as the European nations grow closer together. Already, the legitimation provided by the European Parliament has a supporting effect; this effect could become stronger if the European Parliament were elected by electoral rules consistent in all member states, in accordance with Article 138 (3) of the E.C. Treaty, and if the Parliament's influence on the policies and legislation of the European Community were to increase. The important factor is that the democratic bases of the European Union continue to grow in step with integration, and that as integration proceeds, a democracy thrives in the member states. . . .

If the peoples of the individual states continue to provide democratic legitimation through their national parliaments, then the principle of democracy limits the extension of the European Community's powers and functions. The origin of state power in each member state is the people of that state.

It follows, then, that the Bundestag must retain functions and powers of substantial importance. . . .

3. Since an enfranchised German exercises his right to participate in the democratic legitimation of institutions and agencies entrusted with power by voting in elections for the Bundestag, then the Bundestag must make decisions about German membership in the European Union, and on its continuation and development.

Accordingly, Article 38 of the Constitution is breached if an act opens up the German legal system to the application of the law of the supranational European Communities [if that act] does not establish with sufficient certainty what powers are transferred and how they will be integrated. If it is not clear to what extent and degree the German legislature has assented to the transfer of the exercise of sovereign powers, then it will be possible for the European Community to claim functions and powers that were not [specifically] mentioned. That would be a general authorization and therefore a surrender of powers, something against which Article 38 protects.

NOTE: RULES GOVERNING ELECTIONS. Germany's original electoral laws sought to achieve political stability and fair representation. To this end, German lawmakers adopted a mixed system of political representation. They also sought to prevent the rise of splinter parties by requiring a political party to obtain, as a condition for entering the legislature, a certain percentage of the popular vote under proportional representation. In addition, before gaining access to the ballot, new parties had to produce evidence of electoral support, usually by collecting the signatures of a certain percentage of eligible voters. The Federal Constitutional Court, in several early cases, struck down a number of these restrictions.[20]

The Federal Electoral Act, first enacted in 1956 and last revised in 1993,[21] supersedes major election statutes passed in 1949 and 1953 and governs the conduct of national elections. It incorporates the rulings of several constitutional cases while retaining the major features of the earlier statutes. The most prominent of these features is a mixed electoral system that provides for the election of half of the current 656 members of the Bundestag by a direct vote in single-member constituencies, and half on the basis of proportional representation from party lists put forward by state party organizations. Under this system, each voter casts two ballots, the first for a particular constituency candidate and the second for a specific party list. A federal election committee then distributes the seats among the parties in proportion to the total number of second (party-list) ballots won by them throughout the country. Any party securing at least 5 percent of all second-ballot votes or at least three constituency seats qualifies for parliamentary representation. Other provisions of the Electoral Act specify the conditions for voter eligibility, regulate the process of selecting candidates, and establish rules for casting ballots, challenging election results, and filling vacant seats during a parliamentary term.[22]

NOTE: THE 5 PERCENT CLAUSE. The rule that political parties must obtain 5 percent of the national vote to get into parliament has been a major feature of the electoral system since 1949. Some of the framers wanted to absorb the 5 percent rule into the Basic Law itself,[23] but most felt that the matter should be left to legislation. By 1952, however, the 5 percent rule had been adopted at nearly every level of government. The Second Senate took note of this development in the *Schleswig-Holstein Voters Association* case (1952),[24] which invalidated Schleswig-Holstein's imposition of a 7 percent rule, a hurdle that in the court's view offended the principle of equality as applied to political parties. A very compelling or special reason, said the Second Senate, would have to justify a rule "exceeding the common German value of five percent."

The 5 percent rule was challenged in the *Bavarian Party* case (1957).[25] Strongly represented in Bavaria, the Bavarian party sent several representatives to the Bundestag in 1949. In 1953, however, although it had won 20.9 percent of the vote in Bavaria, the party could garner only 4.2 percent of the national vote, and it was thus excluded from sharing in the distribution of Bundestag seats according to the results of the second ballot. The party claimed that the 5 percent clause violated the Basic Law's provisions on equality (Article 3 [1]), direct elections (Article 38 [1]), and political parties (Article 21 [1]). The court rejected each of the claims. While affirming the equality of all voters in exercising their constitutional right to participate in elections, the court reminded Germans that "the goal of elections is not only to assert the political will of voters as individuals . . . [but] also to create a parliament which is an effective political body."[26] The court added that "if the principle of exact proportional [representation] as the reflection of [all] popular political views were carried to its logical extreme, parliament might be split into many small groups, which would make it more difficult or even impossible to form a majority."[27] The constitutional tasks of parliament require parties that are dedicated to the common good and possess popular mandates large enough to allow them to act. Splinter parties, often extreme in their views and too small to effectively produce legislation, cannot meet this test. The 5 percent clause was vindicated as a reasonable and fair way to establish the ability of parties to act responsibly in the legislature.

The *Bavarian Party* case approved the 5 percent clause as applied to federal elections, but other cases had sustained its application to local elections as well as elections to the European Parliament.[28] In the *Danish Minority* case,[29] decided in 1954, the court even upheld Schleswig-Holstein's application of the rule to the state's Danish minority. The court went on to say, however, that the state parliament could, if it wished, exempt a national minority from the 5 percent requirement, although in its view the Basic Law does not require such special treatment. Schleswig-Holstein took the cue and soon thereafter amended its electoral code to exempt the Danish minority party from the 5 percent rule altogether. Only in the *National Unity Election* case was the 5 percent rule successfully challenged. The objection, however, as noted in the statement of facts, was not to the 5 percent clause itself but to its application to Germany as a whole in the first all-German election, held in December 1990.

5.6 National Unity Election Case (1990)
82 BVerfGE 322

[Considerable controversy greeted the effort to structure the first all-German election on December 2, 1990, following Germany's reunification. The dispute stemmed from the different electoral systems of the two German states. In the old GDR, each voter had only one vote in a system of purely proportional representation — in contrast to the FRG's two-ballot system — and there was no significant threshold requirement for entry into the legislature. East German leaders objected to the 5 percent rule because the political reform groups that had played so critical a role in the GDR's peaceful revolution would be unlikely to win 5 percent of the national vote. In the end, GDR leaders relented on the 5 percent rule, and the two sides worked out a "piggyback" arrangement that would permit smaller parties or groups in East Germany to field candidates in alliance with other, larger parties in the west. This plan, however, favored some small parties at the expense of others. For example, the strength of Bavaria's CSU would carry its sister party, the GDR's DUS (German Social Union) into the Bundestag, whereas the old Communist SED — now dressed up as the PDS — was unlikely to find a willing partner in the FRG to help it win 5 percent of the national vote, whereupon the PDS, together with the Greens and far-right Republicans, petitioned the Constitutional Court to strike down the arrangement.]

Judgment of the Second Senate. . . .

C. The petition and constitutional challenge are well founded.

I. According to the continuing jurisprudence of the Constitutional Court the principle of equal suffrage in the election of a federal parliament must be understood as a guarantee of strict and formal equality. . . . The democratic order established by the Basic Law equalizes the voices of all citizens . . . [and thus] it is impossible, in principle, to give different weights to [different] votes.

Parties are charged with the primary responsibility of organizing citizens into political groups for electoral purposes. In the field of elections and voting, formal equality includes the principle of formal equal opportunity, namely, the opportunity of political parties and voter organizations to compete for electoral support. This right of equal opportunity derives from the constitutional status of [political] parties, the freedom to form political parties, and the principle of a multiparty system which is associated with the concept of a free democracy. The principle of equal opportunity governs the election proper as well as the campaign. Democracy cannot function — as a matter of principle — if the parties are unable to enter an election campaign under the same legal circumstances. In regulating the process of forming the political will of the people, the legislature operates under strict limits. It may not undermine the equal opportunity of parties or voter associations. Differential treatment of parties and voter associations is constitutionally prohibited.

Parliament's discretion is severely limited when legislating on the right to elect representatives to legislative bodies; this [limitation] follows from the principles of formal voter equality and equal opportunity of parties. Any deviation from a system of equal voting must be justified by compelling reasons. One reason sufficiently compelling to justify distinctions between votes in a system of proportional representation—one which this court has repeatedly emphasized—is to ensure the proper functioning of parliament. The very purpose of proportional representation is to have government realistically reflect the political will of the electorate. Such a system may result in splintering the electorate, making it difficult or impossible to form a stable parliamentary majority. Accordingly, the legislature may treat votes differentially in a system of proportional representation if such treatment is required to ensure parliament's ability to act and make decisions.

In principle, the legislature is empowered to ensure the [proper] functioning of parliament by means of a "blocking clause" (if a party does not receive at least 5 percent of the popular vote, it is blocked from being represented in parliament). As a rule, a threshold of 5 percent is constitutionally unobjectionable. This court emphasized early on that the compatibility of a blocking clause with the principle of equality in voting is something that cannot be determined in an abstract manner. Regulations concerning voting rights may be justified in one state at a given time but not in some other state at another time; the circumstances of the state must be taken into account. One thing is certain: a deviation from the customary [five percent rule] — even if only a temporary deviation — may be necessary if the circumstances internal to the state have essentially changed; for instance, if shortly before an election the electoral territory is expanded to include territories that have had a different political structure.

The legislature is obligated to take [such] circumstances into account. In principle, it may disregard the five percent clause, lower it, or resort to other suitable measures. If the legislature finds it advisable to maintain the 5 percent threshold but to mitigate its effects, then the means of mitigation must be constitutional. In particular, the means must respect the principles of voter equality and equality of opportunity for parties. Mitigating the effects of the blocking clause cannot be justified merely because it offers a "special allowance" as compared to its unrestricted application. On the contrary, a regulation has greater constitutional validity if its effects are evenhanded and neutral. . . .

II. The legislative measures objected to in this case [i.e., the unrestricted application of the 5 percent clause and the "piggyback" system] relate to the first all-German parliamentary election. This election is taking place under special, unique circumstances which parliament must take into account when considering the five percent clause. [This election] is different from other elections because the political parties and [electoral] organizations have had such a short time to adapt their strategies to a much larger electoral area, and because some of the newer parties and organizations [in eastern Germany] have had but a few short months to organize and become politically active.

1. Extending the Federal Election Act [and its five percent clause] to the former German Democratic Republic makes it part of the [current] "electoral territory." The first unified German election is taking place one year after the peaceful revolution in the GDR. The day that witnessed the unification of the two territories that had been divided for forty years precedes the election day for the unified territory by only three months. This short period of time fails to give some parties an equal opportunity to become active and to compete equally for votes in the new territories. Prior to the [national] parliamentary election, the parties have had only limited opportunities to participate in the communal or *Land* parliamentary elections and to publicize their platforms and candidates.

(a) In view of these circumstances, the application of the five percent clause to all of unified [Germany] has implications far more severe for those parties that were active only within the GDR than for the parties that were active only within the Federal Republic of Germany. According to the findings of the Parliamentary Committee on German Unity, maintaining the blocking clause for all of unified Germany would mean that former GDR parties would have to poll 23.75 percent of second ballot votes (in their former electoral territory only) in order to clear the five percent hurdle and to be represented in the federal parliament. In contrast, the FRG parties would have to receive only 6 percent of second ballot votes in their former electoral territory to gain parliamentary representation.

An additional circumstance that must be taken into account by the legislature is that political parties and organizations have been able to organize and become active outside their national boundaries only since the revolution in the GDR. Their organizational, personnel, and financial bases have not yet developed sufficiently to cope with this change; they have only a short time to develop their platforms and cooperate with other political groups.

[The court finds that the five percent clause as applied to all of Germany in this first all-German election would result in considerable inequality among the parties, particularly those competing for votes in the old GDR, thus requiring a one-time adjustment or change in the statute to secure a greater measure of equality for these parties.]

III. 1. This matter does not end with our determination that the five percent clause may not constitutionally be applied to the whole electoral territory in this first unified German election. The legislature has weakened the effect of the blocking clause through section 53 (2) of the Federal Elections Act. The legislature intended to assist "parties based in one of the two [former] German states and ill-prepared to organize for an all-German election" by allowing them to form a coalition with a party in the other part of Germany and to present a combined list for the purpose of maximizing their second ballot votes.

Keeping this in mind, the regulation in question must be examined to determine whether it [in fact] removes the particular burden on parties and [voter] organizations that arises from the expansion of the electoral territory and the application of the five percent clause in a manner that is constitutional.

2. This question must be answered in the negative.

(a) Combining lists is restricted by the "competition clause" in section 53 (2) of the Federal Election Act. This clause permits combined lists only for those parties that do not submit joint lists in any one *Land* (except Berlin), with the consequence that more weight is given to votes for a list that has not received 5 percent of the vote. This measure fails to satisfy the requirements of formal equality because it does not benefit all parties in the same way (citing 6 BVerfGE 84).

[The court then considered whether combined lists were constitutionally permissible and found that they were not. After noting that the actual possibilities for combining lists were extremely limited for most parties, the court argued that combined lists violate the principle of equal opportunity by giving more weight to the votes of some parties than others. Similarly, while individual voters may vote for one party on a joint list, both parties may wind up represented in parliament. Next the court considered other alternatives, including lowering the 5 percent threshold and installing a regional blocking clause by which the 5 percent rule would be applied separately in the old FRG and the old GDR. Combining a regional 5 percent rule with the ability of parties to combine their lists for purposes of second ballot voting, said the court, would not satisfy all the requirements of formal equality but it would be constitutionally acceptable. Parliament proceeded forthwith to amend the electoral law accordingly. In a one-time exception to a uniform, national blocking clause, parliament applied the 5 percent rule separately in East and West Germany and allowed small groups in the GDR to form joint tickets to help them over the 5 percent hurdle. The amended statute had the intended effect; some East German groups managed as a consequence to win seats in the Twelfth Bundestag.]

NOTE: THE MEANING OF DIRECT ELECTION. Several early constitutional cases challenged features of the second-ballot system. Proportional representation itself was said to offend the concept of "direct" elections within the meaning of Article 38. In the *State List* case,[30] decided in 1953, the court held that an electoral law would violate the principle of direct suffrage if it permitted a political party to add persons to its nomination list after the election, even if additions were necessary to fill legislative vacancies. The court acknowledged the crucial role of political parties in the electoral process but contended that the final selection of candidates may validly rest only on the "will of the electors." A "direct" election within the meaning of Article 38, declared the court, means "the direct election of representatives, and not merely of their [political] parties."[31] In short, the voter must know precisely for whom he is voting.

Can a statute authorize political parties to change the order of precedence on a party list once an election has taken place? In the *Nachrücker* case (1957), the court declared that this too would violate the direct suffrage clause of Article 38. In still other cases, the fixed list,[32] like proportional representation itself,[33] has been unambiguously sustained by the court.[34] Strands of thought in the political party cases, discussed in the section on political parties and the party state, below, suggest that proportional representation may even be required under the doctrine of the *Parteienstaat*.

NOTE: EQUAL SUFFRAGE. The Basic Law does not prescribe a particular electoral system; this the framers left to parliament's discretion. Germans have often debated whether to modify their system in imitation of the British-American model of single-member, winner-take-all constituencies.[35] In the late 1960s, the grand coalition parties even toyed with the idea of adopting such a system with an eye to eliminating the minor parties whose entry into the Bundestag was made possible by proportional representation.[36] The popular reaction to any manipulation of the electoral process for partisan political purposes was so hostile that the issue was dropped and never raised again. The protection that the Federal Constitutional Court has extended to minor parties in the Federal Republic suggests that any tampering with electoral mechanisms to the significant disadvantage of such parties would be the subject of intensive judicial scrutiny. Indeed, by the 1970s the mixed system of constituency and proportional representation had assumed quasi-constitutional status in the Federal Republic.[37]

Does this mixed system satisfy the principle of equal suffrage? The question seems legitimate because of the way proportional representation works in Germany. If a party wins 55 percent of the second (list) ballot votes, it receives 55 percent of the seats in parliament. The system calls for adding list candidates, in the order of their appearance on a state's second ballot, to those who win constituency seats until the 55 percent figure is reached.[38] Minor parties (e.g., the FDP and the Greens) that fail to win any constituency seats but poll at least 5 percent of all second-ballot votes in the nation as a whole choose their representatives solely from the state lists. Critics complain that this method of counting results in wasted votes if the minor party for which certain citizens vote fails to surmount the 5 percent hurdle.[39] These wasted votes occasionally result in additional, or "overhang," seats for the established parties. Alternatively, a party may win more constituency seats than it is entitled to under proportional representation, in which case it may also receive overhang seats. A voter challenged the validity of these overhang seats in the second *Apportionment* case (1963; no. 5.7).

The Federal Constitutional Court has found that the mixed system is consistent with the principle of equal suffrage so long as the nation's electoral districts are relatively equal in population. In this respect the one-person, one-vote principle is as embedded in the Constitutional Court's jurisprudence as it is in that of the United

States Supreme Court. Yet the court has not insisted on strict mathematical equality among the districts. In *Apportionment I* the court announced that any *significant* differences in population among districts returning single deputies by simple majority vote would clearly violate the principle of equality.[40]

Apportionment II concerns proportional representation as such and the particular problems it creates. This and other apportionment cases are best understood in the light of the section below on political parties and the party state, which examines materials that underscore the court's sensitivity to the rights of minority parties, one of the reasons it embraces proportional representation. The cases illustrate the court's commitment to equal *and effective* representation. The principle of equality, if pushed too far in the interest of stability, could in the court's judgment freeze the status quo by neglecting significant opposition movements (or parties) outside parliament. On the other hand, the court has emphasized that the right to participate in an election is fundamentally a right of the individual, and not that of a political party.[41]

5.7 Apportionment Case II (1963)
16 BVerfGE 130

[The petitioner challenged the validity of the 1961 federal election. He alleged that Schleswig-Holstein had been divided into too many election districts relative to its population, and the result had been three additional direct seats for the CDU. He claimed that no *Land* was entitled to more representatives than warranted by its population. The case offered the Constitutional Court an opportunity to consider the electoral system in general and the principles under the Basic Law on which it must be grounded.]

———————

Judgment of the Second Senate. . . .

B. I. 3. (a) The principle of equal suffrage means that everyone should be able to exercise his right to vote in as formally an equal way as possible. . . . In a pure majority [voting] system consisting of electoral districts of equal size, the weight of each individual vote is equal when all ballots have the same value; electoral equality in a system of proportional representation requires a similar [weighting of votes].

The requirement of fundamental equality in [casting ballots] . . . can also be satisfied when proportional representation is wedded to elements of a [single-district, winner-take-all system] as provided in the Federal Election Act (FEA). By counting district seats as prescribed in section 6 (2) of the FEA and by totaling up the number of seats to which each party is entitled on the basis of second (list) votes in a state, the total number of seats is distributed among the parties regardless of the superimposed majority system so as to correspond to their [respective] sum totals of the second [list] votes. Thus the selection of district candidates by relative majorities within a district does not compromise the basic character of a federal election as one founded on proportional representation. Accordingly, when all district seats have been assigned . . . within the framework of the proportional seat distribution based on second-ballot votes, the size of a district and thus the weight attached to individual votes for the purpose of determining which party-slated candidate will get the nod in a [particular] district has little to do with the principle of electoral equality.

(c) The weight of ballots does differ to a degree in those situations in which, pursuant to section 6 (3) of the FEA, [a party retains all the district seats it has gained even if the seats exceed the total number arrived at under proportional representation]. In the light of the formal principle of equality that governs in a system based on proportional representation, it is not unconditionally permissible to give more weight to these ballots than to those cast for parties which fail to gain district seats in excess of [what they are allowed under proportional representation]. . . .

Rather, such a result is consistent with the principle of electoral equality only to the extent that it represents a necessary consequence of a personalized election system. The Federal Election Act modifies proportional representation [by combining] it with the election of particular individuals in single-member constituencies on the basis of a relative majority. [Indeed, the district ballot precedes the list ballot.] The [primacy] of the single-member-district system is rooted in [this] closer personal relationship between district candidates and their constituencies. This special concern of the personalized proportional election system justifies the [slight inequality] that results from the admission of excessive mandates [under section 6 (3)]. Thus excessive mandates are constitutionally unobjectionable only to the extent that their allocation represents the necessary consequence of the specific purpose of personalized proportional elections. In view of the formal nature of the equality of the right to vote, a differentiation in the weight of ballots that would go beyond this peculiarity of the personalized election system cannot be justified.

For this reason districts with approximately equal population figures must be created when it is technically possible so that no state will end up with more districts than its . . . share of the total population in the federal territory would warrant. If all districts are of approximately the same size, then their appropriate distribution among the states will be guaranteed, thus keeping the number of excessive mandates at a constitutionally permissible minimum.

. . . On the other hand, every district must be a balanced and coherent entity under the terms of the Federal Election Act. But historically rooted administrative boundaries ought also to coincide as much as possible with district boundaries. Demographic figures, of course, do not remain constant. . . . Consequently, the constitutional requirement that district boundaries be adjusted to demographic change in the interest of equality cannot be met completely. Federal legislation has taken these inherent difficulties into account; [for example,] section 3 (3) of the

FEA limits the extremes of permissible deviation from the average population of the constituencies to 33⅓ percent. . . .

4. However, the fact that during the last parliamentary election the districts no longer completely satisfied the required equality of the right to vote does not mean that the division of districts was unconstitutional at that time.

(a) According to the September 4, 1962, report of the Election District Commission, thirty-seven districts as of January 1, 1963, exceeded the limits set forth in section 3 (3) of the FEA. . . . At the same time Scheswig-Holstein had three districts too many while Lower Saxony and Bavaria had a surplus of four; North Rhine–Westphalia, Rhineland-Palatinate, and Baden-Württemberg, on the other hand, were short seven, one, and three seats, respectively. Because these inequalities spilled over to influence the differential weight of votes in Schleswig-Holstein, the current apportionment statute may not [constitutionally] be applied to the next [federal] parliamentary election. [The existing legislative] districting has become unconstitutional because it . . . no longer corresponds to up-to-date demographic figures and because we can no longer expect an automatic readjustment of the current discrepancies. The federal legislature is therefore obliged, during the current legislative period, to reorganize the districts by reducing to a permissible level the deviations in their population from the national average and by adjusting constituency lines to each state's share in the total population.

(b) The unconstitutionality of the apportionment of districts was, however, not so clearly evident on September 17, 1961, as to invalidate the apportionment from that date.

The current apportionment dates from 1949. . . . Since 1949 the population figures of the states have shifted absolutely and increasingly in relation to each other. The greatest differences took place in states particularly affected by the resettlement of refugees and in those affected by internal migration owing to economic developments. . . .

The difficulty in determining the exact point when original constitutional districting becomes unconstitutional stems from changes and trends that are at once continuous and unpredictable. These circumstances . . . rendered it impossible, on the basis of the evidence available, to find any violation against the equality of the right to vote at that time. To be sure a June 20, 1958, report by the Election District Commission clearly showed that even then, districting no longer conformed to the guidelines of section 3 (3) of the FEA — although [only] to a modest extent. In addition, during the parliamentary elections of September 15, 1957, there were three excessive mandates which could have been avoided had the districting been adjusted in time to population shifts. Yet these excessive mandates resulted from two coincidental factors: the relatively small size of the districts in Schleswig-Holstein, and the relative majority of first votes for only one party in all districts — events not likely to have been anticipated to recur again in the 1961 parliamentary elections. . . .

5. Because the apportionment did not violate the principle of equal elections on September 17, 1961, to a degree that would have appeared to jeopardize its constitutionality, one cannot speak of a flaw in the election which would have influenced the 1961 elections in a constitutionally objectionable fashion. Consequently, the Bundestag rightfully rejected the challenge to the validity of the fourth parliamentary election on the ground that the districting system was unconstitutional. . . .

NOTE: CONTESTED ELECTIONS. Article 41 (1) of the Basic Law empowers the Bundestag to examine the validity of elections and to "decide whether a representative has lost his parliamentary seat." Complaints against the decisions of the Bundestag under this paragraph may be lodged with the Federal Constitutional Court under Article 41 (2).[42] Section 48 of the FCCA, however, limits access in such cases to a parliamentary minority (providing the group constitutes at least one-tenth of all representatives), to a representative whose seat is being contested, and to an eligible voter whose election complaint, if denied by the Bundestag, is supported by the signatures of at least one hundred eligible voters.[43] Up to 1990 the Federal Constitutional Court had reviewed about sixty such cases and had sustained the Bundestag's decision in almost all of them. In this respect, the court has construed its authority narrowly, declaring that the proper inquiry in an election dispute within the meaning of Article 41 is "not an injury to a subjective right, but rather the validity of the election as such."[44]

NOTE: ABSENTEE BALLOTING. The *Mayen Absentee Ballot* case (1981) is an example of a Bundestag electoral decision reviewed by the Federal Constitutional Court. More than 16 percent of Mayen's voters cast absentee ballots in the federal election of October 5, 1980. In the absence of proof that officials or voters had violated the Federal Electoral Act, the Bundestag sustained the validity of these ballots. A Mayen voter's constitutional complaint against the Bundestag's decision charged that absentee voting on this scale endangered the freedom and secrecy of elections as secured by Article 38.[45] In rejecting the complaint, the court nevertheless issued a warning:

> Although the Bundestag acted within its constitutional authority in facilitating absentee balloting, it nevertheless has the duty to ensure that the right to vote is safeguarded. Legislators . . . are obligated continuously to review existing regulations dealing with absentee balloting so as to determine whether new situations pose an unexpected danger to the integrity of elections. If abuses are uncovered that adversely affect the freedom and secrecy of elections more than necessary, then the legislature has the constitutional duty to amend or change the original regulations.[46]

Up to now, however, the Bundestag had laid down detailed procedures designed to preserve the secrecy of the ballot and to restrict the conditions under which absentee voting would be permitted. Under these circumstances there could be no valid objection to absentee voting.

German citizens denied the right to vote in federal elections because they lived outside the Federal Republic had a more serious constitutional complaint. Sections 12 (2) and (4) of the Federal Electoral Act extended the right to vote only to civil servants, soldiers, employees, and workers living abroad on orders from their employers. The Second Senate sustained these provisions in the first *Nonresident Voting* case (1973) on the theory that citizens who voluntarily surrender their domicile in Germany to take up residence outside the country no longer have the interest or information necessary to vote in federal elections.[47] Years later, in a case involving the denial of the right to vote to German nationals working as civil servants for the European Union outside Germany, the court had second thoughts about the validity of section 12 (2) and (4). Following its decision in *Nonresident Voting II* (1981), the Bundestag amended the Electoral Act, extending the franchise to German nationals resident in member states of the European Community.[48] The *Foreign Voters* case (1990) represents the next major event in this account of German voting rights.

5.8 Foreign Voters I Case (1990)
83 BVerfGE 37

[Schleswig-Holstein granted its foreign resident aliens the right to vote in municipal elections if these residents were citizens of countries that extended municipal voting rights to German nationals. Thus some seven thousand Danes, Irish, Dutch, Norwegians, Swedes, and Swiss who had resided at least five years in the *Land* would be eligible to vote. Christian Democratic representatives in the Bundestag brought an abstract judicial proceeding in the Constitutional Court claiming that the *Land* law "undermined the democratic right of the German people to self-determination."]

C. The Schleswig-Holstein government's amendment to the Municipal and District Election Act violates Article 28 (1) of the Basic Law. This provision permits the people to elect representatives at communal and district levels; the concept of "the people" is employed in the same way as in Article 20 (2) of the Basic Law, which defines "the people" as the German people. The concept of "the people" within a community and district includes only the German people. Foreigners cannot be given the right to vote at the municipal level.

I. 1. The constitutional assertion that "all state authority shall emanate from the people" (Article 20 (2) of the Basic Law) contains not just the principle of popular sovereignty (evidenced by its location and connection with other norms); it also defines the people who exercise state authority through elections, voting, specific legislative organs, executive power, and the judiciary: it is the body politic of the Federal Republic of Germany. Article 20 (1) through (3) identifies [the republic] as a democratic, social federal state, based on the rule of law and the division of powers; there can be no democratic state without a body politic that is both subject to and object of the state authority vested in it and exercised through its organs. This body politic is the people, from whom all state authority emanates. This does not mean that all state decisions must be approved by the people; rather, it means that the subject of state authority must be a cohesive, unified group.

2. According to the Basic Law, the people, from whom state authority emanates in the Federal Republic of Germany, comprises German citizens and all persons of similar status. Membership in this body politic is determined by citizenship. Citizenship is both the legal precondition for the equal status of individuals and the foundation for equal rights and duties; exercise of legal rights and duties legitimates democratic state authority.

Other provisions of the Basic Law that relate to "the people" are unequivocal in [identifying] the body politic as the German people: the Preamble declares that it is the German people who adopted the Basic Law by virtue of their constituent power; Article 33 (1) and (2) guarantee every German in every *Land* the same political rights and duties; Articles 56 and 64 require the federal president and members of the cabinet to swear that they will dedicate their efforts to the wellbeing of the German people; Article 146 grants the German people the right to adopt a constitution superseding the Basic Law. Notably, the Preamble and Article 146 both declare the German people to be subject and object of the state of the FRG. And Article 116, which attributes the characteristic of being German to so-called status Germans only, derives its meaning from its own definition of the subject of German state authority as all German citizens. The drafters of the Basic Law expressly addressed this issue, even while modifying the principle somewhat in consideration of the circumstances of the post-war era.

3. If the Basic Law conceives being German as necessary to being part of "the people" as the subject of state authority, then it must follow that [being German] is a precondition of the right to vote, which is a direct exercise of the state authority possessed by the people. This does not mean that the legislator is unable to influence the composition of "the people" under Article 20 (2). The Basic Law empowers the legislator to set conditions for gaining or losing citizenship status (see Articles 73 [2] and 116) and thereby to establish the criteria for membership in the body politic. Through the Citizenship Act, the legislator can also change residence requirements to influence political rights. It is incorrect to state that an increase in the population of foreigners within the FRG changes the constitutional concept of "the people." Underlying this misperception is the concept that democracy and the inherent concept of freedom demand [complete] congruence between those who hold democratic rights and those who are subject to state domination. This is the correct starting point, but it cannot eliminate the relationship between being German and being a member of the body politic, and thus vested with state authority.

The Basic Law does not permit such a development. The sole permissible response is regulations that extend citizenship to foreigners who have been in Germany for an extended time and who are legally resident and subject to state authority just like other Germans.

II. So too the state authority granted to the *Länder* under Articles 20 (2) and 28 (1) can be borne only by those who are Germans. The territorially defined unity of Germans living within the area of a *Land* stands in place of, or beside, the body politic of the FRG.

III. 1. Under Article 28 (1) of the Basic Law, the outcome can be no different in the case of popular representation within municipalities and districts. Even the language of the norm, which disregards territorial definitions, uses the concept of "the people" uniformly for *Länder,* districts, and municipalities, pointing out that the concept applies exclusively to Germans and that Germans constitute the people and elect their representatives.

2. This linguistically faithful interpretation of Article 28 (1) corresponds to the Basic Law's meaning and purpose.

(a) This norm establishes that the fundamental constitutional principles of popular sovereignty and democracy, as well as procedures for democratic elections, are valid not only at the federal and *Land* levels, but also for municipalities and community associations. It guarantees a uniform basis of democratic legitimation for all territorial divisions within the FRG. . . .

(c) The drafters of the Constitution had good reasons for locating the democratic legitimation of municipal representatives in the German residents of a community (Article 28 [1]): democratic principles (articulated in Articles 20 [2] and 28) are applied to municipalities and districts through Article 28 of the Basic Law.

NOTE: FOREIGN RESIDENT VOTING AND THE MAASTRICHT TREATY. On the day the Schleswig-Holstein decision came down, the Constitutional Court decided a companion case arising out of the city-state of Hamburg.[49] Here the court nullified, for the same reason, an amendment to Hamburg's constitution conferring the right to vote in county elections on all legally resident aliens, regardless of nationality, provided they had lived in the district for a period of eight years, a change that added ninety thousand persons to Hamburg's voting lists. The Maastricht Treaty, however, extends the franchise to all European Union citizens residing in a member state. Under the provisions of the treaty, Union citizens are now able to vote and stand as candidates in local elections.[50] Accordingly, in December 1992, the Basic Law was amended to grant the nationals of member states the right to vote in county and municipal elections (Article 28 [1]), effectively nullifying the Schleswig-Holstein and Hamburg decisions.

POLITICAL PARTIES AND THE PARTY STATE

In formally recognizing political parties, Article 21 of the Basic Law represents something of a revolution in German constitutional theory. The traditional German view insisted on the separation between state and society. Political parties and other assorted groups represented society and its plurality of interests; society, like political parties, was a source of fragmentation and division. The state, by contrast, represented a higher unity. Staffed by impartial public servants committed to the general interest, the state alone in traditional theory had the capacity to govern creatively within the context of ordered liberty.

Article 21 (1) stood this theory on its head. Now political parties would "participate in forming the political will of the people." Paragraph 1 also declares that the "internal organization [of parties] must conform to democratic principles" just as political parties "shall publicly account for the sources and use of their funds." As if to make good on this promise of internal democracy, paragraph 2 goes on to ban as unconstitutional political parties opposed to the "free democratic basic order."

Out of this sparse language, as we shall see, the Constitutional Court has woven a theory of the party state (*Parteienstaat*) representing "a unique synthesis of Western parliamentarism and the German state tradition."[51] The parliamentary tradition is embodied in the principle of popular sovereignty and the formal institutions of representative democracy. The state tradition, on the other hand, is manifest in the Constitution's formal recognition of political parties as agencies engaged in the process of "will formation" and in their status—one the Constitutional Court has conferred by interpretation—as "integral units of the constitutional state."[52] Yet, as the *Party Finance* cases featured in this section show, the court has not fully resolved the tension between the traditions of democracy and statecraft.

An overlapping tension exists between Articles 21 and 38. On the one hand, political parties in the German view are important, if not necessary, agents of democratic government. They recruit leaders, crystallize issues, aggregate interests, organize governments, and make policies. In the modern nation-state, with millions of voters, political parties are, as the Constitutional Court has recognized, a rational and democratic means for carrying out these functions: rational because they provide the electorate with alternative choices of policy; democratic because they are mechanisms of majority rule and government by consent. Article 38, on the other hand, declares that members of parliament represent the "whole people and are not bound by orders and instructions but subject only to their conscience." The court's jurisprudence in the field of political parties and representation, as noted earlier, is best understood as an attempt to relieve the friction between the two articles.

The experience of the Weimar Republic was uppermost in the minds of the framers when they crafted Article 21. Weimar was a party state in an antiparty constitutional culture. The only mention of political parties in its constitution was the directive instructing civil servants to serve the state, and not political parties.[53]

Under the shattering impact of events too familiar for repetition here, Weimar's democracy degenerated into a regime of warring factions, rendering parliamentary government all but impossible. It was the president, directly elected by the people, who personified the state and ruled in its name in the face of parliamentary breakdown. The Basic Law's framers, themselves party representatives — Christian Democrats and Social Democrats made up the large majority of the delegates — set out to create a stable political system powered mainly by political parties but instead reinforced by shifting power from the president to the chancellor.[54] They built better than they knew, for Germany has developed into a durable democracy marked by high voter turnouts, overwhelming support for the established parties, and a competitive party system capable of producing stable coalitions and alternating governments. The Federal Constitutional Court, for its part, has held firm to the framers' original vision respecting the role of political parties.

NOTE: PARTIES AS CONSTITUTIONAL ORGANS. Early decisions of both senates underscored the critical role of parties in the new polity. In the *Socialist Reich Party* case (no. 5.12), decided in 1952, the First Senate declared that Article 21 (1) "treats political parties as more than mere political-sociological [organizations]; they are [instead] raised to the rank of constitutional institutions." Earlier in the same year, in the *Schleswig-Holstein Voters' Association* case,[55] the Second Senate had emphasized the same point by observing that the "incorporation [of political parties in Article 21] means that parties are not only politico-sociological entities; they are also integral parts of [our] constitutional structure and [our] constitutionally ordered political life."

Finally, in 1954, the Plenum itself ruled that political parties in their capacity as constitutional organs may defend their institutional rights before the Federal Constitutional Court in *Organstreit* proceedings: "By cooperating in the process of forming the political will of the people, parties function as constitutional organs. The parties exercise this right, which is secured by Article 21, primarily through their participation in parliamentary elections. When they are active in this [particular] realm and fight for the rights that flow from this special function in [our] constitutional life, they are entitled to invoke [their own rights as constitutional organs] in constitutional proceedings before [this court]."[56] The *Plenum Party* case (1954) served notice that the court was prepared to protect the equality of political parties as well as their institutional integrity.

5.9 Party Finance Case II (1958)
8 BVerfGE 51

[Federal laws passed in 1954 and 1957, when Christian Democrats were in power, permitted citizens to deduct from their net taxable income a portion of their donations to political parties. The Social Democratic government of

Hesse, joined later by Hamburg and North Rhine–Westphalia, challenged the constitutionality of these deductions in an abstract judicial-review proceeding, claiming that they discriminated in favor of political parties backed by wealthy individuals and large corporations.]

Judgment of the Second Senate. . . .

B. II. . . . By declaring donations to political parties deductible, the federal legislature renounces that part of income or corporate tax which would otherwise accrue. . . . This renunciation benefits political parties. Recognizing donations to political parties as deductible expenses means, therefore, that the government indirectly participates, by the amount of revenue it loses, in financing parties.

When the legislature exercises its authority it is bound by higher constitutional principles. The challenged provision would be unconstitutional if the Basic Law prohibited any direct or indirect governmental financial support of political parties as petitioner claims. But this is not the case. . . .

III. [The challenged provisions of the tax laws,] however, violate the basic right of political parties to equal opportunity. . . .

2. The challenged provisions permit *every taxpayer* who pays income or corporate taxes to donate money to *any political party* and to enjoy the same legal consequences; namely, deductibility of the donation from taxable income. According to its wording, the regulation gives every political party the same chance to obtain donations.

But even if a law avoids unequal treatment on its face . . . , it may be contrary to the principle of equality if its practical application results in an obvious inequality and if this unequal effect is directly due to the legal formulation [of the statute]. It is not the outward form that is decisive, but the substantive legal content. . . .

3. If the legislature interferes with the formation of the political will by enacting a statute which could possibly have even an indirect effect on the equal opportunity of political parties, then it must bear in mind that its discretion in this area is very limited. As a matter of principle, all parties must be treated formally in an equal manner. This principle prohibits [the legislature] from treating parties differently unless [such treatment] is justified by an especially "compelling reason." . . .

Today, all political parties are dependent on donations, due to the huge financial expenditures required by modern electoral campaigns; no party can cover its entire financial needs . . . from member contributions. In a democratic, multiparty state, all political parties are equally called upon to take part in forming the people's political will. . . . It is true that the state need not pass laws to ensure . . . that parties' financial needs are satisfied. However, if the legislature passes any regulation to promote party financing, the provision must be constitutional and, in particular, must not violate parties' basic right of equal opportunity. . . .

Since the income tax rate increases with the size of taxable income, . . . the possibility of deducting donations to a political party from taxable income creates an incentive primarily for corporate taxpayers and those with high incomes to make donations. Pursuant to the new law, these taxpayers can even double their donations without paying more than before, under certain circumstances. Permitting the deductibility of contributions to a political party does not, however, produce greater incentive for taxpayers with low incomes, because the donations that they can afford are usually so small as not to exceed the standard deduction for deductible expenses.

General experience shows that in contrast to donations made for charitable, religious, or scientific purposes, [taxpayers] make donations to a political party with a special interest in mind. . . . Thus a donor will tend to contribute to the party which he believes will foster his special interests on the basis of [the party's] platform and activit[ies]. . . . However, this fact can be of importance only if political parties differ so clearly from each other in their goals and the means to achieve them that the donor must choose one party (or group) over another if he wants to safeguard his interests. Such differences do in fact exist between certain parties in the Federal Republic. . . . The challenged provisions, therefore, favor those parties whose programs and activities appeal to wealthy circles. . . .

NOTE: EQUALITY AND PARTY FINANCE. In 1957, a year before *Party Finance II* was decided, the court nullified another provision of the tax code, disallowing deductions for contributions to political parties unless such parties had elected at least one representative to the national or a *Land* parliament (*Party Finance I* [1957]).[57] In the course of its opinion in *Party Finance II,* the Second Senate acknowledged the financial plight of political parties and their need for funds if they were to play the important role envisioned by the framers of the Basic Law. The senate then suggested that the state might constitutionally fund political parties and election campaigns as a means of ensuring effective competition among the parties and of diminishing their reliance on special interest groups. Funding would be appropriate since parties were now conceived as "constitutional organs" functioning as vital links between state and society. This did not mean, however, that parties would have to be funded equally. Public funding, said the Second Senate, might be adjusted to the popular strength of each party in the community. On the other hand, such funding could not validly accentuate existing *de facto* inequalities among the parties in election campaigns.

The Bundestag responded immediately and eagerly to the court's suggestion by passing the Party Finance Act of 1959. This statute, supported by all the parties in the Bundestag, authorized the use of public funds to finance their "political education" programs.[58] (Shortly thereafter, state and local governments enacted similar statutes.) By 1964 these outlays, divided among the parties in proportion to the number of seats they occupied in the Bundestag, had reached DM 38 million, equivalent to one German mark for each voter. A minor party denied funds under these early appropriations claimed that its exclusion from the act's coverage violated the equal protection clause. In the *All-German Block Party* case (1961),[59] the court rejected that party's application for a temporary injunction to bar the disbursement of such funds, reiterating once again that public financing of political parties is permissible in the light of the crucial representational role assigned to them under the Basic Law. Although specific formulas for the allocation of funding might raise equal protection questions, this decision, together with dicta uttered in *Party Finance II,* seemed to have established the general validity of party financing out of state funds. In *Party Finance III,* however, seemingly alarmed by the enormous annual increases in party funding, the court backed away from the sweeping implications of the earlier cases.

5.10 Party Finance Case III (1966)
20 BVerfGE 56

[The four parties (CDU, CSU, SPD, and FDP) represented in the Bundestag received equal shares of 20 percent of the DM 38 million mentioned above. The rest was apportioned among the parties on the basis of their seat totals in parliament. The Social Democrat–controlled state of Hesse challenged the validity of the law in an abstract judicial-review proceeding. Political parties that had failed to win any seats in parliament and thus ineligible for public funding also challenged the validity of the party finance law within the framework of an *Organstreit* proceeding. One of these parties was the allegedly neo-Nazi National Democratic party. The others were the All-German party and the Bavarian party.]

———————

Judgment of the Second Senate. . . .

C. I. The court said in its judgment of June 24, 1958 [*Party Finance II;* no. 5.9], that political parties are primarily organizations to prepare elections that, for the most part, use their own financial means to serve this purpose. [The court held that] it is permissible for the state to appropriate funds not only for elections but also for political parties that participate in elections, because holding elections is a public function and parties play a decisive role in carrying out this function under the Constitution. Federal and state legislators could have and have understood the court's explanations to mean that it is constitutionally permissible to use public funds to subsidize parties for all political work.

The instant case, however, has convinced the court that to grant subsidies from public funds to parties for everything they do violates Articles 21 and 20 (2). . . . Nonetheless, it is constitutional to use public funds to reimburse political parties that help to form the people's political will by participating in parliamentary elections, but only to the extent of repaying expenditures for a reasonable electoral campaign.

II. 1. By creating a free, democratic basic order, the framers of the Basic Law chose a free and open process of forming the people's opinion and will. It is incompatible with this choice for the state to finance all political activities of parties.

(a) The rights to freedom of expression and of the press, radio, television, and film guaranteed in Article 5 are simply constituent parts of a free democratic system. . . . Article 5 also guarantees the free formation of public opinion. . . . The fundamental right to participate freely in political life follows from the basic right to express one's opinion freely. . . . Freedom of opinion, of association and coalition, of assembly and petition all safeguard the free formation of popular opinion and will. . . . Especially in a democratic system, the formation of the people's will must take place in a free, open, and unregimented manner. . . . The process culminates in a parliamentary election. . . . A distinction must be made between forming the people's will and forming the state's will. . . . Whereas Article 21 (1) deals with forming the people's will, Article 20 (2) concerns the formation of the state's will. The expression of the people's will coincides with forming the state's will only if the people, as the constitutional or creative organ, exercise state authority through elections and voting (Article 20 [2]).

But the people do not express their political will only by voting. A citizen's right to participate in forming the political will can also be manifested in attempts to influence the continuous process of forming the political will or forming "public opinion." . . . Furthermore, groups, associations, and social units of various kinds seek to influence governmental actions . . . to benefit their members' interests. However, political parties are the main ones that influence the decisions of constitutional organs, in particular, decisions of parliaments between elections. . . .

Forming the people's will and forming the state's will are intertwined in various ways. In a democracy, however, forming the popular will must start with the people, and not with the organs of the state. The state's organs are created only through the process of forming the people's political will. . . . This means that state organs are in principle prohibited from becoming active in forming the people's will and opinion; this process must, as a matter of principle, remain "state free." Actions of administrative or legislative organs to influence this process are incompatible with the democratic principle of the free and open formation of popular opinion and are legitimate only if they can be justified by a special reason. . . .

(b) (aa) First, the rule that the state is not obligated to satisfy the financial needs of political parties governs the financial relations between the supreme constitutional organs and political parties; nor is the state obliged to compensate parties, by financial or other measures, on the basis of their different capabilities for influencing the process of forming popular opinion and will. . . .

(bb) Political parties . . . constitute intermediate links between the individual and the state . . . instruments by which the citizens' will can be put into effect even between elections; they are the "mouthpiece" of the people [citing a case]. If parties support the government, they establish and maintain connections between the people and political leadership. As minority parties, they form and make political opposition effective. Parties participate as intermediaries in shaping public opinion. They take note of opinions, interests, and trends relating to political power and the exercise thereof; [parties then] balance [these factors], mold them, and try to bring them to bear in forming the state's will. . . . In a modern mass democracy, political parties decisively influence nominations to the highest governmental positions. . . . They influence the formation of the state's will by working marginally in the state's system of institutions and offices, in particular by influencing decisions and measures taken by parliament. . . .

Precisely because of these party activities, the constitutional rule of the open, "state-free" formation of national opinion and will . . . prohibits the state from consolidating parties into the realm of organized statehood. . . .

The general consensus [of the legal community is that] it is incompatible with the Basic Law to use public funds to cover all or even most of the financial needs of political parties. Partial state financing of parties through annual or monthly payments for all political activities . . . would commit the parties to the care of the state. Through this financing the state would influence the process of forming the people's opinion and will. No special reason can be advanced that would constitutionally legitimate such influence. The financing of political parties provided for in the Federal Budget Law of 1965 is therefore unconstitutional regardless of whether it infringes upon either [the right] of political parties to be free from state interference guaranteed by Article 21 or the principle of equal opportunities for parties. . . .

(1) Further, [the state] cannot justify using public money to fund all political activities of the parties on the ground that Article 21 recognizes the parties as constitutional instruments necessary for building the political will of the people, thus raising parties to the level of a constitutionally protected institution. Since the process of democratically forming opinions and [the people's] will must remain free from state influence, [the fact that] the Constitution recognizes the participation of the parties in this process does not in and of itself furnish justification for constitutional organs to influence this process by financing political parties. . . .

(3) The fact that the members of parliament receive allowances and parliamentary groups receive contributions from state funds does not mean that it is also permissible to grant parties annual subsidies for all their political activit[ies].

The parliamentarian holds an office (Article 48 (2) [1]). Emoluments safeguard his freedom of decision — vis-à-vis his parliamentary group and his party — and enable him to exercise freely the rights and obligations arising from his representative constitutional status (Articles 38 (1) [2], 48 (3) [1]). . . . Emoluments are derived from and justified by the principle of a "liberal representative democracy." . . .

(4) Nor can [petitioners] justify public financing of all political party activities . . . by arguing that subsidies are designed to enable parties to exercise their functions while being less dependent than before on materially unrelated financial sources. . . .

Article 21 guarantees parties' freedom from state interference, but [it] does not protect them from the influence of financially powerful individuals, firms, or associations. The [fact that] Article 21 (1) [4] requires parties publicly to disclose the sources of their funds shows that the Basic Law neither condones nor condemns the influence which large private donors seek to exert on parties; rather the [Constitution] views this as a common way of asserting political interests. . . . It is the responsibility of the parties . . . to resist pressure placed upon them by interested persons. . . . The Constitution does not guarantee freedom from this pressure. Nor should [we] forget that not all large donations are coupled with an attempt to influence party decisions. . . .

III. Additionally, state funds may not be allocated to parties for purposes of "political education." Evidence in this case has confirmed that it is impossible to draw a line between general party work and work for political education. . . .

IV. 1. . . . But reimbursement to political parties for expenses necessary to [fund] an adequate electoral campaign can be constitutionally justified if the principles of parties' freedom and equal opportunity are observed. In this respect we refer to [our] judgment of June 24, 1958 [8 BVerfGE 51]. . . .

In a democratic system, parliamentary elections constitute the crucial act in forming the political will [of the people]. . . .

In a modern mass democracy . . . [the state] could not hold elections without political parties. . . . Active citizens decide on the value of a political party's program and on its influence in forming the state's will primarily through elections. . . . They cannot make decisions sensibly unless the parties have first set forth their platforms and goals in an electoral campaign. The campaign alone induces many voters to cast a ballot and make a decision. The court has emphasized on several occasions that parties are principally organizations for preparing elections and that they take part in forming the people's political will mainly by participating in parliamentary elections. . . .

Because of the special importance of political parties for elections it is constitutionally justifiable for the state to reimburse them for necessary expenditures [incurred during] a reasonable electoral campaign. However, the court need not decide whether the legislature should provide for reimbursement of campaign costs, since this is a political question. . . .

4. (a) The decision that [legislatures] can use federal funds to reimburse political parties for costs incurred in an electoral campaign establishes, on the one hand, the number of those who can benefit from the state subsidies: *only* those parties that have taken part in the electoral campaign. On the other hand, the principle of strict

formal equality of opportunity requires that [the legislature] consider *all* parties which have participated in the campaign when distributing funds. It is inconsistent with the principle of equal opportunity for [the legislature] to provide these funds only to parties already represented in parliament or to those which . . . win seats in parliament. However, this principle does not preclude all differentiations; it permits parties to be treated differently if a special, compelling reason exists. . . . One can predict that reimbursement of campaign costs will encourage the establishment of new political parties. This would promote a development which the 5 percent clause has been counteracting with the approval of the Federal Constitutional Court. . . . The legislature can, however, guard against the formation of splinter parties. . . . It is true that reimbursement of a party's campaign costs cannot be made contingent upon whether or not it received 5 percent of the votes cast. Such a measure would double the effect of the 5 percent clause and would practically prevent a new party from being seated in parliament. . . . [Nevertheless] the legislature can . . . make reimbursement of a party's campaign costs contingent upon its obtaining a certain minimum percentage of votes. This percentage must, however, be considerably lower than 5 percent. . . .

NOTE: TWO VIEWS OF THE PARTY STATE. The result in *Party Finance III* was a compromise between competing views of the relationship between political parties and the state. One view, as already noted, holds that parties are quasi-official agencies of the state. They possess this character because of the critical functions they perform in a modern popular democracy. They are the main engines of state power and political representation, in which capacity they form the "political will of the people" and translate this will into coherent public policy. In the ideal *Parteienstaat,* parties are competitive but also unified, program-oriented organizations of active citizens capable of educating the electorate and representing their interests. The *Parteienstaat* by definition excludes the *Verbändestaat,* a system in which interest groups monopolize the political process and thus undermine majority rule. The state must liberate parties — and itself — from the domination of such interests, and the surest way to achieve this goal is by financing political parties out of public funds.[60]

The competing view is closer to the traditional German attitude toward parties. While accepting the proposition that parties are necessary agencies of modern democracy and that Article 21 looks toward the creation of a *Parteienstaat,* this view does not postulate any fundamental nexus between political parties and the state. Under this interpretation, political parties are voluntary associations with roots in society; they are not part of the state. They may help to form the political will of the people, but they do not represent the will of the state. The state is an independent entity devoted to the public interest, an interest that does not depend on parties for its articulation or implementation.[61]

Party Finance III advances a middle view. The court noted that parties do shape the will of the people in their capacity as electoral organizations. Parties also contribute to shaping the will of the state. But they do not and should not monopolize this process; indeed, the state must remain open to all sorts of influence, including nonparty groups and other social interests. In addition, the court duly noted the significance of Article 38, which provides that legislators are representatives of the whole people. In a nutshell, parties serve as constitutional organs of the state only during election campaigns, when they seek to organize the political will of the people. Accordingly, the Basic Law permits the public funding of political parties only for the purpose of defraying legitimate campaign costs. Funding for the general support of parties is constitutionally impermissible. Finally, the court ruled that under the principle of equality, parties outside parliament are also constitutionally entitled to reimbursement for their campaign expenses.[62]

NOTE: THE POLITICAL PARTIES ACT OF 1967. In numerous decisions handed down between 1952 and 1966 the Federal Constitutional Court created a large and important body of law on political parties and elections. *Party Finance III* finally convinced the Bundestag and the government that they could no longer escape their duty, pursuant to the terms of Article 21 (3), to regulate the details of party life and organization, particularly with respect to the command that parties must "publicly account for the sources of their funds." Having denied a fertile source of general party funding, *Party Finance III* prompted government and parliament, now dominated by the CDU/CSU-SDP Grand Coalition, to collaborate on a new party finance measure within the framework of a general law on political parties. (All previous efforts to pass a general law had failed.) The result, the Political Parties Act of 1967,[63] codified many of the rules on parties and elections laid down by the Federal Constitutional Court over the years.

The Parties Act consisted of seven major sections dealing with the status and functions of parties, their internal organization, the nomination of candidates for election, public financing of parties, the disclosure and auditing of campaign contributions and expenditures, the implementation of the ban on unconstitutional political parties, and concluding provisions amending various tax statutes and provisions of the Civil Code implicating political parties. In one of its most interesting parts (section 1), the act accepted the theory of the *Parteienstaat*. It defined parties as "constitutionally integral units of a free and democratic system of government," confirmed their role in "forming the political will of the people," and charged them with "ensuring continuous, vital links between the people and public authorities." The party finance section, drafted to conform to the ruling in *Party Finance III*, provided that each party would receive DM 2.50 per voter on the basis of its total second-ballot vote, but only for the specific purpose of defraying the "necessary costs of an appropriate election campaign." (This figure was increased to DM 3.50 in 1974, and to DM 5.00 in 1983.) Parties winning at least 2.5 percent of the vote in a state were eligible for these generous payments.

Unlike American campaign finance legislation, the German Parties Act imposed no limits on campaign contributions or expenditures. It did, however, include limited reporting and disclosure requirements on contributions to the parties. The act as originally passed encouraged such donations by allowing annual tax-deductible contributions to a party of up to DM 600 for individuals and corporations and up to DM 1,200 for a married couple. (These sums were raised to DM 1,800 and DM 3,600 in 1980.) Public disclosure was required of all contributions in excess of DM 20,000 for individuals and DM 200,000 for corporations. Legislators expected that these disclosure requirements, by identifying large contributors, would prompt the parties to broaden the base of their financial support and thus avoid the ignominy of being too closely associated in the public eye with wealthy donors. The grand purpose of all these financial provisions was to make the parties as competitive as possible.[64]

NOTE: PARTY FINANCE (1966–1988). The Parties Act prompted several rounds of litigation involving the continuous interplay of court and parliament that has continued down to the present. In fact, the court's intervention in the field of party finance has few parallels in other areas of public policy; it has virtually dictated the rules and regulations governing the public funding of political parties. Barely had the ink dried on the Parties Act when it met its first challenge. Denied funds under the new statute, the German Unity, Peace, and Freedom party questioned the act's definition of a political party, including the provision that strips an association of its status as a party if it has not participated for a period of six years in either a federal or state election with electoral proposals of its own. In sustaining the statutory definition of a political party, the Second Senate ruled that the Freedom party was not a party within the meaning of Article 21 or the Parties Act and was thus incapable of petitioning the Constitutional Court in an *Organstreit* proceeding.[65] The senate went on to say that it is perfectly reasonable for the legislature to require parties to meet certain standards of electoral support and durability as a condition for public financing.

In the fourth *Party Finance IV* case (1968),[66] however, the court found that the National Democratic party, the European party, and the Bavarian State party did qualify as "political parties" within the meaning of the Constitution and the Parties Act. In response to their petitions, the Second Senate examined no fewer than fourteen of the act's funding provisions. With two exceptions the court pronounced each of these provisions valid, including those allowing tax deductions for party contributions, thus sustaining the legislature's basic approach to party financing. The court distinguished the tax deductions allowed here from those invalidated in *Party Finance II* (no. 5.9). The tax-deductible amounts involved here, said the court, were not large enough to offend the principle of equality. By a vote of six to two, however, the Second Senate invalidated statutory provisions that limited funding eligibility to parties securing at least 2.5 percent of the total vote.[67] This numerical requirement, said the senate, is too high, and it therefore violates the equal protection clause of Article 3 as well as the principle of universal and equal suffrage under Article 38 (1). The court then laid down a rule holding that any party securing 0.5 percent of the vote — 167,000 votes on the basis of 1965 election returns — "manifests its seriousness as an election campaign competitor." Finally, over the objection of three justices, the Second Senate invalidated the disclosure limit of DM 200,000 for corporations.[68] Like individuals, corporate donors were required to identify themselves publicly in the relevant party's annual report if their contribution exceeds DM 20,000. The act was promptly amended by parliament to incorporate the holdings of this case.[69]

Can a person running as an independent candidate for a constituency seat claim reimbursement for his or her campaign expenditures? This was the issue in the *Daniels* case (1976).[70] Section 18 of the Parties Act allocates funding only to qualified political parties on the basis of valid second-ballot votes. Section 20 (3) of the Federal Electoral Act, however, permits independents to run in particular constituencies if they secure a minimum number of signatures in support of their candidacies. *Daniels* involved an independent who secured a spot on a constituency ballot and won 20.06 percent of the votes in the 1969 federal election. The Bundestag subsequently denied the candidate's request for reimbursement, a decision later sustained by Cologne's administrative court on the theory that independent candidates are ineligible for funding under the Parties Act.

In a surprising reversal, the Federal Constitutional Court pointed to the tension between Articles 21 and 38, saying: "Article 21 of the Basic Law does indeed expressly recognize that parties participate in forming the political will of the people, but Article 38 of the Basic Law also endorses the [independent status] of representatives. Which principle shall prevail in resolving the tension between these provisions depends on the concrete constitutional question [before the court]."[71] The court noted that the first, or constituency, ballot plays an important role in Germany's system of modified proportional representation. Second-ballot votes, said the Second Senate, are a valid basis of party funding because these votes determine the allocation of parliamentary seats. But particular individuals also stand for election in single-member constituencies. To deny funding to these individuals, whether they were nominated by a party or not, would be inconsistent with Article 38 considered in tandem with the principle of electoral equality.[72]

Party Finance V,[73] decided in 1979, grew out of a major controversy involving irregular party financing. Despite the sums appropriated over the years to defray the costs of election campaigns, the parties were hard-pressed to meet all their expenses during a time of rising expenditures. In addition, the disclosure requirements of the Parties Act appeared to have had a chilling effect on large corporate donations.[74] As a consequence, the parties turned once again to the state treasury, increasing their quadrennial allowances and resorting to stratagems that some commentators described as *Umwegfinanzierung,* or "going around the law." One such stratagem, designed to avoid the reporting and disclosure requirements of the Parties Act, encouraged businessmen and corporations to make large tax-deductible donations to various educational and charitable associations, donations then transferred to political parties. In some instances dummy charitable organizations "laundered" money targeted for specific party treasuries.[75] These and related schemes led to numerous charges of tax fraud and illegal party financing, all topped by the scandalous Flick affair in the early 1980s.[76] (The giant Flick Corporation had contributed enormous sums of money to all of the established parties, expecting in return to receive — as it did — a favorable tax ruling allowing the company to avoid millions of deutsche marks in taxes.) These developments provided the overture to *Party Finance V.*

The constitutional dispute centered once again on the provisions of the Parties Act dealing with tax-deductible contributions to political parties. Recall that in *Party Finance II* (1958) the Constitutional Court invalidated tax-deductible donations because they conferred an unfair advantage on certain parties. Ten years later, however, in *Party Finance IV* (1968), the court sustained the relatively small tax-deductible amounts permitted under sections 34 and 35 of the Parties Act. The present litigation, initiated by the Christian Democratic government of Lower Saxony, featured new arguments designed to reverse the court's holding in the 1958 case and even to force the court to reconsider the limits it imposed on party financing in *Party Finance III* (1966). The treasurers of all the established parties, including the SPD, filed briefs in support of Lower Saxony's claim that the small tax-deductible amounts allowed under the Parties Act were woefully inadequate and in conflict with Article 21 of the Basic Law. They argued that the act's squeamish tax-deductible provisions made it almost impossible for the parties to perform the tasks that the *Parteienstaat* expected of them.

The petitioners advanced a strong case in oral argument before the Constitutional Court: Political parties had changed drastically over the years; they had evolved into catchall parties and mass-membership organizations; membership dues, however, had not kept pace with the rising costs of political education, not to mention the skyrocketing costs of maintaining viable party organizations; existing sources of revenue, apart from reimbursable campaign costs, were severely limited; tax-deductible personal and corporate contributions could supply the parties with ample funds, but this source had dried up because of limits the Constitutional Court had imposed on tax deductibility, resulting in a "fundamental discrepancy" between the role assigned to parties under the Basic Law and the Parties Act, on the one hand, and federal tax policy, on the other. Furthermore, federal law invidiously discriminated against parties because it permitted religious, charitable, and educational associations to receive larger amounts of tax-deductible contributions; after all, political parties in their capacity as constitutional organs were also involved in the critical business of civic and political education; to place them at a disadvantage vis-à-vis these other groups offended the principle of equality and undermined the integrity of the *Parteienstaat.*[77]

The Federal Constitutional Court was unimpressed with this picture of impending financial ruin. Although one begins to detect an undertone of dissatisfaction with the seminal decision in *Party Finance III* (1966), the court reaffirmed the bright line drawn in that case between parties as constitutional organs for electoral purposes and parties as voluntary associations of private citizens. "Parties are not state organs," reiterated the court, "but rather groupings freely organized in an open multiparty system and sustained by their own efforts.... For the state to provide full or even substantial coverage of a party's total financial needs would offend the principle that such funds are to be limited to [those activities] concerning which they play an [official] constitutional role.... [Such financing] would circumvent the function and status of political parties as defined in Article 21 of the Basic Law."[78]

Finally, disturbed by recent scandals and the increasing amounts of public money seeping into party coffers, some of it by *Umwegfinanzierung,* the court instructed the parties to abide by the tax-deductible limits on donations currently embodied in the Federal Parties Act. To the political parties the court appeared to be conveying this message: The state will not bail you out of your financial difficulties; your viability as parties depends on your public appeal, your ability to expand your membership, and your creativity in devising legitimate means of raising money. The Parties Act, particularly the tax-deductible provisions, was designed to stimulate, not inhibit, such voluntary fund-raising activities. Political parties, far from relying on the state, should bring themselves into line with the spirit of the act.

Two additional party funding cases decided in July 1986 emerged from petitions filed by the Green party. The Flick scandal had prompted major changes in the Parties Act. Parties were now defined as "charitable" organizations for tax purposes, allowing individuals to deduct donations up to 5 percent of their income and business up to two mills of their total wages, salaries, and sales. In addition, to solicit the support of smaller parties, an "equalization" (*Chancenausgleich*) scheme was adopted whereby political parties receiving at least 0.5 percent of the votes in a federal election would be entitled to additional funds — beyond the DM 5 per vote received in an election — calculated from the sum of their respective party members, membership dues, and donations. Finally, to encourage small donations to the parties, a tax credit of 50 percent was allowed to individuals and couples up to the respective sums of DM 1,200 and 2,400.

Party Finance VI (1986) sustained most of these amendments.[79] The court did, however, strike down the rise in tax-deductible donations to specified percentages of total income as violative of the equal protection clause. But then, in an unexpectedly generous move, and are seemingly sensitive to the financial plight of the parties, the court said that a maximum corporate tax-deductible amount of DM 100,000 would be constitutionally acceptable. Justices Mahrenholz and Böckenförde dissented from the ruling on two grounds. First, they maintained that only natural persons are entitled to make tax-deductible contributions to the parties. The inclusion of the juristic persons, in their view, would undermine the "citizen's right to equal participation in the formation of [the people's] political will." Second, they argued that the DM 100,000 figure was too high to withstand constitutional analysis. Such a large sum, they maintained, tended to discriminate against parties supported by persons of modest means.[80]

In the *Political Foundations* case, however — decided on the same day — the court sustained the validity of state subsidies allocated to four party-oriented foundations for purposes of "political education."[81] The recipients of these funds were the Konrad Adenauer Foundation (CDU), the Friedrich Nauman Foundation (FDP), the Friedrich Ebert Foundation (SPD), and the Hans Seidel Foundation (CSU), all prominent national organizations with large staffs and overseas branches and well known for their educational and civic contributions, including their sponsorship of student research grants, fellowships, and academic conferences. In 1967, the year after the court decided *Party Finance III,* these foundations received DM 9 million in public subsidies. By 1983 this figure had climbed to an astounding DM 83.3 million, with 37 and 33 percent going, respectively, to the Ebert and Adenauer foundations, while the Nauman and Seidel foundations each received 15 percent of the allocation. The Greens and other critics charged that these subsidies circumvented the holding of *Party Finance III* and constituted a veiled means of financing the total activity of the parties. But after examining the nature and operations of the foundations, the court found them to be legally and organizationally separate from the parties as well as intellectually independent of them. Because they are legitimate civic and educational institutions operating in the public interest, their funding is constitutionally permissible.[82]

Party Finance VI resulted in the fifth revision of the Parties Act. In 1988 the Bundestag raised the disclosure threshold for large donors from DM 20,000 to DM 40,000 and allowed generous tax deductions to individuals and couples for donations up to DM 60,000 and 120,000, respectively. For the benefit of smaller parties, parliament established a base payment (*Sockelbetrag*) that would amount to 6 percent of the total state funds allocated to the parties as reimbursement for their campaign costs in a federal election should they receive 2 percent of the second-ballot votes. In 1988 this amount was about DM 18 million. The *Sockelbetrag* placed millions of marks into the hands of certain minor parties, a provision some observers thought would surely encourage the proliferation of minor parties, thus undercutting the rationale of the 5 percent clause.

NOTE: *PARTY FINANCE VII.* Once again the Green party went to court, this time precipitating a revolutionary change in constitutional policy. On April 9, 1992, finally convinced that it was no longer reasonable or practicable to distinguish between campaign costs and other political party expenditures, the Second Senate unanimously rejected the core of its 1966 decision.[83] In addition, the senate nullified most of the court's holdings from 1968 to 1986. The *Chancengleichheit* and *Sockelbetrag* provisions of the existing statute were declared unconstitutional as violative of the equality clause. In addition, the court revived its 1958 decision by nullifying tax-deductible donations of DM 60,000 and DM 120,000 for individuals and couples and by disallowing tax deductions altogether for donations from businesses. The court also lowered the publicity threshold from DM 40,000 to DM 20,000. Finally, and most significantly, the court declined to distinguish between electoral and other costs. From now on, it declared, state funding and reimbursements could not exceed the total amount raised by the parties themselves. In its parting shot, the court directed the Bundestag to change the Parties Act accordingly by January 1993.[84]

The classic tension between state and society referred to at the outset of this section clearly surfaced in *Party Finance VII*. After the 1990 election, the parties received nearly DM 500 million in state funds, the highest figure ever. Of this total, the two largest parties — the CDU/CSU and SPD — received DM 312 million, and the FDP, in a parliamentary coalition with the CDU/CSU, received DM 46 million. The court seemed worried that the established parties were becoming too entrenched and comfortable, reinforcing their internal bureaucracies at the state's expense, and thus widening the distance between themselves and their voters. Now *Staatsfreiheit* — freedom *from* the state — was being emphasized as the court sought to impose a constitutional policy that would send the parties back into society, where they would have to depend much more than in the past on their own resources and fund-raising capabilities.

5.11 West German Media Case (1962)
14 BVerfGE 121

[The West German Broadcasting Station (WDR), located in Cologne, allocated free broadcasting time to the CDU, SPD, and FDP during the North Rhine–Westphalia state election campaign of 1962. The parties, however, received different amounts of radio and television time. For example, between June 18 and July 7, 1962, WDR assigned thirteen five-minute slots to the CDU, eleven such slots to the SPD, and five to the FDP. After exhausting its administrative remedies, the FDP filed a constitutional complaint before the Federal Constitutional Court, claiming a right to broadcasting time equal to that of the other parties.]

Judgment of the Second Senate. . . .

C. [We] cannot sustain the constitutional complaint.

II. 1. The necessity to officially allot airtime to the political parties is a consequence of the public ownership of radio and television stations in the Federal Republic. Moreover, the availability of airtime that is free of charge is limited. If radio and television were not in the hands of publicly incorporated institutions, election campaign advertising would be at the mercy of the marketplace, as in the case of leaflet propaganda or newspaper advertisements, which are not subject to any restriction. It would be unnecessary to allot airtime officially if all parties were in a position to take advantage of radio and television advertising according to their resources and under equal conditions. The principle of equal opportunity in electoral competition would also be assured if the individual parties enjoyed access to airtime in accordance with their financial situation and other possibilities. The principle of equal opportunity does not require a differential allocation [of radio and television time] depending on the size, [leadership] abilities, and political goals of the parties. It merely demands that the legal order guarantee each party fundamentally equal campaign chances, and thus equal opportunity in their competition for votes.

2. The principle of equal opportunity obligates the publicly incorporated radio and television stations to remain largely neutral in election campaigns. But the principle permits differential time allotments for very significant reasons, just as it would allow equal allotments of time.

(a) In allotting broadcast time [publicly owned radio and television stations] need consider only parties [running candidates] on state lists within the range of a given radio or television station [citing 7 BVerfGE 99]. . . .

(c) Radio and television are, next to the press, the most important means of mass communication by which citizens obtain the knowledge necessary for forming their opinions. Programming must adhere to a minimum standard of balance, objectivity, and mutual respect if it is to do justice to this task in conformity with Article 5 of the Basic Law [citing the *Television I* case]. [Conveying] objective information about the balance among important political, ideological, and social groups is a part of this task. In allotting differential amounts of airtime for purposes of electioneering, radio and television perform [an important] social role by informing [the electorate] of the relative importance of the political parties. . . .

4. Even though differential airtime allotments keyed to the importance of parties are not on principle inadmissible . . . these distinctions are constitutionally limited. [Publicly owned radio and television stations] may not permit the differentiation . . . to seriously jeopardize the basically free competition among all political parties participating in an election. In particular, [they] may not entirely exclude from radio and television propaganda those small groups competing in the election that are within a radio or television station's range.

There is no absolute way of determining the boundary [between a valid and invalid] differentiation in the allotment of airtime. The boundary can be determined only by considering the existing concrete situation.

III. In applying these principles [in the present case] we find that the general manager of WDR did not exceed the discretionary limits set down by the Constitution when he denied the demands of the complainant.

Only the CDU, SPD, and FDP succeeded in the last North Rhine–Westphalian state election, which took place on July 6, 1958. All remaining parties foundered on the 5 percent restrictive clause. The CDU obtained 104, the SPD 81, and the FDP 15 of the 200 available seats. WDR makes 170 minutes available to the political parties on both radio and television. Out of this total, [WDR] distributes 145 minutes [of radio and television time] among the parties represented in parliament. The remaining 25 minutes are reserved for other parties participating in the election. Of the 145 minutes available to the CDU, SPD, and FDP, the CDU received thirteen broadcasts of 5 minutes each, for a total of 65 minutes; the SPD eleven broadcasts of 5 minutes each, for a total of 55 minutes; and the FDP five broadcasts of 5 minutes each, for a total of 25 minutes. In addition, the CDU, SPD, and FDP each received a 25-minute radio spot entitled "Parties on the Line" in which a representative of one party responded to questions by representatives of the other two parties. A purely proportional allotment would have given the CDU 52 percent, the SPD 40.5 percent, and the FDP 7.5 percent of airtime. In reality, the CDU received 41 percent, the SPD 36 percent, and the FDP 23 percent of radio time and, respectively, 45 percent, 38 percent, and 17 percent of television time.

This distribution means that [WDR] equally allotted more than half of the entire radio broadcast time to those parties represented in the parliament. [It] distributed the remainder proportionate to the results of previous elections. This is clearly consistent with the principle of equal opportunity. With respect to television, too, [WDR] did not merely allot the total broadcast time proportionate to the results of previous elections. The FDP obtained more than twice the amount of broadcast time that it would have been entitled to on the basis of its percentage [of the vote]. This distribution is also consistent with the principle of equal opportunity because [WDR] gave the FDP an amount of airtime which, on the one hand, made effective election propaganda possible, and, on the other, corresponded to the party's importance as a party represented in parliament.

The general manager's decision thus remains within the framework outlined in the Constitution because it is dictated by the principle of formal equality of political parties during an election campaign and because by allotting differing time slots it takes into account the varying strengths of the parties involved.

[We] must therefore . . . deny the constitutional complaint.

MILITANT DEMOCRACY

The German Constitution requires the defense of the "free democratic basic order." These terms appear in numerous provisions of the Basic Law, serving generally as a limitation on the exercise of certain freedoms. Fundamental rights may be limited or even forfeited (under the terms of Article 18) if they are used to combat or to abolish the constitutional order. For example, Article 9 (2) of the Basic Law prohibits associations whose "purposes or activities . . . are directed against the constitutional order or the concept of international understanding." Even the freedom to teach "shall not absolve from loyalty to the Constitution" (Article 5 [3]). In short, the exercise of several guaranteed rights under the Basic Law is predicated on certain principles of political obligation.

Article 21 (1), as we have already seen, establishes the so-called party privilege, the principle that secures to all political parties the freedom to organize and mobilize the electorate.[85] This freedom, however, is limited by the terms of paragraph 2: "Parties which, by reason of their aims or the behavior of their adherents, seek to impair or abolish the free democratic basic order or endanger the existence of the Federal Republic of Germany, shall be unconstitutional. The Federal Constitutional Court shall decide on the question of unconstitutionality." This provision was designed to repair a central failing of the Weimar Republic; namely, its tolerance of extremist parties bent on destroying democracy. Recalling the conditions that led to the Hitler state, the founders resolved that the Federal Republic could never be neutral in the face of its mortal enemies. They set out to create what in German constitutional jurisprudence would become known as a "militant democracy."[86]

The language of Article 21, however, is far from clear. What, in truth, is the meaning of "free democratic basic order"? How much resistance to the democratic order is required to trigger a decision of unconstitutionality by the Federal Constitutional Court? Must the danger to the existence of the Federal Republic be clear and present, or is the mere probability of danger sufficient to warrant such a decision? Or is it sufficient for a party to be merely antidemocratic in its general philosophy? But when may a party reasonably be characterized as antidemocratic or anticonstitutional? When it advocates systemic changes in the existing polity? When it advocates criminal activity? When there is a plan of action, however remote, for the overthrow of democracy? These and related questions are the subject of this section.

5.12 Socialist Reich Party Case (1952)
2 BVerfGE 1

[The Socialist Reich Party (SRP) was founded in 1949 as a successor to the rightist *Deutsche Reichspartei* (German Imperial Party). Its publications, campaign appeals, and leadership convinced many people of its neo-Nazi orientation. Finding that the SRP "seeks to impair the liberal democratic order," the federal government petitioned the Federal Constitutional Court to declare the new party unconstitutional under Article 21 (2) of the Basic Law.]

Judgment of the First Senate. . . .

[Political Parties and the Free Democratic Order]
E. . . . German constitutions following World War I hardly mentioned political parties, although even at that time . . . political parties to a large extent determined democratic constitutional life. The reasons for this omission are manifold, but in the final analysis the cause lies in a democratic ideology that refused to recognize groups mediating between the free individual and the will of the entire people composed of the sum of individual wills and represented in parliament by parliamentarians "as representatives of the entire people." . . .

The Basic Law abandoned this viewpoint and, more realistically, expressly recognizes parties as agents — even if not the sole ones — forming the political will of the people.

The Basic Law's attempt to regulate political parties encounters two problems. The first relates to the principle of democracy, which permits any political orientation to manifest itself in political parties, including — to be consistent — antidemocratic orientations. The second relates to a special tension on the parliamentary level: The parliamentarian is to be a free representative of the entire people and at the same time be bound by a concrete party program. [We must] examine the first problem in more detail.

In a free democratic state, as it corresponds to German constitutional development, freedom of political opinion and freedom of association — including political association — are guaranteed to individual citizens as basic rights. On the other hand, part of the nature of every democracy consists in the people exercising their supreme power in elections and voting. In the reality of the large modern democratic state, however, this popular will can emerge only through parties as operating political units. Both fundamental ideas lead to the basic conclusion that the establishment and activity of political parties must not be restrained.

The framers of the German Constitution had to decide whether they could fully implement this conclusion or whether, enlightened by recent experiences, they should instead draw certain limits in this area. They had to consider whether principles governing every democracy should limit the absolute freedom to establish parties on the basis of any political idea, and whether parties seeking to abolish democracy by using formal democratic means should be excluded from political life. [They] also had to take into account the danger that the government might be tempted to eliminate troublesome opposition parties.

Article 21 of the Basic Law has tried to resolve these problems. On the one hand, it establishes the principle that formation of political parties shall be free. On the other hand, it offers a means of preventing activity by "unconstitutional" parties. To avert the danger of an abuse of this power, Article 21 authorizes the Federal Constitutional Court to decide the question of unconstitutionality and attempts to determine as far as possible the factual requirements for this declaration.

At the same time, the fundamental ideas upon which this provision is based furnish important indicators for interpreting Article 21. . . . Because of the special importance of parties in a democratic state, [the court] is justified in eliminating them from the political scene if, but only if, they seek to topple supreme fundamental values of the free democratic order which are embodied in the Basic Law. . . .

[We] have thus stated the crucial determinants of the relationship between Article 21 and Article 9 (2) of the Basic Law [freedom of association subject to certain restrictions]. Conceptually, parties are also "associations" within the meaning of Article 9 (2). Hence, Article 9 (2) would prohibit them under the conditions mentioned there and would subject them to the authority of the executive in general. . . . [But] if an association is a political party, it is [also] entitled to the privileges contained in Article 21 (2) because of the special status granted only to parties. . . .

. . . [We] derive the answer to the question [of the constitutionality of a party] from the consideration that a party may be eliminated from the political process only if it rejects the supreme principles of a free democracy. If a party's internal organization does not correspond to democratic principles, [one] may generally conclude that the party seeks to impose upon the state the structural principles that it has implemented within its own organization. . . . Whether or not this conclusion is justified must be determined in each individual case. . . .

The SRP's Leadership and Organization

[The court analyzed the history of German political parties, especially the NSDAP (Hitler's Nazis), then examined in detail dozens of letters between Socialist Reich party (SRP) leaders and between party leaders and potential recruits. These documents showed that most SRP leaders had been Nazis with positions in such organizations as the SS and SA and that they were actively seeking out other former Nazis.]

G. II. 3. (e) . . . The SRP claims in its defense that other parties have also tried to enlist former National Socialists. . . .

This objection shows that the SRP misunderstands the situation. [We] do not reproach the SRP for having tried to enlist former National Socialists, but rather for collecting the particularly hard-core individuals who have "remained true to themselves." [The SRP recruited these persons] not in order to gain positive forces for democracy, but to preserve and propagate National Socialist ideas. . . .

(f) . . . Both former and active Nazis gather [in the SRP] in order to regain influence. . . . [The SRP] systematically seeks them out and enlists them. . . . They form the core of the SRP. . . . Former Nazis hold key positions in the party to such an extent as to determine its political and intellectual image. [N]o decision can be made against their will.

III. (a) . . . [The SRP's] organization is also similar to that of the Nazi party. . . . Its internal structure is not in keeping with democratic principles (Article 21 (1) [3] of the Basic Law). . . . In brief, a party must be structured from the bottom up; that is, members must not be excluded from decision-making processes, and the basic equality of members as well as the freedom to join or to leave [the party] must be guaranteed. It would also contravene democratic principles . . . either to promise absolute obedience to party leaders or to demand such a promise. . . . [The court then examined the party's bylaws and practices and found that authority flowed from the top down, not from members to leaders.]

(d) (2) The documents . . . show how the selection system under section 4 of the bylaws works. [The SRP] allows only those who fight for the party to become members. [The SRP] does not accept members of trial tribunals, political persecutees, people with serious criminal records, 20th of July people, etc. . . . ["20th of July people" refers to the group of army officers led by Colonel Claus Graf Schenk von Stauffenberg, who tried to assassinate Hitler on July 20, 1944, by placing a bomb in Hitler's headquarters in East Prussia. "Political persecutees" refers to members of the Resistance and opposition parties whom the Nazis persecuted while in power.]

(3) According to the bylaws, a member can be expelled only in an orderly proceeding of the Honorary Council. Numerous documents among the confiscated material prove, however, that the SRP disregarded this provision, and not a single piece of evidence was found to show that the [SRP] implemented the expulsion proceedings in accordance with the bylaws. . . . This practice corresponds exactly with the procedure in the Nazi party. . . .

(e) These facts demonstrate that the SRP was governed in a dictatorial manner from the top down. Several published statements indicate that the SRP was to be organized like a political order based upon the principle of absolute obedience. . . . In a letter of December 25, 1950, the party chairman revealed his intention to organize the party apparatus "according to principles of an officers corps" and to "make a ruthless reorganization in the sense of cadre organizations." . . .

(f) The establishment of affiliated organizations like the Reichsfront, Reichsjugend, and Frauenbund also followed the example of the Nazi party. The Reichsfront was conceived as an elite fighting group along the lines of the SA and SS and was also structured similarly. Its [organization] strongly reflected the Führer principle. The uniforms provided for the Reichsjugend were even the same as those for the Hitler Youth, the only difference being that the color of the shirt was olive green instead of brown. . . .

(g) The statements made . . . in connection with the SRP's clear imitation of the Nazi party's organizational structure necessarily lead [us] to conclude that it seeks to impose its own organizational structure on the nation as soon as it has come into power, just as the Nazi party did. [T]hus [the SRP] seeks to eliminate the free democratic basic order. . . .

[The court next embarked on a similarly exhaustive analysis of the SRP's program and the behavior of its leaders. The program showed that the party was committed to a revival of the mythical notions of an indestructible Reich and German racial superiority. In addition, the speeches and activities of party leaders demonstrated the party's contempt for the officials and institutions of the Federal Republic and their acceptance of the idea of an authoritarian *Führer* state. Finally, the court noted the revival of a vicious anti-Semitism in which "murderers are represented as innocent victims and surviving relatives of victims as criminals against humanity."]

H. I. The SRP is thus unconstitutional within the meaning of Article 21 (2) of the Basic Law. . . . Therefore, the party must be dissolved.

————————

NOTE: THE *COMMUNIST PARTY* CASE AND ITS IMPACT. The *Socialist Reich Party* case gave the court its first opportunity to define the grand purpose of the *Parteienstaat*. Article 21, said the court, confers a special status on political parties (the so-called party privilege); it encourages party organization, recognizes parties as the principal organs of popular democracy, and legitimizes opposition parties. In short, Article 21 seeks to avoid any repetition of the one-party state that molded the Third Reich. The court's decision to declare the Socialist Reich party unconstitutional comforted the Allied powers and occasioned few protests in Germany. After all, the horrors of Nazism were still fresh in the memories of most people, and the new polity was struggling to establish itself in the face of doubts about Germany's commitment to political democracy. Seen in this light, the ban on the Socialist Reich party appeared to be a manifestation of judicial enlightenment.

The *Communist Party* case (1956) was another story.[87] Adenauer's government initiated an Article 21 action against the Communist Party of Germany (KPD) in 1951, the same year it sought a declaration of unconstitutionality against the Socialist Reich party. Yet the *Communist Party* case was not decided until 1956. The delay reflected the growing feeling among some of the justices that the Adenauer government's action against the KPD was premature and that it would be more prudent to allow the party to bury itself in an open political contest than to have it banned by judicial decree. The KPD's electoral strength dipped to 2.3 percent of the national vote in 1953, and by 1956, under the impact of West Germany's astounding economic revival, its popular support had almost vanished. Yet, in the face of rising Soviet-American tensions — tensions exacerbated by the division and rearming of Germany — the *Communist Party* case was important symbolically in the bitterly cold war between East and West Germany. Finally, on August 17, 1956, convinced that the government would not withdraw the case,[88] the court handed down an opinion declaring the Communist party unconstitutional. The opinion consumed 308 pages in the official reports, the longest by far of all the court's opinions.

It was no surprise that the KPD suffered the same fate at the hands of the court as the SRP. The bulk of the opinion consisted of an exhaustive analysis of Marxism-Leninism and the history of German communism, including a survey of the KPD's structure, leadership, campaign literature, and overall political style. The court found, as a matter of ideology and fact, that the KPD directed all of its operations against the existing constitutional system. In interpreting Article 21 (2), the court rejected the contention that illegal activity or some other "concrete undertaking" to abolish the constitutional order is necessary to deprive a party of its constitutional status.[89] On the other hand, the mere advocacy of overthrow is an insufficient basis for banning a political party. What is important, said the court, is whether a party has "a fixed purpose constantly and resolutely to combat the free democratic basic order" and manifests this purpose "in political action according to a fixed plan."[90] This purpose or plan, continued the court, can be gleaned from a party's program, its official declarations, statements of its leaders, and its educational materials. The court's own independent examination of such records convinced it that the KPD was an unconstitutional party within the meaning of Article 21 (2).

In a passage that marked the birth, jurisprudentially, of West Germany's militant democracy, the court set forth the essential meaning of Article 21 (2):

> The Basic Law represents a conscious effort to achieve a synthesis between the principle of tolerance with respect to all political ideas and certain inalienable values of the political system. Article 21 (2) does not contradict any basic principle of the Constitution; it expresses the conviction of the [founding fathers], based on their concrete historical experience, that the state could no longer afford to maintain an attitude of neutrality toward political parties. [The Basic Law] has in this sense created a "militant democracy," a constitutional [value] decision that is binding on the Federal Constitutional Court.[91]

As in the *Socialist Reich Party* case, the court concluded its decision by ordering the dissolution of the Communist party and the confiscation of its property. Dissolution, said the court, is the natural consequence of a judicial finding of unconstitutionality, a finding that authorizes federal and state officials to implement the decree. A final consequence of this decision was that the Communist party lost its seats in both federal and state parliaments.

But this was not all the KPD lost. The court's decree dissolved not only the party itself but all of its surrogate organizations, current and future. In 1961, for example, the newly established Communist Voters' League ran candidates for the Bundestag in North Rhine–Westphalia. In litigation growing out of the state's refusal to put the league on the ballot, the court held that the ban on the KPD extended to all organizations, including the league, that effectively supplanted the banned party.[92]

In the years following the original decree, security officials stepped up their crack-down on subversive activities throughout the Federal Republic while the Office for the Protection of the Constitution proceeded to publicly identify organizations that opposed the constitutional order. At about the same time, postal, railway, and customs officials confiscated millions of subversive publications brought into the country from East Germany and other communist countries.[93]

NOTE: THE *NATIONAL DEMOCRATIC PARTY* CASE (1975). The *Communist Party* case raised the question of how far the state may go in gathering and publishing informa-tion about the activities of anticonstitutional parties or groups. The rise of the National Democratic Party of Germany (NPD), an extreme right-wing party often attacked for its neo-Nazi tendencies, raised the question once again. The NPD, however, had not been declared unconstitutional, and the government did not petition the court to declare it unconstitutional. Nevertheless, the Interior Ministry published a report that described the NPD as a "party engaged in anticonstitutional goals and activity," as "radical right and an enemy of freedom," and as "a danger to the free democratic basic order." The NPD challenged the validity of Interior's "dis-closure" as a violation of the "party privilege" secured by Article 21 (1). A unan-imous senate ruled, however, that state agencies concerned with the protection of the Basic Law were constitutionally permitted, if not required, to make such find-ings about a party engaged in anticonstitutional activities, even if the court has not declared the party unconstitutional.[94]

During the years when the Federal Republic was in its third decade, the gov-ernment seemed increasingly reluctant to mount judicial challenges against "uncon-stitutional" parties. It never did bring an Article 51 action against the NPD; nor did it do so against the reorganized Communist party, now called the German Commu-nist party (DKP). The new party could have been suppressed as a surrogate organi-zation of the banned KPD, but security officials failed to move against the party, and it continued to operate openly. As one commentator noted: "The toleration of the DKP and the NPD probably reflects a sense that it would be improper to move to ban parties that act lawfully within the liberal democratic system, even when they clearly aim to have that system replaced by an illiberal, antidemocratic one."[95] In the *Radi-cal Groups* case (1978), even the Constitutional Court seems to have backed away from its earlier militancy.

5.13 Radical Groups Case (1978)
47 BVerfGE 198

[In various election campaigns (both federal and state) during 1975 and 1976, radio and television stations in three German states denied campaign broadcasting time to three radical left-wing parties. The stations declined to carry the parties' campaign ads because of their extreme revolutionary rhetoric calling for the destruction of the existing political order. Administrative courts sustained the actions of the broadcasters. The affected parties—the Marxist-Leninist German Communist party, the Communist Federation of West Germany, and the German Communist party—brought constitutional complaints against these judicial decisions, alleging a denial of their rights as political parties under Articles 3, 5, and 21 of the Basic Law.]

———————

Judgment of the Second Senate. . . .

The constitutional complaints are valid.

1. The contested decisions are predicated on the fact that the complainants constitute political parties—or units thereof—within the meaning of Article 21 (1) of the Basic Law and section 2 of the Political Parties Act. No constitutional objections have been marshaled against [this predicate].

Under section 2 of the Parties Act, political parties represent associations of citizens who permanently or for an extended period influence the formation of the political will within the Federal Republic or an individual state and who wish to take part in representing the people in the federal or a state parliament if the totality of their [activity]—particularly [as measured by] the size of the party, the stability of its organization, its membership, and public prominence—is sufficient to underscore the seriousness of these goals. This definition harmonizes with Article 21 (1) of the Basic Law and is thus constitutional.

The complainants would wish to exert influence over the formation of the political will [of the people] in the Federal Republic. The stability and size of their organizations, their membership figures, and their public visibility satisfy the threshold requirements for [being treated as] political parties. As the initial proceedings have shown, they were permitted to participate as political parties in federal and state elections, and tried subsequently to win seats during the course of [these] campaigns.

The fact that the complainants were possibly engaged in pursuing unconstitutional goals, especially the abolition of the parliamentary system, does not strip them of their character as political parties. Article 21 (2) states that [political] parties which, by reason of their aims or the behavior of their adherents, seek to impair or to abolish the free democratic basic order or to endanger the existence of the Federal Republic are unconstitutional. This phraseology reveals that a political organization's status as a political party is to be judged independently of its constitutional or unconstitutional nature. If constitutionality were an essential characteristic of political parties, there would be no need for [a section of the Basic Law] authorizing proceedings against unconstitutional parties. . . .

C. The disputed decisions by the administrative courts violate the constitutional rights of the complainants under Article 3 (1) and (3) in connection with Article 21.

1. While the right of all parties to equal opportunity is not expressly mentioned in the Basic Law, [this right] may be inferred from the significance associated with the multiparty principle [sanctioned by the Basic Law] and the [guaranteed] freedom to establish political parties [under Article 21 (1)]. . . . This basic right [to equal treatment] extends not only to the election itself but also, since [elections] are influenced by measures of public authority, to campaign propaganda [the dissemination of which] is so necessary for electioneering in modern mass democracy. . . .

Thus the principle of equal opportunity bars radio and television stations from denying broadcasting time to political parties admitted to participation in the electoral process on the ground that [these] parties are too insignificant or even harmful. On the other hand, the equal opportunity principle does not bar [these stations] from differentiating between parties in allotting broadcasting time so long as they grant small and new parties adequate airtime.

[Another] question raised by the constitutional complaints is whether the principle of equal opportunity is violated where broadcasting stations, after screening ads submitted by political parties, refuse to run them on the ground that the messages [conveyed] have nothing to do with the election or are either anticonstitutional or just plain criminal.

2. The principle of equal opportunity demands that every political party receive fundamentally the same opportunity during the election campaign and during the actual election process, thus maintaining an equal chance in the competition for electoral votes. However, the above-mentioned political parties may plead in this fashion only if they submit messages to the broadcasting stations which really deal with the election. This is the sole purpose of the free allotment of airtime to political parties by radio and television stations. This purpose precludes the use of airtime for purposes other than election campaigning. This limitation corresponds to the right of radio and television stations to examine submitted scripts and to refuse airtime in the event that [the messages] can no longer be considered election advertisements.

At the same time, the definition of what will and what will not constitute an election advertisement must not be interpreted too narrowly. Generally, one may say that it comprises all measures which aim at persuading the citizen to vote for one or the other political party or for a certain candidate. . . .

3. Radio and television stations have no right to refuse broadcasting [time to a party] merely because its election ad contains anticonstitutional ideas. This [view] stands opposed to the provisions of Article 21 (2) as well as to the [spirit] of the Basic Law's principle of equal opportunity.

(a) The principle of equal opportunity bars public authority from any differentiation of treatment among parties . . . unless justified by a special, that is, cogent, reason. . . . Even in the case of political parties whose goal is to destroy the democratic state and to abolish at least in part the constitutional order of the Federal Republic, and which, if they were to win seats in parliament, would constitute a political danger, even then radio and television stations are not authorized to meet this danger by refusing to broadcast election campaign ads simply because they espouse political goals and programs that are unconstitutional. The unwritten political party privilege found in Article 21 will not permit such far-reaching station control over the contents of election campaign messages. . . .

The jurisdictional monopoly of the Federal Constitutional Court categorically precludes administrative action against the existence of a political party, regardless of how anticonstitutional the party's program may be. To be sure, the possibility of political opposition against such a party exists; however, [the party] must be free to act politically without in any way being impeded. The Basic Law tolerates the dangers inherent in the activities of such a political party until it is declared unconstitutional. . . . This [principle] must also be respected by radio and television stations.

(b) . . . In view of these considerations, a violation of a general criminal law must be evident if a [broadcasting station] is to refuse an election campaign ad. There must be no doubt that a concrete and substantial violation of the object of protection by criminal law is apparent. This will always be the case whenever political parties encourage — also indirectly — the commission of criminal acts. . . .

The Federal Constitutional Court has repeatedly ruled that the participation of political parties in elections represents the core of their activity. . . . A denial of airtime to political parties without sufficient reason is a rather severe violation [of the Basic Law]. Such a denial would curtail the process of freely forming the political will [on which] political elections [depend]; citizens would find it difficult or even impossible to exercise their entrusted right to decide on the merits of political party programs. . . .

[After vindicating the right of radical parties to have their political advertisements carried on public broadcasting stations, the court reached the free speech issue. The complaining parties alleged that in refusing to carry their ads because of their content, the public broadcasting stations were engaging in prior censorship. The court rejected this argument. While broadcasting stations may not censor the content of a valid political message, they are authorized, said the court, to determine whether a given text submitted to them qualifies as a campaign advertisement. As autonomous public institutions, stations are allowed to ensure that they are not being used for purposes not sanctioned by law. Because there is no unrestricted right of access to these media, the stations may constitutionally determine whether a political party meets the objective legal conditions for gaining such access.]

NOTE: OTHER ASPECTS OF MILITANT DEMOCRACY. *Radical Groups,* like the *German Media* case, not only expressed a lessening fear of radical parties; it also reflected the court's vigilant defense of minority political parties generally, much in the spirit of the voting and party finance cases. Groups not qualifying as political parties, however, had a tougher time vindicating their rights in the Constitutional Court. Indeed, Article 9 of the Basic Law authorizes security officials to ban anticonstitutional groups (as distinguished from political parties) without the Constitutional Court's intervention. Vigilance over these groups, stemming in part from terrorist activities, was most intense during the 1960s and 1970s. The controversial *Spiegel* case (1966; no. 8.7), like the *Civil Servant Loyalty* case (1975; no. 5.14), emerged from this atmosphere of pervasive concern for internal security. The Constitutional Court's effort to balance freedom and security was a most difficult exercise. The task was complicated by a constitutional text that promotes freedom while simultaneously restricting it to preserve the democratic polity it creates. The *Klass* and *Civil Servant Loyalty* cases illustrate the court's effort to reconcile the values of freedom and security.

The Klass case (1970). In its original version, Article 10 of the Basic Law declared simply: "Privacy of the mail and telecommunications shall be inviolable." In 1968, however, a constitutional amendment restricted this basic right by permitting government agents to tap telephones and break into other private communications without informing the persons involved if the intrusions "serve to protect the free democratic basic order or the existence of the federation or a state." In addition, Article 10 as amended bars aggrieved parties from contesting such invasions of privacy in the courts; instead, commissions appointed by parliament review complaints pursuant to a law that limits the conditions for invading private communications, specifies the agents or officers entrusted with this responsibility, and lays out procedures for reviewing the legality of their activities. Several German citizens, one of them a senior state prosecutor (Gerhard Klass), brought constitutional complaints against the statute and the amendment. They claimed that these measures were null and void under Articles 19 (4) and 79 (3), constitutional provisions that, respectively, guarantee *judicial* review of administrative action encroaching on basic rights and prohibit constitutional amendments infringing "the essential content of a basic right."[96]

In sustaining the validity of both the statute and the amendment, over the dissent of three justices, the First Senate once again invoked the concept of a militant democracy:[97]

> Constitutional provisions must not be interpreted in isolation but rather in a manner consistent with the Basic Law's fundamental principles and its system of values. . . . In the context of this case, it is especially significant that the Constitution . . . has decided in favor of "militant democracy" that does not submit to abuse of basic rights or an attack on the liberal order of the state. Enemies of the Constitution must not be allowed to endanger, impair, or destroy the existence of the state while claiming protection of rights granted by the Basic Law (cf. Article 9 (2), Articles 18 and 21). To protect the

Constitution the Basic Law explicitly provides for an institution, the Office for the Protection of the Constitution (cf. Article 73, no. 10, and Article 87 [1]). When the Basic Law requires the highest constitutional organs of the state to perform a task and sets up a special agency to carry out this task, it may not at the same time deny this agency the means necessary to fulfill its assigned mission.[98]

The First Senate continued by emphasizing the constitutional limits imposed on the individual in the interest of the common good. Finally, the senate held that the substantive limits and procedural safeguards of the statute satisfy the constitutional principles of legality and proportionality while respecting the basic concept of human dignity.[99]

5.14 Civil Servant Loyalty Case (1975)
39 BVerfGE 334

[On January 28, 1972, against a background of violent demonstrations and the determination of radical groups to "march through the institutions" of the Federal Republic, the federal chancellor and all ten state ministers-president issued a loyalty decree setting forth guidelines for the recruitment and dismissal of civil servants. These guidelines barred from public service applicants found to have engaged in "anticonstitutional" activities and permitted the exclusion of persons previously or currently members of organizations pursuing anticonstitutional goals. Schleswig-Holstein invoked these guidelines in refusing to admit a law graduate into the practical phase of his training. Law, like a number of professions in Germany, requires a practical internship. Law graduates who have passed their first state bar examination after successfully completing their university studies are required to apprentice in various state judicial and administrative offices. The appellant was barred from his apprenticeship for having attended meetings of a radical student group (the Red Cell) while a student at Kiel University. He appealed to the Administrative Court of Schleswig-Holstein to vindicate the right to continue his legal education. Doubting the validity of the state's action, the court referred to the Federal Constitutional Court several questions arising under Articles 3 (principle of equality), 5 (freedom of speech), 12 (right to choose a trade), 21 (party privilege), and 33 (rights and duties of civil servants). The court upheld the loyalty requirement over the dissents of Justices Seuffert, Rupp, and Wand. The dissents, which are not included in the extracts below, were based on two principal grounds: that an apprenticeship, especially for a person not planning a career in government service, does not constitute a "civil service" position within the meaning of the Constitution; and that no organization can be regarded as anticonstitutional until the Federal Constitutional Court has so declared.]

Judgment of the Second Senate. . . .

C. Section 6 (1), no. 2, of the Schleswig-Holstein Civil Service Act is compatible with the Constitution and federal law. . . .

I. The rule that civil servants and judges must defend the Constitution they are sworn to uphold is a traditional and respected principle of the professional civil service and of the judicial system, a principle set forth in Article 33 (5) of the Constitution.

> [The court retraced the history of the German civil service. From the end of the eighteenth century to the present, the principal trademark of the civil servant was his duty of loyalty (*Treuepflicht*) to monarch or state. This duty was indeed part of his professionalism. "This traditional loyalty of the civil servant," noted the court, "is explicitly rooted in the text of the Basic Law" and arises out of the conviction that the modern "administrative state" (*Verwaltungsstaat*) requires a "professional civil service loyal to the state and its constitutional order."]

  2. At this point we need not decide ultimately and in detail the full extent of the responsibility expected of the civil servant in the light of the comprehensive duty of loyalty. In any case, it suffices to point out that political loyalty is central to the loyalty of the civil servant. We do not mean an obligation to identify with the goals or with a specific political measure of a particular government. . . . What we do mean, however, is the duty to be willing to identify with the idea of the state for which the civil servant is obliged to work and with the free democratic, social, and legal order of this state based on the rule of law [*Rechtsstaat*]. This does not preclude the right to criticize certain phenomena of this state or to speak up for changes in the status quo within the framework of the Constitution, using constitutionally valid means, so long as the state and its constitutional basis are not questioned under such a pretext. Neither the state nor society is interested in an "uncritical" civil service. Nevertheless, the civil servant has an irrevocable duty to take a positive attitude toward the state — regardless of its deficiencies — and the existing constitutional order. He must consider them worth defending . . . and actively stand up for them. In doing so, the civil servant fulfills his duty of loyalty and, *from this vantage point,* he may criticize [the government] and support attempts to change existing conditions, [but only] within the framework of the constitutional order and by constitutional means. . . . Civil servants are duty-bound to defend the state in times of crisis by fulfilling the tasks entrusted to them in faithful harmony with the spirit of the Constitution along with its system of values and prescriptions. Such loyalty is required of civil servants in the interest of the state's preservation.

  3. The traditional loyalty of the civil servant has a special meaning within the context of the Basic Law. This Constitution is not value free; it regards certain values

as fundamental and . . . charges the state with their protection (Article 1). [The Constitution] takes measures to protect against threats to these values and institutionalizes special procedures to ward off attacks on the constitutional order; [in sum], it creates a militant democracy (Articles 2 [1], 9 [2], 18, 20 [4], 21 [2], 79 [3], 91, 98 [2]). This fundamental decision of the Constitution prevents the state from accepting civil service applicants who reject and oppose the free democratic order, the rule of law, and the social welfare state. The civil servant cannot work within the system of organized government, claim the personal securit[y] and benefits which accompany his position, and at the same time try to destroy the foundation of his professional activities. The free democratic constitutional state cannot and must not hand itself over to its destroyers.

4. These constitutional considerations dictate the following conclusion: A civil servant who contravenes the duty of loyalty demanded of him under Article 33 (5) of the Basic Law violates his professional obligation. . . . [Here the court reviewed federal statutes that govern the behavior of civil servants. The rules laid down in these statutes clearly distinguish between legitimate criticism of existing political conditions and attacks on the constitutional order itself.]

II. When enforcing the legal regulations governing the civil service, Article 21 of the Basic Law does not diminish the public employer's freedom of decision concretely to determine the political loyalty of the civil servant. . . .

3. The loyalty demanded of the civil servant under Article 33 (5) is not contrary to Article 21 (2); Article 33 (5) requires civil servants to support the constitutional order. Article 21 (2), on the other hand, grants to the citizen the freedom to reject the constitutional order and to oppose it politically, so long as he employs permissible means of opposition and operates within a political party that is not prohibited. . . . Whether such loyalty can be expected of applicants for the civil service can be determined by their previous activities. Affiliation with or membership in an anticonstitutional party, whether or not the Federal Constitutional Court has declared it unconstitutional, is an admissible factor in evaluating the credentials of an applicant. . . .

III. The legal position thus far expounded does not conflict with the fundamental right to freedom of expression. . . . Because of his official status [the civil servant] is charged with special duties vis-à-vis the state; at the same time, he is a citizen who may assert his fundamental rights against the state. Thus, two basic values of the Basic Law clash within the person of the civil servant: the assurance that the state will be served by an indispensable and reliable body of civil servants who will support the state and affirm the free democratic basic order . . . and the fundamental right freely to express one's opinion. . . . Article 5 of the Basic Law protects all conduct involving the expression of political opinion [but] only to the extent that it is compatible with the duty of political loyalty required by the civil servant under Article 33 (5). . . .

3. According to Article 3 (3), no person may be "discriminated against or favored because of . . . his political opinions." . . . [Yet] the formal prescription of Article 3 (3) is not absolute. It should be obvious that it is not impermissible to require acknowledgment of a particular creed on the part of a teacher about to be employed at a denominational school, or to give preference to a female for the position of principal at a girl's school. . . . Article 3 prohibits only "purposeful" discrimination; it does not prohibit favorable or prejudicial treatment which is the consequence of a provision based on a totally different purpose (e.g., rules for the protection of the pregnant mother or for the protection of the constitutional order). . . .

Finally, a constitutional provision should not be interpreted in isolation; on the contrary, it must be interpreted within the context of the Constitution itself. With this understanding, it is simply inconceivable that the Constitution which, in the wake of the bitter experience of Weimar's democracy, intended the Federal Republic of Germany to be a strong and valiant democracy should also permit the surrender of this state to its enemies with the aid of Article 3 (3) of the Basic Law. . . .

NOTE: THE PUBLIC SERVANT LOYALTY DECREE. The Loyalty Decree of January 28, 1972, commonly referred to as the extremist resolution (*Extremistenbeschluss*), was one more illustration of West Germany's militant democracy.[100] Chancellor Willy Brandt and all state prime ministers signed the decree against the backdrop of rising political terrorism, violent student demonstrations, and the renewed determination of radical groups to "march through the institutions" of the Federal Republic. The decree did not create anything new. It restated existing policy and sought to ensure the uniform application of the civil service laws throughout the country. It banned from public service persons engaged in anticonstitutional activities as well as members of organizations pursuing anticonstitutional goals. The most controversial paragraph of the decree provided that anyone belonging to an organization committed to anticonstitutional goals was presumptively unfit for public service.

Strictly speaking, the decree was neither the *Berufsverbot* (denial of a profession) nor the "radicals decree" that it was derisively called. It was, however, a failure as an effort to ensure the states' uniform and nondiscriminatory application of national guidelines. Several states, mainly those under CDU/CSU leadership, seized on the decree's "membership" provision to deny public service jobs to aspiring teachers and other low-level bureaucratic personnel. Other states, mainly those under SPD leadership, followed the more liberal policy of not excluding persons from the public service in the absence of real evidence of anticonstitutional behavior on the part of the applicant. Meanwhile, the federal Office for the Protection of the Constitution and its state affiliates stepped up their surveillance of subversive activity and carried out security checks on large numbers of public service applicants. Thousands of persons were swept up in this net of official inquiry, although a mere handful of applicants were actually denied public employment because of their doubtful loyalty.[101]

In its review of other loyalty cases the Constitutional Court continued to hold that the obligation of loyalty under Article 33 constitutes a limitation on the right of expression and the right of access to the civil service. The court tended, however, to pay increasing attention to the circumstances of each case and to focus on the nature of the conduct presumed to render a person unfit for public service. Accordingly, in the *Bar Admission* case,[102] decided in 1983, the court nullified a decision to ban a person from the private practice of law merely because he had been a member of a communist organization. The court held that disbarment was permissible only if it could be shown that the applicant engaged in punishable activity against the free democratic basic order.[103]

NOTE: ANALYSIS AND IMPACT OF *CIVIL SERVANT LOYALTY*. As the court noted in its opinion, loyalty to the established political order has been a hallmark through the ages of the German civil service.[104] Article 33 of the Basic Law carries on this tradition, providing that the "exercise of state authority as a permanent function shall as a rule be entrusted to members of the public service whose status, service, *and loyalty* are guaranteed by public law" (emphasis added). Federal law lays down the guidelines for the organization and conduct of civil servants. These guidelines have long insisted on the allegiance of civil servants to the Constitution. Moreover, they require not merely the passive loyalty implied in a simple oath of allegiance but rather an active loyalty that requires civil servants (*Beamte*) — and more recently employees (*Angestellte* and *Arbeiter*) — to "manifest by [their] entire behavior [their] support for the free democratic basic order within the spirit of the Basic Law."[105] The same provision appears in several state civil service statutes.

The constitutional analysis in the *Loyalty* case was complex. Articles 5 (freedom of expression), 12 (right to choose a trade), 3 (equality under law), and 33 (equal eligibility for public service), together with the principles of *Rechtsstaatlichkeit* and proportionality, were implicated in the case. Complainants rested their arguments on Articles 12 and 33. Article 12 guarantees to all citizens the right "freely to choose their trade, occupation, or profession"; Article 33 (2) proclaims that "every German shall be equally eligible for any public office according to his aptitude, qualifications, and professional achievements." Article 33 (4) provides that the "status, service, and loyalty" of public servants shall be "governed by public law."

Loyalty dealt with several constitutional issues. Is employment in the public service a "trade" or "profession" within the meaning of Article 12? Does Article 33 imply a limitation on the reach of Article 12? Does the term "loyalty" used in Article 33 fall within a reasonable definition of the "aptitude" required under the same article? Does Article 3 confer an entitlement to public service employment, or is such employment a privilege? Is the principle of proportionality violated if limitations on the right to enter the public service cannot be shown to further a compelling state purpose? Should Article 33 be broadly construed — and thus supportive of the complainant — in the light of Article 3 (3), affirming that "no person may be prejudiced or favored because of his . . . political opinions and in light of the free speech provisions of Article 5 (1)"? Or should Article 33 be narrowly construed — and thus damaging to the complainant — in the light of other constitutional doctrines requiring the protection and active support of the free democratic basic order?

After weighing and balancing these considerations, the court sustained the validity of the decree but found fault with its administration. The principle of *Rechtsstaatlichkeit,* said the court, limits the discretion of appointing authorities; they must respect procedural guarantees, including the applicant's right to a fair hearing, to be represented by counsel, and to rebut evidence against him. On the other hand, said the court, the state may consider an applicant's membership in an anticonstitutional organization to determine his loyalty, but cautioned that such membership alone would not be sufficient to exclude a person from the public service. Other facts must be present to substantiate a finding of disloyalty. With the situation of the complainant in mind, the court rebuked state authorities for drawing inferences of disloyalty from statements made and activities carried out in the heat of emotion during the applicant's student days. The three dissenting justices, finally, found that the loyalty decree did in fact amount to a *Berufsverbot,* since lack of in-service training would effectively bar the complainant from a career in the private practice of law. For this reason, they held, the legal educational requirement of in-service training with the state should not be regarded as public service within the meaning of Article 33, though they conceded that this training period could not be used to promote anticonstitutional goals.[106]

The political response to the court's decision was both supportive and swift. The Bundestag passed a resolution affirming the principles laid down in the decision, but over the opposition of the CDU/CSU. On May 19, 1976, the federal government issued a resolution entitled "Principles for Deciding upon a Candidate's Loyalty to the Constitution," which sought to implement all of the procedural protections specified by the Constitutional Court. The states, however, continued to attach different weights to the membership provision of the original decree. Politicians grew weary of the continuing controversy, and Willy Brandt publicly expressed regret for his original support of the decree. In 1979, the decree was fully rescinded in SPD-FDP-governed states.[107]

NOTE: ANTITERRORISM AND THE RIGHTS OF DEFENDANTS. The journey from radicalism to terrorism that characterized a small segment of German youth in the 1960s is a well-known story. The rising tide of politically motivated crimes that besieged the Federal Republic in the 1970s aroused enormous resentment and fear among West Germans. The brutal criminal acts committed by terrorists were, in fact, calculated to spread fear throughout the polity, to undermine the stability of its established order, and to invite the harsh reprisals that would lend credibility to the terrorist critique — such as it was — of the existing society. Aggravating what many German Democrats saw as a serious threat to internal security were the activities of political "radicals,"[108] persons who often sympathized with the aims of the terrorists while rejecting their methods. The tendency of some politicians and police officials to identify radicals and other ideological extremists with political terrorists raised the specter of a potential witch hunt; it was not always clear which of these groups were the targets of antiterrorist legislation.

Antiterrorist legislation passed in the 1970s prohibited certain organizations and forms of advocacy, and laid down new rules limiting the rights of defendants in criminal proceedings. The most controversial of these rules expanded the search-and-seizure authority of the police, extended the grounds for pretrial detention, imposed severe restrictions on the activities of terrorist defendants in pretrial proceedings, regulated client-counsel communications, and excluded defense lawyers from representing terrorist defendants under certain conditions. These provisions supplemented a large body of previous internal security law, a ban on several kinds of antistate activities, and the comprehensive emergency legislation of 1968, especially the controversial statute authorizing wiretaps and other interferences with private communications.[109]

Some of this legislation was hastily drawn and failed to adequately limit the discretion of law enforcement officials. Notable abuses in the execution of these laws were eventually corrected by higher courts in cooperation with the Bundestag. For example, the Federal Constitutional Court ruled that the defense counsel exclusion statute lacked adequate standards to guide prosecutors and judges in applying its provisions.[110] The Bundestag responded to the decision by drafting a more precise statute specifying the conditions under which exclusion of defense attorneys from trial would be permissible.

From the point of view of West German authorities, public criticism of these laws tended to overlook similar provisions in the criminal codes of other European democracies. But responsible foreign critics, such as Amnesty International, seemed more concerned with the potential effect of these laws than with their facial validity. For instance, laws against the advocacy of anticonstitutional activities, if vigorously enforced and expansively interpreted, could chill public discussion of sensitive issues. The zeal of some police officials had already led to raids on left-wing bookstores, and some public prosecutors were known to have filed charges against persons accused of defaming the state. Yet Amnesty International reported in 1980 that "legislation which [could] be used to restrict political criticism and the freedom of speech of the individual has not led to the adoption of anyone as a prisoner of conscience."[111]

NOTE: MILITANT DEMOCRACY AFTER REUNIFICATION. The collapse of the GDR and Germany's reunification might have led to a belief that the need for militancy in defense of democracy was less pressing than in the past. In fact, unification provided the occasion for its reaffirmation. A joint letter released by the foreign ministers of the two German states at the signing of the final peace treaty (Two-Plus-Four Treaty) in Moscow incorporated the language of Article 21 (2). In united Germany, the letter read, "the Constitution will protect the free democratic basic order," thus ensuring "that parties which, by reason of their aims or the behavior of their adherents, seek to impair or abolish the free democratic order . . . can be prohibited." The statement also reproduced the text of Article 9 (1), which bans associations other than political parties "which are directed against the constitutional order or the concept of international understanding." The letter singled out for special attention "parties and associations with National Socialist aims."[112]

Despite this reaffirmation of militant democracy, the level of tolerance for extremist political speech and activity appears to have risen in the Federal Republic as Germans have gained confidence in their democratic institutions and processes. The evolving jurisprudence of free speech over the years provides some evidence of this increasing tolerance (see Chapter 8). The record in recent years is mixed, however, especially in the light of the violence directed against foreign residents in Germany and the proliferation of extremist right-wing groups and parties. There is, of course, a crucial constitutional difference between groups and parties: under Article 21 (2) a political party can be declared unconstitutional only by a decision of the Constitutional Court, whereas a group or association within the meaning of Article 9 (1) that engages in illegal activities can be banned by executive order.

In the early 1990s, numerous organizations associated with neo-Nazi objectives were under investigation following hundreds of attacks on foreigners and their homes. As a warning signal against groups "whose goal is to destroy the democratic order," the federal government banned one of them — the National Front — in November 1992.[113] In 1993, for the first time since the *Communist Party* case, the federal government and the Bundesrat filed petitions under Article 21 (2) to have the Free Democratic Workers party (Freiheitliche Deutsche Arbeiterpartei) declared unconstitutional, and Hamburg's senate filed a similar petition against the National List (Nationale Liste), a neo-Nazi party active in that city-state. The court rejected the petitions in major decisions handed down on November 14, 1994. Given their skeletal structures and lack of electoral participation, these organizations did not qualify as "political parties" within the meaning of Article 21 or the Political Parties Act.[114] Whereupon the respective federal and state governments proceeded to ban the two "parties" on their own authority under Article 9 (1).

Christian Democratic and Social Democratic members of the Bundestag considered bringing an Article 21 (2) action against the far-right Republicans, who had experienced some success in electing their candidates to *Land* and local legislatures in the early 1990s. The idea was dropped out of fear that such an action would make martyrs of the party and its members.[115] It is unlikely that any such action would have succeeded anyway, given the care the Republicans have taken to remain within the parameters of constitutional behavior and to adhere to the organizational, financial, and auditing provisions of the Federal Parties Act.

NOTE: REUNIFICATION AND THE PUBLIC SERVICE. German unification raised a more serious question: What should be done with teachers, judges, and other civil servants who were members of the SED or otherwise implicated in the repressive activities of the former communist state? This issue concerned not the thousands of civil servants dismissed on the ground that they were no longer needed,[116] but those who had compromised themselves politically while serving the state, especially those who worked for or cooperated with the dreaded Ministry of State Security (Stasi). Under the Unification Treaty, an employee found to have violated any human right protected by the Universal Declaration of Human Rights or the UN Covenant on Civil and Political Rights is subject to immediate dismissal.[117] The courts, however, have interpreted this provision narrowly, requiring a "significant violation of the human rights instrument as well as knowledge and consciousness of a violation."[118]

Finally, although this is not the place for an extended treatment of prosecutions against former East German spies whose activities undermined the FRG's democratic constitutional order, the *Markus Wolf* case (1995) must be mentioned for its general significance. After reunification, German prosecutors sought to try former GDR spies for their espionage activities in West Germany. The most dramatic of these trials involved Markus Wolf, the master spy behind three decades of East German intelligence operations. On May 15, 1995, the Constitutional Court ruled by a five-to-three decision that Wolf and other East Germans whose espionage activities against West Germany were carried out on GDR soil could no longer be prosecuted. Such trials, said the court, violated the principle of proportionality because they tended to subject the defendants to an excessive burden relative to the benefits to be obtained from their prosecution in the light of German unification. This was especially so since West Germans who spied on the GDR were not subject to prosecution. The decision amounted to a *de facto* amnesty for thousands of GDR intelligence officers, although the "amnesty" would not apply to West Germans who spied against the FRG on behalf of the GDR.[119]

CONCLUSION

The Federal Constitutional Court is an important custodian of political democracy. It has expanded the rights of voters and furthered equality of opportunity among competing political parties. While guarding the integrity of elections and insisting on the one-person, one-vote principle in single-member election districts, it has also defended the principle of effective representation exemplified in the modified system of proportional representation. In addition, the court has vigilantly shielded minor and unconventional parties against discriminatory legislation, particularly with regard to party financing and requirements for gaining access to the ballot. At the same time, with the single exception of the first all-German election of 1990, it has sustained the 5 percent rule at state and national levels in the interest of overall political stability, just as it has held certain extremist parties unconstitutional in the interest of democracy. In recent years, however, the court has exhibited a more tolerant attitude toward so-called antidemocratic parties, defending their institutional rights with the same vigor with which it safeguards other electoral groups. In addition, the Constitutional Court's decisions in the field of parties and elections seems clearly to reflect, and to have contributed to, the maturity of German democracy.

PART III

BASIC RIGHTS AND LIBERTIES

When the framers devoted the first nineteen articles of the Basic Law to guaranteed rights and liberties, they consciously set out to underscore the priority of individual freedom in the scale of German constitutional values. Articles 1 and 2 proclaim, respectively, the principle of human dignity and the right to life and personal inviolability. On top of these general rights of liberty the Basic Law guarantees equality under law (Article 3), religious liberty (Article 4), freedom of expression (Article 5), parental rights (Article 6), educational rights (Article 7), freedom of assembly (Article 8) and association (Article 9), privacy of posts and telecommunications (Article 10), freedom of movement (Article 11), occupational rights (Article 12), the right to conscientious objection (Article 12a), inviolability of the home (Article 13), and the right to property (Article 14). Articles 15, 16, 16a, and 17 deal, respectively, with public ownership, citizenship, asylum, and the right of petition. Article 18 provides for the forfeiture of certain basic rights if they are used to threaten Germany's political democracy. Article 19, finally, emphasizes the value of these guaranteed rights by declaring that "in no case may [the state] encroach upon the content of a basic right."

These rights, however, have been proclaimed with an important German twist: they are to be exercised responsibly and used to foster human dignity within the framework of ordered liberty. The Basic Law reflects a conscious ordering of individual freedom and the public interest. It resounds with the language of human freedom, but a freedom restrained by certain political values, community norms, and ethical principles. Its image of man is one rooted in and defined by a certain kind of human community. Yet in the German constitutionalist view the person is also a transcendent being far more important than any collectivity. Thus there is a sense in which the Basic Law is both contractarian and communitarian in its foundation: contractarian in that the Constitution carves out an area of human freedom that neither government, private groups, nor individuals may touch; communitarian in the sense that every German citizen is under the obligation to abide, at least in his overt behavior, by the values and principles of the moral and political order. The

Federal Constitutional Court must both safeguard the values of the constitutional order and defend the rights of individuals against governmental intrusion.

The materials in part 3 are devoted to significant constitutional cases in the field of civil rights and liberties. Chapter 6 takes up property and occupational rights, a subject far more prominent in German than in American constitutional law because the Basic Law confers on all Germans the right freely to choose their occupation and place of work. Several cases featured in this chapter, like some of those covered in the previous chapter on voting rights and political parties, are important because they implicate the principle of equality and illustrate the Constitutional Court's approach to its interpretation. Chapter 7 covers a wide variety of cases relating to personal inviolability and individual autonomy. Several of these cases could just as easily have been placed in other chapters, but their inclusion here instead underscores the importance that the Constitutional Court attaches to the general values of person-hood and human dignity.

Chapter 8 focuses on freedom of expression. It deals mainly with political speech and recalls notes already sounded in the section on political parties in chapter 5. Landmark cases on speech and personality also reemphasize lines of thought running through the cases in chapter 7. These overlapping themes illustrate the extent to which two or more constitutional values may converge in a single case. Chapter 8 includes a section on the mass media and concludes with artistic expression. Chapter 9, finally, includes leading cases on church-state relations and religious liberty. It also includes a section on rights associated with marriage and parenthood. These materials do not involve judicial interpretations of the religious clauses of Article 9, but they are nevertheless important for a wider understanding of the role played by religious values and social morality in German constitutionalism.

6

ECONOMIC LIBERTIES

Germans often describe their economic system as a "social market economy" (*soziale Marktwirtschaft*).¹ An outgrowth of German neoliberal and Catholic social thought, the social market economy is predicated on a belief in the compatibility of a free market with a socially conscious state. It seeks to promote a unified political economy based on the principles of personal freedom and social responsibility. But the freedom of the individual and the responsibility of the state are constrained by the constitutional framework within which the economy operates. This framework includes the rights of property and inheritance (Article 14), freedom of choice in the exercise of a trade or profession (Article 12), freedom to form and join economic or trade associations (Article 9 [3]), freedom of commerce and industry flowing from the general right to personality (Article 2), and the principle of the social welfare state (*Sozialstaat*). The principle of the social welfare state is of particular importance because it establishes the boundaries and infuses the meaning of all economic rights created by the Basic Law.² As noted earlier in this volume, the *Sozialstaat* is anchored in two constitutional clauses: Article 20 defines Germany as a "social federal state," and Article 28 (1) requires the states to adopt a constitutional regime faithful to "the principles of republican, democratic, and *social government based on the rule of law*" (emphasis added). The italicized words are a loose translation of *sozialer Rechtsstaat,* a more succinct rendering of which is "social legal state."

Rechtsstaat and *Sozialstaat* thus join in a higher unity under the Basic Law.³ The first, a concept rooted in bourgeois liberalism, protects the individual *from* the state; the second, rooted in the needs of modern industrial society, obligates the state to construct a just social order. In the understanding of some commentators, the *Sozialstaat* places social rights on the same constitutional footing as civil rights.⁴ But the Basic Law is largely silent with regard to the nature of social rights. The entitlement of "every mother . . . to the protection and care of the community" (Article 6 [4]) and the provisions in Article 15 for the nationalization of property are two exceptions to this general silence. Most of the rights expressly secured in the First Section (Articles 1–19) of the Basic Law are rights associated with the tradition of liberal democracy. When the Basic Law was created in 1949, the German public mind appeared committed first and foremost to the *Rechtsstaat*. In its new incarnation under the Basic Law, the *Rechtsstaat* was to be based on law and justice,[5] two standards appearing to need special protection at the time in the light of their debasement by the Nazis.

Nevertheless, the *Sozialstaat* is an established principle of German public law, and it has a good pedigree in German constitutional history.[6] The social welfare provisions of the Basic Law, including the social obligation attached to the right of property, occasioned little debate in the Parliamentary Council.[7] A variety of reasons account for the Constitution's lack of specificity on social rights. The economic liberals among the framers preferred the broad language already alluded to, socialists were confident that a progressive social agenda could be set in place by ordinary legislation under the general rubric of the *Sozialstaat,* and still others were leery of freezing a particular social or economic program into the Constitution. Little wonder, then, that in the march of time the exact content of the *Sozialstaat* has become a matter of dispute among constitutional lawyers and commentators.[8]

The Federal Constitutional Court, on the other hand, has repeatedly called attention to the fundamentality of the social state clause and has often reminded the federation and the states of their constitutional duty to establish a just social order.[9] It has been reluctant, however, to lay down guidelines for the realization of socioeconomic rights or the achievement of other social goals. In this "legal and economic-political realm," the court has said, "the legislature enjoys wide-ranging discretion,"[10] a latitude extending to the nature and extent of the social welfare to be provided as well as the means of its promotion and delivery.[11] And so, while the social welfare state clause has some bite, it does not appear to cut very deeply on behalf of individual litigants seeking relief under its terms. The clause has been used to much greater effect in justifying social welfare legislation against the objection that it interferes with classical individual freedoms such as the right to property.

THE NATURE OF THE ECONOMIC SYSTEM

"The Bonn Basic Law," wrote Ernst Karl Pakuscher, "does not reflect a specific economic system. Thus, it is lawful for the legislature to pursue any economic policy which it deems feasible. Even a socialized economy would not violate the Constitution, since Article 15 allows it under specific conditions."[12] This view is correct, as Pakuscher recognized, but only up to a point, for all economic policies must be enacted within the parameters and in the light of the values of the Constitution. The neo-Marxist claim that the principle of the social state permits the transformation of West Germany into a full-blown socialist society strains the meaning of the Basic Law.[13] Equally untenable is the more influential conservative claim that the Basic Law throws up an impenetrable barrier to socialist legislation.[14] The Federal Constitutional Court's view falls somewhere between these extremes. It proclaims the fundamental neutrality of the Basic Law with respect to economic policy, but undergirds this view with certain assumptions about the nature of man and his relationship to the larger society, in a sense combining elements of the *Rechtsstaat* with those of the *Sozialstaat*.

NOTE: SOCIETY AND ECONOMY IN REUNITED GERMANY. The State Treaty of May 18, 1990, on Monetary, Economic, and Social Union was a major step toward German reunification. The treaty united the social economies of eastern and western Germany within the framework of the FRG's social market economy. It introduced the FRG's currency (DM) into the GDR; incorporated the GDR's command economy into an established and affluent market economy; and transformed an obsolete and inefficient system of industrial management into one of private ownership, competition, and the free movement of goods, capital, and services. The immediate conversion of a planned into a free enterprise economy caused considerable adversity in the GDR, including factory closings, high rates of unemployment, dismissal of personnel from the civil service and other state institutions, and the loss of social benefits not available in the FRG's social welfare state (*Sozialstaat*).[15] These dislocations and other disruptions arising from the policy of restoring expropriated property to their former owners generated a large number of constitutional complaints. Leading cases stemming from these complaints are discussed in subsequent notes.

6.1 Investment Aid I Case (1954)
4 BVerfGE 7

[After World War II the iron and coal industries lacked the necessary capital to finance their reconstruction. On the recommendation of the Common Market the federal parliament enacted the Investment Aid Act in 1952 (as amended in 1953) for the purpose of creating an investment fund to benefit these industries. The fund was created by compulsory contributions from the profits of other manufacturers and traders. Several corporations filed a constitutional complaint, claiming that the legislation imposed a special tax on them in violation of Articles 1, 2, 3, 9, 14, 15, 20, 70, 110, and 115 of the Basic Law.]

Judgment of the First Senate. . . .

D. First, the complainants attack the legislation as a whole.

    1. Some argue that the federal government had no authority to pass this law. The court has already decided this question. . . . The administration derives the

authority for this legislation from Article 74 (11) of the Basic Law. The content and history of this section do not support the interpretation that the legislative authority of the federation is limited to areas of merely organizational import or to the regulation of legal relations of those branches of the economy which are mentioned separately in Article 74 (11). Rather, under Article 74 (11), the federation may also pass laws that intervene in economic life with the purpose of ordering and directing that life. The Investment Aid Act is such a law. Its purpose is to channel capital for investment purposes from one area of the economy to another. . . .

[A. The Basic Law's Image of Man]

2. Complainants allege a violation of the constitutional guarantee of free development of personality because of an alleged limitation on their free entrepreneurial initiative. Article 2 (1) of the Basic Law is not violated. . . . If one views Article 2 (1) only as a limited protection of human freedom without which man cannot exist as a spiritual and moral person, the investment aid law does not reach this area at all. The statute does not touch the autonomous entrepreneurial personality. If one sees in this constitutional right a comprehensive guarantee for freedom of action, such a freedom can, in principle, exist only to the extent that it violates neither the rights of others, nor the constitutional order, nor morality. The image of man in the Basic Law is not that of an isolated, sovereign individual. On the contrary, the Basic Law has resolved the tension between individual and society in favor of coordination and interdependence with the community without touching the intrinsic value of the person. This principle follows from a comprehensive review of Articles 1, 2, 12, 14, 15, 19, and 20 of the Basic Law. The individual has to accept those limits on his freedom of action which the legislature imposes to cultivate and maintain society. In turn, such acceptance depends upon the limits of what can reasonably be demanded in a particular case, provided the autonomy of the person is preserved. The Investment Aid Act falls within these limits. No "charged debtor" is prevented from developing his personality in this sense, even if the law temporarily limits his authority to dispose of the means of production and forces him to enter a legal relationship with certain entrepreneurs. Despite such limitations, there remains ample opportunity for free development of responsible entrepreneurship. . . .

[B. Neutrality of Economy]

5. Complainants further allege that division of the economy into firms which give and those which receive violates the constitutional principle of equality as well as the principle of neutrality in economic policy and the customary economic and social order. Plaintiffs also allege that investment aid is incongruous with a market economy.

The Basic Law guarantees neither the neutrality of the executive or legislative power in economic matters nor a "social market economy." . . . The Basic Law's neutrality in economic matters consists merely in the fact that the "constituent power" has not adopted a specific economic system. This omission enables the legislature to pursue economic policies deemed proper for the circumstances, provided the Basic Law is observed.

Although the present economic and social order is . . . consistent with the Basic Law, it is by no means the only one possible. It is based upon a political decision sustained by the will of the legislature which can be substituted or superseded by a different decision. Consequently, it is constitutionally irrelevant whether the Investment Aid Act fits in with the existing economic and social order and whether the means employed for guiding the economy are congruent with a market system. . . .

The Constitutional Court is not authorized to judge the wisdom of legislation. . . . The Constitutional Court must examine such measures only to the extent of determining whether the legislature has observed the ultimate limits of its discretionary power and whether it has abused that power. . . . The principle of equality does not extend the authority of review granted to the Constitutional Court. The yardstick of Article 3 (1) always remains the same. If one applies this yardstick to the Investment Aid Act, it becomes evident that the legislature did not transgress the ultimate limits of its discretionary power. In this context one has to realize that every directive measure more or less restricts the free play of market forces. . . . In principle, the constitutional authority even includes power to pass laws in the interest of particular groups. Such laws must, however, be aimed at the public welfare, and they must not neglect the interests of others which are worth protecting. The Investment Aid Act makes allowances for such considerations. The charged debtors receive bonds for the amount of their contributions. Those bonds will yield interest and perhaps even dividends. . . . The economic interests of the charged debtors are consequently not arbitrarily impaired even if their own demands for investment must be deferred. . . . Because no violation of the Basic Law has been established, the constitutional complaints must be dismissed as unfounded.

NOTE: TAXATION AND SPECIAL LEVIES. In the years since *Investment Aid I* the Constitutional Court has severely scrutinized special taxes earmarked for particular purposes over long periods of time. Such levies are usually enacted outside the framework of annual budgetary appropriations, which invites the charge that they weaken parliament's control over the allocation of annual tax revenues — thus undermining democratic accountability — and bestow special privileges on the recipients of such levies as well as a special burden on those who must pay them. Professor Paul Kirchhof, Germany's leading tax authority and currently a justice of the Federal Constitutional Court, has noted: "An earmarked levy is a rare exception in the financial system of a State governed by the rule of law and bound by the principle of equality, because [in part it] contradicts the principle of general equality of burdens."[16] This is now the prevailing view of the Constitutional Court.[17] A special levy will survive constitutional analysis if it is justified by a compelling state interest and if its satisfies certain tests of facticity and accountability.[18]

The *Coal Penny* case (1994) is the most recent example of an invalid special levy. Since 1975, the so-called *Kohlepfennig* (coal penny) has been collected as a surcharge on the electricity bills of private households. These revenues, which in 1994 amounted to DM 7.3 billion, were used to offset the price difference between domestic and imported hard coal. The tax was used to subsidize German hard coal to bring the price more in line with world market levels. According to the court's ruling, the coal penny placed an unconstitutional burden on consumers of electricity, thus making this single group bear the expense of satisfying the general interest in the use of coal for the production of electricity. In yet another manifestation of resolute judicial authority, the court instructed parliament to abolish the tax by January 1, 1996.[19]

NOTE: TAX LEGISLATION AND CONSTITUTIONAL LITIGATION. Tax policy has been a major subject of constitutional adjudication in Germany, owing in part to the detailed provisions in the Basic Law on fiscal administration and the apportionment of tax revenue between the federal government and the states. (The tax revenue cases are treated in the section on cooperative federalism in chapter 2.) In addition, several tax laws have been struck down for violating the general equality clause of Article 3 and the marriage and family provisions of Article 6. (For a discussion of the Article 6 cases, see the section on marriage and family rights in chapter 9.)

The *Interest Tax* case (1991), which also implicates the principle of equality, is a classic example of the extent to which tax legislation in Germany is subject to constitutional review. Under German tax law, some interest income was taxable and other interest income — for example, interest payments from banks — was not taxable. The law was also unclear as to when interest income was to be reported for tax purposes and when not, leaving the taxpayer with considerable discretion in reporting his taxable income. In still another illustration of an admonitory decision, the Second Senate held that current tax provisions related to interest income would be held invalid unless parliament corrected the constitutional deficiency by a fixed date. The court emphasized that the tax burden on all taxpayers must be legally and factually equal and that parliament must adopt procedural measures to guarantee an equal tax burden on income from interest payments.[20]

NOTE: NEUTRALITY AND INDUSTRIAL RELATIONS. The Basic Law contains few provisions on the structure of the economic system. The economy may be organized, it seems, in any manner that does not encroach, in the words of Article 19 (2), on the "essential content of a basic right," including the right to property under Article 14. There is a general consensus in Germany that government has a major responsibility for the direction and organization of the economy. Government intervention in the economy is considerable, taking the form of massive investments in industry and major regulatory policies such as the Restraint of Trade Act of 1957, the Economic

Stabilization Act of 1967, and the Codetermination Acts of 1951 and 1976.[21] Yet the relationship between government and industry implicates constitutional concerns that in most other Western democracies are strictly matters of public policy. This is due in part to numerous provisions of the Basic Law that define the government's interest in property.[22] On the other hand, the Basic Law guarantees the right to property (Article 14), the right to choose an occupation (Article 12), and the rights to freedom of contract and economic competition under the Constitutional Court's interpretation of Article 2.[23]

Contending that these personal rights cannot coexist with massive investments by government in private industry or with large state-owned enterprises operating under the rules of a market economy, some commentators have questioned the legitimacy of state-operated commercial activities.[24] While the principle of neutrality leaves much in this field to legislative discretion, the Constitutional Court has observed that "a state economic monopoly is a foreign body in a free economy; such monopolies not only interfere with [economic] activities that individuals could carry out voluntarily, but they also impinge resolutely upon the free development of broader aspects of the economy."[25] The court has uttered similar sentiments with respect to certain economic regulations,[26] a view which in the opinion of one leading scholar "allows the Government actively to carry out . . . economic policies by fiscal means, in fulfillment of its *social-political functions,* without, however, allowing it to interfere with constitutionally protected private activities" (emphasis added).[27]

In spite of these assertions and the *obiter dicta* about "foreign bodies" in the stream of commerce, the Constitutional Court continues to approach general economic policy with great restraint and is unlikely to risk the political backlash that would probably greet significant judicial intervention in this field. In the landmark *Codetermination* case (1978; no. 6.6) the court reiterated the doctrine of neutrality by refusing to treat the social market economy as a constitutionally prescribed principle.[28] According to management, the coparticipation of labor in the management of industry would interfere not only with individual rights essential to entrepreneurial activity but also with the substantive guarantees of the Basic Law. The court's answer, supported in part by the principles of the *Sozialstaat,* was that while the legislature's discretion in shaping the economy is surely bound by the Basic Law, the latter does not incorporate any particular economic framework of organization prior to or independent of guaranteed individual rights. In the court's view, the legislature may pursue any economic policy it chooses so long as particular fundamental rights of the Basic Law are taken into account. Commentators have pointed to the *Volkswagen Denationalization* case (1961) as still another illustration of this posture of neutrality. Article 15 of the Basic Law permits the public ownership of land, natural resources, and the means of production "by a law which shall provide for the nature of and extent of compensation." But if an industry is nationalized under this provision, may it be denationalized at a later time? This was a key issue in *Volkswagen.*

6.2 Volkswagen Denationalization Case (1961)
12 BVerfGE 354

[After World War II the federal government and the state of Lower Saxony inherited the Volkswagen Company. In 1960, with the consent of Lower Saxony, the federal parliament enacted a law denationalizing the firm through the public sale of 60 percent of its stock. To encourage wide public ownership, the statute provided for the sale of the stock at reduced value, limited the number of shares any one person could buy, and allowed the firm's employees to purchase the bulk of the stock. Several groups of people brought constitutional complaints against the denationalization statute, claiming violations of Article 15 and of the principle of equality.]

———————

Judgment of the First Senate. . . .

IV. [A. A Permissible Public Sale]

1. Complainants desire a better position within the framework of denationalization. Before this concern can be examined, the court must decide whether denationalization itself is constitutional. This ruling is imperative not only because of the measure's broad significance for the political system but also because of the effect of such a decision on other cases.

(a) No constitutional principle prohibits sale of purely economic enterprises owned by the federation. This measure lies within the discretion of the federation's political organs, as long as its implementation does not violate constitutional law and, in particular, basic rights [citing the *Investment Aid I* case]. . . . In a modern liberal state different views will always exist as to what broad economic and social policy and what specific measures serve the public interest. The objectives of denationalization may not find general approval; the measure itself may even be partially intended to win the approval of circles which presently still reject the idea. . . . But that sort of compromise cannot be excluded where social, political, or economic measures are concerned. Political compromise is probably inevitable in a modern state that is forced to intervene in social life, and it should not be disapproved for constitutional reasons. . . . In any event, a court cannot, with binding force for the general public, rule that denationalization of Volkswagen cannot serve the public interest. This principle of restraint would apply even if serious doubts existed as to whether the goals pursued . . . could be achieved by means of acquisition of stocks. . . . Confirmation or refutation of the rightness of such measures by their later success or failure is a matter for which responsible political organs will be debited or credited.

[B. The Socialization of Property]

Neither does Article 15 of the Basic Law contain anything to impede dena-

tionalization of Volkswagen. This article contains no constitutional order to social-
ize the economy, but only an authorization for the legislature to do so. Whether and
to what extent the legislature makes use of this authorization must be left to its
political discretion. . . . We must therefore reject the view that enterprises that could
be socialized according to Article 15 cannot be "denationalized" again when they are
public property. Also, one cannot deduce a "tendency toward socialization" from
Article 15, meaning that the legislature, if it wants to regulate property conditions in
branches of the economy which may be socialized, can do so only in the direction
toward socialization. Such fundamental restrictions on the legislature's freedom of
decision in economic policy follow neither from the words nor from the genesis and
the meaning of the provision.

(b) The fundamental constitutionality of denationalization does not exempt
the federation from the obligation . . . to seek an adequate price when selling public
property. Establishment of an adequate price may often be difficult. . . . But if special
goals are pursued along with the sale — e.g., goals of an economic or sociopolitical
nature — deviation from the market price may be justified. So-called political considerations may then also be taken into account if the decision remains within certain
limits and if the principles of a state based on the rule of law are adhered to.
Accordingly, regulation of the sale of Volkswagen stock is not constitutionally
objectionable.

(aa) As the oral proceedings have shown, competent agencies of the federation
proceeded from the assumption that the true value of the enterprise must be the
basis for deciding the sale price of the original stock. To determine this value several
experts whose knowledge and authority are recognized were asked to write detailed
estimates. . . . The responsible federal agencies have adhered to the framework of
considerations which are clearly the basis for the law itself; namely, a compromise
between the optimum capital for the Volkswagen Foundation from high sales proceeds, on the one hand, and certain general sociopolitical purposes, on the other.

In assessing this procedure and its results, the court cannot conclude that the
federal government abused its discretion, even if one acknowledges that the true
value — and thus also the sale price — could have been set higher according to available expert opinions.

The fact that in the open market the price of Volkswagen stock has in the
meantime risen to more than double the sale price does not prove anything to the
contrary. This development was hardly predictable at the time the sale price was
fixed. Prices of stocks . . . are affected by numerous circumstances that often have
nothing to do with the real value of individual stocks, but arise, for example, from
mere speculation. But the law's intent was to interest exactly those persons in acquir-
ing permanent portfolios who would not have been able to buy the stocks if they
had been sold to the highest bidder. Under these circumstances it would hardly have
been justifiable to let the sale price be influenced by the possibility of a considerably
higher market rate. . . .

[In the last section of its opinion the court ruled that the stock sale was consistent with the general equality clause of Article 3. "Government regulations favoring individual groups . . . are permissible," the court said, "if reasonable grounds exist for such distinctions."]

THE RIGHT TO PROPERTY

Article 14 (1) states: "Property and the right of inheritance are guaranteed. Their content and limits shall be determined by the laws." In reading this provision, one is prompted to ask whether the state can later take back by law what the Constitution confers. The content and limits clause, however, is in turn limited by Article 19 (2), which provides that the state "may not encroach upon the essential content of a basic right." In addition, any restriction of a basic right must be, under the terms of Article 19, "by or pursuant to a law" and "must apply generally and not solely to an individual case" and "name the basic right" that is being restricted. Thus, any limitation of the right to property under Article 14 (1) has to contend with the requirements of Article 19 (2). In short, the content and limits of property cannot be redefined in such a way as to interfere with the essence of the right. Property is nevertheless subject to other limitations specified in Article 14. First, there is a social duty associated with the ownership of property. "Property imposes duties," according to paragraph 2, and "its use should also serve the public weal" (words and phrases with exact equivalents, incidentally, in the Weimar Constitution). Second, and according to paragraph 3, property may be taken by "expropriation," but "only in the public weal" and "by or pursuant to a law which shall provide for the nature and extent of the compensation." (American fundamental law, by contrast, does not impose duties on private property or provide that it serve the common good.) The general significance of the right to property and the principles governing the interpretation of Article 14 are set forth in the *Hamburg Flood Control* case.

6.3 Hamburg Flood Control Case (1968)
24 BVerfGE 367

[Owing to damage caused by an enormous flood in 1962, the city-state of Hamburg passed the Dikes and Embankments Act of 1964. The act provided for the conversion of all grassland classified as "dikeland" in the land register into public property. It terminated all private rights over the property and provided compensation to the owners. Several owners of the dikeland property filed constitutional complaints alleging a violation of their fundamental right under Article 14.]

Judgment of the First Senate. . . .

D. I. 1. Article 14 (1) [1] of the Basic Law guarantees property both as a legal institution and as a concrete right held by the individual owner. To hold property is an elementary constitutional right which must be seen in close context with the protection of personal liberty. Within the general system of constitutional rights, its function is to secure for its holder a sphere of liberty in the economic field and thereby enable him to lead a self-governing life. The protection of property as a legal institution serves to secure this basic right. [And] this constitutional right of the individual is conditioned upon the legal institution of "property." Property could not be effectively secured if lawmakers were empowered to replace private property with something no longer deserving the label "ownership." . . . The regulation of property may be adjusted to social and economic conditions. The legislature's task is to regulate property in the light of fundamental constitutional values. The institutional guarantee, however, prohibits any revision of the private legal order which would remove the fundamental catalog of constitutionally protected activities relating to the area of property and which would substantially curtail or suspend the protected sphere of liberty protected by this fundamental right. . . .

[Despite these broad principles protective of the property right, the court went on to hold that the state could legitimately place the dikeland properties under public control. The taking of the lands near the dike did not constitute an abridgment of the right to property guaranteed by Article 14 (1) [1] so long as the property was to be used for a particular public purpose. The public purpose standard was satisfied here because of the pressing need to build an effective system of dikes and embankments to avert a disaster similar to the one that hit Hamburg in 1962. The following extracts underscore the importance of the public purpose doctrine.]

E. III. 1. (a) . . . Article 14 (3) permits the expropriation of real property if the common good requires it. [But] the overriding standard of the common good limits the legal power to take property ordinarily within the protection of Article 14. This standard — and only this standard — permits an expropriation of property under Article 14 (3). . . . The object of a valid taking under Article 14 (3) must be clearly specified in the law. The Basic Law establishes that in the recurring tension between the property interest of the individual and the needs of the public, the public interest may, in case of conflict, take precedence over the legally guaranteed position of the individual. . . . The Constitution does not leave the resolution of this conflict to the legislature but settles the issue itself. If all these relationships are borne in mind, then Article 14 (3) [2], which permits expropriation "only by or pursuant to a law," does not contain a proviso empowering the legislature to restrict the basic right, as required by the terms of Article 19 (1).

(b) The terms of Article 14 (3) [1] [the "common good" requirement] limit the taking of property under the terms of Article 14 (3) [2] [the "by law" and "compensation" requirements]. . . . If these requirements are not met, the basic right to property is violated. The owner's duty to tolerate an intrusion against his right to property is limited to the terms established by the Constitution itself. These limits are fixed and permanent. The legislature is not empowered to change them.

Beyond all this, the right to property as specified in Article 14 (3) is secured by the fact that property may not be taken in the absence of just compensation. The core guarantee under a permissible expropriation is the value of the property in question. Thus the state is obligated to compensate owners whose special rights and privileges are forcibly sacrificed for the common good. If compensation is not compatible with the requirements of Article 14 (3) [3], then the basic right is violated, resulting in an unconstitutional expropriation. By the same token, the legislature is powerless to restrict or deny adequate compensation as provided by the Constitution.

It is essential to understand that the property right guaranteed by Article 14 has far-reaching significance going well beyond the protection afforded by the Weimar Constitution. The function of Article 14 is not primarily to prevent the taking of property without compensation — although in this respect it offers greater protection than Article 153 of the Weimar Constitution — but rather to secure existing property in the hands of its owners. The view propounded under the Weimar Constitution, and to some extent also under Article 14, is that the property guarantee is essentially a guarantee of the value of property and that its expropriation is acceptable so long as the parties are adequately compensated. Yet this view does not reflect the [full] purpose and spirit of Article 14. Because the Weimar Constitution had no provisions for testing the constitutionality of expropriation laws, and because judicial review was [severely] restricted, the judiciary had to be concerned primarily with protecting property owners through compensation. Thus the basic right [of property] emerged more and more into a demand for adequate compensation. By contrast, as already pointed out, the property guarantee under Article 14 (1) [2] must be seen in relationship to the personhood of the owner — i.e., to the realm of freedom within which persons engage in self-defining, responsible activity. The property right is not primarily a material but rather a personal guarantee. The basic right protects the individual against every unjustified infringement of the entire range of protected goods.

NOTE: THE GERMAN APPROACH TO PROPERTY RIGHTS. The *Flood Control* case is important because it underscores the social function of property under the Basic Law. Particularly emphasized in German constitutional law is the subjective character of the property right: Property is associated with liberty and personhood; it provides space for the exercise of autonomy and self-realization. Accordingly, as

Flood Control points out, the state may not change the Civil Code in a way that would constrict or obliterate the core of this freedom. It follows, therefore, that restrictions on property must also respect the constitutional value of personhood underlying individual ownership. The court also requires that any restriction on property be consistent with other basic values of the Constitution, such as the principle of equal protection.[29] *Flood Control,* however, also underlines the institutional character of property. Property in this sense, like other basic decisions of the founding fathers, is an autonomous legal institution, or, to use the standard alternative formulation, an objective constitutional value that the state is obliged affirmatively to preserve and foster. Exactly and precisely what positive duty the state has under this theory has never been laid out in full. But some commentators have suggested recently that the objective character of Article 14 may require environmental protection legislation to preserve the value of property the productive use of which depends on clean water and unspoiled forests.[30]

The social obligation of property. Property, according to Article 14 (2), "imposes duties" and "should serve the public weal." An earlier draft by the Parliamentary Council that harbors the intent of this broad language reads: "Ownership entails a social obligation. Its use shall find its limits in the living necessities of all citizens and in the public order essential to society."[31] This would suggest that the legislature has been given a wide berth for the regulation of property in the public interest. Property may not be used to damage the public interest, just as it may be regulated in the public interest. Yet the regulation of property, as already seen, may not infringe on the essence of ownership. The core of one of the Basic Law's objective values, such as the right to property, may not be infringed even in the interest of social duty.[32] The public interest may have to give way if the power of eminent domain is used to interfere with rights rooted in personhood. For example, the condemnation of private property may fundamentally change the structure of important social and personal relationships. The collectivization of agriculture is possibly one example of such a fundamental change. In this situation, as George Fletcher has suggested, "Article 19 (2) [may possibly] deny to the government the power to recast these relationships, even if it left the wealth of the affected individuals intact."[33]

The standards governing the attempt to balance public and private interests in the field of regulation have actually been worked out by the High Court of Justice for Civil Matters and the Federal Administrative Court.[34] The two main principles involved here are individual sacrifice and regulatory intensity. (The High Court of Justice has tended to emphasize the first, the Federal Administrative Court the second.) If the burden of a regulation falls heavily on an individual owner, depriving him of the use of his property, and if all benefits of the regulation are claimed by the public, the state is then obligated to compensate the owner. On the other hand, no compensation is due if a uniformly imposed regulation confers benefits on all owners while exacting limited costs from all for the sake of the common good. Considerations of equality undergird these approaches. Simply put, the state acts unfairly if it forces a single individual to sacrifice his essential rights for the public good,[35] but if an individual affected by a general regulation is part of the public, and if he benefits from the regulation, he is also expected to bear its costs, in which case his loss is not compensable.

The Federal Constitutional Court has declined to place primary emphasis on one or the other of these principles; it considers them in tandem.[36] The court's essential position, as articulated in the *Vineyard* case (1967),[37] is that property can be regulated but not to an intolerable degree. In *Vineyard* the court sustained a federal restriction on the cultivation of new vineyards not only because the regulation helped to maintain the quality of German wine, but also because it contributed to the economic position of the German wine industry as a whole, particularly grape growers. The burden imposed by the regulation was therefore not excessive. Property, as *Flood Control* shows, is subject to public regulation and taking under the Basic Law. The Constitutional Court has insisted, however, on independently assessing what constitutes a public interest within the meaning of the expropriation clause (Article 14 [3]). In *Flood Control* the court validated the taking of dikeland properties because they were to be used for a particular public purpose. According to Article 14 (3), the extent of compensation "shall be determined by establishing an equitable balance between the public interest and the interests of those affected." The general rule in Germany is that the taking of private property is admissible only when adequate compensation is paid.[38]

The content and limits of property. Article 14 (2) confers on the legislature the authority to determine the "content and limits" of property. Yet, under the terms of Article 19 (2), the Constitutional Court is required to define the essence of the property right if the freedom associated with it is to be protected. The court has tended to approach this problem of definition by considering the property guarantee within the framework of the Constitution as a whole.[39] In reality, however, it has relied more heavily on the historical development of the concept of property in the Civil Code than on any systematic or teleological approach to constitutional interpretation.[40]

In regulating the "content and limits" of property under Article 14 (1), the legislature is required by the Federal Constitutional Court to accord due weight to the framers' fundamental value decision in favor of private property. As with other fundamental rights, balancing is again the order of the day, for any such regulation is subject to certain overarching values that inform the meaning of the entire Constitution. These are the principles of human dignity, personality, and equality, which are enshrined, respectively, in the first three articles of the Basic Law. The legislature's responsibility is to bring these values into some kind of working balance, albeit with a heavy thumb on the property right side of the scale. Finally, the principles of proportionality (*Verhältnismässigkeit*), rule of law (*Rechtsstaatlichkeit*), and social justice (*Sozialstaatlichkeit*) must be fed into the equation. The function of the Constitutional Court in reviewing an alleged intrusion into the right of property is to determine whether lawmakers have adequately considered and properly weighed these competing values.

Other cases illustrate the manner in which the court has adjudicated these often conflicting values. In the *Small Garden Plot* case (1979),[41] the court struck down a federal statute that sought to limit the right of landowners to terminate garden plot leases. Garden plots rented from landowners on the fringes of large cities were a major feature of German social organization and once played a large role in feeding the population. The legislature felt that limiting the landowners' right to terminate garden plot leases was consistent with the social duty of property and an emerging national policy against urban sprawl. But in the light of changed economic conditions and developments in commercial agriculture, the burden on the property owner was deemed by the court to be too heavy relative to the value of the protected interest. In the *Landlord-Tenant* case (1993), on the other hand, the court declared that the right of a tenant to live in a rented apartment constitutes "property" within the meaning of Article 14 (1). The *Landlord* case protects the tenant against termination of a rental contract that is not based on a well-founded interest of the landlord and specified in the contract.[42]

In the *Tenancy and Rent Control* case (1974),[43] the court invalidated several lower court decisions for the similarly harsh manner in which a federal rent control statute had been applied to owners of rental dwelling units. But at the same time the court announced that the social obligation related to property requires lawmakers to accord equal weight to the interests of tenants and owners in defining their respective rights under law. The *Thalidomide* case (1976),[44] on the other hand, is a dramatic example of an important social concern overriding a claim based on a traditional property right. *Thalidomide* sustained a federal plan of benefits to children seriously deformed by a drug marketed in Germany, thus nullifying settlement agreements under private law that did not provide for the special needs of these handicapped children.

In the *Feldmühle* case (1962),[45] finally, the court sustained the validity of a company reorganization statute permitting majority shareholders who owned more than three-fourths of the capital stock of a joint-stock company to convert it into a new company over the objection of minority stockholders. Because the legislature was acting in the general interest by fostering the creation of larger business enterprises, said the court, the three-fourths conversion rule was not "manifestly out of proportion to the severity of the encroachment on the property interest of minority shareholders."

NOTE: PROPERTY AND GERMAN UNIFICATION. On June 15, 1990, the two German governments issued the Joint Declaration on the Settlement of Open Property Issues, an agreement to return expropriated property in the GDR to its original owners or their heirs. Incorporated into the Unification Treaty as Exhibit III,[46] the agreement covered seized businesses and real estate — nearly all the industrial and landed property in the GDR. Property placed under state administration in consequence of forced emigration, renunciation, flight to West Germany, and nonconsensual sale or property appropriated by the state was also to be restored to former owners under the general policy of *Rückgabe vor Entschädigung* (restitution before compensation).[47] Compensation, however, was available as an option.

The joint declaration, however, contained a major exception to the policy of restitution; namely, property seized during the Soviet occupation (May 8, 1945 to October 6, 1949). The Soviet Union and the GDR flatly refused to undo these takings, which chiefly involved the uncompensated seizure of large industrial enterprises and agricultural holdings of 250 acres or more, the latter having been distributed to poor farmers and organized into agricultural production cooperatives. The Soviet Union would not have signed the final peace treaty without this concession on the part of the Allies and the FRG. Former owners of land in eastern Germany challenged the treaty's exemption clause on the ground that it violated their right to property secured by Article 14 (3), their right to equality under Article 3 (1), and the rule of law, an unamendable principle laid down in Article 79 (3).

On April 23, 1991, the Constitutional Court affirmed the validity of the exemption clauses.[48] The decision was an exercise in judicial pragmatism. Faced with the Soviet Union's nonnegotiable stance against any rollback of properties expropriated during the occupation, the court accepted the government's argument that the exemption was a compromise necessary to achieve the higher constitutional goal of reunification.[49] Equally important, the court sustained the validity of Article 143 over the objection that it amounted to an unconstitutional amendment to the Basic Law.[50] (Petitioners claimed that Article 143 eroded the "core" values of Articles 1 and 20.) In point of international law, finally, the court noted that Germany was not responsible for the takings between 1945 and 1949, that the properties were subject to a legal system other than that of the FRG, and that in any event the Basic Law did not enter into force until after the property had been taken.[51]

Many of the related property cases to reach the Federal Constitutional Court in the 1990s involved procedural irregularities. For example, the court granted an injunction in favor of the former owner of expropriated GDR property against its present owner, restraining him from building a home on that property, because the civil court below had failed to grant the former owner a hearing on the validity of his claim, thus violating Article 103 of the Basic Law.[52] On large issues of policy, however, the court continued to sustain the political judgments embodied in various laws and treaties. In 1993, the court reaffirmed its 1990 holding that former owners of land expropriated between 1945 and 1949 as part of an agrarian reform program would not have a right to the return of their property.[53] In addition, the court summarily dismissed a claim by a German citizen that the German-Polish Frontier Treaty of 1990 violated his right to property, noting that Germans could no longer lay claim to expropriated or abandoned property they once owned within the present boundaries of Poland.[54] Finally, in rejecting motions for injunctions that would have undermined the general willingness to invest in the former GDR, the court demonstrated considerable sensitivity to the needs of eastern Germany's economy.[55]

NOTE: INTRODUCTION TO THE *GROUNDWATER* CASE. Relying on traditional protections afforded to property owners under the civil code, the Federal Supreme Court questioned the validity of a federal statute interfering with the right of a property owner to dispose of the groundwater under his property, and in the case before it certified the question to the Constitutional Court. In response, the Federal Constitutional Court declared: "The concept of property as guaranteed by the Constitution must be derived from the Constitution itself. This concept of property in the constitutional sense cannot be derived from legal norms (ordinary statutes) lower in rank than the Constitution, nor can the scope of the concrete property guarantee be determined on the basis of private law regulations."[56] *Groundwater,* probably the most important property rights case since *Flood Control,* appears to have eroded the logic of many of the "regulatory takings" cases discussed earlier. Departing from its own previous orientation, by considering property in the light of its historical development under the Civil Code, the court appears to have widened the boundaries of public control.

6.4 Groundwater Case (1981)
58 BVerfGE 300

[*Groundwater* is a leading case in the constitutional law of contemporary property rights. Earlier cases, including the *Flood Control* case, have emphasized the overriding importance of private law in defining the content and limits of property. *Groundwater* is significant because it attaches almost equal weight to public law in setting boundaries to the use of property. The case emerged out of the Federal Water Resources Act in its amended version of October 16, 1976. Designed to preserve public water supplies against contamination or other uses damaging to the public welfare, the statute required any person whose activities affect the quantity or quality of groundwater to procure a permit granted for limited periods and specified purposes sanctioned by law. The plaintiff owned and operated a gravel pit near Münster. For decades he had freely used the groundwater beneath his property for the purpose of extracting gravel. This unlimited use of groundwater was restricted in 1968 with the creation of a new water conservation district by the city of Rheine. The quarry was located within the district and near the city's water wells. Because these wells were threatened by the quarry operation, the city denied the operator a permit to use the water beneath his property. After exhausting his administrative remedies the plaintiff sued North Rhine–

Westphalia for damages, claiming that the denial of the permit for wet gravel extraction violated his right to property as well as his right to pursue his occupation. He won in the lower court but lost in the state appeals court. The Federal High Court of Justice, doubting the compatibility of the Water Resources Act (as amended) with the right to property secured by Article 14, referred the constitutional question to the Federal Constitutional Court.]

Judgment of the First Senate. . . .

[After a lengthy opening discussion of the power of the legislature to regulate property, the distinction between regulating and taking property, the means by which property may be taken, the remedies available in the event of impermissible takings, and the extent of the reviewing authority of administrative and ordinary courts, the Constitutional Court continued.]

C. II. 2. (a) The referring court [Federal High Court of Justice] proceeds on the assumption that groundwater is part of the owner's property and thus within his rights under section 905 of the Civil Code. [Section 905, in part, declares: "The right of the owner to a piece of land extends to the space above the surface and to the terrestrial body under the surface."] The property right here involved includes the right to dispose of the groundwater found on the premises. The Water Resources Act therefore violates the "right which is indigenous to property."

We do not accept this interpretation of the law. . . .

(b) The referring court adheres to the legal view that the right to property encompasses every possible and economically reasonable utilization of that property the content of which is determined by . . . section 903 of the Civil Code. [This section declares: "The owner of a thing may, to the extent that it is not contrary to law or the rights of third parties, deal with the thing as he pleases and exclude others from any interference."] According to this view, the limits imposed by the Water Resources Act on rights secured by private law unduly restrict the right to property. In the eyes of the referring court, the Water Resources Act amounts to an expropriation of property because of the "infringement here of the private sphere." . . .

The legal view that the right to property conferred by section 903 of the Civil Code takes precedence over regulations of public law — a view sanctioned under the Weimar Constitution — contradicts the Basic Law. The concept of property as guaranteed by the Constitution must be derived from the Constitution itself. This concept of property in the constitutional sense cannot be derived from legal norms [ordinary statutes] lower in rank than the Constitution, nor can the scope of the concrete property guarantee be determined on the basis of private law regulations.

The Basic Law assigns to the legislature the task of defining property law in such a way as to protect the interests of the individual and the public. The legislature has a twofold responsibility: first, to make the rules of private law governing the [protection and transfer] of property; and second, to safeguard public interests — in which every citizen has a stake — mainly through regulations of public law. . . . Both private *and* public law contribute equally to the determination of the constitutional *legal position* of the property owner. The corpus of property law represented in the Civil Code does not exclusively define the content and limits of property. . . . The totality of regulations over property that exist at particular points in time determine what rights the property owner concretely enjoys. If these regulations divest the property owner of a certain control over his property, then this control is not included in his right to property. . . .

3. (b) . . . The Water Resources Act does not constitute expropriation by law, as would have been the case under the old Prussian Water Resources Act, which granted to the owner an absolute right to the water beneath his property. The [current] law merely defines for the future and for the entire Federal Republic of Germany, as a matter of objective law, the content of property in relation to ground-water. Such a change in objective law does not result in a deprivation of a concrete legal interest protected by the institutional guarantee of Article 14 (1) and thus does not constitute an expropriation of property. . . .

III. Further examination reveals that the regulations in question properly define the content and limits of the right to property.

1. When defining the content and limits of property under Article 14 (1) the legislature must acknowledge the constitutional right of private ownership in accordance with Article 14 (1) and the social duty attached to property under Article 14 (2). As emphasized repeatedly by the Federal Constitutional Court, the legislature must observe certain [constitutional] standards when curtailing the right to property. The issue here is whether the legislature has violated the right of ownership when it separates the use of groundwater from the right to property.

(a) First of all, we cannot infer from the terms of Article 14 that groundwater must be legally allocated as a matter of principle to the owner of property because of a presumed natural relationship between groundwater and the property on which it is located. The legislature is not bound to adhere to a concept of ownership which would emanate from "the nature of things" when enacting a set of regulations pertaining to property rights in accordance with the Basic Law.

The institutional guarantee of private property does indeed bar lawmakers from modifying or undermining the core of the right to property embedded in private law in such a way as to remove or substantially reduce the realm of freedom guaranteed by Article 14. But the definition of property is not the exclusive domain of private law. The institutional guarantee is not adversely affected when public law intrudes to protect and defend aspects of property vital to the well-being of the general public. . . .

2. The objections raised against these legal regulations rest on the mistaken

assumption that, constitutionally speaking, groundwater is legally inseparable from the right to property.

(a) First, it is incorrect to assume that the Water Resources Act would lead to an "erosion of the substance of the right to property" because it would be subject to "total control in the interest of society." Property ownership does not result in the loss of usufruct simply because the owner's right to use groundwater is subject to governmental approval. The property owner's right has always been primarily the right to use the surface of the property, whereas the right to take material buried in the ground has always been subject to far-reaching restrictions. Even the right to dispose of [surface] property is in many ways subject to constitutional restriction. The possibility of making meaningful economic use of property does not — as a rule — depend on whether or not groundwater can be brought to the surface or [used by the owner]. The constitutionally guaranteed right to property does not permit the owner to make use of exactly that which promises the greatest possible economic advantage. . . .

> [In the next section of the opinion the court found the Water Resources Act consistent with the principle of equality secured by Article 3. The owner had argued that he was required to sustain an undue economic burden merely because of the proximity of his quarry to the municipal water supply, whereas other quarry operators farther away from the water supply were not so burdened.]

D. The findings of the initial proceedings show that the plaintiff has been quarrying gravel since 1936. The decision in this case, therefore, also hinges on whether the Water Resources Act took away a constitutionally protected legal position to which the plaintiff was entitled prior to the enactment of the Water Resources Act. Thus, the earlier legislation as well as the transitional provision of the Water Resources Act must be taken into consideration. . . .

I. . . . The constitutional test must proceed from the fact that the provisions of the Prussian Water Resources Act did not prevent the owner of the property from quarrying gravel and that the guarantee of the right to property protected the right to use groundwater which had been granted and exercised under the old law. It would be incompatible with the content of the Basic Law if the government were authorized, abruptly and without any transitional period, to prevent the continuation of property rights whose exercise had required substantial initial investments. Such a regulation would devalue labor and capital investment from one day to the next. It would upset confidence in the stability of the legal order, without which responsible structuring and planning of life would be impossible in the area of property ownership. . . . [The court found that section 17 of the Water Resources Act provided the owner with sufficient time to adjust to the new regulations. The transitional provisions of the act are mentioned below.]

II. . . . 2. The Water Resources Act is not constitutionally infirm because it denies the right to the stated use of property and fails to provide the grounds for a claim to compensation.

(a) The constitutional guarantee of ownership exercised by the plaintiff does not imply that a property interest, once granted, would have to be preserved in perpetuity or that it could be taken away again only by way of expropriation. The Federal Constitutional Court has repeatedly ruled that the legislature is not faced with the alternative of either preserving old legal positions or taking them away in exchange for compensation every time a legal area is to be regulated anew. Within the framework of Article 14 (1) the legislature may restructure individual legal positions by issuing an appropriate and reasonable transitional rule whenever the public interest merits precedence over some justified confidence — secured by the guarantee of continuity — in the continuance of a vested right. . . .

(c) . . . Moreover, section 17 (1) [1] of the Water Resources Act afforded the rightful claimant the possibility of continuing his unhindered use of groundwater without a permit for another five (5) years after enactment. Because the Water Resources Act was not implemented until 31 months after its enactment, the affected parties had almost eight (8) years during which to adjust to the changed legal position. The deadline was even extended if an application for a permit to continue the use unhindered had been filed. The right to use groundwater without a permit did not terminate in these cases until a final and conclusive decision had been reached on the petition. As a result, the plaintiff in the initial proceedings was able to continue his gravel pit operation unhindered for seventeen years beyond the point in time when the Water Resources Act had been enacted. . . .

With respect to gravel pit operations begun under the provisions of an earlier law, the transitional provision of the current statute is therefore reasonable since it considers sufficiently the interests of the affected party. This applies also to the effects, if any, it had on his business. . . .

NOTE: THE COPYRIGHT CASES. Five controversial cases decided in 1971 established that artistic and other intellectual creations constitute "property" within the meaning of Article 14.[57] But the nature and extent of the right to copyrighted material or patented objects can be determined by the legislature in the public interest. Although the court invalidated regulations denying fees to authors and composers for the reproduction and distribution of their work, it sustained statutory provisions permitting the use of protected material without authorization in certain kinds of educational or cultural contexts. Here, more than in cases dealing with other kinds of property, the court treats the right to property in tandem with the rights of personality and artistic freedom. But the cases also place a heavy accent on the social character of intellectual property. The *Schoolbook* case, the leading opinion, is presented not only for what it has to say about intellectual property, but also because it brings together many of the standards and principles governing the Constitutional Court's construction of the content and limits clause of Article 14.

6.5 Schoolbook Case (1971)
31 BVerfGE 229

[In 1965 parliament amended the Federal Copyright Act to permit already published "literary and musical works of small extent, single artistic work, or single photographs" to be published in a collection "that assembles the works of a considerable number of authors and is intended, by its nature, exclusively for religious, school, or instructional use" (section 46, Urheberrechtsgesetz, *BGBl* 1 [1965]: 1273). Such collections had to bear a clear statement of their purpose on the title page. In addition, authors had to be notified by registered mail of the use of their work before reproduction and distribution could begin. Several musicians filed constitutional complaints alleging that the amendment violated their property rights under Article 14.]

Judgment of the First Senate. . . .

B. The constitutional complaints are justified.

I. Copyright protects the author with respect to his intellectual and personal relations to his work and also with respect to the utilization of his work. In accordance with this understanding of the content of copyright, the act differentiates between the moral rights of authors and their utilization rights. The question as to the legal relationship between the two aspects of copyright and as to which basic [constitutional] rights govern the personal and intellectual relations of the author to his work need not be elaborated in this case. The constitutional evaluation must focus solely on the economic aspect of the copyright. In this question the Federal Constitutional Court, in accordance with prevailing opinion, proceeds on the ground that the constitutionality of the author's utilization rights must be assessed under Article 14.

The idea and purpose behind the [constitutional] guarantee of freedom of art [Article 5 (3)] is to keep government out of those processes, actions, and decisions rooted in the inherent laws of artistic creation and motivated by aesthetic considerations. Freedom of art prohibits any official attempt to influence the tendency or content of artistic activity, to prescribe universally binding rules for the creative process, or to narrow the field of artistic activity [citing the *Mephisto* case].

In the case of section 46 of the Copyright Act, these [particular] matters are not at issue. This provision presupposes the publication of the works, copies of which are in circulation and are being sold with the consent of the author. Hence this case is concerned neither with artistic activity [as such] nor even with the process of making creative work known to the general public. Critical here is the economic utilization of an intellectual creation. The issue is whether the statutory limitation on the economic rights of authors is compatible with the Constitution, a question within the normal protective range of the property guarantee of Article 14. Considered within the framework of the Constitution as a whole, this guarantee is primarily intended to protect the holder of the basic right to property by granting and affording him control over the utilization and disposition [of his property], and thus to enable him independently to direct his own life [citing the *Flood Control* case]. . . .

The protective and defensive character of the right to property requires us to classify the author's economic rights as "property" within the meaning of the Article 14 and to extend its protection to these rights. In our constitutional assessment, however, we must consider the inextricable link between personal-artistic creation and its economic utilization, together with the special nature and character of the property rights. . . .

II. . . . Section 46 of the Copyright Act is incompatible with the property guarantee of Article 14 (1).

Because there is no preexisting and absolute definition of property, and because the content and function of property need to be adjusted to social and economic change, the Constitution vests the legislature with the authority to define its content and limits. The economic rights of authors, like tangible property rights, are not excluded from being shaped by the legal order. Bound by the Constitution, however, the legislature is not totally free [to dispose of such rights]. In determining the content of the right, the legislature must ensure that the essential core of the right is preserved and conforms to all other constitutional provisions. . . .

Article 14 (1) first and foremost guarantees the legal institution of property. This institution grants to the individual the right to use and dispose privately of his property. In the copyright field the meaning of this is clear; included in the essential elements of copyright as property within the meaning of the Constitution are the author's right, secured by private law, to have the propertylike results of his creative activity attributed to him and his freedom to dispose of his work on his own responsibility. This is the essence of copyright protected by the Constitution.

This fundamental freedom of the author to dispose of the economic rights associated with copyright does not mean, however, that every conceivable use [of his own property] is constitutionally secured. The institutional guarantee ensures a basic set of legal rules that must exist in order to justify a characterization of the right as "private property." In the course of defining the content of copyright under Article 14 (1), the legislature is responsible for laying down standards designed to guarantee the appropriate utilization [of a work of art] that corresponds to the nature and social significance of the right.

Under section 15 of the Copyright Act the author has, *inter alia,* the exclusive right to utilize his work in material form; he is basically at liberty to dispose of his work by way of contractual agreements. This right, however, is not unlimited. There are various limitations on copyright contained in [the act] that are on different levels and of varying degrees. The provision [of the act] at issue here, which allows third parties to use the [author's] work without prior consent and free of charge, is permissible.

In assessing the constitutionality of this provision, the court must keep in mind that the legislature is not only obliged to safeguard the interests of the individual but also to circumscribe individual rights to the extent necessary to secure the public good. It must strive to bring about a fair balance between the sphere of individual liberty and the interests of the public. The validity of the contested provision depends, therefore — apart from whether it is in other respects consistent with the Constitution — on its justification in terms of the public interest.

III. 1. There are no objections against [authorial] rights [with respect to the] collections specified in section 46 (1) [of the Copyright Act]. When a protected work has been published it is no longer at the exclusive disposal of the individual, for [at that point] it simultaneously enters the social sphere and thus becomes an independent factor contributing to the cultural and intellectual climate of the time. Thus the general public has a substantial interest in seeing that young people, in the course of their education, have access to these artistic creations. This also applies to those who participate in such educational programs. The realization of this social task would not be possible if an author were wholly free to bar the use of his work in an [educational] collection. . . . The author's legitimate interests have been taken into account in a reasonable manner in the light of the narrowly defined purposes for which the collections can be used. The inclusion [of his work] in collections to be used for religious reasons is thus justified in view of the special position of churches in [our] public life.

2. The contested provision is not constitutional, however, to the extent that it allows the incorporation of copyrighted material into the aforementioned collections without any compensation.

The denial of [all compensation] for the reproduction and distribution of his work in [such] collections . . . impairs [the author's] right to dispose [of his property] because he is unable to prevent the use of his work or to establish by contract the conditions under which his work is to be used. This limitation results in a substantial impairment of the economic value attached to a copyrighted work if [indeed] the ordinary opportunity to bargain for royalties is not available and if the [legislature fails] to enact [as a substitute for this usual bargaining power] some provision for [authorial] remuneration.

In accord with the property guarantee the author has in principle the right to claim compensation for the economic value of his work insofar as the interests of the general public do not take priority over those of the author. We must remind ourselves that what is involved here is the artist's own intellectual and personal creativity. . . . Thus, not every consideration of public interest justifies the denial of the right to remuneration; in particular the general public's interest in the unrestricted access to the copyrighted works in and of itself does not suffice [as a justification]. The intensity of the limitation on the copyright owner requires [for its justification] a compelling public interest if its validity is to be sustained.

A general public interest of this nature does not exist. . . .

[Here the court considered and rejected various arguments in favor of the law's no remuneration provision. The copyright laws, past and present, exempt materials used in schoolbooks for educational purposes. Citing parliamentary hearings on these laws, the court found that the legislature had serious doubts about the constitutional validity of current policy, which the court viewed as presumptive evidence of a lack of consensus on the matter. Legislators, however, felt that a requirement of remuneration would force school and church officials to use only materials in the public domain, prompting them to exclude more up-to-date works from their institutional materials. They also believed that such a requirement would make the cost of producing such materials prohibitively expensive. The court appeared to reject both of these contentions.]

(d) The reasoning advanced in parliament that authors are duty-bound to permit reproduction of their works free of charge because they owe a special debt of gratitude to the general public is unacceptable. Authors are not the only persons who build "on traditional cultural values" and "the common intellectual property of the people." The same is true for all intellectual and creative persons. What is decisive, however, is that in no other comparable sphere of life is there a legal duty to put the fruits of one's labor at the disposal of the public for purposes of education in the absence of remuneration. Complainants point out correctly that the use of instruments in natural science classes is protected under patent laws. . . .

The author's work is a prerequisite for the production of schoolbook anthologies. His creation is decisive, for without his contribution such collections would be impossible. Yet the full burden of the [statutory] limitation falls on the shoulders of the author; he is expected to donate his services free of charge. [The statute] denies no one else — neither the editor, nor the publisher, nor the printer — his share of compensation for such common efforts. There is thus no convincing justification for this policy.

NOTE: MORE ON INTELLECTUAL PROPERTY. In the *Broadcast Lending* case (1971), the Constitutional Court sustained a provision of law that permitted schools to lend out on a nonprofit basis broadcasts of the single works of authors after equitable remuneration has been provided for the original use.[58] Under the ruling of *School Broadcast* (1971), a companion case, an author need not be paid for each broadcast of his work. This limitation on the author's right to the reproduction of his work is permissible since it may have to be aired several times to reach all of its intended school audiences.[59] In the *Tape Recording I* case (1971), the court sustained a section of the Copyright Act that conferred upon authors a claim against manufacturers of tape recorders capable of being used to reproduce protected works for personal use. The court approved the balance that the legislature had struck here between the interests of manufacturers of tape recorders, producers of tape recordings, retailers, and the ultimate buyers.[60] Finally, in the *Phonograph Record* case, the court upheld a change in the law that limited a recording copyright to twenty-five instead of fifty years, as originally provided.[61] As in *Groundwater,* the court pointed out that compelling public interests may warrant a redefinition of ownership rights so long as proper regard is paid to the principles of certainty and proportionality in the law.

In the well-known *Church Music* case, decided in 1978, the court was again concerned with the tension between the individual and social dimensions of intellectual property.[62] Several composers of church music challenged provisions of the Copyright Act of 1965, which allows the reproduction of a musical score without authorization or payment of royalties if it is played at a nonprofit public event, in a church, or in connection with a religious event. The court ruled that the performance of a musical piece without authorization at a state-sponsored public event may be justified by the "social character of intellectual property." But the court then went on to hold as a general principle that the public or nonprofit character of an event does not always justify a denial of royalties or compensation. The major part of the opinion concentrated on the "church performance" provisions of the law, which the court sustained, although somewhat grudgingly. The right to remuneration can be overridden only when the public interest prevails in a given situation, a balancing act that the lower courts would not be obliged to perform.[63]

OCCUPATIONAL LIBERTIES

The Basic Law is said to be neutral with respect to economic policy. This reigning German view recalls Justice Holmes's dictum, in *Lochner* v. *New York,* that a constitution rooted in liberal democratic theory "is not intended to embody a particular economic theory."[64] Yet the Federal Constitutional Court has been anything but neutral in its approach to socioeconomic legislation. As the materials in this section show, the court has been extremely active in reviewing the constitutionality of laws affecting the liberty of an individual to pursue a business, trade, or occupation. By contrast, the United States Supreme Court has not voided such a law since 1936. The intervention of the German Court is, of course, easily traceable to Article 12 (1) of the Basic Law, which declares: "All Germans shall have the right freely to choose their trade, occupation, or profession, their place of work, and their place of training." This right is, in truth, on a par with the right of property. The right to choose one's trade and place of work, like the right to property, fosters an economy based on entrepreneurship and ownership. Indeed, the protection of these economic rights by the Constitutional Court may be regarded as one manifestation of the *Sozialstaat*, just as the limitation of unbridled entrepreneurship can be seen as another.

The *Codetermination* case is an appropriate link between this section on occupational rights and the previous section on property rights; as the *Groundwater* case illustrates, claims involving the right to property often implicate occupational rights. The *Codetermination* case, however, is also important because it raises the larger question of how far the state may go in regulating the economy as a whole, and thus it allows us to loop back to the related concerns of the nature of the economic system. The Codetermination Act of 1976, although based on historic precedents in Germany, effected a major change in the governance of large industrial enterprises. The Fair Trade and Competition Act of 1957 and the Economic Stabilization Act of 1967 are other examples of major governmental interventions in the economy. But only the Codetermination Act resulted in a spirited constitutional controversy implicating several rights guaranteed by the Basic Law.

6.6 Codetermination Case (1979)
50 BVerfGE 290

[The Codetermination Act of 1976, passed by an overwhelming majority of the Bundestag, provided for the representation of employees on the supervisory boards of business and manufacturing firms with two thousand or more employees. At the time of enactment the act covered no fewer than 476 companies employing 4.1 million persons. The idea of coparticipation by employees in corporate enterprises, as the first part of the opinion shows, has a long history in Germany. The 1976 act, modeled on the Works Constitution Act of 1972 (which entitles employees to one-third of the seats on the supervisory boards of firms with less than two thousand employees), entitles employees and shareholders to equal representation on supervisory boards (section 7). In addition, the act provides (1) that the supervisory board chairman and vice chairman be elected by a two-thirds majority of its members (section 27), (2) that other decisions of the board be taken by a majority of board votes (section 29), and (3) that the legal representatives of the enterprise as well as its labor director be selected by the supervisory board in accordance with prescribed procedures (sections 31 and 33).

Numerous business firms and employer associations lodged constitutional complaints against each of these sections of the Codetermination Act for violating the rights of property (Article 14), association (Article 9), occupation (Article 12), and the freedom of economic activity component of the Basic Law's personality clause (Article 2). The German Protective Association for Security Holders also filed a constitutional complaint against a court ruling upholding the act. Finally, the act was challenged by judicial reference in a concrete judicial-review action. The Constitutional Court heard all of these cases in one consolidated proceeding marked by four days of oral argument.

A battery of corporate and government lawyers armed with thick briefs drafted by distinguished law professors argued their respective positions before the justices of the First Senate. Complainants essentially maintained that codetermination under the 1972 and 1976 acts not only violated the property rights of shareholders but also constituted the first step toward labor's domination of management. Additionally, they argued that the enforced amalgamation of shareholders and employees violated the right of individuals to form associations, just as it violated, under Article 9 (3), the right of trades, professions, and occupations to form associations. Such a major restructuring of the private economy, they maintained, would require a constitutional amendment.

The *Codetermination* case consumes ninety-one pages of the official German reports. In addition, the Federal Constitutional Court's public relations office issued a short summary of the case. Unless otherwise indicated, the following extracts are drawn from this official summary. A full English translation of the case appears in *European Commercial Cases* 2 (1979): 324–86.]

Judgment of the First Senate. . . .

C. IV. [We cannot] sustain the constitutional complaints. The provisions of the Codetermination Act submitted for review are compatible with the Constitution. . . . [This extract is from the opinion of the court.]

[A. History of Codetermination]

1. The idea of coparticipation of workers in the sense of participation in economic and social decisions in works and enterprises dates back in Germany to the beginning of industrialization. It was constitutionally recognized — after initial statutory elaborations — in Articles 156 (2) and 165 (1) of the Weimar Constitution, and it achieved statutory form in the Works Council Act of February 4, 1920, and also in the Law on the Election of Works Council Members to the Supervisory Committee of February 15, 1922. During the period of the [Hitler] regime the National Socialists repealed these statutes. In the course of the reorganization after 1945, some of the German [states] incorporated rules concerning the codetermination and coparticipation rights of workers into their constitutions. The Basic Law essentially limits itself to guaranteeing the classical human and civil rights; it accordingly contains no express rules as to the coparticipation of workers. This matter is the subject of federal legislation. . . . [This extract is from the opinion of the court.]

[In the first part of its opinion the court rejected the employers' assertion that the 1976 act conferred absolute equality of participation on workers and shareholders. The court noted that in the event of a fifty-fifty deadlock between workers and shareholders, the chairman of the board, who is usually a representative of the shareholders, may cast the deciding vote. In so concluding, the court refrained from suggesting that a codetermination based on absolute parity would be unconstitutional. That issue was left to another day, but once again the court observed that in regulating the economy the legislature enjoys wide-ranging discretion. Employers had argued that the cumulative effects of codetermination and related economic policies would eventually burden property and association rights in a manner incompatible with the letter and spirit of the Constitution. The court, however, declined to anticipate the future. Nor would it burden the legislature with the task of predicting the ultimate effects of codetermination. The court was satisfied that the legislature had performed its task carefully, after holding many hearings considering Germany's previous experience with codetermination and giving due regard to the individual freedom of citizens. This was sufficient to override anticipated but unproven assertions of unconstitutionality.]

[B. Right to Property]

The provisions infringe neither the property of the shareholders nor that of the enterprises; on the contrary, they define the content and limits of property in pursuance of the powers conferred upon the legislature under Article 14 (1) [1] of the Basic Law. Admittedly, [the provisions] reduce the powers of the shareholders as members of the supervisory board, although not by half—inasmuch as the shareholders as a whole retain their decisive influence in the enterprise. However, this restriction remains within the ambit of the commitments of property owners to society in general, and these commitments increase in scope as the relationship between the property in question and its social environment as well as its social function narrows. As a rule, the personal relationship conferred by holding shares covered by the Codetermination Act has less of an impact upon the law affecting the right to membership of the supervisory board. On the other hand, these shareholdings have far-reaching social relevance and serve a significant social function, especially since the use of this property always requires the cooperation of the employees whose fundamental rights are affected by such use. To the extent that the property of companies responsible for the undertakings affected by the act is concerned, one cannot assume [solely] on the basis of the legislature's prognosis that extended codetermination will render enterprises unworkable or produce conditions similar to unworkableness.

[The court emphasized that property in shares is controlled by company law. Such law imposes valid limits on the rights of shareholders. Property in shares is not like ordinary property: it cannot be used or disposed of in the manner of tangible property. Moreover, shareholder rights vary according to the particular form of corporate organization and its internal decision-making procedures. In any case, as the court noted, "codetermination was intended in part to bestow a larger measure of social legitimacy upon private enterprise. The Codetermination Act does not promote narrow group interests. Rather, the cooperation and integration served by institutional coparticipation . . . have general importance as social policy; coparticipation is a legitimate political means of safeguarding the market economy. It serves the public welfare and cannot be regarded as an unsuitable means for the achievement of this purpose."]

[C. The Right to Form Associations]

Nor [does the act] impair the fundamental right to form associations. It may even be doubtful that the protected right set out in Article 9 (1) of the Basic Law and the substance of this provision permit an application of the guarantee to larger joint-stock companies. Unlike the type of association and society which the Basic Law primarily safeguards, the personal element in such larger companies dwindles to the point of insignificance. However, this issue can remain unresolved since the contested provisions do not infringe Article 9 (1) of the Basic Law even if we assume in principle that it is applicable in this case. . . .

Sections 7, 27, 29, and 31 of the Codetermination Act are consistent with Article 9 (3) of the Basic Law. Pursuant to the rulings regularly handed down by the Federal Constitutional Court, the Basic Law protects the crucial part of the right of free association. This also includes the general guarantee of autonomy in negotiating collective wage agreements . . . [and the] independence of employers' associations. In view of the justifiable prognosis made by the legislature we cannot assume that the contested provisions of the Codetermination Act will result in the autonomy of concluding collective wage agreements becoming unworkable. If the existing statutory provisions should nevertheless prove insufficient to ensure the fundamental independence of employer associations, the legislature would have to provide a remedy.

[D. Freedom of Trade and the Right to Choose an Occupation]

Furthermore, the contested provisions do not infringe either Article 12 (1) or Article 2 (1) of the Basic Law insofar as these fundamental rights safeguard freedom of economic activity. In view of the size of the enterprises that fall within the scope of the Codetermination Act, freedom of choice with regard to trade, occupation, or profession in such firms largely lacks the personal element forming the real core of the guarantee in this fundamental right. To this extent, freedom of choice with regard to trade, occupation, or profession may be deemed to have a social relationship and a social function in [those] enterprises which can exercise this freedom only through their employees. Hence the contested provisions of the Codetermination Act prove to be admissible limitations of the exercise of one's trade, occupation, or profession. To the extent that Article 2 (1) of the Basic Law remains for [our] consideration, [the act's provisions] do not infringe that fundamental right either. [Complainants] have not shown that the challenged provisions unduly constrain the development of entrepreneurial initiative, thus [adversely] affecting the substance of that freedom of activity enjoyed by companies or shareholders.

NOTE: FREEDOM OF ECONOMIC ASSOCIATION AND THE RIGHTS OF LABOR. Article 9 (1) guarantees to all Germans "the right to form associations and societies." Paragraph 2, however, echoing the jurisprudence of militant democracy, prohibits associations whose "purposes and activities . . . conflict with criminal laws . . . or are directed against the constitutional order or the concept of international understanding." Paragraph 3, finally, confers on "everyone" the right to associate for the purpose of "improving working and economic conditions," and in addition guarantees the right of association "to all trades, occupations, and professions." From an American perspective, the last clause of this paragraph is interesting because it reaches into private contractual relationships. "Agreements which restrict or seek to impair this right [of association]," the clause reads, "shall be null and void." Under this provision, a complainant would have a constitutional cause of action against private parties for any infringement of his or her right to join or not to join an association.

The *Erft Public Corporation* case (1959),[65] in which a mining company challenged its compulsory membership in a state-created association of property owners and industries organized to conserve water resources in the highly industrialized area where they operated, is the leading case under Article 9 (1). The freedom to associate or not to associate, the First Senate said, is a right that Article 9 confers on individual persons, not on associations of persons — i.e., a public-law corporation — created and organized by the state to perform "legitimate public tasks" the fulfillment of which is in the interest of the whole community.[66] Compulsory membership in such an association is constitutionally permissible — and indeed consistent with the spirit of the *Sozialstaat* — so long as the controlling statute conforms to the "constitutional order," satisfies the principle of proportionality, and requires the performance of public tasks that private entities acting alone cannot accomplish or regular state organs are reluctant to undertake. The First Senate noted that a particular company or individual contesting compulsory membership in a corporation organized under public law would have to vindicate the claim to freedom of association under Article 2 (1) of the Basic Law.[67]

In the related *Chamber of Workers* case (1974),[68] the First Senate sustained a state (Bremen) statute requiring all employed persons to join the Chamber of Workers, a public corporation organized to tender advice on labor relations to public authorities and employees and to coordinate the aims of various professional organizations. The First Senate conceded that the performance of a legitimate public function does not always justify a statute such as this, which "in principle constitutes a severe infringement of the individual's freedom of action in economic and social life."[69] Various trade unions also raised constitutional objections to the state-created chamber, arguing that its "arbitrary establishment" imperiled the existence of voluntary associations — here labor unions — that could just as easily perform the public tasks assigned to the chamber. The senate suggested that if, in fact, the activities of a public corporation prevented or inhibited the establishment of a voluntary or private-law association with similar goals, its establishment would be an unconstitutional infringement of the right of economic association within the meaning of Article 9 (3). Here, however, the court found that the Chamber of Workers did not compete with trade unions and that the small fee each employee had to pay for membership in the chamber was an insignificant burden on the right to associate.

The decision in the *Lockout* case (1975),[70] which includes a general restatement of the rights of labor and management under Article 9 (3), resulted from a company's lockout of its employees following a strike and the company's refusal to reinstate certain employees after the strike was settled. The court reaffirmed the legality of both strikes and lockouts, regarding them as legitimate techniques of pressure and counterpressure as well as essential aspects of economic association and associational autonomy. In this case, however, the employer had refused to reinstate employees who were members of the company's works council. Members of such councils, elected by their fellow employees, deal directly with employers over matters affecting safety and working conditions.[71] These councils are an important feature of German labor organization. The court therefore concluded that the members of these councils cannot be dismissed consistent with the protection afforded expressly to the right to associate for the improvement of working and economic conditions.

The *IG-Metall* case (1976) also involved the activity of a member of a works council.[72] The chairman of IG-Metall's works council distributed handbills to employees on the factory grounds urging them to vote for union members (nearly all of whom belonged to the SPD) running for election to the town council in a nearby Bavarian community. The employer then sought and eventually obtained a ruling from a Bavarian labor court excluding the employee who distributed the bills from the works council. The lower court's order was based on a provision of the Works Council Act that provides for such an exclusion if the employee "engages in party politics" on the factory's premises. In response to the employee's complaint, the Federal Constitutional Court ruled that while Article 9 (3) may not secure a general right of association, it does protect the right to organize for the purpose of improving working conditions. On the facts of this case, the court found that the employee's behavior was not a "gross violation" of his legal obligations. The court might have sustained the complaint by a broader construction of Article 9 (3), but chose instead to base its decision on the worker's right to freedom of speech under

Article 5 of the Basic Law. The "political party activity" provision of the Works Constitution Act, said the court, has to be construed narrowly to give the fundamental value of freedom of speech its proper and legitimate scope within the workplace.[73]

In the *Postal Workers Strike* case (1993), finally, the Constitutional Court applied the provisions of Article 9 (3) to government employees (*Angestellte* and *Arbeiter*). After German postal workers struck for higher wages, the Ministry of Post and Telecommunications sought to replace them temporarily with civil servants (*Beamten*), an action sustained by the Federal Labor Court. On the complaint of the German Postal Union, the Constitutional Court reversed, holding that the right of public service workers to strike is a legitimate tool under Article 9 (3) for safeguarding and improving their working conditions, at least in the absence of legislation limiting their right to strike. The Court also emphasized the special character of the civil service and its duty to remain neutral in labor disputes of this kind. Civil servants, who belong to the traditional class of state officials responsible for the day-to-day administration of the *Rechtsstaat,* enjoy a higher status and more privileges than ordinary public employees.[74]

NOTE: JUDICIAL INTERVENTION VERSUS SELF-RESTRAINT. The *Codetermination* case was hailed as a disciplined exercise in judicial self-restraint. This is not an altogether inaccurate characterization. As in the first *Kalkar* case (1978; no. 4.6), the court allowed the legislature considerable leeway (*Prognosespielraum*) in regulating the economic order. Parts of the *Codetermination* opinion, however, reveal that the court may have stayed its hand only temporarily. A significant feature of the opinion is its exacting scrutiny of the coparticipation statute's content and the legislative basis for its enactment. The court recognized that the statute "brings about substantial changes in the economic order" and "regulates a sector of complex interconnections," but nevertheless regarded it as "constitutionally tenable" because parliament paid close attention to the political, economic, and legal aspects of codetermination. The court was doing no less here than examining the adequacy of the legislative process, and finding that the various interests at stake had been adequately considered. The court went on to emphasize, however, that if future developments under codetermination should unduly impinge on property, associational, or occupational rights, parliament will be constitutionally obliged to make the necessary corrections. Any legislative negligence in this regard is presumably subject to further judicial scrutiny.

The *Pharmacy* case (1958) is the leading decision in the field of occupational rights. It is also a leading illustration of the economic "interventionism" that has come to characterize constitutional adjudication under Article 12. The rights vindicated by this article are in full accord with the social market economy, just as they represent a triumph over a once hierarchically organized social structure. In the

Federal Constitutional Court's jurisprudence, however, these rights are ranked as fundamental not only for their value in the promotion of economic growth but also for their intrinsic moral value. Indeed, the court has come close to developing a coherent philosophy of work. Work is seen less as a means of earning a living than as the foundation of human personality. Work is vocation as well as job, and necessary for personal self-realization. Yet these rights, like most rights under the Basic Law, are subject to regulation "by or pursuant to a law" (Article 12 [1], sentence 2).

6.7 Pharmacy Case (1958)
7 BVerfGE 377

[Bavaria restricted the number of pharmacies licensed in any given community. The state's Apothecary Act provided for the issuance of additional licenses only if the new pharmacies would be commercially viable and would cause no economic harm to nearby competitors. In 1955 Bavaria invoked this statute to deny a license to a person who had recently immigrated from East Germany, where he had been a licensed pharmacist. The aggrieved applicant filed a constitutional complaint against the decision of the Bavarian government and the statutory provision under which the action was taken. In striking down the action, the Constitutional Court set forth the general principles governing its interpretation of the right to occupational choice.]

———————————

Judgment of the First Senate. . . .

Section 3 (1) of the Bavarian Apothecary Act of June 16, 1952, as amended on December 10, 1955, is void. . . .

B. IV. Whether Article 3 (1) of the Apothecary Act is consistent with Article 12 (1) requires a discussion of the fundamental propositions concerning the importance of the right to choose a trade.

1. Article 12 (1) protects the citizen's freedom in an area of particular importance to a modern society based on the division of labor. Every individual has the right to take up any activity which he believes himself prepared to undertake as a "profession" — that is, to make [the activity] the very basis of his life. . . . [Article 12 (1)] guarantees the individual more than just the freedom to engage independently in a trade. To be sure, the basic right aims at the protection of economically meaningful work, but it [also] views work as a "vocation" [Beruf]. Work in this sense is seen in terms of its relationship to the human personality as a whole: It is a relationship that shapes and completes the individual over a lifetime of devoted activity; it is the foundation of a person's existence, through which that person simultaneously contributes to the total social product. . . .

2. . . . The idea of a "profession" within the meaning of the Basic Law embraces

not only those occupations identified by custom or by law, but also freely chosen activities that do not correspond to the legal or traditional conception of a trade or profession.

(b) The text of Article 12 (1), when viewed against the backdrop of the real significance of the basic right, suggests that the legislature may regulate the *practice* but not the *choice* of an occupation. But this cannot be the [true] meaning of the provision, for the concepts of "choice" and "practice" are not mutually exclusive. Taking up a profession represents both the choice of an occupation and the beginning of its practice. Indeed, the choice of an occupation may not be manifested until it is practiced. Similarly, the intent to remain in an occupation, expressed through its continued practice, together with the voluntary discontinuance of its practice, are essentially acts of vocational choice as well. Both concepts represent a complex unity and, although viewed from different angles, are incorporated into the notion of "vocational activity."

Thus, an interpretation which would absolutely bar lawmakers from *every* interference with vocational choice cannot be correct. . . . Rather, a legal regulation purporting primarily to limit the *practice* of an occupation would survive constitutional analysis even if it has an indirect effect on the choice of an occupation. This situation occurs primarily where the choice of an occupation is largely dependent upon admission standards. Article 74 (19), authorizing the federation to enact laws governing admission to certain occupations, is evidence that the framers did not intend to summarily exclude legislation pertaining to occupational admission standards. But the history of this provision [citing the original debates in the Parliamentary Council] shows that as a general rule they sought also to curtail this power. . . . To be sure, the framers of the Basic Law fell short of a fully objective and conceptual clarification of these problems. Ultimately they came up with a formulation that closely followed the distinction between "choice" and "practice" familiar in the field of trade law and were content to leave the rest to regulation by law. . . .

In any case, Article 12 (1) is a unified basic right in the sense that the reservation clause of sentence 2 ["The practice of trades, occupations, and professions may be regulated by or pursuant to a law"] grants the legislature the power to make regulations affecting either the choice or the exercise of an occupation. But this does not mean that the legislature is empowered to regulate each of these aspects of vocational activity to the same degree. For it is clear from the text of Article 12 (1) that occupational choice is to remain "free" while the practice of an occupation may be regulated. This language does not permit an interpretation that assumes an equal degree of legislative control over each of these "aspects." The more legislation affects the choice of a profession, the more limited is the regulatory power. This interpretation accords with the basic concepts of the Constitution and the image of man founded on those concepts. The choice of an occupation is an act of self-determination, of the free will of the individual; it must be protected as much as possible from state encroachment. In practicing an occupation, however, the individual immediately affects the life of society; this aspect of [vocational activity] is subject to regulation in the interest of others and of society.

The legislature is thus empowered to make regulations affecting either the choice or the practice of a profession. The more a regulatory power is directed to the choice of a profession, the narrower are its limits; the more it is directed to the practice of a profession, the broader are its limits. . . .

(c) . . . The general principles governing the regulation of vocational activity may be summarized as follows: The practice of an occupation may be restricted by reasonable regulations predicated on considerations of the common good. The freedom to choose an occupation, however, may be restricted only for the sake of a compelling public interest; that is, if, after careful deliberation, the legislature determines that a common interest must be protected, then it may impose restrictions in order to protect that interest — but only to the extent that the protection cannot be accomplished by a lesser restriction on freedom of choice. In the event that an encroachment on freedom of occupational choice is unavoidable, lawmakers must always employ the regulative means least restrictive of the basic right.

A graduated scale of possible restrictions governs the legislature's authority to regulate vocational activity.

Lawmakers are freest when they regulate the practice of an occupation. In regulating such practice, they may broadly consider calculations of utility. Lawmakers may impose limitations on the right to practice a profession so as to prevent detriment and danger to the general public; they may also do so to promote an occupation for the purpose of achieving greater total performance within society. Here the Constitution protects the individual only against excessively onerous and unreasonable encroachments. Apart from these exceptions, such restrictions on the freedom of occupation do not greatly affect the citizen since he already has an occupation and [the statutory restrictions] leave the right to exercise an occupation inviolate.

On the other hand, if [the legislature] conditions the right to take up an occupational activity on the fulfillment of certain requirements, thus impinging on the choice of an occupation, then regulations for the public good are legitimate only when such action is absolutely necessary to protect particularly important community interests; in all such cases the restrictive measures selected must entail the least possible interference. But the nature of a regulation prescribing conditions for admission to a profession depends on whether the legislation deals with individual conditions, such as those of educational background and training, or with objective conditions irrelevant to one's personal qualifications and over which one exercises no control.

The regulation of individual (subjective) conditions [for admission to an occupation] is a legitimate exercise of legislative authority. Only those applicants possessing the proper qualifications, determined in accordance with preestablished formal criteria, will be admitted to a trade or profession. Many occupations require knowledge and skills that can be acquired only through theoretical and practical schooling. Without such preparation the practice of such occupations would be impossible or deficient and perhaps even dangerous to the general public. . . . Thus the limits on freedom of choice here are needed to safeguard the public against certain liabilities and hazards. Such limits are reasonable because applicants for various professions know well in advance of their choice whether or not they have the proper qualifications. The principle of proportionality governs here; any requirements laid down must bear a reasonable relationship to the end pursued [i.e., the safe and orderly practice of a profession].

The situation is different, however, when the state proceeds to control the objective conditions of admission. Here the matter is simply out of the individual's hands. Such restrictions contradict the spirit and purpose of the basic right because even one whom the state has permitted to make his choice by meeting the requirements of admission may nevertheless be barred from an occupation. This encroachment on a person's freedom cuts all the more deeply the longer he has had to attend school and the more specialized his training. . . . Because it is not altogether clear what direct disadvantages for the general public will result when a professionally and morally qualified applicant exercises his occupation, the [legislature] will often not be able to show a connection between the limitation on occupational choice and the desired result. In such situations the danger of impermissible legislative motivations is present. In this case it appears that [the legislature] intends to impose the restriction on admission in order to protect practicing pharmacists from further competition, a motive which, by general consensus, can never justify a restriction on the freedom to choose an occupation. This crude and most radical means of barring professionally and presumably morally qualified applicants from their chosen profession thus violates the individual's right to choose an occupation, quite apart from any possible conflict with the principle of equality. Limits upon the objective conditions of admission are permissible on very narrowly defined terms. Generally speaking, [the legislature] may impose them only when they are needed to demonstrate highly probable dangers to community interests of overriding importance. . . .

V. . . . Public health is doubtless an important community interest [whose] protection may justify encroachments on the freedom of the individual. Additionally, there is no doubt that an orderly supply of drugs is crucial for the protection of public health. "Orderly" in this context means that needed drugs will be available to the general public and that their distribution will also be controlled. . . . The Bavarian legislature presumably had these objectives in mind, but between the lines of the legislation we can also discern the political aims of a pharmacy profession at work to protect its [narrow] interests and the traditional concept of the "apothecary."

The decisive question before us is whether the absence of this restriction on the establishment of new pharmacies would . . . in all probability disrupt the orderly supply of drugs in such a way as to endanger public health.

We are not convinced that this danger is impending.

VII. . . . Section 3 (1) of the Bavarian Apothecary Act is unconstitutional because it violates the basic right of the complainant under Article 12 (1). . . .

NOTE: *PHARMACY* AND ITS PROGENY. The *Pharmacy* case reaffirmed the rule that any restriction imposed on a fundamental right must be accomplished by a specific legislative enactment (*Gesetzesvorbehalt*),[75] and once again indicated the Federal Constitutional Court's preoccupation with proper decision-making methods. *Pharmacy* also set forth for the first time the gradation theory (*Stufentheorie*) for assessing restrictions on occupational choice. Finally, the decision is a resounding affirmation of the dignity of work and its relationship to human personality. The term *Beruf* is broadly construed to relate to any occupational activity an individual may legally choose as his or her life's work. But particular occupations may be regulated in the public interest so long as the freedom to choose an occupation is not thereby unduly burdened. Thus the court clearly differentiates between the choice of an occupation and its practice.

A regulation of occupational choice triggers a higher standard of review than a regulation of practice. Limits on choice must satisfy what the court describes as "subjective" and "objective" needs. Under the standard of subjectivity, the state may regulate choice only to the extent necessary to ensure the proper training of the individual wishing to embark upon a given career. The standard of objectivity relates to the regulation, in the wider public interest, of the trade or occupation itself. A recent case reaffirming these propositions is the *Technician Licensing* case (1992). The court sustained legislation that requires sufficient professional knowledge and expertise before a license can be issued to persons setting themselves up as independent advisors or experts in their specific professional field, but following *Pharmacy* the court denied the state's authority to refuse such a license on the ground that there are enough experts already operating in the field.[76]

An illustration of "objective need" analysis is the *Long-Haul Truck Licensing* case (1975).[77] Transportation officials refused to grant long-haul trucking permits to certain companies because the quota for such permits, fixed by law, had already been filled. Employing the gradation theory, the court found that the restriction was a necessary and proper means of preventing a major threat to compelling public interests. Declared the court: "The federal railroad is indispensable for the national economy. This is true not only for passenger transportation, but for freight traffic as well, whose protection fixed quotas are meant to serve. A modern economy based on the division of labor cannot do without this means of transportation which moves great volumes of freight quickly and over long distances. . . . Supplying the population with vital goods could not be guaranteed without the railroad; thus the railroad helps to safeguard the existence of every individual."[78]

As the *Pharmacy* case indicates, the practice of trades and occupations may be regulated in the public interest. The Federal Constitutional Court has, accordingly, upheld laws (1) imposing reasonable age limits on the practice of a profession, (2) permitting only licensed pharmacists to sell certain drugs, (3) prohibiting general public advertising by physicians, (4) regulating the hours when business establishments may remain open, (5) forbidding bakery shops from operating during certain nighttime hours, and (6) withdrawing an attorney's license if he or she engages in a second occupation that is incompatible with that of an independent lawyer.[79] On the other hand, the court invalidated a law restricting the number of doctors allowed to treat patients covered by a statutory medical insurance fund (*Medical Insurance I* case [1960]),[80] as well as several judicial rulings preventing certain lawyers from serving as defense counsel in particular cases.[81] The *Chocolate Candy* case illustrates the point that even general consumer protection legislation may run afoul of Article 12 (1) if it violates the principle of proportionality.

6.8 Chocolate Candy Case (1980)
53 BVerfGE 135

[A federal consumer protection statute banned the sale of foodstuffs that might be confused with products made of chocolate. The statute was successfully invoked against a producer of Christmas and Easter candy made of puffed rice and coated with chocolate. The company brought a constitutional complaint grounded on Article 12 (1) against a decision of the Federal High Court of Justice sustaining the ban as applied.]

———————

Judgment of the First Senate. . . .

II. The constitutional complaint is justified.

1. Section 14 (2) of the Chocolate Products Act of June 30, 1975, is incompatible with Article 12 (1) to the extent that it imposes an absolute ban on the sale of the designated product. The provision under discussion regulates the practice of an occupation. Under Article 12 (1) a regulation may be imposed only by law or pursuant to a law. If an administrative decree regulates the practice of an occupation, it must be rooted in a delegated power authorized by the Basic Law and must adhere to the confines of this delegated power. Reasonable concerns for the common good must justify the regulation, and the means chosen [to implement the regulation] must be necessary and proper for the achievement of its purpose. Section 14 (2) of the Chocolate Products Act satisfies this requirement only in part. . . .

(c) (aa) In deciding whether a regulation [which limits] the practice of a trade is consistent with the principle of proportionality, we must take into account the discretion which the legislature has — within the framework of its authority — in the sphere of commercial activity. The Basic Law grants the legislature wide latitude in setting economic policy and devising the means necessary to implement it. In the instant case, however, the legislature has exceeded the proper bounds of its discretion, for less restrictive means can easily achieve the purpose of the statute. . . . Statutes like those involved here are designed to protect the consumer from confusion when purchasing food and from threats to his health. . . . Section 14 (2) of the Chocolate Products Act is designed to protect the consumer from deception. This protection is undoubtedly in the public interest and justifies restrictions on the practice of a trade.

To achieve this purpose the legislature has not only required proper labeling but also prohibited the sale of the product. Prohibiting [the sale of a product], however, is one of the most drastic means imaginable of protecting the consumer from confusion and deceptive trade practices. [The regulator] can ordinarily avert these threats to the public interest just as effectively and efficiently by mandating proper labeling. It may indeed be true that a consumer bases his decision to purchase a product not on a careful scrutiny of the product but rather on its external appearance. But this does not justify the presumption that [the regulator] must ban the sale of every form of food product described in section 14 (2) of the statute in order to protect the "flighty" consumer. Nor do other considerations justify the competitive edge given here to pure chocolate products. If a case involves possible confusion between milk and margarine products, then the legislature may indeed adopt measures in the public interest for maintaining a productive farm economy — thus serving a purpose beyond the immediate goal of consumer protection. In the instant case, however, no justifiable grounds exist for [imposing] a broader restriction than is needed to safeguard the consumer from false labeling. Thus, [the regulator] should take only [those] measures which are necessary for the protection of the consumer. To accomplish this end, it would have been enough to require proper labeling.

NOTE: LIMITATIONS ON ENTRY INTO AND CHOICE OF AN OCCUPATION. Consistent with the gradation theory espoused in *Pharmacy,* the court has been notably vigilant with respect to admission and entry standards impinging on occupational choice. Regulations governing entry into a profession generally survive constitutional analysis unless such admission standards violate the principle of proportionality, a test requiring not only a substantial relationship between means and ends but also a compelling reason for the law itself. The *Retail Trade* case (1965) illustrates the compelling reason prong of the proportionality principle. Here the court invalidated statutorily imposed technical educational requirements as applied to a general merchandise dealer. Such knowledge, said the court, was unnecessary to operate a general store in the public interest. The requirement was thus an "undue burden" on freedom of occupational choice.[82] In the *Handicraft Admission* case (1961), however, the court sustained a federal statute introducing an examination requirement before master craftsmen could obtain a certificate of proficiency. The court found this measure a reasonable means of protecting and promoting handicraft trades and small economic enterprises.[83] In a number of other cases the court held that any sudden upgrading of otherwise legitimate admission standards may require a transitional stage during which those disadvantaged by the new standards are given the opportunity to meet them.[84]

Moreover, as *Pharmacy* illustrates, admission to an occupation may not be grounded on any effort to protect existing trades or businesses against competition. The denial of a license to a new taxi concern merely because the local community is already well served by the taxicab trade is therefore invalid.[85] The difference between the result in this case and *Truck Licensing* (discussed above) pivots on the court's assessment of the relative public interests involved. Notaries public may also be limited in number because of their quasi-public status and special relationship to the state.[86] Finally, the *Milk Distributor* case (1958) invalidated a regulation denying a license to a milk distributor unless he could offer for sale a specified minimum quantity of milk.[87]

NOTE: OCCUPATIONAL CHOICE AND HIGHER EDUCATION. The modern German university, built on the Humboldtian reforms of the early nineteenth century,[88] was traditionally an elite institution professionally oriented and hierarchically organized around teaching and research programs monopolized by full professors. "The state provided higher education in the finest tradition of independent inquiry, and students educated in this manner provided the state with enlightened ministers."[89] Controversial political reforms of the 1960s transformed this elite system into a mass system of higher education.[90] The high postwar birthrate and reforms in secondary education — reforms that allowed students from the lower strata of German society to obtain university degrees — drove the number of university students to 533,000 in 1970, almost triple the 1950 figure. By the late 1970s enrollment had surged to nearly 1 million students. These soaring figures prompted several universities to place a limit on the number of students admitted into oversubscribed fields of study such as law, medicine, pharmacy, dentistry, architecture, and veterinary medicine.

Until the mid-1960s, any student in possession of the *Abitur*, the traditional ticket into the German university, was entitled to embark on his chosen field of study in the university of his choice. The *Abitur* certifies that a student is competent to enter the university. It can be obtained only by completing a nine-year course of studies at the *Gymnasium*, an advanced secondary school "neither designed for the pupil of average intelligence nor likely to be recommended for children from [lower-income] families."[91] Most German students attended other secondary schools, oriented toward basic literacy or toward preparing their students for advanced training in a technical school. This tracking system tended to reinforce the elitism of German universities.

When the *numerus clausus* — a numerical limit on admissions to a field of study — was imposed in the late 1960s, several universities modified their admission policies. The *Abitur* remained the most important qualifying factor, but now university admissions officials began to rank students according to their *Abitur* grades, placing those with lower grades on waiting lists. In addition, a limited number of students received preferential treatment. Among these privileged applicants were those who had completed their military duty, those on waiting lists for one or more years, and those resident in the state of the university to which they had applied.

The first *Numerus Clausus* case, involving the medical schools of the Universities of Hamburg and Munich, emerged out of these new admission policies. Students rejected because of these restrictions but otherwise presumptively qualified for admission contested the regulations before the administrative courts in their respective states. Doubting the compatibility of the *numerus clausus* with the right of all Germans to freely choose a trade or an occupation under Article 12, the two courts referred the question to the Federal Constitutional Court.

<h3 style="text-align:center">6.9 Numerus Clausus I Case (1972)
33 BVerfGE 303</h3>

[The relevant facts are contained in the court's opinion. The opinion is preceded by the court's statement of the guiding principles (*Leitsätze*) governing the case.]

———————

[Guiding Principles]. . . .

3. Absolute restrictions for admitting first-year students to a particular field of study are constitutional only if (a) [the legislature] mandates them only when absolutely necessary and when available educational and training capacity have been completely exhausted, and (b) the choice and distribution of applicants takes place according to objective criteria, giving each qualified applicant a [fair] chance and considering the applicant's individual choice of institution of higher education.

4. The legislature alone must decide what conditions must be present to order absolute restrictions on [university] admissions and what criteria for selection [the university] should apply. [The legislature] can authorize institutions of higher education to regulate further particulars within prescribed limits.

5. Section 17 of the Hamburg University Law of April 25, 1969, is incompatible with the federal Constitution because the [state] legislature failed to determine the type and priority of selection criteria for absolute admissions restrictions. . . .

6. Section 3 (2) of the Bavarian Admission Law of July 8, 1970, is incompatible with the Constitution insofar as [it allows] the general admission of applicants with

their legal residence in Bavaria or neighboring states, even when the capacity of [Bavarian] educational institutions is completely exhausted. [The statute is also unconstitutional] insofar as [it] gives these applicants preferential ranking. . . .

7. [The court addresses the issue of] the joint responsibility of federal and state governments for a national agency to distribute openings to study at universities [throughout the country] by using selection criteria. . . .

Judgment of the First Senate. . . .

A. III. 1. In the case which took place in Hamburg, the plaintiff passed his *Abitur* in Itzehoe in May 1969 with a grade point average of 3.25. After unsuccessfully applying for acceptance into medical school during the winter semester of 1969–70, plaintiff reapplied for the summer semester of 1970. [The university] again refused plaintiff's application because of insufficient places for students [studying medicine]. After being informed of his list ranking, plaintiff filed an unsuccessful objection to the [university's] decision and [subsequently] brought an action to ascertain the legality of the [university's] refusal. Plaintiff asserts that it is unconstitutional to restrict admission to study medicine for so many years despite the fact that doctors are urgently needed in various branches of the medical profession. [Plaintiff further claims that the university] admitted considerably more applicants in previous years and sufficient time has been available to expand training and educational capacity. . . .

2. The Administrative Court suspended the procedures under Article 100 (1).

C. The Hamburg and Bavarian university admission policies are not fully consistent with the Basic Law.

I. The primary standard used in assessing the constitutionality of admission restrictions, as established by [our] precedents and in the legal literature, is the guaranteed right of all Germans under Article 12 (1) to choose where they are to be educated.

The inclusion of this right in the Basic Law, and its initial interpretation, clearly indicate that Article 12 (1) was designed as a right of the individual to defend himself from official encroachments on educational freedom. The deliberations of the Parliamentary Council's Main Committee emphasized that the individual would enjoy the freedom to choose among the various universities and to attend the lectures of outstanding professors in order to receive a well-rounded education under all circumstances. . . . Indeed, an important aspect of the protective function of this freedom . . . is circumscribed when the capacity of all educational institutions is exhausted, making the planned distribution of applicants unavoidable.

Overcrowded educational facilities highlight another important aspect of the right to freely choose the place of one's training; that is, the closely related right, also guaranteed by Article 12 (1), to freely choose an occupation. As a rule, education is the first step in taking up a profession; both are integral parts of a coordinated life process. The Federal Constitutional Court's case law under Article 12 (1) has long emphasized not only the inseparability of the choice and the later practice of an occupation, but also the importance of guidelines for occupational training [citing the *Pharmacy* case]. Because of the integral relationship between training for an occupation and practicing it, the Federal Administrative Court has already concluded that [legislators] may not impose limits on admission to professional training as a means of steering the choice of an occupation. This close relationship also leads us to conclude that [we shall] judge any restrictions on the admission to a course of study as stringently as restrictions on the choice of the occupation when the choice of an occupation — e.g., the medical profession — involves a prescribed program of study.

In the field of education the constitutional protection of basic rights is not limited to the function of protection from governmental intervention traditionally ascribed to the basic liberty rights. The Federal Constitutional Court has repeatedly declared that basic rights in their capacity as objective norms also establish a value order that represents a fundamental constitutional decision in all areas of the law. Therefore, [the court has said] that basic rights are not merely defensive rights of the citizen against the state. The more involved a modern state becomes in assuring the social security and cultural advancement of its citizens, the more the complementary demand that participation in governmental services assume the character of a basic right will augment the initial postulate of safeguarding liberty from state intervention. This development is particularly important in the field of education. . . . The freedom to choose an occupation — apart from the special provisions of Article 33 relating to civil service employment — is at present predominantly put into practice in the private sector and is largely directed toward protecting the individual's chosen lifestyle; that is, its purpose is to ensure freedom from any coercion or prohibition with respect to one's choice or practice of a profession. By contrast, freedom of choice with respect to one's place of education is geared, by its very nature, toward free access to institutions; this right would be worthless without the actual ability to exercise it. Accordingly, the proposed federal guidelines for higher education proceed from the initial assumption that every German is entitled to carry out his chosen program of study if he demonstrates the requisite qualifications.

It is not within the discretion of the legislature to recognize this right. We may put aside the question of whether participatory rights [in state benefits] can be partially derived from [the concept that] a social state based on the rule of law takes on a guarantor's obligation to implement the value system of the basic rights. We have determined that the legislature must decide whether and to what extent it will grant participatory rights within the limits of administrative services, even in a modern state based on social justice, and the citizen cannot force the legislature to make this decision. However, when the state has created certain educational institutions, claims of access to these institutions may arise from the principle of equality in tandem with Article 12 (1) and with the principle of the state based on social justice. This is especially true when the state has laid claim to a factual monopoly that cannot easily be abandoned, as in the sphere of education, and when participation in governmental services is also an indispensable precondition for the exercise of basic rights, as in the field of training for academic professions. In a free social welfare state based on the rule of law, [one] cannot leave it to the limited discretion of governmental agencies to determine the circle of beneficiaries and to exclude some citizens from these privileges, especially since this would result in the [government] steering the choice of a profession. On the contrary, every citizen qualified for university studies has the right to share equally in the opportunity being offered. [This] conclusion flows from the fact that the state offers these services. Therefore, Article 12 (1) together with Article 3 (1) [the principle of equality] and the mandate of a social welfare state guarantee any citizen meeting the individual admission requirements the right to be admitted to the [institution of] higher education of his choice.

2. The view is widespread that this right of admission, by its nature, is limited exclusively to a claim of participation in existing educational opportunities. By contrast, the Hamburg Administrative Court, in its reference to this court, maintains that the state must expand educational facilities. Thus any regulation in the form of absolute admission restrictions on entering students would be permissible only if pursuant to a law expressly providing for the fulfillment of this obligation within a specified period of time. Both interpretations, however, neglect aspects necessary for the protection of the basic right in the present context.

The problematic nature of absolute limits on admission lies in the fact that the existing capacity is insufficient to afford an educational opportunity to everyone entitled to it. If, from the outset, [we would] confine [our] scrutiny to [the right to] participate in the educational opportunities that already exist, [our analysis] would miss the crux of the difficulty. Normally, with regard to social services — that is, financial benefits — [the legislature] can to some extent redistribute [funds] to deal with the disadvantageous consequences of confining services to existing means. An absolute restriction on admission to the university, however, leads to the glaring inequality that one class of applicants receives everything and the other receives nothing — at least for a more or less long and possibly decisive period. . . . Because of these effects, absolute admissions restrictions are undisputedly on the edge of constitutional acceptability. In the long run, expanding capacity is the only way to deal with these effects. [As a consequence,] the . . . question arises whether the value decisions manifested in basic rights together with the state's educational monopoly vest a social state with an objective constitutional mandate to provide sufficient educational capacities for all courses of study. [We] need not decide whether this question should be answered in the affirmative or whether, under certain circumstances, an individual citizen can use this constitutional mandate as the basis for an enforceable claim [against the state] to create opportunities for higher study. For constitutional consequences would arise only if that constitutional mandate were manifestly violated. [We] can ascertain no such violation with respect to the field of medical studies today.

Even to the extent that participatory rights are not entirely restricted to existing benefits, they are still subject to the limitation of what is possible, meaning that which the individual may reasonably claim from society. The legislature has the primary responsibility for determining [what may reasonably be claimed]. According to the explicit provision of Article 109 (2), the legislature must consider other public welfare concerns as well as the demands of overall economic balance when setting its spending policy. It is also incumbent on the legislature to decide whether to enlarge [existing facilities] as well as which construction [projects] have priority, considering too that the enlargement and new construction of universities are to be regarded as joint tasks of the federation and the states within the meaning of Article 91.

(a) . . . Any constitutional obligation [of the legislature] that may exist does not include the duty to supply a desired place of education at any time to any applicant. This would make costly investments in the realm of higher education exclusively dependent upon individual demands, which often fluctuate and are influenced by manifold circumstances. It would [also] lead to a misunderstanding of [the concept of] freedom — to a failure to recognize that personal liberty, in the long run, cannot be effectuated in isolation either from its equilibrium or from the ability of the whole to function effectively. The idea that the individual has an unlimited claim [which is enforceable] at the expense of the community as a whole is incompatible with the principle of a social welfare state. . . . It would be contrary to the [state's] mandate [to achieve] social justice as articulated by the principle of equality [if the state] gave only a privileged portion of the population the benefit of limited public financial resources while neglecting other important concerns of the public welfare. . . .

[The court concluded that the states had made adequate efforts to expand the number of openings in medical schools but found that regulations governing admission to existing facilities fell short of constitutional requirements. After noting that under the terms of Article 12 (1) the right to choose an occupation and one's place of training is subject to regulation by law, the court set forth the conditions under which admission might be restricted: the state may limit admissions to the university, but only on the basis of criteria clearly defined by law; every applicant must be given a fair chance to be admitted under specified selection procedures; additionally, the *numerus clausus* would survive constitutional analysis only if the state could demonstrate that all the places in a given academic department were filled.]

(c) In the light of these considerations, any absolute limit on admissions must meet strict requirements. According to the Federal Constitutional Court's gradation theory [citing the *Pharmacy* case], the more the freedom of occupation is affected, the more the regulatory power of the state is limited. The choice of occupation depends upon the choice of education, and absolute restrictions on admissions to a particular educational program resulting from the depleted capacity in the educational facility are equivalent to an objective precondition for admission within the meaning of the gradation theory. Therefore a regulation based on general principles developed under Article 12 (1) is permissible only to combat a demonstrably serious or highly probable threat to an exceedingly important community value. Also, [the legislature] must strictly observe the basic principle of proportionality and not wholly fail to consider objectionable side effects — for example, forcing students to change their programs of study or to study in a foreign country. . . .

In the light of past experience, an absolute restriction on the admission of beginning students is constitutional only if (1) [the legislature] imposes [the restriction only] when absolutely necessary, after having exhausted currently available publicly funded facilities; and (2) [the statute] bases the choice and distribution [of openings] on equitable criteria and provides each applicant with the opportunity to compete [for an opening], devoting the greatest possible attention to where the individual wishes to study. [Bavaria's admission law was also struck down under the equal protection clause of Article 3 (2) since it discriminated unfairly against out-of-state residents.]

1. Both the provision concerning the selection of applicants and the aforementioned order to [impose] admissions restrictions belong to the core of admission procedures for higher education. In terms of substantive law, the problems [in this area] center on [the fact] that some applicants for higher studies will have the privilege of being admitted, and other equally qualified candidates will be rejected and consequently hindered from commencing their studies or possibly from choosing a particular occupation. In this connection we need not discuss either the importance of the *Abitur* as the termination of general schooling or whether this manner of qualifying for higher education should be reformed. In any case, no matter where [one] draws the line for entrance requirements, the absolute restriction of admissions presents the problem of selecting among applicants who fulfill all the individual requirements for acceptance.

Since this selection means unequal treatment of equally qualified persons, the creative leeway in setting the rules of selection normally afforded by the principle of equality is not very great. Of course, the provision may not be arbitrary in the sense of being patently unobjective. Here especially, those responsible for admitting [students] are obliged to make a selection which is reasonably acceptable to rejected applicants, always using the principle of fairness as a guideline. In particular the provision must give every qualified applicant a real chance [to be accepted].

As to the procedural aspect of [this issue], the legislature must establish the rules for selection since the effects of this provision are [so] far-reaching. If the legislature authorizes a delegation of its authority, it must at least determine the selection criteria and their order of importance. The Constitution permits the legislature to delegate its legislative power to others through explicit legal authorization. However, if the regulation interferes with the fundamental rights contained in Article 12 (1), it can have the effect of allocating chances [to shape one's] life. Consequently, in a parliamentary democracy based on the rule of law, the constitutional requirement of a specific enactment, which permits the restriction of basic rights only by statute or on the basis of a statute, can only mean that the legislature must be responsible for the basic elements of this decision.

NOTE: JUDICIAL REVIEW AND UNIVERSITY ADMISSION. *Numerus Clausus I* marks the beginning of major judicial intervention in university governance.[92] The court declared that any absolute numerical limit on admission into a course of study is unconstitutional unless the institution applying it can demonstrate that all available space is completely filled.[93] In so deciding the Constitutional Court accelerated the movement toward central control of higher education. *Numerus Clausus I* prompted the various states, in cooperation with their universities, to create a centralized office for university admissions. Following the court's guidelines, the Central Admissions Office worked out procedures for measuring available space and formulated concrete standards for making admission decisions.

These procedures and standards generated yet another round of judicial decisions. In the *Freiburg University Admissions* case (1975),[94] the Federal Constitutional Court ruled in favor of twenty-two applicants denied admission by the Central Admissions Office to the medical school of the University of Freiburg. The novelty of the case consisted in the court's decision to bypass the Central Admissions Office and order the direct admission of the complaining students.[95] On the same day, in the *Munich University Admissions* case (1975),[96] the court reversed a decision denying admission to a medical school applicant who was able to show that Munich's medical facilities were underused. The Central Admissions Office would now have to find ways of verifying the spatial capacities of the universities if suits against particular schools by disappointed applicants were to be avoided. In 1976, the court handed down two more cases in which it was asked to review the standards governing the imposition of the *numerus clausus*.[97]

Meanwhile, and partly in response to the court's university admissions decision, the federal government passed the University Framework Act of 1976. Its detailed provisions on university admission standards specified criteria for determining teaching capacity, established admission quotas, and laid down general and special selection procedures.[98] The Constitutional Court, however, was still not satisfied. In the *Higher Education Admission* case (1977),[99] the court found deficiencies in the new admission criteria laid down in the University Framework Act. In the court's view there was still too much emphasis on scholastic achievement scores. In 1982 the court even nullified provisions of the act to the extent that they denied students the right to study medicine as a minor subject unless it was meaningfully related to their major course of studies.[100] The provisions were invalidated as applied to an applicant who had begun his studies in the mid-1970s when it was possible to embark on such a minor.

At the cost of harsh public criticism, the Constitutional Court has transformed itself into a veritable ministry of education. With each successive decision the court seemed to narrow the discretion of university officials, forcing legislators to devise increasingly precise and nondiscriminatory standards governing university admissions.[101] In treating the cases discussed in this section, Hans Weiler concluded: "The role of the Federal Constitutional Court has been particularly significant in two respects: (a) in overcoming the vestiges of absolute state discretion in educational matters and in making these matters subject to judicial review; and (b) in reasserting, by way of greater 'parliamentarization' of the policy process, the legitimating role of formal legislative action for 'essential' policy decisions in education."[102]

EQUALITY AND THE SOCIAL ECONOMY

Equality has emerged as an important value in many cases featured in other sections of this book. As in *Numerus Clausus I,* reprinted in this chapter, it is often invoked in tandem with other rights secured by the Basic Law. Egalitarian values have played a central role in several cases dealing with political representation and federal-state relations, and as we shall see in subsequent chapters, they play an equally important role in the areas of free speech, religious liberty, and personality rights. These remarks underscore the principle that no provision of the Basic Law is to be construed in isolation. Consequently, as many of the cases reprinted in this volume show, the equality clauses inform the meaning of other constitutional values just as these other values infuse the meaning and limit the reach of the guaranteed right to equality under Article 3.

Article 3 (1) declares that "all persons shall be equal before the law." Like all other guaranteed basic rights, this general principle of equality before the law applies to "the legislature, the executive, and the judiciary" (Article 1 [3]).[103] In addition, paragraph 2 of Article 3 proclaims that "men and women have equal rights," and paragraph 3 bans particular forms of discrimination, namely, those based on "sex, birth, race, language, national or social origin, faith, religion, or political opinions." In 1994, this list was amended to include disability. Actually, the principle of equal treatment appears in several other provisions of the Basic Law, chief among which are clauses securing equal rights for illegitimate children (Article 6 [5]) and guaranteeing to all Germans "the same civil rights and duties" (Article 33 [1]). This section focuses on the principle of equality as it applies to conditions of employment and the workplace.

Before proceeding to the *Nocturnal Employment* case and the accompanying notes, more needs to be said about Article 3 and its interpretation. In the Constitutional Court's view, the general equality clause (Article 3 [1]) bans arbitrary or unreasonable legislative classifications. This standard, however, is much tougher than the equivalent rule of minimum rationality adopted by the United States Supreme Court in assessing the validity of legal distinctions under the equal protection clause of the Fourteenth Amendment. In applying this standard, the Supreme Court rarely examines whether a classification rooted in a socioeconomic judgment is reasonably related to its purpose; the court simply assumes a rational link between ends and means.[104] The German court, by contrast, commonly examines the connection to determine whether in fact a legislative classification furthers the purpose for which it was enacted.[105] If the classification reasonably advances the purpose, the legal distinction will be sustained.

On the other hand, classifications by the traits enumerated in Article 3 (3) are suspect and thus require a degree of scrutiny substantially higher than mere reasonableness. Before the court will sustain legislation founded on a suspect trait, the state must advance a compelling reason in support of the law. But even if the purpose of the forbidden classification is legitimate, the court still requires a close and substantial relationship between ends and means. As the section below on gender shows, the state has frequently sustained this burden of proof. But once again, other constitutional values may limit the doubtfulness of a proscribed classification. For example, persons may not be discriminated against on the basis of their political opinions, but under Article 18 individuals may nevertheless be required to forfeit their basic rights to speech and press if these rights are used "to undermine the free democratic basic order."

NOTE: GENDER DISCRIMINATION AND EMPLOYMENT. In its original version, Article 3 (2) declared that "men and women shall have equal rights," a provision that on first glance appears superfluous since paragraph 3 includes sex in its list of suspect categories. Paragraph 2, however, places special emphasis on the need for equality between men and women; German law was once riddled with gender classifications, many of which mirrored the traditional patriarchy of German society.[106] Out of this realization emerged Article 117 (1), a transitory provision of the Basic Law requiring the repeal of all legislation inconsistent with Article 3 (2) by March 31, 1953. Taking these provisions seriously, the Constitutional Court served notice early on that in properly litigated cases, it would invalidate laws based on sex if the legislature failed to heed the injunction of Article 117 within the prescribed time.[107]

In the beginning, however, the court moved cautiously, sustaining more gender classifications than it struck down, yet insisting that a gender classification would survive constitutional analysis only when objective biological or functional differences between men and women are substantial enough to warrant their dissimilar treatment.[108] Until the 1970s, the prevailing view on and off the court was that Article 3 required little more than the elimination of legal distinctions based on sex.

In subsequent years, the prevailing view shifted, partially in response to European Community directives to bring about equality in matters of pay and employment, but also in response to a growing feminist movement in Germany. The shift manifested itself in the Fair Employment Act of 1980, an antidiscrimination law banning preferences by sex in hiring, promotion, and dismissal; requiring equal pay for equal work; and exhorting employers to advertise job openings in gender neutral language.[109] In the ensuing years the Constitutional Court too would play a crucial role in dismantling Germany's traditional structure of male dominance in the law.

6.10 Nocturnal Employment Case (1992)
85 BVerfGE 191

[A supervisor in a cake factory was fined for employing women to wrap cakes at night in violation of a statute basically forbidding the employment of women as blue-collar workers (*Arbeiterinnen*) during the night. After exhausting her ordinary judicial remedies, the supervisor filed a constitutional complaint, arguing that the law offended the equality provisions of Article 3 (1) and (3) of the Basic Law.]

––––––––––––

B. . . .

The constitutional complaint is admissible.

The complainant's allegations show a possible violation of her basic rights. It is true that she is not herself discriminated against by the prohibition of night labor by women. Thus there is no violation of her right to equality under Article 3 (3). But her general freedom of action [guaranteed by Article 2 (1) as construed in the *Elfes* case] can be infringed if the prohibition . . . offends Article 3 (1) and (3). In any event, a provision that requires a citizen to treat third persons in a discriminatory manner impinges directly upon her freedom of action. . . .

C. The constitutional complaint is justified. . . . The prohibition of nocturnal employment of women is incompatible with Article 3 (1) and (3). The imposition of a fine on the basis of this unconstitutional law violates the complainant's general freedom of action under Article 2 (1) of the Basic Law.

I. The ban on night work for women . . . offends Article 3 (3).

1. Under this provision no one may be disadvantaged or favored on the basis of sex. This paragraph reinforces the general equality provision of Article 3 (1) by imposing more stringent limitations on legislative judgment. Like the other characteristics listed in paragraph 3, sex basically may not be employed as a basis for unequal treatment. This is true even if the law in question is intended not to establish the forbidden inequality for its own sake but to pursue some independent goal.

With respect to the question whether a law unjustifiably discriminates against women, Article 3 (2) imposes no additional restrictions. What Article 3 (2) adds to the discrimination ban of Article 3 (3) is an affirmative command of equal opportunity [*Gleichberechtigungsgebot*] that extends to the real social world [*die gesellschaftliche Wirklichkeit*]. The provision that "men and women shall have equal rights" is designed not only to do away with legal norms that base advantages or disadvantages on sex but also to bring about equal opportunity for men and women in the future. Its aim is the equalization of living conditions. Thus women must have the same earning opportunities as men. . . . Traditional role conceptions that lead to increased burdens or other disadvantages for women may not be entrenched by state action. . . . De facto disadvantages typically suffered by women may be made up for by rules that favor women. . . .

The present case is concerned not with the equalization of conditions but with the removal of an inequality imposed by law. [The statute] treats women laborers unequally because of their sex. It is true that the rule is addressed to employers. But the consequences of the rule are felt immediately by female workers. Unlike men, they are deprived of the opportunity to work at night. This is an inequality imposed by law on the basis of sex.

2. Not every inequality based on sex offends Article 3 (3). Gender distinctions may be permissible to the extent that they are indispensably necessary [*zwingend erforderlich*] to the solution of problems that by their nature can arise only for women or only for men. But this is not such a case.

(a) The prohibition of nocturnal employment was originally based upon the assumption that women laborers were constitutionally more susceptible to harm from night work than men. Studies in occupational medicine provide no firm basis for this assumption. Working at night is fundamentally harmful to everyone. . . .

(b) Insofar as investigations show that women are more seriously harmed by night work, this conclusion is generally traced to the fact that they are also burdened with housework and child rearing. . . . Women who carry out these duties in addition to night work outside the home . . . obviously suffer the adverse consequences of nocturnal employment to an enhanced degree. . . .

But the present ban on night work for all female laborers cannot be supported on this ground, for the additional burden of housework and child rearing is not a sufficiently gender specific characteristic. For the woman to mind the house and the children does correspond with the traditional division of responsibility between husband and wife, and it cannot be denied that she often fills this role even when she is as busy as her male partner with outside work. But this double burden falls with full weight only upon those women with children requiring care who are single or whose male partners leave child care and housework to them despite their nightly jobs. It falls equally upon single men who bring up children. . . . The undeniable need for protection of night laborers, male and female, who have children to bring up and a household to manage can better be met by rules that focus directly on these circumstances.

(c) In support of the prohibition of night work it is also argued that women are subject to particular dangers on their way to and from their place of nocturnal employment. In many cases that is no doubt true, but it does not justify forbidding all women laborers to work at night. The state may not escape its responsibility to protect women from being attacked in the public streets by restricting their occupational freedom in order to keep them from leaving their houses at night. . . . Furthermore, this argument is not so generally applicable to women laborers as a group as to justify disadvantaging all of them. Particular risks might be avoided, for example, by providing a company bus to take employees to work.

3. The infringement of the discrimination ban of Article 3 (3) is not justified by the equal opportunity command of Article 3 (2). The prohibition of night work . . . does not promote the goals of this provision. It is true that it protects a number of women . . . from nocturnal employment that is hazardous to their health. But this protection is coupled with significant disadvantages: Women are thereby prejudiced in their search for jobs. They may not accept work that must be done even in part at night. In some sectors this has led to a clear reduction in the training and employment of women. In addition, women laborers are not free to dispose as they choose of their own working time. One result of all this may be that women will continue to be more burdened than men by child rearing and housework in addition to work outside the home, and that the traditional division of labor between the sexes may be further entrenched. To this extent the prohibition of night work impedes the elimination of the social disadvantages suffered by women.

II. [The statute] also offends Article 3 (1) of the Basic Law because it treats women laborers [*Arbeiterinnen*] differently from women in clerical positions [*Angestellte*] without sufficient reason.

1. The general equality provision of Article 3 (1) forbids the legislature to treat different classes of persons differently if there are no distinctions between them of such type and significance as to justify the difference in treatment. . . .

2. The unequal treatment of the two classes of female employees could be justified only if women in white-collar jobs were less burdened by night work than those in blue-collar positions. But there is no evidence to support this conclusion. The relevant occupational health studies suggest rather that harmful consequences to health are the same for both groups. . . .

3. Nor can the differential treatment of blue-collar and white-collar employees be justified by differences in the rate of nocturnal employment between the two groups of workers. Figures from 1989 show that between February and April of that year some 478,000 female clerical workers (7.6 percent of the total) were engaged in night work. Thus there can be no suggestion that white-collar women employees are typically spared the burdens of nocturnal employment. In any case women clerical workers are not a group so little affected by night work as to justify the legislature in generalizing to exclude them entirely.

III. . . .

3. The immediate consequence of the finding of unconstitutionality is that offenses against [the statute] may not be punished. The legislature is under an obligation to adopt new rules to protect workers from the harmful effects of nocturnal employment. Such rules are necessary in order to satisfy the objective dimension of the fundamental rights, especially the right to bodily integrity (Article 2 [2], clause 1). This basic right imposes an affirmative duty of protection on the state. . . .

The fact that night work is performed on the basis of voluntary agreements does not obviate the need for statutory protection. The principle of private autonomy that underlies the law of contract can afford adequate protection only to the extent that conditions permit the exercise of free will. When there is a gross inequality of bargaining power between the parties, contract law alone cannot ensure an appropriate accommodation of competing interests. With employment contracts this is typically the case. . . .

To leave [the subject] unregulated . . . would be contrary to the objective dimension of Article 2 (2), clause 1. . . .

NOTE: *NOCTURNAL EMPLOYMENT* IN PERSPECTIVE. The *Nocturnal Employment* case is a major benchmark in the Constitutional Court's equal protection jurisprudence. In a lucid restatement of the theory underlying its interpretation of the equality principle, the court served notice that it would no longer tolerate legal classifications based on sex that perpetuate stereotypical notions of sex roles in society.[110] Three things appear to have influenced the decision in *Nocturnal Employment*. First, the old GDR had no such statute, and in the face of mass unemployment among East German women after reunification, it would have seemed callous to saddle these women with the added burden of a ban on nocturnal work. Second, the First Senate followed a 1991 decision of the European Court of Justice that invalidated a French prohibition on women working at night (The Republic [France] v. Alfred Stoeckel [Case C-345/89]). Finally, the court decided the case within a context of increasing emphasis on social and economic equality between the sexes and mounting political pressures in Germany on behalf of affirmative action.

Nocturnal Employment was actually foreshadowed by the *Family Surname* case, decided in early 1991. In this revolutionary decision, the First Senate fundamentally altered German family law by striking down provisions requiring married couples to adopt the surname of the husband in the event that the spouses fail to agree on using one of their names in common. The court took judicial notice of changing social reality and announced that such classifications lack any basis in "objective differences between the sexes."[111] More recently, in *Fire Brigade II* (1995), the same senate ruled that several state laws requiring men only to serve in local fire brigades or, alternatively, to pay a tax if they fail to volunteer for such service, is incompatible with Article 3. Recalling its by now settled constitutional case law, the senate declared that any legal differentiation between the sexes can only be justified if "unavoidable for the regulation of matters which by nature affect one of the sexes."[112]

NOTE: WOMEN AND AFFIRMATIVE ACTION. The Fair Employment Act of 1980 mentioned in the introduction to this section on equality and social economy applied only to private employers. The act expressed parliament's view that the social state principle (*Sozialstaatsprinzip*) obliges government to adopt antidiscrimination measures designed to ensure formal equality between the sexes. Far more uncertain, however, was whether the principle of the social state, when construed in the light of Article 3 (2), requires affirmative action to abolish the effects of past discrimination. Arguments were being advanced in support of such measures, although their constitutional validity remained in doubt.[113] Legal scholars favoring compensatory legislation received some support from the Constitutional Court's decision in the *Pension Reform* case (1987), which sustained the validity of a provision allowing women to retire earlier than men because of the "double burden" (*Doppelbelastung*) they endured from pregnancy and child care.[114]

In a case of major significance decided on November 16, 1993, however, the First Senate signaled its approval of affirmative action measures.[115] A company had declined to hire a woman as a machinist — she was the only female among forty applicants — because she was inexperienced and as a woman was not strong enough to do the job. In reviewing the decision of the labor court that had rejected her complaint under the 1980 antidiscrimination act, the First Senate ruled that discrimination exists even if sex is only one of several reasons for the rejection. But then the senate went on to rule that the 1980 statute was insufficiently protective of women's rights, suggesting that parliament should broaden the statute to create equal conditions in employment.[116]

It may not have been entirely coincidental that a month after this decision, the Constitutional Court of Hesse upheld a *Land* statute prescribing the use of quotas to increase the representation of women in the public service.[117] In June 1994, parliament passed legislation not only extending the antidiscriminatory features of the 1980 statute to all public employees, but also including special measures to establish four-year plans to promote and hire more female public service employees.[118] Finally, a long-term effort to amend Article 3 (2) succeeded in 1994. The original version proclaimed that "men and women shall have equal rights." The new amendment added these words: "The state shall seek to ensure equal treatment of men and women and to remove existing disadvantages [between them]."[119]

NOTE: PUBLIC EMPLOYMENT AND THE UNITY TREATY. The Unity Treaty authorized the dismissal of public employees no longer needed to staff the reorganized bureaucracies in the five new eastern *Länder*. Many agencies were targeted for dissolution (*Abwicklung*), and other administrative units were restructured in accordance with FRG law. Employees of dissolved agencies were entitled to draw 70 percent of their pay for six to nine months, depending on their age, during which time an effort would be made to find them new jobs in the public service. If they were not reassigned within the prescribed "waiting period" (*Warteschleife*) — and most were not — their government employment would come to an end, making them eligible for unemployment compensation. Hundreds of affected employees filed constitutional complaints, asserting that the treaty provisions authorizing their dismissal deprived them of their property interest in government employment and their freedom to choose an occupation and place of work in violation, respectively, of Articles 14 and 12. All complaints were consolidated for decision in the *Public Servant Dissolution* case.[120]

In confining its extended analysis to Article 12, the Constitutional Court declared that occupational freedom was implicated in the dismissals and that GDR public servants could not be discharged because the East German government had ceased to exist. The Unity Treaty converted the old GDR's public servants into employees of the FRG; hence, any interference with their employment contracts would have to be assessed in the light of Article 12. Choosing a place of work, said the court, is linked to one's guaranteed right to choose an occupation, and the state may not interfere with the exercise of either choice unless for valid reasons related to the public interest. In organizing the public service, however, the state may determine the number of its agencies and their location.

Having made these points, and after examining the Unity Treaty's general waiting period provisions in the glow of the principle of proportionality, the court found that the measures taken under the treaty were necessary to achieve the goals of unification, among which is the establishment of a modern and effective system of public administration in the new states. The court went on, however, to invalidate the dismissal of pregnant women and women on maternity leave as incompatible with the constitutional injunction of Article 6 (4) requiring the care and protection of all mothers. The court also objected to terminating the contracts of single parents, disabled persons, and the elderly, pointing out that because of the special vulnerability of these groups, the state would have to adopt measures to ensure their nondiscriminatory treatment.[121]

Two other cases growing out of postunification social and political reconstruction deserve notice. The first involved the dismantling of East Germany's well-known Academy of Science, a major governmental research organization centrally controlled and consisting of some 24,000 scholars, scientists, and employees organized into disciplinary units. (Article 38 of the Unity Treaty laid down the procedures for dissolving and evaluating the structures of science and research in East Germany. Paragraph 3 designated December 31, 1991, as the day on which many GDR research institutes would cease to exist.) In responding to the petitions of nearly 500 scientists and employees whose jobs and departments were being terminated or reconstituted, the court found, as in *Public Servant Dissolution,* that the procedures employed in dissolving or reordering scientific institutes and reassessing the credentials of individual scholars were necessary to bring research and science up to the traditional standards of academic governance in West Germany. But once again the court invalidated the dismissal of pregnant women and new mothers. In addition, the court extended the employment contracts of persons who were given insufficient notice of their dismissal and thus little time to find alternative employment.[122]

The second case was brought by East German lawyers excluded from the practice of law for having collaborated with the State Security Service (*Stasi*). In July 1992 parliament enacted a statute disbarring any East German lawyer whose activities prior to September 15, 1990, had disregarded the principle of humanity or the rule of law or had involved official or unofficial collaboration with the Stasi.[123] Any such person was considered "unworthy" (*unwürdig*) of membership in the legal profession. In the *East German Disbarment* case, the court narrowed the statute's application. It would apply to former GDR lawyers found guilty of a serious violation of human rights, but not to lawyers whose behavior fell short of that. The court ruled, for example, that Article 12 (1) forbade the disbarment of a lawyer who had done no more than file periodic reports with the Stasi on conversations heard and activities performed in an art gallery, particularly since the reports had not resulted in any serious infringement of human rights.[124]

CONCLUSION

The rights to property and the freedom to choose an occupation are fundamental freedoms under the Basic Law. They are crucial to Germany's scheme of ordered liberty because they are bound up with the development of the human personality. These rights may be limited by law so long as their essence is preserved. Indeed, given their objective character, these rights, like other fundamental value decisions of the Basic Law, warrant affirmative state protection. The state is, in short, obligated to create conditions in which these rights can flourish. As guaranteed rights they can be limited only by law, and any such limitation must be compatible with other constitutional rights, most particularly with the principles of equality and the social state (*Sozialstaatsprinzip*), as recent cases involving sex discrimination and East German employment practices have shown. The legislature has a large measure of discretion in regulating the economy, and even in defining property; but legislation in these matters must be sensitive to social change and the needs of the common good. Above all, legislators must be guided by a constitutional perspective in these matters. If technological, economic, or social change begins to endanger or threaten guaranteed rights, proper corrective measures may be required as a matter of constitutional law.

7

HUMAN DIGNITY AND PERSONHOOD

The Basic Law places human dignity at the center of its scheme of constitutional values. Article 1 (1) declares: "The dignity of man is inviolable. To respect and protect it is the duty of all state authority." Paragraph 2 underlines the inseparability of human dignity and basic rights: "The German people therefore acknowledge inviolable and inalienable human rights as the basis of every community, of peace and justice in the world."[1] Thus basic rights and human dignity as a normative concept embrace one another in German constitutional law. Of primary importance, however, is the human dignity clause. In the view of the Federal Constitutional Court, this clause expresses the highest value of the Basic Law, informing the substance and spirit of the entire document.[2] While encompassing all guaranteed rights, the concept of human dignity also includes a morality of duty that may limit the exercise of a fundamental right. Little wonder, then, that the human dignity clause is such a fertile source of constitutional litigation, rivaling, as it does, the debate over the meaning of the due process clause in American constitutional law.[3]

The human dignity clause is almost always read in tandem with the general liberty interests secured by the personality, inviolability, and right-to-life clauses of Article 2. The relationship between Article 1 and Article 2 is symbiotic; all of their provisions nourish and reinforce one another. As capstones of the Basic Law, they contain ringing declarations of human freedom. The general liberty interests of Article 2, however, are also subject to express limits. Thus, as Article 2 (1) provides: "Everyone shall have the right to the free development of his or her personality," but only "insofar as he or she does not violate the rights of others or offend against the constitutional order or the moral code."[4] Paragraph 2 similarly guarantees to everyone "the right to life and to the inviolability of his or her person," and in addition declares that "the liberty of the individual shall be inviolable." According to the final sentence of this paragraph, however, "these rights may be limited only by law."

THE DIGNITY OF PERSONS

7.1 Microcensus Case (1969)
27 BVerfGE 1

[A federal census statute provided for the periodic collection of normal household and employment statistics. In 1960 the statute was amended to require additional information on vacation and recreational trips taken by household residents. A householder was fined DM 100 for refusing to supply this information. He contested the fine in a judicial proceeding, contending that the compulsory disclosure of private information, even for statistical purposes, violated his constitutional right to human dignity under Article 1 of the Basic Law.]

Judgment of the First Senate. . . .

1. The statute is compatible with the Basic Law. . . .

C. II. A statistical survey on the subject of "vacations and recreational trips" based on a random sample of the population does not violate Article 1 (1), Article 2 (1), or any other provision of the Basic Law.

1. (a) According to Article 1 (1) of the Basic Law, the dignity of man is inviolable and must be respected and protected by all state authority. Human dignity is at the very top of the value order of the Basic Law. This commitment to the dignity of man dominates the spirit of Article 2 (1), as it does all other provisions of the Basic Law. The state may take no measure, not even by law, that violates the dignity of the person beyond the limits specified by Article 2 (1), . . . [which] guarantees to each citizen an inviolable sphere of privacy beyond the reach of public authority.

(b) In the light of this image of man, every human being is entitled to social recognition and respect in the community. The state violates human dignity when it treats persons as mere objects. It would thus be inconsistent with the principle of human dignity to require a person to record and register all aspects of his personality, even though such an effort is carried out anonymously in the form of a statistical survey; [the state] may not treat a person as an object subject to an inventory of any kind. The state has no right to pierce the [protected] sphere of privacy by thoroughly checking into the personal matters of its citizens. [It] must leave the individual with an inner space for the purpose of the free and responsible development of his personality. Within this space the individual is his own master. He can thus "withdraw into himself, alone, to the total exclusion of the outside world, and enjoy the right to solitude" [quotation from Josef Wintrich, a former president of the Federal Constitutional Court, writing in a legal journal]. The state invades this realm when in certain circumstances it takes an action—however value neutral—

that tends to inhibit the free development of personality because of the psychological pressure of general public compliance.

(c) However, not every statistical survey requiring the disclosure of personal data violates the dignity of the individual or impinges upon the right to self-determination in the innermost private areas of life. As a member of society, every person is bound to respond to an official census and to answer certain questions about himself, because such information is necessary for government planning.

[One] can regard a statistical questionnaire as demeaning and as a threat to one's right of self-determination when it intrudes into that intimate realm of personal life which by its very nature is confidential in character. In a modern industrial society there are restrictions against such administrative depersonalization. On the other hand, where an official survey is concerned only with the relation of the person to the world around him, it does not generally intrude on personal privacy. This is true . . . when the information loses its personal character by virtue of its anonymity. The prerequisite for [this conclusion] is that anonymity be adequately preserved. In the present case [two factors] guarantee [anonymity]: a statutory prohibition against the publication of information obtained from individuals, as well as the fact that census takers are bound under penalty of law to maintain the confidentiality of the information. [The census taker] has no statutory duty to report data to internal revenue agencies; moreover, responsible officials may not convey any [census] information to their superiors in an official capacity if they have not been expressly given this power under the law.

(d) The collection of census data regarding vacations and recreational trips does not violate Article 1 (1) of the Basic Law. The questionnaire at issue does implicate the sphere of privacy, but it does not force the individual to reveal intimate details of his personal life. Nor does it allow the state to monitor individual relationships which are not otherwise accessible to the outside world and are consequently of a private nature. [The state] could have obtained data regarding the destination and length of vacation trips, lodging, and transportation without a census, although with much more difficulty. The information solicited does not, therefore, involve that most intimate realm into which the state may not intrude. [The state] may [therefore] use the questionnaire for statistical purposes without violating the individual's dignity or right to self-determination. . . .

[The *Census Act* case, reprinted below as case no. 7.6, is the sequel to *Microcensus. Census Act,* however, is more appropriately placed in the section on the right of personality.]

NOTE: THE BASIS AND ORIGIN OF HUMAN DIGNITY. "The dignity of man is founded upon eternal rights with which every person is endowed by nature," read the first draft of Article 1 produced by the Herrenchiemsee Conference. Later, in the

Main Committee of the Parliamentary Council, Christian Democratic delegates sought to characterize these "eternal rights" as "God-given." Social Democrats and Free Democrats resisted the use of such language because of its implications for constitutional interpretation.[5] The result was a succinct and neutral formulation: "The dignity of man is inviolable." Except for the most dogmatic of legal positivists among the framers, the main party groups (Christian, Social, and Free Democrats) in the council were united in the proposition that human dignity, like other fundamental rights of personhood, is anterior to the state. Such rights belong to persons as persons, and in this sense they were regarded as transcendental. The framers were thus successful in refusing to identify the concept of human dignity with a particular philosophical or religious school of thought. The constitutional text seems fully consistent with a variety of philosophical perspectives, although the *Microcensus* case appears to adopt Kantian language in that persons are always to be treated as ends, and not as mere objects of manipulation. The term "language" is used here because the view that people are ends and not means is certainly shared by non-Kantians such as Christian natural-law theorists. Moreover, as the *Mephisto* case shows, the court's view of human dignity falls far short of any judicial glorification of the concept of personal autonomy. Kantian autonomy, in the court's eyes, includes a strong sense of the "morality of duty."

7.2 Mephisto Case (1971)
30 BVerfGE 173

[While in exile from Nazi Germany in the 1930s, Klaus Mann published *Mephisto,* a satirical novel based on the career of his brother-in-law, Gustaf Gründgens, a Faustian actor who had attained fame and fortune during the Third Reich by renouncing his former liberal views and currying the favor of Nazi leaders. Mann later admitted that for him Gründgens personified "the traitor par excellence, the macabre embodiment of corruption and cynicism . . . who prostitutes his talent for the sake of some tawdry fame and transitory wealth." The fictionalized character, Hendrik Höfgen, was a caricature of the model on which he was based. When *Mephisto* was about to be reissued by a West German publisher in 1964, Gründgens's adopted son secured from the Hamburg Court of Appeals an order banning its distribution. The judgment was affirmed by the High Court of Justice on the ground that the novel dishonored the good name and memory of the now-deceased actor. The publisher filed a constitutional complaint in the Federal Constitutional Court against both judgments on the ground that they contravened Article 5 (3) of the Basic Law, which guarantees the freedom of art and science. The court sought to balance the right to freedom of art against the personality and human dignity clauses of Article 1. The extracts below focus mainly on the balance between speech and dignity.]

_____

Judgment of the First Senate. . . .

The constitutional complaint is rejected.

C. III. 4. . . . [We] must also reject the opinion that the constitutional order, the rights of others, and the moral code may restrict the freedom of the arts pursuant to Article 2 (1), second half of the sentence. This view is inconsistent with the subsidiary relationship of Article 2 (1) to the individual liberty rights specifically mentioned [in the Constitution]. The Federal Constitutional Court has consistently recognized [this relationship] in its case law.

> [The sentences above show how the court uses the concept within the Basic Law's hierarchy of values. See the section in this chapter on the right to personality for a detailed explanation of the subsidiary character of the personality clause of Article 2 (1).]

5. On the other hand, the right of artistic liberty is not unlimited. Like all basic rights, the guarantee of liberty in Article 5 (3) [1] is based on the Basic Law's image of man as an autonomous person who develops freely within the social community. But the [fact that] this basic right contains no limiting proviso means that only the Constitution itself can determine limits on artistic freedom. Since freedom of the arts does not contain a provision entitling the legislature to limit [this basic right], it cannot be curtailed by [provisions of] the general legal system. [If] an indefinite clause that applies when goods necessary for the continued existence of the national community are endangered has no anchor in the Constitution and does not sufficiently [conform] to the principle of the rule of law, it may not limit this right. Rather, [we] must resolve conflict[s] relating to the guarantee of artistic freedom by interpreting the Constitution according to the value order established in the Basic Law and the unity of its fundamental system of values. As a part of the Basic Law's value system, freedom of the arts is closely related to the dignity of man guaranteed in Article 1, which, as the supreme value, governs the entire value system of the Basic Law. But the guarantee of freedom of the arts can conflict with the constitutionally protected sphere of personality because a work of art can also produce social effects. ·

Because a work of art acts not only as an aesthetic reality but also exists in the social world, an artist's use of personal data about people in his environment can affect their rights to societal respect and esteem. . . .

6. The courts [below] properly referred to Article 1 (1) in order to determine the late actor Gründgens's protected sphere of personality. It would be incompatible with the constitutional commandment that human dignity is inviolate — a commandment which acts as the foundation for all basic rights — if a person, possessed of human dignity by virtue of his personhood, could be degraded or debased . . .

even after his death. Accordingly, the obligation that Article 1 (1) imposes on all state authority to afford the individual protection from attacks on his dignity does not end with death. . . .

7. The resolution of the conflict between the protection of one's personality and the right to artistic freedom must therefore take into account not only the effects of a work of art in the extra-artistic social sphere but also art-specific aspects. The guarantee of liberty in Article 5 (3) [1] leaves its mark on the image of man upon which Article 1 (1) is based, just as the value conception of Article 1 (1) in turn influences the guarantee [of artistic freedom]. The individual's right to societal respect and esteem does not have precedence over artistic freedom any more than the arts may disregard a person's general right to respect. . . .

Only after carefully weighing all the facts of individual cases can [one] decide whether an artistic presentation's use of personal data threatens such a grave encroachment upon the protected private sphere of the person it describes that it could preclude publication of the work of art. [One] must take into account whether and to what extent the "image" [of a particular person] appears so independent from the "original" because of the artistic shaping of the material and its incorporation into and subordination to the overall organism of the work of art that the individual, intimate aspects have become objective in the sense of a general, symbolic character of the "figure." If such a study . . . reveals that the artist has given or even wanted to give a "portrait" of the "original," then the [the resolution of this conflict] depends on the extent of artistic abstraction or the extent and importance of the "falsification" of the reputation or memory of the person concerned.

IV. 2. . . . [T]he Hamburg Appeals Court and the Federal High Court of Justice assumed that the protection of Gründgens's right to respect extends to the social sphere. In this regard the Federal High Court correctly considered that the need for protection — and accordingly the obligation to protect — diminishes as the memory of the deceased person fades. . . . On the other hand, the courts also assumed that Klaus Mann's novel constitutes a work of art within the meaning of Article 5 (3). . . . The courts tried to solve this conflict by weighing the conflicting interests against each other. . . .

> [In sustaining the judgment against the complainant, the Constitutional Court stressed the narrow limits of its powers of review. "In particular," said the court, "the establishment and evaluation of facts and the interpretation of laws and their application to individual cases are the business of the regular courts and cannot be reviewed by the Federal Constitutional Court." The Constitutional Court sees its task as one of determining whether the court below did, in fact, properly weigh the conflicting rights of the parties under the Basic Law, and whether it attached the proper significance to the constitutional rights implicated in the case. The court found that the judgment below

was fully and adequately explained. It thus did not "demonstrate any incorrect conception of the essence of the basic right that was defeated."]

Finally, [complainant] cannot challenge the conclusion of the courts . . . by arguing that the ban on publication is disproportional to the encroachment on the late Gustaf Gründgens's right to respect. It is true that the Federal Constitutional Court has repeatedly emphasized that the principle of proportionality has constitutional rank and must therefore be considered whenever state authority encroaches on the citizen's sphere of liberty. But the instant case does not involve such an encroachment. The courts simply had to decide a claim based on private law made by one citizen against another; that is, to give concrete definition to a relationship of private law in an individual case. . . . The primary function of private law is to settle conflicts of interests between persons of equal legal status in a manner as appropriate as possible. . . .

[Chapter 8 includes extracts from *Mephisto* dealing with the free-speech aspects of the case as well as the dissenting opinions of Justices Stein and Rupp–von Brünneck (see no. 8.12).]

NOTE: HUMAN DIGNITY AND THE IMAGE OF MAN AND POLITY. The Constitutional Court's "dignitarian" jurisprudence contains numerous declarations about the nature of the human person and the polity. Indeed, this jurisprudence would be unintelligible without reference to the concepts of person and society on which it is based. In seeking to advance human dignity as a constitutional value, both court and commentators have relied on three politically significant sources of ethical theory in postwar Germany — Christian natural law, Kantian thought, and social democratic thought — present in the constitutional text as a whole. It is hardly surprising, therefore, on the natural-law side, to find the human person described in legal literature and in several constitutional cases as a "spiritual-moral being" entitled to rights found in a "preexisting supra-positive order of justice."[6] On the other hand, as G. P. Fletcher has pointed out,[7] emphasis in the case law on individual autonomy, moral duty, and human rationality manifests equally strong Kantian influences, just as the more socially oriented strands of constitutional thought may be said to reflect egalitarian theory. These orientations have converged in German constitutional case law to produce an integrated conception of the human person as an individual possessing spiritual autonomy, which — in a properly governed society — is to be guided by social discipline and practical reasonableness.[8]

    A strong personalist and communitarian philosophy pervades this conception of the human person. *Mephisto* captures the essence of this philosophy when the opinion refers to "man as an autonomous person who develops freely *within the social community*" (emphasis added).[9] The *Investment Aid I* case (1954; no. 6.1) advanced the concept of man as a community-centered person for the first time:

"The image of man in the Basic Law," declared the court, "is not that of an isolated, sovereign individual; rather, the Basic Law has decided in favor of a relationship between individual and community in the sense of a person's dependence on and commitment to the community, without infringing upon a person's individual value."[10] The morality of duty and the principle of human solidarity implicit in this statement and reflected in parts of the Basic Law bear the clear imprint of Kantian moral theory.[11] Needless to say, however, this theory is also shared by other reputable philosophical traditions in Germany.

Mephisto articulates a vision of the polity which may remind Americans of Lincoln's elevated image of a fraternal democracy.[12] Society, the court affirmed, is more than an aggregation of isolated individuals motivated by self-interest and a desire to manipulate one another for purely personal ends. Neither did the court offer a blanket endorsement of the value of autonomy as against competing social goods. Indeed, the notion of a simple opposition between person and polity is alien to the court's jurisprudence and the political theory of the Basic Law itself. The court's vigilant defense of personal freedom is embodied in the larger context of common life. Human dignity resides not only in individuality but in sociality as well. Such dignity requires the protection of the personality and freedom of the individual, but must also promote the goods of relationship, family, participation, communication, and civility.[13] The Basic Law was framed not for individuals alone but for an organic association of persons expressing its will to live a common social, political, economic, and moral life grounded in the overwhelming ethical principle that human beings must always be treated as ends, never as means. *Mephisto* even goes so far as to include in its vision of community not only the living, but the dead as well. According to the court, the dead — particularly those in living memory — remain in communion with the living, and we, the living, owe them continuing honor and respect.

This highly personalistic conception of human dignity was the focal point of a more recent constitutional attack on the sentence of life imprisonment, even for the crime of murder. The *Life Imprisonment* case (1977) is the closest available analogy to the American death penalty cases, in which the notion of human dignity has also played a significant role in constitutional argument.[14] (Owing to the abolition of capital punishment under Article 102 of the Basic Law, no death penalty cases have arisen in West Germany.) In *Life Imprisonment* the Constitutional Court considered an extensive literature as well as expert testimony on the effects of life imprisonment on the prisoner's dignity and personality. The Kantian injunction that human beings are to be treated as ends, not means, applies as much to closed environments as it does to normal society. Even the use of the polygraph in a criminal proceeding has been invalidated by the court on the basis of human dignity. To elicit the truth by attaching a person to a machine, said the court, is to regard him as an object, and not as a human being capable of telling the truth through ordinary questioning.[15]

7.3 Life Imprisonment Case (1977)
45 BVerfGE 187

[A drug addict threatened to expose the defendant for selling forbidden drugs if he failed to deliver a certain drug already ordered and allegedly paid for. At an appointed time the defendant delivered the drug and then, as the addict was injecting himself with it, shot him in the back of the head three times at close range. The Criminal Code as revised in 1969 prescribed a mandatory penalty of life imprisonment for any person who killed another out of wanton cruelty or to cover up some other criminal activity. The defendant was charged under this statute. The Verden District Court, before which the defendant was to be tried, regarded the penalty as incompatible with the dignity clause of Article 1, whereupon it referred the question to the Constitutional Court. The trial court claimed that mental deterioration would result from the knowledge that one would never be able to return to society, and that the punishment thus conflicted with the legislature's obligation to respect the human dignity to which every human being, even a criminal, is entitled. The lower court argued that mandatory life imprisonment, offering no possibility of reentering society, would reduce the criminal to the state of a mere object.]

Judgment of the First Senate. . . .

A sentence of life imprisonment represents an extraordinarily severe infringement of a person's basic rights. Of all valid punishments in the catalogue of [criminal] penalties, this one is the most invasive of the inviolable right to personal freedom guaranteed by Article 2 (2). . . . In carrying out this penalty, the state not only limits the basic right secured by Article 2 (2), but it also — depending of course on the individual case — implicates numerous other rights guaranteed by the Basic Law. The question posed by this case is therefore of considerable gravity and importance.

Under Article 2 (2) of the Basic Law, the right of personal freedom may be limited by an act of parliament. But parliament's freedom to introduce legislation is limited by the constitution in a number of ways. In exercising its powers the legislature must take account of both the inviolability of human dignity (Article 1 [1]), which is the highest value of the constitutional order, as well as constitutional principles such as equality (Article 3 [1]), the rule of law [*Rechtsstaatlichkeit*], and the social state (Article 20 [1]). Since the freedom of the individual is already such an important legal interest that it may only be limited on grounds that are truly compelling, any lifetime deprivation requires special scrutiny by the standard of the principle of proportionality. . . .

C. I. 2. Life imprisonment has for ages been at the core of criminal sanctions. Its significance in modern times has decreased because the death penalty is now the harshest penalty. The dispute over the death penalty has made life imprisonment an alternative the constitutionality of which has not generally been questioned. A substantial amount of older literature has examined in depth the effect and consequences of life imprisonment on the human personality. Advocates of the death penalty advance the argument that life imprisonment is a more cruel and inhuman punishment than the death penalty. It was not until the furor over the death penalty had subsided that scientists in the late 1960s began to concern themselves with the problems of life imprisonment. Since then, the discussion of this maximum penalty has not died down. In fact, the controversy has in recent years grown more intense in the scientific literature, while the courts have barely concerned themselves with the issue. The criminal courts have presumed that life imprisonment presents no constitutional problem. Only very recently did the First Senate of the Federal High Court of Justice with jurisdiction over criminal cases — probably spurred on by the Verden District Court's reference to us — venture to say: "That the threat of life imprisonment for murder is compatible with the Constitution conforms to the general legal outlook and to our existing jurisprudence; the senate sees no occasion now to depart from this view." [The Federal High Court] summarily declared the constitutional doubt raised on appeal in this case against section 211 of the Criminal Code to be unfounded. The court regarded the penalty of life imprisonment as wholly compatible with the Basic Law. . . .

> [The Constitutional Court reviewed the arguments that led the framers of the Basic Law to abolish the death penalty. In their view, the court found, life imprisonment under some conditions would substitute for the death penalty. In the following extract the court employed sociological analysis while asserting the need for an "objective" approach to constitutional interpretation.]

This determination, however, does not clearly decide the constitutional issue before us. Neither original history nor the ideas and intentions of the framers are of decisive importance in interpreting particular provisions of the Basic Law. Since the adoption of the Basic Law, our understanding of the content, function, and effect of basic rights has deepened. Additionally, the medical, psychological, and sociological effects of life imprisonment have become better known. Current attitudes are important in assessing the constitutionality of life imprisonment. New insights can influence and even change the evaluation of this punishment in terms of human dignity and the principles of a constitutional state.

II. 1. The constitutional principles of the Basic Law embrace the respect and protection of human dignity. The free human person and his dignity are the highest values of the constitutional order. The state in all of its forms is obliged to respect and defend it. This is based on the conception of man as a spiritual-moral being endowed with the freedom to determine and develop himself. This freedom within the meaning of the Basic Law is not that of an isolated and self-regarding individual but rather [that] of a person related to and bound by the community. In the light of this community-boundedness it cannot be "in principle unlimited." The individual must allow those limits on his freedom of action that the legislature deems necessary in the interest of the community's social life; yet the autonomy of the individual has to be protected. This means that [the state] must regard every individual within society with equal worth. It is contrary to human dignity to make persons the mere tools of the state. The principle that "each person must shape his own life" applies unreservedly to all areas of law; the intrinsic dignity of each person depends on his status as an independent personality. In the area of criminal sanctions, which demands the highest degree of justice, Article 1 (1) determines the nature of punishment and the relationship between guilt and atonement. The basic principle *"nulla poena sine culpa"* has the rank of a constitutional norm. Every punishment must justly relate to the severity of the offense and the guilt of the offender. Respect for human dignity especially requires the prohibition of cruel, inhuman, and degrading punishments. [The state] cannot turn the offender into an object of crime prevention to the detriment of his constitutionally protected right to social worth and respect. [It] must preserve the underlying assumptions governing the individual and the social existence of the human person. Thus Article 1 (1) considered in tandem with the principle of the state based on social justice requires the state to guarantee that minimal existence — especially in the execution of criminal penalties — necessary for a life worthy of a human being. If human dignity is understood in this way, it would be intolerable for the state forcefully to deprive a person of his freedom without at least providing him with the chance to someday regain this freedom.

We must never lose sight of the fact that human dignity is not dispensable. [We] cannot separate our recognition of the duty to respect human dignity from its historical development. The history of criminal law shows clearly that milder punishments have replaced those more cruel in character and that the wave of the future is toward more humane and differentiated forms of punishment. Thus any decision defining human dignity in concrete terms must be based on our present understanding of it, and not on any claim to a conception of timeless validity.

2. If these standards are used in assessing the nature and effect of life imprisonment, then there is no violation of Article 1 (1)....

(aa) A sentence of life imprisonment must be supplemented, as is constitutionally required, by meaningful treatment of the prisoner. Regarding those prisoners under life sentences, prisons also have the duty to strive toward their resocialization, to preserve their ability to cope with life and to counteract the negative effects of incarceration and the destructive changes in personality that accompany imprisonment. This task finds its justification in the constitution itself; it can be inferred from the guarantee of the inviolability of human dignity within the meaning of Article 1 (1) of the Basic Law.

In enforcing this punishment in the Federal Republic, state officials are under a duty not merely to incarcerate but also to rehabilitate the prisoner through appropriate treatment, a policy consistent with previous decisions of this court. The court on several occasions has maintained that rehabilitation is constitutionally required in any community that establishes human dignity as its centerpiece and commits itself to the principle of social justice. The [prisoner's] interest in rehabilitation flows from Article 2 (1) in tandem with Article 1. The condemned criminal must be given the chance, after atoning for his crime, to reenter society. The state is obligated within the realm of the possible to take all measures necessary for the achievement of this goal. . . .

III. 4. (a) An assessment of the constitutionality of life imprisonment from the vantage point of Article 1 (1) and the principle of the rule of law shows that a humane enforcement of life imprisonment is possible only when the prisoner is given a concrete and realistically attainable chance to regain his freedom at some later point in time; the state strikes at the very heart of human dignity if [it] treats the prisoner without regard to the development of his personality and strips him of all hope of ever earning his freedom. The legal provisions relating to the granting of pardons do not sufficiently guarantee this hope, which makes the sentence bearable in terms of human dignity. . . .

A new trend was evident in the Justice Ministry's 1974 draft of the fifteenth amendment to the Criminal Code. The draft provides that offenders sentenced to life imprisonment should have their records reviewed, with their consent, after they have served a certain length of time — the draft suggests at least twelve to fifteen years. A review board would then decide whether the prisoner is likely to commit more crimes after his release. An independent parole board would render this decision subject to the approval of a superior appellate court. The foreword to the draft states, of course, that under certain conditions life imprisonment would be enforced if necessary to protect the common good. If needed to protect the common good, [the state] should not only impose such sentences but also carry them out. Experience shows, however, that incarceration for life is not always necessary [to protect] the common good. With regard to murder, [the crime for which] a sentence of life imprisonment is most often imposed, we are dealing with a significant number of persons who in all probability will not repeat their crime. In these cases, where the social prognosis is positive, life imprisonment can hardly be justified. Moreover, the long, continuous lack of freedom is an extraordinary physical and psychological burden that could result in substantial detriment to the prisoner's personality, one good reason for introducing the possibility of release. A sentence of life imprisonment cannot be enforced humanely if the prisoner is denied *a priori* any and every possibility of returning to freedom. Indeed, it has hardly been the rule up to now to require the prisoner to serve out his life term. Yet an individual and case-by-case determination of whether a prisoner merits parole is not a satisfactory solution. Leading officials from the various states noted in their resolution of March 16, 1972, that the situation would have to be corrected by a uniform and coordinated parole policy [throughout the Federal Republic]. . . .

IV. The legislature does not offend the constitutional requirement of sensible and appropriate punishment if it decides to impose life imprisonment for a murder of wanton cruelty. . . .

[The court next described various theories of punishment that inform the criminal law. Noting that current law adheres to the so-called unification theory, which tries to bring all the purposes of punishment — i.e., rehabilitation, retribution, atonement, and prevention of crime — into a balanced relationship, the court rejected the district court's contention that life imprisonment in and of itself effectively serves none of these purposes.]

Seen as a whole, life imprisonment for murder is not a senseless or disproportionate punishment. . . .

(c) The imposition of a life sentence does not contradict the constitutionally based concept of rehabilitation (positive special prevention) in the light of the practice of granting pardons and current legislation governing the criminal process. The murderer sentenced to life usually does have a chance to be released after serving a certain length of time. . . . But for the criminal who remains a threat to society, the goal of rehabilitation may never be fulfilled. It is the particular personal circumstances of the criminal which may rule out successful rehabilitation rather than the sentence of life imprisonment itself. . . .

V. 1. Article 1 (1) and Article 2 (1) (the dignity and responsibility of persons) together with the principle of the rule of law require that guilt be assessed in accord with the idea of justice. [The state] must therefore tailor the threatened punishment to the severity of the crime and the culpability of the offender. . . .

2. The issue here is whether the principle of proportionality requires a penalty other than life imprisonment for "murders of wanton cruelty" or for cases of murder "to conceal another crime." The question is particularly relevant here because, with the exception of murder and genocide, the courts are regularly granted a range of punishment within which the applicable court may ascertain, in accordance with those considerations pertaining to the award of punishment named in section 46 of the Penal Code, the extent of punishment in a concrete case. In the present case the referring court also demands a similar discretion so as not to be forced to impose the mandatory sentence of life imprisonment.

. . . In a serious crime such as murder, substantive justice may warrant the effort to impose a uniform system of punishment. But clearly, the application of a rigid system of punishment may lead to unsatisfactory results in individual cases. The prescription of such harsh sentences would be free of constitutional doubt only when the judge retains some discretion in imposing a penalty that conforms to the constitutional principle of proportionality. But as oral argument before this court has shown, when section 211 of the Penal Code — particularly the wanton cruelty and to conceal another crime provisions — is read in the light of the general section of the Penal Code, these provisions can be interpreted in a constitutionally permissible way. . . .

(c) . . . Thus a literal interpretation of section 211 and its constituent elements is not mandatory. Narrower interpretations permitting proportionate sentences are permissible. Expert testimony and the aforementioned brief support [this approach]. It is ultimately the task of the responsible courts to adjudicate the tension between the principle of proportionality and the punitive sanction [of the law]. . . . This approach is compatible with section 211 (2) and the general purpose [behind the statute]; the constitutionality of the decision is thus affirmed. . . .

NOTE: *LIFE IMPRISONMENT* AND ITS AFTERMATH. *Life Imprisonment* was not the first case to address the question of prisoners' rights. Already in the *Prison Correspondence I* case (1972), the court noted that prisoners would have to be treated in accordance with constitutional principles and that any limitation on this basic right would require an act of parliament.[16] The decision in *Life Imprisonment* did not invalidate life imprisonment for murder as such. What the court said is that a person may not be kept in prison for life as a matter of course. Rather, the state is obligated to consider the particular situation of each prisoner in terms of his or her capacity for rehabilitation and resocialization and in the light of the principles of human dignity, the rule of law, and the social state. (See the *Lebach* case [no. 8.10] for another example of the court's application of these principles.)

Soon after the decision in *Life Imprisonment,* parliament amended the Criminal Code by authorizing courts to suspend a life sentence when the situation warranted the offender's release from prison. Under the revised statute, courts may release an offender for a probationary period of five years if he has served fifteen years of his punishment and if "the gravity of the offender's guilt does not necessitate that he continue to serve his sentence." In determining whether or not to release a person sentenced to life imprisonment, courts must consider the personality of the offender, his behavior in prison, the circumstances of his crime, and his capacity to lead a normal life outside prison.[17]

The *War Criminal* case (1986) raised the issue of whether an offender could be required to serve his life sentence merely because of the gravity of his crime.[18] *War Criminal* involved a former member of the ss sentenced to life imprisonment in 1962 at the age of sixty-six for sending fifty persons, including children and pregnant women, to their deaths in the gas chambers of Auschwitz and Birkenau. Prison officials approved his petition for release in 1982, when he was eighty-eight years old, but the Frankfurt Superior Court disallowed the release because of the gravity of the offender's crime. The Constitutional Court sustained the court's judgment because in the circumstances of 1985, when it had decided the case, the superior court had properly weighed the factors bearing upon a decision to release in the light of the value of human dignity. Yet the court gave a new and liberal twist to *Life Imprisonment* by emphasizing that a judicial balancing of these factors may not place too heavy an emphasis on the gravity of the crime as opposed to the personality, state of mind, and age of the offender.

In *War Criminal* the court made clear, as it did in the seminal case, that life imprisonment as such, assuming guilt and a punishment that fits the crime, is constitutionally unobjectionable. The offender, however, cannot be denied all hope for release, for the ultimate aim of any punishment, including life imprisonment, is the rehabilitation and "resocialization" of the offender. Citing the *Prison Furlough* case (1983), decided three years before *War Criminal,* the court observed: "The right to human dignity may not be denied to an offender, notwithstanding the gravity and barbarity of his crime, if we are to protect the value order of the Constitution."[19] Indeed, the Second Senate concluded its unanimous opinion by noting that in any subsequent proceeding involving the release of the offender in the instant case after he has reached the age of eighty-nine, the court would be obligated to weigh much more heavily than before the personality, age, and prison record of the offender. With this decision the Second Senate established the principle that every offender sentenced to life imprisonment, whatever the nature of his crime, must be allowed to live in the realistic hope of regaining his freedom.

NOTE: HUMAN DIGNITY AS A CONSTITUTIONAL VALUE. Both the court and commentators have characterized human dignity as an objective and subjective right: objective in the sense of imposing an affirmative obligation on the state to establish conditions necessary for the realization of dignity; subjective in the sense of barring the state from any direct interference with the negative freedom of individuals.[20] The court has tended to define the concept of human dignity in personalistic and communal terms; that is, in terms of a personhood that is not merely a projection of the autonomous self but is also oriented to communication with other persons and which reveals itself in the experience of the community. As a working concept of German constitutionalism, however, the meaning of human dignity is best understood in the light of its application to concrete situations. What the court appears to be saying in the cases reprinted above — and in several of those reprinted below — is that everyone, including the state, must respect the rationality and humanity of individual persons, although what is rational and humane may often depend on an interpreter's intuitive understanding of what is right and wrong in particular situations.

At this juncture it is important to note that the concept of human dignity is controversial among the justices and constitutional scholars. The controversy surrounding its meaning and application in Germany is similar to the American debate over the meaning and application of the substantive due-process-of-law clause. In Germany, unlike the United States, "dignitarian" jurisprudence often functions to limit or circumscribe specified rights in the Constitution. *Mephisto,* in which the value of human dignity trumped freedom of the press, is a classic example of this. Another example is the *Tobacco Atheist* case (1960),[21] in which the value of human rationality trumped a claim based on the free exercise of religion. In this case the Constitutional Court sustained a decision of prison officials to deny parole to an inmate (an unreconstructed Nazi) who had persuaded fellow inmates to abandon their Christian beliefs in exchange for tobacco and other gifts. The inmate's behavior, said the court, conflicted with the "general order of values" under the Basic Law. "A person who exploits the special circumstances of penal servitude and promises and rewards someone with luxury goods in order to make him renounce his beliefs does not enjoy the benefit of the protection of Article 4 (1) of the Basic Law." The court added: "It follows from the Basic Law's order of values, especially from the dignity of the human being, that a misuse [of a freedom] is especially apparent whenever the dignity of another person is violated."[22]

Justice Wolfgang Zeidler, a former president of the Federal Constitutional Court, was most resistant to what he had always regarded as the essential subjectivity involved in this process of interpretation. As *Tobacco Atheist* shows, dignitarian jurisprudence has evolved out of the Basic Law's "general order of values," an order of values which in Zeidler's view is presupposed, not substantiated. Phrases equivalent to "general order of values" that turn up repeatedly in constitutional cases involving the application of the principle of human dignity include "supreme basic values," "basic decisions of the Basic Law," and "unwritten elementary constitutional principles." Zeidler and other critics see these broad terms and phrases as a kind of "scaffold" superimposed on the structure of the Constitution, a scaffold that permits interpreters to wash the structure in religious and ideological solvents of their own choosing. In Zeidler's view, the ritual incantation of these broad — and indeterminant — standards of review too often leads to the triumph of general values over positive rights and liberties. "Whoever controls the [meaning of the] order of values," he once remarked, "controls the Constitution."[23]

THE RIGHT TO PERSONALITY

NOTE: THE PERSONALITY CLAUSE. The *Life Imprisonment* case shows that the human dignity clause of Article 1 and the general personality clause of Article 2 (1) are interlinked. The Constitutional Court rarely speaks of the right to personality without referring to human dignity.[24] Unlike the human dignity clause, however, the general right to personality is not a shorthand expression of other guaranteed rights.[25] The personality right is so broad in its phrasing that almost any content could be poured into it, and it could easily function as the first and last resort of constitutional arguments. Recognizing this, the Constitutional Court has sought to confine its reach. As a general rule, the personality clause is subordinate to those positive rights of liberty expressly mentioned in the Basic Law.[26] A complainant may invoke the personality clause only when he or she challenges a governmental act that invades a liberty interest vital to the exercise of personality outside the protection of any particular right.[27] In addition, the personality clause can be invoked only to vindicate a fundamental liberty interest against intrusive state activity. The right to personality is not an objective value like the principle of human dignity, and thus it cannot impose on the state an affirmative obligation to take some particular course of action. Finally, the court has limited the reach of the personality clause by breathing life into its restrictive clauses. As pointed out at the beginning of this chapter, the personality right secured by Article 2 (1) may be restrained in the interest of the rights of others, the moral code, or the constitutional order. If a given statutory restriction on some aspect of human behavior is in accord with the moral code or the constitutional order, the restriction will be sustained.

One of the most controversial of all the court's decisions interpreting the personality clause is the *Hashish Drug* case of 1994. Several lower courts had questioned the constitutionality of prison sentences imposed on the possession, use, or sale of narcotic drugs — so-called "soft drugs" — such as hashish and marijuana. In referring the constitutional issue to the Federal Constitutional Court, the lower courts doubted that the use of these soft drugs could be penalized while allowing the use of alcohol to remain unpunished. Lübeck's district court went so far as to suggest that the right to intoxication, like the right to eat and drink, is part of the liberty protected by Article 2 (1).

In an opinion more advisory than declaratory, the Second Senate sustained the constitutionality of the existing drug laws, but advised parliament, over the partial dissents of two justices, to decriminalize the possession and use of small amounts of these soft drugs. Just as the senate dismissed the extreme claims of the Lübeck court, it rejected any comparison between the consumption of alcohol and the use of narcotic drugs. The majority appeared willing to defer to parliament's judgment in determining the measures needed to curtail drug addiction; nevertheless, the court warned that the means used to achieve this goal should not be out of proportion to the scope of the law's objective, particularly when small amounts of these drugs are consumed without endangering third persons.[28]

Far less controversial was the *Child Legitimacy* case of 1994. Under German law, a child may contest his or her legitimacy in the presence of specified circumstances that might indicate the child's illegitimacy. Section 1598 of the German Civil Code (BGB), however, provides that the child is barred from filing such an action if she fails to contest her legitimacy within two years after coming of age, even if during this time she was unaware of facts which might have raised questions about the legitimacy of her birth. In *Child Legitimacy,* the court held this provision incompatible with the general personality clause. A state governed by the rule of law, said the court, cannot justify such limits on a legitimate interest in the circumstances of one's own birth. As in other cases where the court declines to nullify a provision of law but chooses instead to declare it incompatible (*unvereinbar*) with the Basic Law, the legislature was given a limited period of time to amend the law to remove the constitutional infirmity.[29]

NOTE: FREEDOM OF ACTION. In the *Elfes* case (1957), which is reprinted below, the Constitutional Court interpreted Article 2 (1) as establishing a general freedom of action (*Handlungsfreiheit*). In principle, this comprehensive freedom covers all forms of activity related to the expression of the whole personality. Boundless as this formulation seems, however, the court appears to have confined the freedom-of-action doctrine largely to economic and recreational contexts.[30] A recent application of the right to freedom of action that implicates both economic and recreational rights is the *Falconry License* case (1980).[31] West Germany's Federal Hunting Act requires all applicants for a hunting license to pass oral and written examinations as well as a shooting test. If an applicant hunts with hawks, he must also pass a special hawking test. The *Falconry* case involved a constitutional attack on the shooting test by a hawker who never used a gun. To require a gun test in this situation, held the court, denies the hawker's freedom of action within the meaning of Article 2 (1). "The rule of law, considered in relation to the general presumption of freedom in favor of the citizen," declared the court, "demands that the individual be protected against unnecessary intrusions by public authority. If a statutory intrusion is unavoidable, the means must be appropriate to achieve the legislative end and may not excessively burden the individual."[32]

7.4 Elfes Case (1957)
6 BVerfGE 32

[The complainant, an active member of the Christian Democratic Union (CDU), was elected to the North Rhine–Westphalia parliament in 1947. He was also a leading spokesman of a radical right-wing organization vehemently opposed to the Federal Republic's policies toward military defense and German reunification. He had participated in a number of conferences and demonstrations at home and abroad in which he sharply criticized these policies and for which he was refused a passport to travel abroad. Claiming that the state had violated his freedom of movement under Article 11, he filed a constitutional complaint against judicial decisions sustaining the denial of his passport.]

Judgment of the First Senate. . . .

The constitutional complaint is rejected.

II. 1. The complainant contends that section 7 (1) of the Passport Act of March 4, 1952, is null and void because the right to travel abroad, allegedly based on Article

11 of the Basic Law, is impermissibly limited. That is not so. The Passport Act provision reads: "A passport must be refused if facts justify the supposition that (a) the applicant threatens the internal or external security or other vital interests of the Federal Republic of Germany or one of the German states. . . ."

Article 11 (1) [of the Basic Law] guarantees freedom of movement "throughout the federal territory." This text clearly does not secure a fundamental right to travel outside the federal territory. What is more, the original history of the provision does not provide any support for such an interpretation. . . .

The fundamental right to freedom of movement may be limited only by the express provisions of Article 11 (2). Article 11 (2) states: "This right may be restricted only by or pursuant to a law . . . or in which such restriction is necessary to avert an imminent danger to the existence of the free democratic basic order of the federation or a state, to combat the danger of epidemics, to deal with natural disasters or particularly grave accidents, to protect young people from neglect, or to prevent crime." In providing for these limitations, the framers obviously had in mind freedom of movement within the country; [Article 11 (1)] makes no mention of traditional and relevant limitations on travel outside the country. Many countries (including free democracies) have long denied passports for reasons of state security. Similar restrictions, enforced in Germany since World War I, were carried over essentially unaltered into the Passport Act of 1952. If the framers had desired to incorporate a fundamental right to foreign travel into Article 11, they would not . . . have considered the long historical practice of withholding passports on the ground of state security. They clearly did not intend to guarantee freedom to travel abroad in Article 11. . . . Yet, freedom to travel abroad is not without some degree of constitutional protection as derivative of the basic right to general freedom of action. . . .

2. In its ruling of July 20, 1954 [the *Investment Aid I* case], the Federal Constitutional Court did not decide whether the free development of one's personality includes freedom of action in the widest sense possible, or whether Article 2 (1) is limited to the protection of a minimum amount of this right to freedom of action without which an individual would be unable to develop himself as a spiritual-moral person.

(a) The term "free development of personality" cannot simply mean development within that central area of personality that essentially defines a human person as a spiritual-moral being [i.e., the *Kernbereichstheorie*], for it is inconceivable how development within this core area could offend the moral code, the rights of others, or even the constitutional order of a free democracy. Rather, the limitations imposed on the individual as a member of the political community show that the freedom of action [implicit] in Article 2 (1) is to be broadly construed.

To be sure, the solemn formulation of Article 2 (1) was an inducement to see it in the light of Article 1 and to infer therefrom that its purpose was to embody the Basic Law's image of man. Yet nothing other is suggested than that Article 1 is a fundamental constitutional principle which, like all the provisions of the Basic Law, informs the meaning of Article 2 (1). Legally speaking, it represents a separate, individual basic right that guarantees a person's general right to freedom of action. Linguistic rather than legal considerations prompted the framers to substitute the current language for the original proposal, which read, "Every person is free to do or not to do what he wishes" [citing the original records]. Apparently, the fact that the constitutional order is also mentioned in the second half of the sentence among the permissible limitations on the citizen's development of personality contributed to the theory that Article 2 (1) intended to protect only a limited core area of personality. In the effort to uniformly interpret this term [i.e., "constitutional order"], which appears in other provisions of the Constitution, the constitutional order was viewed as a more restrictive concept than the [concept of a] legal order that conforms to the Constitution. Thus one felt compelled to conclude that the Constitution should protect only a core sphere of personality, and not one's right to freedom of action.

In addition to the general right to freedom of action secured by Article 2 (1), the Basic Law [employs] specific fundamental rights to protect man's self-determination in certain areas of life that were historically subject to encroachment by public authority. These constitutional provisions contain graduated reservation clauses that limit the extent to which [the legislature] may encroach upon a given basic right. The individual may invoke Article 2 (1) in the face of an encroachment upon his freedom by public authority to the extent that fundamental rights do not [specifically] protect such special areas of life. There was no need for a [general] reservation clause here because the extent to which encroachments are possible by the state is easily ascertained from the restriction the constitutional order imposes upon the development of personality. . . .

[The text omitted here is a complicated discussion of constitutional order within the meaning of Article 2 (1). Drawing on original history, the Constitutional Court found that, as used within the context of Article 2, "constitutional order" refers to the "general legal order subject to the substantive and procedural provisions of the Constitution." In other contexts (e.g., Article 9), noted the court, the concept "can be limited to certain elementary principles of the Constitution." The general right to freedom of action is thus limited not only by the Basic Law itself but also "by every procedural and substantive norm that conforms to the Constitution." The court then proceeded to meet the objection of legal scholars that such a broad limitation would turn the personality clause into an empty vessel.]

(c). . . They overlook the fact that legislative power is subject to more stringent constitutional restrictions than under the Weimar Constitution of 1919. . . . [T]he legislature [at that time] could modify or alter constitutional rights [at will]. . . . The Basic Law, on the other hand, erected a value-oriented order that limits public authority. This order guarantees the independence, self-determination, and dignity of man within the political community. The highest principles of this order of values are protected against constitutional change. . . . Laws are not constitutional merely because they have been passed in conformity with procedural provisions. [This refers to the Weimar Constitution's adherence to the positivistic theory of constitutional law. See the section in Chapter 1 on structures and principles of the Basic Law for a discussion of *Begriffsjurisprudenz*.] They must be substantively compatible with the highest values of a free and democratic order — i.e., the constitutional order of values — and must also conform to unwritten fundamental constitutional principles as well as the fundamental decisions of the Basic Law, in particular the principles of the rule of law and the social welfare state. Above all, laws must not violate a person's dignity, which represents the highest value of the Basic Law; nor may they restrict a person's spiritual, political, or economic freedom in a way that would erode the essence of [personhood]. This follows from the constitutional protection afforded to each citizen's sphere of private development; that is, that ultimately inviolable area of human freedom insulated against any intrusion by public authority. . . .

3. Even if the right to leave the country does not specifically belong to the concept of freedom of movement as protected by Article 11, it nevertheless is guaranteed by Article 2 (1), within the limits of the constitutional order (i.e., the legal order that conforms to the Constitution) as a manifestation of the general right to freedom of action. Whether or not the passport law is part of the constitutional order as defined here remains to be decided. The answer is yes.

(a) The Passport Act requires all Germans crossing a foreign border to have a passport — in itself a substantial formal limitation on foreign travel. Because the law, however, by unanimous interpretation confers a legal right to a passport, it preserves the principle of free foreign travel. It does so by permitting the denial of a passport only under specified conditions. Thus the act is cognizant of the fundamental requirements of Article 2 (1).

(b) Section 7 of the Passport Act clearly sets forth the grounds for denying a passport. The provision at issue here is unobjectionable to the extent that it permits denial of a passport on the basis of an internal or external threat to the security of the Federal Republic of Germany. Objections might be raised to the extent that [the provision] allows the apprehension of a threat to "other vital interests" to suffice [for the denial of a passport]. The application of such a substantively indeterminate standard could, of course, lead to an abuse of discretion on the part of passport authorities. . . . [But] that has not occurred here.

> [The court went on to reject the constitutional complaint. It found fault with the passport agency's original refusal to support its denial of a passport with reasons, but sustained its decision because the agency in a subsequent administrative hearing finally offered reasons for the denial and gave the complainant an opportunity to be heard. In considering the scope of review of the

decision below, the Constitutional Court declared that its role was not to review the facts *de novo* but rather to determine whether the facts were sufficient to justify the conclusion that the complainant would threaten "other vital interests" of the Federal Republic. The court also found that the Federal Administrative Court had properly harmonized those terms with the spirit of the Basic Law.]

NOTE: *EQUESTRIAN* AND *PUNITIVE DAMAGE* CASES. The *Equestrian* case produced the first major dissent from the broad interpretation of the concept of "freedom of action" that *Elfes* read into the right to personality secured by Article 2 (1). The petitioner objected to a state regulation, promulgated to further a federal policy, limiting horseback riding in wooded areas to well-defined roadways and trails. He claimed that the restriction interfered with freedom of action under the personality clause. The First Senate adhered to the prevailing view that freedom of action extends to every kind of human activity compatible with the reservation clause of Article 2 (1) and other expressly guaranteed rights. The senate ruled that horseback riding is an activity falling within the protection of Article 2 (1) but that here the restriction constituted a reasonable regulation designed to ensure the repose and safety of persons using forests set aside for leisure and recreation.[33]

Justice Dieter Grimm, dissenting, drew on the original history of Article 2 (1) and contemporary commentary on the provision, to argue that the personality clause should be interpreted to include only those liberty interests that are *fundamental* to the development of the human personality. Article 2 (1), he declared, should no longer be regarded as a "catch-all" right that "captures every conceivable human activity."[34] He insisted that "an end should be put to this trivialization of fundamental rights and the associated flood of constitutional challenges never contemplated by the Basic Law."[35] Any liberty interest not expressly grounded in the constitutional text but which seeks the protection of the general personality clause must rise to the level of the significance of an express right. Instead of accepting this complaint on the ground that the regulation involved was inconsistent with Article 2 (1), he concluded, the court should simply have dismissed it for failing to allege any violation of a fundamental right.

More recently, in a case of international significance, the same senate grappled with a freedom of action claim in an adjudicatory context. An American pharmaceutical firm sought to serve a complaint against a German company located in Berlin to collect punitive damages imposed by an American court on its subsidiary in the United States, a subsidiary incorporated under American law. After German authorities had approved the service of process, the Berlin firm petitioned the Federal Constitutional Court for an injunction against serving the complaint on the ground that punitive damages would limit the company's freedom of action under Article 2 (1). The petitioner also argued that since punitive damages is a concept incompatible with German law, service of process in Germany violated the principles of proportionality and the rule of law. The court regarded the complaint serious enough to issue the injunction pending a full hearing on the merits of the argument.[36] In the main decision, however, the court found that even if one concedes that service of process impinges on Article 2 (1), the intrusion was justified by the common good of the international legal order under the terms of the Hague Convention on the Service of Documents Abroad. The court also concluded that since punitive damages in the context of this case was not incompatible with German law, the principles of the rule of law and proportionality had not been violated.[37]

NOTE: THE INTIMATE SPHERE OF PERSONALITY. There is no case in which the Constitutional Court has defined the full range of personality rights under Article 2. It has preferred to work out the substantive meaning of the personality clause on a case-by-case basis in the light of developing social conditions. The court has, however, posited a private sphere, an ultimate domain of inviolability in which a person is free to shape his life as he or she sees fit. The *Eppler* case (1980) is important for its reassertion of this principle of personal interiority. No clear line of division separates *Eppler* from the constitutional cases included in the next section on privacy and bodily integrity. *Eppler* and these other cases illustrate the protection the court has afforded to personality in various private contexts. *Eppler* is important also because it illustrates the interplay of competing constitutional values, in this case the values of speech and personhood.

7.5 Eppler Case (1980)
54 BVerfGE 148

[During the 1976 state election campaign, the Christian Democratic Union of Baden-Württemberg distributed a draft of a speech to its candidates for the state legislature. Entitled "Socialists at Work," it pointed out that "the proposals of the SPD [Social Democratic party] are clearly and fatally socialistic." In accusing the SPD of harboring a desire to nationalize banks and basic industries, the document alluded to a statement by Erhard Eppler, chairman of the SPD in Baden-Württemberg. The CDU quoted him as having said that the "economy must be tested to the breaking point to determine what social responsibilities the state could bear without an economic collapse." Eppler denied that he had used these words or had implied any such thing and sought to enjoin the CDU from any further attribution of the statement to him. He initiated a constitutional complaint against the decision of Baden-Württemberg's appeals court to deny the injunction. Eppler invoked several constitutional provisions in his defense, including his basic rights to human dignity, personality, equality, and freedom of belief. The court rested its opinion mainly on Article 2 (1) of the Constitution.]

Judgment of the First Senate. . . .

B. . . .

[Once again the Constitutional Court asserted, as it has in other cases, that its function is not to review a lower court's determinations of fact. Rather, it is limited to ascertaining whether lower courts have properly interpreted the Constitution. In particular, it must decide whether the lower court has attached the proper weight to constitutional rights when these rights conflict with general law or other actions by state officials. The constitutional complaint was rejected because the evidence did not clearly indicate whether or not a false utterance had been attributed to the complainant. The court may well have decided for the complainant, notwithstanding the free speech claim, had he been able to clearly show that he had not uttered the words alleged. The extracts below are confined to the court's definition of the intimate sphere of personality.]

II. Considered in the light of these standards, the challenged judicial decision does not violate the Constitution. . . .

1. . . . Article 5 (1) does not protect a person who falsifies the opinion of another. This basic right [to free speech] confers no right to attribute to another an opinion that has not been uttered.

2 (a) We now consider the decision below in terms of the general right to personality secured by Article 2 (1) in conjunction with Article 1 (1). This undefined right to freedom complements those express freedoms, such as freedom of conscience and speech, that also protect the essential elements of personality. Its purpose is to safeguard—consistent with the highest constitutional principle, namely, human dignity (Article 1 [1])—that intimate personal sphere and to maintain basic conditions thereof which are not encompassed by the traditional and more concrete guarantees of freedom. This right is particularly crucial today in view of modern developments and new dangers to the protection of human personality which result from them. . . .

Because of the aforementioned special character of the general right to personality, the Federal Constitutional Court as well as the Federal High Court of Justice have refrained from fully defining the content of the protected right; rather, both have dealt with the right on a case-by-case basis. Thus, [they] have recognized the following aspects of the general right to personality: the right to a private, secret, intimate sphere of life [citing the *Microcensus, Divorce Records, Tape Recording, Transsexual,* and *Sex Education* cases], to personal honor and the rightful portrayal of one's own person [citing the *Lebach* case], to one's own image and spoken word [citing *Tape Recording*], and under certain circumstances, the right not to have statements falsely attributed to oneself [citing the *Princess Soraya* case]. These manifestations of the constitutionally protected right of personality must be duly observed when dealing with court decisions concerning conflicting interests under private law.

(b) The facts alleged in the constitutional complaint do not fall within the aforementioned manifestations of the right to personality under Article 2 (1). The complainant's private, secret, or intimate sphere of life is not involved here. Nor does the statement to which the complainant objects constitute an insult to his honor. The opinion of the court of appeals properly explained this point. It is not dishonorable to demand that the economy be tested to its breaking point. Nor does [this demand] contain a call to unconstitutional action, so that the speaker could be slanderously accused of no longer adhering to the fundamental tenets of the Basic Law. The fact that the complainant is a politician whose political goals may have been harmed by the allegation that he advocated a widely rejected viewpoint does not amount to an assault on his personal honor. Last, the complainant cannot base [his contention] on any right to his spoken words, for in this case he claims to have been accused of an utterance he allegedly did not make.

To be sure, the general personality right guaranteed by Article 2 (1) of the Constitution also protects a person from having statements falsely attributed to him. An example of this would be the publication of a fabricated interview dealing with someone's private life that simultaneously violates an acknowledged and protected value within the ambit of the right to personality—e.g., the private sphere [citing *Soraya*]. Even if there is no actual invasion of privacy, it is an infringement of [an individual's] right to privacy to put words into his mouth which he did not utter and which adversely affect his self-image. This [conclusion] follows from the general right to personality underlying the concept of self-determination. The individual should have the freedom to decide for himself—without any limitation of his private sphere—how he wishes to portray himself to third parties or to the public, as well as whether and to what extent third parties may have access to his personality. In particular, this includes a person's right to decide whether and in what manner he wishes his utterance to be made public. . . . The same goes for the right to privacy in conversation. An individual has the right to determine whether he wants to restrict his utterances solely to his conversational partner or to a certain group, or whether he wants to publicize his remarks. [He may determine] whether someone may reproduce his recorded words, and if so, who. Thus the content of the general right to personality is largely determined by the self-image of its bearer [citing the *Cultural Freedom* case]. Therefore Article 2 (1) would be violated if [one] were to decide the issue in this case—i.e., whether falsely attributing statements to someone infringes upon the personality right—not on the basis of the person's own image of himself but rather on the basis of the image that others have formed or could form of him, whether or not justifiable. Others may be constitutionally justified in creating such images by dint of their right to freedom of speech. Their statements, however, cannot determine the content of the complainant's right to personality if it is not to be robbed of its very essence; i.e., of the absolutely personal and inalienable [core] right deserving of protection.

NOTE: THE RIGHT TO INFORMATIONAL SELF-DETERMINATION. On April 13, 1983, in a remarkable display of judicial activism, the Constitutional Court suspended the execution of a census under the Federal Census Act of 1983 pending a decision on the act's constitutional validity.[38] Eight months later, on December 15, 1983, the First Senate sustained most of the statute's major provisions but required parliament to amend the statute in certain particulars before the census could be carried out, a requirement that delayed the census for another four years, at notable cost to the state. In establishing a new "right of informational self-determination," the senate directed parliament to close all loopholes in the law that might lead to abuses in the collection, storage, use, and transfer of the personal data it collected. While it stunned federal census officials, the decision in the *Census* case did not surprise close students of the court's evolving human dignity jurisprudence. In the personalist universe envisioned by the Constitutional Court, the human person is more than the sum of his parts and more than a biological or physiological organism. Rather, as the court has said on numerous occasions, he is a "spiritual-moral being." The state therefore cannot inventory the individual with respect to every aspect of his being without threatening his personal autonomy.

7.6 Census Act Case (1983)
65 BVerfGE 1

[The Federal Census Act of 1983 provided for the collection of comprehensive data on the Federal Republic's demographic and social structure. In addition to a total population count and the collection of basic personal information (name, address, sex, marital status, religious affiliation, etc.), the act required citizens to fill out detailed questionnaires relating to their sources of income, occupation, supplementary employment, educational background, hours of work, mode of transportation to and from work, and related matters. Sections of the statute provided for the transmission of the statistical data to local governments for purposes of regional planning, surveying, environmental protection, and redrawing election districts. This case represents one of those rare instances in which an individual may lodge a constitutional complaint directly against a statute. The need to exhaust one's legal remedies is not necessary when a statute poses an immediate threat to a fundamental right. In response to complaints from more than one hundred persons, the court temporarily enjoined the execution of the census on the ground that the transmission of data to certain agencies threatened to violate the rights of privacy and personality. The court's final decision, from which the following extract is drawn, was handed down several months later.]

———————

Judgment of the First Senate. . . .

C. To the extent that the constitutional complaints are justiciable, they are valid. . . .

II. The standard primarily to be applied is the general right to the free development of one's personality protected in Article 2 (1) in conjunction with Article 1 (1) of the Basic Law.

    1. (a) The focal point of the order established by the Basic Law is the value and dignity of the individual, who functions as a member of a free society in free self-determination. The general personality right, as laid down in Article 2 (1) in tandem with Article (1), serves to protect these values — along with other, more specific guarantees of freedom — and gains in importance if one bears in mind modern developments with their attendant dangers to the human personality. Our jurisprudence to date has not conclusively settled the scope and content of the personality right. As indicated [in several of our cases], it includes the authority of the individual to decide for himself, on the basis of the idea of self-determination, when and within what limits facts about his personal life shall be disclosed.

    The [individual's decisional] authority needs special protection in view of the present and prospective conditions of automatic data processing. It is particularly endangered because . . . the technical means of storing highly personalized information about particular persons today are practically unlimited, and [information] can be retrieved in a matter of seconds with the aid of automatic data processing, irrespective of distance. Furthermore, such information can be joined to other data collections — particularly when constructing integrated information systems — to produce a partial or virtually complete personality profile, with the person concerned having insufficient means of controlling either its veracity or [its] use. The possibilities of acquiring information and exerting influence have increased to a degree hitherto unknown and may affect the individual's behavior because of the psychological pressure which public awareness may place [upon the individual].

    Even under present conditions of data-processing technology, [the concept of] self-determination presupposes that the individual be given the freedom to decide what actions should be taken, including the freedom to decide whether to implement his own decision. An individual's right to plan and make decisions freely [and] without pressure or influence from others is crucially inhibited if he cannot predict with sufficient certainty what personal information [the state] will release in a given area of his social environment. It would be incompatible with the right to informational self-determination if a legal order should permit a societal structure where the citizen could not be sure who knows something about him, what they know about him, when this information will be released, and what occasions the release of this data. If someone is uncertain whether information about unusual behavior is being stored and recorded permanently in computer banks, or does not know whether it will be used or passed on, he will try not to attract attention by engaging in such behavior. If he expects that [the state] will officially register his attendance at a meeting or participation in a citizens' initiative and [believes] personal risks might result from this, this person may refrain from exercising his rights [of association] (Articles 8 and 9). This would not only impair his chances of development but would also damage the common good, because self-determination is an elementary functional condition of a free democratic community based on its citizens' capacity to act and participate.

Because of this, the individual must be protected from the unlimited collection, storage, use, and transmission of personal data as a condition for free personality development under modern conditions of data processing. Article 2 (1) in tandem with Article 1 (1) of the Basic Law guarantees this protection. This basic right guarantees the right of the individual to determine for himself whether [the state] may divulge or use his personal data.

(b) However, the right to "informational self-determination" is not unlimited. The individual does not possess any absolute, unlimited mastery over "his" data; rather, he is a personality . . . developing within the social community. Even personal information is a reflection of social reality and cannot be associated purely with the individual concerned. The Basic Law has resolved the tension between the individual and society by postulating a community-related and community-bound individual, as the decisions of the Federal Constitutional Court have repeatedly stressed. The individual must in principle accept certain limits on his right to informational self-determination for reasons of compelling public interest.

As section 6 (1) of the Federal Statistics Act correctly recognizes, Article 2 (1) of the Basic Law requires the legislature to specify the [purposes and conditions] of all [official] data-gathering processes so that the citizen may clearly know what information is being collected and why. Such legal authorizations must adhere to the rule of law and be clearly framed so as not to be unconstitutionally vague. In enacting these laws, the legislature must also observe the principle of proportionality. This principle, raised to the level of a constitutional norm, follows from the nature of fundamental rights . . . which the state may limit only to the extent necessary for the protection of public interests. Considering the danger involved [today] in utilizing automatic data processing, the legislature is duty-bound, more so than ever before, to adopt organizational and procedural measures designed to safeguard the individual from any infringement of his right to personality.

[In this lengthy and complex case—a full seventy-one pages in the official reports—the Constitutional Court sustained most of the 1983 Census Act's provisions. The court underscored the legitimacy of a general census for purposes of social planning and the "fulfillment of public tasks." The collection and storage of information that fails to serve these purposes is constitutionally suspect. In the bulk of its opinion the court carefully scrutinized the nature of the information collected, the methods of its storage and transmission, and its particular uses. It noted that a constitutionally sensitive census policy would distinguish clearly between "personality-related data collected and processed in an individualized, identifiable manner and data designated for statistical purposes." The court went on to say that the constitutional right to personality would be violated if automatic data processing under modern conditions and the sharing of statistical data with local and regional authorities could result in the reconstruction or release of the personality profiles of particular individuals. The court insisted that federal and state officials take every precaution to prevent this from happening. The court then proceeded to strike down three minor provisions of the 1983 statute. The most important of these empowered local authorities to compare certain census data with local housing registries. The combination of statistical data and a personalized registry, said the court, could lead to the identification of particular persons and thus violate the core of the personality right. Additionally, the provisions offended the principles of clarity and proportionality for their failure to justify the need for certain information and because some of the data were not necessary to achieve the purposes of local authorities.]

NOTE: THE EXPANDING RIGHT TO PERSONALITY. In one of its earliest decisions the Federal Constitutional Court observed that when the framers inserted the human dignity clause into the Basic Law, they intended to protect the individual against "humiliation, stigmatization, and torture."[39] Today, however, as former Constitutional Court president Ernst Benda noted recently, "man's dignity is not endangered by totalitarian tools of suppression but rather by the complexities of modern life, by the potential invasion of an ever-present welfare state into almost all aspects of private life, or by the helplessness of the individual to understand . . . the political process which greatly affects everybody's personal fate."[40] President Benda continued:

> How can human dignity be protected in the computer age, or when considering the dramatic potential of modern gene technology, in vitro fertilization, or other technical and scientific developments? What does freedom of information mean when not censorship or other means of restricting the flow of information are the reality, but rather the overburdening of the individual with more information than he can possibly understand or digest? What does freedom from the state's interference mean when the individual, for his personal well-being, depends more than ever before on the state's activities?[41]

It should thus come as no surprise to learn that President Benda presided over the First Senate when it handed down its opinion in the *Census Act* case.

PRIVACY AND PHYSICAL INTEGRITY

The Basic Law does not explicitly create a general right of privacy. Three of its provisions, however, do protect privacy interests. The first of these provisions, the main concern of this section, is the personality clause of Article 2. The second, at issue in the *Klass* case (see Chapter 4), is the provision of Article 10 that guarantees "privacy of posts and telecommunications"; and the third is the guarantee of the home's inviolability under Article 13. The initial concern in this section is with the privacy aspect, or the intimate sphere of the general personality right. The *Divorce Records* and *Transsexual* cases, like the cases featured in the previous section, uphold claims based on the personality clause of Article 2 (1). But these and related cases are more appropriately grouped around the concept of privacy. We should note, however, that several cases in other chapters are equally concerned with the intimate aspects of personality. The *Princess Soraya* case (no. 4.2), particularly, should be read in tandem with the cases in this section. *Soraya* might have been included here as a bridge between this and the previous section on the personality clause. (As the background to *Soraya* shows, the regular judiciary, inspired by the personality clause of Article 2, had already begun in the 1950s to award civil damages for the invasion of privacy.)

7.7 Divorce Records Case (1970)
27 BVerfGE 344

[The complainant, a high-level civil servant in a city government, was the subject of an internal administrative disciplinary proceeding because he had carried on an adulterous relationship with his former secretary. During this relationship he brought a divorce action against his wife which he later withdrew, but not before the divorce court had recorded the details of his affair. The chief examiner—the person in charge of investigating the complaint against the civil servant—requested the judicial record of the civil servant's divorce action. That record, which the court released, would presumably verify the charge brought against him in the disciplinary proceeding. After his dismissal from the civil service—a decision based in part on the judicial record turned over to the chief examiner—the complainant brought a constitutional complaint against the judicial decision allowing the release of his divorce file. He claimed that his firing was a violation of his fundamental rights to human dignity and personality.]

———————

Judgment of the First Senate....

The decision of the Hamm Court of Appeals violates . . . the complainant's basic right under Article 2 (1), in tandem with Article 1 (1), of the Constitution.

B. The constitutional complaint is valid.

1. (a) The Federal Constitutional Court has repeatedly recognized that the Constitution protects the individual citizen against any state encroachment upon that inviolable sphere of privacy within which he forms his personality. The constitutionally mandated command to respect this intimate sphere of life has its basis in the well-rounded right to the free development of personality secured by Article 2 (1) of the Constitution. A proper regard for the content and scope of this fundamental right requires the state to respect and protect the inviolability of human dignity. Article 19 (2) reinforces this right by barring public authority from encroaching upon the essential content of a basic right.

(b) Yet, private life in its totality is not entitled to absolute protection under Article 2 (1) in conjunction with Article 1 (1) and Article 19 (2) of the Constitution. Quite the contrary. Citizens are members of and bound to society, and thus all persons are required to accept certain restrictions on [their] privacy on behalf of an overriding public interest — tempered, of course, by strict compliance with the principle of proportionality and by respect for the inviolable sphere of personality. The analysis of this case may therefore proceed on the basis of principles developed by the Federal Constitutional Court with respect to when and under what circumstances the state may encroach upon the physical integrity of the individual. The court places a particularly high value, however, upon the protection of the human person in the spiritual-metaphysical realm.

(c) The records of a divorce proceeding indeed concern the private life of a marriage partner, yet these records are not totally insulated against outside inspection. The applicable law currently requires marriage partners to disclose in court intimate details of their common life under certain conditions. Aspects of private life can be revealed in a judicial proceeding for the purpose of resolving conflicts of rights and interests within a marriage. But any such disclosure must be limited to the persons immediately involved — i.e., the court and parties to the proceeding — and by the purpose behind the action — i.e., eliciting a judicial decision. Divorce records are to be treated confidentially under Article 2 (1) in conjunction with Article 1 (1) of the Constitution. Both partners are entitled to this protection. The contents of such records can be made accessible to outside parties only with the consent of both partners.

(d) The civil service proceeding in this case was based on a legitimate desire to ensure the performance of official and legal functions. Nevertheless, in transmitting the records of this divorce proceeding to the chief examiner, the court encroached upon the rights of personality of the marriage partners. Without their consent such an encroachment can be justified only if it conforms to the principle of proportionality. If it does not accord with this principle, then the disclosure violates Article 2 (1) in conjunction with Article 1 (1) and Article 19 (2) of the Constitution.

[Here the Constitutional Court embarked on a discussion of the principle of proportionality, generally noting that the means adopted by the state in pursuit of a legitimate public purpose must be proportionate to that end. Courts must do more than engage in an abstract or theoretical analysis of the rival claims before them. If the facts and circumstances of a case are not independently assessed in the light of the weight attached by the Constitution to the value of privacy or personality and the principle of proportionality, the challenged decision will not survive constitutional analysis. As so often in the past, the court emphasized that its power of review extends not to an examination of the facts or details of the case below but only to a determination of whether the court below has, in fact, engaged in the proper balancing of constitutional values and whether the standards used in determining that balance are legitimate.]

2. (c) . . . [T]he challenged decision cannot stand because there has been no determination of the necessity [for the disclosure of the records in this case]. The record below is silent on the extent to which the court of appeals examined the contents of the divorce records and whether they yielded information relevant to the disciplinary proceeding. It is not clear what effect the objectionable conduct has had on the civil servant's performance of his official duty or on the public. . . . Material relevant to a judgment concerning the misconduct of the civil servant could be obtained from the divorce records. But this does not authorize the disclosure of the entire contents of the record in a disciplinary proceeding. In such cases the constitutional principle of proportionality demands that only relevant portions of the records be made available to the chief examiner. The court of appeals has clearly not undertaken the balancing required by the Constitution. . . .

As a consequence, the court of appeals has violated the complainant's fundamental right derived from Article 2 (1) in conjunction with Article 1 (1) of the Constitution. . . .

The challenged decision must therefore be vacated and the case remanded to the court of appeals. . . .

———————————

NOTE: OTHER PRIVATE RECORDS CASES. The confidentiality of divorce files was also at issue in the *Theodore K.* case (1972), in which another civil servant involved in a disciplinary proceeding objected to a medical expert's inspection of his divorce files.[42] As in *Divorce Records,* the Constitutional Court emphasized that in certain situations of overriding public interest such files could be used in a judicial proceeding. But here, too, disclosure would have been wholly out of proportion to the degree of the offense and thus in violation of the right to privacy. In the *Medical Confidentiality* case (1972), the court held that the human dignity and personality clauses barred the admissibility of a doctor's records on a patient facing a criminal trial.[43] Even the public's interest in prosecuting crime was insufficient in this case to breach the privacy of the doctor-patient relationship. In the *Adolf M.* case (1972), however, decided a few months later, the Constitutional Court declined to extend the same degree of protection to the testimony of a social worker. The court ruled that while such professionals are personal advisers, they are also agents of the state entrusted with the administration of public assistance.[44] *Tape Recording II* (1973) is yet another landmark in the Constitutional Court's privacy jurisprudence.[45] It barred the use in a criminal proceeding of a secret recording that the victim had made in a conversation with the accused. Again the court noted the importance of balancing the individual's interest in privacy against the public's interest in bringing criminals to justice. The public interest, said the court, might require the admissibility of a secret recording that conveys information not related to the private sphere of an individual's personality. Given the nature of the offense, however, the court balanced the interests in favor of the defendant but appeared at the same time to erect an absolute barrier against the public disclosure of information touching the "inner core" of the human personality.

7.8 Transsexual Case (1979)
49 BVerfGE 286

[The complainant in this case had undergone a surgical procedure that changed "his" sex from male to female. Subsequent thereto, a local civil court in Berlin allowed "him" to change "his" civil status to that of a woman and ordered that it be so entered in the appropriate birth registry. In a decision affirmed by the Federal High Court of Justice, the Berlin District Court, pursuant to an objection by the secretary of state, reversed, with the complainant's status reverting to that of a male. The complainant appealed to the Federal Constitutional Court, claiming a violation of human dignity and personality rights.]

Judgment of the First Senate. . . .

The decision of the Federal High Court of Justice of September 21, 1971, violates the basic right of the complainant arising out of Article 2 (1) in tandem with Article 1 (1) of the Constitution. We reverse and remand the case to the Federal High Court of Justice.

B. I. According to the medical opinion before the court, the complainant is psychologically a woman. Through hormone treatments and operations modern medicine has made it possible to give him the appearance of a member of the female sex. Yet the complainant is treated as a man in the eyes of the law. The possibility of living a normal, healthy, and socially adjusted life as a woman is thus denied to this person. The lack of conformity between his outward appearance and his personal legal status is manifested by the fact that it is not legally possible for him to bear a first name normally associated with the female sex. Because the law on civil status is based on the premise that a person's first name must reveal the sex of its bearer, the complainant can change his name only after the entry of his sex is changed in the birth registry. Even where a gender-neutral name is concerned, the possibility of a complainant being brought into a situation of conflict cannot be ruled out; the spheres these situations touch belong to that most intimate realm of personhood, which is protected against state interference and with which government may interfere only in pursuance of special public concerns [citing cases].

2. (a) Article 1 (1) of the Basic Law protects the dignity of a person as he understands himself in his individuality and self-awareness. This is connected with the idea that each person is responsible for himself and controls his own destiny. Article 2 (1), when seen in relation to Article 1 (1), guarantees the free development of a person's abilities and strengths. Human dignity and the constitutional right to the free development of personality demand, therefore, that one's civil status be governed by the sex with which he is psychologically and physically identified. Our law and society are based on the principle that each person is either "masculine" or "feminine," and that this identification is independent of any possible genitalic anomalies. It is doubtful, however, that the theory of gender immutability, determined by sexual characteristics apparent at birth, can be maintained with the absolute certitude reflected in the decision of the Federal High Court of Justice. Various forms of biological intersexuality are known to modern medicine. Medical research into the phenomenon of twin births has revealed a dissociation between body and spirit that manifests itself most sharply, according to reliable medical knowledge, in transsexuals. . . .

(b) The right to the free development of personality is protected only within the limits of the moral law. In the present case the moral law has not been infringed. Whether an operation, not therapeutically necessary, to change a person's sex should be regarded as immoral is not the issue here. According to the available expert opinions, a sex change operation was deemed necessary by the complainant. Current medical research indicates that transsexuals are seeking not to manipulate their sexuality but rather to find some unity of body and spirit. Therefore the operation can be seen as a partial effort to achieve this goal. The anguish of the transsexual described in medical texts has been confirmed by the medical opinions presented in this case. Accordingly, the sexual change secured by the complainant cannot be considered immoral. . . .

Suffice it to say that the ability of a man to conceive a child or of a woman to bear a child is not a prerequisite for marriage. Under Article 6 (1), marriage represents a lifelong union of man and woman in a basically indissoluble community. The marriage partners form this community on the basis of their own ideas and expectations. It may be that many people reject the idea of a marriage between a male transsexual and a man as something deserving of moral condemnation. Such irrational fears, however, may not stand in the way of a marriage. This view is bolstered by available medical knowledge indicating that male transsexuals do not seek homo-sexual relationships. Rather, they desire normal relations with a heterosexual part-ner and expect, in the aftermath of a successful operation on their genitals, to have normal sexual intercourse with a male partner.

(c) According to the decisions of the Federal Constitutional Court, the state may regulate the private life of the individual insofar as his relations with his fellow men are concerned, but it may not encroach on that inviolable and innermost sphere of life. No public interest is served by the state's refusal to allow an official change in the sex identification of the complainant that would justify an encroachment upon the basic right secured by Article 2 (1) in relation to Article 1 (1) of the Basic Law.

NOTE: BODILY INTEGRITY. Article 2 (2) declares: "Everyone shall have the right to life and to the inviolability of his person." This provision is repeatedly invoked in conjunction with the human dignity and personality clauses as a basis for imposing constitutional restraints on criminal procedures. A person may be duty-bound to submit to certain physical interventions if necessary to a judicial investigation, but the action must be specified in precise terms by a judge applying the law in the light of constitutional values.[46] The intervention must, above all, satisfy the principle of proportionality. Thus, in the *Heinrich P.* case (1956), the Constitutional Court sustained the validity of a judicially ordered blood test to determine parentage in a paternity suit.[47] Other federal courts have likewise sustained compulsory vaccina-tion statutes and even corporal punishment in schools.[48] The personal inviolability clause appears to bar all invasions of the body that would result in unusual physical pain, bodily disfigurement, sterilization, impairment of any bodily function, or any injury to a person's health.[49] As the *Spinal Tap* case (1963) shows, the clause also imposes severe limitations on the technical methods that can be employed in any penetration of the body. In the *Pneumoencephalography* case (1963),[50] decided a few weeks after *Spinal Tap,* the court invalidated a court-ordered puncture of a person's vertebral canal for the purpose of testing his personal responsibility for a crime. The Federal Constitutional and Administrative courts have even invalidated the poly-graph test in criminal investigations.[51] To attach a person to a machine for the purpose of eliciting the truth, these tribunals have suggested, is an inadmissible invasion of a person's innermost self and a violation of human dignity. In short, the human person cannot be treated, consistent with the image of man advanced earlier in this chapter, as an object of experimentation of any kind.

Efforts to apply the personal inviolability clause outside the criminal field have been less successful. In the *Widow's Child Welfare* case (1951) the Constitutional Court ruled that Article 2 (2) does not confer any subjective right to a specific social welfare benefit.[52] In more recent years, however, particularly in the aftermath of the first *Abortion* case (no. 7.10), constitutional litigators have been able to argue with some plausibility that, as an objective value, the right to personal inviolability places "all the organs of the State . . . under a duty to promote and protect—that is, by engaging in affirmative action—the legal values of life and of physical integrity."[53] Indeed, as the *Mülheim-Kärlich* case (1979) shows, the Constitutional Court is becoming increasingly sensitive to such arguments when they are advanced in the interest of a safe environment.[54] Since 1983, numerous persons have filed constitutional complaints with the court in defense of a constitutional right to a safe environment under the personal inviolability clause.[55]

7.9 Spinal Tap Case (1963)
16 BVerfGE 194

[The complainant was the manager of an enterprise associated with the Central Chamber of the Munich Knitting Goods Company. He and his eighty-nine-year-old mother, with whom he lived, owned a small number of shares in the parent company. He refused to properly fill out a Board of Trade questionnaire relating to his business, as he was legally required to do. Instead, he returned the questionnaire with a number of frivolous and nonsensical comments on it, whereupon the Board of Trade fined him DM 500 for his failure to cooperate. He refused to pay the fine, claiming that the board lacked jurisdiction over his business. In an action to collect the fine a district court judge, suspecting a disorder of the complainant's central nervous system, ordered him to undergo a medical test requiring the withdrawal of body fluid for the purpose of determining his mental condition pursuant to section 81a of the Code of Criminal Procedure. The court of appeals sustained the order. The complainant challenged these court orders as violative of his right to a hearing in accordance with law under Article 103 (1) and personal inviolability under Article 2 (2) of the Constitution.]

Judgment of the First Senate. . . .

The district court decision of September 11, 1958, and the superior court decision of October 14, 1958, violate the complainant's basic right under Article 2 (2) of the Constitution. They are quashed and the case is remanded to the Munich District Court. . . .

B. We need not decide whether the court of appeals ruling violates Article 103 (1). The constitutional complaint is sustained because the ruling violates the basic right to physical inviolability (Article 2 [2]).

1. The extraction of cerebral and spinal fluid by means of a cannula is not an insignificant surgical invasion of bodily integrity within the meaning of Article 2 (2) of the Constitution. When conducted in accordance with the standards of modern medicine this procedure is not normally dangerous; yet severe pain and nausea are

possible. In fact, according to a report submitted by the court-appointed expert, approximately 10 percent of the persons undergoing spinal taps experience such severe effects. The extraction of fluids may also lead to serious complications in certain cases. Decades ago — in a different context — the former Reich National Insurance Board repeatedly acknowledged that social security benefits could not be suspended pursuant to a refusal to give one's permission for the extraction of body fluids. Expert testimony had convinced the National Insurance Board that danger to bodily health could be avoided only if a thorough medical examination ruled out the possibility of cerebral swelling. Despite the procedure's relative painlessness, [the board] considered it acceptable only under significant restrictions. The medical report particularly emphasized that the danger of neurotic fixation is even further enhanced when dealing with neurotic persons following surgery in cases where the patient does not authorize the spinal tap. Moreover, the Second Ordinance Concerning the Venereal Disease Law of July 5, 1955, includes the extraction of fluids among those surgical procedures which may be performed only with the patient's consent.

2. The right to physical inviolability can be limited only by general law (Article 2 (2) [3]). Section 81a of the Criminal Procedure Code formally satisfies this requirement. . . .

[In this part of the opinion the court sustained the validity of section 81a over objections that the statute is unduly vague and violates the principle of presumption of innocence. Section 81a authorizes a judge to order a criminal defendant, against his consent, to undergo blood tests and other bodily penetrations if such evidence is necessary in a criminal proceeding. The physical examination can be performed only "by a physician pursuant to the rules of medical science" and only if "no resulting detriment to [the defendant's] health is to be feared." The court pointed out that section 81a could reasonably be construed to require judges to apply the principle of proportionality before authorizing such an examination. Judges must be mindful of constitutional values in the application of this provision.]

(c) When ruling on cases involving the compulsory extraction of body fluids, the judge must — as in all cases involving government encroachment on the sphere of freedom — observe the principle of proportionality relative to ends and means. While the public interest in solving crimes — an interest based on the especially important principle of legality — ordinarily justifies even encroachments on the freedom of the accused, this general interest suffices less the more severe the infringement of freedom. Thus, in order properly to evaluate the relationship between means and end, one must also consider the severity of the criminal offense. This is especially to be considered when determining criminal responsibility pursuant to the serious procedures under sections 81 and 81a of the Criminal Code. An application of the law in the light of the meaning of the basic rights requires that the proposed measure be proportionate to the seriousness of the offense, so that the consequences connected with the detection of the crime will not encumber the criminal more than the expected punishment. The judge therefore has the constitutional duty to weigh an encroachment, in itself legally permissible, against the ban on its excess. . . . The Federal Constitutional Court has repeatedly applied this principle to the process of investigative custody. Therefore an interpretation of section 81a which conforms to the Constitution demands the application of the principle of proportionality consistent with the approach the courts have previously taken.

3. The courts disregarded these principles in the present case. . . . All in all, the matter is a minor offense that might lead to only a light sentence, possibly even an acquittal on account of its insignificance. By comparison, the extraction of fluid is not an insignificant physical procedure. There is no justification for submitting the accused to such a surgical procedure against his will. Because the courts disregarded the principle of proportionality by misunderstanding the range of the basic right provided for by Article 2 (2), [we] will not set aside the contested decisions. [Instead, we will] remand the case to the district court.

———————————

NOTE: PRIVACY OF HOME AND COMMUNICATIONS. Article 13 (1) declares: "The home shall be inviolable." Paragraph 2 authorizes judges to order searches as prescribed by law, and paragraph 3 permits "encroachments" (*Eingriffe*) and "restrictions" (*Beschränkungen*) of the home's inviolability only "to avert a common danger or a mortal danger to individuals or, pursuant to law, to prevent imminent danger to public safety and order." In the *Dry Cleaning* case (1971) the court ruled that the term "home" within the meaning of Article 13 is to be interpreted broadly as a "private living sphere" that would include rooms for study, work, and business.[56] But it drew a sharp distinction between this private sphere and a commercial business office. The state could thus permissibly inspect records that would disclose the exact nature of a business for tax purposes. In the *Bauer Company* case (1976), however, the court laid down carefully circumscribed standards for the judicial authorization of such a search.[57]

Personal correspondence and other private communications are also closely protected under the Basic Law. Complainants have invoked the personality clause of Article 2 on a number of occasions to secure this right,[58] but, as we have already seen in the *Klass* case,[59] its chief safeguard is Article 10. (See Chapter 4 for a discussion of *Klass* and related cases.)

THE RIGHT TO LIFE

The first *Abortion* case (1975) is the leading decision under the right-to-life provision of the Basic Law. Article 2 (2) provides: "Everyone has the right to life and to the inviolability of his person." Any articulation of an unborn child's right to life could clearly be drawn from this declaration. By the same token, any countervailing right of a pregnant woman to choose to have an abortion could just as clearly be drawn from Article 2 (1), which secures the right to the development of personality. *Abortion I* attempts to balance these conflicting rights; it stands in sharp contrast to the doctrinal analysis contained in the American case of *Roe* v. *Wade*.[60]

The *Abortion* case arose out of section 218a of the Abortion Reform Act of 1974. Supported by a coalition of Social Democrats and Free Democrats, the new, liberalized statute provided that an abortion would no longer be punishable if performed by a licensed physician with the consent of the pregnant woman during the first twelve weeks of pregnancy. Prior to seeking an abortion, however, the woman was legally obliged to seek advice from a physician or counseling agency concerning available public and private assistance for pregnant women, mothers, and children. Criminal penalties would continue to be enforced as before with respect to abortions performed after the third month of pregnancy, except in those instances where medical, eugenic, or ethical (i.e., in cases of rape or incest) indications would justify the fetus's destruction. On June 21, 1974, three days after parliament enacted the statute, the Federal Constitutional Court enjoined its enforcement in response to a petition from Baden-Württemberg.[61] At the same time the court reinstated the old law, which imposed criminal penalties on any person performing an abortion at any stage of pregnancy — apart from the law's permissible exceptions — pending a full hearing on the constitutionality of the Abortion Reform Act.

7.10 Abortion I Case (1975)
39 BVerfGE 1

[This case was an abstract judicial-review proceeding. Such a proceeding, as noted with regard to earlier cases, allows members of parliament or a state government to directly challenge the constitutionality of a statute immediately after its passage into law. In this instance 193 members of the Bundestag — mostly Christian Democrats — and five state governments (Baden-Württemberg, Bavaria, Rhineland-Palatinate, Saarland, and Schleswig-Holstein) petitioned the Constitutional Court to review section 218a of the Abortion Reform Act, on the ground that it violated several provisions of the Basic Law, including its human dignity and right-to-life clauses.]

Judgment of the First Senate. . . .

I. Section 218a of the Criminal Code in the Version of the Fifth Law to Reform the Criminal Law of June 18, 1974, is incompatible with Article 2 (2) [1] in conjunction with Article 1 (1) of the Basic Law and is void insofar as it exempts termination of pregnancy from punishment in cases where no reasons exist which — within the meaning of the [present] decisional grounds — have priority over the value order contained in the Basic Law. . . .

[The first part of the opinion is a lengthy discussion of the history of the penal provisions on abortion and the legislative background of the new law. The court then summarized the arguments advanced on both sides of the dispute. Before reaching the merits of the case, the court noted: "The statutory regulation in the Fifth Statute to Reform the Penal Law, which was decided upon after extraordinarily comprehensive preparatory work, can be examined by the Constitutional Court only from the viewpoint of whether it is compatible with the Basic Law, which is the highest valid law in the Federal Republic. The gravity and the seriousness of the constitutional question posed become clear if it is considered that what is involved here is the protection of human life, one of the central values of every legal order. The decision regarding the standards and limits of legislative freedom of decision demands a total view of the constitutional norms and the hierarchy of values contained therein."]

C. I. 1. Article 2 (2) [1] of the Basic Law also protects the life developing within the mother's womb as an independent legal interest.

(a) Unlike the case of the Weimar Constitution, the categorical inclusion of the inherently self-evident right to life in the Basic Law may be explained principally as a reaction to the "destruction of life unworthy to live," the "final solution," and the "liquidations" that the National Socialist regime carried out as governmental measures. Article 2 (2) [1] of the Basic Law implies, as does the repeal of the death penalty by Article 102 of the Basic Law, "an affirmation of the fundamental value of human life and of a state concept which emphatically opposes the views of a political regime for which the individual life had little significance and which therefore practiced unlimited abuse in the name of the arrogated right over life and death of the citizen."

(b) In interpreting Article 2 (2) [1] of the Basic Law, one must proceed from its wording: "Everyone shall have the right to life. . . ." Life in the sense of the developmental existence of a human individual begins, according to established biological-physiological findings, on the fourteenth day after conception (implantation, individuation). The developmental process thus begun is a continuous one which manifests no sharp demarcation and does not permit any precise delimitation of the various developmental stages of the human life. Nor does it end with birth; for instance, the phenomena of consciousness specific to human personality do not appear until some time after birth. Therefore [we] may not limit the protection of Article 2 (2) [1] of the Basic Law either to the "completed" human being after birth or to the independently viable nasciturus. [Article 2 (2) [1]] guarantees the right to life to everyone who "lives"; no distinction can be made between individual stages of the developing life before birth or between prenatal and postnatal life. "Everyone" within the meaning of Article 2 (2) [1] of the Basic Law is "every living human being," or, expressed otherwise, every human individual possessing life; "everyone" therefore also includes the yet unborn human being. . . .

[The court noted that any failure to protect unborn life from its inception (i.e., from the fourteenth day after conception) would place the "security of human existence" generally in jeopardy. The First Senate then recalled the original history of the right-to-life clause and found that the framers of the Basic Law intended it to cover unborn life. On the other hand, said the court, the history of the clause "does not answer the question whether unborn life must be protected by penal law."]

2. Therefore, [we] derive the obligation of the state to protect all human life directly from Article 2 (2) [1] of the Basic Law. Additionally, [this obligation] follows from the express provision of Article 1 (1) of the Basic Law; for the developing life also enjoys the protection which Article 1 (1) accords to the dignity of man. Wherever human life exists, it merits human dignity; whether the subject of this dignity is conscious of it and knows how to safeguard it is not of decisive moment. The potential capabilities inherent in human existence from its inception are adequate to establish human dignity.

3. . . . According to established precedent of the Federal Constitutional Court, the constitutional norms contain not only an individual's subjective defensive rights against the state. They also represent an objective order of values that serves as a basic constitutional decision for all areas of the law and provides guidelines and impulses for legislative, administrative, and judicial practice. . . .

II. 1. The obligation of the state to furnish protection is comprehensive. . . . Human life represents a supreme value within the constitutional order that needs no further justification; it is the vital basis of this human dignity and the prerequisite of all other basic rights.

2. The obligation of the state to take the developing life under its protection also exists in principle with regard to the mother. Undoubtedly, the natural union of the prenatal life with the mother establishes a special type of relationship for which there is no parallel in any other factual situation in life. Pregnancy belongs to the intimate sphere of the woman that is constitutionally protected by Article 2 (1) in conjunction with Article 1 (1) of the Basic Law. If [one] were to regard the embryo only as a part of the maternal organism, the termination of pregnancy would remain within the sphere of [a woman's] private life into which the legislator may not intrude. Because the one about to be born is an independent human being under the protection of the Constitution, termination of pregnancy has a social dimension which makes it accessible to and in need of state regulation. It is true that the right of a woman freely to develop her personality also lays claim to recognition and protection. [This right] includes freedom of action in its comprehensive meaning and

consequently also embraces the woman's responsible decision against parenthood and its attendant duties. But this right is not given without limitation — the rights of others, the constitutional order, and moral law limit it. [The right to personality] can never confer *a priori* the authority to intrude upon the protected legal sphere of another without a justifiable reason, much less the authority to destroy [this sphere] as well as a life, especially because a special responsibility exists precisely for this life.

No compromise is possible that would both guarantee the protection of the unborn life and concede to the pregnant woman the freedom of terminating the pregnancy, because termination of pregnancy always means destruction of the pre-natal life. In the ensuing balancing process, "both constitutional values must be per-ceived in their relation to human dignity as the center of the Constitution's value system." When using Article 1 (1) as a guidepost, the decision must come down in favor of the preeminence of protecting the fetus's life over the right of self-determination of the pregnant woman. Pregnancy, birth, and child-rearing may impair the woman's [right of self-determination] as to many personal developmen-tal potentialities. The termination of pregnancy, however, destroys prenatal life. Pursuant to the principle of carefully balancing competing constitutionally pro-tected positions, and considering the fundamental concept behind Article 19 (2) of the Basic Law, [the state] must give the protection of the unborn child's life priority. In principle, this preeminence lasts for the entire duration of the pregnancy and may not be questioned for any particular phase. . . .

3. [We] may deduce the basic position that the Constitution requires of the legal order from the [aforementioned discussion]. The legal order may not use the woman's right of self-determination as the sole guideline for its regulations. Basi-cally, the state must assume [that a woman has] the duty to carry the pregnancy to term and must consequently consider its termination as a wrong. [It] must clearly express its disapproval of the termination of pregnancy. [The state] must avoid the false impression that terminating a pregnancy involves the same social course of events as, for instance, a trip to the doctor to have an illness healed or even a legally neutral alternative to contraception. . . .

III. First, it is incumbent upon the legislature to decide how the state is to fulfill its obligation effectively to protect the developing life.

1. . . . It is therefore the state's task to use sociopolitical means as well as public assistance to safeguard the developing life. The legislature is largely responsible for organizing what assistance can be effectuated and how these measures are to be implemented in detail. The Constitutional Court generally may not review these decisions. [The legislature's] primary concern will be to strengthen the willingness of the expectant mother to accept the pregnancy as her own responsibility and to bring the fetus to full term. Regardless of how the state fulfills its obligation to protect human life, [we] must not forget that nature has entrusted the protection of the developing life to the mother. The principal goal of the state's endeavor to

protect life should be to reawaken and, if required, to strengthen the maternal will
to protect [the unborn child] where it has been lost. . . .

[A principal issue in this case is whether the Basic Law requires the crim-
inalization of abortion. After noting that the legislature is not obligated
to protect unborn life in the same way that it protects born life, the court
continued:]

2. (a) From time immemorial it has been the task of the criminal law to protect
the elementary values of community life. In the preceding passages [we] established
that the life of every individual human being is among the most important legal
values. The termination of a pregnancy irrevocably destroys human life that has
come into being. [It] is an act of killing. . . . [T]he use of criminal law to punish
"acts of abortion" is undoubtedly legitimate; it is the law in force in most civilized
states — under variously formulated conditions — and is particularly in keeping with
the German legal tradition.

(b) However, punishment should never be an end in itself. Basically, its use is
subject to the decision of the legislature. Nothing prevents the legislature from
expressing the constitutionally required disapprobation of abortion by means other
than the threat of penal sanctions. What is determinative is whether the totality of
those measures serving to protect prenatal life — whether classifiable as measures
of private, public, or, more particularly, of social or criminal law — in fact guarantee protection commensurate with the importance of the legal interest to be
safeguarded. . . .

3. As has been shown, the obligation of the state to protect the developing life
also exists with respect to the mother. Here, however, the use of criminal law gives
rise to special problems which result from the singular situation of the pregnant
woman. The incisive effects of pregnancy upon a woman's physical and mental
condition are immediately apparent and require no further exposition. They often
mean a considerable change in her entire lifestyle and a limitation of potential personal development. This burden is not always or not fully compensated by the fact
that the woman finds new fulfillment in her task as a mother and that the pregnant
woman can claim assistance from the community (Article 6 (4) of the Basic Law).
In individual cases difficult and even life-threatening situations of conflict may arise.
The unborn's right to life may place a substantially greater burden on the woman
than that normally connected with a pregnancy. Thus [we] are confronted with the
question of what she may reasonably be expected to endure; in other words,
whether the state, even in these cases, may compel her to carry the child to term by
means of criminal sanctions. Respect for the unborn life conflicts with the woman's
right not to be forced to sacrifice her own values beyond reasonable expectations.
The legislature must show particular restraint in a situation of conflict which, generally, permits no clear moral evaluation and in which a decision to terminate the

pregnancy may be a question of conscience worthy of respect. If in these cases the legislature does not consider the conduct of the pregnant woman deserving of punishment and forgoes the imposition of criminal sanctions, then this decision must be accepted constitutionally as the result of a judgment incumbent upon the legislature. . . .

It would appear unreasonable to expect [a woman] to continue her pregnancy if the termination proves to be necessary to "avert a danger to the life" of the pregnant woman "or the danger of a grave injury to her health" (section 218b, no. 1, Criminal Code in the Version of the Fifth Law to Reform the Criminal Law). In this case her own "right to life and physical inviolability" (Article 2 (2) [1] of the Basic Law) are at stake, and she cannot be expected to sacrifice it for the unborn life. In addition, the legislature may refrain from imposing penal sanctions for abortions in other cases where pregnancy would subject the woman to extraordinary burdens which, from the viewpoint of what may [reasonably] be expected of her, are as oppressive as those listed in section 218b, no. 1. Special reasons for termination of a pregnancy include those based on eugenic, ethical (criminological), and social [considerations]. [Also included are reasons] based on urgent necessity which are contained in the federal government's draft submitted during the sixth session of the federal parliament and were discussed publicly as well as during the legislative proceedings. In the deliberations of the Special Committee for Criminal Law Reform the representative of the federal government demonstrated at length and with convincing reasons why it might not be reasonable to expect a woman to carry the pregnancy to term in these four cases. The decisive point in these cases is that another interest equally worthy of constitutional protection asserts itself with such urgency that the state's legal order cannot require the pregnant woman always to defer to the right of the unborn.

The legislature may also add [termination of pregnancy] for reasons of general necessity (social reasons) to this [list of reasons]. For the general social situation of the pregnant woman and her family may produce conflicts of such gravity that sacrifices in favor of the unborn life cannot be exacted by the instrumentalities of criminal law. In regulating this case, the legislature must describe the statutory elements of the offense which will not be subject to punishment so that the gravity of the social conflict to be presumed here is clearly recognizable and so that — viewed from the standpoint of what the state may [reasonably] expect [of the parties involved] — congruence of this case with the other reasons [for termination] is assured. In removing genuine cases of this kind of conflict from the protection of penal law, the legislature does not violate its duty to protect life. Even in cases [of real conflict] the state may not be content with merely examining whether the legal prerequisites exist for exempting an abortion from punishment and certifying that they exist, where appropriate. Rather, [we] expect the state to offer counseling and assistance so as to remind the pregnant woman of her fundamental duty to respect the unborn's right to life, to encourage her to go through with the pregnancy, and to support her — particularly in cases of social need — with practical assistance.

In all other cases the termination of pregnancy remains a wrong deserving of punishment; for here the destruction of a legal interest of the highest order is subject to the uncontrolled discretion of another and is not motivated by any necessity. If the legislature had wanted to dispense with criminal sanctions, this [decision] would have been compatible with the protective command of Article 2 (2) [1] of the Basic Law only under the condition that another, equally effective, legal sanction was at its command which would permit the clear recognition of this act as a wrong (disapprobation by the legal order) and which would prevent abortions as effectively as a penal provision.

[In the concluding section of its opinion, after examining abortion as a sociopolitical problem, the Constitutional Court found that the Abortion Reform Act fell short of constitutional standards in several particulars. First, it failed to express disapproval of abortion. The court found that the regulatory scheme as a whole, undergirded by abortion funding through state medical insurance programs, conveyed the impression that abortion, like childbirth, is a normal procedure associated with pregnancy. The law must make clear, said the court, that abortion is an "act of killing." Second, the statute failed to distinguish between valid and invalid abortions, thus ignoring the normative content of the constitutional command to protect life. Third, the counseling procedures were flawed because they failed to deter abortion. "Physicians, on the basis of their professional training," said the court, "have neither the qualifications for such counseling activities nor, generally, the time required for individual counseling." Additionally, the court noted that counseling boards were required only to convey information, not to dissuade women from procuring abortions. Finally, the statute was flawed because the physician who was required to inform the pregnant woman of available social assistance could also perform the abortion. In the light of these statutory deficiencies, the Federal Constitutional Court suspended operation of the time-phase counseling rule pending adoption of a new statute consistent with the value order of the Basic Law. As the extract shows, the Constitutional Court instructed parliament that in addition to permitting abortions for medical, eugenic, and ethical indications, it might also allow women to procure abortions in situations of extreme social hardship. In seeking to balance the right-to-life and personality clauses of the Basic Law, the court concluded that the pregnant woman need "not be forced beyond reasonable expectations to sacrifice her life values in order to foster respect for the [unborn]." But the court clearly condemned any and every policy of abortion on demand and concluded that in the present circumstances abortion would once again have to be punished by law in order to adequately foster the protection of unborn life.]

Justices Rupp-von Brünneck and Simon, dissenting:

The life of every single human being is, of course, a central value of the legal order. It is indisputable that the constitutional obligation to protect this life also encompasses its preliminary state before birth. The discussions in the parliament and before the Federal Constitutional Court did not involve the whether, but only the how of this protection. The decision in this matter is the legislature's responsibility. Under no circumstances can [one] deduce from the Constitution a state obligation to subject the termination of pregnancy to punishment at every stage. The legislature was as free to opt for counseling and the time-phase rule as it was [to opt] for listing reasons for terminating pregnancy.

Any contrary constitutional interpretation is incompatible with the freedom-oriented character of the constitutional norms and, in a measure fraught with consequences, transfers decisional authority to the Federal Constitutional Court. In judging the Fifth Law to Reform the Criminal Law, the majority overlooks the singularity of the termination of pregnancy in relation to other dangers to life. It does not properly appreciate the social problems encountered by the legislature or the goals of the urgent reform. Precisely because every solution remains a patchwork, one should not raise constitutional objections over the fact that the German legislature—consistent with the reforms in other Western civilized states—has given sociopolitical measures priority over largely ineffective penal sanctions. Nowhere does the Constitution prescribe a statutory "disapproval" of morally reprehensible conduct without regard to the protective effect such [disapproval] may actually have.

A. I. The authority of the Federal Constitutional Court to annul decisions of the parliamentary legislator demands restraint in its use in order to avoid a dislocation of power among the constitutional organs. The command of judicial self-restraint, which has been termed the "life-giving elixir" of the judicial function of the Federal Constitutional Court, applies when a case does not involve warding off encroachments by governmental authority but rather involves the court issuing directives for the positive development of the social order to the popularly elected legislature by way of constitutional review. In this instance the Federal Constitutional Court may not succumb to the temptation to assume the functions of the organ to be controlled if, in the long run, the status of constitutional jurisdiction is not to be endangered.

1. The review petitioned for in these proceedings moves beyond the area of classical control by constitutional courts. The fundamental norms at the heart of our Constitution guarantee the citizen defensive rights vis-à-vis the state which [provide him with] a personal sphere where he may take responsibility for the unlimited structuring of his own life. To this extent the classic function of the Federal Constitutional Court consists in repulsing excessive encroachments by state power upon this sphere of freedom. Penal provisions are at the very pinnacle on the scale of possible state encroachment: They order the citizen to behave in a certain way and

subject him [or her] to painful restrictions of freedom or financial burdens in case of noncompliance. When a constitutional court reviews such provisions, it examines whether the enactment or implementation of the penal sanction permissibly encroaches upon the constitutionally protected sphere of freedom [concerned]; whether, therefore, the state is permitted to punish at all or [only] to a certain extent. . . .

2. Because fundamental rights, being defensive rights, are *a priori* unsuitable for preventing the legislature from repealing penal provisions, the majority of the court would find the basis for doing so in the more extensive meaning of fundamental rights as objective value decisions. According to this theory, fundamental rights not only regulate defensive rights of the individual vis-à-vis the state but also contain objective value decisions, which the state must continually implement through affirmative measures. The Federal Constitutional Court has developed this concept through its commendable efforts to impart greater efficacy to fundamental rights in their capacity as rights designed to secure freedom and to aspire to social justice. The majority of the court, however, does not adequately consider the differences between the two aspects of fundamental rights which are so important for control by constitutional courts.

Fundamental rights, in the sense of defensive rights, have a relatively clear, recognizable content; in their interpretation and application, case law has developed practical [and] generally recognized criteria for the control of governmental encroachments — for example, the principle of proportionality. On the other hand, how affirmative legislative measures should effectuate a [constitutional] value decision is ordinarily a most complex question. Value decisions, which of necessity are phrased in general terms, may perhaps be characterized as constitutional mandates which, though they give direction for all acts by the state, nevertheless must necessarily depend upon a translation into binding regulations. Greatly differing solutions are possible, depending on the assessment of factual conditions, concrete goals and their priorities, [and] the suitability of conceivable means and methods. The decision [as to which solution is best] frequently requires compromises and is accomplished by trial and error. In accordance with the fundamental rule of the separation of powers and democratic principles, this decision rests with the legislature upon which the people directly confer legitimacy. . . .

The concept of the objective value decision may not, however, become the vehicle for transferring to the Federal Constitutional Court specifically legislative functions for the development of the social order. Otherwise the court would be forced into a role for which it is neither competent nor equipped. Therefore the Federal Constitutional Court should continue to maintain the restraint it practiced up until the time of the university governance decisions [citing five cases on university admissions and governance policy]. This court should confront the legislature only when the latter has completely disregarded a value decision or when the nature and manner in which it effectuated [the value decision] are obviously erroneous. . . .

II. 1. Our strongest objection is addressed to the fact that, for the first time in the adjudication of a constitutional question, an objective value decision is to serve the purpose of postulating a duty of the legislature to issue penal norms, therefore [postulating] the strongest imaginable interference with the citizen's sphere of freedom. This reverses the function of fundamental rights into a directly opposite one. If the objective value decision contained in a constitutional norm which protects a certain legal interest is enough to serve as a basis for deriving a duty to punish, then fundamental rights may surreptitiously become the basis of a maze of rules for the limitation of freedom instead of a bulwark for securing freedom. What applies to the protection of life may also be enlisted for other legal interests of high rank — such as physical inviolability, freedom, marriage, and family.

The Constitution, of course, presupposes that the state may also use its power of punishment to protect an orderly social life; but fundamental rights are meant not to require state intervention but rather to set limits to it. Thus the Supreme Court of the United States has even considered it a violation of a basic right to punish abortions performed by a physician with the consent of the pregnant woman during the first third of the pregnancy. It is true that this would be going too far under German constitutional law. According to the freedom-oriented character of our Constitution, however, the legislature must have a justification for punishing but not for abstaining from punishment because it thinks that a penal sanction promises no success or appears to be an inappropriate reaction for other reasons. . . .

B. I. 3. . . . Considering the failure of penal sanctions, the legislature could, in choosing this solution, assume that the suitable means for redress are to be sought in the social and societal areas. [It could also assume] that the most important thing is, on the one hand, to make it easier for the mother to carry the child to term by [using] preventive psychological, sociopolitical, and societal-political measures of a supportive nature, and, on the other hand, to strengthen her own willingness to decrease the number of unwanted pregnancies through better information about contraception. Apparently, the majority of the court did not doubt that such measures, viewed as a whole, are the most effective ones and most readily correspond to an effectuation of fundamental rights in the sense of greater freedom and increased social justice.

Understandably, supportive measures of this type can receive only limited inclusion in a criminal statute because of differing governmental authority. To this extent, therefore, the Fifth Law to Reform the Criminal Law merely contains a duty to undergo counseling. According to the legislature's conception, the pregnant woman is to be removed from her isolation — without fear of punishment. Open contacts with her environment and individual counseling attuned to her situation of personal conflict should make it easier for her to cope with her environment. It follows from the statutory materials and the majority vote of the parliament cited in the majority opinion that the prescribed counseling is to serve the protection of the developing life by awakening and strengthening the [woman's] willingness to carry the child to term whenever serious countervailing reasons do not exist. . . .

———————————

NOTE: *ABORTION I* AND ITS AFTERMATH. *Abortion I* is perhaps best understood in the light of other values of the Basic Law that help to flesh out the meaning of human dignity as many Germans understand it. As often noted in this volume, the Constitutional Court has articulated a view of human dignity and personhood which, while protecting an inner core of personal freedom, binds the individual at the same time to certain norms governing the whole of society. One of these norms is contained in Article 6, paragraph 1 of which confers the state's "special protection" on marriage and the family. In addition, Article 6 (4) declares that "every mother is entitled to the protection and care of the community." Even though Article 6 is not an important part of the court's analysis in *Abortion I,* the constitutional case law under Article 6 — with its emphasis on filial commitment within the marital relationship — throws some light on the decision.[62] Relevant too is the principle of the *Sozialstaat,* the state based on social justice. When this principle is considered in tandem with the substantive value judgments of Article 6, the state may be said to be under an obligation to establish an environment within which the family is able to survive and flourish. Indeed, as the court reminded West Germans in *Abortion I,* the legal order exists to instruct its citizens in the moral content of the Basic Law, and that includes substantive values pertaining to the nature of life, personhood, and family.

On the other hand, the dissenting opinion in *Abortion I* is a strong argument against judicial intervention. The controversy among the justices did not turn on whether unborn life constitutes "life" within the meaning of Article 2. They agreed that it does, and also that the state is obligated to protect that life. But who determines how best to secure the protection of unborn life in the face of an apparently intractable social problem? The dissenters felt that the legislature had adequately considered the importance of unborn life in settling on a time-phase rule together with compulsory counseling. The dissenting justices argued that the judicial recriminalization of abortion during the first trimester of pregnancy exceeded the bounds of judicial power since in their view the implementation of the Basic Law's objective values was fundamentally a legislative task.

Another point in need of emphasis is that neither the majority nor the dissenting opinions refer to the fetus as a human person. The terms used are "unborn life," "incipient life," "germinating life" or some equivalent reference. Because the fetus is not a "completed person," the court noted, it does not enjoy the same rights as other human beings. Yet fetal life is an "independent legal value" worthy of protection under the Constitution. The German distinction between fetal life and persons is noteworthy in comparative perspective because it allowed the Constitutional Court to engage in a balancing process largely absent in the seminal American case of *Roe v. Wade*.[63]

In applications to the European Commission on Human Rights, two German women claimed that the Constitutional Court's abortion decision violated the rights of privacy and religion under Articles 8 and 9 of the European Convention of Human Rights. The commission rejected these arguments over the strong dissent of two of its eighteen members.[64] Meanwhile, the German parliament complied almost to the letter with the rulings in *Abortion I*. The revised version of the Abortion Reform Act, passed on May 18, 1976, permitted abortions for medical, eugenic, ethical, and serious social reasons.[65] The period within which abortions could legally be carried out varied with the particular reason for procuring the abortion. Medical abortions carried out in the interest of maternal health could be performed within the first twenty-two weeks of pregnancy; after counseling and proper certification, "ethical" and "social" abortions were permissible within the first twelve weeks.[66]

The court's imposition of an indications solution to the abortion problem troubled many Germans on both sides of the controversy. Anti-abortion spokespersons objected to the high number of abortions being performed for reasons of social hardship. (Eighty percent of all legal abortions fell into this category.) The ease or difficulty of securing an abortion for social reasons depended largely on the counseling practices of the state or region charged with administering the law. "One of the most stinging thorns in the flesh of anti-abortion advocates," wrote one commentator, "was the fact that abortions based on the social indication were covered by public health insurance."[67] Pro-choice activists, on the other hand, claimed that the indications regulation was excessively burdensome, interfered with a woman's decision to choose in early pregnancy, and yet constituted no real deterrent to women determined to have a legal abortion. The rates of criminal prosecution were low and empirical studies showed that the law was not really working as intended by the Constitutional Court's guidelines. Pressures for change soon came about, and German unification would hasten the reform.

NOTE: ABORTION AND REUNIFICATION. The Unification Treaty inserted a new Article 143 into the Basic Law. Article 143 was a transitional provision that allowed the five new eastern *Länder* to deviate from existing constitutional requirements for a period of two years (until December 31, 1992) in policy areas in which ingrained separate practices in the old GDR would not permit the Basic Law's immediate application. Abortion was one of these policy areas. West German law, conforming to the 1975 *Abortion* case, permitted abortions to be performed by licensed physicians only for specified medical, genetic, ethical, and social reasons duly certified by a panel of doctors and other counselors. In the absence of these indications, abortion was, as a general principle, a criminal offense when performed at any stage of pregnancy. East Germany, by contrast, permitted abortion on demand within the first trimester of pregnancy. Stalemated, the two German states agreed to retain their respective abortion policies until an all-German legislature could work out a satisfactory compromise, the Unity Treaty having laid down a December 31, 1992, deadline for the enactment of an all-German law acceptable to both sides.[68]

The first all-German parliament, elected on December 2, 1990, struggled to find a middle ground between the conflicting policies of East and West. By May 1992, a severely fractured Bundestag had before it several proposals ranging from a plan to increase the severity of West Germany's existing policy all the way over to one based on unrestricted freedom of choice. After months of debate and negotiation, the quarreling parties broke the logjam and reached a compromise, passing the Pregnancy and Family Assistance Act by a broad majority (357 to 283 votes).[69]

The act incorporated a time-phase solution with obligatory counseling. The following passage captures the essential features of a detailed and complicated statute:

> The new "counseling model" retained the concept that abortion destroys life and should only be allowed if the continuation of pregnancy would result in an unreasonable burden for the woman. But at the same time it reflected the belief that the State's duty to protect developing life could be better served, in general, by improving the social environment for women and families with children, and in the individual case of unwanted pregnancy, by comprehensive information and counseling, than by threatening punishment and establishing cumbersome procedures for obtaining a permission to abort ("support instead of punishment"). Consequently, the new legislation contained a voluminous package of general social measures on education, birth control, and State assistance in matters of family planning and pregnancy. With respect to the individual woman faced with an unwanted pregnancy, the Act focused on providing not only State assistance in case of financial need but on strengthening the woman's rights and opportunities in education, workplace, career, and housing. Special emphasis was put on "day care."[70]

The new statute departed from the Constitutional Court's earlier ruling in one crucial respect. It decriminalized abortion in the first trimester of pregnancy. In words that would come back to haunt the Bundestag, the new change in the criminal code declared that the interruption of pregnancy in some circumstances was "not illegal" (*nicht rechtswidrig*).[71] Specifically, no criminal penalty would attach to an abortion if performed by a licensed physician after compulsory counseling and a three-day waiting period. If, after such counseling—which would have to be certified in writing and before the twelfth week of pregnancy—the woman still decided that an abortion was in her best interest, a licensed physician could then legally perform the abortion.

7.11 Abortion II Case (1993)
88 BVerfGE 203

[On July 2, 1992, the Bundesrat approved the new abortion reform statute and shortly thereafter the federal president signed it. Within hours of the signing, however, and with the backing of Chancellor Helmut Kohl, 249 Christian Democratic members of the Bundestag—all from the former West Germany—petitioned the Constitutional Court to enjoin the law's enforcement. Bavaria's state government, claiming that several provisions of the statute were unconstitutional, filed a separate petition. In a preliminary hearing, after a full day of oral argument on August 4, 1992, the day before the law would have entered into force, the Second Senate, to the surprise of many constitutional scholars and the chagrin of others, unanimously issued an injunction (86 BVerfGE 390) reinstating the old two-German policy pending a full decision on the merits of the case. In *Abortion II* the court reaffirmed the essential core of *Abortion I* while simultaneously adjusting the character of this protection to meet the needs of post-unification Germany.

The full opinion and two dissenting opinions take up 163 pages of the official reports. The extracts below are limited to the case's headnotes and selected passages from the court's opinion. The headnotes, drafted by the court itself, summarize the main rulings of the decision. Translated by Susanne Walther, the headnotes appear in *German Yearbook of International Law* 36 (1993): 402–4 and are reprinted here with the *Yearbook's* permission.]

---

1. Germany's Basic Law places a duty on the state to protect human life, including that of the unborn. This duty of protection is derived from Article 1, subsection 1 GG (Basic Law). The object and scope of this duty is more specifically governed by Article 2 subsection 2 GG. Unborn life is due human dignity. The legal order must guarantee the proper legal foundation for the development of the unborn in terms of its right to life. The unborn's right to life is not predicated on its acceptance by the mother but exists prior to this point in time.

2. The duty to protect the unborn is a duty owed to each individual, not just to human life in general.

3. The unborn is due legal protection even as against its mother. Such protection can be afforded to the unborn only if the legislature passes a law prohibiting abortion and places a basic legal obligation on women to carry pregnancies to term. The bar on abortion and the basic obligation to carry a pregnancy to term constitute two inseparable elements of this constitutionally required protection.

4. Abortions performed at any point during a pregnancy must be fundamentally considered a wrong and, thus, unlawful. The determination of the right to life

of the unborn must not be delegated to the discretion of a third party who is not bound by law, not even where the third party is the mother herself and no matter how limited the time period may be in which such a right may be exercised.

5. The scope of the duty to protect the unborn is to be determined by weighing its importance and need for protection against the conflicting interests of other objects deserving of legal protection. Those interests which conflict with the unborn's right to life include—starting with a woman's right to have her human dignity protected and respected (Article 2 [1])—above all, a woman's right to life and physical integrity (Article 2 [2]) and her right of personality (Article 2 [1]). The constitutional rights of a woman, however, do not go so far as to allow her to claim under Article 4 (1) a fundamentally protected legal right to kill an unborn [child] by means of abortion.

6. The state must fulfill its duty of protection by adopting adequate measures setting legal and factual standards whose objective—in consideration of conflicting legal interests—is to provide for appropriate and effective protection (minimum protection). For this purpose, it is necessary to create a regulatory scheme which combines elements of preventive as well as repressive protection.

7. The fundamental rights of a woman do not mandate the general suspension of a duty to carry out a pregnancy, even within a limited time frame. However, a woman's constitutional rights permit—and in certain cases might require—recognition of exceptional circumstances under which such a duty shall not be imposed on her. It is up to the legislature to determine the specific criteria of these factual exceptions according to a standard of reasonableness. Those burdens shall constitute exceptions which require such a degree of sacrifice of individual needs by a woman that it would be unreasonable to expect this from her.

8. Under minimum protection the state is precluded from freely dispensing with criminal punishment and its protective effect on human life.

9. The state's duty to protect the unborn also includes protecting the unborn from dangers emanating from the influence of the woman's immediate or general social milieu or both her and her family's present and foreseeable living circumstances and, as such, interfering with the woman's willingness to carry out the pregnancy.

10. The state's duty of care furthermore includes maintaining and raising the public's consciousness of the unborn's legal right of protection.

11. The legislature acts constitutionally when it adopts a regulatory scheme for the protection of the unborn which uses counseling as a means of inducing pregnant women in conflict during the early stage of the pregnancy to carry their pregnancy to term. The legislature also acts within constitutional bounds when it dispenses with criminal prosecution for indicated abortions as well as the determination of such indications by third parties.

12. A counseling-based regulation must comply with underlying constitutional

conditions which impose affirmative duties on women for the benefit of the unborn. The state holds full responsibility for implementing the counseling procedure.

13. The state's duty to protect the unborn requires that the physician cooperate not only in the interest of the woman but also to the benefit of the unborn.

14. It is unconstitutional to define by law the existence of a child as a source of damage or harm (Article 1 [1]). For this reason, it is prohibited to acknowledge a maintenance obligation toward a child as a type of damage or harm.

15. Abortions performed in the absence of a determined indication as prescribed by the counseling regulation may not be deemed justified (not unlawful). According to inalienable fundamental principles of law, an exception can have the effect of a legal justification only if it is incumbent on the state alone to establish the criteria necessary to take the act in question out of the general rule.

16. It is unconstitutional to create an entitlement to statutory health insurance benefits for the performance of an abortion whose lawfulness has not been established. By contrast, it is not unconstitutional to grant social welfare benefits for abortions not incurring criminal liability under the counseling regulation where a woman lacks financial means. Continued payment of salaries or wages in the case of an abortion is also constitutional.

17. The administrative power of the *Länder* remains unqualified where a federal law merely prescribes an obligation to be met by the *Länder* and not the specific regulations which can be implemented and enforced by the governmental administrative authorities of the *Länder.*

Judgment of the Second Senate. . . .

D. I. 1. The Basic Law requires the state to protect human life. Unborn life is human life and thus entitled to the state's protection. The Constitution not only supports direct state intervention on behalf of unborn life but also requires that the state protect unborn life from the illegal intervention of others. This *duty to protect* [unborn life] is found in Article 1 (1) of the Basic Law, which expressly obliges the state to respect and protect human life. . . .

(a) Unborn human life possesses human dignity; [dignity] is not merely an attribute of a fully developed personality or a human being after birth. . . .

(b) The duty to protect human life extends to the life of each individual being, not to human life in general. Any ordered life in common within a state requires that this duty be fulfilled. The Basic Law imposes this duty on all levels of state authority (Article 1 [1]); i.e., on the state in all of its functions, particularly in the exercise of its legislative authority. The duty to protect extends also to the adoption of measures designed to ease the burden of pregnancy as well as to [various] rules of conduct.

2. The state imposes rules of conduct to protect unborn life by means of legal obligations, prohibitions, or duties to act or refrain from acting. These rules must also apply to the protection of the unborn child from its mother, regardless of the

stage of this relationship of duality in unity [*Zweiheit in Einheit*]. [But] the unborn child can only be protected from its mother if the legislature prohibits an abortion and imposes a legal duty on the mother to carry the child to term. The fundamental prohibition on abortion and the fundamental duty to carry the child to term are inseparable elements of the constitutionally required protection.

Moreover, [the state must also protect unborn life] against invasion by third parties, not the least of whom are people within the pregnant woman's family or social circle. These individuals may threaten the unborn child directly or indirectly by denying the pregnant woman the assistance they owe her, creating difficulties for her because of the pregnancy, or pressuring her to terminate the pregnancy.

(a) These [legislatively created] rules of conduct cannot be simply voluntary; they must be imposed by law. The right to life is embodied in the norms of the Basic Law. [This right is special] and thus requires special binding rules for its effective realization. [Criminal] penalties, however, are not the only possible sanctions, although they may sway individuals to respect and obey the requirements of law.

Legal rules of conduct must provide for two kinds of protection. On the one hand, where a protected legal value is harmed or threatened, they must include a regulatory scheme that includes individualized preventive measures or punishment. On the other hand, such rules must [be designed to] strengthen and support popular values and concepts of right and wrong; they must promote the public's consciousness [of the unborn child's] legal right to protection [citing the *Life Imprisonment* case].

(b) But since the Basic Law does not elevate the protection of [unborn] life above all other legal values, the right [of the unborn] to life is not absolute. It is not elevated above all other legal values without exception; this is clear from Article 2 (2) . . . Rather, the scope of the state's duty to protect the unborn is to be determined by weighing its importance and need for protection against other conflicting legal values. The legal values affected by the right to life of the unborn include the woman's right to protection and respect for her own dignity (Article 1 [1]), the rights to life and physical integrity, and the right to personal development (Article 2 [1]).

The legislature has the responsibility of determining the nature and scope of the required protection. To the extent that the legislature is constitutionally bound to act in this area, it must provide the minimum protection necessary to safeguard the relevant constitutional value. The required protection may not fall below this minimum standard [*Untermassverbot*]. . . .

(c) So as not to run afoul of this standard of minimum protection, the protection afforded [the unborn] must satisfy the minimum requirements of the legal order.

(aa) This principle requires that abortion be declared illegal [as a general rule] during all stages of pregnancy [citing *Abortion I*]. If the law does not declare abortion to be illegal, the unborn child's right to life would be trumped by the legally unrestrained decision of the mother or other third party, and the legal protection of its life would no longer be guaranteed. The dignity claims of the woman, and her capacity to make a responsible decision, cannot justify such a devaluation of human life. The right to life itself must define the scope and limits of its permissible infringement; this cannot be left to the [complete] discretion of [third] parties.

. . . Although the right of the unborn to life [is the superior value], it does not extend to the point of eliminating all of the woman's legal rights [to self-determination]. [Her rights] can produce a situation in which it is permissible in exceptional cases — and is even required in some — not to impose a legal duty to carry the child to term.

(bb) The legislature is responsible for defining these exceptional circumstances. So as not to fall below the minimal requirement for protecting a basic right, the legislature must recognize that the conflicting legal values cannot be quantitatively balanced. From the perspective of unborn life, the legislature's choice must be for life itself and may not embrace the mere balancing of losses and gains. Because abortion always results in the death of the unborn child, a [balancing act of the kind suggested] is impossible [citing *Abortion I*]. . . .

This does not mean that the only constitutionally exceptional case where the woman need not carry her fetus to term is when her life or health is endangered. Other exceptions are imaginable. This court has established the standard of an unreasonable burden as the basis for identifying such exceptions [citing *Abortion I*] . . . The unreasonable burden standard is justified because in the light of the unique relationship between mother and child, prohibiting abortion does not end with the imposition of a duty to refrain from violating [altogether] the rights of another. There are further duties that affect the woman's entire existence: the duty to carry and bear the child and to care for it many years after its birth. Given these pregnancy-related responsibilities and the psychic conflict they may evoke, it is possible that many women in the early stages of pregnancy may experience serious, even life-threatening distress; in these circumstances, such urgent interests worthy of legal protection arise that the legal order cannot require the woman to value an unborn being's right to life above all else, regardless of broader moral or religious concerns.

An unreasonable burden cannot arise from the circumstances of a normal pregnancy. Rather, [an unreasonable burden] would have to involve such a measure of sacrifice of existential values as could not be expected of any woman. . . .

In addition to defined medical, criminological, and embryopathic indications that would justify an abortion, there may be other situations where an abortion would also be indicated [as justified]. One such scenario would include a condition of such social or psychological distress that a clear case of an unreasonable burden would be demonstrated.

(cc) Although the unreasonable burden standard limits a woman's duty to carry a child to term, it does not relieve the state from its duty to protect unborn human life. It directs the state to support the woman through counseling and assistance and to try to persuade her to carry the child to term. This is the presumption behind Section 218a (3) of the Criminal Code.

(dd) . . . [But] due to its extreme interventionist character, criminal law need not be the primary means of legal protection. Its application is subject to the requirements of proportionality (citing several cases). The criminal law is used as the *ultima ratio* of this protection . . . Where the legislature has enacted constitutionally adequate, noncriminal measures to protect the unborn, the woman need not be punished for having an unjustified abortion in a limited number of [defined] instances so long as the legal order clearly expresses the view that abortion [as a general rule] is to be prohibited. So long as the law makes the general prohibition [of abortion] clear, this may be constitutionally sufficient [to deter abortions] in this limited set of circumstances. . . .

3. The state's duty to protect unborn life is not satisfied merely by defending it against invasion by others. The state must also take measures to confront dangers threatening the present and future real-life relations of the woman and her family. These relations may influence her decision to carry the child to term. This duty to protect [unborn life] implicates the state's duty to protect [marriage, family, and mothers] under the terms of Article 6 (1) and (4) of the Basic Law. It obliges the state to address problems and difficulties that a woman might experience during pregnancy. Article 6 (1) and (4) expresses a binding commitment of protection embracing the entire sphere of public and private law, extending to the pregnant woman. This [task] is consistent with the commitment to treat motherhood and child-rearing activities as in the public interest and worthy of recognition. . . .

(a) The care that the community owes mothers extends to an effort to prevent abortion in cases of existing material need or those that threaten the woman after the birth of the child. An effort needs to be made to remedy the disadvantages to women in education and employment that may result from [pregnancy and childbirth]. . . .

The duty to protect unborn life, to defend marriage and the family (Article 6), and to secure the equality of men and women in employment (Article 3 [2]), together with Articles 3 and 7 of the International Covenant on Economic, Social, and Cultural Rights, obliges the state, and particularly the legislature, to find a way to balance [the needs of] family and employment and to ensure that child-rearing does not lead to disadvantages [for women].

[In a major departure from *Abortion I,* the court declared that non-indicated abortions in the first twelve weeks of pregnancy, while unjustified, need not be punished. A refined system of counseling oriented toward preserving the life of the fetus could now substitute for the criminal penalty. However, sections of the Criminal Code declaring abortions performed during the first trimester of pregnancy "not illegal" were nullified. Non-indicated abortions must remain illegal even though unpunished. In addition, the court directed the legislature to adopt measures in all spheres of law to support a woman's decision in favor of life over abortion. Sections of the law governing Germany's national health plan, which would have covered abortions not medically indicated, were struck down. Laws mandating that the government keep statistics on abortion in Germany that had been removed from the new legislation were restored. Finally, the court said that the state could not constitutionally deny welfare assistance to poor women who wanted non-indicated abortions but could not afford them.

There were two dissenting opinions. The first, by Ernst Gottfried Mahrenholz, the Second Senate's "chief justice," which Justice Sommer joined, dissented from the majority's view that nonhardship abortions were to be classified as illegal in the Criminal Code. These justices felt that the Pregnancy and Family Assistance Act struck an adequate balance between the rights of life and personality under the Basic Law. Justice Ernst-Wolfgang Böckenförde, whose participation in the case was unsuccessfully challenged by the Social Democrats on the basis of his having once belonged to a right-to-life group, wrote a second dissenting opinion to question the court's ban on paying for "illegal" abortions out of the state's medical insurance program. Whether abortions performed for serious social reasons should be a part of the national health plan was, in his view, a matter of legislative discretion.]

NOTE: AFTERMATH OF *ABORTION II*. In rejecting the 1992 abortion statute, the court tossed the ball back into parliament's court. Until parliament acted to craft a new statute within the guidelines of *Abortion II,* the court's rulings would prevail in all of Germany. It would take parliament another two years to agree on amendments to the 1992 statute. The legislative debate centered on three issues: the nature and extent of obligatory counseling, abortion financing, and the criminal liability of persons within a pregnant woman's social circle who might encourage her to procure an abortion. These issues were being vigorously debated as this volume was going to press.

A compromise bill that commanded the support of a substantial parliamentary majority provided for compulsory counseling along the lines suggested by the Federal Constitutional Court, but it seemed to require less vigorous pro-life counseling than the court had urged. The woman would be informed by a recognized social agency that the unborn child is entitled to the right to life at all stages of pregnancy and that under Germany's legal order a non-indicated abortion, although not punishable if procured after compulsory counseling within the first trimester of pregnancy, would be permissible only in exceptional circumstances. Counselors were required to provide the pregnant woman with all the advice and assistance needed to help her cope with the "conflict situation" in which she found herself, but in doing so they placed a heavy emphasis on her own sense of responsibility.[72]

Parliament also narrowed the Constitutional Court's holding that the state would be obligated to protect the pregnant woman against danger emanating from her friends and neighbors. The compromise bill confined punishment to those persons on whom the woman was dependent for subsistence and who would "reprehensively" misuse this leverage to inveigle her into procuring an abortion.[73] Finally, parliament was struggling to find ways for making it easier for women to secure financial support for abortions through the national health system. Although some Christian Democrats felt that the compromise bill fell short of the Constitutional Court's directives, there seemed to be no desire on anybody's part to mount another judicial challenge against the bill should it be enacted into law.[74]

7.12 Schleyer Kidnapping Case (1977)
46 BVerfGE 160

[On September 5, 1977, terrorists abducted Dr. Hans Martin Schleyer, president of the German Federation of Industries, after brutally slaying four of his aides. The kidnappers threatened to "execute" their hostage if the federal government failed to release from prison eleven of their comrades and ensure their safe exit out of the Federal Republic. When the government refused to comply, Schleyer's son, an attorney, petitioned the Constitutional Court for a temporary injunction on behalf of his father. The motion was brought under Article 30 of the Federal Constitutional Court Act empowering the court to grant temporary injunctions when "urgently needed to avert serious detriment" to fundamental rights. Invoking the right-to-life provision of Article 2 (2), the petitioner argued that state authorities were obligated to meet the terrorists' demands. Refusing to do so, he maintained, would be equivalent to an intentional act against the life and limb of the person abducted. The petitioner also advanced an equal protection argument based on Article 3, because in a previous abduction case involving an important public official the government had released certain prisoners to save the official's life.]

Judgment of the Second Senate. . . .

The motion for a temporary injunction is rejected. . . .

C. I. Article 2 (2) [1] in conjunction with Article 1 (1) [2] of the Constitution commits the state to the protection of each human life. This obligation is comprehensive. It requires the state to support and protect life; this means, principally, to protect it from unlawful interference by others. This precept is mandatory for all state authorities in accordance with their respective specific tasks. Because human life represents a supreme value, the state must take its duty to protect [life] particularly seriously.

II. State authorities are basically free to decide how they should meet their obligation to protect life effectively. It is their task to decide what protective measures are useful and necessary to guarantee effective protection. If they cannot accomplish this by other methods, their discretion in the selection of protective measures may under special circumstances be reduced to the selection of one specific measure. [We] fully understand the petitioner's standpoint. However, contrary to his opinion, no such case is before the court.

The peculiarity of [affording] protection from life-threatening extortion by terrorists is characterized by the fact that protective measures must adapt to a multitude of unique situations. [The government] can neither standardize protective measures in advance nor derive standardized measures from an individual basic right. The Constitution creates an obligation of the state to protect not just the individual but all citizens as a whole. The effective accomplishment of this duty requires that the competent state authorities be in a position to react appropriately to the circumstances of each individual case; this precludes planning specific measures. The Constitution cannot prescribe that predetermined steps be taken, because terrorists would [then] be able to predict how the state will react. Thus the state would no longer be in a position to protect its citizens effectively. This would be contrary to the [state's] task as articulated in Article 2 (2) [1] of the Constitution.

For the same reasons the state cannot systematically make identical decisions in all kidnapping cases pursuant to the general equality clause (Article 3 (1) of the Constitution).

The Federal Constitutional Court, therefore, is not in a position to order the competent state authorities to take any specific action. The government has the responsibility to decide which steps should be taken to fulfill the state's obligation to protect life.

———————————

NOTE: THE RIGHT TO LIFE — AN ADDENDUM. In contexts other than abortion the Federal Constitutional Court has exercised considerable caution in adjudicating claims under the right-to-life clause of Article 2. As in the *Schleyer* case, such caution seems particularly warranted in the face of constitutional complaints against governmental decisions touching the field of international politics.

The *Chemical Weapons* case,[75] decided on October 29, 1987, is a more recent illustration of the court's caution. Several German citizens filed constitutional complaints against the federal government's decision to allow American chemical weapons to be stored on German soil within a few miles of their homes. They claimed that the transportation and storage of nerve gas and other poisonous substances, particularly in the light of the strong statistical probability of an accident or leakages at the storage sites, with life-threatening consequences, violated their right to life within the meaning of Article 2 (2). The petitioners alleged that neither the government nor the Bundestag had taken all the measures required to ensure their safety.

In rejecting the complaints, the Second Senate said:

. . . Because the [legislature] can freely choose how it wants to [fulfill its protective duty under Article 2 (2) [1]], the claim derived from this provision is restricted to the [demand] that public authorities take measures which are not totally inappropriate or wholly insufficient to protect this fundamental right. Only in very special circumstances can one reduce this [legislative] discretion in the choice of means to one particular measure suited to fulfilling the legislature's duty. To meet the procedural requirements for a constitutional complaint based on a violation of the fundamental right in Article 2 (2) [1] of the Basic Law, the complainant must convincingly argue that the public authorities either failed to take any protective precautions or that the regulations and measures they chose were totally inadequate or unsuited for accomplishing this goal. If the complainant wishes to assert that the public authorities can fulfill their duty to protect only by taking one particular measure, he or she must present these arguments convincingly as well as describe the measure to be taken.

The instant constitutional complaints have failed to satisfy this requirement. [This conclusion] holds true independent of whether chemical weapons in West Germany may be used in their entirety, as the government claims, or whether one assumes, as do the complainants, that some of these weapons are unfit for deployment anyway, or whether storing them on West German territory violates objective constitutional law. The complainants have asserted neither that the dangers attendant to the storage of chemical weapons cannot be controlled nor that these dangers cannot be alleviated by safety measures which would satisfy the requirements of Article 2 (2) [1] of the Basic Law. Furthermore, they have not said that [the policy] of keeping secret the details concerning the storage of chemical weapons prevented them from making this argument. The weapons concerned have been on West German territory for some time; the complainants could not name any incidents where concrete injury or danger to the West German people has occurred. In spite of this policy of confidentiality it was not unreasonable to require the complainants to better substantiate their claim that only the efforts of the executive branch to have the weapons removed would satisfy the command of Article 2 (2) [1]. Existing security precautions did not prompt the complainants to substantiate their claims in any greater detail.[76]

In short, the court again acknowledged the state's duty to protect life but went on to say that this duty can be enforced only in exceptional circumstances, a decision that adheres to existing doctrine. *Abortion I* and *II* remain the exception to the doctrine. The majority opinion in the *Chemical Weapons* case prompted Justice Mahrenholz to draft an eloquent dissenting opinion rooted in the Basic Law's right-to-life clause.[77] Significantly, he did not cite *Abortion I* in his defense but rather utterances set forth in *Schleyer, Kalkar I, Mülheim-Kärlich,* and related cases.

CONCLUSION

This chapter underscores the importance of the Basic Law's human dignity clause as a source of constitutional adjudication and interpretation. As the Constitutional Court declared in the *Microcensus* case, human dignity is at the top of the Basic Law's value order. It is *the* formative principle in terms of which all other constitutional values are defined and explained. It occupies the position that liberty may be said to play in the American constitutional order, and in several cases featured in this and the following chapter on freedom of speech, dignity is often locked in significant tension with liberty.

Dignity — as well as the jurisprudence that protects it — is defined by its subjective and objective sides. Subjectively, it secures to the individual rights of personal liberty that the state may not invade; objectively, it sets the boundary to liberties flowing from the rights of personal autonomy, and the state is obligated to see that this line is not overstepped. The concept of dignity that emerges from Germany's constitutional jurisprudence is rooted in a particular image of the human person. This image is not that of an isolated and sovereign individual but rather, as the Constitutional Court has repeatedly avowed, that of a human person whose rights and liberties are tempered by a "sense of [his or her] dependence on and commitment to the community."

8

FREEDOM OF SPEECH

The protection of speech from state suppression is among the highest values of the Basic Law.[1] Strikingly similar to the free speech provisions of the Weimar Constitution, Article 5 provides the following:

> 1. Everyone has the right to freely express and disseminate his opinion orally, in writing, and in pictures, and to inform himself without hindrance from all generally accessible sources. The freedom of the press and the freedom of reporting through radio and film are guaranteed. There is to be no censorship.
>
> 2. These rights find their limits in the rules of the general laws, the statutory provisions for the protection of youth, and in the right to personal honor.
>
> 3. Art and learning, research and teaching are free. The freedom of teaching does not release one from loyalty to the Constitution.

In examining this text one notices that it is cast in declaratory form and that it applies to "everyone." It is not phrased as a prohibition on the state, as in the First Amendment to the United States Constitution. The text raises a question about the impact of the Constitution on private parties. Is state action required to adjudicate a claim to freedom of speech? The text itself provides no clear answer.

A second feature of Article 5 is its specificity. It protects no fewer than seven basic rights of speech and defines what is to be protected, establishes guidelines for limiting speech, and takes into account modern techniques of communication. On further reflection, several questions come to mind. What, for example, is the relationship between the various rights of speech? Do all receive the same level of constitutional protection? Does the emphasis on freedom of opinion (*Meinungsfreiheit*) imply less freedom with respect to the dissemination of information? Can a bright line be drawn between fact and opinion? Should such a line be drawn? Does the right to inform oneself (*Informationsfreiheit*) imply a right to know? Does it impose a duty on government, newspapers, and the electronic media to observe certain standards in reporting the news? How far may the regulation of such standards go? To what extent may the reservation clauses limit the rights of speech? What counts as a "general law" within the meaning of paragraph 2? Is the freedom of art and scholarship absolute since, in contrast to other speech rights, it is un-bounded by a reservation clause? Finally, what is the relationship of Article 5 to other constitutional provisions?

The unity of the Constitution and its hierarchy of values are crowning princi-ples of German constitutional interpretation. Do these principles limit rights of speech? Justice Helmut Steinberger wrote that "Art. 5 operates within an inter-related set of other fundamental rights and liberties, constitutional principles, rules and standards, institutional and procedural devices."[2] And thus, he continued, the freedoms secured by Article 5 need "to be reconciled with the rights and liberties of other persons and groups as well as with other individuals and social interests recognized by the Constitution."[3] But what standards determine which of two competing constitutional values will prevail in a given situation?

German constitutional case law involves many such queries and relationships.[4] But as the detailed provisions of Article 5 might suggest, the case law contains few directive principles of an absolute character. Justice Hugo Black once remarked that the language of the American First Amendment is absolute, and as a consequence, the Supreme Court is foreclosed from any balancing of conflicting interests.[5] What-ever the truth of this proposition as applied to the American Constitution, the German speech clauses, read together and in the light of other constitutional provi-sions, readily yield to a balancing analysis, as many of the cases we will examine in this chapter demonstrate. Indeed, the text itself appears to provide a set of scales on which various interests and values are to be weighed and assessed.

FREEDOM OF EXPRESSION:
GUIDING PRINCIPLES

The *Lüth* case (1958), like *Southwest State* (1951; no. 3.1), is a linchpin of German constitutional law. It laid down for the first time the doctrine of an objective order of values and clarified the relationship between fundamental rights and private law. More particularly, it set forth the basic rationale for a regime of free expression, underscored the individual and social dimensions of speech, specified the purposes served by speech in the public forum, and identified the judicial standard to be applied in weighing the rights of speech against other legally protected interests.

8.1 Lüth Case (1958)
7 BVerfGE 198

[Veit Harlan was a popular film director under the Nazi regime and the producer of the notoriously anti-Semitic film *Jud Süss*. In 1950, several years after he was acquitted of having committed Nazi crimes, he directed a new movie entitled *Immortal Lover*. Erich Lüth, Hamburg's director of information and an active member of a group seeking to heal the wound between Christians and Jews, was outraged by Harlan's reemergence as a film director. Speaking before an audience of motion picture producers and distributors, he urged his listeners to boycott *Immortal Lover*. In his view, the boycott was necessary because of Harlan's Nazi past, as well as the moral condemnation from inside and outside Germany that the film's showing would bring down on the German motion picture industry. The film's producer and distributor secured an order from the Superior Court of Hamburg enjoining Lüth to cease and desist from urging the German public not to see the film and asking theater owners and film distributors not to show it. The court regarded Lüth's action as an incitement in violation of Article 826 of the Civil Code ("Whoever causes damage to another person intentionally and in a manner offensive to good morals is obligated to compensate the other person for the damage"). After the Hamburg Court of Appeals rejected his appeal, Lüth filed a constitutional complaint asserting a violation of his basic right to free speech under Article 5 (1).]

———————

Judgment of the First Senate. . . .

B. II. The complainant claims that the superior court has violated his basic right to free speech as safeguarded by Article 5 (1) [1] of the Constitution.

  1. The decision of the superior court is an act of public authority in the special form of a judicial decision. It can violate a basic right of the complainant only if the court was required to take the right in question into consideration when deciding the case.

  The decision prohibits the complainant from making statements that could influence others to adhere to his opinion regarding Harlan's reappearance [as a film director]. . . . Seen objectively, this limits the complainant's freedom of expression. . . . [But] such a ruling can violate the complainant's basic right under Article 5 (1) only if [a] provision of the Civil Code [Article 826] would be so affected by a basic right as to render it an impossible basis for a decision. . . .

  Whether and to what extent basic rights affect private law is controversial [citing legal literature]. The extreme positions in this dispute are, on the one hand, that basic rights are exclusively directed against the state, and, on the other hand, that the basic rights as such, or at least some, and in any case the more important of them, also apply in civil [i.e., private] law matters against everybody. Neither of these extremes finds support in the Constitutional Court's existing jurisprudence. . . . Nor is there any need here to resolve fully the dispute over the so-called effect of the basic rights on third persons [*Drittwirkung*]. The following discussion is sufficient to resolve this case.

... [T]he primary purpose of the basic rights is to safeguard the liberties of the individual against interferences by public authority. They are defensive rights of the individual against the state. This [purpose] follows from the historical development of the concept of basic rights and from historical developments leading to the inclusion of basic rights in the constitutions of various countries. This also corresponds to the meaning of the basic rights contained in the Basic Law and is underscored by the enumeration of basic rights in the first section of the Constitution, thereby stressing the primacy of the human being and his dignity over the power of the state. This is why the legislature allowed the extraordinary remedy ... of the constitutional complaint to be brought only against acts of public authority.

[An Objective Order of Values]

It is equally true, however, that the Basic Law is not a value-neutral document [citations from numerous decisions]. Its section on basic rights establishes an objective order of values, and this order strongly reinforces the effective power of basic rights. This value system, which centers upon dignity of the human personality developing freely within the social community, must be looked upon as a fundamental constitutional decision affecting all spheres of law [public and private]. It serves as a yardstick for measuring and assessing all actions in the areas of legislation, public administration, and adjudication. Thus it is clear that basic rights also influence [the development of] private law. Every provision of private law must be compatible with this system of values, and every such provision must be interpreted in its spirit.

The legal content of basic rights as objective norms is developed within private law through the medium of the legal provisions directly applicable to this area of the law. Newly enacted statutes must conform to the system of values of the basic rights. The content of existing law also must be brought into harmony with this system of values. This system infuses specific constitutional content into private law, which from that point on determines its interpretation. A dispute between private individuals concerning rights and duties emanating from provisions of private law — provisions influenced by the basic rights — remains substantively and procedurally a private-law dispute. [Courts] apply and interpret private law, but the interpretation must conform to the Constitution.

The influence of the scale of values of the basic rights affects particularly those provisions of private law that contain mandatory rules of law and thus form part of the *ordre public* — in the broad sense of the term — that is, rules which for reasons of the general welfare also are binding on private legal relationships and are removed from the dominion of private intent. Because of their purpose these provisions are closely related to the public law they supplement. Consequently, they are substantially exposed to the influence of constitutional law. In bringing this influence to bear, the courts may invoke the general clauses which, like Article 826 of the Civil Code, refer to standards outside private law. "Good morals" is one such standard. In order to determine what is required by social norms such as these, one has to consider first the ensemble of value concepts that a nation had developed at a certain point in its intellectual and cultural history and laid down in its constitution. That is why the general clauses have rightly been called the points where basic rights have breached the [domain of] private law [citation of Dürig, in Neumann, Nipperdey, and Scheuner, *Die Grundrechte*, 2:525].

[Function of Lower Courts]

The Constitution requires the judge to determine whether the basic rights have influenced the substantive rules of private law in the manner described. [If this influence is present,] he must then, in interpreting and applying these provisions, heed the resulting modification of private law. This follows from Article 1 (3) of the Basic Law [requiring the legislature, judiciary, and executive to enforce basic rights "as directly applicable law"]. If he does not apply these standards and ignores the influence of constitutional law on the rules of private law, he violates objective constitutional law by misunderstanding the content of the basic right (as an objective norm); as a public official, he also violates the basic right whose observance by the courts the citizen can demand on the basis of the Constitution. Apart from remedies available under private law, [citizens] can bring such a judicial decision before the Federal Constitutional Court by means of a constitutional complaint.

The Constitutional Court must ascertain whether an ordinary court has properly evaluated the scope and impact of the basic rights in the field of private law. But this task is strictly limited: It is not up to the Constitutional Court to examine decisions of the private-law judge for any legal error that he might have committed. Rather, the Constitutional Court must confine its inquiry to the "radiating effect" of the basic rights on private law and make sure that the [judge below] has correctly understood the constitutional principle [involved] in the area of law under review. . . .

[Freedom of Speech and General Laws]

2. With regard to the basic right of free speech (Article 5), the problem of the relationship between basic rights and private law is somewhat different. As under the Weimar Constitution (Article 118), this basic right is guaranteed only within the framework of the "general laws" (Article 5 [2]). One might take the view that the Constitution itself, by referring to limits imposed by the general laws, has restricted the legitimate scope of the basic right to that area left open to it by courts in their interpretation of these laws. Such an approach would mean that any general law restricting a basic right would never constitute a violation of that right.

However, this is not the meaning of the reference to "general laws." The basic right to freedom of opinion is the most immediate expression of the human personality [living] in society and, as such, one of the noblest of human rights. . . . It is absolutely basic to a liberal-democratic constitutional order because it alone makes possible the constant intellectual exchange and the contest among opinions that form the lifeblood of such an order; [indeed,] it is "the matrix, the indispensable condition of nearly every other form of freedom" [Cardozo, quoted in English].

Because of the fundamental importance of freedom of speech in the liberal-democratic state, it would be inconsistent to allow the substance of this basic right to be limited by an ordinary law (and thus necessarily by judicial decisions interpreting the law). Rather, the same principle applies here that was discussed above in general terms with regard to the relationship between the basic rights and private law. [Courts] must evaluate the effect of general laws which would limit the basic right in the light of the importance of the basic right. [They] must interpret these laws so as to preserve the significance of the basic right; in a free democracy this process [of interpretation] must assume that fundamentality of freedom of speech in all spheres, particularly in public life. [Courts] may not construe the mutual relationship between basic rights and "general laws" as a unilateral restriction on the applicability of the basic rights by the "general laws"; rather, there is a mutual effect. According to the wording of Article 5, the "general laws" set bounds to the basic right, but, in turn, those laws must be interpreted in the light of the value-establishing significance of this basic right in a free democratic state, and so any limiting effect on the basic right must itself be restricted.

The Federal Constitutional Court is the court of last resort for constitutional complaints relating to the preservation of basic rights. Therefore it must have the legal right to control the decisions of the courts where, in applying a general law, they enter the sphere shaped by basic rights. . . . The Federal Constitutional Court must have the right to enforce a specific value found in the basic rights. [Its authority to exercise such control] extends to all organs of public authority, including the courts. It can thus create an equilibrium, as desired by the Constitution, between the mutually contradictory and restricted tendencies of the basic rights and the "general laws."

[Meaning of General Laws as Applied to Speech]

3. The concept of "general laws" was controversial from the very beginning. . . . In any event, . . . the phrase was interpreted as referring not only to laws that "do not prohibit an opinion or the expression of an opinion as such," but also to those that "are directed toward the protection of legal rights which need such protection regardless of any specific opinion"; in other words, laws that are directed toward the protection of a community value that takes precedence over the exercise of free speech [citations to legal literature]. . . .

If "general laws" is construed in this way, then we can say the following with regard to the purpose and scope of the protection of the basic right: [We] must reject the view that the basic right protects only the expression of an opinion but not the inherent or intended effect on other persons. It is precisely the purpose of an opinion to produce an "intellectual effect on the public, to help form an opinion and a conviction in the community" [citation to a commentary on the Basic Law].

Article 5 (1) of the Basic Law protects value judgments, which are always aimed at having an intellectual impact, namely, at convincing others. Indeed, the protection of the basic right is aimed primarily at the personal opinion of the speaker as expressed in the value judgment. To protect the expression itself but not its effect would make no sense.

If understood in this way, the expression of an opinion in its purely intellectual effect is free. However, if someone else's legal rights are violated [and] the protection of these rights should take precedence over the protection of freedom of opinion, then this violation does not become permissible simply because it was committed through the expression of an opinion. [Courts] must weigh the values to be protected against each other. [They] must deny the right to express an opinion if the exercise of this right would violate a more important interest protected [by private law]. [Courts] must decide whether such interests are present on the basis of the facts of each individual case.

> [In the light of this discussion the court noted that "there is no reason why norms of private law should not also be recognized as 'general laws' within the meaning of Article 5 (2)." The court thus rejected the prevailing view, cited in the literature, that "general laws" embrace only public laws regulating the relations between individuals and the state.]

4. . . . The complainant fears that any restriction upon freedom of speech might excessively limit a citizen's chance to influence public opinion and thus [would] no longer guarantee the indispensable freedom to discuss important issues publicly. . . . This danger is indeed present. . . . To counter the danger, however, it is unnecessary to exclude private law from the category of "general laws." Rather, we must strictly adhere to the character of the basic right as a personal freedom. This is especially important when the speaker is exercising his basic right not within the framework of a private dispute but for the purpose of influencing public opinion. Thus his opinion may possibly have an impact upon another's private rights even though this is not his intention. Here the relationship between ends and means is important. The protection of speech is entitled to less protection where exercised to defend a private interest — particularly when the individual pursues a selfish goal within the economic sector — than speech that contributes to the intellectual struggle of opinions. . . . Here the assumption is in favor of free speech.

To conclude: Decisions of ordinary civil courts that restrict freedom of opinion on the basis of the "general laws" in the field of private law can violate the basic right of Article 5 (1). The private-law judge also is required to weigh the importance of the basic right against the value of the interest protected by the "general laws" to the person allegedly injured by [the utterance of the opinion]. A decision in this respect requires the judge to consider all the circumstances of the individual case. An incorrect balancing of the factors can violate the basic right and provide the basis for a constitutional complaint to the Federal Constitutional Court.

[In section III of its opinion the Constitutional Court examined closely the facts of the case and the judgment of the lower court. In noting that the advocacy of a boycott is not always contrary to "good morals" within the meaning of Article 826 of the Civil Code, the court said: "'Good morals' are not unchangeable principles of pure morality; they are, rather, defined by the views of 'decent people' about what is 'proper' in social intercourse among legal partners." The court then proceeded on its own to weigh Lüth's interests against those of Harlan and the film companies. It held that the district court had given insufficient attention to the motives of the complainant and the historical context of his remarks. The court's concerns are captured in the following extracts.]

2. (b) . . . The complainant's statements must be seen within the context of his general political and cultural efforts. He was moved by the apprehension that Harlan's reappearance might—especially in foreign countries—be interpreted to mean that nothing had changed in German cultural life since the National Socialist period. . . . These apprehensions concerned a very important issue for the German people. . . . Nothing has damaged the German reputation as much as the cruel Nazi persecution of the Jews. A crucial interest exists, therefore, in assuring the world that the German people have abandoned this attitude and condemn it not for reasons of political opportunism but because through an inner conversion they have come to realize its evil. . . .

Because of his especially close personal relation to all that concerned the German-Jewish relationship, the complainant was within his rights to state his view in public. Even at that time he was already known for his efforts toward reestablishing a true inner peace with the Jewish people. . . . It is understandable that he feared all these efforts might be disturbed and thwarted by Harlan's reappearance. . . .

The demand that under these circumstances the complainant should nevertheless have refrained from expressing his opinion out of regard for Harlan's professional interests and the economic interests of the film companies employing him . . . is unjustified. . . . Where the formation of public opinion on a matter important to the general welfare is concerned, private and especially individual economic interests must, in principle, yield. This does not mean that these interests are without protection; after all, the basic right's value is underscored by the fact that it is enjoyed by everyone. Whoever feels injured by the public statements of someone else can make a public reply. Public opinion is formed, like the formation of a personal opinion, only through conflicts of opinion freely expressed. . . .

IV. On the basis of these considerations, the Federal Constitutional Court holds that the superior court, in assessing the behavior of the complainant, has misjudged the special significance of the basic right to freedom of opinion. [Courts] must consider [the significance of this right] when it comes into conflict with the private interests of others. The decision below is thus based on an incorrect application of the standards applying to basic rights and violates the basic right of the complainant under Article 5 (1) of the Basic Law. It must therefore be quashed.

———————————

NOTE: THE SEMINAL CHARACTER OF *LÜTH*. *Lüth* is celebrated not only for its statement of the ruling principles governing the interpretation of Article 5 but also for its restatement of the general character of basic rights under the Constitution.[6] Its pivotal importance warrants a careful summary of its teaching. First, the decision emphasizes the individual and social dimensions of speech. The individual values speech because his intellectual and spiritual natures require dialogue and discussion; society cherishes speech because of its importance to political democracy. Second, speech, like other basic rights, is both negative and positive in character. Its negativity protects the individual against official restraints on speech; its positivity obliges the state and its agents to establish the conditions necessary for the effective exercise of speech rights. Third, political or disinterested speech uttered for public purposes ranks higher on the scale of constitutional protection than self-regarding speech made for private purposes or financial gain. Fourth, *Lüth* solidifies the canonical status of the Basic Law as a hierarchy of objective values.[7] Fifth, and most important, the objective values of the Constitution affect all areas of law, including private law (the so-called *Drittwirkung* [literally, "third-party effect"] of the basic rights). In short, the Basic Law's objective values are to be enforced judicially when private legal relationships implicate constitutional concerns of legitimate interest to the wider public.[8] Finally, the "general laws" within the meaning of Article 5 (1) include provisions of the Civil Code that regulate relations between private parties. Such laws permissibly restrict the exercise of speech when they are designed to preserve traditional (nonspeech) values deemed worthy of legal protection. Accepting the prevailing view under the Weimar Constitution,[9] the Federal Constitutional Court excluded from the category of "general laws" any statute that seeks directly to suppress a particular viewpoint. To regard such a law as a "general law" within the meaning of Article 5 (2) would defeat the purpose behind the speech guaranteed. General laws must also be interpreted against the backdrop of the Basic Law and in the light of its values. When, therefore, constitutional rights conflict with other legitimate social interests within the framework of ordinary civil or criminal litigation, the court applies a general reasonableness or balancing standard of review. The superior court's fatal error in *Lüth* was its failure to engage properly in this balancing process. Its exclusive focus on Harlan's private interest as a motion picture producer was unacceptable in view of the overriding public interest in the dispute generated by Lüth's plea for a boycott.[10]

The Basic Law provides several exceptions to the general rule against the imposition of a content-based abridgment of individual expression; Article 21 (2), which prohibits political parties opposed to the free democratic order, is the most familiar.[11] In addition, Article 5 (3) bars teachers from engaging in disloyal speech, and Article 139 shields the prohibition of speech advocating Nazism and militarism from constitutional attack. Article 18 is the most severe of these bans on the form and content of speech, for any person who abuses the freedoms of speech, press, or teaching "in order to combat the free democratic basic order" may be compelled to forfeit these rights altogether. Politicians might in turn be tempted to abuse the prohibitions of Articles 18 and 21 (2), potentially the most threatening of the Basic Law's antisubversive provisions. To prevent this from happening, the framers provided that actions under these articles could be carried out only with the approval of the Federal Constitutional Court.[12]

8.2 Schmid-Spiegel Case (1961)
12 BVerfGE 113

[In a public appearance in Stuttgart in November 1953, the complainant, a high-ranking state judge, delivered a hard-hitting speech on political strikes. In the course of the speech he remarked that 95 percent of the press in Germany was controlled by employers unfriendly to trade unions. Reacting to the speech, which was later published in a trade union journal, the weekly magazine *Der Spiegel* accused the judge of communist sympathies in an article entitled "Arrested on the Volga," even though it had reliable information to the contrary. Judge Schmid, writing in a daily newspaper, struck back with a violent verbal assault on *Der Spiegel,* accusing the magazine of lying about him and comparing its political reporting to pornography in the field of morals. *Der Spiegel* secured a libel judgment against Schmid in the Göttingen Superior Court, and its decision was affirmed on appeal. Schmid based his constitutional complaint against both decisions on his right to free speech under Article 5.]

———————

Judgment of the First Senate. . . .

III. The constitutional complaint is justified.

In applying the provisions of the Criminal Code relating to insults and defamation, a court adjudicating a libel case applies simple statutory law; its decisions are generally not subject to review by the Federal Constitutional Court. [The court] can review them only when the application of provisions for the protection of personal honor fails to conform to the value order of the Basic Law and thus violates the basic rights of the defendants. This is the case here. The judgments of the Göttingen Superior Court and the Celle Court of Appeals violate the complainant's right under Article 5 (1) because they fail to recognize the constitutional importance of the process of forming public opinion; as a consequence, the influence of the basic right to freedom of expression was inadequately considered in the interpretation and application of the statutory provisions on defamation.

1. In its judgment of January 15, 1958 [the *Lüth* case], the First Senate made clear that the interrelationship between the constitutional right to freedom of expression and the "general laws" must not be seen as a one-sided restriction on the effectiveness of the constitutional right by general laws; "rather, an interplay takes place in the sense that the 'general laws' by their terms set bounds to the constitutional right; however, those laws must, in turn, be interpreted in recognition of the value of this guarantee in a free democratic state, and thus any limiting effect on the basic right must itself be restricted." The Constitution confers heightened significance on the basic right to freedom of expression. The [First] Senate has already declared in earlier cases that, as the most direct expression of the intimate sphere of the human personality in society, freedom of speech is one of our most precious human rights. That in itself confers upon it special value. Beyond that, free speech is a constituent element of a free democratic order, for it guarantees continuous intellectual dispute and the battle of opinions that is its vital element. Only free public discussion about matters of general importance can secure the free formation of public opinion. [I]n a liberal democratic state [this process] necessarily manifests itself "pluralistically" in the expression of opposing views — particularly in [the form of] a dialogue — which result from varying motives. Article 5 (1) [1] guarantees every citizen the right to take part in this public discussion. The press, along with radio and television, is the most important instrument in the formation of public opinion; thus freedom of the press enjoys particular protection under Article 5 (1) [1].

> [Under German law, libel is a criminal offense. Section 193 of the Criminal Code, under which this case was brought, qualifies the offense: "Critical comment on scientific, artistic, or commercial production, as well as expressions made in the exercise or defense of rights, or in order to protect justifiable interests, as well as remonstrances and reprimands from superiors to subordinates, official reports or decisions by a civil servant, and similar cases are punishable only to the extent that an insult arises from the form of the expression or from the circumstances in which it was made." The code also seeks to mitigate the offense in the case of mutual insults. Section 199 declares that if an insult is promptly answered by another insult, the judge may dismiss charges against either or both offenders.]

In determining the range of the constitutional right to free speech in the light of section 193 of the Criminal Code, we must engage — if due consideration is to be given to the role of public opinion — in balancing the values of honor and freedom of expression.

2. The courts below incorrectly viewed the facts and circumstances of this case exclusively from the standpoint of personal honor and the interests affected by the resulting harm without considering the particular nature of the feud carried out in the press and its value as a constituent element in the formation of public opinion. . . .

(c) Complainant [made] his controversial statement to "protect justifiable interests" in the form of a value judgment regarding not just the Volga article but, indeed, if one adheres to the findings of the Superior Court, substantial parts of *Der Spiegel's* publications.

Because the statements were not a spontaneous attack but rather a defense against the Volga article, the legitimacy of the claimed interests depends substantially on what interests were touched by the article. More was involved than the personal honor of the complainant. *Der Spiegel,* by delving into the complainant's political past and raising the issue of his suitability for a high judicial post, took sides in a dispute about the personal politics and trustworthiness of the judge, a debate into which former minister-president Dr. Maier and Justice Minister Dr. Haussmann were drawn; the story was basically consistent with the press's mission to inform citizens about public affairs. But there is a similar public interest in safeguarding the complainant's response in the newspaper. This follows from the right of every citizen under Article 5 (1) to contribute to the formation of public opinion by fully expressing his own opinion. . . .

The superior court determined [that in conveying misleading information about the complainant] . . . *Der Spiegel* had purposely presented to its readers only partial truths under the appearance of the full truth. As the complainant emphasizes, the form of his public reply is justified by the nature of the *Spiegel* report and by his need to counter its impact upon public opinion. To that extent *Der Spiegel* invited [Schmid's] adverse criticism and must therefore tolerate like criticism even at the risk of diminishing its reputation in the public eye. . . .

(d) To sum up: When courts fail to classify the reproach that a magazine uses intellectual disclosures like pornography in order to stimulate readers [as a statement made] in the protection of justifiable interests, they assume that the complainant had a justifiable interest in defending his personal honor only within the meaning of section 193 of the Criminal Code. The effect of Article 5 (1) on this norm, however, requires that courts recognize his legitimate interest in influencing public opinion on an important political issue and that they consider the statement [involved here] as a rightful counterattack against the public presentation of inaccurate information. Because this standard of evaluation is lacking in the judgments under attack, the complainant's constitutional right under Article 5 (1) has been violated.

NOTE: FREEDOM OF OPINION AND FIGHTING WORDS. The Basic Law guarantees to "everyone the right freely to express and disseminate his opinion" and to do so by oral, written, or visual means. As *Schmid-Spiegel* points out, such expression of opinion may not be limited by the fractious character of the words used. The Federal Constitutional Court recognizes, as the American Supreme Court did in *Cohen* v. *California*,[13] that the expression of political views is bound to be emotional as well as rational and that no bright line can be drawn between the two without inhibiting the robust expression of diverse political views. *Schmid-Spiegel* is nevertheless to be understood in the light of its particular facts. The case is important for its acceptance of the so-called counterattack (*Gegenschlag*) theory of speech. A person has the right under the Basic Law, above all in the political arena, to defend himself against acrimonious and misleading criticism by employing equally abusive language if such speech is necessary to offset the rancor and misrepresentation of his attacker's original onslaught.[14]

This approach to constitutional review has prevailed ever since *Schmid-Spiegel*. The *Art Critic* case (1980) is one of several decisions in which the court reasserted its opinion that a sharp attack deserves a stinging rebuke.[15] Here a radio commentator made derogatory remarks about a sculptor who had harshly criticized the practices and policies of art critics and museum directors. Yet, as subsequent cases show, the Basic Law—as interpreted—does not protect all manner of speech, even in the political arena. It protects robust and caustic speech but not always reckless or untruthful speech. *Blinkfüer,* another leading case in German free speech jurisprudence, illustrates a mode of speech that is not protected under the Basic Law.

8.3 Blinkfüer Case (1969)
25 BVerfGE 256

[Like the *Lüth* case, *Blinkfüer* involved a boycott. *Blinkfüer* was a small-circulation, procommunist weekly newspaper that advertised East German radio and television programs. The powerful Axel Springer newspaper company sent a circular to kiosk operators instructing them not to sell *Blinkfüer* and threatened to withdraw its own newspapers from dealers who did not comply with the order. *Blinkfüer* sued Springer successfully in the lower courts on the ground of unfair competition. (The suit was brought under section 823 of the Civil Code, which declares: "A person who, willfully or negligently, unlawfully injures the life, body, health, freedom, property, or other right of another is bound to compensate him for any damage arising therefrom.") The Federal High Court of Justice reversed, holding that the boycott was covered by the free speech provisions of Article 5. The publisher and chief editor of *Blinkfüer* countered with an Article 5 argument of their own in a constitutional complaint before the Federal Constitutional Court.]

———————

Judgment of the First Senate. . . .

B. II. The constitutional complaint is justified.

The proceeding before the lower courts was a civil suit which had to be decided according to the rules and regulations of private law. However, the objective order of values established by the Basic Law in the section on basic rights influences the interpretation of these rules and regulations insofar as they are capable of interpretation in light of constitutional norms [citing the *Lüth* case]. With regard to section 823 (1) of the Civil Code, constitutional law is important in establishing the unlawfulness of the injury. The courts must decide, on the one hand, the extent to which the right to freedom of opinion covers a boycott, and, on the other hand, whether the complainant may claim for himself the constitutional right to freedom of the press. In its review of the contested decision, the Federal High Court of Justice misunderstood the scope of the defendant's right to free expression of opinion; in reviewing the complainant's position, it failed to take into consideration the right to freedom of the press.

   1. The Federal High Court sustained the actions of the defendant—i.e., the request that dealers cease distributing newspapers with East German radio and television listings and the warning that newspaper deliveries might be suspended if they would not comply—on the basis of Article 5. In so doing, the Federal High Court extended the protection [of Article 5] beyond the nature and meaning of the constitutional right.

   As an organized and at least partial attempt to prevent the sale of *Blinkfüer,* the defendant's notice to its newspaper dealers represents a call for a boycott regardless of what the underlying motives may have been. The powerful economic position of the defendant and the threat to suspend deliveries were sufficient to deprive the persons so directed of their ability to decide freely.

   Calls for a boycott based on the expression of a certain opinion and serving as a means in the intellectual struggle to influence public opinion on an issue of fundamental [public] concern fall within the protection of Article 5 (1) [1]. That this is a political, economic, social, or cultural issue of public significance rather than a private dispute is a critical consideration [citing *Lüth*]. The call for a boycott may still enjoy protection from the Constitution even where the caller [of the boycott] competes professionally, economically, or in some other form of business relationship. Such circumstances do not in themselves preclude intellectual controversy. If the advocate of a boycott possesses a certain amount of economic power, his or her influence is likely to be substantial. But this fact in and of itself will not render the call for a boycott inadmissible; the Constitution does not bar the economically more powerful from engaging in the intellectual struggle of opinion.

   However, the means employed by the person who calls for a boycott must be constitutionally acceptable. The basic right to free expression will not protect a call for a boycott if it is not based solely on intellectual arguments; that is, if it is not limited to the persuasive force of the presentation, explanation, or consideration itself but, going beyond these, employs means which deprive those affected [by the boycott] of their ability to draw their conclusions freely and in the absence of economic pressure. The latter [means] especially include threats or announcements of severe disadvantages as well as the exploitation of social or economic dependence designed to lend a special emphasis to the boycott. The freedom of free intellectual dispute is an absolute prerequisite for the functioning of a free democracy because it alone guarantees the public discussion of issues of general public and political concern. [When] the exercise of economic pressure entails severe disadvantages for those affected by it, and is aimed at preventing the constitutionally guaranteed dissemination of opinions and news, it violates equality of opportunity in the process of forming political opinion. It also contradicts the meaning and the nature of the basic right to free expression of opinion, which is intended as a guarantee of the intellectual struggle for public opinion.

An assessment of the conduct of the defendant in the light of these criteria shows that the Federal High Court went too far in its interpretation of the protective scope of the basic right to free expression of opinion. . . .

The defendant used means to achieve the boycott which conflict with the constitutional right guaranteed by Article 5 (1) [1] of the Basic Law. If, for example, the defendant had expressed its opinion concerning the public listing of East German radio and television programs in its newspapers and magazines, and if it had restricted itself to a call for a reader boycott of the newspapers and magazines in question, then its conduct would have been constitutionally unobjectionable. The defendant, identifying public interests with its own, would have addressed those most concerned about the issue under discussion. But because the subjects of the boycott were economically and legally dependent on the defendant, the circular sent to newspaper and magazine dealers was an inappropriate means of generating an intellectual discussion of the admissibility and feasibility of publishing the programs of East German radio and television stations. . . .

In this respect the facts are essentially different from the so-called *Lüth* decision. Lüth's call for a boycott was simply an appeal to the moral and political responsibility of his audience; it was incapable of directly and effectively restricting the human and artistic freedom of movie director Harlan, for Lüth had no means of coercion at his disposal which could lend emphasis to his request. All he could do was appeal to the sense of responsibility and the moral conscience of his audience; whether the people he addressed would follow him or not was a matter of their own free will. By contrast, the defendant's threat to suspend delivery would have been capable of inflicting noticeable and, under certain circumstances, even substantial harm on the newspaper wholesalers and retailers involved here because of his control of the market. . . .

2. . . . The complainant, on the other hand, depended [for his livelihood] on this distribution system. The defendant used mainly economic means to limit freedom of reporting and to suppress the news.

The constitutional complaint is justified as a violation of Article 5 (1) of the Basic Law. Thus there is no need to determine if the contested decision violated other constitutional rights. The decision below is quashed in accordance with section 95 (2) of the FCCA and remanded to the Federal High Court.

NOTE: PRIVATE RIGHTS AND FREEDOM OF INFORMATION. Two recurring themes in German free speech jurisprudence run through *Blinkfüer.* First, the discourse most worthy of protection is speech that contributes to the "intellectual struggle of opinions." In deciding whether such a struggle existed, the court examined not only the content of the communication but also, as in *Lüth,* the motives and purposes of the speaker.[16] Second, the court sees its task as one of balancing interests.[17] In the circumstances of *Blinkfüer,* the right to operate one's business free of economic coercion outweighed the freedom to advocate a boycott. In this respect *Blinkfüer* differs from *Lüth.* In *Lüth* the constitutional value prevailed over a private-law damage award; in *Blinkfüer* the damage award under private law overrode the speech claim of the Springer Company. Still, the constitutional value is important, for the court proceeded to hold that the Springer Company had actually violated *Blinkfüer's* right to disseminate information. In so holding, the court reemphasized the principal teaching of *Lüth;* namely, that constitutional values influence, although indirectly, the interpretation and application of private law. According to Peter Quint, "The result in this case may suggest that, if necessary, *Blinkfüer* could proceed directly against Springer for violation of *Blinkfüer's* basic right of free reporting; at least, under the Court's 'indirect' theory, *Blinkfüer* was constitutionally entitled to an interpretation of the general clauses of the private law that would afford it a remedy against another private individual for a constitutional violation under these circumstances."[18] In stark contrast to the "state action" doctrine of American constitutional law, *Blinkfüer* seems to "require the judiciary to create what is in effect a constitutional cause of action that will allow private individuals to enforce their constitutional interests against other private individuals."[19]

Another major thread running through *Blinkfüer* is solicitude for the recipient of information. Article 5 protects freedom of information from generally available sources. The Weimar Constitution contained no such right. Under the Basic Law, however, the interests of the viewer, reader, or hearer rival those of the speaker. So long as the source of information is "generally available," the reader or would-be recipient of the information is entitled to receive it. In the *Satellite Dish* case (1993), however, a three-judge chamber ruled that this right did not permit a tenant to erect a TV dish on the roof of the building in which his flat was located over the landlord's objection. The landlord had already installed a cable TV connection for all his tenants, and thus, said the chamber, the landlord's interest in keeping "unsightly receiving equipment" off his roof outweighed the tenant's interest in having access to additional programs.[20]

NOTE: *LEIPZIG DAILY NEWSPAPER* CASE. In this case, decided in 1969, the court declared that the right to inform oneself is a guaranteed right independent of the right to express an opinion.[21] The constitutional complaint in *Leipzig* evolved out of the seizure by customs officials of the *Leipzig Tageszeitung,* an East German newspaper thought to contain communist propaganda. (Millions of such publications had been seized over the years at the East German–West German border.) The subscriber in this litigation successfully challenged the court order permitting the newspaper's confiscation.

Building its argument on a theory of self-government, the Constitutional Court found that the right to inform oneself is a necessary foundation of the right to speech itself.[22] But the right to receive information, said the court, does not confer a general right to know. The subscriber in *Leipzig* prevailed because the newspaper was "a generally accessible source of information." But not all sources of information are generally accessible. Accordingly, suggested the court, a citizen would not have a constitutional right of access to a market research report held by a private company. Nor would confidential government reports qualify as generally accessible sources of information.[23] Indeed, as the *Census Act* case (1983; no. 7.6) shows, government may even be obliged to withhold information in its possession if its release would impinge on other constitutional values such as privacy or the personal right to self-development.

Leipzig also implicates the no-censorship clause of Article 5. The ban on censorship largely embraces the rule against prior restraint.[24] Yet newspapers, like films, are subject to seizure under the Criminal Code if they contain subversive propaganda.[25] The *Leipzig Daily* was saved because it was found not to contain such material. In 1972 a divided First Senate narrowly sustained the Film Importation Act of 1961 over the minority's objection that it conflicted with the right to freedom of information and thus constituted *de facto* censorship.[26] (The law forbade the importation of films having a tendency to undermine the free democratic basic order and the concept of international understanding.) It may indeed be suggested that the rule against prior censorship loses much of its clout if written or visual material can be seized before it reaches its intended audience. Nevertheless, the safeguards against prior censorship are substantial. As a matter of constitutional law, any administrative seizure of subversive newspapers or films must be carried out pursuant to a general law, and in any case, all such actions are subject to judicial review.

NOTE: INFORMATION VERSUS OPINION. The *Leipzig* case begs questions about the relationship between opinion and information. As *Leipzig* notes, the right to inform oneself surely includes the right to receive opinions. Effective participation in a democracy, said the court, requires access to all opinions related to the process of governance. But an argument rooted in democracy would restrict the meaning of information to opinions and data having political or social significance. Most German commentators, however, hold that it means much more than that;[27] the Basic Law's protection also extends to certain forms of commercial speech. Indeed, the Constitutional Court held in the *Press Advertising* case (1967) that Article 5 protected a newspaper advertisement informing people of working opportunities abroad even though the ad did not qualify as an "opinion."[28] It would seem, therefore, that the right to inform oneself about opportunities, persons, things, and events is an important aspect of the liberties protected by Article 5. Indeed, as Eric Barendt suggested, the information clause provides a "strong textual argument for holding at least some kinds of commercial speech to be constitutionally protected."[29]

Yet it is possible to play the opinion and information clauses off against one another. In the *Chemist Advertising* case (1980),[30] for example, the Constitutional Court held an advertisement unprotected because it did not constitute an "opinion" within the meaning of Article 5. Here the profit motive behind the advertisement appeared to outweigh the value of the information conveyed, underscoring once again the constitutional relevance of the economic context in which speech is exercised. One could plausibly argue that the right to information, unlike the right to express an opinion freely, is bounded by a requirement of accuracy. Thus, a large amount of commercial advertising, particularly advertising claims about the quality of manufactured products, would probably be excluded from constitutional protection. In any event, commercial advertising cases are more likely to be adjudicated under constitutional provisions dealing with occupational freedom and property rights.[31]

NOTE: PRELUDE TO *CAMPAIGN SLUR* CASE. Twenty-four years separate the *Lüth* and *Campaign Slur* cases. During this period the court's analytical approach to balancing conflicting values changed significantly. In *Lüth* the court itself independently examined the particular facts and interests of the parties. It placed a heavy thumb on the free speech side of the scale, particularly in regard to political speech, and instructed lower courts to attach a similar weight to free speech values when they conflict with social interests rooted in private law. In the ensuing years, however, the court lowered its level of scrutiny. So long as ordinary judges had correctly defined the significance of the relevant constitutional principle, the Constitutional Court declined to interfere with the application of the principle. It was unwilling to substitute its judgment for that of judges trained in the "science" of applying law to facts.[32]

The *Mephisto* (1971; no. 8.12) and *Lebach* (1973; no. 8.10) cases exemplify this deferential approach to judicial review, an approach that prevailed until the mid-1970s. Under this balancing doctrine, as Quint noted, the court generally remitted to private-law courts the weighing of the constitutional value of expression against conflicting values.[33] The result was the frequent victory of personality rights over speech rights. Freedom of expression appeared to have no higher status under the Basic Law than personality rights. In conflicts between personality and speech rights it was perhaps to be expected that judges steeped in the legal culture of the Civil Code would be inclined to use the personality clause of Article 2 (1) to protect rights closely related to traditional private-law values. This approach marked a substantial departure from *Lüth*'s emphasis on the primacy of free speech.

The *Deutschland Magazine* case,[34] decided in 1976, expressed the First Senate's dissatisfaction with the existing standard of constitutional review. It shifted away from the approach of *Mephisto* and *Lebach* and toward heightened judicial scrutiny of certain encroachments on speech. The court reasserted the conventional view that judicial balancing is the task of the lower courts. But now, apparently taking a position between *Lüth* and *Mephisto*, the senate laid down a new standard of review:

> There are no rigid and invariable limits on the court's intervention. We retain a degree of freedom to consider the particular facts of special situations. Important in this regard is the severity of the encroachment upon a basic right: The Constitutional Court may not disturb the judgment of a lower court simply because if it had decided the case it would have balanced the equities differently and therefore arrived at a different conclusion. The Constitutional Court may step in to defend an objective constitutional right at the point where the civil courts have erred in assessing the significance of a basic right. . . . The more a civil court's decision encroaches upon the sphere of protected rights, the more searching must be the Constitutional Court's scrutiny to determine whether the infringement is constitutionally valid; and where the infringement is extremely burdensome [citing *Lebach*] the court may even substitute its judgment for that of the civil courts.[35]

A labor union publication had described the conservative *Deutschland-Magazin* as "a right-radical hate sheet." The magazine's publisher won a libel judgment enjoining the union from repeating this statement "in the same words or in words having the same meaning."[36] On review, the state court of appeals sustained the ban on the original statement but overturned the prohibition of "words having the same meaning." The First Senate, citing *Lüth*, noted that any judicial ruling imposing a severe chill on freedom of expression would invite close scrutiny. Here, however, the chill was not regarded as severe. The union was free to express its opinion of *Deutschland-Magazin* in words equally capable of conveying its animosity without intimating, as the original statement did, that the magazine was advocating unconstitutional goals.

8.4 Campaign Slur Case (1982)
61 BVerfGE 1

[The complainant was an SPD-list candidate for election to the European Parliament. In a campaign speech he denounced Bavaria's majority party, the Christian Social Union (CSU), as "the NPD of Europe." (The reference was to West Germany's extreme right-wing National Democratic party, sometimes described as a neo-Nazi organization.) The CSU won a temporary restraining order enjoining the candidate, under threat of civil damage suit, from publicly repeating his charge. Sustained by the courts below, the judgment was challenged in this constitutional complaint as violative of Articles 5 (1) and 2 (1) of the Basic Law.]

Judgment of the First Senate. . . .

B. The constitutional complaint is permissible and justified.

I. The complaint is directed against a cease-and-desist order granted under the Civil Code. [Courts are authorized under section 1004 of the Civil Code to enjoin interferences with "ownership," a broad concept referring not only to material possessions but also to personal rights such as honor and reputation.] The Federal Constitutional Court is obligated only to decide whether the courts have properly assessed the extent and effect of basic constitutional rights in the area of civil law. Doubtless, the limits of our authority to interfere cannot be established with exact precision, for these limits depend upon the extent to which a basic right is infringed. The more a decision by a civil court encroaches upon a basic right, the more intense the judicial scrutiny of the reasons for the encroachment. . . .

II. In deciding the case below, the appeals court undoubtedly considered the basic right to freedom of expression. But it unjustifiably failed to acknowledge that the statement in question was an expression of opinion within the meaning of the Basic Law. Instead, the appeals court treated it as an incorrect factual assertion, thus disregarding the fundamental value of the basic right secured by Article 5 (1).

1. Contrary to the opinion of the appeals court, Article 5 (1) must be considered in any judicial assessment of the nature of the statement.

(a) This basic right guarantees to all persons the right to freedom of expression, without expressly distinguishing between a value judgment and a statement of fact. Everyone is at liberty to speak his mind freely whether or not he is able to furnish verifiable reasons for his judgment. At the same time the purpose of free speech is to form opinions, persuade, and exert an intellectual influence over other persons. This is why value judgments, always meant to convince others, are protected by Article 5 (1) [1] of the Basic Law. The basic right is designed primarily to protect the speaker's personal opinion. It is irrelevant whether an opinion is valuable or worthless, correct or false, or whether it is emotional or rational. If the opinion in question contributes to the intellectual struggle of opinions on an issue of public concern, it is presumed protected by the principle of free expression. Even caustic and exaggerated statements, particularly those uttered in the heat of an election campaign, are fundamentally within the protection of Article 5 (1) [1]. . . .

This principle does not apply in the same way to assertions of fact. False information is not a protected good. The deliberate utterance of untruth is unprotected by Article 5 (1). The same holds true for incorrect quotations [citing the *Böll* case]. . . . To the extent that incorrect allegations of fact are not automatically placed outside the protection of Article 5 (1) [1], they may be more easily restricted by general law than expressions of opinion.

What mainly determines if an expression of "opinion" is protected by the Basic

Law is whether there is an element of stating a viewpoint, taking a position, or [holding] an opinion within the framework of intellectual disputation. The value, truthfulness, or reasonableness of the opinion does not matter. Strictly speaking, a statement of fact is not an expression of an "opinion." Such a statement is nevertheless protected by the Basic Law because it forms the basis of an opinion. . . .

The concept of "opinion" within the meaning of Article 5 (1) [1] is to be understood as an expression of a viewpoint, the taking of a position, or holding an opinion within the framework of intellectual dispute. This also holds true where such utterances — as frequently happens — are combined with elements of reported facts or allegations of fact, especially in cases where the two cannot be separated. . . .

(b) Accordingly, the statement "The CSU is the NPD of Europe" is part of an election speech and thus an expression of opinion protected by Article 5 (1) [1]. Taken literally, the statement is obviously false because the CSU is not identical with a (nonexistent) NPD of Europe. . . .

. . . No one can derive a concrete and tangible fact from this assertion; rather, it represents a sweeping statement. This becomes particularly clear when we analyze the purpose of the utterance. The complainant tried to convince his audience to vote for the SPD in the elections for the European Parliament. To achieve this goal he employed a typical weapon, namely, polemics against political opponents. [H]is intent was to set [his opponents] apart from his own party by resorting to overstatement. This is basic to every electoral campaign and belongs in principle to the realm of opinion, thus falling within the protection of Article 5 (1) [1] of the Basic Law. The electorate clearly understands that the speaker is merely voicing an opinion to win over the audience. To be sure, one could glean factual elements from the statement in question; for example, that the CSU is an extreme right-wing party. Nonetheless, the value judgment outweighs the factual content [contained in the statement]. . . .

2. The [lower] court was thus at fault in . . . characterizing the utterance of the complainant as an incorrect statement of fact. . . .

(b) In addition, the appeals court neglected to consider the vital importance of the status of the person [or entity] allegedly slandered and the degree to which he or she participated in the process of public opinion formation protected by Article 5 (1). A person who voluntarily exposes himself to public criticism forgoes part of his protected private sphere. This principle, developed with natural persons in mind, is to be applied even more stringently to political parties, for their existence and activities — in contrast to those of private citizens or even individual politicians — are automatically and exclusively understood as being a part of political life. . . . Under the circumstances . . . a political party must endure even caustic remarks rightfully deemed slanderous by any democratic party. [Such remarks] are not unusual in the heat of political battle, especially because the party had the opportunity to defend itself by political means.

3. In the light of these considerations, the appeals court inadequately deter-

mined the range and effects of the basic right to freedom of expression. The judgment on appeal is based upon these errors. . . . The judgment is therefore quashed and the case remanded to the appeals court in accordance with section 95 (2) of the Federal Constitutional Court Act.

NOTE: TREND TOWARD HEIGHTENED JUDICIAL SCRUTINY. In Chapter 5 we found that Article 21 lends credence to the view that the Basic Law's speech clauses were intended primarily to enhance the process of democracy. The cases featured in this chapter reinforce the self-government theory of expression. The Constitutional Court tends to evaluate speech in terms of its contribution to the development of public opinion. While defamatory speech may be tolerated in political circumstances such as those of *Schmid-Spiegel,* a fabricated press interview with a socially prominent person enjoys no such immunity against a libel action.[37] The level of protection thus rises with the increasing public significance of the opinion expressed. In *Campaign Slur* the lower courts failed to recognize that the statement at issue was in fact a contribution to a meaningful public debate.[38]

NOTE: THE *PICTURE POSTCARD* CASE. The decision handed down in *Picture Postcard* (1984) is another example of the court's willingness not only to declare whether a given utterance is an "opinion" within the meaning of Article 5 but also independently to assess the political significance of the opinion. A private security service, objecting to the humorous portrayal of one of its guards on a postcard produced and sold in Munich — the card bore the caption "Law and Order: Munich 1980" — secured a court order against the card's further distribution. The postcard company, which had intended the caricature to be a criticism of private police forces, filed a constitutional complaint against the court order. In sustaining the complaint, the court declared:

> The concise and snappy [caption] does not alter the fact that it constitutes an expression of an opinion. Even as rudimentary a text as this — in combination with a picture, as is the case here — can be a critical opinion concerning the institution of the "black sheriff": the way the picture is cropped, the light conditions, the posture, and the facial expression of the security guard can evoke an association with policemen whose identity is frequently concealed in this fashion in newspaper photographs. In addition, the words "law and order" express what the complainant has in mind; namely, that is the way guardians of public order look when they perform police functions. . . . One cannot entirely trust them because they are hiding behind their identity.[39]

Postcard underscores the court's broad construction of the expression-of-opinion clause when political or public speech is involved. It also involves a clash of constitutional values. The defendant company invoked its general right to an intimate sphere in seeking to restrain the complainant's distribution of a caricature using its insignia and other symbols of identification. The lower court erred in this case by ranking the right to personality ahead of free expression and by failing to recognize that security services of the kind provided by the defendant were a subject of considerable public interest. In the light of an existing public controversy surrounding the alleged criminal behavior of some private security guards, the portrayal contributed to the "intellectual struggle of opinions." The lower court therefore had little choice but to uphold freedom of expression. The Constitutional Court rejected the analogy drawn between *Postcard* and *Schmid-Spiegel*. The commercial interest of the postcard company was obvious, but the sway of that interest receded in the face of the more important fact that in this case the company was genuinely motivated by a desire to influence public opinion.[40]

Yet, as was suggested above in the discussion of the right to information, the Constitutional Court extends the protection of Article 5 to much more than political speech and speech related to the formation of public opinion. The utility of political speech and information is heavily stressed in the German cases. *Lüth,* however, teaches that Article 5 is an end in itself as well as a means to a better polity. The right to inform oneself accurately about persons, things, and events may be necessary for self-government, as *Leipzig Newspaper* points out. But this right is equally necessary for self-awareness and self-determination. "The concept of the spiritual nature and personal dignity of man as an individual," wrote Justice Steinberger, "is at the very core of Article 5."[41]

NOTE: OPINION VERSUS FACT. An Article 5 "opinion" is a value judgment about a person or an event. A fact is an objective datum of information. Facts, of course, are usually arranged according to a preconceived plan and are often assessed in terms of their meaning; such communications qualify as protected speech under the Basic Law. Although *Campaign Slur* acknowledges the difficulty of disentangling expressions of opinion from statements of fact, the Constitutional Court adheres to the view, accepted in *Schmid-Spiegel* and reaffirmed in the *Holocaust Denial* case, that opinion and fact are distinguishable and that the distinction is constitutionally relevant. Some facts may not be distorted with impunity.

8.5 Holocaust Denial Case (1994)
90 BVerfGE 241

[In 1991, a regional association of the far-right National Democratic Party of Germany (NPD) issued invitations to a meeting intended to discuss "Germany's future in the shadow of political blackmail." The featured speaker was to be David Irving, a revisionist historian who argued that the mass extermination of Jews during the Third Reich never happened. The state government in Munich made it a condition of the meeting's being held that the

"Auschwitz Hoax" thesis not be promoted there. The government took this action on the authority of the Public Assembly Act, one provision of which allows the prohibition of meetings when the likelihood exists that things said there will themselves constitute criminal violations. In this case the likely violations were denigration of the memory of the dead, criminal agitation, and, most important, criminal insult, all of which are prohibited by the Criminal Code. The NPD argued that the state's condition was an unconstitutional intrusion on its right to free expression (although the meeting itself took place). The complaint was rejected by the lower courts before being heard by the Federal Constitutional Court.]

Judgment of the First Senate. . . .

B. II. The challenged decisions do not violate Article 5 (1), first sentence, of the Basic Law, which guarantees the right to freedom of expression and dissemination of opinion.

(a) The judicial decisions below must be assessed primarily in terms of this basic right. It is true that the complainant opposes a condition related to a meeting [on grounds that it violates the right to free assembly]. The subject [of the complaint], however, is certain utterances which the complainant, who organized the meeting, was not allowed to make or tolerate. The evaluation of the constitutionality of this situation depends on whether such utterances [ought to be] allowed. An utterance not prohibited on constitutional grounds cannot be subject to a restrictive measure applied to a meeting subject to section 5 (4) of the Assemblies Act. The criteria for this evaluation follow, not from the basic right of freedom of assembly, but from the right of free expression.

(b) Article 5 (1) of the Basic Law protects opinion; free expression and dissemination relates to opinion. Opinion is defined by the individual's subjective relationship to the content of his utterance. Comment and appraisal are elements of opinion. To this extent, demonstrating the truth or untruth [of opinions] is impossible. [Opinions] enjoy the protection of basic rights regardless of whether they are well-founded or deemed emotional or rational, valuable or worthless, dangerous or harmless. The protection of the basic right extends as well to the form of the utterance. An expression of opinion does not lose its protection as a basic right by being sharply or hurtfully worded. . . . [T]he question is only whether, and to what extent, limitations on freedom of expression comport with Article 5 (2) of the Basic Law.

Strictly speaking, representations of fact are not expressions of opinion. In the case of statements of fact it is the objective relationship of the utterance to reality that comes to the fore. Thus, representations of fact are amenable to examination of their truth. But this does not mean that representations of fact are outside the scope of Article 5 (1). Since opinions are usually based on assumptions about facts, or they comment on factual circumstances, [statements of fact] are protected by the basic right to the extent that they are the foundation for opinions, which Article 5 (1) protects as a whole [citing the *Campaign Slur* case].

Consequently, protection of a representation of fact stops only when [the so-called fact] contributes nothing to the constitutionally protected formation of opinion. From this point of view, incorrect information does not constitute an interest worthy of protection. Thus the Federal Constitutional Court has consistently ruled that a deliberate, demonstrably untrue representation of fact is not protected by the guarantee of free expression [citing the *Böll* case]. However, requirements reflecting a duty of truth must not be applied in such a way as to harm freedom of expression, or stifle permissible expression for fear of sanctions [citing the *Böll* and *Campaign Slur* cases].

Distinguishing expressions of opinion from representations of fact can certainly be difficult, because the two are linked and only together give sense to utterances. In this situation, severing the factual from the evaluative elements [of an utterance] is permissible only if in doing so it does not falsify its meaning. Otherwise, in the interest of effectively protecting the basic right, the utterance as a whole must be viewed as an expression of opinion, and thus within the scope of the protection afforded to freedom of expression; to do otherwise would threaten to curtail a basic right.

(c) Freedom of expression, however, is not unconditionally guaranteed. Article 5 (2) limits [such freedom] through general laws and statutory provisions protecting youth and personal honor. We must nevertheless consider the significance of free expression in interpreting and applying laws that limit it [citing the *Lüth* case). This usually requires balancing the limit on the basic right against the legal interest served by the statute that limits it, in the light of pertinent norms and the [facts of the individual case].

In [achieving this balance], the Federal Constitutional Court has developed rules by which freedom of expression does not always take precedence over the protection of personality, as the complainant thinks. On the contrary, when expressions of opinion are seen as a formal insult or vilification, protection of the personality normally comes before freedom of expression [citing the *Wallraff* case]. When expressions of opinion are linked to representations of fact, the [degree of] protection merited depends on the truth of the assumed fact on which [the opinions] are based. If the [assumed facts] are demonstrably untrue, freedom of expression usually gives way to the protection of personality [citing the *Campaign Slur* case]. In general, one must determine which legal interest deserves preference. Here, however, it must be remembered that in questions of importance to the public there is a presumption in favor of free speech [citing the *Lüth* case]. Hence, we must constantly consider this presumption when balancing the legal positions of the parties.

2. Seen in these terms, a breach of Article 5 (1) of the Basic Law manifestly has not been committed. The condition imposed on the complainant as organizer of the meeting (namely, to see to it that there would be no denial of or doubt cast on [the fact of] the persecution of the Jews during the Third Reich) is compatible with the basic right.

(a) The complainant does not dispute the danger foreseen by the authority overseeing the meeting and affirmed by the administrative courts: namely, that utterances of this kind would be made during the meeting. On the contrary, the complainant argues that he should be able to make such statements.

(b) The prohibited utterance (that there was no persecution of the Jews during the Third Reich) is a representation of fact that is demonstrably untrue in the light of innumerable eyewitness accounts, documents, findings of courts in numerous criminal cases, and historical analysis. Taken on its own, therefore, a statement with this content does not enjoy the protection of freedom of expression. There is an important difference between denying the Third Reich's persecution of the Jews and denying German guilt in the outbreak of World War II, the subject of the decision of the Federal Constitutional Court on January 11, 1994 [the *Historical Fabrication* case is discussed below]. Utterances about guilt and responsibility for historical events are always complex evaluations not reducible to representations of fact, while denial of the very existence of an event will normally be a representation of fact.

(c) Even if we do not consider the utterance [in this case] in isolation, but view it in connection with the subject of the meeting and thus as a precondition for forming opinion on the "susceptibility to blackmail" of German politics, the contested decisions will still withstand constitutional review. True, the prohibited utterance does enjoy the protection of Article 5 (1) of the Basic Law, but constitutional law offers no objection to its limitation.

(aa) Such limitation has a lawful basis conforming to the Constitution. . . .

[The court went on to sustain section 5 (4) of the Assemblies Act, which authorizes the state to prohibit meetings that support or provide occasion for uttering views that "form the substance of a serious crime (*Verbrechen*) or a less serious crime (*Vergehen*) prosecutable *ex officio.*" The guarantee of freedom of assembly under Article 8 (1) does, however, require the legislature and government to observe the principle of proportionality. Similarly, the act does not violate freedom of expression since the Auschwitz Hoax thesis had previously been held to constitute the offense of insult under the Criminal Code, the constitutionality of which the court then affirmed.]

There are doubts about the constitutionality of the criminal provisions on which the condition [i.e., the Auschwitz Hoax thesis not be promoted] was based. The laws against defamation protect personal honor, which is expressly mentioned in Article 5 (2) of the Basic Law as a legal interest that justifies limits to freedom of expression. Section 130 of the Criminal Code is a general law within the meaning of

Article 5 (2) serving to protect humanity, ultimately founded on Article 1 (1) [mandating the inviolability of human dignity]. . . .

(1) The administrative authorities and courts based their decisions on the ordinary courts' interpretations of the criminal norm. According to this [interpretation], the Jews living in Germany form an insultable [*beleidigungsfähige*] group in view of their fate under National Socialist rule; denial of the persecution of the Jews is regarded as an insult to Jews as a group. On this point, the Federal Court of Justice had this to say:

> The historical fact itself, that human beings were singled out according to the criteria of the so-called "Nuremberg Laws" and robbed of their individuality for the purpose of extermination, puts Jews living in the Federal Republic in a special, personal relationship vis-à-vis their fellow citizens; what happened [then] is also present in this relationship today. It is part of their personal self-perception to be understood as part of a group of people who stand out by virtue of their fate and in relation to whom there is a special moral responsibility on the part of all others, and that this is part of their dignity. Respect for this self-perception, for each individual, is one of the guarantees against repetition of this kind of discrimination and forms a basic condition of their lives in the Federal Republic. Whoever seeks to deny these events denies vis-à-vis each individual the personal worth of [Jewish persons]. For the person concerned, this is continuing discrimination against the group to which he belongs and, as part of the group, against him.

In the light of this court's jurisprudence, there can be no denial of the fact that these decisions bear witness to a grave violation of the right of personality where the persecution of the Jews is denied. Constitutionally, there is no flaw in the Federal Court of Justice's logical connection between the racially motivated extermination of Jews during the Third Reich and a [current-day] attack on the right to respect and human dignity of today's Jews. In this way, there is also a distinction between denying the persecution of the Jews and denying German war guilt [citing the *Historical Fabrication* case]. At any rate, the latter opinion does not injure the interests of third persons, regardless of its historical questionability. . . .

(2) Balancing defamation, on one hand, against limits on freedom of expression, on the other, does not reveal any constitutional errors. It is the gravity of the injury in each case that is decisive. When insulting opinions that contain representations of fact are voiced, it is crucial whether the representations of fact are true or untrue. Demonstrably incorrect representations of fact do not merit protection. If they are inseparably connected to opinions, they will enjoy the protection of Article 5 (1) of the Basic Law; but from the outset, limits [on demonstrably untrue assertions] are less serious than in cases where the representations of fact have not been proven untrue.

That is the case here. Even if one considers the utterance that the complainant was forbidden to voice an expression of opinion within the context of the meeting, its factual content has been proven false. Hence, interfering with it is not particularly serious. In view of the weight of the insult, there can be no objection to the precedence given the contested decisions' protection of personality over freedom of expression.

[It does not matter] if one sees Germany's attitude toward its National Socialist past and its political consequences (which were the subject of the meeting) as a question concerning the public in an important way. True, in this case there is a presumption in favor of free speech, but this does not apply if the utterance constitutes a formal insult or vilification [of the Jewish people], nor does [the presumption] apply if the offensive utterance rests on demonstrably untrue representations of fact.

This balance, then, does not result in a stretch of the requirements of truth applicable to the core of the utterance in a manner incompatible with Article 5 (1) of the Basic Law. Limiting the duty of care, which is the basis of the Federal Constitutional Court's [limits on] free communication and control over the media, refers to representations of fact still of uncertain accuracy at the time they are uttered, and unverifiable within a short time. But it does not come into play when the falsity of a statement is already established, as in this case.

NOTE: THE *HISTORICAL FABRICATION* CASE. Crucial to the court's judgment in the *Holocaust Denial* case was the distinction between matters of demonstrable fact and matters of interpretation combined with the permissible limitations on free expression that flow from the Basic Law's protection of the right to personality and personal honor. The denial of the Holocaust, a demonstrable historical fact, constituted a denial of the personal identity and dignity of the Jewish people. Different factors were at play in the *Historical Fabrication* case (1994),[42] another instance in which the court grappled with the legacy of national socialism. That case concerned a book called *Truth for Germany: The Question of Guilt for the Second World War.*

The book did not deny the occurrence of the Holocaust. Rather, it argued that Germany was not to blame for the outbreak of the Second World War, but had had war thrust upon her by her enemies. Under the provisions of the Act on Publications Harmful to Young People, this book was listed as "immoral" and "dangerous" to youth, the result being that it could neither be distributed to children nor generally advertised. The Constitutional Court upheld the statute but ruled that the book could not be "listed" merely because it contained a false interpretation of a historical event. The argument at issue, said the court, qualified as an "opinion" — however false — within the meaning of Article 5 (1) and thus constituted protected speech. The court's opinion failed to convince all commentators that it had adequately distinguished its reasoning in *Historical Fabrication* from the argument advanced in support of the suppressed speech in *Holocaust Denial*.

8.6 Tucholsky I Case (1994)
21 *EuGRZ* 463–465

[Kurt Tucholsky was a writer and well-known pacifist who was stripped of his German citizenship in 1933 for his anti-Nazi and antimilitaristic views. He once wrote that "soldiers are murderers," the slogan that would become the rallying cry for pacificists in the Federal Republic of Germany. Tucholsky left Germany early in the Nazi period to take up residence in Sweden. He took his own life in 1935 after Sweden rejected his application for citizenship. The relevant facts of this case are included in the following opinion, which was handed down on August 25, 1994 by the Third Chamber of the First Senate. The chamber consisted of Justices Dieter Grimm, Helga Seibert, and Renate Jaeger.]

Judgment of the First Senate's Third Chamber.

The constitutional complaint involves a criminal conviction based on inciting hatred against and defaming a segment of the population.

I. 1. During the 1991 Gulf War the complainant, a social science teacher and a recognized conscientious objector, pasted a bumper sticker on his car that said "Soldiers Are Murderers." The *t* in the word "*Soldaten*" was formed in the shape of a cross. Appearing under the slogan was a reproduction of Kurt Tucholsky's signature. Next to this sticker were two others, one proclaiming the words "swords into plowshares," the other showing a picture of a soldier hit by a bullet and bearing the inscription "*Warum?*" (Why?). The picture was based on a photograph taken by R. Capa during the Spanish Civil War.

2. (a) The district court fined the complainant DM 70 for each of 120 days. The court justified its sentence with the following argument:

In displaying the slogan "Soldiers Are Murderers," the complainant has assaulted the human dignity of other persons. A reasonable, objective observer of this slogan could only understand it to mean that all soldiers, including members of the Federal Army (Bundeswehr), are murderers. This amounts to an attack on the human dignity of individual soldiers, who also constitute part of the population. The slogan charges soldiers in the Bundeswehr with the commission of serious crimes and thus [identifies them] as unworthy members of the community. Accordingly, the complaint has defamed this segment of the population within the meaning of section 130, paragraph 1, of the Criminal Code, while at the same time holding all soldiers in the Bundeswehr up to malicious contempt within the meaning of section 130 of the Alternative Criminal Code. Whoever accuses members of some segment of the population of [committing] murderous deeds thereby consigns them to the lowest level of society, marking them as unworthy and dishonorable in the eyes of their fellow citizens, making them appear malicious and contemptible.

The element of the offense under section 130 of the Criminal Code has nothing to do with the use of Kurt Tucholsky's signature; that is, conveying the impression that the slogan stems from Kurt Tucholsky. Indeed, in a polemical commentary Kurt Tucholsky did remark that "soldiers are murderers." The complainant, however, has [independently] affirmed this abusive and maliciously disparaging slogan and has [thus] made the slogan his own.

(b) The county court rejected the complainant's appeal and directed that he be sentenced for inciting hatred against a segment of the population.

In this matter of inciting hatred against a segment of the population, the reasoning of the county court is essentially the same as that of the district court. The [county court] noted that the content of the message [i.e., that soldiers are murderers] was not mitigated by the adjoining signs conveying a pacifist message. The county court explained further: The complainant could not appeal to the *Ossietzky* judgment of the Reich Supreme Court (*JW* 1933, p. 972). The Supreme Court's judgment treated Ossietzky's utterance as a nonpunishable offense for a [general] collective defamation. This legal concept is no longer applicable. The offense of inciting hatred against a segment of the population regulated in section 130 of the Criminal Code was first introduced with an amendment [to the code] in 1960. . . .

[Argument of the Complainant]

(c) (3) The complainant alleges that the decisions below violate his right to freedom of belief and conscience under Article 4 (1) and his right to freedom of expression under Article 5 (1). . . .

He claims to have attached the three signs [to his car] at the height of the Gulf War, feeling bound to do so in the light of his deep Christian and pacifist beliefs, and in the conviction that the war was unjust and merited public discussion.

The decisions offend Article 4 (1) because in displaying the Tucholsky sign he was manifesting his faith as a pacifist Christian and a recognized conscientious objector. Such an acknowledgment of one's own convictions is protected by Article 4 (1).

The arguments and conclusions of the criminal courts [below] are also incompatible with Article 5 (1). Kurt Tucholsky was not the first [person] to utter such an opinion; it rather represents a long-lasting pacifist tradition in European history.

. . . The utterance [involved here] cannot be described as implying murder in the strict legal sense, thereby constituting a grave criminal act. The utterance cannot be understood legally as a crime within the meaning of section 211 of the Criminal Code [section 211 defines the crime of murder] but rather as a moral judgment.

The criminal courts should have acknowledged that what was involved here was a group of placards that conveyed the message that soldiers were made to appear not only as offenders but also as victims. Accordingly, the complainant rested his case on the fact that [the courts below], contrary to reality, read far more into the utterance than was actually there, thus violating the basic right to freedom of opinion within the meaning of Article 5 (1). . . .

II. 1. The chamber accepts the constitutional complaint, which it may validly decide under the authority of section 93 (c) of the Constitutional Court Act.

The constitutional complaint is clearly justified. The appealed decisions violate the complainant's basic right to freedom of opinion under Article 5 (1) of the Basic Law. The Federal Constitutional Court has already decided a number of constitutional issues that dictate the result in this constitutional complaint.

2. The basic right to freedom of opinion guarantees to everyone the right to express his opinion. Everyone should be able to say what he thinks, even if he is unable to offer verifiable reasons for his judgment. Article 5 (1) protects freedom of opinion in the interest of individual self-realization as well as in the interest of the democratic process, for which it has constitutive significance. The Basic Law also protects sharp and caustic criticism. Moreover, value judgments enjoy the complete protection of Article 5 (1) without regard to whether they are worthy or worthless, right or wrong, emotional or rational.

To be sure, the basic right to freedom of opinion is not guaranteed unreservedly. Under Article 5 (2) it is limited by the provisions of general law, legal provisions for the protection of youth, and the right to personal honor. These laws and provisions, however, must be interpreted in the light of the restricted basic right so that its significance is preserved in the application of ordinary law. As a rule, this [process of interpretation] involves balancing the importance of the basic right to freedom of opinion against the legal value impaired by the free expression of an opinion. When the utterance contributes to the intellectual clash of opinions with respect to an important public issue, the presumption is in favor of free speech.

The significance of an utterance must be correctly grasped in order to determine whether it enjoys the protection of Article 5 (1) and whether it constitutes a violation of the limits set forth in Article 5 (2). Article 5 (1) requires not only an exacting interpretation and application of those ordinary laws limiting freedom of opinion, but also an understanding and appreciation of the utterance itself. Otherwise, any effective protection of freedom of opinion could not be guaranteed. Thus, a violation of Article 5 (1) occurs not only when an utterance is mistakenly withheld from the protection of the basic right or not adequately considered in the interpretation and application of [ordinary] law; punishment for an utterance already offends Article 5 (1) when it does not possess the meaning that a court reads into it or when the court punishes one meaning [of the utterance] in the face of multiple meanings without [making an effort] convincingly to exclude [these] other possible meanings. In addition, legal terms [such as "murder"] employed in the clash of public opinion may not without further ado be understood in a specialized-technical sense. Moreover, the circumstances will dictate whether a legal term is used in a general or technical [i.e., legalistic] sense.

3. The judgments under attack cannot stand in the light of these principles. The criminal courts based their judgment on meanings that could not reasonably be associated [with the slogan at issue].

(a) The district and county courts were unanimous in holding that the slogan identified soldiers in the Bundeswehr as heavy-handed criminals and thus less than worthy members of society. Their judgments are based on an understanding of "murder" as that term is used in the Criminal Code, that is, an act warranting severe punishment. But the judgments furnish no basis for believing that a reasonable observer of the slogan would understand the utterance in this narrow legalistic sense. In everyday usage, the term "murder" is often used in a more general, non-legal way. Employed legalistically, the term "murder" is customarily understood as an unjustifiable and inexcusable killing of a human person. The criminal courts here failed to understand that the objectionable slogan can be used in a more general sense, one that does not equate the term with the criminal act punishable under section 211 of the Criminal Code, but rather in the sense that the military profession is often associated with the unjustified killing of human beings.

(b) Moreover, in considering the meaning of the Tucholsky slogan, the courts ignored the larger context in which the utterance was made. The district court failed totally to consider the accompanying signs, while the county court failed adequately to consider the meaning of the term "why" on one of them. The complainant claimed to depict "a soldier . . . who threw away his weapon, asking 'Why?'" According to this interpretation the question "Why?" relates to the tossing of the gun. By one interpretation, the slogan depicts a soldier who drops his weapon when struck by a deadly blow. In this context, the word "why" refers to the death of the depicted soldier. Accordingly . . . the portrayal constituted a graphic statement that symbolically depicted a soldier as a victim of an armed conflict, raising the question of the meaning of such a death. So viewed, the offending sticker appears in a different light.

(c) In addition, the district court has imposed a meaning on the offending utterance that it does not objectively have. It bases its judgment on the assumption that the complainant was actually accusing members of the Bundeswehr of committing murder. One cannot, however, derive such a meaning from the utterance displayed on the sticker. In the view of the district court, the members of the Bundeswehr were accused of committing the crime of murder, assuming that the utterances had the character of a factual claim [and that a murder had actually taken place at a particular point in time]. No informed reader in 1991 could so understand [the slogan] even if he had not known that Kurt Tucholsky died on September 21, 1935. Moreover, the average reader knows that since its founding the Bundeswehr has not engaged in any armed conflict; thus no one has been killed in any battle by soldiers of the Bundeswehr. Hence, one may virtually assume that the average reader would not understand the Tucholsky sticker to say that [German] soldiers are actually guilty of committing murder.

(d) The judgment of the county court also violates Article 5 (1) in punishing the complainant for defaming soldiers in the Bundeswehr without considering the significance of the utterance which led to the judgment. In justifying its ruling, the court did not regard the matter as an unpunishable defamatory utterance against [all persons in uniform], because it was apparent that the complainant had the soldiers of the Bundeswehr in mind. If the utterance had been directed against soldiers generally or against all soldiers, one would have to determine whether the soldiers of all armies in the world or only members of the Bundeswehr were to be regarded as the persons under attack. Only by looking at the utterance in this sense can we determine whether it expresses a sharp disapproval of killing in war generally or conveys an expression of contempt for soldiers in the Bundeswehr to the exclusion of all other soldiers. Indeed, in some circumstances it could happen that the utterance in spite of its general formulation might refer to a particular group of persons. No such circumstances, however, are mentioned by the court. The court imposed punishment in this case by simply concluding that the term "soldiers" also referred to the members of the Bundeswehr. That may indeed be so, but it cannot serve as a basis for concluding that the utterance was directed against soldiers in the Bundeswehr rather than being a mere saying traceable to the writer Kurt Tucholsky. . . .

This decision is nonappealable.

———————

NOTE: *TUCHOLSKY I* AND ITS IMPACT. *Tucholsky I* set off a storm of protest. Germany's foreign and defense ministers and other members of parliament expressed their indignation over the decision on the floor of the Bundestag. Letters to the nation's newspapers thundered with outrage. Some prominent constitutional scholars added their own voices of disapproval. A former director of the well-known Max Planck Institute of Comparative and International Public Law deplored the "unlimited individual freedom" that he believed *Tucholsky I* had sanctioned in Germany's value-ordered society. Echoing parliamentary criticism, he charged that the slogan, soldiers are murderers, "poisons the international atmosphere" and undermines the international community's efforts to maintain peace and order in the world.[43] Many Germans, particularly social and political conservatives, found it hard to reconcile the court's opinion with Germany's respect for the traditional values of honor and reputation.

Ernst Benda, former president of the Federal Constitutional Court, also entered the fray. In a letter to the *Frankfurter Allgemeine Zeitung*, he remarked that the three-judge "chamber would have been well advised to have referred [the *Tucholsky* case] to the full senate," a move he believed "might have produced a more composed and perhaps better grounded judgment."[44] He then tried to calm the public tempest by noting that the chamber had done nothing revolutionary. He conceded that in its recent jurisprudence the court manifested a clear tendency to prefer freedom of expression over personality rights,[45] but that this in no way justified the popular view that members of the armed services could be defamed or vilified with impunity. Benda noted that the three-judge chamber had quashed the judgments below because of their failure to properly weigh the constitutional values at stake, a situation that required the court to remand the case back to the lower courts for determination in the light of the proper weights to be attached to these values.

NOTE: *TUCHOLSKY II* CASE. Whether influenced by Benda's suggestion or not, the full senate revisited the "soldiers are murderers" controversy in four related cases that the senate consolidated for decision in *Tucholsky II.* In each case, the complainant had displayed a banner, distributed a leaflet, or published a letter accusing soldiers of being "murderers" or "potential murderers." Over the dissent of Justice Evelyn Haas, the senate vindicated freedom of speech once again but sought to clarify questions not fully adumbrated in the chamber decision. (*Tucholsky II,* handed down on October 10, 1995, merits full translation, but it appeared too late for reprinting in this volume.) As in the first judgment, *Tucholsky II* implicated provisions of the criminal code. Sections 185 and 194 (3) provide for the punishment of insults directed at members of the armed forces, public officials, and government institutions. Under section 193, however, critical comments on certain public matters that "protect justifiable interests" are punishable "only to the extent that the insult arises from the form of expression or from the circumstances in which it was made." In addition, the reservation clause of Article 5 (2) of the Basic Law permits limits on speech in the interest of protecting personal honor.[46]

Once again, according to the senate, the lower courts misconstrued the intent of the criminal code and neglected to attach the proper weight to the Basic Law's free speech values. "By saying that soldiers are murderers or potential murderers," said the senate, "the complainants did not claim that readily identifiable soldiers had committed murder. Rather, they expressed a general opinion about soldiers and the military profession whose activities occasionally require the killing of other human beings." In short, the complainants were expressing an opinion rather than making allegations of fact. In accord with many of its previous rulings, the senate placed a heavy thumb on the free speech side of the scale, even going so far as to say that "governmental institutions do not possess 'personal honor,' nor do they enjoy a general right of privacy." Yet the senate found no fault with the criminal provisions under inquiry. Public institutions, said the court, are legitimate subjects of legal protection. The senate noted:

> Public institutions cannot discharge their functions without a minimum measure of societal acceptance; therefore, they can be protected from verbal attacks which potentially undermine [their social acceptance]. Still, the penal

code must not shield public institutions from public criticism, no matter how harsh, since such criticism is expressly guaranteed by the constitutional right of freedom of expression. . . . The values of Article 5 (1) preclude an interpretation of Section 185 of the penal code that either expands the concept of insult to outstrip the conditions for protecting the honor of individuals and the integrity of institutions, or that leaves no room for any consideration of freedom of expression. Article 5 (1) forbids interpreting Section 185 et seq. of the penal code in a way that would deter the exercise of the basic right to freedom of expression or inhibit even admissible criticism for fear of sanctions.

The court added that punishable criticism must be aimed at defaming the actual character of "soldiers as people" and "exceed the limits of polemical or exaggerated criticism." In examining the particular circumstances of the pending cases, the senate concluded that the lower courts read the disputed remarks too literally as if the soldiers referred to actually committed murder within the meaning of the criminal code. The remarks could have been interpreted in other ways. They might have been intended to remind draftees and soldiers of "their personal responsibility for conduct that is universally reprehensible." The killing of innocent persons, the disputed remarks might also have suggested, is "an accepted consequence of maintaining armies and their readiness to wage war regardless of whether it serves offensive or defensive purposes."

The court went on to make clear that defamatory remarks about particular institutions do not always qualify as protected speech under Article 5. Insults or degrading remarks might be used in a context that would actually assault the honor and integrity of all the members of that institution. Criminal courts, said the court, "may constitutionally regard a defamatory remark against the federal armed forces as a punishable insult if it is tied to a characteristic that clearly or typically applies to all members of the collective body." Here, however, the utterances were indiscriminately directed at all soldiers within a context of general criticism of military violence. So long as it is possible contextually to interpret the words used as broad criticism within the protection of the free speech clauses of Article 5 (1), it is this interpretation that must prevail. With this analysis, the court labored to preserve a rigorous regime of free speech while validating the concept of group libel as incorporated in the criminal code.

Even this carefully crafted opinion failed to quell the public chafing over the "soldier" cases. *Tucholsky II* triggered another round of court-bashing in and out of parliament, with most of the criticism emanating from the governing coalition in Bonn and from the right-of-center political establishment. The passage of time failed to diminish the intensity of the criticism, and in February 1996 Federal Minister of Justice Edzard Schmidt-Jortzig presented a draft bill to the federal cabinet that would make criticism of the armed forces punishable under certain circumstances.

The proposed law sought to characterize chants or statements that soldiers are murderers as judgments on the personal character of soldiers on active duty.[47]

NOTE: RELATED FREEDOM OF EXPRESSION CASES. In the *Darmstadt Signals* case (1993), the Third Chamber of the First Senate ruled that a soldier could not be punished or demoted for signing a statement declaring that soldiers are "potential murderers."[48] As in *Tucholsky I,* the chamber placed a heavy burden of proof on the state seeking to suppress the communication of a political message. As the *Dissident Officer*'s case (1970) shows, however, the context within which a remark is uttered is crucial. Here the Federal Administrative Court had sustained the court-martial of an officer who in the presence of the men under his command faulted the Federal Republic for suppressing freedom of speech.[49]

Context also made the difference in the *Peter W.* case (1970), which concerns a soldier punished for writing a letter to a newspaper in which he criticized the remarks of his superior officer on German military policy. The case recalls the *Gegenschlag* theory of *Blinkfüer.* The officer's speech, critical of an organization of conscientious objectors and certain antimilitaristic groups, was reported in the press. The soldier sought to put the record straight by writing a letter to the editor challenging the accuracy of the officer's account. In overturning his court-martial for breaching military discipline, the Constitutional Court ruled that once the officer's speech had been reported in the press, thus injecting the matter into the forum of public discussion, the soldier in question could likewise state his opinion in the same forum. In such situations, said the court, the Basic Law is oblivious to military rank.[50]

In other situations, however, speech rights may have to give way to values such as fidelity to one's employer and professional decorum and objectivity. Yet, loyalty and discipline do not override all speech interests. In the *Werner* case (1970), the Federal Constitutional Court ruled that while a government employee can generally be required to exhaust grievance procedures within his agency before going public with a complaint of unconstitutional behavior on the part of his employer, he would be justified in bringing "a clear and particularly serious violation of the Constitution" to the immediate attention of parliament or the public.[51] Here we find the court laboring simultaneously to do justice to the fundamental right of speech and to the government's interest in maintaining the fidelity of its employees.

The *Prison Privacy* case (1976) raises the issue of order and discipline in still another context. A criminal defendant held in custody pending his trial had written a letter to his wife bitterly complaining about the judges presiding over cases such as his. He described these judges as "prodigious clowns" who, if they had any conscience, would be unable "to sleep peacefully at night." The presiding judge ordered the letter confiscated on the ground that it contained gross insults against the judiciary and undermined prison discipline. The defendant's constitutional complaint presented the court with an opportunity to reaffirm the value of privacy guaranteed by the right to develop one's personality freely, reinforced in this case by the constitutional protection of marriage and the family under Article 6. However, the court based its decision on freedom of expression. This freedom, said the court, includes the right of a person detained in custody to express his opinion fully, however inaccurate or intemperate, on a pending trial in a private communication to his spouse.[52]

NOTE: THE RIGHT TO DEMONSTRATE AS AN ASPECT OF FREEDOM OF SPEECH. In addition to the rights of speech secured by Article 5 of the Basic Law, Article 8 (1) confers on "all Germans" "the right to assemble peaceably and unarmed without prior notification." In the well-known *Brokdorf* case,[53] decided in 1985, the Constitutional Court affirmed that the right to demonstrate is derivative of the right to shape public opinion by means of speech and assembly. The case arose out of an effort by a number of environmentalist groups to stage a massive outdoor demonstration against the continued construction of a nuclear power plant in Brokdorf, West Germany. Federal law requires a permit for such demonstrations and authorizes local officials to regulate them in the interest of public safety and security.[54] In this instance officials granted the permit but confined the demonstration to a relatively restricted area some distance away from the power station. An administrative court of appeals reinstated this order after a local administrative court had overturned it, whereupon individual demonstrators filed constitutional complaints against the decision of the court of appeals. They challenged the validity of the notification requirement under federal law as well as the conditions that local officials had attached to the permit.

The court sustained the federal statute and at the same time invalidated the decision of the court of appeals. While underscoring the significance of the individual and collective right to demonstrate in a liberal democracy, the First Senate noted that in the case of outdoor demonstrations involving thousands of persons — some of whom may be prone to violence (as was shown here) — local officials may impose, pursuant to law, reasonable regulations designed to balance the freedom to demonstrate against the public need for peace and security. The court of appeals, however, had violated Article 8 (1) in conjunction with the principle of the rule of law (*Rechtsstaatsprinzip*) by its failure to examine independently, as required by the Administrative Procedure Act, the dangers posed by the demonstration. The fact that a few small groups may cause violence, said the court, may not be used as an excuse to hold down the size of a demonstration or to dampen the desire to demonstrate. In short, the court of appeals in its disposition of the case had not attached the proper weight to the values of Article 8 (1).[55]

THE MASS MEDIA

The principles discussed in the previous section also apply to freedom of the press. Indeed, most of the cases featured in this chapter evolved out of actions by or against the print and broadcast media. Accordingly, this section emphasizes only those aspects of Article 5 that relate directly to the media *qua* media.

The right to a free press is a separate and independent freedom under Article 5. When the founding fathers provided expressly for the "freedom of reporting by means of broadcasts and films," they clearly anticipated the role of the electronic media and their increasing importance in the life of an information-oriented society. Whether they were equally conscious of the dangers to free speech posed by advancing media technology is not so clear. To what extent may government regulate the press, together with the organization and programming of the electronic media, in the interest of promoting the values underlying Article 5? German constitutional scholars continue to wrestle with this issue.[56]

The *Spiegel* case (1966) set forth the general principle governing the role of the press in a democratic society as well as some of the conditions under which it might be regulated in the public interest. Its prominence as one of the Constitutional Court's most controversial decisions is owing to its dramatic setting and dashing cast of characters.[57] The case is interesting not only for its doctrinal statements on freedom of the press but also for the form in which the opinion appears. *Spiegel* represents the first reported opinion in which the Constitutional Court was openly split on the merits of a controversy. Half the justices held that there was probable cause for the original proceedings against the defendant, and thus that there was no violation of a free press; the other half held that freedom of the press had been violated. In these circumstances, according to the FCCA (section 15 [2]), the Federal Constitutional Court may not declare an infringement of the Basic Law. The effect of the decision, therefore, was to sustain the Federal High Court's decision to dismiss the case for lack of evidence. The unprecedented publication of both sets of views in this case laid the basis for the eventual adoption by law of personalized dissenting opinions.[58] Bear in mind, however, that in the opinion that follows the justices were unanimous with respect to the general principles governing the role of the press in the German polity.

8.7 Spiegel Case (1966)
20 BVerfGE 162

[Late at night on October 26, 1962, squads of West German federal and state policemen mounted a coordinated raid on the premises of the popular weekly *Der Spiegel*. The magazine's editors were arrested, and boxes of papers and documents were carted away to police headquarters. The arrest and seizure followed the publication of *Der Spiegel*'s cover story on a NATO exercise designed to underscore West Germany's military weakness and to attack Defense Minister Franz Josef Strauss's attempt to equip the German army with tactical atomic weapons. The story included an astoundingly detailed account of the NATO maneuvers, the lackluster performance of German troops, and the military plans of both NATO and West Germany. The editors were charged with knowingly and willfully disclosing state secrets and conspiring to expose secret information from the Ministry of Defense.

After three years of legal skirmishing, the Third Senate (Criminal Division) of the Federal High Court of Justice dismissed the charges against the defendants for lack of evidence. The editors then filed constitutional complaints with the Federal Constitutional Court, claiming that the original search and arrest warrants authorized by the courts, together with the ensuing investigative proceedings, violated Article 5 and the rule of law. The complainants did not directly challenge the validity of the treason statutes under which they were charged. They claimed instead that the "mosaic" theory of treason read into the statutes by the government conflicted with Article 5. As it turned out, there was no proof that classified military secrets had been divulged. But it was presumptively possible at the time to commit treason in Germany by taking fragments of information found in widely accessible places, including previously published material, and piecing them together in such a way as to present a coherent picture of military strategy that would be useful to the enemy and dangerous to the existence of the Federal Republic.]

Judgment of the First Senate. . . .

C. 1. A free press, untrammeled by governmental control and censorship, is an essential element of a free society; a free, politically active, regularly published press is particularly indispensable in a modern democracy. If citizens are to make political decisions, they must be thoroughly informed; they must also be acquainted with the opinions of others in order to weigh alternative courses of action. The press enlivens this continuing discussion; it supplies information and takes positions with respect to it, and thereby orients public debate. The press articulates public opinion and clarifies public issues, facilitating the citizen's judgment. . . .

This "public task" of the press is important; it cannot be fulfilled by established governmental authority. Publishing companies must be able to organize freely within the social sphere. They operate according to the principles of the free market and in the organizational form of private enterprise. They compete intellectually and economically with other publishing enterprises, a process in which the state must not intervene.

2. The function of a free press in the democratic state corresponds to its legal position under the Basic Law. Article 5 guarantees freedom of the press. The location of the guarantee within the system of the Basic Law, together with the traditional meaning of [this guarantee], underscores the subjective character of the right. This means that persons and companies are free to function without official

interference. [The subjective aspect of this right] confers upon the press, in certain respects, a favored legal position. Freedom of the press also has an objective side; i.e., it guarantees the existence of the institution of a "free press." Independent of the personal rights of individuals, the state is duty-bound in all areas of the legal system to respect the principle of a free press wherever a regulation might concern it. The freedom to engage in a publishing enterprise, free access to the journalistic profession, and the duty of public agencies to divulge information are all manifestations of this principle. In addition, the state may have a positive duty to take action against the development of monopolies of opinion.

The independence of the press guaranteed by Article 5 of the Basic Law extends from the accumulation of information to the dissemination of news and opinion. Thus the protection of the relationship of trust between the press and its private informants is an integral part of a free press. Because the press cannot function without private sources of information, this protection is indispensable. Sources of information will flow freely only when editorial privilege is respected.

3. Freedom of the press carries with it the possibility of conflict with other values also protected by the Basic Law; it can come into conflict with the rights of individuals, groups, or the community in general. The Basic Law gives the legal system, to which the press is also subject, the task of regulating this conflict; it must respect the legal rights and interests of others as well as of the general public whenever those interests are at least as worthy of protection as those of the press. The privileged position of the members of the press is granted them solely because of their function and only so far as this function reaches. It is not a question of personal privileges; the freeing of individuals from generally valid norms must be justified against this background.

Reference to the legal order is made in Article 5 (2) of the Basic Law, according to which the freedom of the press is limited by the general laws. This court, in its decision of January 15, 1958 [citing the *Lüth* case], addressed itself to the relationship between freedom of opinion and general laws. We said that although freedom of opinion may be restricted by the general laws, these laws themselves are to be interpreted in the light of the concept of freedom of opinion, and hence that this restriction is itself correspondingly restricted. These principles are also valid with respect to freedom of the press; in fact, they gain particular significance here because statements in the press as a rule are intended to contribute to the formation of public opinion and therefore carry a presumption of permissibility, even if they infringe on other people's rights. . . .

4. The provisions on treason (sections 99 and 110, Penal Code) are "general laws" within the meaning of Article 5 (2) of the Basic Law. They are constitutionally valid legal provisions. . . . The protection of the Federal Republic from its external enemies — the purpose of the treason laws — conflicts with the notion of a free press when the press publishes facts, subject matter, or observations whose secrecy would serve the national defense. [Courts] cannot summarily resolve this conflict [by

adhering to a policy of prior censorship] with the argument that a free press presupposes the existence of the Federal Republic and would also perish if the nation were
destroyed. The free democratic order . . . [also] requires a vigilant press willing to
criticize the affairs of state, including the structure and policy of the military.

From this point of view, the necessity of military secrecy for state security and
the freedom of the press are not mutually exclusive principles. Rather, they are
complementary, in that both are meant to preserve the Federal Republic — as this is
properly to be understood. It is with an eye to this goal that [courts] are to resolve
conflicts between these two necessities. Therefore courts must consider the significance of the disclosed facts for the potential enemy as well as for the formation of
public opinion. [They] must balance the dangers to the security of the country that
may arise from the publication against the need to be informed of important events,
even [those] in the field of national defense. In this sense, Article 5 (1) of the Basic
Law exercises a basic limiting influence on the construction of the penal statute.

> [The remainder of the opinion examines the facts and circumstances sur-
> rounding the issuance of the search and arrest warrants. Four justices con-
> cluded that on the basis of all the evidence, no unconstitutional action had
> been taken against the complainants. The other four justices concluded that
> the facts did not constitutionally warrant the judicial and investigative pro-
> ceedings against *Der Spiegel*. The first set of justices constituted the effective
> "majority," however, because an even split cannot lead to a finding that the
> Basic Law has been violated. The following extract is from the opinion of the
> "dissenting" justices. The opinion is largely based on the so-called mosaic
> theory of treason. The four justices on the prevailing side refused to concede
> that the seizure and the investigation of *Der Spiegel* were in fact based on any
> such theory.]

1. . . . [One] must distinguish between the publication of state secrets by the
press and a case of "ordinary treason" by agents or spies. The military sphere cannot
be removed from that free and public discussion so vital to a democratic system
of government. . . . The discussion of the government's basic defense policy, the
strength of the country's armed forces, the general effectiveness or ineffectiveness of
the measures taken to ensure defensive capability, and the proper application of
public funds for military purposes is a legitimate function of the press. Its duty is to
inform the public about these issues and provide the facts necessary for each citizen
to make up his mind [about these issues]. Obviously, this does not include the
publication of all details; nevertheless, the boundary between the permissible and
the impermissible in the publication of military facts . . . must be drawn more
liberally when press reports are concerned than in ordinary cases of treason. . . .

Hence the interpretation of section 99 (1) of the Penal Code, which has come
to be known as the mosaic theory, is basically inapplicable to treason by publication.
According to this theory, treason takes place when, through the systematic gather-

ing and compilation of facts either commonly known or available from generally accessible sources, [a person] gives a full and accurate account of some important matter pertaining to national defense. [The compilation of facts constitutes treason] because the total picture creates new information which is viewed as a separate state secret. This interpretation arose in response to acts of treason committed by secret agents and may well have its use in that context. . . . [But] the application of this theory to treason by publication would excessively limit the role of the press, for the press's normal task is to gather and organize the news into a coherent account of a given event or phenomenon [or] to analyze single pieces of information, assemble them into a pattern, and then draw conclusions. The prior disclosure of such facts excludes as a matter of principle the possibility of treason by publication. If this were not the case, the ability of the press to inform the public about essential questions of national defense and to stimulate public discussion about [these matters] would be decidedly inhibited. . . .

2. The *Spiegel* article contributes to the discussion, already familiar to the public, concerning two contrary defense concepts; it contributes especially to the debate between those who would equip the army with atomic weapons and those who would strengthen it with conventional weapons. . . . In applying these principles of construction, we must consider first whether the published military facts were already current in public discussion and whether they were known or generally accessible, either individually or in connection with other publications. . . .

This examination, required under Article 5 (1) [2], was not carried out when the search warrant was granted. The investigating judge, who was not an expert in military matters, found the facts sufficient to justify the search on the basis of the opinion of Defense Ministry officials. . . . By relying exclusively on the opinion of the Defense Ministry, the investigative judge failed to construe section 99 of the Penal Code in the light of the radiating effect of Article 5 (1) [2]. . . . The court uncritically accepted the findings of the Defense Ministry. . . . Similarly, the [High Court's] degree of October 31, 1963, assumes the [validity of these findings] in the absence of any corroborating evidence and of any examination of the effect of the Basic Law.

———————————

NOTE: THE MOSAIC THEORY AND THE PERILS OF BALANCING. The *Spiegel* case reaffirmed the validity of the balancing test set forth in *Lüth*.[59] On this issue the Constitutional Court was unanimous. Yet, curiously, in *Spiegel* the court did not employ a balancing analysis. The "majority"—the four justices who found no constitutional violation in the original proceedings against *Der Spiegel*—rested on a point of law: They conceded that a newspaper or magazine, given its special institutional role in a liberal democracy, cannot be suppressed under the mosaic theory of treason. (By framing their position in this way, incidentally, the justices seemed to imply that the magazine might have been guilty of treason under some other interpretation of the statute.) The "majority" announced that, on the facts of the case, the courts below did not predicate the original search-and-seizure proceedings on the mosaic theory. As a consequence, they felt no need to engage in a balancing process or to rule on the constitutionality of the mosaic theory. Nor did they find the lower courts in error—most notably the Federal High Court—for their failure to engage in the balancing analysis required by *Lüth*. One critic of the *Spiegel* case, Herbert Bernstein, commented:

> It is submitted that the *Spiegel* case may well be read to mark a serious crisis in the development of the doctrine enunciated in the *Lüth* case a decade ago. Critics of the Federal Constitutional Court have repeatedly called attention to the well-nigh complete absence of guidelines for the balancing-of-interests process that *Lüth* requires the lower courts to follow. The *Spiegel* case will lend further support to this criticism. . . . [E]ven the most sympathetic observer of the Court cannot escape the conclusion that it has still a long way to go in order to achieve a more structured application of the *Lüth* test. Unless this is accomplished, the sanctuary that the Basic Law is supposed to have created for free speech and a free press continues to suffer from poorly defined boundaries.[60]

NOTE: THE RIGHTS AND RESPONSIBILITIES OF THE PRESS. The *Spiegel* case is important for underscoring the objective character of the right to a free press. Article 5 not only incorporates a subjective right of the press against governmental encroachment but also confers on the press an affirmative constitutional right to institutional autonomy and independence. The press enjoys this special status under the Basic Law because it performs a critical "public role" in the life of a liberal democracy.[61] Its primary purposes are to collect information, distribute the news, and contribute to the development of public opinion. Indeed, it is the government's responsibility to legislate norms designed to maintain and facilitate these institutional functions. The *Television I* case (1961; no. 8.8) suggests that the legislature may in certain instances even be obliged to protect the press from societal forces or pressures likely to endanger its freedom.

Each of the German *Länder*, including the five states of the old GDR, has enacted laws defining the rights and duties of the press.[62] Many of these laws have codified a number of the Constitutional Court's holdings, including those that protect editorial secrecy and the right of journalists not to disclose, even in criminal proceedings, their sources of information.[63] Hamburg's Press Act, some of whose provisions would be constitutionally suspect in the United States, exemplifies these statutes. It affirms the principle of a free press by prohibiting licensing or equivalent measures; it defines the public role of the press, emphasizing its responsibility to procure and disseminate the news as well as to voice its opinion on public policy; it imposes a correlative duty on the part of public officials to supply the press with information of value to it in the fulfillment of its public role; it obligates the press in turn to check the content, origin, and truth of all the news prior to its publication; it sets forth the conditions under which publishers and editors are to grant citizens a right of reply; finally, it defines in great detail the responsibility of the press under the Criminal Code.[64]

In addition, and in the interest of journalistic fairness, the German Press Council has adopted a set of guidelines for editors and publishers. One such guideline reads: "The publication of specific news and information in word and picture must be carefully checked in respect of accuracy in the light of existing circumstances. Its sense must not be distorted or falsified by editing, title, or picture captions. Documents must be accurately reproduced. . . . When reproducing symbolic photographs, it must be clear from the caption that these are not documentary pictures."[65] Other guidelines deal with the correction of publishing errors; the publication of names and photographs; reports of suicides, accidents, crimes, and threats of violence; and the publication of the names and photographs of criminals and accused persons. Although promulgated by an association of publishers and journalists, the guidelines adhere to the spirit of the laws governing the press as well as the admonitions of the Federal Constitutional Court.

NOTE: THE *STERN MAGAZINE* CASE. One recently challenged provision of the Criminal Code prohibits the press from publishing the exact wording of a criminal charge before it is presented in a public trial. The statute does not bar other comments about a case or even a summary of an indictment. The *Stern* case, decided in 1985,[66] arose from an action against the weekly magazine *Stern* for publishing, before trial, the text of a criminal charge in the famous Flick party-funding affair. The Hamburg District Court, before which the magazine was haled for violating the code provision, referred the question of its validity to the Constitutional Court, which sustained the rule as a valid limitation on freedom of the press under the general-law clause of Article 5 (2). The court explained:

> By forbidding the publication of the exact wording of court records in criminal proceedings before their disclosure at trial, the legislature was concerned that such publications would be more prejudicial to defendants and other participants in the trial than the mere reporting of the case in other than direct quotations. . . . The literal reproduction of statements knowingly uttered as such is a particularly sharp weapon in the battle of opinions. Such quotations add credence to the charge, almost serving as a statement of fact [citing the *Böll* case]. This is true not only of the literal reproduction of expressions of opinion but also of the literal reproduction of communications based on fact. A word-for-word reproduction of parts of documents conveys, and rightly so, the impression of official authenticity to the disadvantage of defendant in a criminal suit.[67]

The Constitutional Court demonstrated once again that general law may seek to protect certain values — in this case the integrity of the defendant and the objectivity of the criminal law process — so long as the law in question is not directed at a particular opinion.

8.8 Television I Case (1961)
12 BVerfGE 205

[The facts of the case are provided in Chapter 3, case no. 3.2. Portions of the opinion described in Chapter 3 deal with the issue of federalism. The court held that the federal government's creation of a national television station violated the reserved powers of the states. The court then considered issues arising under Article 5.]

Judgment of the Second Senate. . . .

E. III. Article 5 contains more than just the citizen's individual, basic right to a sphere of liberty free from state interference in which he can unrestrictedly express his opinions. In particular, Article 5 (1) [2] guarantees the institutional self-sufficiency of the press — from gathering information to disseminating news and opinions. The state would encroach upon this guarantee if it directly or indirectly sought either to regulate or to steer the press or any of its subdivisions. The constitutional guarantee of press freedom would permit governmental interference only if, because of competition from the abundance of independent newspapers and magazines, it would leave the image of the free press essentially unaltered.

[We] cannot appreciate the significance which Article 5 has for broadcasting without considering the aforementioned statements concerning the content of Article 5. Notwithstanding a peculiarity of broadcasting yet to be discussed, broadcasting, like the press, is among the indispensable means of modern mass communications that influence and help to shape public opinion. Broadcasting is more than a mere "medium" for the formation of public opinion; it is a critical factor in that process. The participation in forming public opinion is by no means limited to news programs, political commentary, or series about past, present, or future political problems; it also occurs in radio plays, musical presentations, the transmission of cabaret shows, and even in the way scenes are presented within a program. . . . These observations clearly illustrate that . . . institutional freedom is no less important for broadcasting than for the press. This is unambiguously expressed in Article 5, where paragraph 1, clause 2, grants "the freedom of reporting by broadcasting and film" in addition to the freedom of the press.

These [precepts] do not tell us how to ensure freedom of broadcasting generally and, more specifically, freedom of reporting in order to satisfy [the requirements] of Article 5. The peculiarity that distinguishes broadcasting from the press becomes significant at this point. To be sure, it is not true that newspapers, newspaper publishing houses, and printing houses can be established in unlimited numbers. But the distinction between press and broadcasting lies in the fact that a relatively large number of independent publications exist in the German press which cover a broad spectrum of political and ideological views, while in the broadcasting realm the number of stations must remain small both for technical reasons and because of the unusually high costs of broadcasting. Because of the unique situation in the broadcasting field, [stations] must take special precautions to effectuate and maintain the broadcasting freedom afforded by Article 5. The principle according to which the existing broadcasting facilities were structured provides one way of accomplishing this purpose: A statute creates a legal entity under public law which is responsible for producing programs to be broadcast [but] removed from state influence or at most subject to limited state supervision; its governing boards are actually composed of representatives from all significant political, philosophical, and social groups; they have the power to supervise those in charge of programming and to ensure compliance with statutory provisions requiring that an appropriate proportion of interested persons be involved [in programming]. Under the present technical conditions, it does not contravene Article 5 to grant an institution a broadcasting monopoly at the state level if it has these reins on its power; but Article 5 by no means mandates the establishment of such a monopoly.

In any case, Article 5 does not require that broadcasting stations be set up as specified by state and federal laws in order to ensure broadcasting freedom. In particular, the federal Constitution does not require that broadcasting companies only be incorporated, public-law institutions. An incorporated company under private law could be responsible for broadcasting programs if its organization, like that of a public broadcasting company, offered sufficient assurance that all socially relevant interests would have the opportunity to express themselves, and that freedom of reporting would remain unimpaired. For example, it would be constitutional for a law to allow the creation of a private company which would guarantee that the specific purpose of the broadcasting media, and particularly its institutional freedom, be maintained. Thus any company engaged in broadcasting and meeting these statutory requirements would be subject to state supervision similar to that over banks or insurance companies.

In any case, Article 5 of the Constitution requires that this modern instrument of opinion formation should be neither at the mercy of the state nor [at the mercy of] of one single social group. Therefore, broadcasting companies must be organized to allow all interests worthy of consideration to exert influence on their governing boards and to express themselves in the overall programming. They must be organized so that binding guidelines ensure that programs contain a minimum of balance, objectivity, and reciprocal respect. Only a statute can guarantee that the organizational and objective principles will be generally applicable. Thus Article 5 requires that such laws be passed.

[We] cannot deduce from Article 5 the requirement that those responsible for programming either own or be authorized to operate the technical broadcasting facilities. Article 5 does not prevent representatives of the state from sitting on the boards of "neutral" companies in a reasonable proportion to [other board members]. By contrast, Article 5 does preclude the state from controlling directly or indirectly an institution or company that broadcasts programs.

The German Television Company, Ltd., founded on July 25, 1960, by notarized contract with the purpose of "broadcasting radio and television programs which will convey a comprehensive picture of Germany both abroad and at home," consisted originally of the Federal Republic and federal minister Schaeffer as partners. Schaeffer's departure places . . . control solely in the hands of the Federal Republic. The company is totally under state control and is thus an instrument of the federation. . . . Accordingly, both the founding and existence of the German Television Company violate Article 5 of the Basic Law.

NOTE: THE MEDIA AND THE BASIC LAW. *Internal pluralism and public monopoly.* *Television I* has been characterized as the "Magna Carta of broadcasting."[68] It demonstrated the Constitutional Court's determination to extend the same freedom to broadcasting that it had to newspapers and magazines. But the court noted that the distinctive features of broadcasting require special legislative attention: "Article 5 of the Constitution requires that this modern instrument of opinion formation should be at the mercy of neither the government nor one single social group."[69] In 1961 this seemed to imply a regulatory structure requiring pluralistic representation on the governing boards of broadcasting stations. The membership of such boards includes representatives of political parties, religious denominations, trade unions and employer groups, educational institutions, various levels of government, and other professional and communal associations.[70] And while *Television I* did not rule out the possibility of private radio and television stations, provided they were carefully monitored to serve the public interest, it placed the Constitutional Court's stamp of approval on policies aimed at public monopoly of the broadcast media.

NOTE: *TELEVISION II* CASE (1971). The original creation in postwar Germany of the public nonprofit broadcast corporation was designed to keep the electronic media free of state control and out of the hands of private economic interests. As a consequence, the public broadcasting corporations were not supported by state funds; instead, they were financed largely through fees imposed on television users. Viewed as an inviting source of tax revenue, these fees were taxed as business income. The tax was successfully challenged in *Television II* (1971).[71] The Federal Constitutional Court held that the broadcasting corporations were public institutions, not commercial enterprises, and thus were beyond the taxing power of federal and state governments.[72] The dissenting opinion, while arguing that the tax should be sustained as a legitimate levy for services rendered, joined the majority in underscoring the public character of broadcasting.[73] Proceeding from an analysis of Article 5 and relying heavily on general propositions set forth in the *Spiegel* case, the justices emphasized the essential link between broadcasting and liberal democracy. Broadcasting is a public trust and a powerful instrument in the formation of public opinion; internal pluralistic control is thus necessary to avoid any kind of state monopoly over program content. But the court was equally concerned with keeping radio and television independent of private control: "As a result of developments in television technology, broadcasting has become one of the most powerful means of mass communications, which, because of its wide-reaching effect and possibilities as well as the danger of misuse for one-sided propagandizing, cannot be left to the free play of [market] forces."[74]

The philosophy of *Television I* and *Television II* was aptly summarized in a Bundestag report on the condition of the press and broadcasting in the Federal Republic:

> The federal government reiterated in the Government Declaration of December 16, 1976, that the private-law character of the press should continue to be upheld in the same way as the public-law character of broadcasting. These are two mutually complementary principles on which the system of the media in the Federal Republic is based. Both organizational solutions must be seen in terms of the aim based in the Constitution that every individual be guaranteed the highest level of freedoms and of possibilities in the media. The individual must have a central place [here so that] he [may] be able to inform himself comprehensively and fully, and to form his own opinion freely and to express it, thereby enabling him to have independent, responsible participation in the development of a democratic community.[75]

NOTE: PRELUDE TO THE *TELEVISION III* CASE. With the emergence of satellite television, cable networks, and other developments in communications technology in the 1970s, a fierce debate broke out in Germany over the propriety and even the constitutionality of an exclusively state-chartered public-law broadcasting system. For one thing, the development of cable television and other new media technology weakened arguments in favor of state control. Other arguments questioned whether the internal pluralistic structure of existing carriers really succeeded in producing a diversity of viewpoints reflective of the wider society. Critics pointed to what they regarded as the excessive influence of political parties in the current structure of representation, the absence of certain socially relevant groups from this structure, and the serious problem of determining which social groups are entitled to representation. Many persons contended that private radio and television stations would offer the German public a broader range of social and political views, and that in any event, competition from private carriers would expand and enliven the arena of public debate. Finally, newspaper publishers were themselves lobbying for access to the new media, often for reasons of economic survival.[76]

8.9 Television III Case (1981)
57 BVerfGE 295

[In 1967 Saarland became the first state in the Federal Republic to provide for the licensing of privately owned radio stations. Under an amendment to its broadcasting law, the Saarland legislature permitted the organization of a private station known as Freier Rundfunk AG (Free Broadcasting, Inc.; FRAG). The state government, however, refused to grant the station a license, whereupon FRAG sued, and lost, in Saarland's administrative court. Several years of complicated appellate litigation ensued, culminating in Saarland's final rejection of FRAG's license application because it feared that a private station would endanger the existence of public stations. Freier Rundfunk AG appealed once more to the administrative court, which on this occasion referred the case to the Federal Constitutional Court. The statute subjected private broadcasters to the same principles governing public broadcasting stations, including pluralistic representation on their governing boards. A private station was required to be supervised by a thirteen-member advisory board consisting of Catholic and Protestant representatives and other public members. But the statute neither specified the advisory board's duties nor identified the groups from which other board members were to be recruited. The Constitutional Court was asked to review the validity of these provisions. The case presented the court with another opportunity to clarify the constitutional conditions required for the establishment and licensing of broadcast media.]

Judgment of the First Senate. . . .

C. II. Article 5 (1) [2] requires the state to regulate private broadcasting. Such regulation is needed to guarantee broadcasting freedom.

1. The effective exercise of the liberty of broadcasting constitutionally guaranteed in Article 5 (2) [1] requires that [the state] pass statutes to flesh out the contours of this right. This [conclusion] results from the purpose and character of the guarantee. . . .

(a) Broadcasting freedom serves the same purpose as do all of the guarantees of Article 5 (1): to secure the freedom of the individual to influence the free formation of individual and public opinion in the comprehensive sense . . . of being able to communicate all information and opinions. The free formation of opinions occurs within a process of communication. It implies, on the one hand, the freedom to express and disseminate an opinion, and, on the other, the freedom to hear opinions and be informed. By treating the freedoms of expression and dissemination of opinion as well as the freedom of information as human rights, Article 5 (1) also seeks to safeguard the integrity of this process. To this extent, it creates individual rights . . . [as well as] an objective principle which is part of the entire legal order [citing the *Lüth* case].

Broadcasting is both a "medium" and a "factor" in this constitutionally protected process of free opinion formation [citing *Television I*]. Accordingly, broadcasting liberty primarily serves freedom of opinion making in terms of subjective as well as objective law: Under the conditions of modern mass communication, [broadcasting liberty] necessarily supplements and reinforces freedom [of opinion making]; it serves the function of guaranteeing free and comprehensive opinion formation through broadcasting.

This function determines the character and the importance of broadcasting freedom: First, the free formation of individual and public opinion requires that broadcasting be free of governmental domination and influence. To this extent, broadcasting liberty, like the classic rights of freedom, has a defensive significance. But that is not sufficient to guarantee [broadcasting freedom]. For mere freedom from governmental influence does not by itself imply that the broadcasting [industry] can freely engage in the comprehensive shaping of opinion making; defensive regulation alone cannot accomplish this task. Rather, [the accomplishment] of this task requires that a system be created to ensure that the diversity of existing opinions finds its greatest possible breadth and completeness through broadcasting, and that, as a consequence, comprehensive information will be offered to the public. In order to reach this goal the legislature must enact substantive, organizational, and procedural provisions designed to effectuate the function of broadcasting liberty and to secure what Article 5 (1) guarantees. . . .

[In this part of the opinion the court criticized the legislature's failure to specify the conditions that would ensure that broadcasting freedom would be maintained and conflicting values or interests properly balanced. Neither administrative officials nor the broadcasters themselves can be entrusted with the task of guaranteeing the freedom of broadcasting. The policies governing the broadcast industry must be set forth in statutory form. To the argument that modern technology has undermined the older rationale governing the regulation of the broadcast media the court responded as follows.]

(c) Even if the special situation caused by the shortage of transmitting frequencies and by the great expense of broadcasting production no longer exists, statutory regulation will still be necessary. Up to now the jurisprudence of the Federal Constitutional Court has presupposed the existence of this special situation; what the [court] will do in the absence of this situation remains an open question. But even if this case [should arise], the Constitution would still require statutory regulation to safeguard the liberty of broadcasting. . . .

Even if the previous limitations [on broadcasting] were to disappear, there would be no certainty that the unwritten laws of the marketplace would produce a selection of programs which would live up to the standards of broadcasting freedom. Certainly one can argue that the variety [of programming] offered to the public would then be similar to that now existing in the nationwide newspaper market. However, this is only a possibility. While the historical development of the press has resulted in a certain balance that is basically sufficient to guarantee that [citizens] continue to receive comprehensive information and can form opinions, [one] cannot assume that the same holds true for private broadcasting — at least, not at present. There is no assurance, however, that remedying the existing deficiency of "programming selection" . . . will enable all or at least a significant number of social groups and ideological movements to express their opinions; that is, [there is no way of knowing] whether a "market of opinions" will arise in which diverse opinions may be expressed without being edited. . . . [We] must confront the danger that [private broadcasters] might exclude opinions deserving of dissemination from the public opinion-making process and that opinion holders in possession of broadcast frequencies and financial resources might exert a dominant influence on the public opinion-making process.

2. (b) . . . In any event, . . . [the introduction of private broadcasting] requires a statutory basis . . . to ensure that broadcasting is not controlled by any single group and that eligible groups will have the opportunity to be heard in the total programming. . . .

To the extent that the legislature has decided to create a structure of "internal pluralism" within the broadcasting industry, . . . it must objectively determine, on the basis of the existing constellation of social forces [in the society], which groups are to be represented in its programming.

The legislature may, however, choose to structure [private broadcasting stations] differently as long as it takes measures to ensure that the program selection corresponds to the existing diversity of opinion. . . . The statute must also regulate the content of administrative activity; it may not merely confine itself to [setting forth] general principles. This applies most particularly to standards governing the revocation of broadcasting licenses. . . .

NOTE: *TELEVISION III* AND ITS IMPLICATIONS. The Constitutional Court found the Saarland statute deficient in several respects, including (1) its failure to specify the procedures private firms must follow in applying for a broadcasting license; (2) its lack of standards for determining the suitability of a private broadcast applicant; (3) its lack of procedures for handling multiple applications for private licenses; and, most important, (4) its failure to provide for full societal representation in the station's governing structure. In the court's view, detailed legislation in each of these areas is constitutionally necessary to ensure that broadcasting stations, private and public, perform the public functions required of them under the prevailing interpretation of Article 5. The First Senate rejected the argument that broadcast freedom within the meaning of Article 5 could be realized by a system of control powered or dominated by the "unwritten law of the marketplace."[77] *Television III* reinforced, in the strongest possible terms, the court's earlier view that the Basic Law bars any interest group monopoly over radio and television. For all these reasons the state is obligated to produce a regulatory scheme that ensures that broadcasting will contribute to the formation of public opinion while simultaneously reflecting its diversity.

NOTE: BROADCASTING AND THE VALUES OF ARTICLE 5 (1). The first three television cases show the extent to which the Federal Constitutional Court was prepared to supervise and even to insist on the detailed regulation of the German broadcasting industry. It might be noted that the court's intervention in this field is fully comparable to the directives it has imposed on campaign financing, a subject discussed at length in Chapter 5. In any event, broadcasting cases continued to command the court's attention in the 1980s and 1990s, largely in response to the decision of state governments to introduce private broadcasting, a movement strongly resisted by Social Democratic members of the Bundestag and by the public broadcasting stations. Most of the cases discussed in this section were initiated by one or another of these petitioners.

The *Television IV* case (1986) arose out of Lower Saxony's statute regulating private broadcasting stations. Stimulated in part by the development of a European broadcasting market, Lower Saxony, like most of the German *Länder*, began in the early 1980s to license private television channels on an experimental basis. In reorganizing its broadcasting system, Lower Saxony sought to ensure the balanced programming required by the Constitutional Court's previous decisions. The *Land*'s new policy required public broadcasting stations to maintain their structure of "internal pluralism"—meaning their governance by an independent council composed of representatives of major social, economic, religious, and cultural groups—but allowed the new private stations to adjust their internal structure and program selections to the forces of the free market so long as the overall effect of both public and private broadcasting was one of multiplicity and balance. "This dual system," said the court in *Television IV*, "may be regarded as a transitional stage on the way to a possible system of full external pluralism in which market forces and an adequate number of suppliers satisfy the constitutional requirements of freedom of expression."[78]

In this abstract judicial-review case brought by Social Democratic members of the Bundestag, the court sought to clarify the relationship between public and private television.[79] The court's analysis underscored the primacy of public broadcasting and its crucial importance in the democracy created by the Basic Law. The national coverage and universal viewership of the public stations, said the First

Senate, require that *they* perform the "basic service" (*Grundversorgung*) of balanced programming throughout Germany. In the *Freelance Writers* case (1982), the court made clear that this constitutionally required service can be carried out by means of news programs and documentaries as well as through radio and television plays, musical programs, and entertainment shows.[80] To ensure that this basic service is carried out, the state must maintain a system of *public* broadcasting and see to its adequate financing.

Television IV makes clear, however, that private broadcasting supported by commercial advertising is compatible with Article 5 (1) of the Basic Law. Indeed private broadcasting, with its ability to broaden and deepen the basic service mission of the public stations, is a valued complement to rather than a competitor of the latter. But once a *Land* government decides to license private broadcasters, the principles of *Staatsfreiheit* and balanced programming apply. The state may no more censure or dictate the programming of private than of public broadcasters. In fact, *Television IV* sustained the constitutionality of Lower Saxony's refusal to permit political parties, public employees, or public law organizations (apart from religious associations) from operating or owning private stations.[81] The court agreed with the *Land*'s view that the nexus between these groups and the state threatened to undermine the principle of *Staatsfreiheit* (i.e., freedom from state control).

As for balanced programming, the court did not object to the *Land*'s failure to hold private broadcasters to the organizational and procedural standards constitutionally required of public broadcasters. Under established doctrine, the *Länder* must regulate all public broadcast stations in the interest of diversity and internal pluralistic governance. Private broadcasters *could* be regulated in the same way, said the court, but they need not be in the light of their specialized programs, targeted audiences, and dependence on advertising revenue. They are bound, however, by the principle of "external pluralism." The state must see to it that private broadcasters in their totality — as opposed to each and every station or channel — provide an overall balance in program offerings.[82]

Although upholding the essentials of Lower Saxony's Broadcasting Act, the Constitutional Court found certain omissions in the statute incompatible with the Basic Law. One of these omissions was the *Land*'s failure to lay down detailed guidelines for the achievement of overall balance and impartiality in private broadcasting. Another of the law's features singled out as unconstitutional was the unlimited discretion conferred on the *Land* government in allocating permits and frequencies. The state's right to decide who and how many stations or channels to license would, said the court, threaten the freedom of private broadcasters as well as undermine the principles of balance and diversity in programming. The state itself may not grant or withhold a license depending on its own indiscriminate judgment of the program content to be offered by the supplier. Structures as well as detailed guidelines must be laid down to avoid any threat to the autonomy and objectivity of the licensing process.[83]

Three additional cases, all dealing with the financing of public and private television, were decided between 1987 and 1992. In the *Television V* case (1987), the First Senate upheld Baden-Württemberg's ban on all advertising on local and regional public television channels. The objective of the ban was to reserve advertising revenues for both the printed press and private stations. So long as public television receives the funding it needs to perform its mission, said the court, the state is free to prescribe the funding source of both public and private channels.[84] In the *Television VII* case (1992), the court also sustained Hesse's decision to ban advertising on its Third Television Station but only because it was evident that the public station could fulfill its mission by means of the user fee.[85]

In sustaining major amendments to North Rhine–Westphalia's broadcasting statute of 1985, the *Television VI* case (1991) reaffirmed several of the principles laid down in *Television IV* and *Television V.* The court approved various cooperative arrangements, particularly in financing, between private and public television stations while also approving the *Land* government's decision to authorize public broadcasting stations to experiment with cable and satellite transmission as well as beaming out programs from a central tower if these experiments would help them fulfill their duties under Article 5 (1).[86] *Television VI* also confirmed parliament's authority to determine which groups are entitled to be represented on the boards of public broadcasting stations.[87] (In this instance, refugee and women's organizations were denied representation.) However, groups that do receive representation are not to serve their own interests but rather to govern broadcasting in the interest of the common good, a duty which the court insisted must be set forth in law.

NOTE: THE *CABLE PENNY* CASE (1994). *Cable Penny,* the most recent of a long line of television cases, was a concrete judicial-review proceeding emerging from a reference by the Bavarian Administrative Court of Appeals.[88] The plaintiffs below were television viewers in Bavaria. They objected to provisions of an interstate compact on broadcasting that required 20 percent of the broadcasting user fee to be spent on financing pilot projects in commercially owned cable television technology. Television viewers claimed that cable's assigned share of each German mark (DM 0.20, the so-called cable penny) constituted a separate levy that would have to be calculated and assessed on its own merits apart from and independent of the general user fee imposed for the benefit of public broadcasting stations. They also claimed that the levy was unconstitutional because it was designed to serve the commercial interests of private broadcasters. The appeals court certified these issues to the Constitutional Court and also the question of the constitutionality of user fees structured and determined by the state alone.

The First Senate's unanimous opinion sustained the validity of the cable penny as a legitimate effort to improve broadcasting as a whole. Even though the cable penny was levied against the fees of users not hooked up to cable television, the goal of the pilot projects was to benefit all viewers and listeners in conformity with the requirements of Article 5 (1). Given the particular facts of this case, the senate declined to decide whether user fees may be employed to promote private broadcasting. Instead, the bulk of the opinion dealt with the questions of *who* determines the user fee and *what* criteria are to be used in fixing its amount.

Once again the court recapitulated established doctrine worthy of repetition here. Article 5 (1) guarantees the freedom to broadcast, which is a communicative freedom designed to inform and develop public opinion in the interest of a "democratic constitutional order." This freedom guarantees to broadcasters the right to determine the content of their programs. But this freedom is positive as well as negative. The state may not interfere with the public broadcaster's right to communicate, but at the same time Article 5 (1) "calls for a positive legal order that ensures that broadcasters address and convey the variety of topics and opinions which play a role in society."[89] As the court has so often emphasized, such programming is the primary duty of *public* broadcasting. Public broadcasting, however, needs to be regulated — substantively, organizationally, and procedurally — to ensure the fulfillment of the Basic Law's normative goals. Up to now, the court has placed its stamp of approval on the user fee as the most appropriate way of financing public television and furthering the values of diversity and pluralism required by Article 5 (1). Commercial advertising on public television is permitted so long as it is limited and advertisers have no influence over broadcasters.

With respect to private broadcasting, the First Senate recalled its precedents by asserting that private radio and television stations are compatible with Article 5 (1) if they do not interfere with or threaten the constitutional mandate imposed on public stations. In short, a dual system of public and private broadcasting is constitutionally permissible so long as public stations and channels are able to fulfill their duties under Article 5 (1) and remain competitive with private broadcasters. In *Cable Penny* the court adhered to its earlier view that private broadcasters do not enjoy an affirmative constitutional right to compete with public broadcasters; yet, consistent with its previous case law, the court conceded that private broadcasters — while not subject to the same degree of regulation required of public broadcasters — have enriched and expanded the program offerings available to the German people, thus contributing significantly to the overall "informing" mission of the broadcasting industry. Under existing constitutional doctrine, private broadcasting could never replace public broadcasting, but the creative complementarity built into the dual system is consistent with the letter and spirit of the Basic Law.

Having set forth these principles, the First Senate proceeded to raise serious questions about the funding scheme laid down in the interstate compact under review. Adequate funding, said the court, must be provided if public broadcasting stations are to fulfill their constitutional mandate. The present scheme failed to meet constitutional standards because the fee imposed under the compact was "a purely political decision made by the heads of [state] governments and [ratified] by *Länder* parliaments," thus posing the threat of state influence over public broadcast programming.[90] Accordingly, the fee was incompatible with Article 5 (1) of the Basic Law. The court noted that the level of funding affects broadcasting freedom. For this reason, said the court, not even the legislature can be given a free hand in setting user fees. A free hand would threaten the autonomy of public broadcasters and might ignore the legitimate interests of viewers and listeners. On the other hand, broadcasters cannot be given total autonomy either, lest they fail to carry out the mandate required by Article 5 (1). The legislature's task is to balance these interests as equitably as possible.

As noted in Chapter 2, the court may declare a law or practice incompatible (*unvereinbar*) with the Basic Law without holding it null and void (*nichtig*). To have voided the funding scheme would have nullified the entire system, resulting in even greater constitutional harm. The decision of incompatibility kept the existing system in place but required it to be amended forthwith, in which respect the court laid down the following principles. First, procedural safeguards must be adopted to ensure that the constitutional interests of public broadcasting will be protected, particularly in the light of the competition stemming from the emergence of cable television. The court remarked that public broadcasting has lost more than half of its advertising revenue because of the increasing prominence of commercial television, requiring a studied reassessment of public broadcasting needs.

Second, legislation must set forth detailed criteria for assessing the needs of public broadcasting, and the criteria must be such as to guarantee its continued vitality and constitutional mission. Finally, the structuring of such a system is to be laid out in a general broadcasting statute — thus meeting the requirements of both democracy and the rule of law — at the discretion of the legislature. The court did say, however, that state parliaments could delegate the task of setting user fees to an independent board or commission so long as the power conferred is "clear and definite."[91] Once again the court vindicated and reaffirmed the role of public broadcasting in Germany's constitutional democracy without encroaching on the state's power to experiment with and promote commercial broadcasting.[92]

SPEECH, PERSONHOOD, AND SOCIAL MORALITY

Article 5 (2) provides that freedom of expression finds its "limits in the rules of the general laws, statutory provisions for the protection of youth, and in the right to personal honor." This text provides little basis for elevating speech into an absolute value capable of trumping other personal interests protected by the Constitution. Moreover, as noted elsewhere in this chapter, the speech clauses invite interpretation in the light of other basic value decisions of the Constitution whose effect is often to confine the range or intensity of speech. Prominent among these value decisions are the human dignity clause of Article 1 and the personality clause of Article 2. The Constitution thus "requires a kind of dialectical method of interpretation and a general as well as concrete balancing of . . . constitutionally protected values."[93] We have already seen this balancing process at work in numerous areas of German constitutional law.

The two cases reprinted in this section represent successful efforts to vindicate the fundamental rights to personal integrity and privacy. In *Lebach* (1973) the court sought to balance freedom of broadcasting against a prisoner's interest in the restoration of his character and reputation. In *Böll* (1980; no. 8.11) the court was called upon to engage in a related analysis and to return to the problem — treated earlier in this chapter — of separating truth from falsehood in the hurly-burly of politics. (Compare these cases with *Eppler* [no. 7.5; decided in 1976].)

8.10 Lebach Case (1973)
35 BVerfGE 202

[The complainant participated in an armed robbery of a German armed forces barracks in the course of which several soldiers on guard duty were killed or severely wounded. After his arrest and conviction as an accessory, he was sentenced to six years' imprisonment. The crime and trial of the defendants attracted considerable public attention. Some years later, several months before the complainant was to be released from prison, a German television station planned to run a documentary play based on the crime. The program would display Lebach's photograph, use his name, and make reference to his homosexual tendencies. The complainant sought an injunction prohibiting the television company from broadcasting the play. Citing the broadcasting freedom provision of Article 5, the Superior Court of Mainz dismissed the case. After weighing the interests of the complainant in the light of constitutional standards, the Koblenz Court of Appeals sustained the dismissal. Claiming that his right of personality under Article 2 was being infringed, the complainant filed a constitutional complaint against the decisions.]

Judgment of the First Senate. . . .

B. II. In the present case the court of appeals has held correctly that several fundamental rights affect the application of private law and that they pull in opposite directions. The right to one's personality guaranteed by Article 2 (1) in conjunction with Article 1 (1) of the Basic Law conflicts with the freedom of broadcasting stations to provide information under Article 5 (1) [2] of the Basic Law.

1. On the one hand, a televised broadcast of the kind at issue concerning the origin, execution, and detection of a crime which mentions the name of the criminal and contains a representation of his likeness necessarily touches the area of his fundamental rights guaranteed by Article 2 (1) in conjunction with Article 1 (1) of the Basic Law. The rights to the free development of one's personality and human

dignity secure for everyone an autonomous sphere in which to shape one's private life by developing and protecting one's individuality. This includes the right to remain alone, to be oneself within this sphere, and to exclude the intrusion of or the inspection by others. It also encompasses the right to one's own likeness and utterances, especially the right to decide what to do with pictures of oneself. In principle, everyone has the right to determine for himself whether and to what extent others may make public an account of either certain incidents from his life or his entire life story.

The decisions of the Federal Constitutional Court have not, however, extended the absolute protection of the above-mentioned fundamental rights to the entire sphere of private life. If an individual as a member of a community enters into relations with others, influences others by his existence or behavior, and thereby impinges upon the personal sphere of other people or upon the interests of communal life, his exclusive right to be master of his own private sphere may become subject to restrictions unless his inviolable, innermost sphere of life is involved. Any such social involvement, if sufficiently strong, may justify measures taken by public authorities in the interest of the public as a whole; for example, publishing pictures of a suspect in order to facilitate a criminal investigation. However, neither the state's interest in solving crimes nor any other public interest invariably justifies an infringement of the personal sphere. Instead, the preeminent importance of the right freely to develop and [command] respect for the personality, closely connected with the supreme constitutional value of human dignity, demands that any encroachment upon the right to personality which may appear necessary always be balanced against the protective rule laid down in Article 2 (1) in conjunction with Article 1 (1) of the Basic Law. . . .

III. 2. . . . In resolving the conflict [between the freedom to broadcast and the right of personality, one] must remember that . . . both constitutional concerns are essential aspects of the free democratic order of the Basic Law, the result being that neither can claim precedence in principle. . . . In case of conflict [the court] must adjust both constitutional values, if possible; if this cannot be achieved, [the court] must determine which interest will defer to the other in the light of the nature of the case and [its] special circumstances. In so doing, the [court] must consider both constitutional values in their relation to human dignity as the nucleus of the Constitution's value system. Accordingly, the freedom to broadcast may have the effect of restricting claims based on the right to personality; however, any damage to "personality" resulting from a public broadcast may not be disproportionate to the significance of the publication to free communication. . . . [The court must also consider] the extent to which the [legitimate] interest served by the broadcast can be satisfied without such a far-reaching invasion of the intimate sphere.

IV. 1. In the light of these general principles the following criteria are constitutionally relevant in assessing televised broadcasts of the kind involved here.

(a) A public report of a crime in which the name, likeness, or representation of the accused is provided will always constitute a severe intrusion into his intimate sphere, given that it publicizes his misdeeds and conveys a negative image of his person in the eyes of the public. . . .

2. On the other hand, weighty considerations suggest that the public should be fully informed of the commission of crimes, including the identity of the accused and the events which led to the act. Crimes are also part of contemporary history, the presentation of which is the quintessential task of the media. . . .

3. In balancing these interests, . . . the public interest in receiving information must generally prevail when current crimes are being reported. If someone breaches the peace by attacking or injuring fellow citizens or the legally protected interests of the community, he must not only suffer the criminal punishment provided by the law; he must also accept, as a matter of principle, that in a community committed to freedom of communication the public has an interest in receiving information through normal channels about a [criminal] act he himself caused. . . .

However, the interest in receiving information is not absolute. The central importance of the right to personality requires not only vigilance on behalf of the inviolable, innermost personal sphere [of the accused] but also a strict regard for the principle of proportionality. The invasion of the personal sphere is limited to the need to satisfy adequately the [public's] interest in receiving information, while the harm inflicted upon the accused must be proportional to the seriousness of the offense or to its importance otherwise for the public. Consequently, it is not always permissible to disclose the name, release a picture, or use some other means of identifying the perpetrator. . . .

4. The radiating effect of the constitutional guarantee of the right of personality does not, however, permit the media, over and above reporting on contemporary events, to intrude indefinitely upon the person and private sphere of the criminal. Instead, when the public's interest in receiving current information [about the crime] has been satisfied, the criminal's right to be left alone increases in importance, [thus] limiting the extent to which the media and the public may convert the individual sphere of his life into an object of discussion or entertainment. . . . Once a criminal court has prosecuted and convicted a defendant for an act that has attracted public attention, and he has experienced the just reaction of the community, any further or repeated invasion of the criminal's personal sphere cannot normally be justified.

5 (a) [We] cannot generally and precisely state when the legitimate reporting of current events loses its [contemporary vitality] and is thus no longer a permissible subject of [public] discussion. . . . The decisive criterion is whether the report in question is likely to inflict upon the criminal new or additional harm, compared with information that is already available.

(b) [Courts] may treat the criminal's interest in rehabilitation or in recovering his position in society as a decisive factor in determining the limits on broadcasting. . . .

(e) In any case, a televised report concerning a serious crime that is no longer justified by the public's interest in receiving information about current events may not be rebroadcast if it endangers the social rehabilitation of the criminal. The criminal's vital interest in being reintegrated into society and the interest of the community in restoring him to his social position must generally have precedence over the public's interest in a further discussion of the crime. . . .

V. 2. A proper assessment of the relevant constitutional provisions involved in this case leads us to the conclusion that the petition of the complainant must prevail.

NOTE: THE CONSTITUTIONALIZATION OF PRIVATE LAW. The topical organization of the cases in this chapter may obscure the significance of an important doctrinal development in German constitutional law. If the cases were organized chronologically and listed with the cases discussed in the section on the right to personality in Chapter 7, they would show an enormous expansion in the 1970s of the right to personal development, a trend that continued into the next decade,[94] reaching its peak in the *Census Act* case of 1983 (no. 7.6). In this respect the Constitutional Court followed the lead of the Federal High Court of Justice. The latter, in an early decision, imported a new right of personality into section 823 of the Civil Code,[95] a creation prompted by the Basic Law's provisions on human dignity and personality. The constitutional reach of these concepts increased steadily over the years, often defeating claims based on freedom of speech and press. *Mephisto* (1971) was an expression of the Federal Constitutional Court's deference to private-law values. *Princess Soraya* (1973) and *Lebach* (1973), in what has been described as "a somewhat strained — but in any event successful — interpretation of the [Bonn] Constitution,"[96] carried such deference to new heights. The *Böll* case (1980), reprinted below, reaffirmed the influence of constitutional values on the law dealing with defamation and privacy.

A similar interaction between private law and constitutional law has taken place in the United States. The Supreme Court, however, has tended to defend free speech at the expense of private-law values such as reputation and privacy. As B. S. Markesinis has suggested, German decisions "and indeed the [personality clause of Article 2] can only be fully understood if one bears in mind the utter contempt shown towards human dignity by the Nazi regime."[97] In *Princess Soraya* — a decision that endorsed the Federal High Court's expansive interpretation of the Civil Code — the Federal Constitutional Court said:

> The personality and dignity of an individual, to be freely enjoyed and developed within a societal and communal framework, stand at the very center of

the value order reflected in the fundamental rights protected by the Constitution. Thus an individual's interest in his personality and dignity must be respected, and must be protected by all organs of the state (see Articles 1 and 2 of the Constitution). Such protection should be extended, above all, to a person's private sphere; i.e., the sphere in which he desires to be left alone, to make . . . his own decisions, and to remain free from any outside interference. Within the area of private law such protection is provided, *inter alia,* by the legal rules relating to the general right of personality.[98]

Accordingly, the court sustained a monetary damage award against a newspaper for violating the personality rights of a prominent socialite (see case no. 4.2).[99]

8.11 Böll Case (1980)
54 BVerfGE 208

[Heinrich Böll, a renowned author, brought suit against a well-known commentator for remarks made about him in a television editorial on the occasion of the funeral of the president of the Berlin Court of Appeals, who had been murdered by terrorists. The commentator lamented the political climate in Germany and complained about the attitude of intellectuals and politicians toward the problem of terrorism. In the course of his remarks he singled out Böll, accusing him of having laid the groundwork for political terrorism. He quoted Böll as having characterized the state against which the terrorists were fighting as a "dung heap defended with ratlike rage by the remnants of rotten power." Böll sued for damages in the civil courts, alleging a violation of his honor. He argued that the quotations were false, or so ripped from context as to give them a meaning he had never intended. He won his damage suit in a lower court, but the judgment was quashed by the Federal High Court of Justice. That court concluded that while the quotation was incorrect, the commentary was justified as a reasonable interpretation of the author's past statements and was thus within the protection of the free speech provisions of Article 5. Invoking his right to personal integrity guaranteed by the dignity and personality clauses of the Basic Law, Böll brought this constitutional complaint against the High Court's denial of his claim.]

Judgment of the First Senate. . . .

B. The constitutional complaint is valid.

II. The challenged decision violates Article 2 (1) in tandem with Article 1 (1) of the Basic Law; the form and manner in which the controversial statement of the complainant was reproduced in the [television] commentary is not protected by the free speech provisions of Article 5.

1. (a) The attacks upon the complainant in the commentary were of such a nature as to impair his constitutionally guaranteed general right to an intimate sphere. Among other things this right includes personal honor and the right to one's own words; it also protects the bearer of these rights against having statements attributed to him which he did not make and which impair his self-defined claim to social recognition.

The individual may also invoke his right to personality to the extent that his statements are falsified, distorted, or rendered inaccurate. . . . As the Federal High Court of Justice explained, a quotation does not involve the discussion of the critic's subjective opinion but rather a fact for which the person being criticized must be held accountable. For this reason a quotation used as evidence of criticism is an especially potent weapon in the battle of opinions: Unlike the easily recognizable expression of an opinion, this particular quotation is perceived as a fact, with the same power [of a fact] to convince and persuade. If the quotation is incorrect, distorted, or false, then it encroaches that much more upon the speaker's right to an intimate sphere, because he is thus led onto the battlefield as a witness against himself.

(b) The [news] commentator's opinion that the complainant sympathized with those who perpetrated terrorist acts is a public disparagement of the complainant and an attack on his personal honor. The attack is particularly serious because it is based on a direct quotation. If the defendant falsely claimed, as charged, that the complainant described the state as a "dung heap," then he violated [the author's] general right to an intimate sphere as well as assaulting his personal honor. The same is true if the complainant's statements were presented in an altered form. The Federal High Court rightly states that one may not allow criticism to seep into one's citation so as to distort the content of what the speaker actually said. To do so is a violation of the speaker's right to his own words and the [correlative] right to determine how he will present himself to another person or to the public. . . .

2. (a) . . . Because value judgments are so much at issue in public discussion, freedom of speech must be allowed in the interest of furthering the formation of public opinion and without regard to the content of individual judgments [citing the *Lüth* case]. But this protection does not extend to false statements of fact. Incorrect information does not merit protection under the rubric of freedom of opinion, because it does not contribute to the constitutionally guaranteed process of forming public opinion [citing the *Schmid-Spiegel* case]; [on the other hand], the duty to tell the truth cannot be enforced in such a way as to jeopardize the process of forming public opinion. An exaggerated emphasis upon the duty to tell the truth, with the consequent levying of burdensome sanctions, could restrict and even cripple the media by preventing them, because of the unreasonable risks involved, from fulfilling their function, particularly in serving as a public check against government abuses. But neither democracy nor the task of forming public opinion will suffer if the media are required to quote [someone] correctly. Indeed, the task of providing

information in the interest of forming public opinion will not be fulfilled in the absence of the duty to report correctly and accurately. The pressures of time and the difficulties of proof do not play the significant role here [where quotations are concerned] as might be the case with other statements of fact. One who transmits a statement is not substantially or unreasonably burdened by the obligation to quote someone correctly. Thus, if by a misquotation one impairs another's general right to personality, this misdeed is not protected under Article 5 (1) of the Basic Law. Otherwise the media would have a license to treat the truth lightly and to ignore without cause or necessity the rights of the party involved.

(b) To be sure, the courts may find it difficult in particular cases to be certain whether a [quoted] statement is properly rendered. The test applied by the Federal High Court is constitutionally doubtful; i.e., how the average reader or listener understands both the statement of the person criticized and the quotation, and whether he also judges as correct a quotation that follows some other plausible meaning of the statement within the standard of evaluation used [by the commentator]. This standard would protect a broad spectrum of possible meanings even though they do not correspond to the actual intent of the speaker. Thus [the media] could present to the reader or listener statements clearly objectionable by the customary principles of correct quotation as statements of the person being criticized with the corresponding appearance of truth and objectivity. . . . In any event, the constitutional right of free speech does not justify presenting one interpretation of a complex statement made by the person criticized as if it were a direct quotation without making it clear that this is only the critic's interpretation.

[The court next turned to a brief discussion of the relationship between the freedoms of expression and an intimate sphere.] The use of a direct quotation as proof of a critical evaluation is, as indicated, a particularly sharp weapon in the battle of opinions and very effective in undermining the personality right of the person being criticized. This is especially true with regard to criticism in the press, radio, and television, for the effects here are far-reaching. To rule out any possibility of invading the personality right in these situations, the person quoting someone else is duty-bound to make it clear that he is employing his own interpretation of a statement open to several interpretations. The statement would then be placed in proper context; namely, out of the realm of fact and into that of opinion, where it belongs. The listener or reader would then be able to recognize that what is quoted is a statement of opinion, and not the communication of a fact. He will then be accurately informed and have a reliable basis for making up his own mind.

Article 5 (1) does not alter the duty to protect the right of personality. [Further], there is no evidence that requiring a journalist to state clearly when he is presenting an exact repetition of an interpretation will restrict the flow of public information or impair the process of freely forming public opinion, or that the freedom to make public criticism would be unduly hampered. . . . To this extent the commentator was required to make clear that he was only giving his interpretation.

Instead, he conveyed the impression that he reproduced the complainant's unequiv-ocal statement. Article 5 (1) does not protect either the form or manner of this reproduction. . . .

NOTE: BALANCING SPEECH AND PERSONALITY. In the *Deutschland Magazine* case (1976),[100] the Constitutional Court served notice that it would intensify its scrutiny of lower court balancing in cases of conflict between speech interests and values protected by private law (i.e., the Civil Code). Under the *Deutschland* test, a serious invasion of speech resulting from a lower court judgment would invite heightened judicial scrutiny of that judgment. In the 1980s, however, the Constitutional Court tended to view with equal gravity serious invasions of the constitutional values of human dignity (Article 1) and personality (Article 2). *Lebach* foreshadowed this tendency. Even though the complainant had projected himself into public view, creating a newsworthy event by his criminal activity, his interest in privacy increased as his public profile receded. *Mephisto* extended the same protection to a deceased public figure. In both cases the court resolved, in acts of delicate and sensitive balancing, the tension between the values of personality (Article 2) and speech (Article 5) in favor of personality. *Mephisto* elicited a strong rebuke from Justice Rupp-von Brünneck (see no. 8.12), who felt that the court was woefully inattentive to the importance of speech in a democratic society.[101]

The *Böll* case seemed actually to enhance the importance of personality under the Basic Law. *Böll* differed from *Mephisto, Deutschland Magazine, Lüth,* and other cases because, as Peter Quint has noted, the constitutional complaint was lodged not against a court-imposed penalty but against the failure of the court, on free speech grounds, to impose a penalty.[102] The First Senate regarded this failure as a serious threat to the right of personality that called for heightened judicial review. The novelty of *Böll* consists in the Constitutional Court's declaration that the Fed-eral High Court's reversal of the damage award constituted a serious threat to Böll's right of personality within the meaning of Articles 1 and 2 of the Basic Law.

The *Wallraff* case (1984) followed the judicial approach employed in *Böll*.[103] Reflecting an elevated scrutiny that would increasingly characterize the court's deci-sional approach in the late 1980s and 1990s, the First Senate engaged in a careful and sensitive examination of the facts and circumstances of the case. The conflict here was between competing claims under Article 5 (1). In this libel action the ultracon-servative newspaper *Bildzeitung* sued Wallraff, an investigative reporter, for publish-ing damaging information about *Bild*'s editorial practices, information that he had collected while working for the newspaper under an assumed name. Lower courts sustained Wallraff's free speech claim in light of the importance of the newspaper's shady practices. In the circumstances of this case, however, the First Senate placed a higher value on editorial confidentiality, which it regarded as an important element of a free press.[104] The balancing process engaged in here has lately resulted in frequent victories for freedom of speech and press, particularly when the subject of the utterance is an important matter of public policy.[105]

NOTE: FREEDOM OF OPINION AND PERSONAL HONOR: A RECAPITULATION. When *Lüth* and *Mephisto* are considered in tandem with more recent cases such as *Tucholsky* and *Holocaust Denial,* we can discern the outline of the court's prevailing approach to free speech analysis. First, the value of personal honor always trumps the right to utter untrue statements of fact made with knowledge of their falsity. If, on the other hand, untrue statements are made about a person after an effort was made to check for accuracy, the court will balance the conflicting rights and decide accordingly. Second, if true statements of fact invade the intimate personal sphere of an individual, the right to personal honor trumps freedom of speech. But if such truths implicate the social sphere, the court once again resorts to balancing. Finally, if the expression of an opinion—as opposed to fact—constitutes a serious affront to the dignity of a person, the value of personal honor triumphs over speech. But if the damage to reputation is slight, then again the outcome of the case will depend on careful judicial balancing.[106]

NOTE: FREEDOM OF EXPRESSION AND PORNOGRAPHY. German constitutional law has largely bypassed the thorny ground of pornography, avoiding the dilemmas of American jurisprudence with its tangle of rules and standards. The problems involved in the regulation of pornography in Germany are both simpler and more complicated than in the United States: simpler because Article 5 (2) allows for the limitation of the right to free expression "in the provisions of general laws, in statutory provisions for the protection of youth, and in the right to respect for personal honor"; more complicated because Article 5 (1) extends the right of free expression to writing and pictures. The Federal Constitutional Court, however, has never challenged the right of the legislature to regulate pornography.[107] Most such regulation has aimed at the protection of youth.[108]

Before 1974, West German pornography laws virtually outlawed commercial pornography. These laws were challenged in several state courts and sustained. In 1974, the legislature liberalized antipornography laws on its own initiative, and the making and sale of most "hard-core" pornography became legal. The new law did prohibit the sale of pornography to minors; the public display, broadcasting, or unsolicited mailing of advertisements containing pornography (as a way of protecting the rights of those who do not wish to be confronted with pornography); and the production and sale of pornography involving sexual violence, children, and depictions of sex between humans and animals. The first prohibition, intended to prevent children's exposure to pornography, entailed the prohibition of the distribution of pornography through the mails or in general movie theaters, since effective age control of patrons is virtually impossible in these areas. Pornography is similarly regulated under provisions of the Act on the Dissemination of Publications

Posing a Danger to Young People.[109] This statute provides for publications deemed dangerous to the morals of children to be listed by the Federal Assessment Office. Materials so listed cannot be distributed to children, disseminated outside business premises, or advertised.

One should note that the German youth protection statute is much broader in its sweep than the American practice of denying protection to material deemed obscene. The German statute is meant to protect children from writings that are "immoral, have a brutalizing effect, encourage violence, crime, or racial hatred, and those which glorify war." Thus German courts have largely ignored the problem of defining obscenity. Rather, in the course of statutory interpretation, German judges have developed a concept of pornography that views it in the light of the Basic Law's primary injunction to protect human dignity. In a case that centered on the infamous *Fanny Hill,* the Federal High Court (Bundesgerichtshof) declined to pronounce the book pornographic since it presented sexuality in the broader context of human life. Rather than deploying a subjective standard that attempts to determine the extent to which a particular work offends the viewer or reader,[110] the German court analyzed the presentation of sexuality in its human context. Mathias Reimann summarized the characteristically Kantian German approach:

> The Court essentially asks whether the material presents the characters truly as human beings with a value in and of themselves. If the material does, the Court will find the sexual explicitness acceptable because sex forms a natural part of life. If, on the other hand, the material basically employs its characters only as objects for other purposes, notably sexual stimulation, the Court will find the depiction of sex unacceptable because the work treats the characters not as humans, but only as objects. Such a work denies the characters their human individuality and personhood. The approach of the German Court thus concerns itself not with the viewer's prurient interest but — ultimately — with human dignity.[111]

The regulation of pornography, then — whether done under the limited provisions of the criminal law or the somewhat broader provisions of the youth protection statute — is, like so much else in German constitutional law, centered on the protection of dignity under Article 1.

The *Mutzenbacher* case,[112] decided in 1990, illustrates these general principles as well as an increasing judicial commitment to freedom of expression. *Mutzenbacher,* which anticipates the materials in the next section on artistic expression, overruled a Federal Administrative Court decision sustaining a ban on the pornographic novel, *Josefine Mutzenbacher — The Life of a Viennese Prostitute as Told by Herself.* The First Senate overturned the ban because the administrative court had inadequately considered the book's artistic merit. Article 5 (3) protects artistic expression. Unlike Article 5 (1), this provision is not subject to a reservation clause and thus can be limited only by competing constitutional values. These competing values are to be found in the human dignity (Article 1 [1]) and personality (Article 2 [1]) clauses of the Basic Law as well as in Article 6 (2), which affirms the natural right of parents to the care and upbringing of their children and includes, according to the court, "the right to determine what children can and cannot read."[113] The court rejected the complainant's view that government must base its judgment on empirical proof that certain publications are harmful to youth; in view of the lack of consensus in this area, value judgments are inevitable and permissible. On the other hand, the court noted that "pornography and art are not mutually exclusive," and it can be plausibly argued that the disputed novel, while containing graphic descriptions of sexual encounters, is a work of art.[114]

As the materials in the next section show, artistic expression is subject to regulation. At the same time, however, artistic expression warrants a heavy presumption in its favor. Accordingly, lower courts are not at liberty to ignore the artistic merits of a creative work in deciding whether it has been validly indexed under the Youth Protection Act. According to the court, when such "artistic expression collides with other constitutional rights, the merits of both must be appropriately weighed in an effort to achieve an optimal compromise between them."[115] The lower administrative courts were found to have erred in failing to follow this interpretive principle of concordance. There is even some suggestion in the case that the lower courts failed sufficiently to consider whether in banning *Mutzenbacher* the government had interfered with the right of parents under Article 6 to monitor the reading habits of their children.[116]

ARTISTIC AND ACADEMIC FREEDOM

The ancestry of the rights guaranteed in Article 5 (3) of the Basic Law can be traced to the Constitution of 1849. The Frankfurt Parliament, heavily influenced by professors and intellectuals,[117] declared in Article 152 of its abortive constitution that "the teaching of art and science is free." Article 142 of the Weimar Constitution reinforced this declaration: "The state guarantees the protection and support of research and scholarship." Article 5 (3) of the Basic Law similarly proclaims that "art and learning, research and teaching are free," with the proviso that "freedom of teaching shall not absolve [one] from loyalty to the Constitution." These provisions express the traditional view of the German university as an autonomous institution of public life organized primarily to train an intellectual elite for service to the state.[118]

Article 5 (3) has been the subject of considerable commentary and litigation in the Federal Republic.[119] The litigation has arisen in various administrative tribunals and has raised issues ranging from whether, in the light of the objective nature of the right, an artist or scholar is entitled to affirmative state support of his activities, to whether, under the subjective aspect of the right, a university professor can be forced out of his chair when he reaches the age of retirement. The commentators and courts are united in their opinion that the state may not constitutionally use its power or influence to favor one art form over another, but it does have a positive duty to preserve an environment in which art and science can flourish. The constitutional view is that all plants in the garden of art and science must be given an equal chance to blossom.[120] The posture of the state must also be one of neutrality toward competing notions of art. Yet, as the *Mephisto* case demonstrates, this neutrality does not relieve the courts of the duty to distinguish between art and nonart in certain situations.

8.12 Mephisto Case (1971)
30 BVerfGE 173

[For the facts of the *Mephisto* case, see Chapter 7, case no. 7.2. In the opening extract, which follows, the court focused on the essential meaning of Article 5, emphasizing the independent and autonomous character of the right to artistic expression.]

―――――――――

Judgment of the First Senate. . . .

C. III. . . . First, Article 5 (3) [1] contains an objective norm that determines values and regulates the relationship between the realm of art and the state. At the same time this provision guarantees every person active in this sphere an individual right to freedom.

    1. . . . The essential characteristic of artistic activity is the artist's free and creative shaping of impressions, experiences, and events for direct display through a specific language of shapes. . . .

    2. . . . Even if the artist describes actual occurrences, this reality is "poeticized" in a work of art. The real event is detached from empirical historical reality and brought into a new context that is governed . . . by artistic rules of graphic description. The truthfulness of an individual event can and sometimes must be sacrificed to artistic uniformity. The essence and purpose of the basic right contained in Article 5 (3) [1] are to keep free from state interference those processes, modes of behavior, and decisions based on the inherent laws of art and determined by aesthetic considerations. If the process of artistic creation is to develop freely, then [the state] may not prescribe how an artist should encounter reality and describe this event. Only the artist himself can decide the rightness of his way of portraying reality. In this respect the guarantee of artistic freedom constitutes a prohibition against influencing methods, contents, and tendencies of artistic activity, and in particular against restricting the sphere of artistic creativity or prescribing generally binding rules for this creative process. For the narrative work of art, the constitutional guarantee includes free choice of subject and free presentation of that subject. . . .

3. Article 5 (3) [1] comprehensively guarantees freedom of artistic activity. To the extent that the publishing media are needed to establish relations between the artist and the public, the guarantee of artistic freedom also protects these intermediaries. . . . The complainant, as the publisher of the novel, can therefore rely on the basic right derived from Article 5 (3) [1]. . . .

4. Article 5 guarantees autonomy of the arts without reservation. In view of the unambiguous text of Article 5 (3) [1], [one] may not restrict this guarantee by narrowing the concept of art on evaluative grounds, broadly interpreting other restrictive clauses in constitutional provisions, or analogizing restrictive clauses to the case of [artistic freedom].

5. On the other hand, the right of artistic liberty is not unlimited. Like all basic rights, the guarantee of liberty in Article 5 (3) [1] is based on the Basic Law's image of man as an autonomous person developing freely within the social community. But the unconditional nature of [this] basic right means that limits on artistic freedom can be determined only by the Constitution itself. Since freedom of the arts does not grant the legislature the authority to restrict this right, this freedom may not be curtailed either by the general legal system or [by] an indefinite clause that permits [limitations on artistic expression] if values necessary for the existence of a national community are endangered. [Courts] must resolve a conflict involving artistic freedom by interpreting the Constitution according to the value order established in the Basic Law and the unity of its fundamental system of values. Freedom of the arts is closely related to the dignity of man, guaranteed in Article 1, which, as the supreme value, governs the entire value system of the Basic Law. Nonetheless, the guarantee of freedom of the arts may conflict with the latter constitutionally protected sphere because a work of art can also produce social effects. Because a work of art acts not only as an aesthetic reality but also exists in the social world, an artist's use of personal data about people in his environment can affect their social rights to respect and esteem. . . .

6. The courts properly referred to Article 1 (1) of the Basic Law in judging the protective effects arising from the personality sphere of the late actor Gründgens. It would be inconsistent with the constitutionally guaranteed right of the inviolability of human dignity, which forms the basis for all basic rights, if a person . . . could be degraded or debased even after his death. Accordingly, the obligation which Article 1 (1) imposes on all state authority to protect the individual against attacks on his dignity does not end with death. . . .

[The conflict in this case is between two constitutional rights: artistic freedom (Article 5 (3) [1]) and human dignity (Article 1 [1]). The courts below resolved the conflict in favor of Gründgens and against the publisher. On review, the First Senate held firm to its standard approach: It would not disturb the result below if the lower courts had properly assessed the importance of the basic rights in conflict. In the majority's view, these tribunals had not only attached the proper significance to the values of human dignity and artistic freedom, they also had engaged in a meticulous examination of the facts and laws applicable to the case in the light of constitutional values. Justices Stein and Rupp-von Brünneck, dissenting separately, rejected the majority's deferential approach. They argued that the court should have examined the facts for itself to ensure a result consistent with the Constitution's value hierarchy. They also maintained that the court had failed to adequately define the scope of artistic freedom.]

Justice Stein, dissenting:

II. 1. The required weighing of interests . . . must correspond in all respects to the Constitution's value decisions. If the obligatory balancing of interests disregards this specific, constitutionally imposed relationship, as in [the official opinion], freedom of the arts as guaranteed by Article 5 (3) [1] is violated. The evaluation of the interests . . . by the Hamburg Court of Appeals and the Federal High Court of Justice fundamentally misjudged this relationship to art which the Constitution demands. . . .

Neither court sufficiently considered that a work of art . . . has reality not only in the extra-artistic sphere . . . but predominantly on the aesthetic level. The courts one-sidedly considered only tensions in the social sphere and, in so doing, ignored the novel's aesthetic aspect. This one-sided consideration affected the weighing of interests: . . . [T]hey compared the appearance and behavior of the fictitious Hendrik Höfgen with the personality of Gustaf Gründgens solely from the viewpoint of readers who see the novel as reality. . . .

This approach may be appropriate for a documentary or biography. . . . But a novel's artistic intent is not a realistic, truth-oriented description of historical events but rather a substantial, descriptive presentation of material based on the writer's imagination. An evaluation of a novel based solely on the effects that it produces outside its aesthetic existence neglects the specific relationship of art with reality and thus unlawfully restricts the right guaranteed by Article 5. . . .

4. Furthermore, the Federal High Court and the Appeals Court of Hamburg overemphasized the detrimental effects of the novel on the protected sphere of Gustaf Gründgens's personality when they undertook the required balancing of interests. . . .

In this connection one must also consider that the danger of an adverse effect on the protected personal sphere decreases as the memory of the deceased person fades. Although [the courts] emphasized these factors in the challenged decisions, they ignored the fact that general interest in persons like Gustaf Gründgens, who are not part of general contemporary history but became prominent in a narrower field of the public life of their time, decreases more quickly after their deaths, thus diminishing the danger of an identification of Gustaf Gründgens with the novel's character Hendrik Höfgen. . . .

[Justice Rupp-von Brünneck joined Justice Stein's dissent. She pointed out that the court had narrowed its usual standard of review by refusing to balance the conflicting values. In so doing, the court acted in contravention of all its past decisions. But the crux of Justice Rupp-von Brünneck's dissent focused on the lower courts' failure to consider Klaus Mann's position as a member of the resistance to the Nazi regime. Forced to emigrate, Mann used his writing to contribute to the intellectual opposition to the Nazi system. Rupp-von Brünneck maintained that Mann's use of Gründgens as a vehicle through which to address the larger political issue was questionable. She argued, however, that the existing emergency in Germany justified Mann's actions.]

NOTE: *POSTHUMOUS LIBEL* CASE (1993). A German writer authored a scathing review of the work of the deceased author Heinrich Böll in which he made derogatory remarks about Böll's character and personality, remarks later classified as defamatory by a court of law. The complainant alleged that his review was "art" within the meaning of Article 5 (3) and thus insulated against legal action. The Constitutional Court disagreed. A three-judge chamber of the First Senate held that literary reviews are not in themselves works of art and thus fall outside the protection of Article 5 (3). The chamber was following the rule set down in *Mephisto* that even the dead are entitled to honor and respect.[121]

NOTE: THE SCOPE OF ARTISTIC FREEDOM. *Mephisto* remains the seminal case decided under Article 5 (3). It presented the Constitutional Court with its first major opportunity to underscore the unique character of freedom of art and learning. For one thing, Article 5 (3) is independent of the general free speech provisions of Article 5 (1). Indeed, under the Weimar Constitution, the art-and-learning clause was contained in the section on education and schools, and not in the section on fundamental rights. The Constitutional Court has in like manner declined to treat the art-and-learning provision of the Basic Law as a subcategory of free speech, for art, learning, and research are not subject to the reservation clauses of Article 5 (2). Only teaching is a limited right under Article 5 (3); it may not be employed as a vehicle for attacking the Constitution. But as *Mephisto* illustrates, the right to artistic freedom may conflict with the human dignity and personal inviolability clauses of Articles 1 and 2. Any conflict between these rights triggers the usual balancing test that courts are obliged to apply in such cases. In the course of time, as noted in the previous section, the court retreated from this extremely deferential position. In *Street Theater* (1984) the court took an expanded view of artistic freedom, exemplifying its increasing tolerance of hard-hitting political speech during the 1980s.

8.13 Street Theater Case (1984)
67 BVerfGE 213

[During the 1980 federal election campaign, a group of German citizens staged a theatrical procession through the streets of various cities and towns in the Federal Republic. Mockingly portrayed as a procession on behalf of freedom and democracy, the motorcade — joined by pedestrians and a "military band" — consisted of army vehicles, passenger cars, and three black limousines draped with slogans derisive of Christian Democratic campaign themes. The cars and limousines carried black-uniformed members of a "private security police force" and members of a "people's court." The end of the caravan featured a "puppet" show in an open vehicle. A person bearing the likeness of Franz Josef Strauss, the Christian Democratic candidate for chancellor, was seated in the vehicle, alongside his chauffeur and accompanied by masked "party comrades" with the faces of well-known Nazi leaders representing the forces of stupidity, leprosy, fraud, murder, robbery, and suppression. The idea for the procession and the narration accompanying the puppet show were taken directly from Bertolt Brecht's 1947 poem "Der anachronistische Zug oder Freiheit und Democracy," in which these same symbols were used to portray the decadence of certain representative establishment figures responsible for Germany's downfall. The Kempten (Allgäu) District Court fined the person who portrayed Strauss and the organizer of the caravan for defaming the would-be chancellor, a judgment sustained by the Bavarian Supreme Court. The defendants lodged constitutional complaints against both decisions, alleging a violation of artistic freedom under Article 5 (3) of the Basic Law.]

Judgment of the First Senate. . . .

A. 1. 1. In 1947 the poet Bertolt Brecht wrote "Der anachronistische Zug oder Freiheit und Democracy," an imitation of Percy Bysshe Shelley's poem "The Masque of Anarchy: Written on the Occasion of the Massacre in Manchester," composed in 1819–20. Shelley wrote the poem in reaction to the bloody suppression of the workers' rebellion at Peterloo. In his poem Brecht describes a procession across a Germany laid in ruins. The procession follows two standard-bearers with signs entitled "Freedom" and "Democracy." The participants include a pastor who walks beneath a swastika, the upturned corners of which are pasted over to form a cross; a representative of the armaments industry; teachers who advocate the right to teach German youth the virtue of killing; doctors who demand Communists for their experiments; designers of gas chambers; "de-Nazified" officials holding high offices; editors of the *Stormtrooper,* who demand freedom of the press; a judge who acquits everyone of the charge of "Hitlerism"; and "all the good people who suddenly are not responsible for what happened."

In the "Capital [city] of the Movement" six "party members" join the procession: Suppression, Leprosy, Fraud, Stupidity, Murder, and Robbery; they also demand freedom and democracy, described by Brecht in the following way:

> With bony hand upon the whip
> *Suppression* leads the tide
> In armored cart from top to tip
> From industry a gift
>
> All greet, in rusty tank,
> *Leprosy* of sickly skin
> Modestly, the wind to stop
> Wraps bandages to its chin
>
> *Fraud* comes with swaying step
> Great tankard of brew he holds
> For free to sip — a fair exchange
> Your children must be sold
>
> Like a mountain aged, old
> Yet active even so
> *Stupidity* 'mongst the fold
> On *Fraud* its gaze bestows
>
> O'er wagon side it hangs
> Its arm, thus *Murder* joins the spree
> Stretches, contented is the beast,
> Sings: sweet dream of liberty
>
> Though yester's shock disturbs it still
> Drives *Robbery* in full girth
> In Junker's garb for field marshals
> Its lap enfolds the earth
>
> Of these great six every one
> Entrenched and without mercy
> In turn demand to have at once
> Freedom and democracy

2. During the 1980 federal election campaign, this poem by Brecht gave the political opponents of then-chancellor and candidate of the CDU/CSU, the Bavarian minister-president Franz Josef Strauss, an idea for political street theater. . . . While driving across the Federal Republic from September 15 to October 4, 1980, the

participants acted out these scenes and recited the poem in villages and cities along the way. . . .

C. The constitutional complaint is justified. The contested decisions violate the complainant's constitutional rights under Article 5 (3) [1] of the Basic Law.

> [In section I the Constitutional Court set forth again the conditions under which it will rectify the decisions of lower courts. The court asserted the conventional view that its intervention is necessary when the courts below have erred in the interpretation of the significance of a constitutional right. This case, however, involved a criminal penalty and an interpretation of a right unrestrained by a reservation clause. Because of the chilling effect that a criminal penalty could have on artistic freedom, the court declared its readiness not only to review mistakes with respect to a lower court's view of the significance of Article 5 (3) but also to define the substance of this right.]

II. Staging the "anachronistic procession" falls within the protective sphere of the constitutional right to free artistic expression (Article 5 (3) [1]) against which the contested decisions must be measured.

  1. The guarantee of artistic freedom . . . contains an objective, basic norm which controls the relationship between the sphere of "art" and the state. At the same time it guarantees to everyone active in this sphere an individual right to freedom. This provision protects the "creative sphere" of artistic endeavor as well as the presentation and dissemination of a work of art to the general public [citing the *Mephisto* case]. . . .

  2. (a) . . . The fact that art theoreticians cannot agree on objective criteria for measuring art is due to a special characteristic of artistic life: The avant-garde actually seeks to expand the borders of art. . . . An expansive concept of art must guide the [court's deliberations in cases such as this]. . . .

  (b) However, the impossibility of generally defining art will not relieve us of the constitutional duty to protect freedom in the artistic sphere. . . .

  3. (a) The Federal Constitutional Court emphasized as essential to artistic activity the "free creative expression through which the artist conveys impressions, experiences, and events through a specific language of shapes." All artistic endeavors are a "symphony of conscious and unconscious events which cannot be separated rationally." The artistic process is "a combination of intuition, fantasy, and knowledge of art. It is not primarily a form of communication but rather a most direct expression of the individual personality of the artist" [citing *Mephisto*]. Similar attempts at substantive and value-oriented description in legal literature also emphasize the creative characteristics, the expression of personal experiences, and the casting into a specific form, as well as the communicative conveyance of meaning.

  The description of the "anachronistic procession" meets these criteria. There are creative elements not only in Brecht's poem but also in the manner of his imaging technique. [We] consider the poem as well as its presentation sufficiently "formed." [The artwork] should express and directly illustrate general and personal historical experiences with respect to actual political circumstances. . . .

(c) . . . The special form of the street theater described leads [us] to conclude that the spectators are at a distance and clearly realize that they are confronted with "theater." Certainly the poem, which can be interpreted in many ways, becomes more specific in its message as a result of its timely allusions to contemporary events and persons. Yet its message remains ambiguous, particularly because this message is not directly conveyed but again is indirectly composed of various elements. . . .

(d) Therefore, if the performance of the "anachronistic procession" is protected by Article 5 (3) [1] of the Basic Law, then the primarily political intentions of the organizers do not change this [fact]. Even when an artist becomes involved in contemporary events, no binding rules and evaluations may inhibit artistic activity. The area of so-called politically involved art is no exception to this guarantee of freedom.

III. 1. Article 5 (3) of the Basic Law guarantees freedom of art in its autonomy and without limitation. Neither the "triad of limitations" contained in Article 2 (1) nor the limitations of Article 5 (2) restrict this freedom, whether directly or by analogy [citing *Mephisto*]. Only other constitutional provisions protecting an equally valued interest within the constitutional order can directly limit the freedom of artistic expression. This applies expressly to the right of personality protected by Article 2 (1) in conjunction with Article 1 (1) of the Basic Law. However, [courts] may not be content merely to ascertain that an encroachment on the right of personality — here in the form of defamation — has taken place. They must determine whether the right of personality is so seriously compromised that the right to artistic freedom must defer to it. In view of the overriding significance of artistic freedom, a negligible encroachment [on the right of personality] or the mere possibility of an encroachment will not suffice. . . .

2. The district court failed to recognize the constitutional requirements resulting from this [discussion].

(a) Artistic expressions can be interpreted and are in need of interpretation. An indispensable element of this interpretation is that the work of art be viewed in its entirety. One may not take individual parts of the work out of context and examine them separately to see if they merit criminal sanctions. Consequently, the district court contravened the Constitution when it determined that the incriminating events took place outside of the actual performance and concluded that Article 5 (3) [1] did not apply. This determination fails to acknowledge the very practical need for preparations (assembling the procession) and regrouping (events in Kassel). Furthermore, modern theater often includes visible stage preparations as part of its overall artistic concept.

(b) Moreover, the district court failed to see that such an overall view would have permitted several different interpretations. . . .

In any case, the district court impermissibly chose from possible interpretations suggested by the [lower court's] statement of facts (further possibilities appear by no means to be precluded) only the interpretation relevant to criminal law. [The interpretation relating to criminal law] uses the construction of the reasonable passerby and focuses on [the impressions of] a fleeting, naive observer who ignores the "struggle" with the six plagues. This too is a violation of Article 5 (3) [1] of the Basic Law.

3. The contested decisions are based on these errors. [We] cannot preclude the possibility that the courts would have decided differently had they observed the constitutional requirements set forth [in this opinion]. Therefore we set aside the decisions and remand them to the district court. The court must consider the principles discussed in this decision relating to the relationship between the freedom of artistic expression and the general right to personality when it reconsiders this case.

NOTE: THE *POLITICAL SATIRE, FLAG DESECRATION,* AND *NATIONAL ANTHEM* CASES. In *Political Satire* (1987),[122] unlike *Street Theater,* the First Senate found the gravity of the offense sufficient to overcome any claim based on artistic freedom. Franz Josef Strauss was again the victim of a savage caricature. The magazine *Concrete* portrayed him pictorially as a sexually active pig copulating with another pig in judicial robes. The captions accompanying the sketches, like the sketches themselves, were unambiguously directed against the intimate sphere and political integrity of Bavaria's minister-president. A lower court convicted the accused of an "insult" within the meaning of section 185 of the German Penal Code, a decision that was sustained by the Hamburg Court of Appeals and against which *Concrete* filed a constitutional complaint alleging a violation of Article 5.

Resting its argument heavily on *Street Theater,* the First Senate held that the portrayals involved here did indeed constitute art within the meaning of Article 5 (3) [1], but a legitimate artwork may offend the value of human dignity if it constitutes a serious encroachment on the personal honor of a particular individual. The court recognized that gross exaggeration of personal features and foibles exceeds the boundaries of fair criticism, but satire in this vein may not be punished by statutory law. It may, however, offend a constitutional value of equal rank, such as human dignity, in which event the lower courts are to balance the competing interests of dignity and speech in the light of their ranking within the hierarchy of constitutional values and against the backdrop of all the circumstances. In the instant case, ruled the Federal Constitutional Court, the lower courts had adequately engaged in this balancing process.[123]

In the *Flag Desecration* case (1990),[124] which may be compared with the American case of *Texas* v. *Johnson,*[125] the Constitutional Court struck the balance in favor of freedom of art. Here, however, a book distributor had sold copies of a work entitled *Just Leave Me in Peace,* a compilation of antimilitary prose and poetry. The back cover of the book contained a photomontage depicting a soldier urinating on the spread-out flag of the Federal Republic. The book distributor's conviction was based on section 90a of the Criminal Code, which punishes the "disparagement of the colors, flag, coat of arms, or anthem of the Federal Republic of Germany or one of its regional states." A lower court fined the defendant DM 4,500, a judgment he assailed in a complaint before the Federal Constitutional Court.

The First Senate ruled that the drawing constituted "artistic freedom" within the meaning of Article 5 (3). This being the case, only a high-ranking value of the Basic Law itself, not a statute, could trump the claimed freedom. The protection of the flag as a state symbol, said the court, does not derive its legitimacy exclusively from Article 22 of the Basic Law, which merely specifies its colors. Yet the flag is "an important integration device," and its "disparagement can thus impair the necessary authority of the state." Nevertheless, the protection that law accords to state symbols cannot insulate the state against criticism or disapproval. In any event, the court found that the drawing in question did not constitute disparagement of the flag within the meaning of section 90a but was rather a satirical attack on German militarism. Taken as a whole, the montage was actually directed against "the governmental ceremony for the swearing in of soldiers," and the state was "the target of attack only because of its responsibility for instituting military service and conferring special legitimation on this process by the use of the [state's] symbols."[126] In this context, artistic freedom was too important a value to be overridden by a criminal prosecution.

National Anthem, finally, is of a piece with *Flag Desecration.* The editor of magazine *Plärrer,* published a scornful version of the national anthem. One of its verses read:

> German Turks and German Pershings
> German Big Macs, German punk
> Should maintain their familiar ring
> Throughout the entire world
> German cola, German peepshows
> Should inspire us to noble acts
> All throughout our entire lives.[127]

In this case, too, the court held that the satirical verses, in terms of their form and structure, constituted "art" under Article 5 (3). The message communicated, said the court, "takes the form of an altered version of the national anthem in which our lifestyle is transformed into an extremely negative description — into its exact opposite — by means of changing the meter, approximating the phonetics of the original, and alienating the original text."[128] The senate faulted the lower court for ignoring the "expressive core of the satire" captured in "the collection of contradictions between expectation and reality."[129] Punishment for disparaging the anthem is compatible with artistic freedom, the senate concluded, but in balancing the interests here the lower courts failed to give appropriate weight to the value protected by Article 5 (3).

8.14 Group University Case (1973)
35 BVerfGE 79

[In 1971 Lower Saxony changed its system of governance for higher education. The legislature of Lower Saxony conferred extensive rights of codetermination on certain nonprofessional groups within the university who were not entitled to professorial status. At the major universities, for example, including Göttingen University, the academic council was to consist of twenty-four professors, twenty-four research assistants, twenty-four students, and sixteen nonacademic employees. Other collegial bodies within the university were similarly organized. No fewer than 398 professors from Lower Saxony claimed in a constitutional complaint that the new rules of university governance encroached on the freedom of research and teaching in violation of Article 5 (3) [1]. Federal and state education officials filed briefs in support of the statute, while the West German Rectors' Conference and other faculty organizations were arrayed against it. The latter, in alliance with the professoriate, argued that the inclusion of insufficiently qualified persons in the governing councils of the university threatened the faculty's preeminent decision-making authority in the areas of science, research, and teaching. In December 1972 the Constitutional Court (First Senate) presided over three days of oral argument in the case. The six-to-two decision was handed down on May 29, 1973.]

Judgment of the First Senate. . . .

C. The constitutional complaints are justified only in part.

II. 1. The right contained in Article 5 (3) to engage freely in scholarly activity is a right that the state is bound to respect. . . . Everyone engaged in science, research, and teaching . . . enjoys a defensive right against every state encroachment upon the discovery and dissemination of knowledge. . . . The world of scholarship is one of personal and autonomous responsibility for the individual scholar, and the state may not dictate in this realm. Article 5 (3) protects no single conception or theory of scholarship but rather every form of scholarly activity; that is, everything that in content and form can be regarded as a serious and systematic attempt to discover the truth. . . .

2. The fundamental rights provisions of the Basic Law also incorporate an objective order of values. . . . Article 5 (3) contains one such value decision. Its key

function is to guarantee free scholarly activity both in the interest of the individual scholar's self-realization and for the benefit of the entire society. . . . The state is therefore obliged as a civilized nation to defend a system of free scholarly inquiry and to affirmatively provide for an institutional framework in which such inquiry can be carried out. . . .

(a) . . . This command of the Constitution is particularly important because without a satisfactory institutional structure and corresponding financial support, which only the state can provide, scholarly research and teaching in broad areas of scholarship, particularly in the field of natural science, could no longer take place. . . .

(b) [The individual scholar also] has a right to state support, including that of an organizational kind, necessary to adequately safeguard his constitutionally protected sphere of freedom, because only such support enables him to engage in scholarly activity. . . .

III. This does not mean, however, that academic freedom can be achieved only at German universities of a traditional nature or that [the Constitution] prescribes how scholarly activity in universities is to be organized. The legislature has the discretion, within certain limits, to organize universities in conformity with today's social and sociological realities.

[In this part of the opinion the court recounted the history of the German university and its tradition of faculty self-governance. Notwithstanding its increasing dependence on the state and the many changes in university structure wrought by the state in the last two centuries, the Humboldtian principle that research and teaching should remain free of government influence has been a steadfast and sacred pillar of German academic life. The court found the principle of academic self-governance to be rooted in early nineteenth-century university statutes as well as in various national and state constitutions. States reserved the right to oversee the appointment of university professors, noted the court, but this traditional practice seldom interfered with the essential autonomy of the scholarly enterprise or the self-governance of the university.]

IV. 1. Thus, in the area of university organization, the legislature enjoys considerable leeway in shaping university policy. This discretion, however, is driven and limited by the right to freedom secured by Article 5 (3) and the value judgment contained therein. On the basis of these constitutional considerations, we are [obliged] to assess the organizational features of laws dealing with institutions of higher learning by determining whether and to what extent they favor or impede either the basic right of every individual scholar to research and teach freely or the functional capacity of an institution dedicated to "free scholarship" to operate. . . .

V. 1. The "group university" as such is compatible with the value decision of Article 5 (3). In itself it is not "alien to scholarship"; for to allow all members of the university a say [in its affairs] does not necessarily lead to procedures or policies in opposition to freedom of research and teaching. Such a system may serve as a [proper] instrument for the resolution of group conflict in the university and also as a means for mobilizing the expertise of individual groups for the purpose of reaching better decisions in the administration of the university. Whether this system is the most useful form of university organization is not a matter for the Federal Constitutional Court to decide.

(a) The right of academic assistants to a voice in [university affairs] needs no further justification; they are as much entitled to the rights secured by Article 5 (3) with reference to their research activities as university professors. Whether students are constitutionally entitled to participate in academic self-governance need not be decided here. There is, however, no constitutional objection to their having a say in academic administration so long as and to the extent that they are participating in research and teaching. Even though only a relatively small percentage of students may reach a level of active participation in the research process, study at a university is itself nevertheless understood to include such participation. . . .

(b) Neither does the involvement of nonacademic staff in university self-governance conflict basically with the constitutional pledge of academic freedom. . . . This group includes experts whose practical experience can be particularly beneficial in the administrative area of universities. Academic activity at universities is coming to depend on these experts in increasing measure. They create the technical and administrative conditions which make teaching and research possible and carry corresponding responsibility. . . .

2. University professors, however, enjoy a special position in research and teaching. . . . By virtue of their office and commitment they bear a particularly heavy responsibility for the smooth running and academic status of the university. . . . In view of the current structure of the university they hold a key position in academic life. . . .

The state is obliged to keep this special position [of the professoriate] in mind when it shapes the organization of academic administration. This [task] requires due attention to the value decision contained in Article 5 (3) in tandem with the general-equality clause, which [in turn] forbids . . . treating those groups equally which are essentially unequal. . . . The legislature is thus required to confer on the professoriate [that degree of authority and responsibility necessary] to fulfill their scholarly mission in light of the functions of the university. It must ensure an organizational framework that does not allow . . . other groups to hinder or interfere with their free scholarly activity. . . .

3. The legislature, while basically at liberty to prescribe the voting strength of various groups in the decision-making councils of the "group university," must nevertheless consider the special position of university professors and [ensure that their strength is proportionate to their status and functions]. . . .

[The court noted that conflicting interests have made their presence felt within the group university "partly because of the long overdue radical reforms in higher education, responsibility for which must be shared by the universities." Yet, "specialized academic knowledge" must not "be overplayed in reaching decisions on questions of research and teaching in academic decision-making bodies. Professors, students, and staff are all entitled to representation in university governance proportionate to the importance of their respective roles within the university." The court then moved on to define these roles.]

4. Given all of these considerations, [we] cannot deduce that the representatives of university teachers are constitutionally entitled to a "clear majority" on university governing boards. In view of the aforementioned constitutional considerations, [we] see no justification for this limitation of the legislature's creative freedom. . . .

[Teaching]

(a) Where teaching is concerned, it is not only the university teachers who fulfill essential functions but also teaching and research assistants. Granted, their participation in discharging teaching tasks in the modern mass university is not always the same when compared on divisional, departmental, and sectional levels, but their share is nevertheless quantitatively significant and qualitatively important. When dealing with decisions directly affecting teaching, they possess the kind of factual knowledge and interest that readily justifies their rights to codetermination.

Teaching matters also directly affect the interests of students. Moreover, appropriate decisions can often be reached only if the experiences and arguments of both teachers and learners are taken into consideration and settled. There are [thus] no constitutional objections to the participation of student representatives when deciding such issues.

However, the unrestricted participation of nonresearch and nonteaching administrative personnel in decisions pertaining to teaching cannot be justified by any of the aforementioned considerations (i.e., qualifications, functions, responsibilities, and involvement).

The legislature must guarantee that within this framework university teachers retain the degree of influence corresponding to their position in the area of teaching.

[Research]

(b) One must employ stricter criteria when determining the extent of codetermination by various groups in matters pertaining directly to research. Research decisions presuppose the ability to assess the current status of research in a given field and the urgency of an individual research project in the light of social needs, as well as to understand clearly the technical, financial, and personnel possibilities in individual areas of research. The responsibility which issues from such decisions becomes particularly clear when large amounts of money are needed for expensive special facilities required by modern research, or when research facilities are established or expanded. Research assistants cannot be denied the right to cooperate with specialists in making such decisions. As a rule, nonresearch personnel do not possess such qualifications. Neither will the large majority of students possess the qualifications necessary for participation in research decisions. Yet, based on their level of education and qualifications, one cannot completely rule out the fact that students contribute to some extent to these decisions. In view of these circumstances there are therefore no constitutional objections against allowing students a certain degree of codetermination, particularly because decisions affecting research may also have an eventual effect on teaching. Yet the value judgment of Article 5 (3) in conjunction with Article 3 (1) of the Basic Law demands that university teachers retain the privilege of having a decisive influence in decisions pertaining directly to research. Because of their qualifications, functions, and responsibilities, university teachers must be able to prevail against other groups in this special area. . . .

> [The court concluded that in university councils concerned with teaching, professors are constitutionally entitled to at least 50 percent of the votes. In matters pertaining to research, however, the influence of university professors must be "decisive." This means, according to the court, that university professors must have substantially more than 50 percent of the votes so that they can "assert themselves against the combined opposition of other groups."]

Justices Simon and Rupp-von Brünneck, dissenting:

Both the result and the findings of the decision rest largely on consistent constitutional arguments. We specifically share the view that Article 5 (3) embraces a negative right against any concrete state intrusion upon academic freedom. . . . We also agree with the majority in holding that there are significant differences between university groups, and we agree that these groups cannot be leveled on the basis of one person, one vote. On the other hand, we consider it untenable to conclude directly from the Basic Law detailed organizational requirements for the autonomy of the university.

To be sure, the majority opinion concedes that the legislature is not locked into the traditional structure of the university under the Basic Law. . . . Rather, the participation of all members of a university in academic self-government is fundamentally compatible with the Constitution, even in the case of the so-called group university. Furthermore, in this "body of teachers and learners" none of the groups concerned is generally and inherently entitled to a majority position. Nevertheless, the senate majority believes that it must distinguish among the groups who enjoy the constitutional right and confer on one of these groups a privileged position in the form of [giving added] weight to their votes.

As a result of this decision, the Federal Constitutional Court exceeds its function and places itself in the position of the legislature. The senate majority converts the seemingly universally recognized creative freedom of the democratically legit-imized legislature in matters of academic organization into an originally impercepti-ble but, finally, clearly recognizable process of erosion. . . .

II. 1. (b) In our opinion the legislature of the state of Lower Saxony cannot be accused of exceeding its creative discretion in its alleged violation of the aforemen-tioned obligations; for in Lower Saxony, too, university teachers are assured within the realm of their creative activity in the service of the common good a position which is possibly unique when compared with the situation of other groups of society.

CONCLUSION

Freedom of speech enjoys wide protection under the Basic Law, particularly when political speech is implicated. Apart from principles of political obligation that require allegiance to the existing constitutional order, the uncommon protection accorded *political* speech is fully consistent with the Basic Law's commitment to representative democracy and universal suffrage. The general rights to speech and press, however, cannot be interpreted in isolation from other constitutional provi-sions. Article 5 (1) is bound by the reservation clauses in Article 5 (2), but in addition, the principle of the Constitution's unity and its incorporation of a hier-archical order of values, the highest of which is human dignity, compels a contex-tual — that is, systematic — approach to constitutional interpretation. The structures and values prescribed in the Basic Law are numerous and complex, and they result in the delicate balancing that typifies many of the cases featured in this chapter. And yet, when viewed comparatively, the German court's record in defense of freedom of speech, particularly in recent years, easily rivals that of most of the world's advanced constitutional democracies.

9

FREEDOM OF CONSCIENCE

AND RELIGION

The multiplicity of the Basic Law's provisions on church-state relations contrasts sharply with the simple command of the United States Constitution that bars Congress from making any law "respecting an establishment of religion or prohibiting the free exercise thereof." In addition, Article 140 incorporates into the Basic Law Articles 136, 137, 138, 139, and 141 of the Weimar Constitution. The incorporation of these church-state provisions into the Basic Law was a compromise flowing from the inability of the framers to agree on new proposals for regulating the relationship between church and state.[1] All of these provisions — the Weimar articles and the religious clauses of the Basic Law — may be loosely arranged around the notions of "free exercise" and "establishment."

Article 4 is the centerpiece of provisions relating to free exercise. It declares:

    1. Freedom of faith, of conscience, and freedom of creed, religious or ideological [*weltanschaulich*], shall be inviolable.

    2. The undisturbed practice of religion is guaranteed.

    3. No one may be compelled against his conscience to render military service involving the use of arms. Details shall be regulated by federal law.

These clauses underscore the fundamental importance of religious freedom under the Basic Law. Indeed, this particular liberty is undiminished by the reservation clauses that qualify other constitutional rights. By the same token, as the text of the article suggests, religious expression cannot be reduced to an aspect of some other right such as speech (Article 5), association (Article 9), or even personal inviolability (Article 2). Religious expression is speech and association of a *special* kind; it rises above ordinary expression because it deals with the innermost convictions of the human person, and thus it merits special protection under the Basic Law.

Other provisions of the Basic Law prohibit discrimination based on religious belief or association. Article 3 (3) declares that persons may not be favored or disfavored because of their "faith" or "religious opinions." In addition, Article 33 (3), like Weimar's Article 136, confers equal civil and political rights on all Germans and guarantees their equal eligibility for public office and the civil service regardless of "religious affiliation." Another clause in Article 136 bans compulsory disclosure of one's religious convictions or participation in a religious exercise, including the mandatory taking of a religious oath. Finally, Article 56, which contains a reference to God in the oath of office prescribed for the federal president, allows the oath to be taken "without a religious affirmation."

The establishment clauses, on the other hand, embrace a complicated scheme of church-state relations. While including the principle of state neutrality toward religion, these clauses — found mainly in the Weimar articles — accord to organized churches an important role in the nation's public life. Article 137 defines churches as "religious bodies under public law" and clothes them with corporate privileges and rights, including the power to levy taxes for the support of religious activities. The Constitution also provides for religious instruction in the public schools, although most commentators see this practice as a manifestation of the free exercise of religion and a corollary of the constitutional right of parents, rooted in Article 7 (2), to determine whether their children "shall receive religious instruction" in the public schools. The Weimar Constitution's injunction: "There shall be no state church" (Article 137 [1]) is the core the Basic Law's nonestablishment provisions. As other church-state clauses show, however, the meaning of the term "nonestablishment" in Germany differs significantly from its meaning in the United States.[2]

The family relations and school provisions of the Basic Law were designed to protect the institution of marriage and to guarantee certain rights to mothers and children. Article 7 (1) celebrates marriage and the family by placing them under "the special protection of the state." The Basic Law's solicitude for mothers is equally strong, for they too "shall be entitled to the protection and care of the community" (Article 7 [4]). The protection afforded to mothers under the Basic Law, together with the provision that provides illegitimate children "with the same opportunities for their physical and spiritual development as are enjoyed by legitimate children" (Article 7 [5]), was mainly achieved by Social Democrats.[3] Christian Democrats, on the other hand, were mainly responsible for including parental rights in the Basic Law. The most important of these are secured by Articles 6 (2) and 7 (2): the first proclaims that the "care and upbringing of children are the natural right of and a duty primarily incumbent on parents"; and the second secures to parents the right to have their children educated in the faith of their choice.[4]

THE FREE EXERCISE OF RELIGION

Religious tolerance came late to German public life. From the peace of Augsburg in 1555 to the Napoleonic conquest in 1806 the principle *cuius regio, eius religio* governed religious life in Germany. Lessing's plea for religious liberty, powerfully set forth in his *Nathan the Wise* (1779), was drowned out, along with other voices of the German Enlightenment, by floodwaters of religious intolerance that rushed, unabated, far into the nineteenth century. These waters finally receded with the ending of Bismarck's *Kulturkampf* against the Catholic church. Still, during most of the nineteenth century, and indeed until the Weimar Constitution of 1919, ties between church and state were close and religious discrimination was widespread. Lutheranism was effectively the official religion in most of the German states. Although Roman Catholics made up one-third of Germany's population, they were virtually excluded from all high positions in the Reich government, and Jews, despite their uncommon educational attainments, were systematically barred from the public service and the army.[5]

As noted above, Article 4 embraces the principle of religious and ideological freedom as well as the "undisturbed practice" of religion. On first reading, these words and phrases may seem redundant. But freedom of faith (*Freiheit des Glaubens*) in German history has not always implied the freedom corporately to express a creed or, at the individual level, one's inner convictions. In addition, German constitutionalism distinguished historically between the dominant churches (e.g., Catholic, Evangelical, and Reformed) and minor religious sects. Prior to 1848 the right to the public expression of religion was extended mainly to the former.[6] Following the libertarian impulses of the Frankfurt and Weimar constitutions, Article 4 as well as the nondiscriminatory provisions of the Basic Law set out to ensure the protection of all belief systems, religious and ideological.[7]

9.1 Rumpelkammer Case (1968)
24 BVerfGE 236

[A Catholic youth association organized a charitable drive to collect old clothes and other secondhand goods, which were to be sold to obtain money for needy young people in underdeveloped countries. The campaign to collect such goods was announced from the pulpits of Catholic churches and publicized in the press. A scrap dealer engaged in the collection and sale of the same goods and financially hurt by the voluntary drive secured an order from a Düsseldorf superior court prohibiting any further publicity of the drive from the pulpit. The youth association lodged a constitutional complaint against the order, alleging a violation of Article 4 (2), which guarantees the "free exercise of religion."]

Judgment of the First Senate. . . .

III. The constitutional complaint is justified. The challenged decision violates the association's fundamental right to the exercise of freedom of religion (Article 4 [2] of the Basic Law) because the court did not sufficiently consider the scope and significance of this fundamental right in interpreting and applying the concept of "good morals" [within the meaning of section 826 of the Civil Code] to market transactions. . . .

2. (a) The fundamental right to the free exercise of religion (Article 2 [2] of the Basic Law) is included within the concept of freedom of belief. This concept — whether it concerns a religious creed or a belief unrelated to religion — embraces not only the personal freedom to believe or not to believe (i.e., to profess a faith, to keep it secret, to renounce a former belief and uphold another), but also the freedom to worship publicly, to proselytize, and to compete openly with other religions [citing a case]. To this extent the unfettered exercise of religion is merely a component of the freedom to believe accorded to individuals as well as denominational and ideological groups. At least since the Weimar Constitution the right to the free exercise of religion has been merged with freedom of belief. The particular guarantee of the free exercise of religion secured by Article 4 (2) of the Constitution against encroachments by the state can be explained historically. The right originated as a rejection of the disruptions of free religious exercise which occurred under National Socialist rule. The historical development clearly shows that Article 4 (2) also protects the basic rights of associations. Their religious existence and right to engage in public activity are protected in a variety of forms and modes of participation. . . .

Because the "exercise of religion" has central significance for every belief and denomination, this concept must be expansively interpreted vis-à-vis its historical content. In support of this view, religious freedom can no longer be restricted by an express provision of the law, in contrast to Article 135 of the Constitution of the Weimar Republic, nor is it tied to other regulations concerning the relationship of church and state. The right is not subject to forfeiture under Article 18 of the Constitution. Moreover, several other constitutional provisions protect this right (e.g., Articles 3 (3), 33 (3), 7 (3) [3], 7 (2) of the Basic Law; and Article 140 of the Basic Law, which incorporates Articles 136 (3) [1] and 136 (4) of the Weimar Constitution into the Basic Law). The right to free exercise extends not only to Christian churches but also to other religious creeds and ideological associations. This is a consequence of the ideological-religious neutrality to which the state is bound and the principle of equality with respect to churches and denominations. Thus there is no justification for interpreting the freedom to perform the rituals associated with religious beliefs more narrowly than freedom of belief or creed.

Accordingly, the exercise of religion includes not only worship and practices such as the observance of religious customs like Sunday services, church collections, prayers, reception of the sacraments, processions, display of church flags, and the ringing of church bells, but also religious education and ceremonies of nonestablished religions and atheists as well as other expressions of religious and ideological life.

(b) The basic right secured by Article 4 (1) and (2) of the Basic Law is accorded not only to established churches, religious communities, and associations united by a particular creed, but also to associations only partially devoted to fostering the religious or ideological life of their members. It is essential only that the organization be directed toward the attainment of a religious goal. . . .

The complainant association is not organizationally incorporated into the Catholic church, but it is institutionally connected with it. Priests are represented on its board of directors, and diocesan bishops place their stamp of approval on the articles of association. The complainant's goals are also within the sphere of church activities. Its articles of association expressly provide that the association is to serve the living church in its mission of alleviating through material support the spiritual and corporeal needs of people throughout the world. The fundamental right to the free exercise of religion pertains, therefore, to this association.

(c) Collections organized by the complainant for religious motives, including announcements from the pulpit occasioned by the collection, are protected religious activities under Article 4 (2) of the Constitution.

In determining what is to be regarded as the free exercise of religion, we must consider the self-image of the religious or ideological community. Indeed, the state, which [strives to remain] neutral in religious matters, must interpret basic constitutional concepts in terms of neutral, generally applicable viewpoints, and not on the basis of viewpoints associated with a particular confession or creed. However, in a pluralistic society in which the legal order considers the religious or ideological self-image [of the individual] as well as the self-image of those performing rituals associated with a particular belief, the state would violate the independence of ideological associations and their internal freedom to organize accorded by the Constitution if it did not consider the way these associations see themselves when interpreting religious activity resulting from a specific confession or creed.

The Catholic and Evangelical churches view the exercise of religion as encompassing not only the freedom to worship and believe but also the freedom to act on those beliefs in the real world. The active love of neighbor is, according to the New Testament, an essential duty for the Christian and is understood by both Catholic and Evangelical churches as a fundamental religious duty. . . .

. . . It follows from the nature of religious freedom outlined here that a charitable collection has a religious character and may claim the protection of Article 4 (2) of the Constitution only if it meets certain conditions.

Donors must make their contributions to the collection free of charge; the gift must flow from a particular religious attitude or ideology of the donor, whether mercy or love of one's neighbor or an expression of personal commitment to a just and good cause based upon ideological convictions. To church members Christian love is more than a mere social transaction designed to provide the poor and needy with the minimum existence necessary for a life of human dignity. It follows from this characterization that Christian love means caring for the poor within the broad framework of religious consciousness. [Organizers of the clothing collection] must inform donors of the purpose and use of the collected goods to prevent false expectations and deceptive publicity. . . .

(d) The collection organized by the complainant, together with the announcement of the campaign from the pulpit, is within the framework of these general requirements.

The collection of donated articles for the support of the needy is part of the traditional function of the deaconate. The method of sale here envisioned was justified by the facts of the case and reflects the particular relationships involved. Because the donations were intended for the needy overseas, [the association] could better attain the maximum effective assistance through sale of the collected items than through costly transport of articles such as usable clothing. . . .

Further, the contention of the complainant scrap dealer that 90 percent of the textile collectors would have to discontinue their operation as a consequence of such charitable collections is immaterial for the evaluation of the Rumpelkammer project as a religious activity. Complainant association's collection was permissible in scope according to the evaluation of the superior court, which the Federal Constitutional Court found determinative. [Complainant scrap dealer] has not established whether the decline in rag collecting is not traceable to a general change in the economic structure and would have to tolerate even a structural change in this commercial branch. In the free market economy a businessman does not have an absolute constitutional right to the preservation of the level of his business and the assurance of business opportunities.

(e) Because the complainant's collection [of used clothing and secondhand goods] is part of the exercise of religion protected by Article 4 (2) of the Basic Law, the superior court should also have taken into consideration the emanations of this fundamental right in its evaluation of the announcement from the pulpit as an "unethical market transaction."

If the collection itself enjoys special protection because of its religious-charitable purpose and character, that protection also must extend to supporting activities within the framework of normal religious life such as the announcements from the pulpit. . . . Because the collection was conducted within the sphere of protected religious activities, there is no doubt as to the validity of the solicitations. In the interpretation of the concept "unethical" market transaction, the superior court should have recognized that competition between a tradesman and a religious association is much different from competition between solely commercial entities. The religious association bases its activity on the constitutional right to the unfettered exercise of religion, a right more highly valued than the right to compete in the marketplace. In considering the instant fact constellation, the court should not have termed the collection unethical. Insofar as the state court has barred the complainant, the judgment must be reversed. . . .

NOTE: FREE EXERCISE AND ITS REGULATION. Article 4 contains no reservation clause that would allow the regulation of religion by law. It therefore imposes an absolute ban on any law regulating religious belief. Equally absolute is the ban on any direct regulation of the free exercise of religion. Moreover, as *Rumpelkammer* teaches, if freedom of religion is to be rendered an effective right under the Basic Law, its expression cannot be limited to the sanctuary. It manifests itself in social work within the community and other practices in society that represent the expression of religious idealism and commitment.[8] In addition, the guarantee of free exercise applies to individuals as well as to religious communities.

It is of interest to note that while paragraph 1 of Article 4 refers to both religious and ideological freedoms, paragraph 2 guarantees simply the "undisturbed practice of religion." The court, however, has interpreted the term "religion" broadly;[9] it includes nonreligious and antireligious as well as religious beliefs. Where, however, legislation enacted in the interest of the general peace and safety of the community conflicts with the free exercise of religion, the job of the courts is to balance the interests of the individual and society. If in the context of a particular case the individual's claim can be sustained without significantly burdening the good order of the community, the claim should usually be upheld. The *Blood Transfusion* case (1971) is an illustration of this balancing process.

9.2 Blood Transfusion Case (1971)
32 BVerfGE 98

[The defendant's wife died because he honored her refusal, on religious grounds, to have a blood transfusion necessitated by the birth of the family's fourth child. Both husband and wife were members of the Association of Evangelical Brotherhood and held the same belief with respect to blood transfusions. The husband's original conviction of negligent homicide was reversed on appeal for failure to show that his wife's death was caused by his refusal to transfer her to a hospital. Later, he was convicted of a misdemeanor for his failure to provide his spouse with necessary assistance. He had allowed a doctor to be summoned when irregularities in the birth occurred, but he left the decision with respect to transfusion and hospitalization to his wife, who was conscious and mentally competent until her death. His faith did not specifically prohibit blood transfusions, but he nevertheless claimed that his conduct accorded with his religious beliefs. He challenged trial and appellate court decisions sustaining the charges against him in a constitutional complaint, claiming a violation of the free exercise clause of Article 4 of the Basic Law.]

Judgment of the First Senate. . . .

B. II. A review of the challenged decisions indicates that they have impermissibly violated the complainant's fundamental right to freedom of faith and creed (Article 4 (1) of the Basic Law).

1. The Constitution guarantees freedom of religion not only to members of recognized churches and religious societies but also to members of other religious organizations. The exercise of religious freedom depends neither upon an association's numerical size nor upon its social relevance. This follows from the command binding the state to ideological and religious neutrality and from the principle of parity of churches and creeds.

2. In a state in which human dignity is the highest value, and in which the free self-determination of the individual is also recognized as an important community value, freedom of belief affords the individual a legal realm free of state interference in which a person may live his life according to his convictions. In this respect freedom of belief is more than religious tolerance, i.e., the mere suffering of religious creeds or ideological convictions. It encompasses not only the internal freedom to believe or not to believe but also the external freedom to manifest, profess, and propagate one's belief. This includes the right of the individual to orient his conduct on the teachings of his religion and to act according to his internal convictions. Freedom of belief protects not only convictions based upon imperative principles of faith; it also encompasses religious convictions which, while not requiring an exclusively religious response to a concrete situation, nevertheless view this response as the best and most appropriate means to deal with the situation in keeping with this belief. Otherwise the fundamental right to freedom of religion could not develop fully.

3. Yet, freedom of belief is not unlimited. . . .

(b) The freedom guaranteed by Article 4 (1) of the Basic Law, like all the fundamental rights, has as its point of departure the view of man in the Constitution; i.e., man as a responsible personality, developing freely within the social community. These community ties of the individual recognized by the Constitution impose formal limits on even those fundamental rights which are guaranteed unreservedly. The limits on the freedom of religion, however, like those on the freedom of artistic expression, can be determined only by the Constitution itself. Because the freedom of religion cannot be limited by the legislature, it can be restricted neither by the general legal order nor by an indefinite provision which, without constitutional anchor and sufficient safeguards for the rule of law, permits [the limitation of a constitutional right] when community goods are endangered. Rather, [we] must resolve a conflict within the framework of the guarantee of freedom of religion in light of the Basic Law's value order and under consideration of the unity of this fundamental value system. Freedom of religion, as part of that value system, is also a part of the mandate of tolerance, especially in reference to the guarantee of human dignity in Article 1 (1) of the Basic Law, which governs the entire value system of fundamental rights as its paramount value.

For these reasons the state cannot subject activities and modes of behavior which flow from a particular religious view to the same sanctions that it provides for such behavior independent of religious motivation. The effect radiating from the fundamental right contained in Article 4 (1) is such that it can influence the type and extent of permissible state sanctions.

With respect to criminal law, one who acts or fails to act on the basis of a religious conviction may find himself in conflict with the governing morality and the legal obligations flowing from this morality. When someone commits a punishable act on the basis of his religion, then a conflict arises between Article 4 (1) of the Basic Law and the goals of criminal law. This offender is not resisting the legal order out of any lack of respect for that order; he too wishes to preserve the legal value embodied in that penal law. He sees himself, however, as being in a borderline situation where the general legal order is competing with the dictates of his personal belief, and he feels an obligation to follow the higher dictates of faith. Even if this personal decision objectively conflicts with the values governing society, it is not so reprehensible as to justify the use of society's harshest weapon, the criminal justice system, to punish the offender. Criminal punishment, no matter what the sentence, is an inappropriate sanction for this constellation of facts under any goal of the criminal justice system (retribution, prevention, rehabilitation of the offender). The duty of all public authority to respect serious religious convictions, [as] contained in Article 4 (1) of the Basic Law, must lead to a relaxation of criminal laws when an actual conflict between a generally accepted legal duty and a dictate of faith results in a spiritual crisis for the offender that, in view of the punishment labeling him a criminal, would represent an excessive social reaction violative of his human dignity.

4. The application of these principles to the present case reveals that the superior court and Stuttgart Court of Appeals misinterpreted the significance of Article 4 (1) of the Basic Law in the construction and application of section 330c of the Criminal Code. One cannot reproach the complainant for not trying to convince his wife to give up their shared convictions. He was bound to her by their common conviction that prayer was the "better way." His behavior, and that of his wife, was a profession of their shared faith. It was supported by mutual respect for each other's opinions in a question concerning life and death, and by the faith that this opinion was right. In this type of case, criminal law cannot require two people with the same beliefs to influence one another so as to convince themselves of the danger of their religious decision.

Nor did the complainant have the duty to substitute his decision for that of his wife. This would be a consideration only if she had no longer been able to decide for herself. Her conviction that she should refuse hospital treatment was based on her freedom of action protected by Article 2 (1) of the Basic Law; during the period which criminal law holds relevant, she exercised her free will — unencumbered up until her death.

5. Additionally, the duties of family members under Article 6 of the Basic Law

do not curb the effects of Article 4 (1) on the interpretation and application of section 330c of the Criminal Code. With respect to whether one spouse is obligated to interfere with the other partner's free decision for his or her own good, [we] must recognize that two autonomous individuals are involved in a marriage, both with a right to the free development of their personalities. This basic realm of freedom for both partners encompasses, above all, the freedom to adhere to one's own convictions according to one's belief and to arrange one's life to correspond to this belief. . . .

The duties which the complainant owes to his children would lead to a different conclusion if, under the pretext of his own convictions, the complainant had allowed his wife to die, thus depriving the children of their mother. This is exactly what the complainant did not want. He was certain that prayer was the most effective way of saving his wife. His duties to the children do not extend so far, even in compliance with Article 6 (2) of the Basic Law, that he would have had to abandon what he thought was a more promising aid in favor of medical treatment which he believed would be ineffectual without God's help.

Admittedly, society's moral standards would dictate that the complainant follow both paths simultaneously. However, because his religious convictions would not permit him [to use both ways to save his wife], imposing criminal sanctions against him was not justified.

NOTE: THE *TOBACCO ATHEIST* AND *COURTROOM CRUCIFIX* CASES. The absence of a reservation clause in Article 4 means that only some other competing constitutional right or value can directly limit the free exercise of religion. *Tobacco Atheist* (1960) illustrates this teaching.[10] Here, the court sustained the denial of parole to a prisoner because he tried to persuade his fellow inmates to abandon the Christian church by offering them tobacco. The First Senate declared:

One who violates limitations erected by the Basic Law's general order of values cannot claim freedom of belief. The Basic Law does not protect every manifestation of belief but only those historically developed among civilized people on the basis of certain fundamental moral opinions. . . . The religiously neutral state cannot and should not define in detail the content of this freedom, because it is not allowed to evaluate its citizens' beliefs or nonbeliefs. Nevertheless, it must prevent misuse of this freedom. It follows from the Basic Law's order of values, especially from the dignity of the human being, that a misuse is especially apparent whenever the dignity of another person is violated. Recruiting for a belief and convincing someone to turn from another belief, normally legal activities, become misuses of the basic right if a person tries, directly or indirectly, to use a base or immoral instrument to lure other persons from their beliefs. . . . A person who exploits the special circumstances of penal servitude and promises and rewards someone with luxury goods in order to make him renounce his beliefs does not enjoy the benefit of the protection of Article 4 of the Basic Law.[11]

As noted in an earlier chapter, *Tobacco Atheist* underscores the importance of the relationship between particular rights of liberty and the general value order of the Basic Law.

The *Courtroom Crucifix* case (1973) is another important milestone in the development of the Constitutional Court's free exercise jurisprudence. The judges of a Düsseldorf administrative court insisted on keeping crucifixes in their courtroom, over the objection of a Jewish litigant appearing before them. The court stepped gingerly in this case, refusing to hand down a ruling that would absolutely bar a crucifix from adorning a courtroom. "The mere presence of a crucifix in a courtroom," said the First Senate, "does not demand any identification with the ideas and institutions symbolically embodied therein or compel any specific behavior in accordance thereof."[12] In the context of this case, however — two crucifixes were in view, one of them on the bench itself — the senate found that the presence of the crucifix was offensively obtrusive and virtually placed the legal proceeding and the oath administered to the litigant "under the cross," thus violating her right to freedom of belief and conscience. The First Senate nevertheless reaffirmed the general principle that the state is obligated to remain neutral with respect to competing religious and ideological values.[13]

9.3 Religious Oath Case (1972)
33 BVerfGE 23

[The essential facts are stated in the opinion.]

Judgment of the First Senate. . . .

A. I. An evangelical pastor testified as a witness in a criminal proceeding before the Düsseldorf Superior Court. Citing his fundamental right of religious freedom, he refused to be sworn in because, according to Christ's words from the Sermon on the Mount (Matthew 5:33–37), he was not allowed to take any oaths. The Superior Court of Düsseldorf, referring to Article 140 of the Basic Law in conjunction with Article 136 (4) of the Weimar Constitution of August 11, 1919, held that the pastor was not justified in refusing to take the oath and sentenced him to a penalty of DM 20 or two days in jail as well as expenses caused by the refusal. . . .

The Düsseldorf Court of Appeals dismissed the appeal of the superior court's decision in its order of July 22, 1966. . . .

B. The appeal on this constitutional issue is both permissible and legally justified.

The oath of a witness, when sworn without using God's name pursuant to section 66c (2) Code of Criminal Procedure, is purely a worldly affirmation of the

truth of a statement without religious or in any way transcendental reference according to the value order of the Basic Law. The differing view of the complainant is
nonetheless protected by Article 4 (1) of the Basic Law. Therefore, the complainant
was justified in refusing to take the oath. . . .

II. The fundamental right of religious freedom under Article 4 (1) of the Basic Law
protects the complainant's convictions. His conviction does not coincide with this
interpretation of the Constitution and statute. [Complainant] continues to view
today's oath even in its nonreligious form as a deed with religious reference, the
swearing of which God forbids according to the words of the Sermon on the
Mount. He did not refuse to take the oath without "legal grounds" in the sense used
in section 70 (1) of the Code of Criminal Procedure, and consequently may not be
prevented from following the dictates of his faith — not even indirectly by the imposition of a penalty.

1. Religious freedom under Article 4 (1) of the Basic Law guarantees the
individual a legal sphere in which he may adopt the lifestyle that corresponds to his
convictions. This encompasses not only the (internal) freedom to believe or not to
believe but also the individual's right to align his behavior with the precepts of his
faith and to act in accordance with his internal convictions. It follows from the
command of ideological-religious neutrality that binds the state and from the principle of the parity of churches and creeds that the numerical strength of a particular
faith or its relevance in society cannot be determinative. Article 4 (1) of the Basic
Law, as a specific expression of human dignity guaranteed by Article 1 (1), protects
those infrequently occurring convictions which diverge from the teachings of the
churches and religious communities. The state may neither favor certain creeds nor
evaluate the beliefs or lack of faith of its citizens.

The Constitution grants the right of religious freedom unreservedly — restricted neither by the general legal system nor by an undefined provision mandating a balancing of concrete interests. Its limits may be drawn only by the Constitution itself; that is, according to the directives of the constitutional value order and
the unity of this fundamental value system. In particular, the close relationship
between religious freedom and human dignity as the supreme value in the system of
fundamental rights precludes the state from sanctioning activities and behavior
which flow from a particular belief, independent of its ideological motivation. A
distinctive characteristic of a state which has proclaimed human dignity to be its
highest constitutional value and which guarantees the inalienable freedom of religion and conscience unrestricted by statute is that it permits even outsiders and sects
to develop their personalities in keeping with their subjective convictions, free of
harassment. [This freedom is granted them] so long as they do not contradict other
values of constitutional rank and their behavior does not palpably encroach upon
the community or the fundamental rights of others.

2. (a) The complainant refused to take an oath as a witness on the basis of his

own conviction derived from the Bible. According to his understanding of his faith, all oaths are forbidden by God's words. In his view, the act of swearing as such is incompatible with Christian teachings and results in damnation according to various concepts of magic if the oath is broken. This viewpoint finds some support from the text of the Bible (Matthew 5:33–37) and is espoused by a school of newer theology—Gollwitzer, for example. For this reason alone, [one] must not fail to consider this viewpoint within the framework of Article 4 (1) of the Basic Law. The state may not evaluate its citizens' religious convictions or characterize these beliefs as right or wrong.

(b) The complainant's refusal to take the oath goes beyond the internal area of belief fundamentally shut off from state intervention and conflicts with the duty the governmental community places as a matter of principle on all citizens in the interest of an effective administration of justice. As a rule, the legislature views the witness's oath in a criminal proceeding as an indispensable means of finding the truth, and consequently has as a starting point the principle of mandatory oaths for witnesses. . . .

. . . Nonetheless, the complainant's overriding fundamental right to refuse to take an oath according to his understanding of his faith, and his right not to be forced indirectly by means of a penalty to commit an act contrary to this understanding, is not subject to any limitation derived from the value system of the Basic Law itself.

More particularly, no such restriction may be derived from Article 136 of the Weimar Constitution in conjunction with Article 140 of the Basic Law. The relation in which this provision, taken from the Weimar Constitution and incorporated into the Basic Law, stands today to the fundamental right of religious freedom does not justify the reverse conclusion drawn from Article 136 (4) of the Weimar Constitution in the appeals court's contested order; that is, that everyone may be forced to use a nonreligious form of oath. The framers of the Basic Law removed the freedom of religion and conscience from the context of the article on churches in the Weimar Constitution and inserted this right—insulated from restriction by simple statute—into the catalog of directly binding fundamental rights which are paramount in the Constitution. Consequently, [one] must interpret Article 136 of the Weimar Constitution in the light of the substantially increased impact of the fundamental right of the freedom of religion and conscience in contrast with earlier times; according to its meaning and internal weight in the context of the system of the Basic Law, Article 136 is superseded by Article 4 (1) of the Basic Law. Under the Basic Law, [one] may determine which duties within the meaning of Article 136 (1) of the Weimar Constitution the state may enforce vis-à-vis the right contained in Article 4 (1) only according to the provisions of the value decision embodied in Article 4 (1).

[We] cannot conclude from the fact that Articles 56 and 64 of the Basic Law require the federal president and other constitutional organs to swear oaths of office that a systemic constitutional obstacle exists which precludes us from accepting complainant's decision concerning the oath. These obligations flow from the voluntary decision to accept the election to office as an organ of the Constitution. [Holding such an office] entails directly representing the state in a particularly marked way and requires, as a matter of principle, the total identification of the elected person with the values set forth in the Constitution. By contrast, everyone must testify in court and swear to the veracity of his or her testimony according to the provisions of the law. The means of compulsion provided for in the law may be used to enforce the duty to take an oath (compare section 70, Code of Criminal Procedure; section 390, Code of Civil Procedure). When a court orders a witness who rejects the oath for ideological reasons to be sworn in, this citizen is confronted with an unavoidable conflict. The fundamental difference between the oath of a witness and the oath of office alone precludes treating both types of oaths as analogous. . . .

(c) The complainant can ask to be absolved from fulfilling his duty to swear an oath pursuant to Article 4 (1) of the Basic Law on the ground that his religious convictions forbid this act. . . .

The interest of the governmental community in an efficiently functioning administration of the law, which has its place in the value system of the Basic Law (compare Article 92 of the Basic Law), should not be undervalued, because in the final analysis every court decision serves to safeguard fundamental rights. But accepting a decision [not to be sworn in] based on someone's conviction that swearing an oath is not permissible in an individual case does not impair this interest. The affirmation of the veracity of a witness's testimony, viewed by lawmakers as an indispensable means of truth finding, need not necessarily take place exclusively in the form of an oath using the word "swear." . . .

3. . . . As long as the legislature has not regulated the witness's power to refuse to swear an oath on religious grounds in a manner consistent with Article 4 (1) of the Basic Law, this fundamental right will produce a direct and, if necessary, corrective effect in the area of the existing law of criminal procedure. Consequently, [courts] must interpret section 70 (1) of the Code of Criminal Procedure in conformity with the Constitution so that . . . in a particular case the fundamental right contained in Article 4 (1) of the Basic Law may relieve a witness from the duty of swearing to the truth of his testimony.

Justice von Schlabrendorff, dissenting:

With respect to the issue of a witness refusing to take an oath, I do not agree with the decision reached by the majority of the senate. My dissenting opinion is grounded upon the following reasons: . . .

2. The complainant bases his view upon the Sermon on the Mount. The majority of the senate believes that the complainant's argument finds some support in this text. This circumstance compels an examination of the sense and meaning of the Sermon on the Mount.

Thomas Aquinas, on behalf of the Catholic church, as well as Martin Luther and Calvin on behalf of the Protestant church, left no doubt that the Sermon on the Mount does not apply to the state. This sermon is not a law and, above all, is not a law for the earthly millennium. . . . As a consequence, one may read and understand the Sermon on the Mount only from the standpoint of eschatology. If one fails to take this to heart, one runs the risk of becoming allied with religious fanatics who, in reliance upon the Sermon on the Mount, believe it their duty to change the world into a pseudoparadise. Only those living beyond this world live in the truth. People in the earthly eon live in the world of facts. But the Sermon on the Mount does direct their glance toward the world beyond. . . .

Those who interpret the Sermon on the Mount positivistically have no sense of history and increase the danger of political irresponsibility. Those who think like the Christian complainant renounce the worldly regiment of God by rejecting the oath but fail to appreciate the meaning both of salvation and of the Sermon on the Mount. According to the Gospel of Matthew, Jesus of Nazareth, too, swore an oath before the High Council — he, who as a religious personality has no equal in the history of the world. To state this more clearly, the view of the majority of the senate, as far as it is expressed in the words "the complainant's view finds some support in the Sermon on the Mount," is a serious misinterpretation of this text and the term "faith."

Admittedly, the majority of the senate is correct in saying that some modern theologians no longer share the opinions of Thomas Aquinas and the reformers. That, however, is a question of the correct or incorrect interpretation of the Sermon on the Mount. Consequently, the assumption seems reasonable that the complainant's behavior contained not an act of faith but rather a misinterpretation. A citizen who, according to his own statement, ascribes to the Christian belief and makes an obvious misinterpretation has no claim to the protection of Article 4 of the Basic Law. . . .

4. The Preamble of our Basic Law states that the German people have chosen a new system in the awareness of their responsibility to God and mankind. The result is that our Constitution recognizes and affirms [the existence of] God. Therefore, the tendency to secularism in our people has not extinguished the concept of God. Every person and every country believes in God. The person who denies God believes in false gods. The same applies to a country. . . .

. . . At issue is not how many people reject the oath. Article 4 of the Basic Law also protects the individual's belief if it remains within the limits of the order that preserves the state. Nor does this case involve either a psychological or sociological issue concerning whether or not the oath today is still a suitable means of finding out the truth. The oath is a question of ethical principles. The following realization is important and decisive: Neither a human being nor a people nor a country can live without God. Consequently, the century-old tradition of our German people mandates that we maintain this religious basis as well as the oath while simultaneously exercising neutrality toward all churches and ideological communities.

5. We Germans can never again renounce the rights of freedom. The state, too, can ill afford to dispense with self-preservation. Therefore we must try to find a balance between the individual's right to freedom and the state's right to exist. The Americans recognized this [problem] very early. As a result, the Supreme Court in Washington sought and found a balancing formula. The Court says: An individual's claim to a right of freedom violates the Constitution if it creates a clear and present danger for the good of the public. Although this pragmatic reasoning encounters objections in Europe, it is better to sacrifice erudition for the sake of the body politic's existence.

NOTE: CONSCIENTIOUS OBJECTION. The Basic Law ranks alone among modern constitutions in protecting conscientious objectors. Article 4 (3) declares: "No one may be compelled against his conscience to perform service in war involving the use of arms." Most commentators regard this freedom, as does the Constitutional Court itself, as a concrete manifestation of the general freedom of conscience secured by paragraph 1 of Article 4.[14] The court has exalted this freedom in sonorous terms, relating it to the fundamental dignity of the human personality. Its decisions emphasize three things: (1) freedom of conscience within the meaning of Article 4 (3) extends to persons motivated by religious and nonreligious values, (2) the state is absolutely bound to respect this freedom, and (3) freedom of conscience is to be given priority over any countervailing interest of the community.[15]

Article 4 (3) lay dormant in the first years of the Federal Republic's life. It emerged from its slumber when the Allies decided to rearm West Germany, and when in response the Bundestag enacted the Universal Military Service Act (1956),[16] section 25 of which requires conscientious objectors to perform alternative civilian service. In 1968, when West Germans inserted into the Basic Law a new section on national defense (Articles 115a–l), they also added Article 12a to the section on basic rights. The amendment constitutionalized the principle of compulsory alternative service for conscientious objectors and stipulated that the length of such service "shall not exceed the duration of military service" (Article 12a [2]).[17]

Conscience: its meaning and application. The *Conscientious Objector I* case (1960) is the seminal decision under Article 4 (3).[18] In a rather strict interpretation of this provision the First Senate ruled that it applies only to military service involving the use of weapons. In addition, a person's refusal to bear arms must be rooted in his conscientious objection to all war. Selective objection to a particular war or to the use of a specific weapon is impermissible. The senate then looked into the nature of conscientious objection. "Conscience," declared the senate, "is to be understood as an experiential and spiritual phenomenon that absolutely compels a person, in demonstrating his concern for fellow human beings, to commit himself unreservedly to an ideal."[19] The touchstone of conscientious objection, the senate continued, is whether a person experiences "an inner moral command against the use of arms of any kind and in all circumstances, an interior force that touches the very depths of his personality, steering him away from evil and toward the good."[20] It makes no difference whether this interior moral force springs from religious, philosophical, ethical, or even emotional considerations. Courts may not, therefore, consider the logic of a conscientious objector's claim. Yet reason alone is insufficient to support such a claim; it must truly be the result of an interior commitment, one that would cause exceptional grief and suffering for the person forced to take up arms.

Article 4 (3) confines conscientious objection to "service in war involving the use of arms." The court, however, has extended the reach of this clause, together with the corresponding provision of Article 12a (2), to military service involving the use of arms in time of peace. In practice this has resulted in exempting conscientious objectors from military service of any kind, including service without weapons. On the other hand, Article 4 (3) does not exempt a conscript from being compelled to work in an armaments factory.[21]

Alternative service. Several important cases arising under Article 4 (3) have involved challenges to various aspects of the requirement for alternative service. Early on, before the inclusion in the Basic Law of Article 12a (requiring alternative service), the Constitutional Court had sustained, over the religious objection of a Jehovah's Witness, a statutory requirement of alternative civilian service.[22] In subsequent cases, also involving Jehovah's Witnesses, the issue shifted to the form and duration of punishment that could be inflicted on persons who refused to perform civilian service. While establishing that reasonable punishment may be inflicted after the first refusal to perform alternative service, the court ruled that successive convictions and imprisonment arising out of repeated refusals to perform such service are unconstitutional.[23]

For many years federal law required all conscientious objectors to submit to an oral test of conscience before a local draft board, a cumbersome procedure increasingly complicated by rising numbers of young men seeking conscientious objector status (from 3,311 in 1963 to 32,565 in 1975). Approximately 75 percent of these satisfied the test.[24] In 1977 the SPD-FDP coalition government simplified this procedure. Under an amendment to the Military and Civilian Service acts, potential conscripts could now achieve conscientious objector status simply by notifying local officials in writing that they are opposed to bearing arms as a matter of conscience, thus allowing such persons to choose civilian over military service without submitting themselves to scrutiny before an examining board.[25] As a consequence, the number of applicants for conscientious objector status shot up in the following months to 75,000.[26] By the end of 1977, according to one report, 130,000 conscientious objectors were still waiting to be assigned to civilian duty.[27] This situation exploded into a major political controversy when 214 Christian Democratic members of the Bundestag sought and won from the Constitutional Court a temporary injunction against any further implementation of the notification provision pending a decision on its constitutionality.[28]

These facts and figures furnished the background to the *Conscientious Objector II* case (1978),[29] the product of an abstract judicial-review proceeding. Over the single dissent of Justice Martin Hirsch, the Second Senate invalidated the law, reasoning as follows: The Basic Law empowers the federal government to legislate in the field of national defense (Article 73 [1]), to establish the armed forces for purposes of defense (Article 87a), and to introduce universal conscription (Article 12a). The defense of the country is therefore a constitutional duty, and Article 12a, reinforced and undergirded by Article 3 (1) (the general equality clause), imposes this duty equally on all citizens except for those who under Article 4 (3) refuse combat duty on the ground of conscience, in which case they must perform alternative civilian service for a time not exceeding the length of military service. This principle of equality requires legislation that ensures that those assigned to alternative service within the framework of Article 12a are in fact conscientious objectors within the meaning of Article 4 (3). The notification statute fails to meet this criterion because it contains no adequate test of conscience. Rather, "it opens the door to an abuse of the appeal to conscience and thus permits violations of a community duty in a manner antithetical to the constitutional concept of parity."[30]

Extended Alternative Service case. An abstract judicial-review proceeding initiated by Christian Democrats resulted in the nullification of the 1977 notification statute. In 1983, with Christian Democrats in power, parliament with the consent of the Bundesrat passed a new law that dispensed with the oral hearing before an examining board. It also extended the period of compulsory civilian service to twenty months, five months longer than the fifteen months required of military conscripts.[31] Legislators felt that the longer period of civilian service for conscientious objectors, together with a requirement for more detailed information to be filed in written form with a federal agency, would be as effective in screening out fraudulent claims under Article 4 (3) as an oral hearing. They assumed that a person willing to spend the additional time (one-third longer) in civilian service is in all likelihood conscientiously opposed to military service. But the measure seemed to contradict Article 12a, which says explicitly that the duration of civilian service shall not exceed that of military service. It was now the Social Democrats' turn to contest the constitutionality of the statute in an abstract review proceeding before the Constitutional Court.[32]

Over the strong dissents of Justices Böckenförde and Mahrenholz the Second Senate rejected arguments against the statute based on the principle of equality under Article 3 (1), freedom of conscience under Article 4 (3), and Article 12a (2). In a broad and loose construction of Article 12a, the senate held that, given the harsher conditions of military service and the additional months (nine altogether) of required reserve duty, not to mention the possibility that the reserves may be called up for active duty in the event of a crisis, the longer period of civilian service, which ends after a determinate period, is effectively equal to the time spent in military service. So long as the time for civilian service does not exceed twenty-four months (equivalent to the total commitment of military conscripts: fifteen months in basic training and nine on reserve duty), said the senate, the legislature is free to consider such matters and lay down durational requirements that seek to balance the burdens of military and nonmilitary service. In so doing, the legislature has achieved the normative goal of Article 12a without impinging on freedom of conscience under Article 4 (3).[33]

ESTABLISHMENT

The *School Prayer* case (1979; no. 9.4) concerns the question of religious freedom in West Germany and the extent to which this freedom appears to collide with the principle of nonestablishment. It contrasts sharply with the outcome of similar American cases.[34] The German tribunal feels that a policy of equal respect and concern for the religious values of each student in the educational context requires not the suppression of a devotional exercise reflecting those values but rather tolerance in the face of such expression, particularly when it is performed voluntarily and outside the teaching curriculum. Although a voluntary prayer led by a teacher within the limited confines of a school may cause tension between principles of free exercise and nonestablishment, in the light of the values set forth in Articles 4 (1) and 7 (1), it is a tension that seems inescapable under the terms of the Basic Law.[35]

In its church-state jurisprudence generally, the court has recognized both the negative and positive characters of religious freedom. Negative freedom includes the freedom of unbelief as well as the freedom not to disclose one's religious beliefs. Positive freedom includes the right to express one's belief in public. The idea of negative and positive freedoms is analogous to the concept of subjective and objective rights in the general sphere of fundamental rights and liberties. Freedom of religion in the negative sense means that the state must respect those inner convictions which belong to the domain of the self. Freedom of religion in the positive sense implies an obligation on the part of the state to create a social order in which it is possible for the religious personality to develop and flourish conveniently and easily.[36]

9.4 School Prayer Case (1979)
52 BVerfGE 223

[This case concerns the permissibility of school prayer apart from religious instruction when the parents of a pupil object to its exercise. Two cases were combined in this decision. The first presented the complaint of a parent who maintained that the administrative prohibition of prayer violated his constitutional rights; the second complainant claimed that being forced to pray in school over his objection violated his fundamental rights. In the first case the

Hesse Constitutional Court found that school prayer was not permitted if a pupil or his parents objected to it. The court based this holding on the "negative freedom of confession," an aspect of religious freedom said to protect the right to abstain from religious worship. Consequently, if a pupil disagreed with school prayer, he or she could not be put in a position where the only recourse was not participating in the exercise. Because the school considered in this decision was a state school, the prayer could not be viewed as an element of school instruction.

The second complaint involved a denominational school in North Rhine–Westphalia. The Federal Administrative Court held that "negative freedom of confession" could not be granted precedence over "positive religious freedom"; i.e., the right to remain silent could not be construed to prohibit others from expressing their beliefs through school prayer. Because the Basic Law leaves the formation of the school system to the states and permits the establishment of "religion-affiliated" schools, neither a parent's nor a pupil's objection may serve as a basis for prohibiting school prayer.]

Judgment of the First Senate. . . .

A. The two decisions, combined into one constitutional complaint, touch upon the issue of whether school prayer outside religion class should be permitted in compulsory state schools when a pupil's parents object to the prayer.

C. I. 1. The standards for judging the constitutional questions raised by the issue of school prayer are set forth primarily in Article 6 (2) [1] of the Basic Law [the parent's right of control concerning the care and custody of minors], Articles 4 (1) and 4 (2) of the Basic Law [freedom of religion and the right to practice one's faith without harassment], as well as Article 7 (1) of the Basic Law [the state's mandate to establish educational systems].

Article 6 (2) [1] of the Basic Law accords parents the right and duty to freely determine the care and education of their children. This right has precedence over the rights of other educational institutions but is subject to the limitations of Article 7 of the Basic Law. This [parental right] also includes the right to educate one's child in religious and ideological respects. Paragraphs 1 and 2 of Article 4 encompass parents' right to teach their children those religious and ideological convictions which they believe to be true.

On the other hand, Article 7 (1) of the Basic Law confers a constitutional mandate upon the state to establish schools. The state's power to shape the school system, vested in the eleven German states, includes not only the power to organize the school structure but also [the power] to determine course content and objectives. Consequently, the state can pursue its own educational goals in the classroom, goals which may be fundamentally independent of parental aims. The state's mandate to establish a school system is autonomous and stands on the same footing as parents' right to control the education and upbringing of their children; neither has an absolute priority over the other.

2. The problem of school prayer must first be seen in the broader framework of whether religious references are ever permissible in (compulsory) interdenominational state schools, or whether the state within its authority to structure the school system is confined to making religious or ideological references in religion classes, which are expressly guaranteed in Article 7 (3) of the Basic Law.

The Federal Constitutional Court considered this question in depth in its decisions of December 17, 1975, concerning Baden's interdenominational schools as well as the Bavarian interdenominational schools. . . .

Pursuant to those decisions, the incorporation of Christian references is not absolutely forbidden when establishing public schools, even though a minority of parents may not desire religious instruction for their children and may have no choice but to send their children to the school in question. However, the school may not be a missionary school and may not demand commitment to articles of Christian faith. [State] schools also must be open to other ideological and religious ideas and values. They may not limit their educational goals to those belonging to a Christian denomination except in religion classes, which no one can be forced to attend. Affirming Christianity within the context of secular disciplines refers primarily to the recognition of Christianity as a formative cultural and educational factor which has developed in Western history. It does not refer to the truth of the belief. With respect to non-Christians, this affirmation obtains legitimacy as a progression of historical fact. Christianity's educational and cultural aspects include not insignificantly the notion of tolerance for those holding other beliefs. . . .

3. If religious references are permissible in compulsory state schools within the principles and guidelines developed by the Federal Constitutional Court, then praying in school is not fundamentally and constitutionally objectionable. However, the performance of the prayer also must comply with the limits of the states' right to establish school systems under Article 7 (1) of the Basic Law and not violate other constitutional precepts, in particular the individual rights of participants derived from Article 4 of the Basic Law.

(a) School prayer, in the sense in which it is the subject matter of this constitutional complaint, represents a supradenominational (ecumenical) invocation of God based upon Christian beliefs. . . .

As an act of religious avowal made outside religion class, school prayer is not part of the general school curriculum taught within the framework of the states' mandate to establish an educational system for children. It is neither instruction typical of teaching a course nor the imparting of knowledge to pupils. Nor is it a goal-oriented, pedagogical exercise of influence on the part of the school and teacher upon the children. Rather, it is a religious activity undertaken, as a rule, in concert with the teacher. Thus it does not fall into the category of conveying Christian cultural and educational values, which the Federal Constitutional Court has deemed permissible within the framework of general instruction in Christian inter-denominational schools. The constitutional permissibility of school prayer does not necessarily follow from the permissibility of these schools.

(b) Because school prayer is not a part of teaching a class in the sense of scholastic instruction, it cannot be a component of a binding lesson plan. Its performance must be completely voluntary. This is universally undisputed in view of the provisions of Articles 4 (1) and 4 (2) of the Basic Law as well as Article 140 of the Basic Law in conjunction with Article 136 (4) of the Weimar Constitution. [Voluntary participation] applies not only to pupils but also to teachers of every class in which a school prayer takes place (compare Article 7 (3) [3] of the Basic Law). . . .

Even if school prayer is not and cannot be part of the mandatory, regulated class instruction, it remains a school event attributable to the state in each of the forms named—especially when school prayer takes place upon the teacher's instigation during class time. To be sure, the state's role is limited to creating the organizational setting for school prayer and permitting the prayer at the request of the parents or pupils or on its own initiative. The state does not issue an order in this case; it makes an offer which the school class may accept.

(c) If the state, in the sense described, permits school prayer outside religion classes as a religious exercise and as a "school event," then certainly it is encouraging belief in Christianity and thus encouraging a religious element in the school which exceeds religious references flowing from the recognition of the formative factor of Christianity upon culture and education. Even in its transdenominational form, prayer is connected to the truth of a belief; specifically, that God can grant that which is requested. Nonetheless, permitting this religious element in (compulsory) interdenominational schools with the safeguard of voluntary participation still remains within the scope of creative freedom granted to the states as bearers of supreme authority in school matters pursuant to Article 7 (1) of the Basic Law. Indeed, this result remains the same even if in trying to reach an optimization of the conflicting interests, the fundamental right of those professing other beliefs under Article 4 of the Basic Law is included in the assessment.

Article 4 of the Basic Law grants not only freedom of belief but also the external freedom publicly to acknowledge one's belief. In this sense Articles 4 (1) and 4 (2) of the Basic Law guarantee a sphere in which to express these convictions actively. If the state permits school prayer in interdenominational state schools, then it does nothing more than exercise its right to establish a school system pursuant to Article 7 (1) of the Basic Law, so that pupils who wish to do so may acknowledge their religious beliefs, even if only in the limited form of a universal and transdenominational appeal to God. . . .

To be sure, the state must balance this affirmative freedom to worship as expressed by permitting school prayer with the negative freedom of confession of other parents and pupils opposed to school prayer. Basically, [schools] may achieve this balance by guaranteeing that participation be voluntary for pupils and teachers. . . .

4. Although the states are free to allow school prayer in the sense discussed here within their authority for the establishment of the educational system, they are not always compelled to permit prayer in public schools.

Under the Constitution, the states are bound to provide religious instruction as a regular subject of instruction in all state schools (except strictly secular schools). But parents have neither an affirmative right to demand that schools allow prayers nor a right to demand that the state establish schools of a particular religious or ideological character. . . .

II. Although in principle [we] see no constitutional impediments to school prayer, [we] could reach a different conclusion if, in a specific case, a pupil or his parents object to praying at school. Both the Hesse Constitutional Court and the Münster Administrative Appeals Court . . . took this view, but for different reasons. The deliberations of neither court may be upheld.

1. The Hesse Constitutional Court believes that [schools] must forbid school prayer upon the objection of a pupil because the pupil may not be placed in the position of having to proclaim to the world his religiously or ideologically motivated rejection of the prayer through his nonparticipation. . . .

3. The objection of a pupil holding other beliefs or of his parents or guardians could lead to the prohibition of school prayer only if the [school] did not guarantee the dissenting pupil's right to decide freely and without compulsion whether to participate in the prayer. As a rule, however, a pupil can find an acceptable way to avoid participating in the prayer so as to decide with complete freedom not to participate.

(a) Pupils can avoid praying in the following ways. The pupil can stay out of the classroom while the prayer is being said; for example, he or she can enter the room only after the end of the prayer or leave the room at the end of class, before the closing prayer is spoken. The pupil holding other beliefs may also remain in the classroom during the prayer but not say the prayer along with the others; he may then remain seated at his desk, unlike his fellow pupils saying the prayer.

(b) Admittedly, whenever the class prays, each of these alternatives will have the effect of distinguishing the pupil in question from the praying pupils — especially if only one pupil professes other beliefs. His behavior is visibly different from that of the other pupils. This distinction could be unbearable for the person concerned if it should place him in the role of an outsider and serve to discriminate against him as opposed to the rest of the class. Indeed, the pupil in a classroom is in a different, much more difficult position than an adult who publicly discloses his dissenting conviction by not participating in certain events. This is especially true of the younger schoolchild, who is hardly capable of critically asserting himself against his environment. With respect to the issue of school prayer, the child will generally be involved in a conflict not of his own choosing, but rather one carried on by his parents, on the one hand, and the parents of the other schoolchildren or teachers, on the other hand.

4. Nonetheless, one cannot assume that abstaining from school prayer will generally or even in a substantial number of cases force a dissenting pupil into an unbearable position as an outsider. An assessment of the conditions under which the prayer is to occur, the function that the teacher has in connection with this exercise, and the actual conditions in the school leads us to conclude that we need not fear discrimination against a pupil who does not participate in the prayer. . . .

———————

NOTE: CHURCH-STATE RELATIONS AND THE DOCTRINE OF NEUTRALITY. Neutrality is a central concept in German church-state relations.[37] This follows from constitutional provisions banning legislative classifications based on religious opinions (Article 3 [3]), guaranteeing freedom of conscience (Article 4 [1]), and barring the establishment of a state church (Article 140 [Weimar 137 (1)]). Yet the Constitution permits religious instruction in the public schools (Article 7 [3]), recognizes the churches as "corporate bodies under public law" (Article 140 [Weimar 137 (5)]), and authorizes such bodies to tax their members (Article 140 [Weimar Article 139]). Clearly, neutrality in Germany means something very different than it does in the United States.

Cole Durham, drawing on a rich literature, has identified the various senses in which Germans have understood the notion of neutrality.[38] He identified these "models of neutrality" as nonintervention, nonidentification, equality, and cooperation. Nonintervention requires the state's disentanglement from religious organizations in the interest of preserving their autonomy; nonidentification requires the state to refrain from taking sides in religious conflicts and from endorsing any religion or ideology; equality requires, at the level of the institutional church, that the denominations share equally in the distribution of public benefits and burdens; cooperation, finally, implies accommodation or joint action in various fields of activity.

Each of these definitions of neutrality is capable of gravitating to the pole of separation or cooperation. "Despite considerable advocacy of the notion of a more separationist model of neutrality in Germany, the predominant view among German constitutional scholars is that separation in the French or American sense is clearly not mandated by the Fundamental Law."[39] The theory of nonintervention comes close to the American doctrine of neutrality, but, as Durham remarked, "if exaggerated into absolute non-concern, [it] might have the effect of inadvertently favoring anti-religious outlooks and thereby becoming an unacceptable type of passive intervention."[40] By the same token, nonidentification construed as "wide-ranging state indifference to religious affairs . . . tends to be rejected on the grounds that it fails to recognize the level of church-state cooperation the German scheme permits and that it could degenerate into effectual identification of the state with a secular Weltanschauung, which would be equally impermissible."[41]

9.5 Interdenominational School Case (1975)
41 BVerfGE 29

[In 1967 Baden-Württemberg amended Article 15 (1) of its constitution to establish Christian interdenominational schools as the uniform type of public grade school within the state. The complainants, whose children attended school in this state, asserted a violation of their right to religious freedom under Article 4 (1) of the Basic Law. They objected to their children being educated according to any religious or ideological precepts. Complainants also alleged a violation of their parental right to determine the care and upbringing of their children pursuant to Article 6 of the Basic Law.]

Judgment of the First Senate

C. I. 1. (a) Article 6 (2) of the Basic Law guarantees the complainants the right to rear their children in every respect; and this includes raising them in accordance with ideological or religious principles. However, this provision contains no exclusive parental claim to the education and upbringing [of their child]. The state, which supervises the entire school system under Article 7 (1) of the Basic Law, exercises its own educational mandate in the area of school education autonomously and, in this realm, on the same footing with the parents.

As did the Federal Constitutional Court in the *Concordat* decision, the Basic Law presupposes the organizational freedom of the states in educational matters. Article 7 . . . establishes the principles for the denominational organization of schools. Accordingly, persons charged with child-rearing have the right to determine if the child may participate in a religion class (Article 7 (2) of the Basic Law) that is offered as a regular subject in state schools, with the exception of non-denominational schools (Article 7 (3) [1]). If no state elementary school of this type exists in the local community, a private elementary school is to be licensed as an interdenominational, denominational, or ideological school (Article 7 (5) of the Basic Law). Article 7 does not provide for more far-reaching parental influence on the denominational organization of the state school. To this extent this constitutional norm differs substantially from the so-called school compromise of the Weimar Constitution. [In that document] Article 146 (2) determined that, upon parental petition, [the state was to establish] elementary schools of the parents' denomination or ideology within the community as long as the orderly operation of the school was not affected. It also provided that the wishes of the parents be respected as much as possible.

(b) The history of Article 7 of the Basic Law illustrates that the states were intended to be largely independent with respect to the ideological and denominational character of state schools. This is primarily a manifestation of the principle of federalism. During preliminary deliberations on Article 7, [the framers of the Basic Law] rejected proposals suggesting more extensive parental rights (parental rights concerning religion) in the form of a constitutional guarantee of denominational schools. . . . That is why the state legislature was granted extensive freedom to make democratic decisions concerning the actual organization of school systems.

Accordingly, Article 7 (3) of the Basic Law does not require the establishment of a specific type of school. Rather, it presupposes that the various school types of a religious or ideological nature are legally possible. Similarly, Article 7 (5) of the Basic Law assumes that state elementary schools can be established as interdenominational, denominational, or ideological schools. According to this provision, a private elementary school is to be licensed as an interdenominational, denominational, or ideological school if no state elementary school of this type exists within the community. Thus, the Basic Law assumes that any of these types of state elementary schools are permissible.

As a result, the state legislature is basically free to select one of the aforementioned forms or even a mixture of them. Neither the parental right in Article 6 (2) [1] nor other provisions of the Basic Law set forth an affirmative right of control on the basis of which parents could demand that the state establish schools of a particular religious or ideological character. Nor do complainants claim this right, as they specifically state. To this extent the Basic Law refers the parents to private schools. Basically, it allows the states to decide whether they want to grant parents an affirmative right to control and participate in the denominational organization of public schools beyond the scope set forth in Article 7 of the Basic Law. . . .

2. (a) Insofar as the denominational nature of the state elementary school encroaches upon religious freedom, it is primarily the constitutional position of the child who must attend such a school which is affected. But parents' constitutional rights can also be affected when they are compelled to expose their school-age children to an education which does not correspond to their own ideas of religion and ideology. The ideological education of their children demanded by complainants is an inseparable part of the parent-child relationship, which the Basic Law specifically protects by guaranteeing the [institution of the] family (Article 6 (1) of the Basic Law) and the parents' right to rear their children (Article 6 (2) of the Basic Law). Considering the special weight to which the ideological and religious elements of parental child-rearing [are] entitled — at least until the child reaches the age of religious majority — a school education based on a different denomination can severely tax the entire parent-child relationship. Because of the inseparable connection between the educator's task and his ideological and religious beliefs, the burden on the parent-child relationship brings the educator into conflict with his religious or ideological convictions and thus infringes upon the protected sphere of his fundamental right to religious freedom under Article 4 of the Basic Law. Conse-

quently, this fundamental right also includes the right of parents to pass on to their children the kind of religious and ideological convictions they consider right. It is true that parents cannot derive from this right a claim against the state to have their children educated in the desired ideology. However, parents' obligation to allow their children to be exposed to ideological and religious influences which contradict their own convictions may adversely affect this right. Those charged with the child's upbringing may, by virtue of their right to freedom under Article 4 of the Basic Law, protect themselves from governmental actions which adversely affect their personal, constitutionally protected sphere. . . .

(b) . . . Article 4 of the Basic Law protects the negative as well as the positive manifestation of religious freedom against encroachments by the state. This freedom especially affects the organization of those areas of life which, because of their social necessity or political aims, are not left to the free play of social forces but have been taken into the care of the state. Additionally, where compulsory school attendance is at issue, the education of young persons is involved — an area in which religious and ideological ideas have always been relevant. In the instant case the complainants' request to keep the education of their children free from all religious influences, based on Articles 4 (1) and 4 (2) of the Basic Law, must inevitably conflict with the desire of other citizens to afford their children a religious education, also based on Article 4 of the Basic Law. There is a tension here between "negative" and "positive" religious freedom. The elimination of all ideological and religious references would not neutralize the existing ideological tensions and conflicts, but would disadvantage parents who desire a Christian education for their children and would result in compelling them to send their children to a lay school that would roughly correspond with the complainants' wishes. . . .

(c) Because life in a pluralistic society makes it practically impossible to take into consideration the wishes of all parents in the ideological organization of compulsory state schools, [we] must assume that the individual cannot assert his right to freedom pursuant to Article 4 of the Basic Law free of any limitation at all. To this extent the individual is limited in the exercise of his basic right by the countervailing basic rights of persons with different views. In school matters the task of resolving the inevitable tension between negative and positive religious freedom falls to the democratic state legislature. In the process of making public policy, the legislature must seek a compromise which is reasonable for all while considering the varying views. As a guideline for its regulation, it can consider, on the one hand, that Article 7 of the Basic Law permits ideological and religious influences in the area of school matters, and, on the other hand, that Article 4 mandates the elimination of ideological and religious coercion as far as possible in choosing a particular form of school. When interpreting these provisions, one must see them together and harmonize them with one another because only the "concordance" of the legal values protected in both articles does justice to the decision of the Basic Law. None of these norms and principles takes precedence over the others *a priori,* even though the individual aspects differ in significance and internal weight. One can resolve this [problem] only by assessing the conflicting interests through a balancing [process] and categorizing the constitutional aspects previously discussed. At the same time one must take into consideration the constitutional commandment of tolerance (compare Article 3 (3), Article 33 (3) of the Basic Law) as well as the safeguarding of state independence in matters of school organization. Further, one must keep in mind that individual states may pass differing regulations due to differences in school traditions, the denominational composition of the population, and its religious roots.

3. As a result, the state legislature is not absolutely prohibited from incorporating Christian references when it establishes a state elementary school, even though a minority of parents have no choice but to send their children to this school and may not desire any religious education for their children. However, the [legislature] must choose a type of school which, insofar as it can influence children's decisions concerning faith and conscience, contains only a minimum of coercive elements. Thus the school may not be a missionary school and may not demand commitment to Christian articles of faith. Also, it must remain open to other ideological and religious ideas and values. The [legislature] may not limit a school's educational goals to those belonging to a Christian denomination, except in religion classes, which no one can be forced to attend. Affirming Christianity within the context of secular disciplines refers primarily to the recognition of Christianity as a formative cultural and educational factor which has developed in Western civilization. It does not refer to the truth of the belief. With respect to non-Christians, this affirmation obtains legitimacy as a progression of historical fact. . . . Confronting non-Christians with a view of the world in which the formative power of Christian thought is affirmed does not cause discrimination either against minorities not affiliated with Christianity or against their ideology — at least, not if the issue focuses on striving to develop the autonomous personality in the ideological and religious realm according to the basic decision of Article 4 rather than focusing on an absolute claim to the truth of a belief. A school which permits an objective discussion of all ideological and religious views, even if based on a particular ideological orientation, does not create an unreasonable conflict of faith and conscience for parents and children under constitutional law. Parents have sufficient freedom to educate their children religiously and ideologically and to communicate to their offspring why they have affirmed or rejected commitments of faith and conscience.

NOTE: RELIGION AND THE SCHOOLS. During most of the nineteenth and early twentieth centuries, confessional schools, usually Catholic or Protestant, predominated in Germany, a practice rooted in the historical association of education with the churches.[42] This situation changed when the Basic Law placed the entire educational system under the authority of the individual states. Today, elementary and secondary schools are of three kinds — confessional, interdenominational (*Gemein-schaftschulen*), and secular (*bekenntnisfrei*) — but all are public schools fully financed by the state. The interdenominational school, the standard form that most states have chosen to adopt, is a Christian-oriented school designed to serve students of all denominations. In many states, however, confessional schools exist side by side with interdenominational schools, and in some areas the former actually predominate. Secular schools follow a wholly nonreligious curriculum and are the preferred form in northern cities such as Bremen and Berlin. But even these schools often have religion classes, although attendance is voluntary and they are taught by persons who are not regular members of the faculty.[43]

The *Concordat* case (1957; no. 3.4) vindicated the states' reserved right to establish the school systems of their choice, even when these systems contravene the terms of an international treaty. Lower Saxony ignored the German-Vatican Concordat of 1933 when it decided in 1955 to adopt the interdenominational school as the standard form of elementary and secondary education, thus violating the agreement to have Catholic children placed in their own confessional schools. Article 7 (2), however, guarantees to parents the right to decide whether to have their children taught in the religion of their choice. In addition, pursuant to paragraph 3, "religious instruction shall form part of the regular curriculum in state and municipal schools," although "teachers may [not] be obliged against [their] will to provide religious instruction." Children whose parents object to their participation in religion classes need not attend them. Students choosing to enroll in such courses take their instruction from a regular member of the faculty who is a member of their faith and teaches in accordance with the tenets of that faith.

The teaching of religion in the public schools is relatively noncontroversial in Germany. Article 7 (3) of the Basic Law, which prescribes religious instruction in the public schools, follows a practice that prevailed under the imperial and Weimar constitutions. It must also be pointed out, however, that freedom of religion in Germany, like freedom of the press, is an institutional as well as an individual right. Article 7 (3) is one manifestation of the institutional guarantee. Under this guarantee the churches direct the program of religious instruction under the general supervision of the state. This too is noncontroversial. What *is* controversial is whether minority religious sects, particularly non-Christian, non-Jewish religions, shall also be entitled to religion classes in state-supported schools. Recently, for example, North Rhine–Westphalia, with the support of the Turkish government, introduced special Islamic classes for Moslem children attending public schools.[44] The state took this step over the objection of both the German mainline churches and the private Islamic schools, whose teachers demand the exclusive right to instruct students in the Koran.

As the *School Prayer* case demonstrates, religious practices that take place in the public schools over and beyond the formal classes on religion may also lead to

controversy. Much of the litigation in this area, however, occurs in state constitutional tribunals.[45] (These tribunals decide disputes arising under their respective state constitutions.) The predominant German view is that such practices constitute an important aspect of religious liberty so long as freedom of choice prevails.
Ernst Christian Helmreich, an American authority on religious education in Germany, wrote: "At least these [religious] services give public expression to what
the people have written into their fundamental laws: that the schools are, with due
respect and tolerance for representatives of other Weltanschauungen, to be organized on a Christian basis, and are to teach reverence for God in the spirit of Christian brotherhood."[46]

9.6 Classroom Crucifix II Case (1995)
93 BVerfGE 1

[A Bavarian school ordinance required the display of the crucifix in every
elementary school classroom. The parents of children attending one of these
schools objected to the display of the crucifix in classrooms. The parents,
members of a cult known as anthroposophy, which is based on the naturalis-
tic quasi-religious teachings of Rudolf Steiner, claimed that the display of the
crucifix offended their childrens' religious beliefs and thus violated the Basic
Law. School officials sought to resolve the conflict by removing the large
crucifix that had been on display and replacing it with a small cross absent the
figure of Christ. This compromise, however, was not respected by school
authorities when the next child of the complainants started school. The parents then filed an action in the Bavarian Administrative Court for the removal
of the cross. The court's rejection of their motion was sustained by Bavaria's
High Administrative Court. Shortly thereafter, on November 5, 1991, the
Federal Constitutional Court rejected the parents' application for a temporary injunction against the practice of displaying the cross in elementary public school classrooms (*Classroom Crucifix I*, 85 BVerfGE 94). The present case
was decided four years later on its merits following the submission of briefs
by Catholic and Protestant groups as well as Bavaria's government. As usual,
most of the citations have been removed from the edited version of this
translation. Throughout the majority and dissenting opinions, however, the
justices repeatedly cited two cases in support of their respective opinions,
namely, the *Interdenominational School* case (1975; no. 9.5) and the *School
Prayer* case (1979; no. 9.4).]

Judgment of the First Senate

C. The constitutional complaint is well founded. The rejection of the plaintiff's
claim is incompatible with Article 4 (1) and Article 6 (2). . . .

[In the first part of its opinion the court addressed constitutional issues arising under Article 19 (4) of the Basic Law. This provision guarantees legal redress and effective protection against any claimed violation of a subjective constitutional right. The majority opinion noted that the Bavarian administrative courts had failed to appreciate the significance of the constitutional violation and had placed the burden on the plaintiffs to work out a compromise with school administrators. The plaintiffs seemed ready to compromise, and thus to avoid legal action, but school administrators failed to make any final concession to the parents. In these circumstances, said the court, the administrative courts should have acted promptly to protect the children and their parents against any further delay in vindicating their liberty interest under the Basic Law.]

II. The decisions also violate the basic rights of complainants under Article 4 (1) in tandem with Article 6 (2) of the Basic Law. . . . [These decisions] are based on section 13 (1.3) of Bavaria's Elementary School Ordinance, which in turn is incompatible with the Basic Law and thus void.

   1. Article 4 (1) of the Basic Law protects freedom of belief. Whether under this provision one is for or against a particular belief is an affair of the individual, not the state. The state must neither prescribe nor forbid a religion or a religious belief. Freedom of belief includes not only the freedom to uphold a faith but also the freedom to live and act according to one's own religious convictions. In particular, freedom of faith guarantees the right to participate in cultish activities which a specific belief prescribes or in which it expresses itself. It likewise guarantees the right to refrain from participating in such activities. Article 4 also applies to symbols that incorporate a belief or a religion. It allows individuals to decide for themselves which religious symbols they wish to acknowledge or venerate and which they wish to reject. To be sure, in a society that tolerates a wide variety of faith commitments, the individual clearly has no right to be spared exposure to quaint religious manifestations, cultish activities, or religious symbols. However, a different situation arises when the state itself exposes an individual to the influence of a given faith, without giving the child a chance to avoid such influence, or to the symbols through which such a faith represents itself. Article 4 (1) safeguards precisely those areas of life which enjoy the special protection of the state, . . . a safeguard reinforced by Article 140 of the Basic Law in tandem with Article 136 (4) of the Weimar Constitution. These provisions prohibit the state from forcing anyone to participate in religious practices.

   Article 4 (1) does not simply command the state to refrain from interfering in the faith commitments of individuals or religious communities. It also obliges the state to secure for them a realm of freedom in which they can realize their personalities within an ideological and religious context. The state is thus committed to protect the individual from attacks or obstructions by adherents of different beliefs or competing religious groups. Article 4 (1), however, grants neither to the individual nor to religious communities the right to have their faith commitments supported by the state. On the contrary, freedom of faith as guaranteed by Article 4 (1) of the Basic Law requires the state to remain neutral in matters of faith and religion. A state in which members of various or even conflicting religious and ideological convictions must live together can guarantee peaceful coexistence only if it remains neutral in matters of religious belief. Therefore, the state must be wary of independently endangering religious peace in society. This mandate finds its basis not only in Article 4 (1) of the Basic Law, but also in Article 3 (3), Article 33 (1), and Article 140, which incorporates into the Basic Law Articles 136 (1) and (4) and 137 (1) of the Weimar Constitution. These articles prohibit the establishment of official churches and forbid the state from granting special privileges to members of certain faiths. The numerical strength or social importance [of a religious community] has no relevance. Rather, the state is obligated to treat various religious and ideological communities with an even hand. And when the state supports or works together with [these religious communities], it must take care not to identify itself with a particular community.

Article 4 (1), when considered in relation to Article 6 (2) of the Basic Law, which confers on parents the natural right to take care of and to raise their children, also embraces the right of parents to educate their children in accord with their religious and ideological convictions. It is up to the parents to transmit to their children those commitments of faith and ideology which they accept as true. Similarly, they have the right to shield their children from religious beliefs they consider false or harmful.

2. Section 13 (1.3) of the Bavarian Elementary School Ordinance and the disputed [judicial] decisions based on this provision encroach on this basic right.

(a) Section 13 (1.3) of the Bavarian Elementary School Ordinance prescribes the display of the crucifix in all elementary school classrooms in Bavaria. According to the interpretation of the courts involved in the initial proceedings, the term "cross" represents both a simple cross and one adorned with the figure of Christ. Our examination of the ordinance, therefore, must consider the significance of both the cross and the crucifix. In their action before the administrative court, the complainants had requested that only the crucifixes be removed; the court below, however, insisted that the motion might also include [a simple] cross without the figure of Christ. . . .

Given the context of compulsory education, the presence of crosses in classrooms amounts to state-enforced "learning under the cross," with no possibility to avoid seeing it. This constitutes the crucial difference between the display of the cross in a classroom and the religious symbols people frequently encounter in their daily lives. Encounters of the latter type are not the result of any state action but are merely a consequence of the pervasive presence of various faith commitments and religious communities in society. In addition, the latter situation does not admit to the same degree of compulsion. Admittedly, persons who walk the streets, use public transportation, or enter buildings have no control over such encounters with religious symbols and manifestations. But as a rule, these encounters are fleeting, and even if they are not, they are still not the result of any state preference backed by sanctions. . . .

(b) The cross is the symbol of a particular religious conviction, and not merely an expression of cultural values that have been influenced by Christianity.

Admittedly, numerous Christian traditions have found their way into the general culture of our society over the centuries, and these traditions cannot be denied even by the adversaries of Christianity and its historical heritage. However, these traditions must be distinguished from the particular tenets of the Christian religion, and especially from a particular Christian faith together with its ritual and symbolic representations. Any support of these faith tenets by the state would undermine freedom of religion, a matter already determined by the Federal Constitutional Court in its ruling on the constitutionality of so-called biconfessional public elementary schools [*Simultanschulen*] (citing 41 BVerfGE 29, 52). In affirming the Christian character of these schools, the court ruled that the state may legitimately recognize Christianity's imprint on culture and education over the course of Western history, but not the particular tenets of the Christian religion. Only if the parameters of its continued historical impact are delineated can the affirmation of Christianity be legally justified in the eyes of non-Christians.

The cross now as before represents a specific tenet of Christianity; it constitutes its most significant faith symbol. It symbolizes man's redemption from original sin through Christ's sacrifice just as it represents Christ's victory over Satan and death and his power over the world. Accordingly, the cross symbolizes both suffering and triumph. For believing Christians, it is the object of veneration and practiced piety. To this day, the presence of a cross in a home or room is understood as an expression of the dweller's Christian faith. On the other hand, because of the significance Christianity attributes to the cross, non-Christians and atheists perceive it to be the symbolic expression of certain faith convictions and a symbol of missionary zeal. To see the cross as nothing more than a cultural artifact of the Western tradition without any particular religious meaning would amount to a profanation contrary to the self-understanding of Christians and the Christian church. Section 13 (1) of the Bavarian ordinance also makes clear the religious significance of the cross.

(c) One cannot deny, as do the challenged decisions of the administrative courts, that the cross also has an effect on students.

Needless to say, the presence of the cross in classrooms does not force children to identify with or to venerate the cross, or to conduct themselves in certain ways. Similarly, the cross has no influence on the teaching of secular subjects, and no religious belief or practice is required in learning these subjects. But the cross does exert influence in other ways. Education is more than just transmitting fundamental cultural values and developing cognitive facilities. It also involves the development of pupils' emotional and affective abilities. The mission of the school is to develop and promote a pupil's personality and to influence his or her social behavior. In this context, the display of the cross in classrooms takes on critical significance. Its presence constitutes a deeply moving appeal; it underscores the faith commitment it symbolizes, thus making that faith exemplary and worthy of being followed. This is particularly true with young and impressionable people who are still learning to develop their critical capacities and principles of right conduct.

While the decisions below acknowledge the appeal of the cross, they do not suggest that it has a specific Christian meaning for students of different faiths. According to the lower courts it is an essential expression of faith only for the Christian pupils. Similarly, although the Bavarian prime minister was of the opinion that the cross has no distinctive religious meaning during periods of ordinary instruction, he conceded that the cross transforms itself into a distinct symbol of faith when students are engaged in reciting prayer and during periods of religious instruction.

3. The basic right to religious freedom is unconditionally guaranteed, but this guarantee does not imply that there is no limitation on this right. Any limitation, however, must be rooted in the Constitution. Legislatures are not free to restrict [religious] liberty in the absence of such limiting provisions in the Basic Law itself. In short, there is no constitutional justification for the limitation imposed here. . . .

[Bavaria and the dissenting justices argued that Article 7 (1) of the Basic Law confers exclusive jurisdiction over educational matters on the state. In this section of its opinion, the majority conceded that under the Basic Law the state is entrusted with the duty of establishing schools and setting educational goals and courses of study, and that these requirements may often conflict with the religious and ideological convictions of students and their parents. Here, however, the court invoked the interpretive principle of "practical concordance" (*praktische Konkordanz*), which requires the court to reconcile or harmonize conflicting values as much as possible in any given set of circumstances. Accordingly, the majority saw its task as one of preserving, to the extent possible, the values of both Articles 4 and 7.]

In working out such a compromise, the state need not abandon all references to religion or ideology in meeting the educational mission mandated by Article 7 (1) of the Basic Law. No state, even one that universally guarantees freedom of religion and is committed to religious and ideological neutrality, is in a position completely to divest itself of the cultural and historical values on which social cohesion and the attainment of public goals depend. The Christian religion and the Christian churches have always exerted a tremendous influence in our society, regardless of how this influence is evaluated today. The intellectual traditions rooted in their heritage, the meaning of life and the patterns of behavior transmitted by them cannot simply be dismissed by the state as irrelevant. This applies particularly to education since it constitutes a unique setting for perpetuating our traditions and renewing the cultural foundations of society. Furthermore, any state that requires children to attend state schools must respect the religious freedom of those parents who want their children to receive a religiously based education. Article 7 (5) of the Basic Law acknowledges this parental right by permitting the establishment of public ideological and confessional schools and by making religious instruction a regular part of the curriculum in state schools (Article 7 [3]). Additionally, the Basic Law also leaves room for the exercise of a student's faith commitment.

In a pluralistic society, needless to say, the state, in setting up a system of compulsory public school instruction, cannot possibly satisfy all educational goals or needs. Problems will always arise, and it will be particularly difficult to implement the negative as well as the positive aspects of religious freedom in one and the same public institution. So far as education is concerned, no one can claim an absolute right under Article 4 (1) of the Basic Law.

In resolving the inevitable tension between the negative and positive aspects of religious freedom, and in seeking to promote the tolerance that the Basic Law mandates, the state, in forming the public will, must strive to bring about an acceptable compromise. On the one hand, Article 7 of the Basic Law acknowledges the role of religious and ideological influences in education; on the other hand, Article 4 of the Basic Law mandates — to the extent possible — that religious and ideological pressures be removed from decisions favoring a certain type of school. Each article must be interpreted in the light of the other, and the two must be harmonized in such a way as to protect the interests that they were originally designed to safeguard.

The Federal Constitutional Court has concluded [in its previous case law] that the state legislature is not forbidden to introduce Christian values into the organization of public elementary schools, even if parents who cannot avoid sending their children to this type of school reject all forms of religious education. This presupposes, however, that coercion is to be reduced to an indispensable minimum. In particular, the school must not proselytize on behalf of a particular religious doctrine or actively promote the tenets of the Christian faith. Christianity's influence on culture and education may be affirmed and recognized, but not particular articles of faith. Christianity as a cultural force incorporates in particular the idea of tolerance toward people of different persuasions. Confrontation with a Christian worldview will not lead to discrimination or devaluation of a non-Christian ideology so long as the state does not impose the values of the Christian faith on non-Christians; indeed, the state must foster the autonomous thinking that Article 4 of the Basic Law secures within the religious and ideological realms. In the light of these principles we have already sustained the validity of the establishment of Christian community schools under Article 135 (2) of the Bavarian Constitution; the court has likewise upheld the constitutionality of the biconfessional public elementary schools of Baden-Württemberg. These schools were based on traditions prevailing in the region of Baden [and were designed to serve the needs of the major denominations without interfering with the religious liberty of any student or parent].

The display of crosses in classrooms, however, exceeds [these guidelines and constitutional limits]. As noted earlier, the cross cannot be separated from its reference to a particular tenet of Christianity; far from being a mere symbol of Western culture, it symbolizes the core of the Christian faith, one that has admittedly shaped the Western world in multiple ways but which is not commonly shared by all members of society. . . . The display of the cross in public compulsory school thus violates Article 4 (1) of the Basic Law. This rule, of course, does not apply to [state-supported] Christian confessional schools.

(b) Parents and pupils who adhere to the Christian faith cannot justify the display of the cross by invoking their positive freedom of religious liberty. All parents and pupils are equally entitled to the positive freedom of faith, not just Christian parents and pupils. The resulting conflict cannot be resolved on the basis of majority rule since the constitutional right to freedom of faith is particularly designed to protect the rights of religious minorities. Moreover, Article 4 (1) does not provide the holders of the constitutional right with an unrestricted right to affirm their faith commitments within the framework of public institutions. Inasmuch as schools heed the Constitution, leaving room for religious instruction, school prayer, and other religious events, all of these activities must be conducted on a voluntary basis and the school must ensure that students who do not wish to participate in these activities are excused from them and suffer no discrimination because of their decision not to participate. The situation is different with respect to the display of the cross. Students who do not share the same faith are unable to remove themselves from its presence and message. Finally, it would be incompatible with the principle of practical concordance to suppress completely the feelings of people of different beliefs in order to enable the pupils of Christian belief not only to have religious instruction and voluntary prayer in the public schools, but also to learn under the symbol of their faith even when instructed in secular subjects.

D. The provision of section 13 (1.3) of the Bavarian Community School Ordinance, which is the subject of this opinion, is incompatible with the Basic Law and therefore unconstitutional.

Justices Otto Seidl, Alfred Söllner, and Evelyn Haas, dissenting.

We do not share the senate majority's opinion that section 13 (1.3) of the Bavarian Elementary School Ordinance, which mandates the display of crosses in all classrooms, violates the Basic Law. The challenged decisions . . . do not violate the complainants' basic rights guaranteed by Article 4 (1) and (3) in tandem with Article 6 (2) of the Basic Law.

I. 1. According to Article 7 (1) of the Basic Law, . . . the right to establish schools is conferred exclusively on the individual states. . . . The right to establish and operate schools is unlisted among the powers [conferred exclusively on the national government]. In contrast to the Weimar Constitution, which assigned legislative authority in educational matters to the Reich, the Basic Law confers no legislative or administrative authority on the federal government in the field of education. The history of Article 7 shows that the individual states were to enjoy extensive power over the ideological and religious character of public schools. This was one manifestation of the federal principle. . . . The founders repeatedly said that educational policy would remain in the hands of the [individual] states.

2. Therefore, the constitutional issue raised by the complaints must be considered in the light of the special situation in the *Land* of Bavaria. . . .

[Article 131 (2) of] the Bavarian Constitution of December 2, 1946, defines the state's educational objectives as follows:

(2) The highest goals of the educational system are: Fear of God; respect for the religious convictions of all; the dignity of the human person; self-control; willingness to accept responsibility; readiness to assist others; an open mind in matters of truth, goodness, and beauty; and a sense of responsibility for nature and the environment.

The last clause on environmental responsibility was added to the Constitution on June 20, 1984. The other objectives listed in Article 131 have remained unchanged since the Constitution entered into force in 1946.

As for elementary education, Article 135 of the Bavarian Constitution initially provided for confessional and community schools, with some degree of preference given to confessional schools. In the course of time, however, the people of Bavaria changed this policy. On July 22, 1968, they voted — in a plebiscite — to amend Article 135 of the state constitution. [Article 135] now reads as follows:

All children subject to compulsory elementary education shall attend common public schools. These schools shall instruct and educate their pupils in accordance with the principles of the Christian faith. Details shall be regulated by law.

According to Article 135 (2) of the amended Bavarian Constitution, Christianity is not to be understood in a confessional sense. Rather, the principles of the Christian faith within the meaning of this provision encompass those values common to all Christian denominations as well as the ethical norms on which they are based. These values and norms are characteristically Christian and are widely recognized as such. Instruction in these principles is intended to lead pupils toward the educational goals described in Article 131 (2) of the Bavarian Constitution. Bavaria's constitution, however, does not mandate a specific Christian faith commitment. In affirming Christianity, the state is merely acknowledging the West's cultural and educational indebtedness to Christianity. [This acknowledgment], as borne out by the history of Western civilization, is warranted even in the eyes of non-Christians.

Given these considerations, there can be no constitutional objection to the type of Christian community school provided for under Article 135 (2) of the Bavarian Constitution.

3. Under Article 7 (1) and (5) of the Basic Law, individual states enjoy a large measure of discretion in determining the [nature] and organization of elementary schools. . . . The rule that mandates the display of a cross in every classroom does not exceed that discretion. Since the state legislature is permitted to establish a Christian community school, it cannot be prevented from expressing, through the symbol of the cross, the values and ideals which characterize this type of school.

(a) Section 13 (1.3) of the Bavarian Elementary School Ordinance implements the organization of the Christian community school. For teachers and students alike, the display of the cross in classrooms symbolizes Western values and ethical norms that transcend confessional considerations and are to be taught in this type of school. In enacting this law, the state legislature was permitted to consider the fact that the majority of citizens residing in Bavaria belong to one or another form of the Christian church. Furthermore, the state legislature was permitted to assume that the display of a cross would be welcomed, or at least respected, by the majority of persons unaffiliated with any of the aforementioned churches; [it could legitimately be assumed that the] cross's symbolic character — representing nondenominational Western values and norms — would be accepted by all. Indeed, the majority of the population approved the Bavarian Constitution's provisions on Christian community schools. . . .

4. The state has a constitutional mandate to remain neutral in religious and ideological matters. But the principle of neutrality must not be construed as indifference toward such matters. The church-state articles of the Weimar Constitution, which have been incorporated into Article 140 of the Basic Law, envision neutrality in the sense of cooperation between the state, churches, and religious communities. These articles [may even require the state] to support churches and religious communities.

In its decisions regarding the constitutional admissibility of Christian community schools, the Federal Constitutional Court, following the constitutional command of neutrality [in religious affairs], declared that the school may exercise only minimal influence in those areas where it is in a position to influence children in matters of faith and conscience. Furthermore, a public school must not be missionary in nature, nor is the school permitted to demand the obligatory acceptance of Christian faith commitments; schools must remain open to influences from other ideological and religious ideas and values (citing 41 BVerfGE 29, 51).

The provisions of section 13 (1.3) of the Bavarian Elementary School Ordinance that the senate struck down as unconstitutional meet every one of these criteria. The mere presence of the cross demands no particular mode of conduct and does not convert the school into a missionary enterprise. Nor does the cross change the character of the Christian community school; rather, as a symbol shared by all Christian faiths, the cross is uniquely suited to illustrate the constitutionally permitted educational subject matter of this type of school. The display of the cross does not exclude consideration of other ideological or religious norms and values. In addition, Article 136 (1) of the Bavarian Constitution requires the schools to respect the religious sensibilities of all persons.

II. Contrary to the view of the senate majority, the display of the cross in school classrooms does not interfere with religious freedom. . . .

The undisturbed *practice* of religion secured by Article 4 (2) reinforces and accentuates the religious freedom that Article 4 (1) guarantees, a fact that the senate majority entirely overlooks. Together these two paragraphs provide the individual with a space in which actively to practice his or her faith. If therefore one cannot object constitutionally to participation in voluntary nondenominational prayer, then surely this holds equally true of the display of the cross in school classrooms. Thus the state provides space for positive freedom of creed in areas for which it has assumed complete responsibility and in which religious and ideological views have traditionally been relevant (citing 41 BVerfGE 29, 49; and 52 BVerfGE 223, 241).

2. Thus there has been no violation of religious freedom.

(a) The complainants have not invoked the freedom to practice their religion under Article 4 (2) of the Basic Law, nor have they claimed that the state has violated their positive freedom of faith under Article 4 (1); they merely assert a violation of their negative freedom of religion, a freedom Article 4 (1) also guarantees. In fact, they do not demand the display of a symbol of their own faith or ideology next to or in place of the cross. Rather, they request the removal of crucifixes, which they perceive to be symbols of a religious doctrine to which they do not adhere. In our ruling of November 5, 1991 (citing 85 BVerfGE 94), which rejected the complainants' request for a temporary injunction, we formulated the constitutional issue — even more pointedly than in the present ruling — as follows: "Under what circumstances does the display of religious symbols in schools implicate the negative right to freedom of religion and to what extent must a minority be expected to tolerate [such a display] in the interest of the majority's right to practice its religion?"

This issue . . . deals with the question of how the positive and negative freedoms of religion of pupils and their parents can be generally reconciled in the public compulsory school arena. To find a solution to the inevitable tension between the negative and positive freedoms of religion is the task of the democratic state legislature; the legislature is required to work out a compromise that honors the various opinions and values present during the formation of the public will (citing 41 BVerfGE 29, 50). In the process, the negative freedom of religion must not be allowed to negate the positive right to manifest one's religious freedom in the event that the two conflict. The principle of religious liberty implies no right to have religious expression banned altogether. The key principle here is tolerance. This principle requires the reconciliation of opposing views on religious freedom.

(b) Section 13 (3) of the Bavarian Elementary School Ordinance satisfies these principles and requirements. The recommended balancing [that has taken place here] fully complies with the Basic Law.

(aa) In evaluating and assessing the concerns of the parties to this case, the senate majority has mistakenly identified the cross with a Christian theological view. What matters instead is the effect that the sight of the cross has on individual pupils. Admittedly, the Christian pupil may see the cross in the religious light suggested by the majority. The nonbelieving pupil, however, cannot be assumed to share the same view. From his or her point of view, the cross is less a symbol of the Christian faith than of the values reflected in the Christian community school, namely, those values associated with a Western culture deeply rooted in Christian ideas. . . .

(bb) In view of the cross's symbolic character, non-Christian pupils and their parents are obligated to accept its presence in the classroom. The principle of tolerance requires as much, and the display of the cross does not constitute an unacceptable burden [on the religious conscience of non-Christian pupils].

The psychological effect that exposure to the cross has on non-Christian pupils is relatively mild. The mental burden here is minimal, for pupils are not required to behave in a given way or to participate in religious practices before the cross. In contrast to [compulsory] school prayer, pupils are not forced to reveal their ideological or religious convictions through nonparticipation. This precludes any discrimination against them.

In addition, the cross does not imply any kind of missionary activity. As noted above, its [narrow] religious significance has no impact on the course of instruction. Moreover, the particular situation in Bavaria must be considered. Even outside the narrow confines of the church, pupils are exposed daily to the sight of crosses in many areas of life. We need only mention the presence of crosses along roadways, their exhibition on secular buildings (such as hospitals, nursing homes, and even hotels and restaurants), and their display in private homes. Under these circumstances, the presence of the cross in schoolrooms is nothing unusual; it has nothing to do with anything [that could remotely be regarded as] missionary.

Justice Evelyn Haas, dissenting. . . .

[Justice Haas dissented mainly on the ground that the constitutional complaint was inadmissible. Five years had elapsed since the First Senate's denial of the request for a temporary injunction. Meanwhile, the students involved in this case had changed schools, and thus there was no longer any urgency or good reason to interfere with the judgments of the courts below.]

NOTE: THE IMPACT OF THE *CRUCIFIX* CASE. *Crucifix II* case triggered a storm of protest throughout Germany. Chancellor Helmut Kohl called the decision "incomprehensible." Conservative newspapers bashed the Constitutional Court for overriding the popular will. Church leaders uniformly condemned the decision, calling it a threat to Germany's Christian culture. Many constitutional lawyers, including a former president of the Constitutional Court, chastised the justices for their infirm reasoning. The decision produced the strongest denunciation in Bavaria. Holding crucifixes aloft, demonstrators in Munich and other communities marched in defiance of the Karlsruhe court as their political leaders called on state officials not to enforce the decision.[47] It was the most negative reaction to a judicial decision in the history of the Federal Republic and the only instance of clear and open defiance of a ruling by the Federal Constitutional Court.

The duration and intensity of the protest worried Germany's judicial establishment. The German Judges' Association warned that the rule of law was at stake and that any refusal to obey the *Crucifix* ruling would endanger the Federal Republic's constitutional democracy.[48] Justice Dieter Grimm, one of the five justices in the *Crucifix* majority, was prompted to answer the court's critics in the *Frankfurter Allgemeine Zeitung,* Germany's newspaper of record. Grimm's prominently displayed letter was published under the caption "Why a Judicial Ruling Merits Respect" and deserves to be reproduced in full:

UNDER THE LAW
Why a Judicial Ruling Merits Respect

In a system that sets forth its political and social order in a constitution and establishes a constitutional court to protect that document, political and social conflicts are bound to arise in the form of constitutional disputes. Unlike the political arena, the court is unable to sidestep such disputes by refusing to decide them. It has to decide the conflicts, yet not on its own initiative and according to the justices' individual preferences or the supposed wishes of a popular majority, but according to the preestablished provisions of the Basic Law. Not everyone will be satisfied with the court's decision, but that is in the nature of the judicial resolution of conflicts; and, at times, the majority will be the disappointed party. This is what constitutionalism is all about; its purpose is to safeguard the rights of minorities against encroachment by the majority.

Under these circumstances constitutional Court decisions cannot always be greeted with universal approval. Criticism of such decisions is normal and in the interest of the court's own reflections about its role as the final arbiter of the Constitution; indeed, such criticism is necessary. Disagreement with a decision, however, does not relieve the critic of the duty to comply with it. This is the basic premise of the entire system of constitutional governance. The process of decision making must be established in a way that gives room to the different viewpoints. The result of the process is valid notwithstanding one's disagreement with it. If in the light of the *Crucifix* case, state or church officials create the impression that this is not so, they threaten to disrupt the Federal Republic's generally stable history of postwar constitutional governance and are likely to shake the foundations of social peace.

Those who insist on disobeying the court's decision or encouraging resistance to it act on the maxim that the law is to be respected only if we agree with it. At risk here is nothing less than the unitary force of the law. This binding force constitutes the foundation of the rule of law and political order, at least within the constitutional state. Anyone who encourages others to defy a judicial ruling today because he or she fails to approve of it will be unable to explain tomorrow why others should obey laws or administrative orders of which they disapprove. If politicians continue on their chosen path, they will not only undermine the foundation of the constitutional state, they will also make it impossible to conduct their own affairs [of state]. This is meanwhile the issue of the Federal Constitutional Court's crucifix ruling.[49]

Justice Grimm's views were shared by numerous spokespersons in the Social Democratic Party and by most left-of-center political parties and groups. The SPD's legal experts and the justice ministers of several German *Länder* warned against excessive criticism of the court out of fear that such criticism would undermine the court's integrity as an institution.[50] A lead editorial in the *Frankfurter Allgemeine Zeitung* by Friedrich Karl Fromme, one of Germany's most respected commentators on the Federal Constitutional Court, expressed the views of many of the court's responsible critics. First, he noted, the court's opinion was thought to be inconsistent with the *Interdenominational School* case (1975; no. 9.5), which had upheld the validity of Christian community schools. Second, the court was faulted for the broad scope of its ruling and the "laicist enthusiasm" of its reasoning.[51]

Much of the early critical reaction to *Classroom Crucifix* was in response to the headnotes (*Leitsätze*) which accompanied the release of the decision. The headnotes seemed to suggest that the court was mandating the removal of all crucifixes from all elementary school classrooms. If this is what *Classroom Crucifix* required, it would indeed be a revolutionary decision, amounting to a reversal of *Interdenominational School*. Perhaps in response to the public outcry, the court appeared to back away from this interpretation, indicating in a press release that the headnotes were not fully consistent with the reasoning of the case.[52] This was taken to mean, as Bavarian school officials had already maintained, that a crucifix would have to be removed only in the presence of students objecting to it on religious grounds. Nevertheless, the debate continued as Bavarian state officials were preparing "corrective" legislation in defiance of the court's ruling.[53]

NOTE: THE CHURCH TAX. Among the provisions of the Weimar Constitution absorbed into the Basic Law is the clause empowering religious societies incorporated under public law "to levy taxes in accordance with state law on the basis of the civil taxation lists." The primary beneficiaries of this constitutional policy are the Catholic and Protestant (Reformed and Evangelical) churches and the relatively small Jewish religious community. Church finance offices can collect the tax directly, but most churches delegate this function to their respective state governments. The tax or-dinarily takes the form of a surcharge, usually 8 to 10 percent, on the assessed income tax of resident individuals whose names appear on the baptismal records of those churches or religious communities. It is limited, however, to a fixed percent-age of taxable income. As with the income tax, the employer withholds and remits the church tax to a state revenue office, after which the state distributes the funds to the churches in amounts proportionate to their total membership.[54] These cash payments amount to tens of millions of deutsche marks per year and enable the churches not only to build new facilities—from chapels to advanced academies of continuing education—but also to operate and maintain, as they have traditionally done, thousands of schools, nursing homes, hospitals, and charitable organizations.

Any person whose name appears in a church registry is automatically subject to the tax. To be relieved of the tax, a wage earner must formally resign or withdraw from his or her church, and approximately 175,000 persons do so each year. Need-less to say, the church tax "goes to the very core of the church-state relationship as it most directly affects the individual."[55] The constitutional validity of the tax, how-ever, is unquestioned. The Constitutional Court has written:

> [In the light of Article 137 (6) of the Weimar Constitution], the state is obligated to establish the conditions for the levying of [church] taxes, thus providing for the possibility of their compulsory collection. This sovereign right to tax collection granted by the state is quite different from the process of collecting contributions [from parishioners], which is an internal affair of the church. Pursuant to Article 137 (3) [of the Weimar Constitution], re-ligious societies are able to impose fees and contribution requirements with-out state interference. The levy of the church tax, on the other hand, is a common affair of both church and state. Here the state makes its own admin-istrative apparatus available to the church for the collection of the tax. State regulation is necessary to administer the tax. For that reason, the levying of the church tax is also subject to judicial review.[56]

The typical challenge to the church tax revolves around questions such as these: Who precisely is subject to the tax? Juristic or natural persons? What determines church membership for purposes of the tax? Who makes the determination? May the tax be levied for the full year in which a wage earner withdraws from his or her church? What constitutes a church or religious society entitled to cash payments derived from the tax? Which church receives tax proceeds collected from spouses joined in religiously mixed marriages? What portion of a joint income tax return is subject to the tax if only one of the marriage partners belongs to a church?

In 1965 the Constitutional Court decided a number of seminal cases involving the church tax and answered several of the questions posed in the previous para-graph.[57] One major theme runs through these cases: The state may lawfully apply the tax only to salaried persons who are church members. Once again the court has emphasized that "the state as the home of all citizens is bound by ideological and religious neutrality, [which] means that the state is not permitted to confer on a religious society any sovereign authority over individuals who are not among its members."[58] With regard to the church tax specifically, the First Senate said that

> religious societies exercise sovereign authority, however, when pursuant to state law they tax persons who are not among their members. . . . In the exercise of this authority the state, by means of its taxing power, is effectively providing financial support for religious societies. This the state may not do when the taxing power reaches persons who do not belong to those religious societies. The churches in their corporate character may obligate only their own members through the power of taxation.
>
> No significance is to be derived from the historical fact that religious societies once held a privileged position under the law. State churches in the sense that they were formerly known no longer exist in the light of the prohibition against an official church. Churches no longer have the legal capacity unilaterally to enroll persons, without regard to their wishes, who settle within their territorial jurisdiction. Indeed, the Weimar Constitution had already deprived them of any such territorial control; rather, their authority was to extend only to persons within their membership.[59]

Mixed-Marriage Church Tax I (1965) applied these principles to a mixed marriage involving one spouse who belonged to a church and the other who was not a member.

9.7 Mixed-Marriage Church Tax Case I (1965)
19 BVerfGE 226

[Baden-Württemberg's Church Tax Act permitted the spouse of a church member to be taxed even though he or she might not be a church member. Two employees who were not church members initiated an action to reclaim taxes withheld from their paychecks. The employees were taxed because their wives were church members. After the lower tax court rejected their claims, they appealed to the Federal Finance Court. The court, seriously doubting the constitutionality of the act as applied to nonmember spouses, referred the constitutional question to the Federal Constitutional Court pursuant to Article 100 (1) of the Basic Law. The two cases were consolidated in the following judgment.]

Judgment of the First Senate. . . .

2. [The Baden-Württemberg statute] . . . is null and void with respect to paragraph 2 of the sentence reading "or the spouse of the member."

C. I. 1. As the Federal Constitutional Court has determined, . . . Articles 136, 139, and 141 of the Weimar Constitution have been incorporated to form constituent parts of the Basic Law. They form an organic whole and must consequently be interpreted according to the meaning and spirit of the constitutional value system. This means that state laws promulgated on the basis of Article 137 (6) of the Weimar Constitution concerning the collection of church taxes must adhere to constitutional principles, that is, the fundamental rights of the Basic Law. The state legislators may not disregard the value system expressed in these constitutional norms. . . .

2. Section 6 (2) of the Church Tax Act violates the fundamental right of an employee who is not a member of a religious association as derived from Article 2 (1) of the Basic Law.

(a) According to this act, all employees "are subject to" a church tax on wages if they or their spouses belong to a religious association authorized to tax. Contrary to the opinion of the state ministry of Baden-Württemberg, this provision can be understood to determine who must pay the tax (section 97 (1) of the Tax Code, section 38 (3) of the Income Tax Act). An employee is required to pay the church tax simply because his spouse is a church member. Thus, because of the state law, the employee must pay the church tax although he does not belong to a church authorized to tax him.

As this court has said, a law may not be viewed as part of the constitutional order if it obligates a person to pay financial benefits to a religious association of which he or she is not a member. Because the nonmember employee has no legal way of avoiding this tax liability, the Church Tax Act impermissibly interferes with his right to personality under Article 2 (1) of the Basic Law.

(b) The legal rule which states that state law may not impose a church tax upon a third person not belonging to that church must also apply to the regulation of married persons' liability for church taxes when only one of them is a church member. The argument is erroneous that subjecting the nonmember spouse to the church tax may be justified because of the nature of marriage as a permanent union of the partners into a complete community of all aspects of life.

In a mixed-faith marriage, no community exists in the exact areas being considered—i.e., religious convictions and beliefs. The marital community is not based upon mutual recognition of religious articles of faith, values, and obligations. Consequently, it would be unreasonable and would contradict the libertarian constitutional system of the Basic Law if one wished to force the nonmember spouse to establish direct relations—even if only financial ones—to a religious community by imposing unavoidable legal sanctions. If, as the Federal Constitutional Court and the Federal High Court of Justice have said, each partner may believe what he chooses and may even convert to another religious belief without being guilty of a marital transgression, then one partner's connection with a church does not obligate the other partner. Hence it is impermissible to argue that because the nonmember spouse made the decision to marry his spouse he should not assert a violation of his religious freedom when he is forced to pay his spouse's church tax obligation. Each partner must decide if he wants and is able to make concessions in religious and ideological matters. The tolerance that married persons of different faiths owe one another may not lead to the creation of legal ties to third parties, especially not to churches and other religious associations.

(c) Marriage may be linked with economic legal consequences only if these consequences are related to the sphere of life being regulated. This is not the case here. The liability for church tax is the economic equivalent and consequence of church membership; that is, it results from a strictly personal relationship. However, the tax relationship to be regulated is, by its nature, an individual one. Even if both partners were unlimitedly liable for the tax, the marital status may not be used as the basis for discriminating against married persons. This applies even more forcefully if marital status is used as a reason for creating a tax obligation which one spouse would otherwise not owe to the tax creditor, the church. Accordingly, we see no reason to disadvantage married persons by deviating from the individual taxation statutorily anchored in section 27 of the Church Law and to impose the obligation to pay the church tax on an employee solely because his or her spouse is a church member.

3. Section 6 (2) of the Church Tax Act also would be unconstitutional if it burdened a nonmember spouse with the liability for his member spouse's obligation to pay the church tax.

(a) For the same constitutional reasons that prohibit a nonmember spouse from being held responsible as a tax debtor, this spouse may also not be made liable for his spouse's church taxes. Liability in the sense of answering for someone else's debt creates a direct relationship between the nonmember spouse and the other spouse's church authorized to tax, by virtue of which the church has direct access to the income of the nonmember spouse. . . .

(b) The attempt to derive the nonmember spouse's liability for the church tax debt of his spouse from their mutual obligation to support each other is misdirected.

First, it is incompatible with the concept of a marital community to treat the married persons' obligation to support and maintain each other as performance in exchange for valuable consideration similar to bilateral contractual obligations. This obligation is part of a web of reciprocal, often disparate rights and duties which, in their totality, are basically of equal value and are precluded from being weighed arithmetically one against the other. Apart from this, the husband is no longer solely responsible for support and maintenance pursuant to section 1360 *et seq.* of the Civil Code as amended by the act according equal rights to women of June 18, 1957; rather, both partners have the mutual obligation of maintenance and support. To the extent that one spouse must maintain and support the other, he or she must supply the other with the means required to satisfy that spouse's personal needs (section 1360a (1), Civil Code). The cultivation of religious, spiritual, political, cultural, or athletic interests are unanimously counted as personal needs. Accordingly, the spouse obligated to pay support must supply the other with the means needed to fulfill his religious obligations. . . . It is not the legal relationship between married persons that is at issue but rather their relationship to an institution existing outside of the marriage. The problem of the husband's obligation to support his wife is important only for the question of who, as between the marriage partners, must raise the means for the tax burden arising from the person of the wife. Consequently, if the members of a church levy a tax which is and can only be connected to the fact of church membership, then the husband's obligation to pay this tax based on his duty of support possibly exists toward his wife, but not toward the church. On the other hand, someone may not be subject to a tax only because he is obligated to support someone else. This would mean viewing the husband's spousal support payments as market economy income in the sense used by the Income Tax Act and taxing them accordingly.

II. Thus section 6 (2) of the Church Tax Law is unconstitutional insofar as it subjects employees to a church wage tax when only their spouses belong to the religious corporation; therefore it violates the fundamental right derived from Article 2 (1) of the Basic Law. The phrase "or his spouse" is therefore null and void. . . .

NOTE: CHURCH AND STATE IN GERMANY. As the materials in this chapter show, religion plays an important role in German society. There are historical reasons for the high value the Basic Law attaches to the place of religious societies in the nation's public life. Altar and throne were joined throughout most of German history before the establishment of the Weimar Republic.[60] Two central principles informed the church-state articles of the 1919 Constitution: the denominational neutrality of the state in religious matters, and the autonomy of religious societies with respect to their internal affairs. In practice, however, the established churches have continued to enjoy a preferred position in society as past institutional arrangements persist into the present. The church tax is such an arrangement, as is the provision of the Weimar Constitution (Article 137 [5]) carried over into the Basic Law, which treats the main churches as corporate bodies under public law.

Provisions such as these trace their origins to the medieval tradition of the "two swords," in which the royal and the sacred powers, each supreme in its respective sphere, shared in the governance of society. The view that church and state are equal partners in the social order was manifested in the first half of the twentieth century by the theory of coordination (*Gleichordnung*).[61] According to this theory, church and state settled their disputes by negotiation, with church-state treaties and concordats serving as common instruments through which they regulated their relationship. Indeed, treaties and concordats are still a principal method of accommodation between church and state.[62] As these treaties demonstrate, the German notion of neutrality, which continues to shape the law of church-state relations in the Federal Republic, is one that emphasizes a cooperative rather than a strict separationist model of this relationship.

Coordination versus cooperation. The framers of the Basic Law were unwilling to renounce the *modus vivendi* between church and state established by the Weimar articles. The continuity represented by these articles was more than a mindless or reluctant adherence to tradition. Contemporary circumstances helped to support the tradition. The religious divisions of the past had virtually disappeared as new forms of political and social cooperation emerged out of the common struggle of the major churches against national socialism. The state collapsed, but the churches survived the war with their organizations intact and their reputations far less sullied than other institutions of society. As a consequence, the churches were poised to assist in the work of reconstruction, both material and moral. The common good, as then understood, dictated not only the juridical recognition of religion as uniquely important to contemporary society but also the fostering of cooperation between church and state.

Whether or not the incorporation of the Weimar articles into the Basic Law implies the continuing validity of the coordination theory is hotly disputed among German constitutional scholars. Some hold fast to the theory of equal partnership; others maintain the legal superiority of the state over religious communities. The constitutionally recognized status of the churches, argue the latter, is no more than an affirmation of their independence as influential social groups. This position relegates the churches to the same rank as other groups competing with each other in a pluralistic society. These critics acknowledge the utility and even propriety of church-state treaties but claim that the subjects of such agreements could be regulated by ordinary law. Most commentators, however, seem reluctant to freeze either of these polar views into the meaning of the Basic Law. The middle view says that constitutional interpretation should take into account the evolving and dynamic character of the church-state relationship, including the increasing diversity and secularization of society and even changes in the churches' conception of their own role in society.[63]

The Federal Constitutional Court has taken a position midway between the theory of equal partnership and the pluralistic view. In the *Clergyman in Public Office* case (1976), the Second Senate, citing a number of leading authorities on church-state issues, rejected the view that the church is simply one group among many and thus subject to the limits of general law. A unanimous senate declared that churches bear a "qualitatively different relationship to the state than do other large social groups. This is because these groups represent only partial interests, whereas the church, like the state, represents persons as a whole in all fields of endeavor and behavior (legal or moral-religious). The church's unique character stems from its spiritual and religious mission [in the world]."[64] In the same opinion the court characterized the relationship between church and state as an "imperfect separation" and a "relationship of reciprocal independence,"[65] underscoring once again that the relationship is one not of rivalry but of cooperation.

The Basic Law does not explicitly recognize churches as such. Except for the provision that bars the establishment of a state church, the Weimar articles make no mention of a church or denomination. They speak, rather, of "religious bodies." Historically, however, this term has been taken to mean religious organizations or denominations characterized by institutional permanence and relatively stable memberships. The mainline Protestant and Catholic churches clearly qualify as religious bodies in this sense, rendering them, as a consequence, "corporate bodies under public law" with certain rights and privileges. German law also distinguishes between churches and minority religious sects, particularly those of recent vintage. Although the latter do not enjoy the corporate rights of the mainline churches, the Basic Law secures their freedom and autonomy.[66] Finally, Article 137 (7) declares that "associations whose purpose is the cultivation of a philosophical ideology shall have the same status as religious bodies." According to Article 137 (5), however, the granting of such status would depend, as in the case of religious bodies other than the mainline churches, on whether the constitution and membership of these associations "offers an assurance of their permanency."[67]

9.8 Evangelical Church Case (1965)
18 BVerfGE 385

[The essential facts are contained in the opinion.]

Judgment of the First Senate. . . .

The constitutional complaint is rejected.

I. The complainant is a congregation of the Evangelical church in Hesse and Nassau. On March 4, 1963, the leaders of this church decided to split the congregation and form a new parish from the members living north of the Frankfurt-Main–Main-Höchst train line. On November 26, 1964, the [Evangelical] church's Constitutional and Administrative Court denied the complainant's petition against this decision.

The congregation alleges in its complaint that the judgment of the ecclesiastical court violates Articles 2, 3, and 14 of the Basic Law. The complaint alleges that Article 2 is offended because the congregation has been divided against the will of its members, and that this [in turn] is not permitted under the basic rules of the Evangelical church. Article 3 is also violated, so the argument runs, because the decision was made on arbitrary grounds. Finally, the complaint alleges that Article 14 is implicated because the church's decision tramples upon the complainant's property right.

The complainant has moved for a temporary injunction because the division of the congregation, scheduled to take place on January 1, 1965, threatens seriously to disadvantage the [affected members of the congregation].

II. A constitutional complaint under section 90 (1) of the FCCA may be brought only against a violation of a basic right by "public authority." Public authority within the meaning of this provision does not include purely internal church measures.

1. There can be no state church under the system of church-state relations prescribed by the Basic Law. Every religious community has the right to order and administer its affairs independently within the limits of generally applicable law. Neither the state nor the civic community may involve itself in the selection of church officials (Article 140 of the Basic Law and Article 137 (1) and (3) of the Weimar Constitution). Churches are institutions endowed with the right of self-determination. Their nature is such that they do not derive their authority from the state and are independent of state influence. Thus the state may not interfere in their internal affairs.

The Constitution defines churches as corporate bodies under public law (Article 140 of the Basic Law and Article 137 of the Weimar Constitution). But this status does not compromise their independence. In light of the religious and confessional neutrality of the state under the Basic Law, this legal characterization does not signify an equality in status to other public-law corporations within the organic structure of the state. It is only a recognition of their public status. That status, while higher than that of religious societies organized under private law, does not subordinate the churches to the supreme authority of the state or to close administrative supervision [citing legal literature]. As a result of the public legal position and public effect of the churches, which they derive from their special mission and through which they are fundamentally differentiated from other societal organizations, ecclesiastical authority is indeed public [in nature] but does not exercise state authority. Only insofar as the churches exercise power conferred by the state, adopt measures beyond their authority as church bodies, or intrude into the sphere of the state do they indirectly exercise state authority, the consequence of which is to limit their self-determination depending on the [particular] facts of the case. In this connection we need not decide whether and to what extent basic rights can influence the self-determination of churches as it relates to [their treatment] of individual believers.

2. Whether an ecclesiastical measure is an internal church affair or is based on authority conferred by the state or affects the sphere of the state is to be decided — to the extent that a union of church and state does not result [therefrom] — by what is substantively to be regarded as a church affair, by the nature of the subject matter or by the purpose of the subject [under consideration]. If the church's activity has been confined to the sphere of internal church affairs, then no act of public authority has taken place against which a constitutional complaint may be brought. The inde-

pendence and autonomy of ecclesiastical authority recognized by the Constitution would be diminished if the state were to grant courts the right to examine whether internal church measures that do not spill over into the state's sphere of competence are compatible with the Basic Law. . . .

3. The challenged judgment of the ecclesiastical court . . . relates only to a dispute in the area of internal ecclesiastical affairs. The establishment and location of ecclesiastical assemblages, as provided for in section 14 of the Hesse-Nassau Church Congregation Order of March 25, 1954, belong to this sphere because they are matters pertaining to the constitution and organization of the church. Whether the [church tribunal's] decision violates the congregational principle of the Evangelical church is a question for the church itself to decide. . . . [To be sure], Article 4 of the Hesse Church Agreement of February 18, 1960, provides that decisions concerning the formation and alteration of congregational boundaries must be reported to the minister of culture and a copy of the organizational charter submitted to him. However, this participation of the state does not furnish a basis for a state agency to exert its influence. Article 4 of the Church Agreement involves no veto power by the minister of culture or the state government. The duty to report [in this instance] is based on a voluntary agreement between church and state. Thus the church's right to self-determination has not been limited.

4. Because on these grounds the challenged ecclesiastical judgment is not an exercise of public authority within the meaning of section 90 (1) of the FCCA, the constitutional complaint is inadmissible. Therefore the complainant's motion for a temporary restraining order is rejected.

NOTE: THE AUTONOMY OF THE CHURCH. Article 137 (3) of the Weimar Constitution, absorbed into the Basic Law under the terms of Article 140, declares that all religious organizations "shall regulate and administer [their] affairs independently within the limits of the law valid for all." Even apart from this provision, the principle of neutrality would seem to guarantee the independence of the churches or any other organization that describes itself as religious. The independence or institutional autonomy of such an organization is, of course, an aspect of religious freedom, a principle set forth in the *Rumpelkammer* case, in which the Constitutional Court extended the protection of the religious exercise clause (Article 4) to the collection of goods for charity because the activity was carried out for religious reasons.[68]

The Federal Constitutional Court has decided a number of cases involving the principle of church autonomy. The *Clergyman in Public Office* case arose out of a rule the Bremen Evangelical church laid down for its ministers. According to the rule, any clergyman elected to the Bundestag or any other state or local legislative body would be required to take a leave of absence from his official church duties during the period for which he was elected. Bremen's constitutional court invalidated the regulation as a violation of Article 48 (2) of the Basic Law, in which persons elected to the Bundestag are protected from being prevented from taking up their legislative duties or dismissed from their employment because of their intention to serve in parliament. The Federal Constitutional Court ruled in turn that this decision was an unauthorized interference with the internal affairs of a religious body.[69]

The *Catholic Hospital Abortion* case (1985) vindicated the right of a religiously affiliated hospital to determine its internal employment policies.[70] A Catholic hospital had dismissed a physician after he announced publicly that he was against the church's stand on abortion. (A companion case involved a Catholic youth center which dismissed an accountant after the center learned that he had left the church.) The hospital lodged a constitutional complaint against a decision of the Federal Labor Court invalidating the dismissal for contravening a public labor law. The Constitutional Court, while recognizing the universal applicability of public laws designed to protect employees against unlawful dismissal, nevertheless invalidated the Federal Labor Court's decision because it had not attached sufficient weight to the significance of the constitutional right of religious organizations to self-determination.

The court held that the hospital involved here was an "affair" of the church, and thus subject to church regulation. "This right of self-government," said the court, "embraces all the measures that [the hospital] takes in carrying out the charitable and pastoral tasks prescribed by its fundamental ecclesiastical mandate." This mandate "includes the choice of staff, [particularly when such a choice] is inseparably linked . . . to the 'religious dimension' of the work according to the church's own understanding [of its mission]."[71] In short, public law applies to all employer-employee relationships, but where the churches are concerned, this relationship can be shaped by the demands of their religious mission as they understand it. "By laying down such duties of loyalty in a contract of employment," continued the Second Senate, "the ecclesiastical employer not only relies on the general freedom of contract, he simultaneously makes use of his constitutional right to self-determination, [thus] permitting churches to shape [their social activity], even when regulated by contracts of employment according to a particular vision of Christian community service shared by their members."[72]

The Second Senate went on to emphasize that church autonomy is anything but absolute:

> The church employer's right under Article 137 (3) to shape the employment relationship established by contract is subject to the reservation that it must respect the law valid for all. This law includes . . . labor laws protecting persons against unlawful dismissal. But these laws do not trump the church's right to self-determination in every instance. The church-state provisions of the Weimar Constitution form an organic unity with the Basic Law, requiring [the courts] to balance and weigh the different interests and values at stake in

the relationship between the freedom of the churches and the limits imposed on this freedom.[73]

Here the Federal Labor Court had failed to adequately consider the "serious and significant" nature of the church's own law. That law — i.e., canon law — treats abortion as the killing of innocent human life and "a major crime warranting automatic excommunication." To require the church to retain the services of a doctor who rejects this teaching, said the court, would undermine its religious mission in the provision of hospital services.[74]

MARRIAGE AND FAMILY RIGHTS

Article 6 of the Basic Law extends special protection to marriage and the family. It is worth quoting in full:

1. Marriage and family shall enjoy the special protection of the state.

2. The care and upbringing of children are a natural right of, and a duty primarily incumbent on, the parents. The national community shall watch over their endeavors in this respect.

3. Children may not be separated from their families against the will of the persons entitled to bring them up, except pursuant to a law, if those so entitled fail, or the children are otherwise threatened with neglect.

4. Every mother shall be entitled to the protection and care of the community.

5. Illegitimate children shall be provided by legislation with the same opportunities for their physical and spiritual development and their place in society as are enjoyed by legitimate children.

Article 6 represents one of the framers' fundamental value decisions (*wertentscheidende Grundsatznorm*).[75] It constitutionalizes the right to marry and raises marriage and the family to the level of an institutional guarantee (*Institutsgarantie*). Marriage, like the right to property and freedom of the press, is an institution that the state must protect and preserve. The two cases reprinted below illustrate the importance the Constitutional Court attaches to the basic values of Article 6, values closely connected to the freedoms of conscience and religion.[76]

9.9 Joint Income Tax Case (1957)
6 BVerfGE 55

[Section 26 of the Income Tax Act of 1951 provided that if a wife earns money other than by a regular salary, she and her husband will have their incomes assessed together for tax purposes. Thus, because of progressive rates of taxation, she and her husband might have to pay more than they would if they were allowed to file separate returns. One of the legislative justifications for this regulation was that it would encourage women to stay at home. The Federal Fiscal Court at Munich thought that the provision violated Articles 3 (equality of the sexes) and 6 (special protection of marriage) of the Basic Law and sent the case directly to the Constitutional Court.]

––––––––––––––

Judgment of the First Senate. . . .

D. II. Placing a heavier tax burden on married couples . . . violates Article 6 (1) of the Basic Law.

1. In contrast to Article 134 of the Weimar Constitution, the Basic Law contains no express provision requiring citizens to share public expenses. But there is no doubt that the legislature is bound by the principle of fair taxation that follows from Article 3 (1) of the Basic Law.

The Federal Constitutional Court has said that the meaning of Article 3 (1) lies "to an essential extent in the fact that not all actual differences merit different treatment by the law; only those actual inequalities that have distinguishing legal significance [should be treated differently]. The legislature is primarily responsible for deciding these matters." However, the legislature's discretion finds its limitation not only in prohibitions against arbitrariness and "concretizations" of the general principle of equality (in particular Article 3 (2) and (3)) but also in other norms that establish principles and express a choice of values made by the framers for certain areas of the legal and social order. . . . Because section 26 of the Income Tax Act is connected with the fact of marriage, its constitutionality is primarily to be determined by Article 6 (1) of the Basic Law.

2. Article 6 (1) is a norm that establishes a principle and enunciates a decision about values. It regards marriage and family as the core of any human community, the significance of which cannot be compared with any other human bond, and places it under the special protection of the public order.

First, Article 6 involves a provision in the sense of classical basic rights, which, in view of experiences under National Socialist rule, are intended to protect the specific private sphere of marriage and family from external restraints by the state. . . .

At the same time the constitutional recognition of marriage and family indisputably encompasses a guarantee for both ways of arranging one's life. . . . In this capacity it guarantees the essential structure of marriage and family, so that its legal effect is to provide a constitutional guarantee for a core of norms in marriage and family law.

But these functions do not exhaust the legal impact of Article 6 (1). Like a number of constitutional norms—in particular, norms that regulate relationships between citizen and state or that order life in a society—Article 6 (1) fulfills several functions that overlap and are interconnected. Constitutional interpretation has the task of deducing the various functions of constitutional norms, especially basic rights. In performing this task, [interpreters] are to give preference to the interpretation which "most strongly develops the legal effectiveness of the particular norm." . . .

Interpreting Article 6 (1) according to these principles means that it contains not only a declaration of belief and an institutional guarantee but is also a norm which establishes a principle; that is, a binding basic standard for the entire area of civil and public law concerning marriage and the family. . . .

3. The function of Article 6 (1) as a principle-establishing norm imposes legal limits on legislative discretion.

Just like any other constitutional norm, Article 6 (1) is binding upon the legislature only to the extent that its formulation is precise enough for a norm of inferior rank to be measured against it. The precision of this article follows from the term "protection"; its literal meaning implies advancement of the object to be protected, defense against disturbances or injuries, and, above all, the state's renunciation of disturbing interferences on its own part. Thus the special state protection for marriage and the family in Article 6 (1) has two aspects: the positive task of the state not only to protect marriage and family from interference by other forces but also to advance these institutions through appropriate measures; and the negative aspect that prohibits the state itself from injuring or otherwise impairing marriage. . . .

4. The effect of Article 6 (1) as an actual protective norm is of decisive importance in evaluating the constitutionality of section 26 of the Income Tax Act of 1951; for joint tax assessment of spouses' income violates the principle of individual taxation, and does so to the disadvantage of married people, thus constituting a disruptive interference in marriage. . . .

Joint assessment is to serve the purpose of "bringing the wife back to her home" — the so-called educational effect — by imposing a heavier tax burden to keep wives from working. . . . In principle it is constitutionally permissible to impose a tax for other purposes besides collecting revenue. But this is possible only if these secondary purposes are themselves constitutionally neutral and are pursued with constitutionally valid taxes. With respect to the joint assessment of spouses, the educational effect is relied upon, on the one hand, to justify a provision that is already unconstitutional for other reasons. On the other hand, the educational purpose relates to an area which has already been circumscribed by decisions of the Constitution. In this area the legislature is therefore no longer completely free to choose [other] values. This reasoning follows from Article 6 (1) as well as from Article 3 (2) and (3).

. . . In the sense of classical basic rights, paragraphs 2 and 3 of Article 6 are an acknowledgment of the freedom of the specific private sphere of marriage and family; it corresponds with a guiding idea of our Constitution; namely, the basically limited authority of all public power to affect the free individual. . . . Spouses' freedom of decision in private matters also includes the decision concerning whether the wife should devote herself exclusively to the household, assist her husband with his job, or earn her own income. The goal used to justify joint assessment — that is, to "bring" the working wife "back to the home" — articulates a definite notion of the best way to arrange a marriage. But the mandate to protect marriage and family in Article 6 (1) includes any marriage . . . and thus leaves formation of the private sphere within this framework to the spouses themselves. . . . If this direct compulsion is unconstitutional, then that same goal cannot legitimate a measure which, like joint assessment, attempts to serve that goal indirectly.

The failure of the so-called educational effect to justify joint assessment also follows from the principle of equal rights of the two sexes (Article 3, paragraphs 2 and 3). The Basic Law presupposes that equality of rights is compatible with the protection of marriage and family. . . . However, equal rights for women include the opportunity for each woman to have the same legal chance to earn an income as any male citizen. To regard a wife's gainful economic activity as destructive to marriage is inconsistent not only with that principle but also with the text of Article 3 (2). . . .

5. It follows from all this that section 26 of the Income Tax Act of 1951 discriminates against married persons and thus violates the value decision of Article 6 (1) to the detriment of [the institution] of marriage. . . .

NOTE: THE FUNDAMENTAL RIGHT TO MARRY. The *Joint Income Tax* case underscores the fundamental nature of the right to marry, a right the court strongly reaffirmed in subsequent cases.[77] The *Spanish Marriage* case (1971) is perhaps the strongest re-affirmation of the right to marry under Article 6. *Spanish Marriage* is important because it vindicated the right to marry over the objection that a contrary rule of foreign law took precedence over the domestic constitutional right to marry. The case involved a Spanish national, resident in the Federal Republic for nearly ten years, who applied for a license to marry a German woman divorced in a German court pursuant to German law. Spanish authorities, however, refused to grant him the certificate of eligibility for marriage required under German law because his fiancée's divorce was not recognized under Spanish law. In applying international private law to this case, German courts sustained the denial of the marriage license. The couple involved filed constitutional complaints against the lower court decisions, claiming an infringement of their right to marry under Article 6.

The Constitutional Court held that Spanish law, which did not recognize divorce, could not be enforced in Germany in the light of the basic value decision of Article 6 (1). "The freedom to marry and the right derived from it to protection against infringement by the state," declared the court, "applies not only to Germans within the meaning of Article 116 of the Basic Law but also to foreigners and stateless persons."[78] Given the fundamental nature of the right to marry, the court was unwilling to follow a conflict-of-laws rule that impinged unduly on this right. The First Senate concluded that the "contested [judicial] decisions are an excessive and unreasonable infringement of the right to marry . . . and can be justified only by a higher interest worthy of recognition." The court made it clear that very few interests rank higher in the constellation of German constitutional values than the decision of a man and a woman to spend their lives together in matrimony.

Despite its resounding defense of the constitutional right to marry, *Spanish Marriage* nevertheless conceded that the state has wide discretion in regulating marital and family relationships. Indeed, in the late 1970s the West German parliament substantially amended its family law code, particularly in the areas of divorce, property settlement, and adoptions.[79] One revision in the law changed the basis of divorce from a fault to a no-fault principle, the constitutionality of which several family courts questioned. In the *Divorce* case (1980) the First Senate sustained the validity of the no-fault principle over the objection that it undermines the institutional guarantee of marriage.[80] The specific provision at issue here was the law's "conclusive presumption [that a marriage has failed] when the spouses have been separated for three years."[81]

More controversial was the new family code's hardship clause, which prohibited divorce when "special reasons in the interest of minor children born of the marriage" are present or when the divorce would result in a severe hardship "owing to exceptional circumstances";[82] this provision did not apply if the spouses have lived apart for more than five years. In the *Divorce* case the First Senate split four to four over the validity of this provision, leaving the matter temporarily unresolved. Several months later, however, in the *Divorce Hardship* case (1980),[83] the court invalidated the five-year clause as applied to a woman in ill health and still burdened with minor children born of the marriage. The five-year clause, said the court, was incompatible with Article 6 (1) to the extent that it permitted the immediate dissolution of the marriage upon the application of one spouse, without considering the extraordinary hardship that the divorce may impose on the other spouse. Article 6 (1) thus applied to a failed as well as to an intact marriage. Marriage, the court noted, entails certain continuing responsibilities, and the legislature must ensure that these responsibilities are met in order to prevent unreasonable hardship for one of the spouses.[84]

NOTE: MARRIAGE, FAMILY, AND WELFARE LEGISLATION. The *Joint Income Tax* case is one example of how closely the court monitors tax legislation deemed to conflict with the Basic Law's fundamental commitment to the institutions of marriage and family. The *Orphan Pension* case (1970) shows that the court takes an equally vigilant stance when welfare legislation impinges on these institutions.[85] *Orphan Pension* and related cases established the principle that state benefits — in this case for orphaned children — may not automatically be withdrawn from such children when they decide to marry.[86] Under the statute, unmarried orphans eighteen years old and older (up to the age of twenty-five) are entitled to support payment if they are still in school or training for a job, but such payments terminate when they marry. Under the court's analysis, values derived from the equality clauses of Article 3 (1) and the social state principle embodied in Article 20 (1) combine with the institutional guarantee of Article 6 (1) to render the withdrawal of benefits after marriage unconstitutional if the person affected derives no support from his spouse. The orphan's benefit, said the court, "is intended to compensate the child for the loss of his familial community (the natural economic structure of the familial household)."[87] The parental duty of support does not pass automatically to the spouse of the child. The benefit allowance is genuinely related to the basic needs of the child and compensates him in part for the death of his parents.[88]

NOTE: CHANGING NATURE OF FAMILY RELATIONSHIPS. In the 1990s the Constitutional Court mounted a virtual revolution in certain areas of family law and in two instances overruled its earlier decisions. In one of these instances, relying on the personality clause of Article 2 (1), the court invalidated a long-established rule that a married woman adopt the surname of her husband in the event that the spouses cannot agree on a single common surname.[89] The court also ruled that if parents disagree over whether to give their child the surname of the father or the premarital name of the mother, the child should be given the names of both parents in hyphenated form. The legislature was instructed to modify the civil code accordingly and to apply the court's ruling retroactively.[90]

On May 7, 1991, the court overruled its 1981 decision sustaining a law that granted the mother but not the father legal custody of an illegitimate child.[91] In *Child Custody II,* the court held that the law discriminated against illegitimate children in violation of Article 6 (5) of the Basic Law. Both father and mother, declared the court, are entitled to joint custody of the child if they continue to live together and assume joint responsibility for the child's welfare. *Child Custody II* represented the first judicial application of Article 6 to a nonmarital union. In October 1993, however, the court rejected an appeal from a homosexual couple who claimed that current law abridged their freedom to marry. The justices observed that the appeal had "no constitutional relevance" since marriage within the meaning of the Basic Law refers to a union between a man and woman.[92]

9.10 Sex Education Case (1977)
47 BVerfGE 46

[In 1970 Hamburg school officials promulgated a series of guidelines for sex education in the schools. The guidelines were based on the recommendations of the Conference of Cultural Ministers of the Federal Republic. While recognizing the primary responsibility of parents for sex education, the conference also regarded such education as a legitimate subject of academic instruction. Carried out within the framework of existing courses and adjusted to the age and maturity of the students, the program covered such subjects as sexual development during puberty, the biological aspects of human reproduction, various problems of sexuality, and the responsibilities of parenthood. Constitutional complaints challenged the program as violative of the rights of parents under Article 6 of the Basic Law.]

Judgment of the First Senate. . . .

The constitutional complaints are rejected.

C. I. 2. (a) Article 6 (2) of the Basic Law designates the care and upbringing of children as the "natural right of, and a duty primarily incumbent on, the parents." The national community's task is "to watch over their endeavors in this respect." The parents' "right and duty to organize freely the care and upbringing of their children according to their own ideas takes precedence over the right of any other guardians of education, subject to the provisions of Article 7 of the Basic Law. The parental freedom to choose ways in which to meet their responsibility is constitutionally protected against encroachments by the state, providing that such encroachments are not within the ambit of the state's mandate as guardian of the national community pursuant to Article 6 (2) [2] of the Basic Law."

Concerning the issue of parental rights in sexual matters, the conference of educational ministers declared succinctly: "Sex education is primarily the task of the parents." There are, indeed, good reasons why individual sex education should be assigned primarily to the sphere of the parental home and the natural right of parents according to Article 6 (2) of the Basic Law. Instruction in sex matters takes place most naturally within the protected and sheltered atmosphere of the family. . . .

(b) With this in mind, one must ask whether the state is ever permitted to get involved in sex education in school, and if so, to what extent it may do so. The conference recommendations note the following: "Based on their mandate to raise and educate children, schools have an obligation to participate in sex education." The mandate to raise and educate children has its constitutional foundation in Article 7 (1) of the Basic Law. In any case, as the Federal Constitutional Court has pointed out, the state supervision provided in Article 7 (1) of the Basic Law incorporates the authority to plan and organize the educational system with the objective of affording all young citizens educational opportunities geared to contemporary life in [this] society and commensurate with their abilities. This authority to arrange the school system includes not only the organizational structuring of the schools but also the determination of the content of the courses of study and educational goals. That is why the state may pursue its own educational goals independent of the parents. The general mandate of the school to raise and educate children is not classified as inferior but, rather, equal to the parents' right. Neither the parental right nor the state's mandate has absolute priority over the other. Contrary to an opinion found in the case literature, the mandate to raise and educate children is not restricted merely to the act of imparting knowledge. Rather, this mandate, presupposed by Article 7 (1) of the Basic Law, also includes [the premise] that every single child must be brought up to be a responsible member of society. Therefore the tasks of the schools exist in the realm of child-rearing. As explained above, much may be said in favor of sex education in the home as an ideal setting, but one must also take into consideration that human sexuality involves numerous social references. Sexual behavior is a part of the general behavioral pattern of human beings. For this reason the state must be allowed to treat sex education as an important element of the general education of a young person. Included in this also is the duty to warn and guard the children against sexual dangers. . . .

(c) Sex education in schools also affects the rights of the child provided for in Article 2 (1) of the Basic Law.

The Basic Law places intimate and sexual matters, as a part of a person's private sphere, under the protection of Article 2 (1) in conjunction with Article 1 (1) of the Constitution. These statutes assure each person of the right to determine his or her own sexual attitudes. A person may regulate his or her own sexual conduct and basically decide whether, within which limits, and with what goals he or she wants to accept third parties' influence upon his or her attitudes. If, however, a person's relationship to sexual matters is under constitutional protection, then each individual young person must have the same rights derived from Article 2 (1) in conjunction with Article 1 (1) of the Basic Law. A person's intimate sphere may be vitally affected by the methods of sex education in school. A youngster is not only the object of parental and state education. Rather, from the very beginning, a child becomes and continues to be at an ever-increasing rate his or her own person, protected by Article 1 (1) of the Basic Law. Experience has shown that youngsters in particular may sustain psychological damage and be seriously hampered in their development as a result of misconceived educational models.

3. As a result, sex education is in a very special way the source of tension between the parents' right under Article 6 (2) of the Basic Law, the child's personality right pursuant to Article 2 (1) of the Basic Law, and the state's mandate to raise and educate children in accordance with the provisions of Article 7 (1) of the Basic Law. . . .

(b) There must be a balancing process between the implementation of sex education in school and sex education at home, whereby the responsible parties may raise demands and voice criticisms according to the special rights assigned them but must also make concessions to each other. Thus sex education must be planned and implemented with the greatest possible cooperation between parents and school. The recommendations of the Conference of Ministers of Education and Cultural Matters provide that parents should have the opportunity to discuss these issues at gatherings of parents and teachers. According to Article 6 (2) of the Basic Law, parents have a right to request timely and accurate information about the content and teaching methods employed in sex education courses in order for them to be sure that their children are being taught in accordance with the parents' own ideas and convictions on the topics discussed in school. Thus, at the same time the state is fulfilling its obligation, parents may assert their individual right to raise their children, guaranteed them by the Basic Law.

A parental right of collaboration in the structure and format of sex education in school, however, must be rejected on the grounds of Article 6 (2) of the Basic Law. Article 6 (2) of the Basic Law is an individual right which is singly guaranteed to every parent. It may not be exercised by majority rule. In a pluralistic society it is practically impossible for schools to take into account the wishes of all parents and to consider them in establishing educational goals and curricula, as well as in actual classroom implementation. . . . Therefore, in this area parents may not refer to their rights under Article 6 (2) of the Basic Law without any limitation. The conflicting basic rights of people whose opinions and views differ restrict parents in the exercise of their basic rights.

To be sure, parents are entitled to demand necessary restraint and tolerance in sex education based on provisions of the Basic Law (Articles 4, 3 (3), and 33 (3) [2] of the Basic Law). School[s] must refrain from attempting to indoctrinate pupils for the purpose of advocating or opposing certain forms of sexual behavior. They must respect the natural modesty of children and must generally consider the religious and ideological convictions of parents as they manifest themselves in the sexual sphere. If these boundaries are sometimes overstepped in isolated cases, then the responsible school boards must intervene and ensure that the constitutionally mandated limitations are observed. In these cases parents may also initiate the necessary action. . . .

. . . Because sex education is to be taught in the aforementioned spirit of restraint and tolerance, it is unconstitutional to require either parents or older pupils to consent. Moreover, an exemption [from instruction] would significantly complicate interdisciplinary sex education, as provided for today by all states, primarily in such subjects as biology, history, religion, art, etc. This educational model in particular appears most suited to avoid disadvantages, because instruction does not concentrate just on the subject of sex education, and because it is not the responsibility of only one teacher. [We] need not address the issue of whether or not the legal situation would have to be judged differently if sex education were taught as a separate subject or by a special teaching unit. The legislature's task is primarily to establish rules which will deal fairly with parental rights under Article 6 (3) of the Basic Law and possible moral conflicts.

NOTE: THE *OBLIGATORY SCHOOL* CASE. As *Sex Education* shows, there is considerable tension between the "natural right of parents" to provide for the education of their children under Article 6 (2) and the duty of the state to supervise the "entire educational system" under the terms of Article 7 (2). The *Obligatory School* case

(1972) is an example of a particularly sharp conflict between these constitutional values.[93] In the mid-1950s the state of Hesse set up, on an experimental basis, the so-called comprehensive school (*Gesamtschule*). Under the traditional system of education in Germany, students are channeled into one of three major secondary schools (*Gymnasium, Realschule,* or *Hauptschule*) after they have completed four years of common elementary education. Hesse established two additional years of common schooling designed as a compulsory observational stage (*Förderstufe*) during which students were to be channeled into special courses and tracks based on interest and ability. Students' progress would be closely monitored, and on that basis they would then be advised, following consultation with teachers and parents, as to their future course of studies. This program deprived parents of the option of sending their children, after the fourth grade, directly to the *Gymnasium,* the highly demanding school whose nine-year classical and scientific curriculum has served as the main route to a university education in Germany. Several parents filed constitutional complaints against the new system because the *Förderstufe* limited their freedom of choice with respect to both schools and courses of study for their children.

The First Senate, recognizing the "far-reaching creative freedom of the individual states" in the field of education, sustained the validity of the new system as well as the *Förderstufe*'s processes of student selection and advancement. This creative authority, said the senate, "extends not only to the organizational structuring of schools but also to the determination of educational goals and course content."[94] Yet this authority is limited by and equal to the constitutionally guaranteed right of parents under Article 6 (2). "The state must therefore respect the responsibility of parents for the total plan of education for their children and lend a sympathetic ear to the variety of opinion[s] expressed on educational matters so long as this is compatible with an orderly school system organized by the state."[95] After carefully examining the statute and the history that led to its enactment, the senate concluded that the state had not unconstitutionally invaded the rights of parents. The state's interest prevailed over any exclusive right on the parents' part to dictate the school or curriculum of their children at this formative stage (the fifth and sixth grades) of educational development. But the state's interest is controlling only as long as parents were not deprived of the right to send their children to a private school or of the right generally to be consulted with respect to the placement and training of their children in the *Förderstufe*.[96]

CONCLUSION

Strong historical forces have molded the practice of church-state relations in Germany. The religious clauses of the Basic Law command the state to remain neutral in the sphere of ideological or religious values and to follow a policy of equal treatment with respect to churches and creeds. At the same time, the religious clauses imply more than mere tolerance of religious diversity. As interpreted, they require the state to bestow special protection on religiously motivated behavior so long as such conduct does not endanger an otherwise valid community interest or the rights of others. By the same token, the principle of state neutrality in church-state relations, as understood by Germans, permits a measurable degree of cooperation between church and state. Contrary to the strong separationist mold of American church-state relations, the Basic Law accords religion a special role in the nation's public life, a role manifested in constitutional provisions on parental rights and religious instruction in the public schools.

German constitutionalism in the field of church-state relations, like other basic rights areas treated in this volume, represents a delicate balance between competing rights and values, both personal and communal. The Basic Law itself often requires the Federal Constitutional Court to balance clauses against one another, although the weight attached to a particular clause (i.e., a right or value) depends on its location within the hierarchical ordering of values that the court has discovered in the Constitution. This general approach to interpretation, in church-state as well as other areas, means that no particular constitutional choice should be allowed to entirely negate a competing constitutional right, value, or interest. In the German constitutionalist view, the task of the interpreter is to optimize each constitutional value that is at stake in a given set of circumstances.

APPENDIX A

SELECTED PROVISIONS OF

THE BASIC LAW

I. BASIC RIGHTS

Article 1

(1) Human dignity shall be inviolable. To respect and protect it shall be the duty of all state authority.

(2) The German people therefore acknowledge inviolable and inalienable human rights as the basis of every community, of peace, and of justice in the world.

(3) The following basic rights shall bind the legislature, the executive, and the judiciary as directly enforceable law.

Article 2

(1) Everyone shall have the right to the free development of his personality insofar as he does not violate the rights of others or offend against the constitutional order or the moral code.

(2) Everyone shall have the right to life and to inviolability of his person. The liberty of the individual shall be inviolable. These rights may be encroached upon only pursuant to a law.

Article 3

(1) All persons shall be equal before the law.

(2) Men and women shall have equal rights. The state shall seek to ensure equal treatment of men and women and to remove existing disadvantages.

(3) No one may be prejudiced or favored because of his sex, his parentage, his race, his language, his homeland and origin, his faith, or his religious or political opinions. Persons may not be discriminated against because of their disability.

Article 4

(1) Freedom of faith, of conscience, and of creed, religious or ideological, shall be inviolable.

(2) The undisturbed practice of religion is guaranteed.

(3) No one may be compelled against his conscience to render military service involving the use of arms. Details shall be regulated by a federal law.

Article 5

(1) Everyone shall have the right freely to express and disseminate his opinion by speech, writing, and pictures and freely to inform himself from generally accessible sources. Freedom

of the press and freedom of reporting by means of broadcasts and films are guaranteed. There shall be no censorship.

(2) These rights are limited by the provisions of the general laws, the provisions of law for the protection of youth, and by the right to inviolability of personal honor.

(3) Arts and science, research and teaching shall not absolve from loyalty to the Constitution.

Article 6

(1) Marriage and family shall enjoy the special protection of the state.

(2) The care and upbringing of children are a natural right of, and a duty primarily incumbent on, the parents. The national community shall watch over their endeavors in this respect.

(3) Children may not be separated from their families against the will of the persons entitled to bring them up, except pursuant to a law, if those so entitled fail, or the children are otherwise threatened with neglect.

(4) Every mother shall be entitled to the protection and care of the community.

(5) Illegitimate children shall be provided by legislation with the same opportunities for their physical and spiritual development and their place in society as are enjoyed by legitimate children.

Article 7

(1) The entire educational system shall be under the supervision of the state.

(2) The persons entitled to bring up a child have the right to decide whether it shall receive religious instruction.

(3) Religious instruction shall form part of the ordinary curriculum in state and municipal schools, except in secular [bekenntinsfrei] schools. Without prejudice to the state's right of supervision, religious instruction shall be given in accordance with the tenets of the religious communities. No teacher may be obliged against his will to give religious instruction.

(4) The right to establish private schools is guaranteed. Private schools, as a substitute for state or municipal schools, shall require the approval of the state and shall be subject to the laws of the Länder. Such approval must be given if private schools are not inferior to the state or municipal schools in their educational aims, their facilities, and the professional training of their teaching staff, and if segregation of pupils according to the means of the parents is not promoted thereby. Approval must be withheld if the economic and legal position of the teaching staff is not sufficiently assured.

(5) A private elementary school shall be permitted only if the education authority finds that it serves a special pedagogic interest, or if, on the application of persons entitled to bring up children, it is to be established as an interdenominational or denominational or ideological school, and a state or municipal elementary school of this type does not exist in the commune [Gemeinde]. . . .

Article 8

(1) All Germans shall have the right to assemble peaceably and unarmed without prior notification or permission.

(2) With regard to open-air meetings this right may be restricted by or pursuant to a law.

Article 9

(1) All Germans shall have the right to form associations and societies.

(2) Associations whose purposes or activities conflict with criminal laws or are directed against the constitutional order or the concept of international understanding are prohibited.

(3) The right to form associations to safeguard and improve working and economic conditions is guaranteed to everyone and to all trades, occupations, and professions. Agreements which restrict or seek to impair this right shall be null and void; measures directed to this end shall be illegal. Measures taken pursuant to Article 12a, to paragraphs 2 and 3 of Article 35, to paragraph 4 of Article 87a, or to Article 91 may not be directed against any industrial conflicts engaged in by associations within the meaning of the first sentence of this paragraph in order to safeguard and improve working and economic conditions.

Article 10

(1) Privacy of posts and telecommunications shall be inviolable.

(2) This right may be restricted only pursuant to a law. Such law may lay down that the person affected shall not be informed of any such restriction if it serves to protect the free democratic basic order or the existence or security of the Federation or a *Land,* and that recourse to the courts shall be replaced by a review of the case by bodies and auxiliary bodies appointed by parliament.

Article 11

(1) All Germans shall enjoy freedom of movement throughout the federal territory.

(2) This right may be restricted only by or pursuant to a law and only in cases . . . in which such restriction is necessary to avert an imminent danger to the existence or the free democratic basic order of the Federation or a *Land,* to combat the danger of epidemics, to deal with natural disasters or particularly grave accidents, to protect young people from neglect, or to prevent crime.

Article 12

(1) All Germans shall have the right freely to choose their trade, occupation, or profession, their place of work, and their place of training. The practice of trades, occupations, and professions may be regulated by or pursuant to a law.

(2) No specific occupation may be imposed on any person except within the framework of a traditional compulsory public service that applies generally and equally to all.

(3) Forced labor may be imposed only on persons deprived of their liberty by court sentence.

Article 12a

(1) Men who have attained the age of eighteen years may be required to serve in the Armed Forces, in the Federal Border Guard, or in a Civil Defense organization.

(2) A person who refuses, on grounds of conscience, to render war service involving the use of arms may be required to render a substitute service. The duration of such substitute service shall not exceed the duration of military service. Details shall be regulated by a law which shall not interfere with the freedom of conscience and must also provide for the possibility of a substitute service not connected with units of the Armed Forces or of the Federal Border Guard.

Article 13

(1) The home shall be inviolable.

(2) Searches may be ordered only by a judge or, in the event of danger in delay, by other organs as provided by law and may be carried out only in the form prescribed by law.

Article 14

(1) Property and the right of inheritance are guaranteed. Their content and limits shall be determined by the laws.

(2) Property imposes duties. Its use should also serve the public weal.

(3) Expropriation shall be permitted only in the public weal. It may be effected only by or pursuant to a law which shall provide for the nature and extent of the compensation; recourse may be had to the ordinary courts.

Article 15

Land, natural resources, and means of production may for the purpose of socialization be transferred to public ownership or other forms of publicly controlled economy by a law which shall provide for the nature and extent of compensation. In respect of such compensation the third and fourth sentences of paragraph 3 of Article 14 shall apply mutatis mutandis.

Article 18

Whoever abuses freedom of expression of opinion, in particular freedom of the press (paragraph 1 of Article 5), freedom of teaching (paragraph 3 of Article 5), freedom of assembly (Article 8), freedom of association (Article 9), privacy of posts and telecommunications (Article 10), property (Article 14), or the right of asylum (paragraph 2 of Article 16) in order to combat the free democratic basic order shall forfeit these basic rights. Such forfeiture and the extent thereof shall be pronounced by the Federal Constitutional Court.

Article 19

(1) Insofar as a basic right may, under this Basic Law, be restricted by or pursuant to a law, such law must apply generally and not solely to an individual case. Furthermore, such law must name the basic right, indicating the article concerned.

(2) In no case may the essential content of a basic right be encroached upon.

(3) The basic rights shall apply also to domestic juristic persons to the extent that the nature of such rights permits.

(4) Should any person's right be violated by public authority, recourse to the court shall be open to him. If jurisdiction is not specified, recourse shall be open to the ordinary courts. The second sentence of paragraph 2 of Article 10 shall be affected by the provisions of this paragraph.

II. THE FEDERATION AND THE STATES

Article 20

(1) The Federal Republic of Germany is a democratic and social federal state.

(2) All state authority emanates from the people. It shall be exercised by the people by means of elections and voting and by specific legislative, executive, and judicial organs.

(3) Legislation shall be subject to the constitutional order; the executive and judiciary shall be bound by law and justice.

(4) All Germans shall have the right to resist any person or persons seeking to abolish that constitutional order, should no other remedy be possible.

Article 20a

The state, aware of its responsibility for present and future generations, shall protect the natural sources of life within the framework of the constitutional order through the legislature and, in accordance with the law and principles of justice, the executive and the judiciary.

Article 21

(1) The political parties shall participate in the formation of the political will of the people. They may be freely established. Their internal organization must conform to democratic principles. They must publicly account for the sources and use of their funds and assets.

(2) Parties which, by reason of their aims or the behavior of their adherents, seek to impair or abolish the free democratic basic order or to endanger the existence of the Federal Republic of Germany shall be unconstitutional. The Federal Constitutional Court shall decide on the question of unconstitutionality.

(3) Details shall be regulated by federal law.

Article 23

(1) With a view to establishing a united Europe, the Federal Republic of Germany shall participate in the development of the European Union, which is committed to democratic, rule-of-law social and federal principles as well as the principle of subsidiarity, and ensures protection of basic rights comparable in substance to that afforded by this Basic Law. To this end the Federation may transfer sovereign powers by law with the consent of the Bundesrat. The establishment of the European Union as well as amendments to its statutory foundations and comparable regulations which amend or supplement the content of this Basic Law or make such amendments or supplements possible shall be subject to the provisions of paragraphs 2 and 3 of Article 79. . . .

Article 24

(1) The Federation may by legislation transfer sovereign powers to international organizations. . . .

(2) With a view to maintaining peace the Federation may become a party to a system of collective security; in doing so it shall consent to such limitations upon its sovereign powers as will bring about and secure a peaceful and lasting order in Europe and among the nations of the world.

Article 25

The general rules of international law shall be an integral part of federal law. They shall override laws and directly establish rights and obligations for the inhabitants of the federal territory.

Article 26

(1) Any activities apt or intended to disturb peaceful international relations, especially preparations for military aggression, shall be unconstitutional. They shall be made a criminal offense.

Article 28

(1) The constitutional order in the *Länder* must conform to the principles of republican, democratic, and social government based on the rule of law, within the meaning of this Basic Law. In each of the *Länder,* counties, and municipalities, the people shall be represented by a body chosen in general, direct, free, equal, and secret elections. In the county and municipal elections, persons who are nationals of member states of the European Community are also entitled to vote and are eligible for election in accordance with European Community law. . . .

III. THE BUNDESTAG

Article 30

The exercise of governmental powers and the discharge of governmental functions shall be incumbent on the *Länder* insofar as this Basic Law does not otherwise prescribe or permit.

Article 31

Federal law shall override *Land* law.

Article 32

(1) Relations with foreign states shall be conducted by the Federation.

(2) Before a treaty which affects the specific circumstances of a German *Land* is concluded, that *Land* shall be consulted in good time.

(3) Insofar as the *Länder* have power to legislate, they may, with the consent of the federal government, conclude treaties with foreign states.

Article 38

(1) The deputies to the German Bundestag shall be elected in general, direct, free, equal, and secret elections. They shall be representatives of the whole people, not bound by orders and instructions, and shall be subject only to their conscience.

(2) Anyone who has attained the age of eighteen years shall be entitled to vote; anyone who has attained full legal age shall be eligible for election.

(3) Details shall be regulated by federal law.

Article 39

(1) The Bundestag shall be elected for a four-year term. Its legislative term shall end with the assembly of a new Bundestag. The new election shall be held at the earliest forty-five, at the latest forty-seven, months after the beginning of the legislative term. If the Bundestag is dissolved, the new election shall be held within sixty days.

Article 41

(1) Scrutiny of elections shall be the responsibility of the Bundestag. It shall also decide whether a member's seat is forfeited.

(2) Complaints against such decisions of the Bundestag may be lodged with the Federal Constitutional Court.

Article 44

(1) The Bundestag has the right, and upon the motion of one-quarter of its members the obligation, to set up committees of inquiry which shall hear evidence at public hearings. The public may be excluded.

Article 45a

(1) The Bundestag shall appoint a Committee on Foreign Affairs and a Committee on Defense.

(2) The Committee on Defense also has the powers of a committee of inquiry. Upon the motion of one-quarter of its members it shall be obliged to investigate a specific matter.

IV. THE BUNDESRAT

Article 50

The *Länder* shall participate through the Bundesrat in the legislation and administration of the Federation and in matters concerning the European Union.

Article 51

(1) The Bundesrat shall consist of members of the *Land* governments, which appoint and recall them. Other members of such governments may act as substitutes.

(2) Each *Land* shall have at least three votes; *Länder* with more than two million inhabitants shall have four, *Länder* with more than six million inhabitants five, and *Länder* with more than seven million inhabitants six votes.

(3) Each *Land* may appoint as many members as it has votes. The votes of each *Land* may be cast only as a bloc vote and only by members present or their substitutes.

V. THE FEDERAL PRESIDENT

Article 54

(1) The Federal President shall be elected by the Federal Convention without debate. . . .

(3) The Federal Convention shall consist of the members of the Bundestag and an equal number of members elected by the *Land* parliaments on the basis of proportional representation.

Article 59

(1) The Federal President represents the Federation in its international relations. He concludes treaties with foreign states on its behalf. He accredits and receives envoys.

(2) Treaties which regulate the political relations of the Federation or relate to matters of federal legislation shall require the approval or participation of the appropriate legislative body in the form of a federal law. . . .

VI. THE FEDERAL GOVERNMENT

Article 62

The federal government shall consist of the Federal Chancellor and the Federal Ministers.

Article 63

(1) The Federal Chancellor shall be elected, without debate, by the Bundestag upon the proposal of the Federal President.
(2) The person obtaining the votes of the majority of the members of the Bundestag shall be elected. The person elected must be appointed by the Federal President.
(3) If the person proposed is not elected, the Bundestag may elect within fourteen days of the ballot a Federal Chancellor by more than one-half of its members.
(4) If no candidate has been elected within this period, a new ballot shall take place without delay, in which the person obtaining the largest number of votes shall be elected. If the person elected has obtained the votes of the majority of the members of the Bundestag, the Federal President must appoint him within seven days of the election. If the person elected did not obtain such a majority, the Federal President must within seven days either appoint him or dissolve the Bundestag.

Article 67

(1) The Bundestag may express its lack of confidence in the Federal Chancellor only be electing a successor with the majority of its members and by requesting the Federal President to dismiss the Federal Chancellor. The Federal President must comply with the request and appoint the person elected.
(2) Forty-eight hours must elapse between the motion and the election.

Article 68

(1) If the motion of the Federal Chancellor for a vote of confidence is not assented to by the majority of the members of the Bundestag, the Federal President may, upon the proposal of the Federal Chancellor, dissolve the Bundestag within twenty-one days. The right to dissolve shall lapse as soon as the Bundestag with the majority of its members elects another Federal Chancellor.
(2) Forty-eight hours must elapse between the motion and the vote thereon.

VII. FEDERAL LEGISLATION

Article 70

(1) The *Länder* shall have the right to legislate insofar as this Basic Law does not confer legislative power on the Federation.
(2) The division of competence between the Federation and the *Länder* shall be determined by the provisions of this Basic Law concerning exclusive and concurrent legislative powers.

Article 71

In matters within the exclusive legislative power of the Federation the *Länder* shall have power to legislate only when and to the extent that a federal law explicitly so authorizes them.

Article 72

(1) Where concurrent legislation is concerned the *Länder* have the right to legislate as long as and to the extent that the Federation has not exercised its right to legislate.

(2) The Federation has the right to legislate on such matters if a need for federal legislation exists because a matter cannot be effectively regulated by the legislation of individual *Länder* or . . . [because] the maintenance of uniformity of living conditions beyond the territory of any one *Land* necessitates such regulation.

Article 73

The Federation shall have exclusive legislative jurisdiction in respect of
    1. foreign affairs and defense including protection of the civilian population. . . .

Article 79

(3) Amendments to this Basic Law affecting the division of the Federation into *Länder,* their participation in the legislative process, or the principles laid down in Articles 1 and 20 shall be prohibited.

VII. IMPLEMENTATION OF FEDERAL LEGISLATION

Article 83

The *Länder* shall execute federal laws as matters of their own concern insofar as this Basic Law does not otherwise provide or permit.

Article 87a

(1) The Federation shall establish armed forces for defense purposes. Their numerical strength and general organizational structure shall be shown in the budget.

(2) Other than for defense purposes the armed forces may be employed only to the extent explicitly permitted by this Basic Law.

VIIIa. JOINT RESPONSIBILITIES

Article 91a

(1) The Federation shall participate in discharge of the following responsibilities of the *Länder,* provided that such responsibilities are important to society as a whole and that federal participation is necessary for the improvement of living conditions (joint tasks):
    1. extension and construction of institutions of higher education, including university clinics;
    2. improvement of regional economic structures;
    3. improvement of the agrarian structure and of coast preservation.

IX. ADMINISTRATION OF JUSTICE

Article 92

Judicial power shall be vested in the judges; it shall be exercised by the Federal Constitutional Court, by the federal courts provided for in this Basic Law, and by the courts of the *Länder.*

Article 93

(1) The Federal Constitutional Court shall decide:

1. on the interpretation of this Basic Law in the event of disputes concerning the extent of the rights and duties of a highest federal organ or of other parties concerned who have been vested with rights of their own by this Basic Law or by rules of procedure of a highest federal organ;

2. in case of differences of opinion or doubts on the formal and material compatibility of federal law or *Land* law with this Basic Law, or on the compatibility of *Land* law with other federal law, at the request of the federal government, of a *Land* government, or of one-third of the Bundestag's members;

3. in case of differences of opinion on the rights and duties of the Federation and the *Länder,* particularly in the execution of federal law by the *Länder* and in the exercise of federal supervision;

4. on other disputes involving public law, between the Federation and the *Länder,* between different *Länder,* or within a *Land,* unless recourse to another court exists;

4a. on complaints of unconstitutionality, which may be entered by any person who claims that one of his basic rights or one of his rights under paragraph 4 of Article 20 or under Article 33, 38, 101, 103, or 104 has been violated by public authority;

4b. on complaints of unconstitutionality, entered by communes or associations of communes on the ground that their right to self-government under Article 28 has been violated by a law other than a *Land* law open to complaint to the respective *Land* constitutional court.

5. in the other cases provided for in this Basic Law.

(2) The Federal Constitutional Court shall also act in such other cases as are assigned to it by federal legislation.

Article 94

(1) The Federal Constitutional Court shall consist of federal judges and other members. Half of the members of the Federal Constitutional Court shall be elected by the Bundestag and half by the Bundesrat. They may not be members of the Bundestag, the Bundesrat, the federal government, nor any of the corresponding organs of a *Land.*

(2) The constitution and procedure of the Federal Constitutional Court shall be regulated by a federal law which shall specify in what cases its decisions shall have the force of law. Such law may require that all other legal remedies must have been exhausted before any such complaint of unconstitutionality can be entered, and may make provision for a special procedure as to admissibility.

Article 95

(1) For the purposes of ordinary, administrative, fiscal, labor, and social jurisdiction, the Federation shall establish as highest courts of justice the Federal Court of Justice, the Federal

Administrative Court, the Federal Fiscal Court, the Federal Labor Court, and the Federal Social Court.

(2) The judges of each of these courts shall be selected jointly by the competent federal minister and a committee for the selection of judges consisting of the competent *Land* ministers and an equal number of members elected by the Bundestag.

(3) In order to preserve uniformity of jurisdiction, a joint panel of the courts specified in paragraph 1 of this Article shall be set up. Details shall be regulated by a federal law.

Article 97

(1) The judges shall be independent and subject only to the law.

(2) Judges appointed permanently on a full-time basis in established positions cannot against their will be dismissed or permanently or temporarily suspended from office or given a different function or retired before the expiration of their term of office except by virtue of a judicial decision, and only on the grounds and in the form provided for by law. Legislation may set age limits for the retirement of judges appointed for life. In the event of changes in the structure of courts or in districts of jurisdiction, judges may be transferred to another court or removed from office, provided they retain their full salary.

Article 99

The decision on constitutional disputes within a *Land* may be assigned by *Land* legislation to the Federal Constitutional Court, and the decision of last instance in matters involving the application of *Land* law, to the highest courts of justice referred to in paragraph 1 of Article 95.

Article 101

(1) Extraordinary courts shall be inadmissible. No one may be removed from the jurisdiction of his lawful judge.

(2) Courts for special fields may be established only by legislation.

Article 102

Capital punishment shall be abolished.

Article 140

The provisions of Articles 136, 137, 138, 139, and 141 of the German Constitution of August 11, 1919, shall be an integral part of this Basic Law.

APPENDIX TO THE BASIC LAW (WEIMAR ARTICLES)

Article 136

(1) Civil and political rights and duties shall be neither dependent on nor restricted by the exercise of the freedom of religion.

(2) The enjoyment of civil and political rights and eligibility for public office shall be independent of religious creed.

(3) No one shall be bound to disclose his religious convictions. The authorities shall not have

the right to inquire into a person's membership of a religious body except to the extent that rights or duties depend thereon or that a statistical survey ordered by law makes it necessary.

(4) No one may be compelled to perform any religious act or ceremony or to participate in religious exercises or to use a religious oath.

Article 137

(1) There shall be no state church.

(2) Freedom of association to form religious bodies is guaranteed. The union of religious bodies within the territory of the Reich shall not be subject to any restrictions.

(3) Every religious body shall regulate and administer its affairs independently within the limits of the law valid for all. It shall confer its offices without the participation of the state or the civil community.

(4) Religious bodies shall acquire legal capacity according to the general provisions of civil law.

(5) Religious bodies shall remain corporate bodies under public law insofar as they have been such heretofore. The other religious bodies shall be granted like rights upon application, if their constitution and the number of their members offer an assurance of their permanency. If several such religious bodies under public law unite in one organization, such organization shall also be a corporate body under public law.

(6) Religious bodies that are corporate bodies under public law shall be entitled to levy taxes in accordance with *Land* law on the basis of civil taxation lists.

(7) Associations whose purpose is the cultivation of a philosophical ideology shall have the same status as religious bodies.

(8) Such further regulation as may be required for the implementation of these provisions shall be incumbent on *Land* legislation.

Article 138

(1) State contributions to religious bodies, based on law or contract or special legal title, shall be redeemed by means of *Land* legislation. The principles for such redemptions shall be established by the Reich.

(2) The right to own property and other rights of religious bodies or associations in respect of their institutions, foundations, and other assets destined for purposes of worship, education, or charity are guaranteed.

Article 139

Sunday and the public holidays recognized by the state shall remain under legal protection as days of rest from work and of spiritual edification.

Article 141

To the extent that there exists a need for religious services and spiritual care in the army, in hospitals, in prisons, or in other public institutions, the religious bodies shall be permitted to perform religious acts; in this connection, there shall be no compulsion of any kind.

APPENDIX B

JUSTICES OF THE FEDERAL

CONSTITUTIONAL COURT, 1951–1995

Justice		Position

FIRST SENATE: BUNDESTAG ELECTED

	Justice	Position
Seat 1	Höpker-Aschoff, Hermann† (1951–54)	President
	Wintrich, Josef† (1954–58)	President
	Müller, Gebhard† (1959–71)	President
	Benda, Ernst (1971–83)	President
	Herzog, Roman (1984–87)	Vice President
	by Bundesrat (1987–94)	President
	Haas, Evelyn (1995–2007)	Justice
Seat 2	Zweigert, Kurt† (1951–52)	Justice
	Heck, Karl† (1954–64)	Justice
	Böhmer, Werner (1965–83)	Justice
	Niedermaier, Franz† (1983–86)	Justice
	Seidl, Otto (1986–95)	Justice
	(1995–98)	Vice President
Seat 3	Heiland, Gerhard† (1951–61)	Justice
	Haager, Karl (1962–79)	Justice
	Heussner, Hermann† (1979–89)	Justice
	Kühling, Jürgen (1989–2001)	Justice
Seat 4	Scholtissek, Herbert† (1951–67)	Justice
	Brox, Hans (1967–75)	Justice
	Katzenstein, Dietrich† (1975–87)	Justice
	Söllner, Alfred (1987–95)	Justice
	Steiner, Udo (1995–2007)	Justice
Seat 5	Zweigert, Konrad† (1951–56)	Justice
	Seat abolished in 1956	
Seat 6	Lehmann, Joachim† (1951–63)	Justice
	Seat abolished in 1963	

Justice	Position

FIRST SENATE: BUNDESRAT ELECTED

Seat 1	Stein, Erwin† (1951–71)	Justice
	Faller, Hans (1971–83)	Justice
	Henschel, Johann Friedrich (1983–93)	Justice
	(1994–95)	Vice President
	Hömig, Dieter (1995–2007)	Justice
Seat 2	Wessel, Franz† (1951–58)	Justice
	Berger, Hugo† (1959–67)	Justice
	Zeidler, Wolfgang† (1967–70)	Justice
	Simon, Helmut (1970–87)	Justice
	Dieterich, Thomas (1987–94)	Justice
	Jäger, Renate (1994–2006)	Justice
Seat 3	Scheffler, Erna† (1951–63)	Justice
	Rupp-von Brünnick, Wiltraut† (1963–77)	Justice
	Niemeyer, Gisela (1977–89)	Justice
	Siebert, Helga (1989–2001)	Justice
Seat 4	Ritterspach, Theodor (1951–75)	Justice
	Hesse, Konrad (1975–87)	Justice
	Grimm, Dieter (1987–99)	Justice
Seat 5	Ellinghaus, Wilhelm† (1951–55)	Justice
	Kutscher, Hans† (1955–56)	Justice
	Seat abolished in 1956	
Seat 6	Drath, Martin† (1951–63)	Justice
	Seat abolished in 1963	

SECOND SENATE: BUNDESTAG ELECTED

Seat 1	Rupp, Hans† (1951–75)	Justice
	Zeidler, Wolfgang† (1975–83)	Vice President
	(1983–87)	President
	Franssen, Everhardt (1987–91)	Justice
	Sommer, Thomas (1991–2003)	Justice
Seat 2	Hennecka, Anton† (1951–68)	Justice
	Rinck, Hans-Justus† (1968–86)	Justice
	Grasshof, Karin (1968–98)	Justice
Seat 3	Federer, Julius† (1951–67)	Justice
	von Schlabrendorff, Fabian† (1967–75)	Justice
	Niebler, Engelbert (1975–87)	Justice
	Kruis, Konrad (1987–99)	Justice

	Justice	Position
Seat 4	Liebholz, Gerhard† (1951–71)	Justice
	Hirsch, Martin† (1971–81)	Justice
	Mahrenholz, Ernst Gottfried (1981–87)	Justice
	(1987–93)	Vice President
Seat 5	Roediger, Conrad Frederick† (1951–56)	Justice
	Seat abolished in 1956	
Seat 6	Klas, Walter† (1951–63)	Justice
	Seat abolished in 1963	

SECOND SENATE: BUNDESRAT ELECTED

Seat 1	Katz, Rudolf† (1951–61)	Vice President
	Wagner, Friedrich Wilhelm† (1961–67)	Vice President
	Seuffert, Walter† (1967–75)	Vice President
	Steinberger, Helmut (1975–87)	Justice
	Kirchhof, Paul (1987–99)	Justice
Seat 2	Geiger, Willi† (1951–77)	Justice
	Träger, Ernst (1977–89)	Justice
	Winter, Klaus (1989–2001)	Justice
Seat 3	Frölich, Georg† (1951–56)	Justice
	Kutscher, Hans† (1956–70)	Justice
	Wand, Walter Rudi† (1970–83)	Justice
	Klein, Hans Hugo (1983–95)	Justice
Seat 4	Leussner, Carl† (1951–52)	Justice
	Schunck, Egon† (1952–63)	Justice
	Geller, Gregor† (1963–71)	Justice
	Rottmann, Joachim† (1971–83)	Justice
	Böckenförde, Ernst-Wolfgang (1983–95)	Justice
Seat 5	Wolff, Bernhard† (1951–56)	Justice
	Seat abolished in 1956	
Seat 6	Friesenhahn, Ernst† (1951–63)	Justice
	Seat abolished in 1963	

†deceased

NOTES

1 THE FEDERAL CONSTITUTIONAL COURT

1 For a general discussion of centralized and decentralized systems of judicial review, see Mauro Cappelletti and William Cohen, *Comparative Constitutional Law* (Indianapolis: Bobbs-Merrill, 1979), 73–90. See also Mauro Cappelletti, *Judicial Review in Comparative Perspective* (Oxford: Clarendon Press, 1989), 136–46.

2 Gerhard Leibholz, *Politics and Law* (Leiden: A. W. Sythoff, 1965), 329.

3 For an excellent overview of the German judicial system, see Wolfgang Heyde, *Justice and the Law in the Federal Republic of Germany* (Heidelberg: C. F. Müller Juristischer Verlag, 1994), 38–65. See also Nigel Foster, *German Law and Legal System* (London: Blackstone Press, 1993), 36–45.

4 Arnold J. Heidenheimer and Donald P. Kommers, *The Governments of Germany,* 4th ed. (New York: Thomas Y. Crowell, 1975), 264.

5 See Rupert Emerson, *State and Society in Modern Germany* (New Haven: Yale University Press, 1928).

6 The first major scholarly study of constitutional and judicial review in Germany appears to be Friedrich Dahlmann, ed., *Gutachten der Juristenfakultäten in Heidelberg, Jena, und Tübingen: Die Hannoversche Verfassungsfrage* (Jena: Friedrich Frommann, 1839). Dahlmann, a liberal intellectual who played a major role in the constitutional assembly of 1849, was dismissed from his professorship at Göttingen University for defending the Hanoverian Constitution. In defense of his position Dahlmann enlisted several university law professors to write briefs in support of constitutional government in Hanover. These were published in the cited work. In the course of their briefs they traced the history of constitutional review in Germany. We learn among other things that the Imperial Court not only deprived the prince of Mecklenburg of his throne for constitutional violations but also on several occasions reviewed the constitutionality of state statutes. For a general treatment of constitutional review in German history, see also Robert C. Binkley, "The Holy Roman Empire versus the United States: Patterns for Constitution-Making in Central Europe," in *The Constitution Reconsidered,* ed. Conyers Read (New York: Columbia University Press, 1938), 274; Otto Kimminich, *Deutsche Verfassungsgeschichte* (Frankfurt: Athenäum Verlag, 1970), 237–40; and Karl August Betterman, Hans Carl Nipperday, and Ulrich Scheuner, eds., *Die Grundrechte* (Berlin: Duncker and Humboldt, 1959), 3:645–58.

7 Modern German constitutionalism began with the establishment of the German Confederation of 1815, created by the Congress of Vienna nine years after Napoleon's invading armies had demolished the loose alliance known as the Holy Roman Empire of the
German Nation. The fusion of countless kingdoms and principalities into a more compact confederation — consisting now of thirty-four sovereign states and four free cities —
set the stage for a century of constitution making in Germany at both state and national
levels. It also marked the beginning of a century-long conflict between the monarchical
and republican traditions. One of the best treatments in English of German constitutionalism since 1800 is John A. Hawgood, *Modern Constitutions since 1787* (London:
Macmillan, 1939), 111–26, 197–214, 230–47, and 346–65.

8 Such conflicts are currently resolved by the Federal Constitutional Court under Article 93
(1) [3] and [41] of the Basic Law. These provisions trace their nineteenth-century roots
to Article 11 of the Vienna Constitution (1815) and Article 61 of the Vienna Accords
(Schlussakte) of 1820. Article 11 obligated the states (i.e., the sovereign principalities and
free cities) to submit their constitutional disputes to the National (Reich) Assembly for
peaceful resolution; Article 61 authorized the states to submit even their internal constitutional conflicts (e.g., between the princes and their estates) to the same body if they could
not be resolved within their borders. See Deutsche Bundesakte, Article 11, and Wiener
Schlussakte, Article 61, in Ernst R. Huber, ed., *Dokumente zur Deutschen Verfassungsgeschichte* (Stuttgart: Verlag W. Kohlhammer, 1978), 1:87, 99. Almost identical provisions
appear in the national constitutions of 1849 (Article 126 [Frankfurt Constitution]), 1867
(Article 76 [North German Confederation]), 1871 (Articles 19 and 76 [Imperial Consti-
tution]), and 1919 (Article 19 [Weimar Constitution]). English translations of the 1849,
1871, and 1919 constitutions appear in Elmar M. Hucko, ed., *The Democratic Tradition:
Four German Constitutions* (Leamington Spa, England: Berg, 1987).

9 When deciding federal-state disputes over the administration of national law, the Staatsgerichtshof consisted of a special seven-judge panel composed of the president and three
additional judges of the Reichsgericht chosen by the court as a whole, and one judge each
elected by the Prussian, Bavarian, and Saxon administrative courts of appeal. For the
settlement of cases perceived as more political in character, the Staatsgerichtshof also
consisted of a seven-person bench headed by the president of the Reichsgericht, but
parliament chose four of its members. When presiding over impeachment cases, the most
political of all, it consisted of a much larger panel of fifteen judges with even wider public
representation. See *Reichsgesetzblatt* 1 (1921): 907, secs. 3, 18, and 31.

10 Hideo Wada, "Continental Systems Of Judicial Review," *Jahrbuch des Öffentlichen Rechts*
31 (1982): 35; see also Mauro Cappelletti and John C. Adams, "Judicial Review of
Legislation: European Antecedents and Adaptations," *Harvard Law Review* 79 (1966):
1207–24.

11 Franz W. Jerusalem, *Die Staatsgerichtsbarkeit* (Tübingen: J. C. B. Mohr [Paul Siebeck],
1930), 50–51; see also Mahendra P. Singh, *German Administrative Law* (Berlin: Springer
Verlag, 1985), 8–12.

12 By the second half of the nineteenth century, German legal scholars accepted a limited
form of judicial review. Then as now they distinguished sharply between a law's procedural and substantive constitutionality. In their view, courts might refuse to enforce
laws that had not been enacted and promulgated in strict accordance with procedures laid

down in the Constitution, but they were not authorized to invalidate laws for any substantive reason. For a general historical treatment of judicial review in Germany, see Christoph Gusy, *Richterliches Prüfungsrecht: Eine verfassungsgeschichtliche Untersuchung* (Berlin: Duncker and Humboldt, 1985).

13 Robert von Mohl, *Staatsrecht, Völkerrecht und Politik* (Tübingen: Buchhandlung Laupp, 1860), 1:66–95.

14 *Verhandlungen des dritten deutschen Juristentages* (Berlin: Druck- und Commissionsverlag von G. Jansen, 1863), 2:61.

15 The one recorded instance of judicial review during this period was greeted as a reckless act. In overturning a decision of the Hanseatic Court of Appeals (see Seuffert's *Archiv für Entscheidungen der Obersten Gerichte* [Munich: Rudolf Odenbourg, 1876], 32:129–31) declaring a local tax law unconstitutional, the German Imperial Court reasserted the conventional doctrine: "The constitutional provision that well-acquired rights must not be injured is to be understood only as a rule for the legislative power itself to interpret and does not signify that a command given by the legislative power should be disregarded by the judge because [he believes] it injures well-acquired rights." (See Decision of February 17, 1883, 9 RGZ 235. This decision [*K. v. Dyke Board of Niedervieland*] is translated in Brinton Coxe, *An Essay on Judicial Power and Unconstitutional Legislation* [Philadelphia: Kay and Brother, 1893].) In 1910 Otto von Gierke remarked: "It is a fundamental deficiency of our public law that there exists no protection of constitutional principles by an independent court of justice"; see "German Constitutional Law in Its Relation to the American Constitution," *Harvard Law Review* 23 (1909–10): 284.

16 The "free law" movement, led by Rudolf von Ihering, Josef Kohler, Ernst Zitelmann, Eugen Ehrlich, Hermann Kantorowicz, and Ernst Fuchs, was an assault on philological and deductive methods of judicial reasoning that foreshadowed the legal realist movement in the United States. These scholars were skeptical of a jurisprudence founded exclusively on the formal rules of code law. Arguing in favor of judicial creativity, they stressed the importance of a judicial process informed by a knowledge of society and economics as well as formal legal rules. The free law, or realist, movement started in Germany around 1900, reached its zenith prior to World War I, and then ebbed late in the Weimar Republic. For an excellent discussion of the impact of the free law school in Germany, see Albert S. Fouilkes, "On the German Free Law School (Freirechtsschule)," *Archiv für Rechts- und Sozialphilosophie* 55 (1969): 367–417. For a discussion of legal realism, see James E. Herget and Stephen Wallace, "The German Free Law Movement as the Source of American Legal Realism," *Virginia Law Review* 73 (1987): 399–439.

17 Legal scholars were deeply split over the question of judicial review. Gerhard Anschütz, Weimar's leading constitutional authority, maintained that courts had no power to examine the constitutionality of laws. Under Article 70 of the Constitution, according to Anschütz, only the president of the republic had the authority to review the constitutionality of Reich legislation, and even he was limited to reviewing the constitutionality of laws on procedural grounds. See Gerhard Anschütz, *Die Verfassung des deutschen Reichs* (Berlin: Verlag von Georg Stilke, 1932), 367. Anschütz was joined in this view by other authoritative commentators such as Walter Jellinek, Richard Thoma, Julius Hatschek, Friedrich Giese, Gustav Radbruch, Franz W. Jerusalem, and Carl Schmitt. See Georg Jellinek, *Gesetz und Verordnung* (Tübingen: J. C. B. Mohr, 1919), 395–412; Richard

Thoma, "Zur Frage des richterlichen Prüfungsrechts," *Deutsche Juristenzeitung* 27 (1922): 729; Julius Hatschek, *Deutsches und preussisches Staatsrecht* (Berlin: Verlag von Georg Stilke, 1923), 2:96–97; Friedreich Giese, *Verfassung des deutschen Reiches* (Berlin: Carl Heymanns Verlag, 1926), 210–11; Gustav Radbruch, "Richterliches Prüfungsrecht," *Die Justiz* 1 (1915): 12–16; Jerusalem, supra note 11, at 18; and Carl Schmitt, "Das Reichsgericht als Hüter der Verfassung," *Archiv des Öffentlichen Rechts*, n.s., 16 (1929): 161–237. Equally strong voices in support of judicial review were Hans Fritz Abraham, Hans Nawiasky, Fritz Pötzsch, Eduard Hubrich, Rudolf Stammler, and Heinrich Triepel. See Hans Fritz Abraham, "Die Anklage gegen das Reichsgericht," *Deutsche Juristenzeitung* (1918): 295; Hans Nawiasky, *Bayerisches Verfassungsrecht* (Munich: J. Schweitzer Verlag, 1913), 268–377; Fritz Pötzsch-Heffter, *Handkommentar der Reichsverfassung* (Berlin: Verlag von Otto Leibmann, 1928), 310–11; Eduard Hubrich, *Demokratisches Verfassungsrecht des deutschen Reiches* (Griefswald: von Bruncken, 1921), 150; Rudolf Stammler, *Der Richter* (Berlin: Tageswerkverlag, 1924), 32; Heinrich Triepel, "Der Weg der Gesetzgebung nach der neuen Reichsverfassung," *Archiv des Öffentlichen Rechts* 39 (1919): 534. Jellinek, incidentally, reported that a majority on the constitutional committee in the Weimar Constituent Assembly that considered judicial review was against it. See Walter Jellinek, "Verfassungswidrige Reichsgesetze," *Deutsche Juristenzeitung* 26 (1921): 753.

18 See Carl J. Friedrich, "The Issue of Judicial Review in Germany," *Political Science Quarterly* 43 (1928): 190. Hugo Preuss was a liberal democrat and one of the fathers of the Weimar Constitution. According to Friedrich, Preuss and his colleagues in the National Assembly did not fully understand the implications of judicial review: "Careful consideration of the various arguments would seem to indicate that there existed no very clear idea as to just what was to be understood by judicial review. There is little doubt that the special significance of the question was realized by only a few in the committee" (ibid., 190–91). For a good treatment in English of judicial review as practiced in the Weimar Republic, see J. J. Lenoir, "Judicial Review in Germany under the Weimar Constitution," *Tulane Law Review* 14 (1940): 361–83.

19 5 *Sammlung der Entscheidungen und Gutachten des Reichsfinanzhofs* 233–36 (1921); Decision of December 15, 1921, 56 *Entscheidungen des Reichsgerichts in Strafsachen* 179–91, 182 (1922); and Decision of October 21, 1924, 4 *Entscheidungen des Reichsversorgungsgerichts* 168 (1925).

20 See "Erklärung des Richtervereins beim Reichsgericht zur Aufwertungsfrage," in Huber, supra note 8, at 3:383–84.

21 107 RGZ 377–81, 379 (1924).

22 See Bavarian Constitution of 1919, Article 72, and Schamburg-Lippe Constitution of 1922, Article 47, in Otto Ruthenberg, *Verfassungsgesetze des deutschen Reichs und der deutschen Länder* (Berlin: Verlag von Franz Vahlen, 1926), 78–79, 204. The willingness of judges to nullify laws reflected the judiciary's distrust of, even opposition to, democracy. They often asserted the power of judicial review, as the U.S. Supreme Court was doing at about the same time, when legislation threatened property rights. Walter C. Simon, president of the Reichsgerichtshof from 1922 to 1929 and the regular judiciary's chief spokesman on behalf of the American doctrine of judicial review, betrayed his own feelings toward the Republic when he spoke of the need to check "the overbearing power of parliamentarianism and the secret influence of ministerial bureaucracy." This check, he

insisted, would never come about "if the Supreme Court is not perfectly independent and on the same footing with both the other powers of the state. Until now," he lamented, "the Reichsgerichtshof has not found a Chief Justice Marshall" (Walter Simon, "Relation of the German Judiciary to the Executive and Legislative Branches," *American Bar Association Journal* 15 [1929]: 762).

23 *Germany 1947–1949: The Story in Documents.* U.S. Department of State Publication 3556 (Washington, D.C.: U.S. Department of State, 1950), 49.

24 In an aide-mémoire sent to the framers of the Basic Law, the military governors noted: "The constitution should provide for an independent judiciary to review federal legislation, to review the exercise of federal executive power, and to adjudicate conflicts between federal and *Land* authorities as well as between *Land* authorities, and to protect the civil rights and freedom of the individual." See Aide-Mémoire on German Political Organization Presented by the United States, United Kingdom, and French Military Governors, November 22, 1948, in *Germany 1947–1949*, supra note 23, at 278.

25 See Donald P. Kommers, *Judicial Politics in West Germany: A Study of the Federal Constitutional Court* (Beverly Hills, Calif.: Sage Publications, 1976), 70.

26 For a discussion of the background of the participants in the Herrenchiemsee Conference, see Heinz Laufer, *Verfassungsgerichtsbarkeit und politischer Prozess* (Tübingen: J. C. B. Mohr [Paul Siebeck], 1968), 35–38.

27 *Bericht über den Verfassungskonvent auf Herrenchiemsee vom 10. bis 23. August 1948* (Munich: Richard Plaum Verlag, n.d.), especially articles 98 and 99.

28 For a description of constitutional review in Austria and Kelsen's influence, see Cappelletti and Cohen, supra note 1, at 86–90. See also Mauro Cappelletti, *Judicial Review in the Contemporary World* (Indianapolis: Bobbs-Merrill, 1971), 90–93; and Cappelletti, review of *Supreme Courts and Judicial Law-Making: Constitutional Tribunals and Constitutional Review*, by E. McWhinney, in *American Journal of International Law* 82 (1988): 422.

29 Laufer, supra note 26, at 38–39.

30 For an account of the structure and powers of the Staatsgerichtshof, see Frederick E. Blachly and Miriam Oatman, *The Government and Administration of Germany* (Baltimore: Johns Hopkins University Press, 1928), 441–46.

31 *Bericht Herrenchiemsee,* supra note 27, Article 100.

32 A plan modeled on Weimar's Staatsgerichtshof would have proposed a part-time tribunal consisting of judges chosen from various federal and state appellate courts who would meet at specified times to resolve pending constitutional disputes. See Blachly and Oatman, *Government of Germany,* supra note 30.

33 The constitutional convention was known as the Parliamentary Council (West German Constituent Assembly). It convened in Bonn on September 1, 1948. Its 65 delegates, elected by the state parliaments, consisted of 27 Christian Democrats, 27 Social Democrats, 5 Free Democrats, and 6 additional delegates representing (2 each) the Center party, the German party, and the Communist party. An excellent account of its proceedings in English is John E. Golay, *The Founding of the Federal Republic of Germany* (Chicago: University of Chicago Press, 1958). See also Peter H. Merkl, *The Origin of the West German Republic* (New York: Oxford University Press, 1963).

34 Parlamentarischer Rat, *Verhandlungen des Hauptausschusses* (Bonn, 1950) (mimeograph; 1948–49), 275.

35   For a detailed discussion of this debate, see Kommers, supra note 25, at 72–77. See also Laufer, supra note 26, at 52–59; and Hans Lietzmann, *Das Bundesverfassungsgericht: Eine soziowissenschaftliche Studie* (Opladen: Leake and Budrich, 1988), 46–49.

36   The conflict is described in Kommers, supra note 25, at 78–82; and Laufer, supra note 26, at 93–139.

37   Gesetz über das Bundesverfassungsgericht (Federal Constitutional Court Act) in the version of March 12, 1951, *Bundesgesetzblatt* [hereafter *BGBl*] 1:243 (hereinafter cited as FCCA). This statute has been amended frequently since its original enactment. All subsequent references to the FCCA are based on the amended statute up to and including the amendments of August 11, 1993 (*BGBl* 1:1473). For an excellent discussion of the FCCA's genesis, see Willi Geiger, *Gesetz über das Bundesverfassungsgericht* (Berlin: Verlag Franz Vahlen GmbH, 1951), iii–xxv; and Laufer, supra note 26, at 97–139. See also Wolfgang Kralewski and Karl Heinz Neunreiter, *Oppositionelles Verhalten im ersten deutschen Bundestag 1949–1953* (Cologne: Westdeutscher Verlag, 1963), 192–204. These treatments of the politics surrounding the establishment of the Federal Constitutional Court are based on the debates and proceedings of the Bundestag's Legal and Constitutional Affairs Committee. The protocols are included in Ausschuss für Rechtswesen und Verfassungsrecht, *Die Verfassungsgericht des (23.) Ausschusses für Rechtswesen und Verfassungsrecht über das Gesetz über das Bundesverfassungsgericht,* Deutscher Bundestag, 1. Wahlperiode (1950; mimeograph).

38   1 Cranch 137 (1803).

39   The FCCA allocates mutually exclusive jurisdiction to each senate. Under section 14 (1) the First Senate is responsible for the abstract and concrete review of laws involving cases dealing with claims to a fundamental right arising under Articles 1 through 19 and with rights secured by Articles 33 (equal right to employment in the civil service), 101 (ban on extraordinary courts), 103 (fair hearing, ban on ex post facto laws and double jeopardy), and 104 (other specified legal guarantees prior to incarceration). The First Senate also has jurisdiction over all constitutional complaints except those dealing with electoral law or the claims of municipalities and local governments. All remaining jurisdiction is vested in the Second Senate. (Originally, the FCCA authorized the Plenum to hand down advisory opinions requested by the federal government or the federal president. On the court's own recommendation, parliament repealed this jurisdiction early on in the midst of a severe conflict within the court over whether an advisory opinion by the Plenum would be binding on each of the senates.)

Under the FCCA's section 14 (4), however, the Plenum is authorized to change this distribution of authority if necessary to relieve one of the senates of a severely overburdened docket. The change, in effect as of January 1, 1994, shifts to the Second Senate constitutional complaints as well as abstract and concrete review cases involving rights and privileges secured by Articles 19 (4), 33, 101, 103, and 104. These articles, as noted in the previous paragraph, deal mainly with the rights and obligations of civil servants and elected officials together with procedural issues arising in the normal course of civil and criminal proceedings, leaving to the First Senate all cases involving mainly the interpretation of substantive rights under the Basic Law. The Plenum also shifted to the Second Senate constitutional complaints and judicial review cases involving an interpretation of international law, and cases dealing with asylum and citizenship law, the disciplining of public servants, liability for military service and conscientious objector claims, income and church tax law, and summary proceedings concerning administrative penalties. See Plenum Decision of November 15, 1993, *BGBl* 1:1473.

40   See Socialist Reich Party Case, 2 BVerfGE 1 (1952); and Communist Party Case, 5 BVerfGE 85 (1956).

41   See National List Case, 91 BVerfGE 262 (1994) and Free German Workers Party Case, 91 BVerfGE 276 (1994).

42   See Dieter Lorenz, "Der Organstreit vor dem Bundesverfassungsgericht," in *Bundesverfassungsgericht und Grundgesetz,* ed. Christian Starck (Tübingen: J. C. B. Mohr, 1976), 1:255–59.

43   With respect to the Bundestag, these units would include the Committees on Foreign Affairs and Defense (Article 45a), the parliamentary commissioner (Article 45b), the Petitions Committee (Article 45c), and even individual deputies deprived of rights or entitlements under Articles 46, 47, and 48.

44   See, for example, Judgment of June 8, 1982, 60 BVerfGE 374, in which a member of the Bundestag unsuccessfully sought to challenge a ruling of the chamber's presiding officer reprimanding him for certain remarks made on the floor of the house. See also Judgment of June 13, 1989, 80 BVerfGE 188, sustaining the right of a nonparty delegate to speak on the floor of the Bundestag.

45   See Judgment of July 14, 1986, 73 BVerfGE 40. For a general discussion of decisions affecting the rights of parliamentary parties, see Gerald Kretschmer, *Fraktionen: Parteien im Parliament,* 2d ed. (Heidelberg, 1992). Parliamentary political parties may initiate an *Organstreit* proceeding to vindicate their status as parliamentary parties.

46   Plenum Jurisdiction Case, 4 BVerfGE 27 (1954).

47   See Party Finance Case I, 20 BVerfGE 56, 98 (1966).

48   For a general discussion of the court's jurisdiction over constitutional controversies involving the highest organs of the Federal Republic, see Dieter C. Umbach and Thomas Clemens, *Bundesverfassungsgerichtsgesetz* (Heidelberg: C. F. Müller Verlag, 1992), 821–907. See also Julius Federer, "Aufbau, Zuständigkeit, und Verfahren des Bundesverfassungsgerichts," in *Das Bundesverfassungsgericht 1951–1971,* rev. ed. (Karlsruhe: Verlag C. F. Müller, 1971), 64–66.

49   FCCA, sec. 67. See also Umbach and Clemens, supra note 48, at 914–16.

50   FCCA, secs. 63–67.

51   See Umbach and Clemens, supra note 48, at 1033–34. See also the *Preliminary Judgment* case, in which the court held inadmissible a request by a lower court to issue a preliminary judgment on the validity of a statute the latter regarded as null and void in view of the fact that the lower court had not fully evaluated the question and failed to consider the possibility of construing the statute in such a way as to render it valid under the Basic Law (85 BVerfGE 329 [1992]). In 1993, the chambers were authorized to dismiss judicial referrals if the three justices unanimously voted to dismiss. The full senate must decide, however, if the referral comes from a state constitutional court or one of the high federal courts (FCCA, sec. 81a).

52   Basic Law, Article 93.

53 FCCA, sec. 31 (2).

54 Klaus Schlaich, *Das Bundesverfassungsgericht,* 2d ed. (Munich: C. H. Beck'sche Verlags-buchhandlung, 1991), 77.

55 There is one exception to the exhaustion rule. The court may accept a constitutional complaint before all remedies have been exhausted "if recourse to other courts would entail a serious and unavoidable disadvantage to the complainant" (FCCA, sec. 90 [2]).

56 FCCA, sec. 93. A person who wishes to challenge a judicial decision must file the complaint within one month of receiving notification of the decision. But if a statute is under attack, the complaint must be filed within one year of its enactment. As indicated, ordinarily the complainant must exhaust all other legal remedies before petitioning the Constitutional Court. Laws and ordinances, however, are subject to direct attack if they require no independent act of execution, an example being the person who is threatened by a criminal statute but does not wish to violate the law as a condition of contesting its validity. The court's own standards, finally, require the complainant to have personally suffered a clear, present, and cognizable injury directly resulting from the governmental action complained of. A detailed discussion of the constitutional complaint procedure in English is Michael Singer, "The Constitutional Court of the German Federal Republic: Jurisdiction over Individual Complaints," *International and Comparative Law Quarterly* 31 (1982): 331–36. See also Walter Seuffert, "Die Verfassungsbeschwerde in der Verfassungsgerichtsbarkeit," in *Bundesverfassungsgericht 1957–1971,* supra note 48, at 159–69.

57 FCCA, sec. 93a (2).

58 Basic Law, Article 93 (1) [4b].

59 The popularity of the constitutional complaint and the willingness of German citizens to resort to it was illustrated in 1983 when more than a hundred persons filed separate complaints against the constitutionality of the Federal Census Act of 1983. These complaints resulted in one of the most important cases decided by the court in recent years. See *Census Act* case (no. 7.b).

60 Public address by Justice Wolfgang Zeidler (undated and unpublished typescript).

61 See, respectively, Mental Deficiency Case, 1 BVerfGE 87 (1951); Firma L. and Company Case, 3 BVerfGE 359 (1954); and Bank Standing Case, 23 BVerfGE 153 (1968). The court has also granted "standing" to public broadcasting stations claiming free speech rights under Article 5. See State Radio Cases, 31 BVerfGE 314 (1971).

62 Wine Export Case, 18 BVerfGE 399 (1965).

63 FCCA, sec. 93c.

64 German reunification contributed heavily to the swelling number of complaints filed in the 1990s. About 10 percent of the complaints filed in 1994 originated in the new East German states. See *Frankfurter Allgemeine Zeitung,* February 20, 1995, 5.

65 For a general discussion of the court's status, see Gerhard Leibholz, "Der Status des Bundesverfassungsgerichts," in *Bundesverfassungsgericht 1951–1971,* supra note 48, at 31–57; see also Kommers, supra note 25, at 83–86.

66 "Bericht an das Plenum des Bundesverfassungsgerichts zur 'Status Frage'" [March 21, 1952], in *Jahrbuch des Öffentlichen Rechts* 6 (1957): 120–37. For other views on the court's status, see "Denkschrift des Bundesverfassungsgerichts" [June 27, 1952], in ibid., 144–48; and Richard Thoma, "Rechtsgutachten betreffend die Stellung des Bundesverfassungsgerichts" [March 15, 1962], in ibid., 161–94.

67 "Denkschrift," ibid., 148. For an assessment of Höpker-Aschoff's contribution to the early development of the Constitutional Court, see Theo Ritterspach, "Hermann Höpker Aschoff: Der erste Präsident des Bundesverfassungsgerichts 1883–1954," *Jahrbuch des Öffentlichen Rechts* 32 (1983): 55–62.

68 See Leibholz, supra note 65, at 31–57; see also Laufer, supra note 26, at 254–334.

69 Deutsches Richtergesetz in the version of September 8, 1961, *BGBl* 1:1665. See also Wilhelm K. Geck, "Zum Status des Bundesverfassungsrichter: Besoldungs und Versorgungsrecht," in *Festschrift für Wolfgang Zeidler,* ed. Walther Fürst, Roman Herzog, and Dieter C. Umbach, 2 vols. (Berlin: Walter de Gruyter Verlag, 1987), 1:189–218.

70 Basic Law, Article 115h.

71 The Constitutional Court's organization, procedures, and jurisdiction are regulated by the FCCA. The court's internal administration (i.e., budget, administrative duties of judges, authority and procedures of the Plenum, selection and responsibilities of law clerks, judicial conference procedures, and the rules governing oral argument and preparation of written opinions) is regulated by the court's Standing Rules of Procedure. See Geschäftsordnung des Bundesverfassungsgerichts [Rules of procedure of the Federal Constitutional Court], Law of September 2, 1975, *BGBl* 1:2515 (hereinafter cited as GO-BVerfGE). The court's organization and internal administration are treated at considerable length in Kommers, supra note 25, at 69–108.

72 For a discussion of these internal administrative matters, see Laufer, supra note 26, at 315–29.

73 Jurisdiction over cases involving the constitutionality of political parties was originally vested in the First Senate. With the backing of the Adenauer-led government, however, the Bundesrat transferred this jurisdiction to the Second Senate in 1957. The transfer grew out of the government's impatience and dissatisfaction with the First Senate's handling of the *Communist Party* case. See Kommers, supra note 25, at 1990–91.

74 For an excellent survey of the functioning of concrete judicial review, see Karl August Bettermann, "Die konkrete Normenkontrolle und sonstige Gerichtsvorlagen," in Starck, supra note 42, at 323–73.

75 See *BGBl* 1 (1956): 1735. Decisions of the Plenum redistributing the court's internal workload must be published in the *Federal Law Gazette* (*Bundesgesetzblatt*).

76 FCCA, sec. 2 (a).

77 See Donald P. Kommers, *Judicial Politics in Germany* (Beverly Hills, Calif.: Sage Publications, 1976), 128–44.

78 FCCA, sec. 15 (a).

79 Law of July 21, 1956, *BGBl* 1:662. FCCA, sec. 93a (earlier version of the statute). The procedures for establishing these committees were initially laid down in GO-BVerfGE, secs. 38 and 39.

80 FCCA, sec. 15a (1).

81 FCCA, sec. 93b (2).

82 GO-BVerfGE, sec. 40 (1).

83 FCCA, sec. 93d (3).

84 This discussion of the complaint procedure relies heavily on Hans Spanner, "Die Beschwerdebefugnis bei der Verfassungsbeschwerde," in Starck, supra note 42, at 374–95; and Hans H. Zacker, "Die Selektion der Verfassungsbeschwerden — die Siebfunktion der

Vorprüfung, des Erfordernisses der Rechtswegerschöpfung und des Kriteriums der unmittelbaren und gegenwärtigen Betroffenheit des Beschwerdeführers," in ibid., 396–431.

85 FCCA, sec. 93b (2). More recently, and again provided all three justices agree, the FCCA authorized the chambers to reject as "inadmissible" referrals on concrete review from other courts. Only the full senate, however, may reject a referral for lack of admissibility if it originates in a state constitutional court or one of the high federal courts. FCCA, sec. 81a.

86 FCCA, sec. 93c (1).

87 FCCA, sec. 93d (1).

88 These "unofficial" opinions constitute a large and growing body of constitutional decisions. The original complaints from which these published opinions emerge are often prepared by legal counsel and arguably raise issues of constitutional significance. The justices feel obligated to respond to such arguments notwithstanding their dismissal of the complaint on the ground of its probable lack of success. An illustration is the judgment of October 11, 1985, by Justices Zeidler, Steinberger, and Böckenförde involving a constitutional complaint against a procedural ruling of a Stuttgart court allegedly incompatible with a decision of the European Court of Human Rights, and thus in conflict with a general rule of international law within the meaning of the Basic Law's Article 25. In a rather detailed nine-page opinion the committee cited several decisions of the European Human Rights Court to sustain its conclusion that the complaint would not succeed if accepted and decided by the full senate. Chamber Judgment of October 11, 1985, 2 BvR 336/85 (typescript).

89 GO-BVerfGE, sec. 41 (2).

90 See, for example, 49 BVerfGE 375 (1978); 54 BVerfGE 39 (1980); and 56 BVerfGE 247 (1981).

91 The release of these opinions is usually at the discretion of the chamber or the rapporteur in the case. See Umbach and Clemens, supra note 48, at 1333. Some of these opinions are extremely controversial. See, for example, the *Tucholsky* case, reprinted in chapter 8, case no. 8.6. A chamber composed of Justices Grimm, Seibert, and Jaeger ruled that the public display of a sign saying that soldiers are murderers is protected against punishment under the free speech provisions of the Basic Law.

92 In practice, however, the chambers do notify, often in formal opinions running to several pages, close to 75 percent of all complainants of their reasons for declining petitions. The 75 percent figure is from Justice Helmut Steinberger, interview with the author, October 9, 1986. An example of such a rejected petition is the complaint brought by the academic council of Oldenburg University's social science faculty. The Federal Office of Political Education had denied the faculty permission to inspect its records under a rule requiring such documents to remain classified for a period of thirty years. The complaint challenged the constitutional validity of the ruling and several administrative court decisions sustaining it. On January 30, 1986, a chamber consisting of Justices Herzog, Katzenstein, and Henschel dismissed the complaint over the objection that the federal office had interfered with the freedom of information and the freedom of research and teaching secured, respectively, by paragraphs 1 and 3 of Article 5 of the Basic Law. Citing precedent as well as authoritative commentary, the committee explained in detail why the full senate would not decide the case on its merits. Chamber Judgment of January 30, 1986, 1 BvR 1352/85 (typescript).

93 FCCA, sec. 34 (5) (old version). As a result of 1993 amendments to the statute, this provision now appears in FCCA, sec. 34 (2).

94 FCCA, sec. 34a (3). In 1993 the chambers imposed "nonacceptance" fees in 9.24 percent of all cases, amounting to DM 121,310 ($86,850), and "abuse" fees in 0.25 percent of all cases, totaling DM 19,310 ($13,792) ("Gesamtstatistik des Bundesverfassungsgerichts für das Geschäftsjahr 1993" [unpublished report, 1994], p. 12). See also Ernst Gottfried Mahrenholz, "Kammerbeschlüsse — Nichtannahmegebühren," in *Zeidler Festschrift,* supra note 69, at 2:1361–77.

95 Three-Justice Committee Case I, 7 BVerfGE 241 (1958); Three-Justice Committee Case II, 18 BVerfGE 440 (1965); and Three-Justice Committee Case III, 19 BVerfGE 88 (1965).

96 Three-Justice Committee Case I, 7 BVerfGE 241 (1958).

97 Singer, supra note 56, at 338.

98 Ibid., 332.

99 On the relationship between the senates and their respective chambers, see Ernst Gottfried Mahrenholz, "Kammerbeschlüsse — Nichtannahmegewehren," in *Zeidler Festschrift,* supra note 69, at 2:1364–65.

100 Deutsches Richtergesetz, sec. 5.

101 FCCA, sec. 3 (4).

102 FCCA, sec. 4 (1).

103 Influential in the adoption of the dissenting opinion was the detailed study by Konrad Zweigert, a former justice of the Federal Constitutional Court; see *Empfiehlt es sich, die Bekanntgabe der abweichenden Meinungen des überstimmten Richters [dissenting opinion] in den deutschen Verfahrensordnungen zuzulassen?* Gutachten für den 47. *Deutschen Juristentag,* pt. D, vol. 1 (Munich: C. H. Beck'sche Verlagsbuchhandlung, 1968).

104 See Kommers, supra note 25, at 195–98; Wilhelm K. Geck, *Wahl und Amtsrecht der Bundesverfassungsrichter* (Baden-Baden: Nomos Verlagsgesellschaft, 1986).

105 FCCA, sec. 6 (2). The JSC is unique among Bundestag committees. For one thing, its decisions are, in effect, the decisions of the Bundestag. For another, only parliamentary parties may submit lists of candidates for committee membership. Several parliamentary parties may agree on a common list, as is usually done, so long as the Bundestag has at least two competing lists to vote for. No changes in these lists are permitted from the floor. The JSC's proceedings take place behind closed doors, and its members are obliged by law "to keep secret the personal circumstances of candidates which became known to them as a result of their [inquiries]"; see FCCA, sec. 6 (4). This rule of secrecy has been challenged in recent years. Critics of the system would prefer open hearings on judicial nominees like those conducted by the Judiciary Committee of the U.S. Senate. In 1957 Professor Richard Thoma, a distinguished professor of public law, questioned the constitutionality of the JSC itself because the Basic Law provides for the election of the justices by the Bundestag as a whole. This view, however, has attracted little support among constitutional lawyers. See also infra note 110.

106 FCCA, sec. 7.

107 FCCA, sec. 5.

108 For a discussion of the political problems raised by this alternation rule, see Friedrich Karl Fromme, "Zwei Nachfolger für Herzog," *Frankfurter Allgemeine Zeitung,* August 27, 1994, 8.

109 FCCA, sec. 7a.

110 As indicated above (supra note 105), there are no public hearings on judicial nominees in Germany. As a consequence, many of the persons elected to the court are unknown to the public at large. In any event, as the SPD magazine, *Vorwärts,* noted on the occasion of the election of six new justices in November 1987, public hearings reminiscent of the congressional inquiry into the background and qualifications of Robert Bork for a seat on the Supreme Court of the United States "would be unthinkable in the Federal Republic" (*Vorwärts,* November 21, 1987, 14). Many Germans would regard such hearings as an assault on the institutional integrity of the Constitutional Court itself. Any public fixation on how a judicial nominee would vote in a particular case or in a wide range of cases would be seen as a potential threat to the independence of that nominee. By the same token, any interest group lobbying on behalf of a particular judicial nominee, accompanied by threats of retaliation against legislators who vote the wrong way, would be regarded as interference with the independence of those entrusted with the duty of selecting justices. Finally, the public exposure of every facet of a judicial nominee's life and personality would be regarded as an egregious intrusion on his or her privacy. Nevertheless, the secrecy of the JSC's deliberations is occasionally the subject of severe criticism in the German press. See *Der Spiegel* 34 (1987): 30–32; and Roll Lamprecht, "Kungelei hinter den Kulissen," *Deutsche Richterzeitung* 64 (August 1986): 314.

111 In 1971, for example, Christian Democrats were in conflict over a judicial appointment. Minister-President Hans Filbinger of Baden-Württemberg worked hard in the Bundesrat for the appointment of his aide, Paul Feuchte, to a vacancy on the First Senate; Christian Democrats on the JSC preferred Hans Faller, a judge of the High Court of Justice (Bundesgerichtshof). What finally tipped the scale in favor of Faller — a former Constitutional Court law clerk — was the court's own "intervention" on his behalf. A majority of the justices issued a statement claiming that the member in question must be chosen from the federal bench, a highly dubious proposition because the First Senate was already staffed with three justices recruited from the high federal courts. The Bundesrat, however, yielded to this view and elected Faller. More recently, in the Henschel Judicial Selection Case, 65 BVerfGE 152 (1983), the First Senate had to decide whether one of its own members had been legally elected. Johann Friedrich Henschel, a lawyer, was chosen by the Bundesrat to succeed Faller. The court rejected the argument that because Faller was a federal judge his successor would have to be elected from the federal bench. This action was necessary to ensure the legitimacy of the court's proceedings in the light of the constitutional provision (Article 101) that prohibits the removal of any person from the jurisdiction of his lawful judge. On the role of the Federal Constitutional Court in the judicial selection process, see Henning Frank, "Die Mitwirkung des Bundesverfassungsgerichts an den Richterwahlen," in *Festschrift: Hans Joachim Faller,* ed. Wolfgang Zeidler et al. (Munich: C. H. Beck'sche Verlagsbuchhandlung, 1984), 37–52.

112 *BGBl* 1 (1975): 2095.

113 FCCA, sec. 13.

114 FCCA, secs. 17–35.

115 FCCA, sec. 18.

116 FCCA, sec. 19.

117 20 BVerfGE 56 (1966).

118 36 BVerfGE 1 (1973).

119 See Leibholz Exclusion Case, 20 BVerfGE 1 (1966); and Rottmann Exclusion Case, 35 BVerfGE 246 (1973).

120 FCCA, sec. 30.

121 FCCA, sec. 31 (2).

122 Any jurisdictional dispute between the senates at this stage of the decision-making process would be resolved by a committee composed of the president, the vice president, and two justices from each senate. The president casts the deciding vote in the event of a deadlock. FCCA, sec. 14 (5).

123 Kommers, supra note 25, at 178.

124 An illustration is the Green Party Exclusion Case, 70 BVerfGe 324 (1986), in which spokesmen for parliament and the Greens were given two days to present their respective views. The Green party challenged the legality of a Bundestag decision to deny it representation on a budgetary control committee concerned with secret service activities. The first day was consumed in argument on procedural issues, the second on whether the exclusion violated the principle of parliamentary democracy. The senate even permitted a leader of the Green parliamentary party, a nonlawyer, to read a lengthy statement at the oral proceeding. The author was present at these hearings.

125 Kommers, supra note 25, at 179–81.

126 Ibid., 181–91. This description of the judicial dynamics on the Constitutional Court, based originally on interviews with twenty-four justices in 1968, was confirmed by additional interviews with selected justices in 1986.

127 GO-BVerfGE, sec. 59.

128 GO-BVerfGe, sec. 60.

129 Unpublished Federal Constitutional Court statistics for 1993.

130 Kommers, supra note 25, at 173.

131 See the concluding section of Chapter 2.

132 See Donald P. Kommers, "The Federal Constitutional Court in the German Political System," *Comparative Political Studies* 26 (January 1994): 470–92.

133 For a detailed discussion and analysis of the constitutional cases decided in the aftermath of German reunification, see Peter E. Quint, *The Imperfect Union: Constitutional Structures and German Unification* (Princeton: Princeton University Press, 1996), 194–215.

134 See, for example, Rudolf Dolzer, *Die staatstheoretische und staatsrechtliche Stellung des Bundesverfassungsgerichts* (Berlin: Duncker and Humblot, 1972), 114–18.

2 THE BASIC LAW AND ITS INTERPRETATION

1 GG (Grundgesetz or Basic Law), Article 146.

2 For a different view of the East German perspective, see Arthur Benz, "A Forum of Constitutional Deliberation: A Critical Analysis of the Joint Constitutional Commission," *German Politics* 3 (1994): 99–117.

3 For a detailed account of these amendments, see Peter E. Quint, *The Imperfect Union: Constitutional Structures and German Unification* (Princeton: Princeton University Press, 1996), 115–23.

4   A superior treatment of this "common enterprise" is John Ford Golay, *The Founding of the Federal Republic of Germany* (Chicago: University of Chicago Press, 1958).

5   See Theodore Maunz and Rheinhold Zippelius, *Deutsches Staatsrecht,* 25th ed. (Munich: C. H. Beck'sche Verlagsbuchhandlung, 1983), 181–84; see also Christian Starck, "Menschenwürde als Verfassungsgarantie im modernen Staat," *Juristenzeitung* 36 (1981): 457–64. For a critical assessment of the concept of human dignity, see Hans S. Stoecker, "Menschenwürde und kritische Jurisprudenz," *Juristenzeitung* 23 (1968): 685–91.

6   See Johannes Mattern, *Principles of the Constitutional Jurisprudence of the German National Republic* (Baltimore: Johns Hopkins University Press, 1928), 614–25.

7   "Die Grundrechte im Entstehungszusammenhang der bürgerlichen Gesellschaft," in Dieter Grimm, *Die Zukunft der Verfassung* (Frankfurt am Main: Suhrkamp Verlag, 1991), 86–90.

8   Leonard Krieger, *The German Idea of Freedom* (Boston: Beacon Press, 1957), 121.

9   Georg W. Friedrich Hegel, *Hegel's Philosophy of Right,* trans. with note by T. M. Knox (Oxford: Clarendon Press, 1942), 279.

10   Georg Wilhelm Friedrich Hegel, *The Philosophy of History,* trans. J. Sibree (New York: Willey Book Company, 1944), 19.

11   For accounts of this tradition, see J. G. A. Pocock, *The Machiavellian Moment* (Princeton: Princeton University Press, 1975); Gary Wills, *Explaining America: The Federalist* (Garden City, N.Y.: Doubleday, 1980); and Gordon Wood, *The Creation of the American Republic* (Chapel Hill: University of North Carolina Press, 1969).

12   Krieger, supra note 8, at 470.

13   See below, pp. 47–48

14   For a commentary on Article 28, see Ingo von Münch, *Grundgesetz-Kommentar* (Munich: C. H. Beck'sche Verlagsbuchhandlung, 1983), Article 28.

15   See Chapter 4 (separation of powers), pp. 117–22.

16   See Konrad Hesse, "Die verfassungsrechtliche Stellung der Parteien im modernen Staat," *Veröffentlichungen der Vereinigung der Deutschen Staatsrechtslehrer* 17 (1959): 11–47; Hans Justus Rinck, "Der verfassungsrechtliche Status der politischen Parteien in der Bundesrepublik," in *Die Moderne Demokratie und ihr Recht,* 2 vols. (Tübingen: J. C. B. Mohr [Paul Siebeck], 1966), 1:305–30; and Gerhard Leibholz, *Strukturprobleme der modernen Demokratie* (Karlsruhe: Verlag C. F. Müller, 1958).

17   See Gerhard Leibholz, "Parteienstaat und repräsentative Demokratie: Eine Betrachtung z. Art. 21 und 38 des Bonnet Grundgesetzes," *Deutsches Verwaltungsblatt* 66 (1951): 1–8.

18   See Maunz and Zippelius, supra note 5, at 96–97.

19   See Ernst Forsthoff, *Rechtsstaatlichkeit und Sozialstaatlichkeit* (Darmstadt: Wissenschaftliche Buchgesellschaft, 1968).

20   See Ernst Benda, "Der soziale Rechtsstaat," in *Handbuch des Verfassungsrechts* (Berlin: Walter de Gruyter, 1984), 477–544.

21   See Ernst Forsthoff, "Begriff und Wesen sozialen Rechtsstaates," in *Rechtsstaat im Wandel* (Stuttgart, 1964), 27–56; and Ernst Forsthoff, "Grenze des Sozialstaat," *Deutsche Zeitung* (June 7, 1974), 2. For a criticism of the Forsthoffian view, see Ernst Benda, Werner Maihofer, and Han-Jochen Vogel, *Handbuch des Verfassungsrechts,* vol. 1 (Berlin: Walter de Gruyter, 1984), 509–12; cf. Peter Caldwell, "Ernst Forsthoff and the Legacy of Radical

Conservative State Theory in the Federal Republic of Germany," *History of Political Thought* 15 (1994): 631–39.

22   For a particularly clear historical overview of the development of the idea of the *Rechtsstaat,* see Ernst-Wolfgang Böckenförde, "The Origin and Development of the Concept of the *Rechtsstaat,*" in Böckenförde, *State, Society and Liberty* (New York: Berg Publishers, 1991), 47–70. The brief recapitulation of the history of the idea of the *Rechstsstaat* that follows draws heavily on Böckenförde's analysis.

23   For a discussion of the use and meaning of these terms and the difficulty of interpretation that they present, see Erhard Denninger, "Judicial Review Revisited: The German Experience," *Tulane Law Review* 59 (1985): 1015–17.

24   It is of interest to note that the original version of Article 1 (3) made the basic rights binding only on the executive and the judiciary. A 1956 amendment added the legislature to this provision. Under the older conception of the *Rechtsstaat,* the principle of equal protection under law was understood to bind the executive in the administration of law and the judiciary in its interpretation, but not the legislature. During the Weimar period, Gerhard Leibholz, who in 1951 would be among the first appointees to the Federal Constitutional Court, vigorously challenged the notion that the legislature was not bound by the constitutional principle of equality. See his *Die Gleichheit vor dem Gesetz* (Berlin: Liebmann, 1925). Leibholz continued his assault on this notion in the early years of the Federal Republic and was largely responsible for persuading the German legal community that the principle of equality and other basic rights bind the legislature as well as other branches of government. See Christian Starck, "Die Anwendung des Gleichheitsatzes," in *Der Gleichheitssatz im modernen Verfassungsstaat,* ed. Christoph Link (Baden-Baden: Nomos Verlagsgesellschaft, 1982), 53–54.

25   Böckenförde, *State, Society and Liberty,* supra note 22, at 67.

26   For a discussion of this case, see Chapter 5, pp. 222–24.

27   Gregory H. Fox and Georg Nolte, "Intolerant Democracies," *Harvard International Law Journal* 36 (1995): 32.

28   For a commentary on Article 18, see Ingo von Münch and Philip Kunig, *Grundgesetz-Kommentar,* 3 vols. (Munich: C. H. Beck'sche Verlagsbuchhandlung, 1992), 1:967–83. Article 9 represents still another expression of militant democracy. It prohibits all associations whose activities are directed against the constitutional order (ibid., 593–94).

29   For an excellent discussion of this essentially neo-Kantian approach to constitutional law, heavily influenced by the work of Hans Kelsen, see Rupert Emerson, *State and Sovereignty in Modern Germany* (New Haven: Yale University Press, 1928), 159–208. Many contemporary legal scholars find no incompatibility between the Basic Law and the tradition of legal positivism, for they read the Constitution as applicable law. A useful discussion is Ernst-Wolfgang Böckenförde, "Methoden der Verfassungsinterpretation," *Neue Juristiche Wochenschrift* 29 (1976): 2089–99.

30   William F. Harris II, "Bonding Word and Polity: The Logic of American Constitutionalism," *American Political Science Review* 76 (1982): 34.

31   Some American constitutional scholars have also seen the U.S. Constitution as embodying a preferred way of life. See Sotirios A. Barber, *On What the Constitution Means* (Baltimore: Johns Hopkins University Press, 1984).

32 Eckhart Klein, "The Concept of the Basic Law," in *Main Principles of the German Basic Law,* ed. Christian Starck (Baden-Baden: Nomos Verlagsgesellschaft, 1983), 15–35.

33 Gerhard Leibholz, "Constitutional Law and Constitutional Reality," in *Festschrift für Karl Löwenstein* (Tübingen: J. C. B. Mohr [Paul Siebeck], 1971), 308.

34 Karl Heinrich Friauf, "Techniques for the Interpretation of Constitutions in German Law," in *Proceedings of the Fifth International Symposium on Comparative Law* (Ottawa: University of Ottawa Press, 1968), 9.

35 Modern German *Begriffsjurisprudenz* is heavily indebted to the teaching of Hans Kelsen; see his *Pure Theory of Law,* trans. Max Knight (Berkeley: University of California Press, 1967), 1. See also Arthur Kaufman and Winfried Hassemer, "Enacted Law and Judicial Decision in German Jurisprudential Thought," *University of Toronto Law Journal* 19 (1969): 469–76.

36 Clarence J. Mann, *The Function of Judicial Decision in European Economic Integration* (The Hague: Martinus Nijhoff, 1971), 95. For an excellent treatment of law so conceived, see Philippe Nonet and Philip Selznick, *Law and Society in Transition* (New York: Octagon Books, 1974), 53–72.

37 Oliver W. Holmes, *The Common Law* (Boston: Little, Brown, 1881), 1. For an excellent contrast between the role of courts in civil- and common-law systems, see J. G. Sauve-Planne, *Codified and Judge-Made Law* (Amsterdam: North-Holland Publishing, 1982).

38 Leading representatives of this approach to judicial decision are Benjamin Cardozo, *The Nature of the Judicial Process* (New Haven: Yale University Press, 1921), and Roscoe Pound, *Justice according to Law* (London: Cumberlege, 1951). In recent constitutional theory, two competing strands of American constitutionalism have been identified. One strand is the liberalism associated with Hobbes and Locke; the other is the tradition of republican virtue identified most prominently with the early antifederalists. See Mark Tushnet, "Anti-Formalism in Recent Constitutional Theory," *Michigan Law Review* 83 (1985): 1507–8.

39 See, especially, James Willard Hurst, *Law and the Conditions of Freedom* (Madison: University of Wisconsin, 1956).

40 Holmes, supra note 37; Pound, supra note 38; Karl Llewellyn, *Common Law Tradition* (Boston: Little, Brown, 1960); Jerome Frank, *Law and the Modern Mind* (New York: Tudor Publishing, 1936); Cardozo, supra note 38; and Learned Hand, *The Bill of Rights* (Cambridge: Harvard University Press, 1958).

41 Georg Jellinek, *Gesetz und Verordnung* (Tübingen: J. C. B. Mohr, 1919); Gerhard Anschütz, *Die Verfassung des deutschen Reichs* (Berlin: Verlag Georg Stilke, 1932); Franz W. Jerusalem, *Die Staatsgerichtsbarkeit* (Tübingen: J. C. B. Mohr [Paul Siebeck], 1930); Georg Friedrich Puchta, *Kursus der Institutionen,* 9th ed., ed. Paul Fruger (Leipzig, 1881); Karl Bergbohm, *Jurisprudenz und Rechtsphilosophie,* 2 vols. (Leipzig: Duncker and Humboldt, 1892); and Gustav Radbruch, *Rechtsphilosophie* (Stuttgart: K. E. Kochlet Verlag, 1963).

42 See Alphons Beitzinger, *A History of American Political Thought* (New York: Dodd, Mead, 1972), 204–9.

43 See Leonard Krieger, supra note 8, at 86–138, 182–87. See also W. Friedmann, *Legal Theory* (New York: Columbia University Press, 1967), 157–70.

44 Mann, supra note 36, at 96–97.

45 Various versions of historicism in German law are discussed in Hendrik Jan van Eikema Hommes, *Major Trends in the History of Legal Philosophy* (Amsterdam: North-Holland Publishing, 1979), 185–205.

46 See Friedmann, supra note 43, at 332–36. *Interessenjurisprudenz,* or "jurisprudence of interests," set forth and encouraged an interest-balancing approach to judicial decision making.

47 See Hommes, supra note 45, at 229–66.

48 A general discussion of the emergence and impact of natural-law doctrine in Germany after World War II and during the early years of the Federal Republic can be found in Heinrich Rommen, "Natural Law in Decisions of the Federal Supreme Court and of the Constitutional Courts in Germany," *Natural Law Forum* 4 (1959): 1–25. See also Ernst von Hippel, "The Role of Natural Law in the Legal Decisions of the German Federal Republic," *Natural Law Forum* 4 (1959): 106–18; and Gottfried Dietze, "Natural Law in Modern European Constitutions," *Natural Law Forum* 1 (1956): 73–91.

49 For a discussion of the attempt to convert law into a science in nineteenth-century America, see Morton J. Horowitz, *The Growth of American Law* (Boston: Little, Brown, 1950), 269–76. Examples of the late twentieth-century attempt to "objectify" constitutional decision making in terms of moral principle are Ronald S. Dworkin, *A Matter of Principle* (Cambridge: Harvard University Press, 1986); Michael Perry, *The Constitution, the Courts, and Human Rights* (New Haven: Yale University Press, 1982); and David A. J. Richards, *The Moral Critique of the Law* (Belmont, Calif.: Dickenson Publishing, 1977).

50 A standard description of these techniques is found in Bruno Schmidt-Bleibtreu and Franz Klein, *Kommentar zum Grundgesetz für die Bundesrepublik Deutschland,* 5th ed. (Darmstadt: Verlag Luchterhand, 1980), 109–18. See also Gerd Roellecke, "Prinzipien der Verfassungsinterpretation in der Rechtsprechung des Bundesverfassungsgerichts," in *Bundesverfassungsgericht und Grundgesetz,* ed. Christian Starck, 2 vols. (Tübingen: J. C. B. Mohr [Paul Siebeck], 1976), 2:22–49; and Böckenförde, "Methoden der Verfassungsinterpretation," supra note 29, at 2089–99.

51 See, for example, Ralph Drier and Friedreich Schwegmann, eds., *Probleme der Verfassungsinterpretation: Dokumentation einer Kontroverse* (Baden-Baden: Nomos Verlagsgesellschaft, 1976).

52 Friauf, supra note 34, at 9–22. See the Constitutional Court's discussion of these techniques in Reich Tax Levy Case, 11 BverfGE 126, 129–32 (1960). For an excellent comparison of these approaches with American methods of judicial interpretation, see Winfried Brugger, "Legal Interpretation, Schools of Jurisprudence, and Anthropology: Some Remarks from a German Point of View," *American Journal of Comparative Law* 42 (1994): 396–402. Cf. Kaufmann and Hassemer, "Enacted Law and Judicial Decision," supra note 35, at 465–66.

53 Konrad Hesse, *Grundzüge des Verfassungsrechts für die Bundesrepublik Deutschland,* 16th ed. (Karlsruhe: Verlag C. F. Müller, 1988), 23.

54 My colleague, Sotirios Barber, finds this interesting in light of the argument of the New Right that original intent is the only way to restrain the exercise of judicial review in the United States. See also Stephen Macedo, *The New Right v. The Constitution* (Washington, D.C.: Cato Institute, 1987).

55 See Homosexuality Case, 6 BVerfGE 389, 431 (1957); and Special Federal Aid Program

Case, 41 BVerfGE 291, 309 (1976). This principle derives from the conventional approach to statutory interpretation in Germany. As Gustav Radbruch noted, "the state does not speak through the personal opinions of those who drafted the law, but rather through the law itself." See his *Rechtsphilosophie*, 4th ed. (Stuttgart: K. E. Koehler Verlag, 1963), 210.

56 This, at least, is the prevailing theory of German constitutional interpretation. Yet historical arguments are frequently advanced in German constitutional opinions, and some decisions seem actually to be grounded in such arguments. See, for example, Soviet Zone Case, 2 BVerfGE 266, 276 (1953); Extradition Case, 4 BVerfGE 299, 304–5 (1955); and Medical Practice Case, 33 BVerfGE 125, 153–55 (1972). In the United States, by contrast, historical arguments based on the will of the founders of the Constitution — if this will can be discovered — are of "decisive importance." For Germans the objective meaning of the text itself takes clear priority over the subjective will of the framers. See Hans Joachim Koch and Helmut Rüssmann, *Juristische Begründungslehre* (Munich: C. H. Beck, 1982), 21–25.

57 Friauf, supra note 34, at 13.

58 Hesse, *Grundzüge*, supra note 53, at 22. It may be of interest to note here that some German writers have recently sought to reformulate the approach to constitutional interpretation by resorting to analytic philosophy. See Koch and Rüssmann, *Juristische Begründungslehre*, supra note 56; and Robert Alexy, *Theorie der Grundrechte* (Baden-Baden: Nomos Verlagsgesellschaft, 1985). Alexy has drawn inspiration from Ronald Dworkin's work in this seminal effort to articulate a theory of rights under the Basic Law.

59 Siegfried Magiera, "The Interpretation of the Basic Law," in Starck, *Main Principles*, supra note 32, at 93. See also Hesse, *Grundzüge*, supra note 53, at 21–24. Hesse cites a large number of cases in which the court has deviated from the customary methods of interpretation.

60 For an excellent discussion of *Normgebundenheitstheorie*, see Mann, supra note 36, at 153–62.

61 Ernst Friesenhahn, "Wesen und Grenzen der Verfassungsgerichtsbarkeit," *Zeitschrift für Schweizerisches Recht* 73 (1954): 158.

62 Ibid., 153. This statement parallels the view of Justice Owen Roberts: "When an act of Congress is appropriately challenged in the courts as not conforming to the constitutional mandate, the judicial branch of the Government has only one duty — to lay the article of the Constitution which is invoked beside the statute which is challenged and to decide whether the latter squares with the former. All the court does, or can do, is to announce its considered judgment upon the question. The only power it has, if such it may be called, is the power of judgment" (United States v. Butler, 297 U.S. 1, 62–63 [1936]).

63 Gerhard Leibholz, *Politics and Law* (Leiden: A. W. Sythoff, 1965), 276.

64 Ibid., 275. This "truth-finding" theory of judicial decision is compatible with the declaratory character of most German constitutional cases. "The judgments of a constitutional court," Justice Leibholz observed, "have mostly a meaning which transcends the actual case itself; their significance affects the general weal and interest. They bind the State as a whole" (ibid., 274).

65 Ibid., 274.

66 See Helmut Simon, "Verfassungsgerichtsbarkeit," in *Handbuch des Verfassungsrechts*, ed.

Ernst Benda, Werner Maihofer, and Hans-Jochen Vogel (Berlin: Walter de Gruyter, 1984), 1282.

67 Hesse, *Grundzüge*, supra note 53, at 21. See also the classic criticism of conventional legal methodology by Josef Esser, *Vorverständnis und Methodenwahl in der richterlichen Rechtsbildung des Privatrechts*, 3d ed. (Tübingen: J. C. B. Mohr, 1974).

68 Ernst-Wolfgang Böckenförde, "Grundrechtstheorie und Grundrechtsinterpretation," *Neue Juristische Wochenschrift* 27 (1974): 1530–38.

69 Comment by Dieter Grimm in symposium discussion. See Christine Landfried, ed., *Constitutional Review and Legislation: An International Comparison* (Baden-Baden: Nomos Verlagsgesellschaft, 1988), 169.

70 Leibholz, *Politics and Law,* supra note 63, at 276.

71 "Constitutional Law and Constitutional Polity," in *Festschrift für Karl Löwenstein*, supra note 33, at 308. Leibholz expressed his ultimate view of the judicial task as fundamentally creative when he said: "It must be the task of the constitutional lawyer to reconcile rules of law and constitutional reality in such a way that the existing dialectical conflict between rule and reality can be removed as far as possible by creative interpretation of the Constitution without doing violence thereby either to reality in favor of the rule, or to the rule in favor of reality" (ibid.).

72 See Donald P. Kommers, *Judicial Politics in West Germany: A Study of the Federal Constitutional Court* (Beverly Hills, Calif.: Sage Publications, 1976), 182–91; see also Peter Wittig, "Politische Rücksichten in der Rechtsprechung des Bundesverfassungsgerichts," *Der Staat* 8 (1969): 137–58.

73 Leibholz, *Politics and Law,* supra note 63, at 276–77.

74 Justice Zeidler, interview with the author, April 9, 1986.

75 Kommers, supra note 72, at 185.

76 1 BVerfGE 14, 32 (1951).

77 Ibid.

78 Leibholz, *Politics and Law,* supra note 63, at 289.

79 Rudolf Smend, *Verfassung und Verfassungsrecht* (1928), 188–89.

80 Smend's theory has influenced numerous constitutional theorists. See, for example, Ekkehart Stein, *Staatsrecht,* 8th ed. (Tübingen: J. C. B. Mohr [Paul Siebeck], 1982), 250–53. For a critical assessment of the theory as applied by the Federal Constitutional Court, see Friedrich Müller, *Juristische Methodik,* 3d ed. (Berlin: Duncker and Humboldt, 1989), 217–19.

81 Hesse, *Grundzüge,* supra note 53, at 27.

82 Eberhard Grabitz, "Der Grundsatz der Verhältnismassigkeit in der Rechtsprechung des Bundesverfassungsgesetzes," *Archiv des Öffentlichen Rechts* 98 (1973): 568–616; see also Ingo von Münch, *Staatsrecht,* 5th ed. (Stuttgart: Verlag W. Kohlhammer, 1993), 367–68.

83 The proximate source of this notion of the Constitution as substantive or material rather than a formal or procedural entity is the Bavarian Constitutional Court's decision of June 10, 1949, interpreting the postwar constitution of Bavaria as a substantive unity. The Federal Constitutional Court cited the case at length in its famous *Southwest State* case (reprinted in Chapter 3), one of the court's earliest judgments and a seminal opinion fully comparable in importance to *Marbury* v. *Madison* in American constitutional law. See 1 BVerfGE 14, 32–35 (1951).

84 Peter E. Quint put it this way: "These [objective] values are not only specified rights of individuals but are also part of the general legal order, benefiting not only individuals who may be in a certain relationship with the state but possessing relevance for all legal relationships" ("Free Speech and Private Law in German Constitutional Theory," *Maryland Law Review* 48 [1989]: 261).

85 The objective value theory and its adoption by the Federal Constitutional Court are the subjects of a large literature in Germany. Critics see the objective value approach as a disingenuous means for importing the personal values of the justices into constitutional law. See, for example, Helmut Goerlich, *Wertordnung und Grundgesetz* (Baden-Baden: Nomos Verlagsgesellschaft, 1973). A related view refers to the constant incantation of values as a "tyranny of values" — see Carl Schmitt, "Die Tyrannei der Werte," in *Säkularization und Utopie: Ernst Forsthoff zum 65. Geburtstag,* ed. Karl Doehring and Wilhelm G. Greve (Stuttgart: Verlag W. Kohlhammer, 1967) — and a substitute for hard reasoning and the difficult task of legal justification. See also Erhard Denninger, "Freiheitsordnung-Wertordnung-Pflichtordnung," *Juristenzeitung* 30 (1975): 545–47. It is said that the mere designation of one basic right as ranking higher than another often foreordains without argument a given result. The *Abortion I* and *Mephisto* cases are often cited as illustrations of this process at work. See Roellecke, supra note 50, at 37. For strong defenses of the basic values approach, see Koch and Rüssmann, supra note 56; and Alexy, supra note 58.

86 Mann, supra note 36, at 159.

87 Article 117 Case, 3 BVerfGE 225, 232 (1953).

88 Ibid., 233. The opinion quotes with approval Gustav Radbruch's affirmation of natural-law theory in the 1950 edition of his *Rechtsphilosophie*. A leading defender of legal positivism in the 1920s, Radbruch eventually renounced legal positivism in the light of the Nazi regime; see his *Der Mensch in Recht* (Göttingen: Vandenhoeck and Ruprecht, 1957), 105ff.

89 In the Parental Control Case, 10 BVerfGE 59, 81 (1959), the court explicitly forswore reliance on natural-law doctrine in the light of what it regarded as adequate guidelines within the text of the Basic Law itself. A recent reference to justice as a valid interpretive norm is contained in the Stern Case, 54 BVerfGE 53, 67 (1980).

90 The notion of an unconstitutional constitutional amendment first surfaced in an *obiter dictum* in the Southwest State Case, 1 BVerfGE 14, 32 (1951). It appears to have originated with the Bavarian Constitutional Court, which noted in its decision of April 24, 1950: "It is not conceptually impossible to regard a constitutional provision as void even though it is part of the Constitution. Some constitutional principles are so basic and so much the expression of a legal principle which antedates the Constitution that they bind the constitutional framer himself. Other constitutional provisions which are not of equal rank may be void if they contravene them" (quoted in an advisory opinion prepared for the Federal Constitutional Court by the First Civil Senate of the Federal High Court of Justice, 6 *Entscheidungen des Bayerischen Verfassungsgerichtshofes* 47). The best critical treatment of this principle is Otto Bachof, "Verfassungswidrige Verfassungsnormen," in Bachof, *Wege zum Rechtsstaat* (Königstein: Athenäum Verlag, 1979), 1–48.

91 3 BVerfGE 225, 234 (1953).

92 30 BVerfGE 1, 33–47 (1970).

93   Lüth Case, 7 BVerfGE 198 (1958).

94   See Böckenförde, "Grundrechtstheorie und Grundrechtsinterpretation," supra note 68, at 1530; see also Alexy, supra note, 58, at 29–31.

95   Examples of prominent constitutional cases which rest, at least in part, on these respective theories are the Codetermination Case, 50 BVerfGe 290 (1979) (liberal theory); First Television Case, 12 BVerfGE 205 (1961) (democratic theory); and *Numerus Clausus* Case, 33 BVerfGE 303 (1972) (social theory).

96   See Milton C. Regan, Jr., "Community and Justice in Constitutional Theory," *Wisconsin Law Review* (1985): 1074.

97   See, for example, Peter Häberle, *Verfassungsgerichtsbarkeit zwischen Politik und Rechtswissenschaft* (Königstein: Athenäum Verlag, 1980); Christian Starck, *Das Bundesverfassungsgericht im politischen Prozess der Bundesrepublik* (Tübingen: J. C. B. Mohr [Paul Siebeck], 1976); Rolf Lamprecht and Wolfgang Malanowski, *Richter machen Politik* (Frankfurt am Main: Fischer, 1978); Heinz Laufer, *Verfassungsgerichtsbarkeit und politischer Prozess* (Tübingen: J. C. B. Mohr [Paul Siebeck], 1968); Wiltraut Rupp-von Brünneck, "Verfassungsgerichtsbarkeit und gesetzgebende Gewalt: Wechselseitiges Verhältnis zwischen Verfassungsgericht und Parlament," *Archiv des Öffentlichen Rechts* 102 (1977): 1–26; Klaus Stern, *Verfassungsgerichtsbarkeit zwischen Recht und Politik* (Opladen: Westdeutscher Verlag, 1980); and Christine Landfried, *Bundesverfassungsgericht und Gesetzgeber* (Baden-Baden: Nomos Verlagsgesellschaft, 1984).

98   Hans G. Rupp, "Some Remarks on Judicial Self-Restraint," *Ohio State Law Journal* 21 (1960): 507.

99   29 U.S. 288, 345–48 (1936). Justice Hans Rupp, an original appointee to the Federal Constitutional Court, compared the American "*Ashwander* rules" to practices developed by the court in the first ten years of its work. See his "Remarks on Judicial Self-Restraint," supra note 98, at 503–15. Justice Rupp, who studied at the Harvard Law School in the 1930s, was thoroughly acquainted with the Supreme Court and the American legal system, and he kept abreast of the Supreme Court's work during his tenure (1951–75) on the Second Senate. Another excellent article in English on the theme of judicial self-restraint was written by Wiltraut Rupp–von Brünneck, a justice of the First Senate and the wife of Justice Rupp; see "Admonitory Functions of the Constitutional Court," *American Journal of Comparative Law* 22 (1972): 387–403. The first two subsections of this section rely heavily on these two articles.

100   The *Steam Boiler* case is an illustration of this rule; see 11 BVerfGE 6 (1960).

101   See, for example, the Christmas Bonus Case, 3 BVerfGE 52, 55–58 (1953). The FCCA authorizes the court to grant a temporary injunction only "if this is urgently needed to avert serious detriment, to ward off imminent force, or for any other important reasons concerning the commonweal" (FCCA, section 32 [1]).

102   Constitutional cases establishing this principle are numberless; many are enumerated in G. Leibholz and H. J. Rinck, *Grundgesetz für die Bundesrepublik Deutschland: Kommentar an Hand der Rechtsprechung des Bundesverfassungsgerichts,* 6th ed. (Cologne: Verlag Dr. Otto Schmidt KG, 1970), 7. See also Dieter C. Umbach and Thomas Clemens, eds., *Bundesverfassungsgerichtsgesetz* (Heidelberg: C. F. Müller Juristischer Verlag, 1992), sec. 80, 1044–46.

103 See, for example, Saar Treaty Case, 4 BVerfGE 157, 168 (1955); and Conscientious Objector II Case, 48 BVerfGE 127, 160 (1978).

104 50 BVerfGE 290 (1979); and 49 BVerfGE 89 (1978).

105 See, for example, Soviet Zone Case, 2 BVerfGE 266, 271 (1953); Mineral Oil Case, 7 BVerfGE 171, 173–75 (1957); and Country Road Law Case, 51 BVerfGE 401, 403 (1979).

106 A good discussion in English of these rules is Jörn Ipsen, "Constitutional Review of Laws," in Starck, *Main Principles,* supra note 32, at 114–17.

107 Judicial Reference Case, 80 BVerfGE 54, 58–59 (1989). On the problems associated with the process of referring questions to the Constitutional Court, see Karl-Georg Zierlein, "Zur Prozessverantwortung der Fachgerichte im Lichte der Verwerfungskompetenz des Bundesverfassungsgerichts nach Artikel 100 Abs. 1 GG," in *Grundrechte, soziale Ordnung und Verfassungsgerichtsbarkeit: Festschrift für Ernst Benda,* ed. Eckart Klein (Heidelberg: C. F. Müller Juristische Verlag, 1995), 458–98.

108 The Constitutional Court affirmed the subordinate status of these preconstitutional laws in the Reich Tax Levy Case, 11 BVerfGe 126, 131–36 (1960).

109 Ipsen, supra note 106, at 119.

110 See, for example, Inge H. Case, 42 BVerfGE 64 (1976); and Unlawfulness of Arbitrary Rule Case, 70 BVerfGE 93 (1985).

111 This principle is illustrated in numerous cases reproduced in this book. The best example is the *Mephisto* case (no. 7.2.).

112 A study published in 1979 includes a list of all federal legal provisions invalidated by the Constitutional Court up to and including the year 1978. This ambitious project, undertaken by Professor Ernst Benda, a former president of the Constitutional Court, presents an interesting profile of the constitutional cases nullifying these provisions. Of the 112 cases listed, 51 were the direct result of constitutional complaints and 47 were referrals by lower courts under the procedure of concrete judicial review. Fifty-five cases implicated one or more of the equality clauses of Article 3, often in connection with the principle of the social welfare state (*Sozialstaat*) or one of the provisions of Article 6 on marriage and the family, and dealt mainly with tax and social welfare legislation. Twenty-three cases involved occupational rights under Article 12, and in 10 cases statutes were struck down because they violated the principle of *Rechtsstaatlichkeit*. See Ernst Benda, *Grundrechtswidrige Gesetze* (Baden-Baden: Nomos Verlagsgesellschaft, 1979), 64–75; see also Klaus von Beyme, *Das Politische System der Bundesrepublik Deutschland nach der Vereinigung* (Munich: R. Piper, 1991), 382.

113 See FCCA, sec. 31 (2).

114 Official statistics of the Federal Constitutional Court, 1993.

115 See Umbach and Clemens, supra note 102, sec. 78, 1008–9.

116 For good treatments in English of these admonitory decisions, see Rupp-von Brünneck, supra note 99; and Wolfgang Zeidler, "The Federal Constitutional Court of the Federal Republic of Germany: Decisions on the Constitutionality of Legal Norms," *Notre Dame Law Review* 62 (1987): 508–20.

117 An illustration is the Rendsburg Illegitimacy Case, 25 BVerfGE 167, 181–88 (1969). After an earlier decision (Marburg Illegitimacy Case, 8 BVerfGE 210 [1958]) in which the court admonished the legislature, unsuccessfully, to repeal all discriminatory statutes

against illegitimate children consistent with Article 6 (5) of the Basic Law, the court declared in the 1969 case that "at the end of the current legislative term (autumn 1969) — all discriminatory statutes would become automatically unconstitutional and void; and in case of further delay by the legislature, it would be up to the courts to implement the constitutional requirement: i.e., they would have to decide which of the old provisions were clearly in violation of the constitution and to close the gap with judge-made law" (Rupp-von Brünneck, supra note 99, at 388). The pending crisis was avoided, however, when the legislature proceeded forthwith to carry out the court's instructions. Recent examples of such cases are the Short Work Week Case, 52 BVerfGE 369, 379 (1979); Social Security Discrimination Case, 57 BVerfGE 335, 346 (1981); Severance Notice Case, 62 BVerfGE 256, 289 (1982); and Household Head Tax Case, 61 BVerfGE 319 (1982).

118   See, for example, Apportionment Case II, 16 BVerfGE 130, 141 (1963); Sales Tax Case, 21 BVerfGE 12, 39–42 (1966); Securities Tax Case, 23 BVerfGE 242 (1968); Civil Servant Pension Tax Case, 54 BVerfGE 11 (1980); and Widower's Pension Case, 39 BVerfGE 169 (1975).

119   Party Finance Case II, 24 BVerfGE 300 (1968).

120   This binding force has even been applied to state-owned enterprises such as radio and television; see Equal Time Case, 7 BVerfGE 99 (1957).

121   See Laufen District Court Case, 40 BVerfGE 88 (1975); and Strasskirchen Case, 69 BVerfGE 112 (1985).

122   FCCA, sec. 79 (1).

123   See Illegitimacy Discrimination Case, 37 BVerfGE 217, 261 (1974).

124   FCCA, sec. 79 (2).

125   See Alexander M. Bickel, *The Least Dangerous Branch* (Indianapolis: Bobbs-Merrill, 1962).

126   Rudolf Smend, "Festvortrag zur Feier des zehnjährigen Bestehens des Bundesverfassungsgerichts am 26. Januar 1962," in *Das Bundesverfassungsgericht* (Karlsruhe: Verlag C. F. Müller, 1963), 24.

127   Christian Starck, *Das Bundesverfassungsgericht im politischen Prozess, Recht und Staat in Geschichte und Gegenwart,* Hefts 466–67 (Tübingen: J. C. B. Mohr, 1976) 17. To say that the court is the capstone of the constitutional state is not to suggest that it is the *suprema potestas,* or even that it should have the last word on the meaning of the Constitution. On ceremonial occasions such as those just mentioned, high public officials customarily refer to the court's coordinate status alongside the Bundestag, Bundesrat, federal president, and federal government. Conventional wisdom holds that each of these constitutional organs is responsible for actualizing the Basic Law; each interprets the Basic Law with respect to its assigned functions and duties. Just as the Bundestag, for example, is the institutional manifestation of the principle of parliamentary democracy and the Bundesrat of federalism, the Constitutional Court represents the principle of the "state based on the rule of law" (*Rechtsstaat*). The court's job, then, is not to control these other constitutional organs as much as it is to safeguard and preserve their legitimate roles within the constitutionally prescribed structure of separate and divided powers. Federal president Walter Scheel uttered the conventional view in his address on the occasion of the Constitutional Court's twenty-fifth anniversary; see *25 Jahre Bundesver-*

fassungsgericht 1951–76 (Heidelberg: C. F. Müller Juristischer Verlag, 1976), 12. See Peter Häberle, *Die Verfassung des Pluralismus* (Königstein: Athenäum Verlag GmbH, 1980), for a lengthy treatment of this more restrictive view of the Constitutional Court's role.

128   Much of this literature is cited in Peter Häberle, "Verfassungsgerichtsbarkeit als politische Kraft," in *Verfassungsgerichtsbarkeit zwischen Politik und Rechtswissenschaft,* supra note 97, at 59–79. See also Richard Hässler, *Der Konflikt zwischen Bundesverfassungsgericht und politische Führung* (Berlin: Duncker and Humboldt, 1994).

129   See, especially, Lamprecht and Malanowski, *Richter machen Politik,* supra note 97, in which several of these decisions are treated and criticized. See also Christine Landfried, "The Impact of the German Federal Constitutional Court on Politics and Policy Output," *Government and Opposition* 20 (1985): 522–41; Friedhelm Hase and Matthias Ruete, "Constitutional Court and Constitutional Ideology in West Germany," *International Journal of the Sociology of Law* 10 (1982): 267–76; and Barend van Niekerk, "Social Engineering in the German Constitutional Court," *South African Law Journal* 92 (1975): 298–313.

130   See Landfried, *Bundesverfassungsgericht und Gesetzgeber,* supra note 97, at 47–146, for several case studies of this process at work. Justice Wiltraut Rupp–von Brünneck addressed the problem in "Verfassungsgerichtsbarkeit und gesetzgebende Gewalt," supra note 97, at 9.

131   See, for example, Uwe Wesel, "Nach Karlsruhe gehen," *Kursbuch* 77 (1984): 123–44; also Friedhelm Hase and Matthias Ruete, "Constitutional Court and Constitutional Ideology in West Germany," supra note 129; and Ulrich Preuss, "Political Concepts of Order for Mass Society," in *Observations on the "Spiritual Situation of the Age,"* ed. Jürgen Habermas (Cambridge: MIT Press, 1984), 89–121.

132   Landfried, *Bundesverfassungsgericht und Gesetzgeber,* supra note 97, at 152.

133   See, particularly, Rudolf Dolzer, *Die staatstheoretische und staatsrechtliche Stellung des Bundesverfassungsgerichts* (Berlin: Duncker and Humboldt, 1972), 114–18. Christine Landfried reported that in her recent interviews with all of the court's members, twelve of the justices favored retention of abstract judicial review; see *Bundesverfassungsgericht und Gesetzgeber,* supra note 97, at 177.

134   See Häberle, "Recht aus Rezensionen," in *Verfassungsgerichtsbarkeit,* supra note 97, at 1–53, in which the author classifies and assesses the importance of this literature. For an overview of current commentary on the U.S. Supreme Court, see Laurence E. Wiseman, "The New Supreme Court Commentators: The Principled, the Political, and the Philosophical," *Hastings Constitutional Law Quarterly* 10 (1983): 315–431.

135   See Häberle, "Recht aus Rezensionen," in *Verfassungsgerichtsbarkeit,* supra note 97, at 24–27.

136   See *25 Jahre Bundesverfassungsgericht,* supra note 127, at 39–40.

137   Ibid., 41.

3   FEDERALISM

1   For treatments of this movement toward unity, see Egmont Zechlin, *Die deutsche Einheitsbewegung* (Frankfurt am Main: Ullstein, 1967); Arnold Brecht, *Federalism and Regional-*

ism in Germany (New York: Oxford University Press, 1945); Peter Rassow, *Deutsche Geschichte* (Stuttgart: J. B. Metzlersche Verlagsbuchhandlung, 1987), 403–645; and H. W. Koch, *A Constitutional History of Germany* (London: Longman, 1984), 105–63.

2   For a succinct discussion of Germany's increasingly integrated economy, see Jochen Abr. Frowein, "Integration and the Federal Experience in Germany and Switzerland," in *Integration through Law. Vol. 1: Methods, Tools and Institutions,* ed. Mauro Cappelletti et al. (Berlin: Walter de Gruyter, 1986), 574–81.

3   The most important of these plans, submitted to the Brandt government in 1975, was considered by the Ernst Commission on the Reorganization of the Federal Territory (see infra note 12). The goal of the plan was to create five or six states of roughly equal size, population, and economic structure. See *Neugliederung des Bundesgebietes: Kurzfassung des Berichts der Sachverständigenkommission für die Neugliederung des Bundesgebietes* (Bonn: Carl Heymanns Verlag KG, n.d.); see also Rudolph Hebek, "Das Problem der Neugliederung des Bundesgebietes," *Aus Politik und Zeitgeschichte,* no. 46 (November 13, 1971).

4   Philip M. Blair, *Federalism and Judicial Review in West Germany* (Oxford: Clarendon Press, 1981), 4; see also Roger H. Wells, *The States in West Germany: A Study in Federal-State Relations, 1949–1960* (New York: Bookman, 1961).

5   Baden-Württemberg was formed out of the original states of Württemberg-Baden, Württemberg-Hohenzollern, and Baden. For an excellent discussion of the formation of the new southwestern state, see Theodor Eschenburg, "The Formation of the State of Baden-Württemberg," in *The German Southwest* (Berlin: Verlag W. Kohlhammer, 1990), 37–57.

6   For an excellent discussion of this dispute, see Arthur T. von Mehren, "Constitutionalism in Germany — The First Decision of the New Constitutional Court," *American Journal of Comparative Law* 1 (1952): 71–85.

7   1 Cranch 137 (1803). See von Mehren, supra note 6, at 70–94; Gerhard Leibholz, "The German Constitutional Federal Court and the *Southwest* Case," *American Political Science Review* 46 (1953): 723–31; and Franz W. Jerusalem, "Das Urteil des Bundesverfassungsgerichts über den Südweststaat-Streit," *Neue Juristische Wochenschrift* 5 (1952): 45–48. For an account of the proceedings and arguments before the court in the *Southwest State* case, see *Der Kampf um den Südweststaat* (Munich: Isar Verlag, 1952).

8   1 BVerfGE 14, 32 (1951).

9   See Charles Groves Haines, *The Role of the Supreme Court in American Government and Politics 1783–1835* (Berkeley: University of California Press, 1944), 256–65.

10 Leibholz, supra note 7.

11 13 BVerfGE 54 (1961).

12 The federal minister of the interior formed a state boundary study group in 1972 known as the Ernst Commission. Its recommendation that the eleven existing states be reduced to five or six in the interest of greater social and economic integration fell on deaf ears; see *Sachverständigenkommission für die Neugliederung des Bundesgebietes* (Bonn: Federal Interior Ministry, 1973); and supra note 3.

13 The entire procedure for reorganizing the federal territory was changed as a result of 1968 and 1976 amendments to Article 29. A principal change was the repeal of the original provision requiring a national referendum in the event that a proposed reorganization of the federal territory should be rejected by a majority of voters in one area of the state.

Measures for reorganizing the federal territory must still be introduced by federal law subject to confirmation by referendum in the state or area concerned. The current provisions of Article 29 specify the various conditions and percentages of the votes required in local referenda before territorial changes go into effect.

14   49 BVerfGE 10 (1978).

15   Konrad Hesse, *Der unitarische Bundesstaat* (Karlsruhe: C. F. Müller Verlag, 1962).

16   Ulrich Scheuner, "Struktur und Aufgabe des Bundesstaates in der Gegenwart," *Die Öffentliche Verwaltung* 15 (1962): 641–48.

17   Theodore Maunz, Günter Dürig, and Roman Herzog, *Grundgesetz: Kommentar* (Munich: C. H. Beck'sche Verlagsbuchhandlung, 1973), Art. 20, p. 6. For a discussion of these differing conceptions of the federal state, see Ekkehart Stein, *Staatsrecht,* 9th ed. (Tübingen: J. C. B. Mohr, 1984), 287–88.

18   13 BVerfGE 54, 77 (1961). For a general treatment of West German federalism, see Heinz Laufer, *Das Föderative System der Bundesrepublik Deutschland* (Munich: Bayerische Landeszentrale für politische Bildungsarbeit, 1981).

19   See Blair's discussion of the cases, supra note 4, at 157–62.

20   1 BVerfGE 299 (1952) (involving a federal law allocating funds to the various states for housing construction).

21   1 BVerfGE 117 (1952).

22   See Housing Funding Case, 1 BVerfGE 299 (1952); Christmas Bonus Case, 3 BVerfGE 52 (1953); and North Rhine–Westphalia Salaries Case, 4 BVerfGE 115 (1954).

23   6 BVerfGE 309 (1957); and 8 BVerfGE 105 (1958).

24   Blair, supra note 4, at 164.

25   For documentation of this development, see Waldemar Schreckenberger, "Intergovernmental Relations," in *Public Administration in the Federal Republic of Germany,* ed. Klaus König et al. (Netherlands: Kluwer-Venenter, 1983), 78–80.

26   81 BVerfGE 310, 337 (1990).

27   86 BVerfGE 148, 258–70 (1992).

28   Bavaria originally asked for a temporary injunction against the cabinet's decision. It was rejected for lack of urgency. Broadcast Injunction Case, 80 BVerfGE 74 (1989).

29   Television Programming Case, 92 BVerfGE 203 (1995).

30   Atomic Weapons Referenda Case II, 8 BVerfGE 122 (1958). See Frido Wagener, "The External Structure of Administration in the Federal Republic of Germany," in König et al., supra note 25, at 49–64.

31   One example of such a response is the 1969 amendment to the Basic Law conferring on the federal government the authority to enact "general principles governing higher education" (Article 75, [1a]). The *First Television* case (1961), which emphasized the primacy of the states in the field of cultural policy, prompted the introduction of this amendment.

32   Under the new Article 87e, ratified in 1993, "federal railways shall be operated as private enterprises," although the "construction, maintenance, and operation of tracks" shall remain under federal control and ownership. Under Article 87d as amended in 1992, parliament may authorize the privitization of the airlines.

33   Amnesty Legislation Case, 2 BVerfGE 213 (1953).

34   North Rhine–Westphalia Salaries Case, 4 BVerfGE 115 (1954).

35 Explosives Control Case, 13 BVerfGE 367, 371–72 (1962). Cf. Water Pollution Case, 15 BVerfGE 1 (1962); and Federal-State Salary Case, 34 BVerfGE 9 (1972).

36 8 BVerfGE 122 (1958).

37 See Hans-Justus Rinck, "Der verfassungsrechtliche Status der politischen Parteien in der Bundesrepublik," in *Die moderne Demokratie und ihr Recht,* ed. Karl Dietrich Braeher et al. 2 vols. (Tübingen: J. C. B. Mohr [Paul Siebeck], 1966), 2:305–30.

38 8 BVerfGE 122, 140 (1958).

39 This provision traces its origin to Articles 17 and 127 of the Weimar Constitution. See, generally, Ingo von Münch, *Grundgesetz-Kommentar,* 3 vols. (Munich: C. H. Beck'sche Verlagsbuchhandlung, 1983), 2:196–200.

40 60 BVerfGE 175.

41 Ibid., 207–8.

42 Ibid., 209.

43 For a discussion of this case, see Edward McWhinney, "Constitutional Law and Treaty-Making Power — German Vatican Concordat of 1933 — Decision of the West German Federal Constitutional Court," *Canadian Bar Review* 35 (1957): 842–48.

44 252 U.S. 416 (1920).

45 For an excellent description of these various levels of administration, see Arthur B. Gunlicks, *Local Government in the German Federal System* (Durham: Duke University Press, 1986), 84–118.

46 See Chimney Sweep Case, 63 BVerfGE 1 (1983).

47 See Klaus Stem, *Das Staatsrecht der Bundesrepublik Deutschland* (Munich: C. H. Beck'sche Verlagsbuchhandlung, 1980), 2:832–33.

48 Blair, supra note 4, at 246. Examples of such decisions are the Road Traffic Case, 27 BVerfGE 18 (1969) (upholding a federal law regulating road traffic); Casino Tax Case, 28 BVerfGE 119 (1970) (voiding a federal tax on casinos); Freight Traffic Case, 38 BVerfGE 61 (1974) (sustaining a federal tax on road freight traffic); and Wine Tax Case, 37 BVerfGE 1 (1974) (sustaining a federal tax on wine). The following cases upheld state taxes on various kinds of entertainment: Pleasure Tax Case, 14 BVerfGE 76 (1962); Music Box Tax Case, 31 BVerfGE 119 (1971).

49 61 BVerfGE 149 (1982).

50 See the discussion of local government finance in Gunlicks, *Local Government,* supra note 45, at 119–42; see also Manfred Timmerman, "Budgetary and Financial Planning," in König et al., supra note 25, at 189–203. For a general discussion of cooperative federalism, see Jost Pietzscher, "Landesbericht Bundesrepublik Deutschland," in *Zusammenarbeit der Gliedstaaten im Bundesstaat,* ed. Christian Starck (Baden-Baden: Nomos Verlagsgesellschaft, 1988), 17–76.

51 1 BVerfGE 117, 131 (1952).

52 72 BVerfGE 330 (1986).

53 86 BVerfGE 148 (1992).

54 55 BVerfGE 274 (1980).

55 These special levies have also raised constitutional issues under the tax provisions of the Basic Law. See Paul Kirchhof, "Budgeting Levies Earmarked for the Achievement of Social Policies," in *Reports on German Public Law and Public International Law,* ed. Rudolf

Bernhardt and Ulrich Beyerlin (Heidelberg: C. F. Müller Juristischer Verlag, 1986), 139–54.

56 Beamtenrechtsrahmengesetz, *BGBl* (January 6, 1977): 23ff.; and Hochschulrahmengesetz, *BGBl* 1 (1976): 85ff.

57 University Governance Case II, 66 BVerfGE 291 (1984). Cf. University Governance Case I, 66 BVerfGE 270 (1984). In the *Professorial Title* case, on the other hand, the court struck down a provision of the Higher Education Act that established pay scales for different instructional ranks in universities but labeled the instructors in each category "professors," thus interfering with the state's statutory authority to distinguish between professorial ranks in the tradition of the professional civil service (64 BVerfGE 323 [1983]).

58 Blair, commenting on the *North Rhine–Westphalia Salaries* case, supra note 4, at 82. In the *Salaries* case the federal government had established a fixed salary schedule for its own civil servants. Shortly thereafter, North Rhine–Westphalia passed a law providing its own employees with higher salaries. The federal government contested the validity of the state law. In applying the balancing test mentioned in the text, the Second Senate sustained the validity of the state's salary schedule. The court upheld similar statutes enacted by two other states even though the push of federal policy here was toward greater overall uniformity. See Schleswig-Holstein Salaries Case, 18 BVerfGE 159 (1964); and Hamburg Salaries Case, 30 BVerfGE 90 (1970); cf. Judicial Title Case, 38 BVerfGE 1 (1974).

59 Widow's Pension Case, 25 BVerfGE 142, 152 (1969) and North Rhine–Westphalia Salaries Case, 4 BVerfGE 115 (1954).

60 For a detailed discussion of this crisis, see Peter J. Katzenstein, *Policy and Politics in West Germany* (Philadelphia: Temple University Press, 1987), 296–324.

61 See Blair, supra note 4, at 207–45.

62 39 BVerfGE 1 (1975); and 48 BVerfGE 127 (1978).

63 Article 87b (2) declares: "Federal laws concerning defense, including recruitment for military service and protection of the civilian population, may, with the consent of the Bundesrat, provide for their implementation by the federation itself . . . or by the states on behalf of the federation."

64 48 BVerfGE 127, 129 (1978).

65 Price Law Case, 8 BVerfGE 274 (1958); see also Income and Corporation Tax Administration Case, 1 BVerfGE 76 (1951) (requiring the Bundesrat's consent when federal law lays down procedures to be used by a state in collecting federal revenue).

66 Conscientious Objector Case, 12 BVerfGE 45 (1960).

67 David P. Conradt, *The German Polity,* 3d ed. (New York: Longman, 1986), 154, see also Uwe Thaysen, *The Bundesrat, the Länder and the German Federation* (Washington, D.C.: American Institute for Contemporary German Studies, 1994), 37.

68 See Konrad Reuter, *Föderalismus: Grundlagen und Wirkungen in der Bundesrepublik Deutschland,* 4th ed. (Heidelberg: Decker and Müller, 1991).

69 Gunlicks, *Local Government,* supra note 45, at xi.

70 The development of local government in German history is treated in Gunlicks, *Local Government,* supra note 45, at 5–31.

71 Municipal Financial Autonomy Case, 71 BVerfGE 25 (1985).

72 Laatzen Case, 50 BVerfGE 50 (1978). Recently, however, the court held hearings in a case involving municipal boundary changes in Thuringia. Thuringia enacted a redistricting

law designed to incorporate certain municipalities into larger units of government. The court rejected a request by the affected municipalities to suspend the law, but nevertheless reinstated some of their local prerogatives pending a full hearing on whether the reorganization measure violated the rights of municipalities under Article 28 of the Basic Law. See Isserstedt Case, 91 BVerfGE 70 (1994). See also Papenburg Case, 82 BVerfGE 310 (1990).

73 Arthur B. Gunlicks, "Constitutional Law and the Protection of Subnational Governments in the United States and West Germany," *Publius* 18 (1988): 151.

74 Ibid.

75 426 U.S. 833 (1976).

76 Garcia v. San Antonio Metropolitan Transit Authority, 469 U.S. 528 (1985).

77 Gunlicks, "Constitutional Law," supra note 73, at 22.

78 79 BVerfGE 127, 143 (1988).

79 Ibid., 145.

80 The Bundestag passed the Act of Succession to the Union Treaty on December 2, 1992, by 543 of 568 votes cast (Sten. Bericht 12/126, p. 10879). The Bundesrat assented unanimously to the act on December 18, 1992. See BR Drucks. 810/92, Sten. Ber. der 650. Sitzung, December 18, 1992. The act was published in the *Bundesgesetzblatt* on December 30, 1992. *BGBl* 2:1251.

81 The new Article 23 replaced the old "accession" article repealed by the Unification Treaty. See discussion below in the section of German federalism and the European Union.

82 The guaranteed personal rights allegedly under attack were human dignity (Article 1 [1]), freedom of action (Article 2 [1]), freedom of speech (Article 5 [1]), freedom of association (Article 9 [1]), the right to choose one's occupation or trade (Article 12 [1]), and the right to property (Article 14 [1]). All of these claims were ruled inadmissible.

83 See Helmut Lecheler, *Das Subsidiaritätsprinzip* (Berlin: Duncker and Humboldt, 1993), 46–55.

84 10 BVerfGE 59, 83 (1959).

85 Judith A. Dwyer, *The New Dictionary of Catholic Social Thought* (Collegeville, Minn.: Liturgical Press, 1994), 927. In his 1931 encyclical, *Quadragesimo Anno,* Pius XI wrote: "Just as it is gravely wrong to take from individuals what they can accomplish by their own initiative and industry and give it to the community, so also it is an injustice and at the same time a grave evil and disturbance of right order to assign to a greater or higher association what lesser and subordinate organizations can do" (paragraph 79).

86 Lecheler, supra note 83, at 50–51.

87 Ibid., 19.

88 See Helmut Steinberger, "Anmerkungen zum Maastricht-Urteil des Bundesverfassungsgerichts" in *Der Staatenverbund der Europäischen Union,* ed. Peter Hommelhof and Paul Kirchhof (Heidelberg: C. F. Müller Juristischer Verlag, 1994), 25–33.

4 SEPARATION OF POWERS

1 References to the tripartite structure of government appear in two other constitutional provisions: Article 20 (3) binds the executive and the judiciary to "law and justice" while

subjecting legislation "to the constitutional order"; and Article 1 (3) commands that constitutionally guaranteed fundamental rights of persons "shall bind the legislature, the executive, and the judiciary as directly enforceable law." Provisions subjecting the powers of government to principles of liberty and justice reflect the Basic Law's premise that separation of powers is not alone sufficient to ensure limited government.

2   See Veterans Assistance Case, 7 BVerfGE 183, 188 (1957); Bremen Civil Servant Case, 9 BVerfGE 268, 280 (1959); and Fiscal Administration Case, 22 BVerfGE 106, 111 (1967).

3   The Federal Constitutional Court has ruled that the Basic Law's scheme of separated powers is a "fundamental principle of the liberal democratic basic order." See Graf Compensation Case, 3 BVerfGE 4, 13 (1953); Equality of Rights Case, 3 BVerfGE 225, 239 (1953); and Hessian Judges Act Case, 34 BVerfGE 52, 59 (1972). For a general discussion of separation of powers, see H. J. Hahn, "Über die Gewaltenteilung in der Wertwelt des Grundgesetzes," *Jahrbuch des Öffentlichen Rechts* 14 (1965): 15–44; and Klaus Stern, *Staatsrecht der Bundesrepublik Deutschland* 2 vols. (Munich: C. K. Beck'sche Verlagsbuchhandlung, 1980), 2:513–46.

4   These special units would include constitutionally created committees such as the Committee on Foreign Affairs and Defense (Article 45a), the Petitions Committee (Article 45c), and the Bundestag's Defense Commissioner (Article 45b). In addition, the Federal Constitutional Court has conferred independent constitutional status on political party groups within the Bundestag. A minority party, for example, may vindicate its rights as a parliamentary party in a proper proceeding before the Federal Constitutional Court; see Party Finance Case II, 24 BVerfGE 300 (1968).

5   As suggested in note 4, intrabranch disputes may also be the subject of an *Organstreit* proceeding. For example, a political party represented in parliament would be permitted to initiate an *Organstreit* proceeding against the Bundestag if the latter denied it a right to which it is entitled as a constituent unit of the parent body; see the Green Party Exclusion Case, 70 BVerfGE 324 (1986). Even an individual legislator would be able to bring such an action if the Bundestag were to deprive him of certain entitlements guaranteed under Articles 46, 47, and 48.

6   See Peter Haungs, "Kanzlerdemokratie in der Bundesrepublik Deutschland: Von Adenauer bis Kohl," *Zeitschrift für Politik* 33 (1986): 44–66.

7   Werner Maihofer, "Abschliessende Äusserungen," in *Handbuch der Verfassungsrechts*, 2 vols., ed. Ernst Benda et al. (Berlin: Walter de Gruyter, 1984), 2:1412.

8   See Dieter Grimm, *Einführung in das öffentliche Recht* (Heidelberg: C. F. Müller Juristischer Verlag, 1985), 15.

9   For studies of the Bundestag, see Gerard Braunthal, *The West German Legislative Process* (Ithaca: Cornell University Press, 1972); Gerhard Loewenberg, *Parliament in the West German Political System* (Ithaca: Cornell University Press, 1966); and Friedrich Schaefer, *Der Bundestag* (Opladen: Westdeutscher Verlag, 1982). For studies heavily touching on the relationship between the chancellor and the federal parliament, see R. Rausch, *Bundestag und Bundesregierung* (Munich: C. H. Beck, 1976); E. U. Junker, *Die Richtlinienkompetenz des Bundeskanzlers* (Tübingen: J. C. B. Mohr, 1965); and Nevil Johnson, *Government in the Federal Republic of Germany* (Oxford: Pergamon Press, 1973). For studies of parliamentary state secretaries and the presidency, see Heinz Laufer, *Der Parlamen-*

tarische Staatssekretär (Munich: C. H. Beck, 1969); and H. Rausch, *Der Bundespräsident* (Munich: Bayerische Landeszentrale für Politische Bildungsarbeit, 1979).

10 For detailed discussions of this process, see Klaus von Beyme and Manfred G. Schmidt, *Policy and Politics in the Federal Republic of Germany* (New York: St. Martin's Press, 1985).

11 Gustav Heinemann, federal president from 1969 to 1974, once threatened not to sign any measure seeking to restore capital punishment in Germany. In 1970 he actually did refuse to sign a law regulating architects, and thus prevented it from coming into force. In this instance he based his refusal on the Federal Constitutional Court's judgment in the Engineer's Case, 26 BVerfGE 246 (1969), which invalidated a similar statute on the ground that the federation is not empowered under the Basic Law to legislate for the protection of the professions.

12 Karl Carstens, interview with the author, October 19, 1986, Washington, D.C.

13 Mary Lovik, "The Constitutional Court Reviews the Early Dissolution of the West German Parliament," *Hastings International and Comparative Law Review* 7 (1983): 116.

14 In spite of the favorable way things worked out, the dissolution order has been the topic of continuing controversy among constitutional scholars. For a critical view of the case by a former justice of the Federal Constitutional Court, see Willi Geiger, "Die Auflösung des Bundestages," *Jahrbuch des Öffentlichen Rechts* 33 (1984): 41–61. For a complete record of the case, see Wolfgang Hyde and Gotthard Wöhrmann, *Auflösung und Neuwahl des Bundestages 1983 vor dem Bundesverfassungsgericht* (Heidelberg: C. F. Müller Juristischer Verlag, 1984).

15 See, for example, Klaus von Beyme, *The Political System of the Federal Republic of Germany* (New York: St. Martin's Press, 1983), 186. The author cited, in particular, the Group University Case, 35 BVerfGE 79 (1973) (invalidating a measure requiring the participation of several groups in university governance); the East-West Basic Treaty Case, 36 BVerfGE 1 (1973) (requiring foreign policymakers to adhere to the goal of German reunification); the Abortion Case, 39 BVerfGE 1 (1975) (invalidating a liberal abortion law); the Widower's Pension Case, 39 BVerfGE 169 (1975) (instructing parliament to find a fairer method of transferring a wife's pension entitlement to her surviving husband by the end of 1984); and the Legislative Pay Case, 40 BVerfGE 296 (1975) (effectively ordering parliament to increase the salaries of legislative representatives). These cases, remarked the author, "have deeply interfered with the prerogatives of the other constitutional powers." For a critical discussion of these and other cases, see Christine Landfried, *Bundesverfassungsgericht und Gesetzgeber* (Baden-Baden: Nomos Verlagsgesellschaft, 1984), 51–123; and idem., "The Impact of the German Constitutional Court," *Government and Opposition* 20 (1985): 522–41.

16 See, respectively, Youngstown Sheet & Tube Co. v. Sawyer, 343 U.S. 579 (1952); and Immigration and Naturalization Service v. Chadha, 462 U.S. 919 (1983).

17 418 U.S. 683 (1974).

18 67 BVerfGE 100, 129 (1984).

19 45 BVerfGE 1 (1977).

20 Ibid., 35.

21 30 BVerfGE 1 (1970), at 27–28. This translation is from Walter F. Murphy and Joseph Tanenhaus, *Comparative Constitutional Law* (New York: St. Martin's Press, 1977), 662.

22 For a general discussion of judicial independence in Germany, see Peter Gilles, "Germany: Judicial Independence and the Involvement of Judges in Party Politics and Trade Union Activities," in *Judicial Independence: The Contemporary Debate,* ed. Shimon Shetreet and Jules Deschenes (Dordrecht: Martinus Nijhoff, 1985), 96–116.

23 See Ernst K. Pakuscher, "Administrative Law in Germany — Citizen and State," *American Journal of Comparative Law* 16 (1968): 312–14.

24 57 BVerfGE 250 (1981).

25 10 BVerfGE 200 (1959).

26 Disciplinary Court Case, 18 BVerfGE 241 (1964); see also Lawyer's Disciplinary Case, 26 BVerfGE 186 (1969); and Social Court Case, 27 BVerfGE 312 (1969).

27 38 BVerfGE 326 (1975).

28 See Gerhard Loewenberg, *Parliament in the German Political System* (Ithaca: Cornell University Press, 1966), 48–53.

29 32 BVerfGE 157, 163–69 (1971).

30 See, for example, Armin Dittmann, "Unvereinbarkeit von Regierungsamt und Abgeordnetenmandat — eine unliebsame Konsequencz des Diatenurteils?" *Zeitschrift für Rechtspolitik* 11 (1978): 52–55; Willi Geiger, "Der Abgeordnete und sein Beruf: Eine kritische Auseinandersetzung mit folgenreichen Missdeutungen eines Urteils," *Zeitschrift für Parlamentsfragen* 9 (1978): 32–56; and Rupert Hoffmann, "Abgeordnetenfreiheit und parlamentarischer Abstimmungsmodus," *Zeitschrift für Politik* (1978): 32–56. For a list of scholarly articles as well as newspaper and magazine commentary on this case, see Josef Mackert and Franz Schneider, *Bibliographie zur Verfassungsgerichtsbarkeit des Bundes und der Länder* (Tübingen: J. C. B. Mohr, 1982), 3:374–80.

31 Gerhard Loewenberg and Samuel C. Patterson, *Comparing Legislatures* (Boston: Little, Brown, 1979), 107.

32 The Weimar Constitution contained no provision expressly regulating the delegation of legal authority to the executive. This lack of a check on the executive is what allowed Hitler to legally dissolve the Reichstag. Article 80 was the framers' reaction to this experience. See Ingo von Münch, *Grundgesetz Kommentar,* 3 vols. (Munich: C. H. Beck'sche Verlagsbuchhandlung, 1983), 3:246. For a general discussion of this, see Dieter Wilke, "Bundesverfassungsgericht und Rechtsveränderung," *Archiv des Öffentlichen Rechts* 98 (1973): 196–247.

33 For a discussion of the ordinance power of the national government under the Weimar Republic and the various kinds of ordinances issued by executive officials, see Johannes Mattern, *The Constitutional Law of the German National Republic* (Baltimore: Johns Hopkins University Press, 1928), 453–507.

34 Pakuscher, supra note 23, at 321–24.

35 Klaus Bosselmann, "Protection of Constitutional Rights and Reform of Nuclear Power Plant Licensing Procedures in West Germany: An Interim Assessment," *Hastings International and Comparative Law Review* 6 (1983): 555.

36 53 BVerfGE 30 (1979).

37 For an American view almost identical with this German perspective, see Kenneth L. Karst, "Legislative Facts in Constitutional Litigation," *The Supreme Court Review* (1960): 75–112.

38   17 BVerfGE 1 (1963).

39   Widower's Pension Case, 39 BVerfGE 169 (1975).

40   53 BVerfGE 30 (1979).

41   See Thomas Giller, "Decommissioning Nuclear Power Plants: The United States, West Germany, and Canada," *Hastings International and Comparative Law Review* 6 (1983): 490–98.

42   Bosselmann, supra note 35, at 559–64.

43   20 BVerfGE 257, 269 (1966).

44   Under Article 67, in a procedure known as a constructive vote of no-confidence, parliament can dismiss the chancellor provided it simultaneously elects his successor.

45   1 BVerfGE 351 (1952).

46   See Thomas M. Franck, *Political Questions/Judicial Answers* (Princeton: Princeton University Press, 1992), especially chap. 7, pp. 107–25.

47   55 BVerfGE 349 (1980).

48   See Rudolf Dolzer, *Verfassungskonkretisierung durch das Bundesverfassungsgericht und durch politische Verfassungsorgane* (Heidelberg: Decker and Müller, 1982).

49   Ibid., 365.

50   46 BVerfGE 160 (1977).

51   An example of such a proceeding is the often-cited Iranian Embassy Case, 16 BVerfGE 27 (1963). A company in Cologne filed suit with the Cologne District Court against Iran to compel payment for the repair of a heating installation in the Iranian embassy. The local court declined to serve the bill of complaint because the Iranian Empire as a sovereign state was exempt from German jurisdiction in accordance with a general rule of public international law. The firm appealed, and the Cologne Superior Court certified the question to the Constitutional Court. After examining in detail the practice of other national courts, the Constitutional Court concluded that general international law does not grant a foreign state immunity from domestic jurisdiction for nonsovereign acts of a private-law character.

52   Two Plus Four Settlement of September 12, 1990, Article 2. See *The Unification of Germany in 1990: A Documentation* (Bonn: Press and Information Office, 1991), 100.

53   66 BVerfGE 39, at 65.

54   68 BVerfGE 1 (1984).

55   Ibid., 85–87, an edited version of the English translation in *Decisions of the Bundesverfassungsgericht,* vol. 1, pt. 2 (Baden-Baden: Nomos Verlagsgesellschaft, 1992), 518–19.

56   Ibid., 90.

57   Ibid., 99.

58   Ibid., 100.

59   Ibid., 100–108.

60   The SPD's petition would plunge the Constitutional Court into the middle of a two-year constitutional struggle over German rearmament. On May 15, 1952, the First Senate rejected the SPD's application for a preventive injunction against further German negotiations over the EDC; see European Defense Community Case, 1 BVerfGE 281 (1952). This case was the first of several attempts on the part of both government and opposition to pressure the court into accepting their respective positions. See Karl Loewenstein, "The

Bonn Constitution and the European Defense Community Treaties: A Study in Judicial Frustration," *Yale Law Journal* 64 (1955): 805–839, and Donald P. Kommers, *Judicial Politics in Germany* (Beverly Hills, Calif.: Sage Publications, 1976), pp. 282–86.

61 See, for example, Louis Henkin, *Constitutionalism, Democracy, and Foreign Affairs* (New York: Columbia University Press, 1990); John Hart Ely, *War and Responsibility* (Princeton: Princeton University Press, 1993); and Miroslav Nincic, *Democracy and Foreign Policy* (New York: Columbia University Press, 1992).

62 See Franck, supra note 46.

63 90 BVerfGE 286 (1994).

64 For an excellent discussion of the debate over the meaning of Article 87a (2), see Daniel-Erasmus Kahn and Markus Zöckler, "Germans to the Front, or Le malade imaginaire," *European Journal of International Law* 3 (1992):163–77.

65 NATO-AWACS Case, 88 BVerfGE 173 (1993).

66 Somalia Military Mission Case, 89 BVerfGE 38 (1993).

67 90 BVerfGE 286 (1994).

68 Critics would point out that the court took a very different approach to its interpretation of the Maastricht Treaty. As the *Maastricht* case (no. 3.10) shows, the court had few qualms about finding serious deficiencies in the treaty, flaws that would have to be corrected by the European Union over the course of time if parliament's rightful powers were to be protected.

69 For excellent discussions of the *Military Deployment* case, see W. Heintschel von Heinegg and U. R. Haltern, "The Decision of the German Federal Constitutional Court of 12 July 1994 in Re Deployment of the German Armed Forces 'Out of Area,'" *Netherlands International Law Review* 41 (1994):285–311; and Manfred H. Wiegandt, "Germany's International Integration: The Rulings of the German Federal Constitutional Court on the Maastricht Treaty and the Out-of-Area Deployment of German Troops," *American University Journal of International Law and Policy* 10 (1995): 889–916.

70 See Konrad Hesse, *Grundzüge des Verfassungsrechts der Bundesrepublik Deutschland,* 16th ed. (Heidelberg: C. F. Müller Juristischer Verlag, 1987), 184–86.

71 *Federalist,* ed. E. Mead Earle (New York: Modern Library, 1941), no. 51, at 336 (J. Madison).

72 Ibid., no. 71, at 465 (A. Hamilton).

5 POLITICAL REPRESENTATION AND DEMOCRACY

1 Southwest State Case, 1 BVerfGE 14, 41 (1951); see also Baden Home Association Case, 5 BVerfGE 34, 42 (1956).

2 Article 28 (1) also requires the states to embrace "the principles of republican, democratic, and social government based on the rule of law." These provisions set forth the fundamental structural principles of the German state, principles which under the terms of Article 79 (3) may not be amended out of the Constitution. For a discussion of these structural principles, see Ingo von Münch, *Grundgesetz-Kommentar,* 3d ed., 3 vols. (Munich: Verlag C. H. Beck, 1985), 1:814–27.

3   See, especially, Klaus Stern, *Das Staatsrecht der Bundesrepublik Deutschland,* 2d ed., 2 vols. (Munich: Verlag C. H. Beck, 1983), 1:587–635. See pp. 583–87 for an extensive bibliography on the democratic principle underlying the Basic Law.

4   For a detailed discussion in English of each of these aspects of Germany's system of political representation, see Helmut Steinberger, "Political Representation in Germany" in *Germany and Its Basic Law,* ed. Paul Kirchhof and Donald P. Kommers (Baden-Baden: Nomos Verlagsgesellschaft, 1993), 121–72.

5   See Martin Kriele, "Das demokratische Prinzip im Grundgesetz," *Veröffentlichungen der Vereinigung der deutschen Staatsrechtslehrer* 29 (1971): 48.

6   For a list and discussion of some thirty constitutional cases dealing with the rights of parliamentary parties (*Fraktionen*), see Gerald Kretschmer, "Selbständige Rechtspersonen der Parlamentsrechts," *Das Parlament,* May 22–29, 1992, 12–14.

7   See James M. Markham, "Germany's Volatile Greens," *New York Times Magazine,* February 13, 1983, 37ff; Wilhelm Bürklin, "The German Greens: The Post-Industrial Non-Establishment and the Party System," *International Political Science Review* 6 (1985): 463–81; E. Gene Frankland, "The Role of the Greens in West German Parliamentary Politics, 1980–1987," *Review of Politics* 50 (1988): 99–122; and Gerd Langguth, *The Green Factor in German Politics* (Boulder: Westview Press, 1986).

8   See Reinhard Brückner Case, 65 BVerfGE 101 (1983); Political Foundations Case, 73 BVerfGE 1 (1986); and Party Finance I Case, 73 BVerfGE 40 (1986). On December 15, 1983, the court rejected the Green party's application for a temporary injunction against the Bundestag's exclusion decision. See Hubert Kleinert Case, 66 BVerfGE 26 (1983).

9   See Party Finance I Case, 73 BVerfGE 40 (1986).

10   Ibid., 117. See the section below on political parties and the party state for a discussion of this and related cases dealing with the financing of political parties.

11   See Hans-Georg Betz, "Alliance 90/Greens: From Fundamental Opposition to Black-Green," in *Germany's New Politics,* ed. David Conradt et al. (Tempe, Ariz.: German Studies Review, 1995), 177–92.

12   Geschäftsordnung des Bundestages, as amended November 12, 1990, *BGBl* 1:2555.

13   73 BVerfGE 40, 117 (1986).

14   See remarks of Ernst Benda in "Herausforderungen an die parlamentarische Demokratie," *Verhandlungen des fünfundfünfzigsten Deutschen Juristentages,* pt. P (Munich: C. H. Beck'sche Verlagsbuchhandlung, 1984), 2:9.

15   See *Frankfurter Allgemeine Zeitung,* June 6, 1992, 1.

16   See remarks of former federal minister of interior Werner Maihofer, in ibid., 10.

17   Recall the *Atomic Weapons Referenda I* case (no. 3.3), in which the court nullified state legislation providing for advisory referenda on arming the Bundeswehr with atomic weapons. For a general discussion of the constitutional implications of the various forms of direct democracy, see Peter Krause, "Verfassungsrechtliche Möglichkeiten unmittelbarer Demokratie," in *Handbuch des Staatsrechts,* 8 vols., ed. Josef Isensee and Paul Kirchhof (Heidelberg: C. F. Müller Juristischer Verlag, 1987), 2:313–37.

18   See Albert Bleckmann, "Die Zulässigkeit des Volksentscheides nach dem Grundgesetz," *Juristenzeitung* 33 (1978): 217–23; and Christian Graf von Pestalozza, *Der Popularvor-*

behalt (Berlin: Walter de Gruyter, 1981). For a vigorous discussion of this problem, see the record of the panel discussion at the Fifty-fifth Annual Meeting of the German Lawyers Association. The participants were Professors Klaus Stern (University of Cologne), Ernst Benda (Freiburg University), Christian Graf von Krockow (Göttingen University), Werner Maihofer (European University Institute [Florence]), and Christian Graf von Pestalozza (Free University Berlin). In *Verhandlungen,* supra note 14, at 5–48. Another spirited discussion took place in the panel discussion at the meeting of the German Association of Municipal and Local Government, in *Bürgerinitiativen — Wege oder Irrwege der Parlamentarischen Demokratie* (Göttingen: Verlag Otto Schwartz, 1977). See also Klaus G. Troitzsch, *Volksbegehren und Volksentschied* (Meisenheim am Glan: Verlag Anton Hain, 1979).

19 See also Peoples Ballot Case, 74 BVerfGE 96–101 (1986). An organization known as Abstimmungsinitiative für Volksentscheid (AIV) tried to qualify for a position on the ballot in the federal elections of January 25, 1987. The group's main objective was to secure a referendum that would allow citizens to vote on particular measures without regard to party identification. The effort was unsuccessful because the group failed to qualify as a party under section 2 of the Federal Parties Act. It was not, therefore, an "eligible electoral organization" within the meaning of section 18 of the Federal Electoral Act. Instead of running candidates for office, the AIV would have placed certain issues on the ballot. The AIV was particularly interested in securing votes on nuclear plant closings, the stationing of nuclear missiles in Germany, and a peace treaty between East and West.

20 See Non-Party List Case, 5 BVerfGE 77 (1956); and Ballot Admission Case, 3 BVerfGE 19 (1953). *Ballot Admission* nullified a provision of federal law requiring new parties to produce the signatures of five hundred voters in each electoral district prior to securing a position on the ballot, whereas parties already seated in the Bundestag or a *Land* parliament needed only the signatures of the members of the state party executive committee. "Even though treatment differentiating between new parties and those represented in parliament for the purpose of their admissibility to elections is basically compatible with the principle of equality," said the court, "the particular provision is so onerous on new parties aspiring to parliamentary representation that the legislature must be held to have acted unreasonably and in excess of its discretionary latitude" (3 BVerfGE 19, 29 [1953]).

The court has been particularly vigilant when new political groups challenge local restrictions on access to the ballot. In the *Stoevesandt* case (1960), for example, the court nullified a Lower Saxony statute requiring a minimum number of signatures to secure a ballot position for a candidate nominated by local voters' groups (in this case the Independent Voters Association) while exempting political parties from this requirement. The court recognized that such regulations served the legitimate purpose of admitting only nominations supported by a politically significant group, but in this case the equality clause of Article 3 (1) combined with the principle of municipal autonomy under Article 28 to invalidate the measure. Declared the court: "The principle of equality means equal voting rights for all citizens. In the field of election law the legislature enjoys only a narrow range of options. Differentiations in the field always require a *particularly compelling* justification. The guarantee of communal autonomy secured by Article 28 (2) makes it even plainer that in communities and [election] districts, locally oriented city council groups and voters' associations are to be accorded essentially the same legal [rights] as political parties. Citizens are therefore entitled to submit candidacies on behalf of voters' associations under essentially the same conditions and in the same manner as political parties" (12 BVerfGE 10, 25 [1960]).

21 See Federal Election Act (Bundeswahlgesetz) in the version of July 21, 1993, *BGBl* 1:1217.

22 For a detailed description of developments in German electoral law from 1949 to 1983, see Eckhard Jesse, *Wahlrecht zwischen Kontinuität und Reform* (Düsseldorf: Droste Verlag, 1985). A massive bibliography on German election law and electoral politics appears at pp. 383–432. See also Heino Kaack, *Zwischen Verhältniswahl und Mehrheitswahl* (Opladen: C. W. Leske, 1967). For a good description in English of the German election system, see U. W. Kitzinger, *German Electoral Politics* (Oxford: Clarendon Press, 1960), 17–37. See also Wolfgang Schreiber, *Handbuch des Wahlrechts zum Deutschen Bundestag,* 3d ed. (Cologne: Carl Heymann Verlag, 1986), 50–53.

23 Gebhart Müller, minister-president of Württemberg-Hohenzollern, was one of those who urged his fellow delegates in the Parliamentary Council to anchor the 5 percent rule in the Basic Law; see Jesse, supra note 22, at 222. (Gebhart Müller became the president of the Federal Constitutional Court in 1959 and served in that capacity until his retirement in 1971.) For another discussion of the 5 percent clause, see Hans Meyer, *Wahlsystem und Verfassungsordnung* (Frankfurt am Main: Alfred Metzner Verlag, 1973), 225–54; Gerhard Leibholz, *Strukturprobleme der modernen Demokratie,* 3d ed. (Karlsruhe: Verlag C. F. Müller, 1967), 41–54.

24 1 BVerfGE 208, 247–61 (1952).

25 6 BVerfGE 84 (1957).

26 Ibid., 92.

27 Ibid., 92–93.

28 See All-German Party Case, 6 BVerfGE 99 (1957); and European Parliament Case, 51 BVerfGE 222, 237 (1979). For a detailed study of the legality and effects of the 5 percent clause at all levels of government, see Ulrich Werner, *Sperrklauseln im Wahlrecht der Bundesrepublik Deutschland* (Frankfurt am Main: Peter Lang, 1986).

29 4 BVerfGE 31 (1954).

30 3 BVerfGE 45 (1953).

31 Ibid., 50. See also Territorial Reorganization Case, 13 BVerfGE 54, 82 (1961).

32 Fritz M. Case, 7 BVerfGE 63 (1957).

33 Bundestag Election Case, 21 BVerfGE 355 (1967).

34 For a comprehensive discussion of these rulings, see Hans Meyer, "Wahlgrundsätze und Wahlverfahren" in Isensee and Kirchhof, supra note 17, at 269–311.

35 See, for example, Hans Rass, "Die Mehrheitswahl—und was dann?" *Der Monat* (September 1965): 204; and Ferdinand A. Hermens, "Das Wahlrecht und die politische Stabilität," *Die Politische Meinung* 4 (1959): 33–43; also Kaack, supra note 22.

36 See Jesse, supra note 22, at 164–71.

37 The Constitutional Court has always maintained that *effective* political representation depends to some extent on the proportional system of counting votes. See, for example, European Parliament Case, 51 BVerfGE 222, 253 (1978).

38 This is the so-called Hare-Niemeyer system of calculating votes. The mathematics of the process are described in Schreiber, supra note 22, at 141–43.

39   See Meyer, supra note 23, at 244–45.

40   See 13 BVerfGE 127 (1961).

41   See Rhineland-Palatinate Apportionment Case, 34 BVerfGE 81, 98 (1972); Daniels Case, 41 BVerfGE 399, 413 (1976); District Representation Case, 47 BVerfGE 253, 269 (1978); European Parliament Case, 51 BVerfGE 222, 232 (1979); and Sehnde Communal Election Case, 57 BVerfGE 43, 58 (1981). A leading commentator is critical of these cases because they were decided under the general equality clause of Article 3. In his view the standards of the general equality clause do not control the principle of equal elections within the meaning of Article 3 (1); see von Münch, supra note 2, at 2:477.

42   The Bundestag has enacted, pursuant to Article 41, the Election Review Act (Wahlprüfungsgesetz). See amended version of June 24, 1975, *BGBl* 1:166. The text is included in Schreiber, supra note 22, at 654–58. Schreiber discusses the competence of the Bundestag to review election disputes at pp. 561–62.

43   For an overview of the court's jurisprudence under Article 41, see von Münch, supra note 2, at 2:553–69.

44   Schleswig-Holstein Voters' Association Case, 1 BVerfGE 208, 238 (1952). For other limits the court has imposed on its power of review, see Joseph C. Case, 1 BVerfGE 430 (1952); Democratic Economic Community Case, 2 BVerfGE 300 (1953); and Mail Ballot Case, 59 BVerfGE 111 (1981).

45   59 BVerfGE 119 (1981).

46   Ibid., 127.

47   36 BVerfGE 139 (1973).

48   58 BVerfGE 202 (1981). For a discussion of this case, see Robert Hilworth and Frank Montag, "The Right to Vote of Non-Resident Citizens: A Comparative Study of the Federal Republic of Germany and the United States of America," *Georgia Journal of International and Comparative Law* 12 (1982): 269–79. The change in the Electoral Act also extended the franchise to German nationals resident in countries outside the European Community provided they have maintained a residence in Germany within ten years of casting their ballots.

49   Foreign Voters Case II, 83 BVerfGE 60 (1990).

50   Treaty on European Union, Article 8b (1) (February 7, 1992). See also 31 *International Legal Materials* 259 (1992).

51   Michaela Richter, "The Basic Law and the Democratic Party State: Constitutional Theory and Political Practice," in *Cornerstone of Democracy: The West German Grundgesetz, 1949–89*. Occasional Paper No. 13 (Washington D.C.: German Historical Institute, 1995), 37. The theory of the *Parteienstaat* traces its origin to the work and advocacy of Gerhard Leibholz, a justice of the Constitutional Court from 1951 to 1971. See Gerhard Leibholz, "Der moderne Parteienstaat," in Leibholz, *Verfassungsstaat — Verfassungsrecht* (Stuttgart: Verlag W. Kohlhammer, 1973), 68–94.

52   Schleswig-Holstein Voters' Association Case, 1 BVerfGE 208, 225 (1952).

53   Weimar Constitution, Article 130.

54   See John F. Golay, *The Founding of the Federal Republic of Germany* (Chicago: University of Chicago Press, 1958), 138–58.

55   1 BVerfGE 208, 240–241 (1952)

56   Plenum Party Case, 4 BVerfGE 27 (1954).

57   6 BVerfGE 273 (1957).

58   See Party Finance Case III, 20 BVerfGE 56, 60 (1966). In it, the court described in detail the history and provisions of the Party Finance Act. See also All-German Party Finance Case, 20 BVerfGE 116 (1966); and National Democratic Party Finance Case, 20 BVerfGE 134 (1966). For a detailed analysis of *Party Finance III* (1966), see Henning Zwirner, "Die Rechtsprechung des Bundesverfassungsgerichts zur Parteifinanzierung," *Archiv des Öffentlichen Rechts* 93 (1968): 81–135.

59   12 BVerfGE 276 (1961).

60   See Leibholz, "Die moderne Parteienstaat," supra note 51, at 68–94.

61   See Donald P. Kommers, "Politics and Jurisprudence in West Germany," *American Journal of Jurisprudence* 16 (1971): 223–41.

62   A fuller discussion of this case is contained in ibid., 228–41.

63   See Political Parties Act (Parteiengesetz) in amended version of February 15, 1984, *BGBl* 1:242.

64   A recent discussion of party finance in West Germany is Arthur B. Gunlicks, "Campaign Finance in the West German 'Party State,'" *Review of Politics* 50 (1988): 30–49. See also Wolfgang Hoffmann, *Die Finanzen der Parteien* (Munich: Praeger, 1973).

65   24 BVerfGE 260 (1968).

66   24 BVerfGE 300 (1968).

67   Ibid., 342.

68   Ibid., 357.

69   Law of July 22, 1969 [1969], *BGBl* 1:925.

70   41 BVerfGE 399 (1976).

71   Ibid., 416.

72   For a commentary on this case, see Ludger-Anselm Verstegle, "Zur Wahlkampfkostenerstattung unabhängiger Wahlkreisbewerber," *Zeitschrift für Parlamentsfragen* 4 (1976): 528–30. The *Daniels* case also led to a change in the Parties Act. Section 18 (4) and (5) now provides for the funding of independent candidacies. In the *Montabaur* case, 42 BVerfGE 53, also decided in 1976, the court sustained a denial of funds to an organization that had campaigned on behalf of a referendum proposal to detach Montabaur from Rhineland-Palatinate and incorporate it into Hesse. The referendum failed, whereupon the Hesse-Nassau Heimatbund challenged the validity of the balloting because it had received no state financial assistance to carry out an "adequate campaign" on behalf of the measure. Rhineland-Palatinate had used its own resources to oppose the referendum. In its complaint to the Constitutional Court, the Heimatbund charged that the state had offended the principle of equality through its failure to furnish roughly equal support to the opposition. In the course of its opinion the court reiterated its long-held view that the Basic Law does not require the public funding of any political activity, but if it *is* granted, the principle of equality must be observed. The principle, however, was not offended in this case because no funding of any kind had been provided for campaigns carried on in connection with referenda on federal reorganization held under the authority of Article 29 of the Basic Law.

73   52 BVerfGE 63 (1979).

74   Thomas F. Gede, "Comparative Study of U.S. and West German Political Finance Regulation: The Question of Contribution Controls," *Hastings International and Comparative Law Review* 4 (1981): 575.

75   Gunlicks, "Campaign Finance," supra note 64, at 36–40.

76   Ibid., 39–40. See also the Flick Case, 67 BVerfGE 100 (1984).

77   These arguments are summarized in the Party Finance V Case, 52 BVerfGE 63 (1979), at 67–74.

78   Ibid., 85.

79   73 BVerfGE 40 (1986).

80   Ibid., 103–17.

81   73 BVerfGE 1 (1986).

82   For a detailed discussion of these foundations, see Henning von Vieregge, "Die Partei-Stiftungen: Ihre Rolle im politischen System," in *Parteienfinanzierung und politischer Wettbewerb,* ed. Göttrik Wewer (Opladen: Westdeutscher Verlag, 1990), 164–94.

83   85 BVerfGE 264 (1992).

84   The new law entered into force on time. See Sechstes Gesetz zur Änderung des Parteiengesetzes und anderer Gesetze vom 28 January 1994, *BGBl* 1 (1994): 142. For a discussion of this statute and the events leading up to it, see Arthur Gunlicks, "The New Germany Party Finance Law," *German Politics* 4 (1994): 101–21.

85   See Horst Rapp, *Das Parteienprivileg des Grundgesetzes und seine Auswirkungen auf das Strafrecht* (Tübingen: J. C. B. Mohr, 1970), 6–65.

86   For a discussion of this concept and the effect of its application, see Gerhard Leibholz, "Freiheitliche demokratische Grundordnung und das Bonner Grundgesetz," in *Grundprobleme der Demokratie* (Darmstadt: Wissenschaftliche Buchgesellschaft, 1973); Johannes Lameyer, *Streitbare Demokratie: eine verfassungshermeneutische Untersuchung* (Berlin: Duncker and Humblot, 1978); Eckhard Jesse, *Streitbare Demokratie* (Berlin: Colloquium Verlag, 1980); and Martin Kutscha, *Verfassung und "streitbare Demokratie"* (Cologne: Pahl-Regenstein Verlag, 1979).

87   5 BVerfGE 85 (1956). For commentaries on the *Communist Party* case, see Edward McWhinney, "The German Federal Constitutional Court and the Communist Party Decision," *Indiana Law Journal* 32 (1957): 295–312; and Paul Franz, "Unconstitutional and Outlawed Political Parties: A German-American Comparison," *Boston College International and Comparative Law Review* 5 (1982): 51–89. For an extremely critical view of the case, see Wolfgang Abendroth, "Das KPD-Verbotsurteil des Bundesverfassungsgerichts," in Abendroth, *Antagonistische Gesellschaft und politische Demokratie* (Neuwied: Hermann Luchterhand Verlag, 1967), 139–74. For a communist view, see *The Karlsruhe Trial for Banning the Communist Party of Germany* (London: Lawrence and Wishart, 1956).

88   Donald P. Kommers, *Judicial Politics in West Germany* (Beverly Hills, Calif.: Sage Publications, 1976), 190–91.

89   5 BVerfGE 85, 141–42 (1956).

90   Ibid., 142.

91   Ibid., 139.

92   Communist Voters' League Case, 16 BVerfGE 4 (1963).

93   The Film Propaganda Case, 33 BVerfGE 52 (1972), arose out of these antisubversive activities. The Film Censorship Act of 1961, aimed mainly at East European countries,

authorized the seizure of films containing "propaganda against the free democratic basic order or the concept of international understanding." The court sustained the statute over the complainant's objection that an imported film — a documentary highly critical of capitalism — that he purchased in East Germany was a work of art within the protection of Article 5 (3) and that the mandatory screening of imported films violated the no censorship clause of Article 5 (1). For a vigorous defense of the state's fight against subversive propaganda and anticonstitutional activities, see Günter Willms, *Das Staatsschutzkonzept und seine Bewährung* (Karlsruhe: C. F. Müller, 1974). See also Ulrich Probst, "Die kommunistischen Parteien der Bundesrepublik Deutschland," *Zeitschrift für Politik* (1979): 59–96; and Otto Schönfeldt, "KPD Verbot — ein fortwirkendes Übel," in *Die KPD* (Verlag Marxistische Blätter, 1978), 111–44. For a complete history of radical movements and the extraparliamentary opposition in Germany, see Hans M. Beck, *Geschichte des "linken Radikalismus" in Deutschland: Ein Versuch* (Frankfurt am Main, 1976); and Giselher Schmidt, *Hitlers und Maos Söhne* (Frankfurt am Main, 1969).

94   40 BVerfGE 287 (1975).

95   Dan Gordon, "Limits on Extreme Political Parties: A Comparison of Israeli Jurisprudence with that of the U.S. and the Federal Republic of Germany," *Hastings International and Comparative Law Review* 10 (1987): 376.

96   An important procedural issue was whether or not the individual complainants had the right to petition the Constitutional Court. Ordinarily a statute cannot be attacked directly, in the absence of its enforcement, unless it constitutes a *direct and immediate* violation of a person's fundamental rights. Klass and his fellow complainants could claim no such violation. The court nevertheless accepted the complaints because in the circumstances of any secret surveillance the complainants could not know whether in truth the state was invading their rights. The complaints and the abstract review petitions were thus consolidated for purposes of its judgment.

97   30 BVerfGE 1 (1970).

98   Ibid., 19–20. Justices Geller, von Schlabrendorff, and Rupp, dissenting, argued that Article 10 as amended conflicts with Articles 19 (4) and 79 (3) because it deprives individuals of their essential right to judicial protection when the state encroaches on a basic right (in this instance, privacy). This right, being absolute, cannot be abrogated under any circumstances. Article 10 as amended violates the foundation principles of Articles 1 (human dignity) and 20 (legality and separation of powers). The amendment, like the statute passed pursuant to it, they concluded, is therefore itself unconstitutional (ibid., 33–47).

99   Having lost in the Federal Constitutional Court, Klass and his fellow complainants, claiming that the court's judgment violated Articles 6 (right of access to courts of justice), 8 (privacy of home and correspondence), and 13 (national remedy for breach of basic rights) of the European Convention on Human Rights, appealed to the European Human Rights Commission. In a unanimous holding, and after its detailed review of the Constitutional Court's decision, together with an equally extensive examination of the statute at issue and its administration, the commission ruled that the West German government had not breached any of these articles. See *Klass v. Federal Republic of Germany, European Human Rights Reports* 2 (1978): 214.

100 For a discussion and a documentary collection of materials related to the antiradicals

decree and the *Loyalty* case, see Peter Frisch, *Extremistenbeschluss* (Leverkusen: Heggen Verlag, 1976). See also Kenneth H. F. Dyson, "Anti-Communism in the Federal Republic of Germany: The Case of the Berufsverbot," *Parliamentary Affairs* 27 (1975): 51–67.

101   A few of these denials became causes célèbres, eliciting strong public outcries from literary figures, students, clergymen, and other intellectuals who attacked the decree as a pernicious attempt to stifle dissent and block social change. Some politicians and editorial writers responded by questioning the loyalty of the critics, seeming to confirm the latter's charge that fear and distrust were sweeping the land. Other commentators saw the whole enterprise as a cycle of overreaction: the government overreacting to the security threat in the first place, the critics responding with gross exaggerations of the decree's impact, and the critics of the critics retaliating in language far more robust than enlightening. The commentary on the *Loyalty* case and its aftermath is extensive. For a list of articles related to the case, see Josef Mackert and Franz Schneider, *Bibliographie zur Verfassungsgerichtsbarkeit des Bundes und der Länder,* 3 vols. (Tübingen: J. C. B. Mohr, 1982), 3:342–55.

102   See 63 BVerfGE 266 (1983).

103   Persons seeking civil service employment, however, did not fare so well. In the aftermath of *Civil Servant Loyalty* the court rejected several constitutional complaints against actions denying civil service jobs to particular persons on the ground of loyalty. The court — in this case a three-judge panel — rejected these complaints because they did not offer sufficient prospects of success. In this event, the only remaining recourse was an appeal to the European Commission or Court of Human Rights. One such case involved the dismissal of an assistant research professor from the physics faculty of Heidelberg University for his membership and activity in the NPD (alleged to be a neo-Nazi party). In a split decision (ten to seven) the Commission on Human Rights sustained Baden-Württemberg's action. See *K. v. Germany, European Human Rights Reports* 6 (1984): 519–31. Two years later the European Court of Human Rights sustained North Rhine–Westphalia's dismissal of a grammar school teacher because of her allegedly procommunist activity, once again vindicating West German policy under the European Convention on Human Rights. See *Glasenapp* v. *Germany, European Human Rights Reports* 9 (1986): 25–55.

104   The *Civil Servant Loyalty* case describes this history at great length; see 39 BVerfGE 334, 357–71 (1975).

105   39 BVerfGE 334, 348 (1975).

106   39 BVerfGE 334, 386–389 (1975) (Justice Wand, dissenting).

107   For a more detailed account of these events, see Donald P. Kommers, "Public Policy: Domestic and Foreign Affairs," in *Introduction to Comparative Government,* ed. Michael Curtis (New York: Harper and Row, 1985), 260–64.

108   See Hans Dahs, "Anti-Terroristen-Gesetz — eine Niederlage der Rechtsstaats," *Neue Juristische Wochenschrift* 47 (1976): 2145–51.

109   For the text of the decree and the implementing resolutions adopted by the several states, see Frisch, supra note 100, at 142–76. The Anti-constitutional Advocacy Act is included in the Fourteenth Law on the Reform of the Criminal Code of April 22, 1976, *BGBl* 1:1056–57. A large number of antiterrorist amendments to the German Criminal

Code and the Criminal Procedure Code were also passed between 1972 and 1978; see *BGBl* 1 (December 11, 1974): 3393; *BGBl* 1 (December 28, 1974): 3686; *BGBl* 1 (January 7, 1975): 44; *BGBl* 1 (January 11, 1975): 129; *BGBl* 1 (April 24, 1976): 1056; *BGBl* 1 (May 21, 1976): 1213; *BGBl* 1 (August 20, 1976): 2181; and *BGBl* 1 (October 1, 1977): 1877. The most controversial of these laws expand the search-and-seizure authority of the police, extend the grounds for detention prior to trial, impose severe restrictions on the activity of terrorist defendants in pretrial proceedings, regulate client-counsel communications, and exclude defense lawyers from representing terrorist defendants under certain conditions. For a description and sharp critical review of these restrictions, see the cover story "Wird der Rechtsstaat abgebaut?" and related articles in *Der Spiegel,* no. 50, December 5, 1977, 32–70.

110 Contact Ban Case, 49 BVerfGE 24 (1978).

111 *Amnesty International Report 1980* (London: Amnesty International Publications, 1980), 272.

112 Joint Letter of Hans-Dietrich Genscher, Minister for Foreign Affairs of the Federal Republic of Germany, and the Acting Foreign Minister of the GDR, Prime Minister Lothar de Maiziere, to the Foreign Ministers of the Four Powers on the Occasion of the Signing of the Two-Plus-Four Treaty in Moscow, 12 September 1990. Reproduced in English in *The Unification of Germany: A Documentation* (Bonn: Press and Information Office, 1991), 111.

113 *New York Times,* November 28, 1992, 1.

114 Free German Workers Party Case, 91 BVerfGE 246 (1994); and National List Case, 91 BVerfGE 262 (1994). See Judgments of the Second Senate, November 17, 1994. As of this writing the cases have not yet appeared in the official reports.

115 *Frankfurter Allgemeine Zeitung,* June 3, 1994, 1.

116 See, in this connection, the Public Servant Dissolution Case, 84 BVerfGE 133, in Chapter 6 at pp. 296–97.

117 Unification Treaty, Attachment I, chap. 29 (A), para. 3 (1), sec. 5 (1).

118 See Peter Quint, *The Imperfect Union: Constitutional Structures and German Unification* (Princeton: Princeton University Press, 1996), 172.

119 For a critical treatment of united Germany's effort to prosecute former GDR spies and other East Germans accused of human rights violations, see Quint, supra note 118 at 210–14; see also A. James McAdams, "The Honecker Trial and the German Future," *Review of Politics* 58 (1996): 53–80. The Markus Wolf case has not yet appeared in the official reports. The full text of the opinion appears in *Europäische Grundrechte Zeitschrift* 22 (June 2, 1995): 202–26. For an excellent summary of the case, see David Currie, "The Pains of Growing Together: The Case of the East-German Spies," *East European Constitutional Review* 4 (1995): 66–70.

6 ECONOMIC LIBERTIES

1 See, for example, Martin Kriele, *Legitimitätsprobleme der Bundesrepublik* (Munich: Verlag C. H. Beck, 1972), 115–20.

2 One of the best treatments of the background and current interpretation of the social

welfare state principle is Ernst Benda, "Der soziale Rechtsstaat," in *Handbuch des Verfassungsrechts,* 2 vols., ed. Ernst Benda, Werner Maihofer, and Hans-Jochen Vogel (Berlin: Walter de Gruyter, 1984), 1:477–553. See also Peter Badura, "Die Rechtsprechung des Bundesverfassungsgerichts zu den verfassungsrechtlichen Grenzen wirtschaftspolitischer Gesetzgebung im sozialen Rechtsstaat," *Archiv des Öffentlichen Rechts* 92 (1967): 382–407.

3 See Hans F. Zacher, "Die soziale Staatsziel," in *Handbuch des Staatsrechts der Bundesrepublik Deutschland,* 8 vols., ed. Josef Isensee and Paul Kirchhof (Heidelberg: C. F. Müller Juristischer Verlag, 1987), 1:1101–4.

4 See Erhard Denninger et al., *Kommentar zum Grundgesetz für die Bundesrepublik Deutschland* (Neuwied: Hermann Luchterhand Verlag, 1984), 1380–86.

5 For an excellent overview of the history of the concept of the *Rechtsstaat,* see Ernst-Wolfgang Böckenförde, *State, Society and Liberty,* trans. J. A. Underwood (Oxford: Bey, 1991), 47–70.

6 This is particularly true of the concept of social democracy; see Zacher, supra note 3, at 1096–1101.

7 See, for example, the protocols of the Main Committee of December 4, 1948, 18th session (first reading) (typescript), 216ff. Some scholars have severely criticized Social Democratic delegates for not fighting for a bill of social rights in the Parliamentary Council. See Hans Hermann Hartwich, *Sozialstaatspostulat und gesellschaftlichen Status Quo* (Opladen: Westdeutscher Verlag, 1970), 27–33.

8 See Zacher, supra note 3, at 1101–4.

9 See Subsidiary Case, 22 BVerfGE 180, 204 (1967); Allied Property Damage Case, 27 BVerfGE 253, 283 (1969); and Lebach Case, 35 BVerfGE 202, 235 (1973). In addition, the court has specifically recognized the importance of the individual's constitutional interest in securing work, housing, and health care. See Employment Agency Case, 21 BVerfGE 245, 251 (1967) (concerning work); Tenant Security Case, 18 BVerfGE 121, 132 (1964) (concerning housing); and the Mülheim-Kärlich Case, 36 BVerfGE 237, 245 (1973). *Mülheim-Kärlich* deals mainly with the right to life and bodily security. The state's obligation to promote and safeguard the health of its citizens is implied in this case.

10 See Heinz B. Case, 10 BVerfGE 354, 372 (1960); and Medical Insurance Case II, 18 BVerfGE 257, 273 (1964).

11 See, for example, the Subsidiarity Case, 22 BVerfGE 180 (1967). The court sustained, over the objection of several states, a federal grant-in-aid program (Youth Welfare Act of 1961) that sought to enlist the support of various private organizations in caring for young people at risk.

12 Ernst Karl Pakuscher, "Judicial Review of Executive Acts in Economic Affairs in Germany," *Journal of Public Law* 20 (1971): 274.

13 Such a theory has been suggested by W. Abendroth et al., *Der Kampf um das Grundgesetz: Über die politische Bedeutung der Verfassungsinterpretation* (Frankfurt: Syndikat, 1977).

14 See Ernst Forsthoff, ed., *Rechsstaatlichkeit und Sozialstaatlichkeit* (Darmstadt: Wissenschaftliche Buchgesellschaft, 1968), 171.

15 For an excellent discussion of developments in the social economy of the old GDR, see Eric Owen Smith, *The German Economy* (London and New York: Routledge, 1994), 254–318 and 416–542.

16 Paul Kirchhof, "Budgeting Levies Earmarked for the Achievement of Social Policies," in

Reports on German Public Law and Public International Law, ed. Rudolf Bernhardt and Ulrich Beyerlin (Heidelberg: C. F. Müller Juristischer Verlag, 1986), 146.

17 See Vocational Training Act Case, 55 BVerfGE 274, 297 (1980).

18 The court applies a five-part test in these cases: first, the group burdened by the levy must be readily identifiable and clearly distinguishable from the public at large; second, there must be a special relationship between the taxed group and the purpose of the tax; third, the group taxed must bear a special responsibility for the situation to be remedied by the levy; fourth, there must be a substantial relationship between the burden imposed and the benefit secured by the levy; and fifth, the legislature must periodically review the situation and *reenact* the levy when conditions require its continuance. The court enunciated these tests in the *Vocational Training Act* case. These standards were also applied in Handicapped Tax Act Case, 57 BVerfGE 139 (1981); and Investment Aid Case II, 67 BVerfGE 256 (1984).

19 91 BVerfGE 186 (1994).

20 84 BVerfGE 239 (1991).

21 Partial translations of these acts appear in Carl-Christoph Schweitzer et al., *Politics and Government in the Federal Republic of Germany 1944–1994: Basic Documents,* 2nd ed. (Oxford: Berghahn, 1995), 411–12 and 417–19.

22 Articles 134 and 135, for example, the residue of economic arrangements going back to Bismarck's time, transfer Reich property and Prussian commercial enterprises to the federation. Article 110 specifically refers to revenues earned by "federal enterprises," and Article 15 provides for the socialization of natural resources and means of production.

23 See Elfes Case, 6 BVerfGE 32, 41–45 (1957).

24 See Georg Ress, "Government and Industry in the Federal Republic of Germany," *International and Comparative Law Quarterly* 29 (1980): 90. Some commentators maintain that governmental enterprises operating under private law are entitled to the same entrepreneurial liberty that Article 12 confers on private concerns; others take a more restrictive view of their legality; and still others would sanction their existence so long as they serve a "public interest beyond purely commercial purposes" (ibid., 88–92).

25 Employment Agency Case, 21 BVerfGE 245, 249 (1967).

26 See Milk and Butterfat Case, 18 BVerfGE 315, 327 (1965).

27 Ress, "Government and Industry," supra note 24, at 91–92.

28 For comments on this case, see Fritz Rittner, "A New Constitution for German Big Business: The Codetermination Act of 1976," *Hastings International and Comparative Law Review* 1977 (1977): 113–22, and Herbert Wiedemann, "Codetermination by Workers in German Enterprises, *American Journal of Comparative Law* 28 (1980): 79–92.

29 Compensation Exclusion Case, 34 BVerfGE 118 (1972). An excellent overview of the right to property in German constitutional law is Peter Badura, "Eigentum," in *Handbuch des Verfassungsrechts,* ed. Ernst Benda et al. (Berlin: Walter de Gruyter, 1984), 653–96.

30 See P. Kunig, "German Constitutional Law and the Environment," *Adelaide Law Review* 8 (1983): 326–27; and Georg Ress, "The Right to Property under the Constitution of the Federal Republic of Germany" (Paper delivered at Notre Dame German-American Constitutional Law Conference, April 1986), 10.

31 Rudolf Dolzer, *Property and Environment: The Social Obligation Inherent in Ownership* (Marges, Switzerland: International Union for the Conservation of Nature and Natural

Resources, 1976), 17. See also Klaus-Berto Doemming, Rudolph Werner Füsslein, and Werner Matz, "Entstehungsgeschichte der Artikel des Grundgesetzes," *Jahrbuch des Öffentlichen Rechts*, n.s., 1 (1951): 144f.

32   Feldmühle Case, 14 BVerfGE 263 (1962).

33   George Fletcher, "Troubled by Takings: An Inquiry into Constitutional Theory in West Germany and the United States" (Paper presented at Conference on Comparative Constitutional Law, University of Southern California, April 5–7, 1979), 11.

34   Ordinarily only one set of courts in Germany has jurisdiction over a given subject area of law. In the field of property, however, jurisdiction is divided between administrative and ordinary courts: the former have authority to decide whether property has been taken, the latter to decide the amount of compensation. Because these issues are interlinked, both tribunals have been forced to define a "public good" and a "compensable taking." This discussion relies heavily on Dolzer, supra note 31; Badura, "Eigentum," supra note 29; and Fletcher, supra note 33.

35   Regulatory takings are much less likely to be compensated in American than in German law. Fletcher found these contrasting approaches to regulatory takings to be rooted in differing postures toward the doctrine of sovereign immunity. The doctrine has a strong lineage in the Anglo-American legal tradition but is severely limited by Article 34 of the Basic Law. (Article 34, which has no equivalent in the U.S. Constitution, renders the state liable for injuries caused by the negligence of public officials.) Under German tort theory, on the other hand, a landowner forced to sacrifice a property interest for the sake of the higher social good of his neighbor is also a victim entitled to compensation. The principle of justice behind the theory — "the party benefiting from the justified intrusion must bear the risk of the resulting harm" — permeates the constitutional law of regulatory takings: The state is obligated to compensate owners whose special rights and privileges are forcibly sacrificed for the common good. See "Troubled by Takings," supra note 33, at 15–20.

36   Lower Saxony Dikeland Case, 25 BVerfGE 112, 121 (1969).

37   21 BVerfGE 150 (1967).

38   See Württemberg-Baden Civil Servant Case, 4 BVerfGE 219 (1955).

39   Thalidomide Case, 42 BVerfGE 263, 292 (1976).

40   See Ress, "Property under the Constitution," supra note 28, at 6. One problem in this field was the continuing tendency of the Federal Supreme Court (Bundesgerichtshof) to define the right to property more broadly than the Federal Constitutional Court, occasionally bringing the two tribunals into confrontation. For example, in upholding a federal law denying former civil servants tainted by their Nazi records reinstatement in their former positions, the Constitutional Court declined the Supreme Court's invitation to regard civil service tenure and its associated job benefits as "property" within the meaning of the Basic Law; see Civil Servant Case, 3 BVerfGE 58 (1953). For a detailed discussion of this and related cases, see Hans W. Baade, "Social Science Evidence and the Federal Constitutional Court of West Germany," *Journal of Politics* 23 (1961): 421–61. See also Gestapo Case, 6 BVerfGE 132 (1957), discussed in Hans W. Baade, "Haagan's History — A West German Case Study in the Judicial Evaluation of History," *American Journal of Comparative Law* 16 (1965): 398–99.

41   52 BVerfGE 300 (1981).

42 Judgment of October 18, 1993 (1 BvR 1335/91) (Chamber opinion), *Neue Justiz* (1994): 25.

43 37 BVerfGE 132 (1974).

44 42 BVerfGE 263 (1976).

45 14 BVerfGE 263 (1962).

46 Unification Treaty, Article 41 (1), in tandem with Exhibit III, Einigungsvertrag, Bulletin no. 104 (Bonn: Presse-und Informationsamt der Bundesrepublik, September 6, 1990), 1:119–20.

47 For more detailed discussion, see Peter Quint, *The Imperfect Union: Constitutional Structures of German Unification* (Princeton, N.J.: Princeton University Press, 1996), chap. 11, pp. 124–53.

48 84 BVerfGE 90.

49 Ibid., 127–28.

50 Ibid., 117–21.

51 Ibid., 122–25.

52 Dresden Property Case, 84 BVerfGE 286 (1991).

53 *Property Confiscation II* case, Chamber decision of April 15, 1993 (1 BvR 1885/92), *Neue Juristische Wochenschrift* (1993), 366.

54 *German-Polish Frontier Treaty* case, Chamber decision of June 5, 1992, *Europäische Grundrecht Zeitung* 19 (1992).

55 See Berlin Property Case, 85 BVerfGE 130 (1991) (refusing to stop the sale of a former owner's property to a third party for development) and Real Estate Case, Chamber decision of April 21, 1993 (1 BvR 1422/92) (refusing to bar the Treuhandanstalt, the agency charged with privatizing state-owned property in the old GDR and clarifying questions of ownership, from implementing a contract by which it had sold property for investment purposes and thus to prevent the loss of a legal position the previous owner might have until the applicant's main claim in respect of the property was decided upon).

56 58 BVerfGE 300 (1981).

57 See Schoolbook Case, 31 BVerfGE 229 (1971); Broadcast Lending Case, 31 BVerfGE 248 (1971); Tape Recording Case, 31 BVerfGE 255 (1971); School Broadcast Case, 31 BVerfGE 270 (1971); and Phonograph Record Case, 31 BVerfGE 275 (1971).

58 31 BVerfGE 248 (1971).

59 31 BVerfGE 270 (1971).

60 31 BVerfGE 255 (1971).

61 31 BVerfGE 275 (1971).

62 49 BVerfGE 382 (1978).

63 The *Church Music* case is marked by still another nuance. "The Constitution not only protects the different proprietary rights laid down in the Copyright Act," said the court, "*but also protects potential property rights* and the right of exploitation [*Verwertungsrecht*]. The legislature is, in principle, required to vest in the author economic control over his creative work and to allow him the freedom to dispose of it on his own responsibility." Notwithstanding the self-restraint exhibited by the court in this case, there is some suggestion here that the justices are prepared independently to determine, apart from legislative policy, what kind of intellectual property is deserving of protection under Article 14.

64 Lochner v. New York, 198 U.S. 45, 75; 25 S.Ct. 539, 547; 49 L.Ed. 937, 949 (1905).

65 10 BVerfGE 89 (1959).

66 Ibid., 102.

67 For a detailed consideration of Article 2 (1), see the section on the right to personality in Chapter 7.

68 38 BVerfGE 281 (1974).

69 Ibid., 301–2.

70 38 BVerfGE 386 (1975).

71 The functions and rights of these councils are set forth in the Works Constitution Act (Betriebsverfassungsgesetz) of 1972, *BGBl* 1:13, the statute that confers on labor certain limited rights of codetermination within industry and laid the groundwork for the Co-determination Act of 1976.

72 See 42 BVerfGE 133 (1976).

73 This approach to constitutional interpretation anticipates the materials in Chapter 8 dealing with the impact of constitutional values in the private sphere.

74 88 BVerfGE 103 (1993).

75 The *Medical Practice* case, which concerns the right of a doctor to label himself a specialist, is an illustration of this principle. The court ruled that the activities of medical specialists cannot be controlled by a medical association. Any such regulation would require an act of the legislature; see 33 BVerfGE 125 (1972); see also Adult Education Expulsion Case, 41 BVerfGE 251 (1973).

76 86 BVerfGE 28 (1992).

77 40 BVerfGE 196 (1975).

78 Ibid., 227–28.

79 See, respectively, Midwife Case, 9 BVerfGE 338 (1959); Drug Order Case, 9 BVerfGE 73 (1959); Medical Advertising Case, 9 BVerfGE 213 (1959); Shop Closing Case, 59 BVerfGE 336 (1982); Baking Working Hours Case, 23 BVerfGE 50 (1968); and Attorney Regulation Case, 87 BVerfGE 287 (1992).

80 11 BVerfGE 30 (1960).

81 See Defense Counsel Case, 16 BVerfGE 214 (1963); Kaul Case, 22 BVerfGE 114 (1967); and Ensolin Case, 34 BVerfGE 293 (1973). These cases involved, respectively, judicial rulings (1) preventing a lawyer from serving as defense counsel in a case merely because he was called as a witness by the prosecution, (2) barring an East Berlin lawyer from continuing as defense counsel in a case because of his membership in East Germany's Socialist Unity party, and (3) preventing an attorney from defending his client on the ground of his suspected complicity in the crime for which his client was on trial. *Ensolin* held that any such restriction on the role of defense counsel would require "unequivocal statutory authorization." In response, parliament amended the Criminal Code in 1974 to bar an attorney from serving as defense counsel in proceedings where he or she is strongly suspected of participation in the act that is the subject of the trial.

82 19 BVerfGE 330 (1965).

83 13 BVerfGE 97 (1961).

84 See Tax Agent Case, 21 BVerfGE 173 (1967); Pharmaceutical Technical Assistant Case, 32 BVerfGE 1 (1971); and Tax Consultant Case, 21 BVerfGE 227 (1967).

85 Taxi Case, 11 BVerfGE 168 (1960).

86 17 BVerfGE 371 (1964).

87 9 BVerfGE 39 (1958).

88 See Fritz K. Ringer, "Higher Education in Germany in the Nineteenth Century," *Journal of Contemporary History* 2 (1967): 123–38.

89 Daniel Fallon, *The German University: A Heroic Ideal in Conflict with the Modern World* (Boulder: Colorado Associated University Press, 1980), 24.

90 For an account of these reforms, see Peter J. Katzenbach, *Policy and Politics in West Germany* (Philadelphia: Temple University Press, 1987), 296–325. See also Donald P. Kommers, "The Government of West Germany," in *Introduction to Comparative Government,* ed. Michael Curtis et al. (New York: Harper and Row, 1985), 267–73.

91 Richard Merritt, "The Courts, the Universities and the Right of Admission in the Federal Republic of Germany," *Minerva* 22 (1979): 7.

92 For other studies of judicial intervention in the field of German education, see David J. Jung and David Kirp, "Law as an Instrument of Education Policy-Making," *American Journal of Comparative Law* 32 (1984): 625; Hans Weiler, "Equal Protection, Legitimacy, and the Legalization of Education: The Role of the Federal Constitutional Court in West Germany," *Review of Politics* 47 (1985): 66–91; and Joyce Marie Mushaben, "The State v. the University: Juridicalization and the Politics of Higher Education at the Free University of Berlin 1969–1979" (Ph.D. diss., Indiana University, 1981).

93 As Richard Merritt noted, this principle has been traced back to the *Pharmacy* case. See "Courts and Universities," supra note 91, at 10, fn. 13. See also Ulrich Karpen, "Zulassungsbeschränkungen und Neuordnung des Hochschulzuganges," *Die deutsche Universitätszeitung* 30 (1975): 823.

94 39 BVerfGE 276 (1975).

95 "This ruling in effect threw the universities to the wolves. Those denied admission by the central admissions office did not have to sue that institution itself, but could turn directly to individual universities to dig up and take advantage of lapses in the latter's measurement or reporting of unfilled places" (Richard Merritt, supra note 91, at 24).

96 39 BVerfGE 258 (1975).

97 See *Numerus Clausus* Case II, 43 BVerfGE 34 (1976); and *Numerus Clausus* Case III, 43 BVerfGE 47 (1976).

98 These general requirements once again emphasized that every German student who furnishes proof that he holds the requisite qualifications is entitled to pursue his chosen course of study. The statute requires the states to lay down admission quotas for each institution of higher learning and to coordinate their regulations with the activities of the Central Admissions Office, which is now bound by the state rules. *Abitur* scores and scholastic achievement are the main criteria of admission. Fixed quotas, however, are established for foreign students, hardship cases (i.e., applicants whose denial of admission would constitute an unusual hardship), students on waiting lists, and those who have finished their military obligation or substitute service in a noncombatant occupation. Residence in a particular state, finally, does not constitute a basis of admission. The full text of this statute is available in English. See *Framework Act for Higher Education* (Hochschulrahmengesetz) (Bonn: Ministry of Education and Science, 1976).

99 43 BVerfGE 291 (1977).

100 Double-Track Admissions Case, 62 BVerfGE 117 (1982).

101 In 1976, consistent with its view that any limitation on a basic right requires a statutory

basis, the court ruled that graduation requirements were to be regulated by law and that administrative decrees with respect to this matter would be valid only during a transitional period. University Ordinance Case, 41 BVerfGE 251 (1976).

102   Hans N. Weiler, "Equal Protection and Education," *Review of Politics* 47 (1985): 67.

103   Under the Weimar Constitution, by contrast, the principle of equality bound the executive in the administration of law but not the lawmakers themselves. In an early decision, the Constitutional Court affirmed that the principle of equal treatment is indeed a binding element of the FRG's legal order — i.e., an objective value as well as a subjective right — and is thus applicable to all state activity (1 BVerfGE 14, 52 [1951]).

104   See United States v. Caroline Products Co., 304 U.S. 144 (1938).

105   See, for example, the tax cases discussed earlier in this chapter. See also Fire Fighting Case I, 9 BVerfGE 291 (1959) (striking down a state fire brigade statute requiring males between the ages of eighteen and sixty to perform voluntary fire service but imposing a tax on those in this age group who chose not to engage in such service); Medical Society Case, 43 BVerfGE 58 (1976) (invalidating a sales tax levied against commercial medical laboratories but exempting doctors who pool their resources to establish their own laboratories); and Educational Training Act Case, 91 BVerfGE 389 (1995) (striking down a provision of federal law that treated the assets and income of a spouse, whether permanently separated or not, in determining the amount of financial assistance a person could receive under the law).

106   For an excellent treatment of Germany's patriarchal tradition, see Gordon Craig's chapter on women in *The Germans* (New York: G. P. Putnam's Sons, 1982), 147–69.

107   See 3 BVerfGE 225, 237–48 (1953).

108   Under this standard, the court invalidated laws favoring males in matters related to child rearing and inheritance (see, respectively, Parental Control Case, 10 BVerfGE 59, 72–81 [1959]; and Male Inheritance Case, 15 BVerfGE 337 [1963]), but sustained laws limiting for health reasons the kind of work women could perform (Female Workplace Case, 5 BVerfGE 9, 11–12 [1956]), punishing male but not female homosexuality (Homosexuality Case, 6 BVerfGE 389 [1957]), and limiting the military draft to men (Conscientious Objector Case I, 12 BVerfGE 45, 52–53 [1960]). In a series of social security cases, the court also sustained laws advantaging men in the allocation of death and retirement benefits; see, respectively, Social Security Case I, 17 BVerfGE 1, 17–26 (1963); and Social Security Case III, 48 BVerfGE 346 (1978). See also Social Security Case II, 43 BVerfGE 213, 225–230 (1977) (requiring widowers but not widows to prove dependency as a condition for receiving death benefits). For a further listing and discussion of cases, see Ingo von Münch and Philip Kunig, *Grundgesetz Kommentar*, 4th ed. (Munich: C. H. Beck'sche Verlagsbuchhandlung, 1992), 282–90.

109   *Arbeitsrechtliches EG-Anpassungsgesetz, BGBl* (1980): 1308.

110   Nocturnal Employment Case, 87 BVerfGE 363 (1992).

111   84 BVerfGE 9 (1991). For a discussion of this and related cases on family law, see Rainer Frank, "Germany: Revolution from the Federal Constitutional Court," *University of Louisville Journal of Family Law* 31 (1992–93): 347–54.

112   Common Marital Name Case, 78 BVerfGE 38 (1988).

113   See Slupik, *Die Entscheidung des Grundgesetzes für Parität im Geschlechterverhältnis* (1988).

114   74 BVerfGE 163 (1987).

115   See Frankfurt Labor Court Case, 89 BVerfGE 276 (1993).

116   Ibid., 290–91.

117   *Frankfurter Allgemeine Zeitung,* December 23, 1993, p. 4.

118   Gesetz zur Durchsetzung der Gleichberechtigung von Frauen und Männern, art. 1, sec. 2, BGBl I (1994): 1406.

119   For a more detailed analysis of the nondiscriminatory provisions of Article 3, see David P. Currie, *The Constitution of the Federal Republic of Germany* (Chicago: University of Chicago Press, 1995), 322–38.

120   84 BVerfGE 133 (1991).

121   For a much more detailed discussion of this case and other decisions treated in this section, see Quint, supra note 47 at 168–71.

122   Academy of Science Case II, 85 BVerfGE 360 (1992). Three months earlier the court had issued a temporary injunction to the same effect; see Academy of Science Case I, 85 BVerfGE 167 (1991). See also Agricultural Academy Case, 86 BVerfGE 81 (1992).

123   Gesetz zur Prüfung von Rechtsanwaltzulassungen of July 24, 1992, *BGBl* 1:1386.

124   1 BvR 2263/94 (slip opinion, August 9, 1995).

7   HUMAN DIGNITY AND PERSONHOOD

1   The framers lifted this language almost verbatim from the Universal Declaration of Human Rights. The declaration's preamble acknowledges that "the inherent dignity and . . . the equal and inalienable rights of all members of the human family [are] the foundation of freedom, justice and peace of the world," just as Article 1 affirms that "all human beings are born free and equal in dignity and rights" (Universal Declaration of Human Rights, December 10, 1948 [U.N. Doc. A/811]).

2   See Peter Häberle, "Die Menschenwürde als Grundlage der staatlichen Gemeinschaft," in *Handbuch des Staatsrechts der Bundesrepublik Deutschland,* 8 vols., ed. Josef Isensee and Paul Kirchhof (Heidelberg: C. F. Müller Juristischer Verlag, 1987), 1:815–61. See also Karl Doehring, *Staatsrecht der Bundesrepublik Deutschland,* 3d ed. (Frankfurt am Main: Alfred Metzner Verlag, 1984), 280–84.

3   See Erhard Denninger, "Verfassungsrechtliche Schlüsselbegriffe," in *Festschrift für Rudolf Wassermann zum 60. Geburtstag,* ed. Christian Broda et al. (Neuwied: Hermann Luchterhand Verlag, 1985), 279–98.

4   For a discussion of the meaning of the term "moral code," see the note that follows the *Transsexual* case (no. 7.8).

5   For a brief overview of the debate in English, see John Ford Golay, *The Founding of the Federal Republic of Germany* (Chicago: University of Chicago Press, 1958), 175–80.

6   The term "spiritual-moral being" appears in the Life Imprisonment Case, 45 BVerfGE 187, 227. Such references to the transcendental character of the human personality flow mainly from the prolific pens of justices and commentators associated with the natural-law tradition. See, for example, Josef Wintrich, "Die Bedeutung der Menschenrechten für die Anwendung des Rechts," *Bayerische Verwaltungsblätter* 5 (1957): 137–40; Willi Geiger, *Gesetz über das Bundesverfassungsgericht* (Berlin: Verlag Franz Vahlen GmbH, 1952), 134; Ernst Benda, Werner Maihofer, and Hans-Jochen Vogel, "Die Menschen-

würde," *Handbuch des Verfassungsrechts,* 2 vols. (Berlin: Walter de Gruyter, 1984), 1:110; Christian Starck, "Menschenwürde als Verfassungsgarantie im modernen Staat," *Juristenzeitung* 36 (1981): 457–64; and Theodore Maunz, Gunter Dürig, and Roman Herzog, *Grundgesetz: Kommentar,* 3d ed. (Munich: C. H. Beck'sche Verlagsbuchhandlung, 1973), Article 1 (1), p. 3. Wintrich, Geiger, and Benda were enormously influential leaders in their respective senates. Wintrich and Benda served as president (chief justice) and presiding officer of the First Senate for a total of sixteen years; Geiger was one of the most articulate members of the Second Senate for twenty years.

7   See G. P. Fletcher, "Human Dignity as a Constitutional Value," *University of Western Ontario Law Review* 22 (1984): 178–82; see also Peter Badura, "Generalprävention und Würde der Menschen," *Juristenzeitung* 19 (1964): 337–44.

8   See Winfried Brugger, "Elemente verfassungsliberaler Grundrechtstheorie," *Juristenzeitung* 42 (1987): 633–40.

9   30 BVerfGE 173, 193 (1971).

10   4 BVerfGE 7, 15–16 (1954); see also Conscientious Objector Case I, 12 BVerfGE 45, 51 (1960); and Klass Case, 30 BVerfGE 1, 20 (1970).

11   Fletcher, supra note 7, at 14, noted that American commentators have discovered in Kantian rationalism a proper foundation for the primacy of rights and personal autonomy in American constitutionalism. In Fletcher's view, this overemphasizes Kant's individualistic legal theory to the neglect of his "communitarian moral theory." Fletcher sees the Basic Law as an effort to "integrate Kant's communitarian moral theory into a liberal legal order."

12   Robert H. Wieber, "Lincoln's Fraternal Democracy," in *Abraham Lincoln and the American Political Tradition,* ed. John L. Thomas (Amherst: University of Massachusetts Press, 1986), 11–30.

13   Ernst Benda, writing in 1983 upon his retirement as president, uttered the conventional German view in noting that the Basic Law rejects the "individualistic conception of man derived from classical liberalism as well as the [more modern] collectivistic view" (see "Die Menschenwürde," supra note 6, at 107).

14   See Furman v. Georgia, 408 U.S. 238 (1972); and Gregg v. Georgia, 428 U.S. 153 (1976).

15   Polygraph Case, 2 BvR 166/81, decision of August 18, 1981, in *Neue Juristische Wochenschrift* 35 (1982): 375.

16   33 BVerfGE 1 (1972).

17   *Penal Code of the Federal Republic of Germany,* trans. Joseph J. Darby (London: Sweet and Maxwell, 1987), secs. 57 and 57a.

18   72 BVerfGE 105 (1986).

19   64 BVerfGE 261, 284 (1983). This case also involved a concentration camp official convicted and sentenced to fifteen years for his complicity in the murder of hundreds of persons. In 1977, at the age of seventy-eight and after serving thirteen years of his sentence, he applied for a ten-day release from prison under a federal statute permitting such furloughs each year after the offender has spent six months in prison or ten years in the case of someone sentenced to life imprisonment. Frankfurt's superior court denied the release in this case because of the gravity of the offender's crime, notwithstanding the offender's advanced age, the serious condition of his health, and his exemplary prison record. The Second Senate, over the dissenting opinion of Justice Mahrenholz, ruled that

the lower court's decision was incompatible with Article 2 (1) considered in tandem with the human dignity clause of Article 1 (1).

20 See Bruno Schmidt-Bleibtreu and Franz Klein, *Kommentar zum Grundgesetz für die Bundesrepublik Deutschland,* 5th ed. (Neuwied: Hermann Luchterhand Verlag, 1980), 141–43.

21 12 BVerfGE 1 (1960). A partial translation of this case appears in Walter F. Murphy and Joseph Tanenhaus, *Comparative Constitutional Law* (New York: St. Martin's Press, 1977), 466–67.

22 Ibid., 4.

23 These remarks are drawn from an unpublished paper by President Zeidler (undated typescript on file in the archives of the Federal Constitutional Court). See also Wolfgang Zeidler, "Grundrechte und Grundentscheidungen der Verfassung im Widerstreit," in *Verhandlungen des 53. Deutschen Juristentages* (Berlin: 1980), 1:1–29.

24 As the court noted in the *Lebach* case, "the preeminent importance of the right to the free development and respect of personality . . . follows from its close connection with the supreme value enshrined in the Constitution, i.e., human dignity" (see 35 BVerfGE 202, 221 [1973]). For a general discussion of the Constitutional Court's interpretation of the personality clause, see R. Scholz, "Das Grundrecht der freien Entfaltung der Persönlichkeit in der Rechtsprechung des Bundesverfassungsgerichts," *Archiv des Öffentlichen Rechts* 100 (1975): 80–130, 265–90.

25 See, for example, the Christian Friedrich Case, 4 BVerfGE 52, 56 (1954).

26 Ekkehart Stein, *Staatsrecht,* 9th ed. (Tübingen: J. C. B. Mohr, 1984), 217. See also Doehring, supra note 2, at 284–85.

27 Some commentators, such as Hans Peters, have adopted a narrower view of the personality clause. This view, which may be described as "Christocentric," is that persons have been created in the image of God. They are fundamentally spiritual beings responsible before God within the larger community. Accordingly, their rights under the human dignity and personality clauses are confined to those liberties which are expressive of this "inner core" of the God-oriented human person; this is sometimes known as the *Kernbereichstheorie* of the personality clause, as opposed to the prevailing and broader *Persönlichkeitskerntheorie.* See Hans Peters, *Das Recht auf freie Entfaltung der Persönlichkeit in der höchstrichterlichen Rechtsprechung* (Opladen: Westdeutscher Verlag, 1963). For a general discussion in English of the right to personality in Germany, see Harry D. Krause, "The Right to Privacy in Germany—Pointers for American Legislation?" *Duke Law Journal* (1965): 481–530.

28 90 BVerfGE 145 (1994).

29 90 BVerfGE 263 (1994).

30 The right to personality, incidentally, has not been confined to natural persons. Freedom of action has been extended by interpretation to corporations and legal persons. See Erfurt Public Corporation Case, 10 BVerfGE 89 (1959); and Accident Insurance Case, 23 BVerfGE 12 (1967).

31 55 BVerfGE 159 (1980).

32 In still another licensing case—the Public Assembly Case, 20 BVerfGE 150 (1956)—the court held that freedom of action protected by Article 2 (1) was violated by a standardless and arbitrary denial of a license to an organization wishing to assemble in public and

solit funds for its activities. We have also seen from the materials in Chapter 5 that freedom of action as an expression of personality includes economic rights to the extent that such rights are not fully secured by other basic rights. See Small Garden Plot Case, 10 BVerfGE 221 (1959); Kurt L. Case, 30 BVerfGE 250 (1971).

33 80 BVerfGE 137 (1989).

34 Ibid., 166.

35 Ibid., 168.

36 91 BVerfGE 140 (1994).

37 91 BVerfGE 335, 339–340 (1994).

38 Census Injunction Case, 64 BVerfGE 67 (1983).

39 Widow's Child Welfare Case, 1 BVerfGE 97 (1951).

40 "Fundamental Rights: A Comparative Analysis" (Lecture presented at the Center for Contemporary German Studies, Johns Hopkins University, Washington, D.C., September 23, 1987), 6.

41 Ibid.

42 34 BVerfGE 205 (1972).

43 32 BVerfGE 373 (1972).

44 33 BVerfGE 367 (1972).

45 34 BVerfGE 238 (1973).

46 Schmidt-Bleibtreu and Klein, supra note 20, at 167–68.

47 5 BVerfGE 13 (1956).

48 See Decision of Federal Administrative Court, 9 BVerfGE 78 (1959); and *Neue Juristische Wochenschrift* (1958): 800.

49 Schmidt-Bleibtreu and Klein, supra note 20, at 168.

50 17 BVerfGE 108 (1963).

51 Polygraph Case, supra note 15. See also 17 BVerfGE 347 (1963).

52 1 BVerfGE 97 (1951).

53 See P. Kunig, "German Constitutional Law and the Environment," *Adelaide Law Review* 8 (1983): 329.

54 53 BVerfGE 62 (1979).

55 See Wolfgang Koch, "Pollution Cases Go to Court," *Kölner-Stadt-Anzeiger,* July 22, 1983. The *Chemical Weapons* case, decided in 1987, was the most important of these cases. Michel M. Bothe, professor of constitutional law at Hanover University, filed the original complaint — an unusually detailed eighty-nine-page typewritten brief — on behalf of sixteen German citizens on July 1, 1983. See the discussion of this case that follows the Schleyer Kidnapping case (no. 7.12).

56 32 BVerfGE 54 (1971).

57 42 BVerfGE 212 (1976). For a general overview of Article 13 jurisprudence, see Schmidt-Bleibtreu and Klein, supra note 20, at 300–304.

58 The personality clause figured prominently in the *Klaus K.* case, involving the inspection of a letter a wife had sent to her husband being held in pretrial detention. The judge responsible for checking such correspondence, said the court, must attach "special importance" to this freely written communication in light of the constitutional requirement of respect for personal privacy (35 BVerfGE 35 [1973]). With respect to correspondence between prisoners, see Prison Correspondence Case, 35 BVerfGE 311 (1973).

59 30 BVerfGE 1 (1970).

60 410 U.S. 113 (1973). For a detailed comparison of the American and German abortion cases, see Donald P. Kommers, "Liberty and Community in Constitutional Law: The Abortion Cases in Comparative Perspective," *Brigham Young Law Review* 1985 (1985): 371–409. See also Winfried Brugger, "A Constitutional Duty to Outlaw Abortion? A Comparative Analysis of the American and German Abortion Decisions," *Jahrbuch des Öffentlichen Rechts der Gegenwart* 36 (1987): 49–66.

61 Abortion Injunction Case, 37 BVerfGE 324 (1974).

62 See Wolfgang Zeidler, "Ehe und Familie," in *Handbuch des Verfassungsrechts der Bundesrepublik Deutschland* (Berlin: Walter de Gruyter, 1983), 556–607.

63 See Brugger, supra note 60, at 50–55. For a comprehensive discussion of the American jurisprudence, see Laurence H. Tribe, *American Constitutional Law*, 2d ed. (Mineola, N.Y.: Foundation Press, 1988), 1337–62.

64 See Brüggemann and Scheuten v. Federal Republic of Germany, *European Human Rights Reports* 3 (1977): 244.

65 *BGBl* 1 (1976): 1213.

66 For a discussion of the impact of *Abortion I* on the frequency of abortion in Germany, see *Bericht der Kommission zur Auswertung der Erfahrungen mit dem reformierten Sec. 218 des Strafgesetzbuches,* Deutscher Bundestag, 8. Wahlperiode, Drucksache 8/3630 (January 31, 1980). See also Evert Ketting and Philip van Praag, *Schwangerschaftsabbruch* (Tübingen: Deutsche Gesellschaft für Verhaltenstherapie, 1985).

67 Susanne Walther, "Thou Shalt not (but thou mayest): Abortion After the German Constitutional Court's 1993 Landmark Decision," *German Yearbook of International Law* 36 (1993): 387.

68 Unification Treaty, Article 31 (4). This paragraph borrows heavily from my essay "The Basic Law under Strain: Constitutional Dilemmas and Challenges," in *The Domestic Politics of German Unification,* ed. Christopher Anderson et al. (Boulder, Col.: Lynne Rienner, 1993), 142–43.

69 Article 13 of the Pregnancy and Family Assistance Act amended sections 218 and 219 of the German Criminal Code. These amended sections (*Änderung des Strafgesetzbuches*) constitute the Abortion Reform Act of 1992. Strafgesetzbuchreform [*StGBR*], article 13 (1992).

70 See Walther, supra note 67, at 389.

71 *StGBR,* sec. 218a (2).

72 *Frankfurter Allgemeine Zeitung,* June 27, p. 2.

73 *Frankfurter Allgemeine Zeitung,* June 30, p. 1.

74 Recent articles commenting on *Abortion II* are Donald P. Kommers, "The Constitutional Law of Abortion in Germany: Should Americans Pay Attention?" *Journal of Contemporary Health Law and Society* 10 (1994): 1–32; Gerald L. Neuman, "*Casey* in the Mirror: Abortion, Abuse and the Right to Protection in the United States and Germany," *American Journal of Comparative Law* 43 (1995): 273–314; and Walther, supra note 67, at 384–402.

75 77 BVerfGE 170 (1987).

76 Ibid., 215–16.

77 Ibid., 234–40.

8 FREEDOM OF SPEECH

1   Konrad Hesse, *Grundzüge des Verfassungsrechts der Bundesrepublik Deutschland,* 13th ed. (Heidelberg: C. F. Müller Juristischer Verlag, 1982), 151–55. For a comprehensive discussion and survey of the Federal Constitutional Court's free speech jurisprudence, see David P. Currie, *The Constitution of the Federal Republic of Germany* (Chicago: University of Chicago Press, 1994), 174–243.

2   See Helmut Steinberger, "Freedom of the Press and of Broadcasting and Prior Restraints," in *Völkerrecht als Rechtsordnung, Internationale Gerichtsbarkeit, Menschenrechte, Festschrift für Hermann Mosler,* ed. Rudolf Bernhardt et al. (Berlin: Springer Verlag, 1983), 913.

3   Ibid.

4   For a comprehensive overview of the Federal Constitutional Court's case law, see Walter Schmidt-Glaeser, "Die Meinungsfreiheit in der Rechtsprechung des BVerfGE," *Archiv des Öffentlichen Rechts* 97 (1972): 60–123; see also Christian Starck, "Meinungs- und Wissenschaftsfreiheit," in *Festschrift für Wolfgang Zeidler* (Berlin: Walter de Gruyter, 1987), 1539–59. For a short review of the struggle to vindicate freedom of opinion in the history of German constitutionalism, see Wolfram Sielmann, *Kampf um Meinungsfreiheit im deutschen Konstitutionalismus* (Strassburg: N. P. Engel Verlag, 1986), 173–88.

5   Barenblatt v. United States, 360 U.S. 109 (1960) (J. Black, dissenting).

6   See Helmut Goerlich, *Wertordnung und Grundgesetz* (Baden-Baden: Nomos Verlagsgesellschaft, 1973), 51–60.

7   See also Turnover Tax Record Case, 36 BVerfGE 321, 331 (1974); and Abortion Case I, 39 BVerfGE 1, 41 (1975).

8   For the most recent application of *Drittwirkung,* see Possessory Title Case, 89 BVerfGE 1, 9 (1993) (invoking the right to property in a dispute between owner and tenant). The Parliamentary Council did not appear to share the Federal Constitutional Court's view of the relationship between constitutional and private law. According to the most authoritative account of the council's proceedings, the Basic Law was meant to apply to public, not private, law. See Hermann von Mangoldt, *Das Bonner Grundgesetz,* 4 vols. (Munich: Verlag Franz Vahlen, 1953), 1:34–42. The other view—that basic rights guarantees would apply to private legal relationships as well as to the relationship between individuals and the state—was strongly advocated by Günter Dürig. See his "Grundrechte und Zivilrechtsprechung," in *Vom Bonner Grundgesetz zur gesamtdeutschen Verfassung. Festschrift zum 75. Geburtstag von Hans Nawiasky,* ed. Theodor Maunz (Munich: ISAR Verlag, 1956), 157–90. See also Hans Nipperdey, "Grundrechte und Privatrecht," in *Festschrift für Erich Molitor zum 75. Geburtstag* (Munich: C. H. Beck, 1962), 17–33.

9   See Häntzschel, "Das Grundrecht der freien Meinungsäusserung und die Schranken der allgemeinen Gesetze des Artikel 18 der Reichsverfassung," *Archiv des Öffentlichen Rechts* 49 (1926): 228–37; see also Frede Castberg, *Freedom of Speech in the West* (New York: Oceana Publications, 1960), 322–25.

10 For additional commentaries on the *Lüth* case, see Gerhard Casper, *Redefreiheit und Ehrenschutz* (Karlsruhe: Verlag C. F. Müller, 1971), 30–39; Günter Dürig, "Zum 'Lüth Urteil' des Bundesverfassungsgerichts vom 15.1.1958," *Die Öffentliche Verwaltung* 11 (1958):

184–97; and Peter Lerche, "Zur verfassungsgerichtlichen Deutung der Meinungsfreiheit," in *Festschrift für Gebhard Müller* (Tübingen: J. C. B. Mohr, 1970): 197–215. For an excellent critical analysis of *Lüth* in English, see Peter Quint, "Free Speech and Private Law in German Constitutional Theory," *Maryland Law Review* 48 (1989): 252–65.

11 For a fuller discussion, see the section on delegation of legislative power in Chapter 5.

12 For an overview of the limits to free speech in West Germany's "fighting democracy," see Hella Mandt, "Demokratie und Toleranz," in *Res Publica,* ed. Peter Haungs (Munich: Wilhelm Fink Verlag, 1977), 233–60. See also the following cases of the Federal Constitutional Court: Socialist Reich Party Case, 2 BVerfGE 1, 12–15 (1952); Communist Party Case, 5 BVerfGE 85, 140–46 (1956); and Election Propaganda Case, 44 BVerfGE 125, 145–46 (1977).

13 403 U.S. 15 (1971).

14 For related cases, see the Art Critic Case, 54 BVerfGE 129 (1980); and Credit Shark Case, 60 BVerfGE 234 (1982).

15 54 BVerfGE 129 (1980).

16 The motive behind a call for a boycott continues to color the court's view of whether such advocacy is constitutionally protected; see Supermarket Boycott Case, 62 BVerfGE 230 (1982).

17 For a more recent application of the balancing test, see Physician Advertising Case, 71 BVerfGE 162, 175 (1985).

18 See Quint, supra note 10, at 277.

19 Ibid. See also Kenneth M. Levan, "The Significance of Constitutional Rights for Private Law: Theory and Practice in West Germany," *International and Comparative Law Quarterly* 17 (1968): 587–88.

20 See Chamber Judgment of March 10, 1993 [1 BvR 1192/92], 20 *EuGRZ* 302–3 (1993).

21 27 BVerfGE 71 (1969).

22 For a related decision, see the Demokrat Case, 27 BVerfGE 88 (1969).

23 See Ingo von Münch, *Grundgesetz Kommentar,* 3 vols. 3d ed. (Munich: C. H. Beck'sche Verlagsbuchhandlung, 1981), 1:271–72.

24 Film Propaganda Case, 33 BVerfGE 52 (1972); see also Radical Groups Case, 47 BVerfGE 198 (1978).

25 The validity of such confiscations was sustained in the Demokrat Case, 27 BVerfGE 88 (1969).

26 See Film Propaganda Case, 33 BVerfGE 52 (1972). For a discussion of the act, see Steinberger, "Freedom of the Press," supra note 2, at 925–27.

27 Bruno Schmidt-Bleibtreu and Franz Klein, *Kommentar zum Grundgesetz für die Bundesrepublik Deutschland,* 5th ed. (Neuwied: Hermann Luchterhand Verlag, 1980), 205; Gerhard Leibholz and Hans Justus Rinck, *Grundgesetz für die Bundesrepublik Deutschland,* 6th ed. (Cologne: Verlag Dr. Otto Schmidt, 1979), 217–18; and von Münch, supra note 23, at 271–72.

28 21 BVerfGE 271 (1967).

29 Eric Barendt, *Freedom of Speech* (Oxford: Clarendon Press, 1985), 59.

30 53 BVerfGE 96 (1980).

31 See, for example, Lawyer Advertising Cases I and II, 76 BVerfGE 171 and 196 (1987).

32   Quint, supra note 10, at 325–30.

33   Ibid., at 302–7.

34   42 BVerfGE 143 (1976).

35   Ibid., at 148–49.

36   Ibid., at 144–46.

37   Soraya Case, 34 BVerfGE 269 (1973).

38   See also Political Defamation Case, 43 BVerfGE 130 (1976); and Credit Shark Case, 60 BVerfGE 234 (1982).

39   68 BVerfGE 226, 230 (1984).

40   More recently, in the Old Age Home Case, 85 BVerfGE 23 (1991), the court vindicated a newspaper's right to express its opinion in a series of rhetorical questions about alleged abuses in old age homes even though the questions were impliedly defamatory.

41   See Steinberger, "Freedom of the Press," supra note 2, at 913.

42   90 BVerfGE 1 (1994). For examples of other cases in which the court was unwilling to sacrifice freedom of speech on the basis of a sharp distinction between fact and opinion, see the Bayer Pharmaceutical Case, 85 BVerfGE 1 (1991) (reversing a judgment punishing statements made about the drug company's business practices) and Nursing Home Case, 85 BVerfGE 1 (1991) (reversing a judgment against published criticism of the quality of care in a nursing home).

43   *Frankfurter Allgemeine Zeitung,* January 20, 1995, p. 12.

44   *Frankfurter Allgemeine Zeitung,* September 28, 1994, p. 12.

45   Recent cases in which the right to freedom of expression prevailed over the right to dignity or personality are the Stern-Strauss Interview Case, 82 BVerfGE 277 (1990) (nullifying a damage award against a reporter who called Franz Josef Strauss an "opportunistic democrat"); Anti-Strauss Placard Case, 82 BVerfGE 43 (1990) (overruling a damage award against persons who displayed placards accusing Strauss of protecting Fascists); Magazine Titanic Case, 86 BVerfGE 1 (1992) (reversing a judgment satirizing a crippled person for expressing his wish to serve in the armed forces). Justice Dieter Grimm, a member of the chamber that handed down the *Tucholsky* judgment, defended these and related decisions in a magazine interview. See *Zeitschrift für Rechtspolitik* (1994): 276–79. See also Deiter Grimm, "Die Meinungsfreiheit in der Rechtsprechung des Bundesverfassungsgerichts," *Neue Juristische Wochenschrift* 27 (1995): 1697–1705.

46   For relevant provisions of the criminal code see *The Penal Code of the Federal Republic of Germany,* trans. Joseph J. Darby (London: Sweet and Maxwell, 1987), secs. 185, 193, and 194 (3).

47   *Frankfurter Allgemeine Zeitung,* March 2, 1996, p. 4, and March 9, p. 1.

48   Chamber Decision of July 10, 1992, 20 *Europäische Grundrechte Zeitung* (1993): 28–37.

49   See *Neue Juristische Wochenschrift* 23 (May 14, 1970): 908–10.

50   Peter W. Case, 28 BVerfGE 55 (1970).

51   28 BVerfGE 191, 205 (1970).

52   42 BVerfGE 234 (1976).

53   69 BVerfGE 344 (1985).

54   See sections 14 and 15 of the Assembly Act of November 15, 1978, *BGBl* 1 (1978): 1790.

55   For related decisions, see Bitburg Case, 71 BVerfGE 158 (1985); and Mutlangen Case, 73 BVerfGE 206 (1986).

56 See Wolfgang Hoffmann-Riem, "Massenmedien," in *Handbuch des Verfassungsrechts,* ed. Ernst Benda, Werner Maihofer, and Hans-Jochen Vogel (Berlin: Walter de Gruyter, 1984), 389–496. This excellent study includes citations to nearly all of the relevant literature and judicial decisions dealing with Article 5 and the media.

57 The political turmoil surrounding the *Spiegel* case is described in Donald P. Kommers, "The *Spiegel* Affair: A Case Study in Judicial Politics," in *Political Trials,* ed. Theodore L. Becker (Indianapolis: Bobbs-Merrill, 1971), 5–33; and David Schoenbaum, *The* Spiegel *Affair* (Garden City, N.J.: Doubleday, 1968).

58 Donald P. Kommers, *Judicial Politics in West Germany* (Beverly Hills, Calif.: Sage Publications, 1976), 152–53.

59 The balancing approach was reaffirmed again in the Journalist Treason Case, 21 BVerfGE 239 (1967).

60 Herbert Bernstein, "Reflections on the *Spiegel* Case," *American Journal of Comparative Law* 14 (1967): 560–61.

61 One of the strongest endorsements of the "public function" doctrine appeared in the Press Forfeiture Case, 10 BVerfGE 118, 121 (1959). North Rhine–Westphalia sought to bar publishers and editors from their profession who disseminated materials advocating socialism, militarism, totalitarianism, and racial discrimination. The Constitutional Court declared that the act was violative of freedom of the press and incompatible with Article 18. Under Article 18, only the Federal Constitutional Court is authorized to order the forfeiture of basic rights.

62 For a list of the press laws of each of the sixteen *Länder,* see *Press Laws,* 3d ed. (Bonn: Inter Nationes, 1993), 10–11.

63 See, generally, Film Propaganda Case, 33 BVerfGE 52 (1972); Tax Consultant Advertising Case, 64 BVerfGE 108 (1983); and Liebesgrotte Case, 51 BVerfGE 304 (1979).

64 The English text of this statute appears in *Press Laws,* supra note 57, at 22–23.

65 *Press Laws,* supra note 57, at 25.

66 71 BVerfGE 206 (1985).

67 Ibid., 216.

68 12 BVerfGE 205 (1961).

69 Ibid., 260.

70 See, for example, the representation of interest groups on the television board of the Second German Television Station in C. C. Schweitzer et al., *Politics and Government in the Federal Republic of Germany: Basic Documents* (Leamington Spa: Berg, 1984), 256–57.

71 31 BVerfGE 328 (1971).

72 Ibid., 330.

73 Ibid., 343 (Geiger, Rinck, and Wand, dissenting).

74 Ibid., 325. The translation is from Christopher Witteman, "West German Television Law: An Argument for Media as Instrument of Self-Government," *Hastings International and Comparative Law Review* 7 (1983): 154.

75 See Schweitzer et al., *Basic Documents,* supra note 70, at 258.

76 Good treatments in English of the German broadcasting industry and the media debate are Witteman, supra note 74, at 145–210; Arthur Williams, *Broadcasting and Democracy in West Germany* (Philadelphia: Temple University Press, 1977); Marcellus Snow, "Telecommunications and Media Policy in West Germany," *Journal of Communications* 32

(1982): 9; Peter J. Tettinger, "New Mass Media and German Constitutional Law," *Public Law Forum* 5 (1986): 125–35; and Michael Zoeller, "Public Control — Cause or Consequence of Scarcity? The Example of Regulating Electronic Media in the United States and in Germany," in *The Political Economy of Freedom*, ed. Kurt R. Leube and Albert H. Zlabinger (Munich: Philosophia Verlag, 1984), 143–57.

77   57 BVerfGE 295, 322.

78   73 BVerfGE 118, 125 (1986).

79   Ibid.

80   59 BVerfGE 231 (1982).

81   73 BVerfGE 118, 182–90 (1986).

82   Ibid., 157–59.

83   Ibid., 182–84.

84   74 BVerfGE 297 (1987).

85   87 BVerfGE 181 (1992).

86   83 BVerfGE 238 (1991).

87   Ibid., 332–33. Several years earlier, in the *FDP Broadcasting* case, the court sustained the constitutionality of Hamburg and Lower Saxony's decision to exclude the Free Democratic party from representation on the board of the North German Broadcasting Station; see 60 BVerfGE 53 (1982).

88   90 BVerfGE 60 (1994).

89   Ibid., 88.

90   Ibid., 98.

91   Ibid., 103.

92   For a detailed treatment of many of the developments discussed in this section, see Eric Barendt, "The Influence of the German and Italian Constitutional Courts on their National Broadcasting Systems," *Public Law* (1991): 93–115; and his book *Broadcasting Law* (Oxford: Clarendon Press, 1993).

93   Steinberger, "Freedom of the Press," supra note 2, at 917.

94   For a general discussion of the right to personality in Germany, see B. S. Markesinis, *A Comparative Introduction to the German Law of Torts,* 3d ed. (Oxford: Clarendon Press, 1994), 63–68. For important cases vindicating the right to personality, see pp. 321–24 and 380–410.

95   Ibid., 376–80. Section 823 (1) reads: "A person who, willfully or negligently, unlawfully injures the life, body, health, freedom, property, or other right of another is bound to compensate him for any damage arising therefrom" (translation from Ian S. Forrester et al., *The German Civil Code* [South Hackensack, N.J.: Fred B. Rothman, 1975], 134).

96   Markesinis, supra note 94, at 410.

97   Ibid.

98   Translation from Rudolf Schlesinger, *Comparative Law,* 4th ed. (Mineola, N.Y.: Foundation Press, 1980), 586.

99   The *Princess Soraya* case (no. 4.2) involved a similar constitutional analysis. Here, a popular newspaper published a fictitious "exclusive interview" with a well-known socialite that revealed certain "facts" about her private life. The Federal Constitutional Court sustained her successful libel action over the newspaper's objection that the story was protected by the guarantee of a free press. The court was sensitive to the claim that

high damage awards in cases such as this could impair freedom of the press, but it found the award proportionate to the injury to reputation sustained by the complainant. The right to personal honor trumped freedom of the press in this instance because the newspaper in question was not objectively covering a matter of public interest or seriously contributing to the formation of public opinion but rather pandering to the public desire for frivolous entertainment. Under these circumstances, freedom of the press receded before the principle of personal integrity embodied in Articles 1 and 2 of the Basic Law.

100 42 BVerfGE 143 (1976).

101 30 BVerfGE 173, 218–27. Her dissent here, as in the *Deutschland Magazine* case, echoes the theme of "uninhibited, robust, and wide-open" debate on public issues sounded in New York Times v. Sullivan, 376 U.S. 254, 270 (1964).

102 Quint, supra note 10, at 332.

103 66 BVerfGE 116 (1984).

104 Ibid., 135.

105 See cases and sources cited in supra note 45.

106 See Grimm, "Meinungsfreiheit," supra note 45.

107 Adult Theatre Case, 47 BVerfGE 109 (1978). See also Mathias Reimann, "Prurient Interest and Human Dignity: Pornography Regulation in West Germany and the U.S.," *University of Michigan Journal of Law Reform* 21 (1987–88): 201–53. The discussion in this section relies heavily on this article.

108 See Nudist Colony Case, 7 BVerfGE 320 (1958) (sustaining the Youth Protection Act but vindicating the right of parents to educate their children in a nudist culture); Heinrich Case, 11 BVerfGE 234 (1960) (upholding the right of the Federal Censorship Office to list materials morally harmful to children); and Nudist Magazine Case, 30 BVerfGE 336 (1971) (invalidating the application of the Youth Protection Act to a magazine promoting nudism).

109 *BGBl* I (1953): 377. This statute was at issue in the *Historical Fabrication* case, discussed above at 385–86.

110 This was the approach of the U.S. Supreme Court in Memoirs v. Massachusetts, 383 U.S. 413 (1966).

111 Reimann, supra note 107 at 229.

112 87 BVerfGE 209 (1990).

113 Ibid.

114 In this connection the court noted that "the heroine could be viewed as the incarnation of every man's sexual phantasy which is presented here as a response to an up-bringing whose objective was the suppression of sexual matters. There is even evidence of parody." Ibid.

115 Ibid.

116 *Horror Film* is a related case in which free speech was vindicated. *Horror Film* involved the seizure under the Youth Protection Act of an American film because of its excessive violence. The court acknowledged that the state is permitted to safeguard the dignity of youth by shielding them against films exhibiting excessive or gratuitous violence, but in this instance the seizure was nullified because it occurred prior to being listed as "harmful" under the Act's rating guidelines. This, said the court, is prior restraint in violation of the censorship clause of Article 5 (1). See 87 BVerfGE 209 (1992).

117 See Elmar M. Hucko, *The Democratic Tradition* (Leamington Spa, England: Berg, 1987), 3–21.

118 For a description of the university system, see Peter J. Katzenstein, *Policy and Politics in West Germany* (Philadelphia: Temple University Press, 1987), 296–302.

119 See Henning Zwirner, "Zum Grundrecht der Wissenschaftsfreiheit," *Archiv des Öffentlichen Rechts* 98 (1973): 313; see also *Kommentar zum Grundgesetz für die Bundesrepublik Deutschland* (Neuwied: Hermann Luchterhand Verlag, 1984), 590–651. For an extensive bibliography on the freedom of scientific and scholarly inquiry, see pp. 584–89.

120 von Münch, supra note 23, at 294.

121 Posthumous (Böll) Libel Case (1993), 20 *EuGRZ* 146–47.

122 Political Satire Case, 75 BVerfGE 369 (1987).

123 Ibid. See also Flag Desecration Case, 81 BVerfGE 278, 290–298 (1990).

124 81 BVerfGE 278 (1990).

125 491 U.S. 397 (1989). For an insightful comparison of the two cases, see Peter E. Quint, "The Comparative Law of Flag Desecration: The United States and the Federal Republic of Germany," *Hastings International and Comparative Law Review* 15 (1992): 613–38.

126 81 BVerfGE 278, 297 (1990).

127 Ibid., 299–300.

128 Ibid., 307.

129 Ibid.

9 FREEDOM OF CONSCIENCE AND RELIGION

1 Bruno Schmidt-Bleibtreu and Franz Klein, *Kommentar zum Grundgesetz für die Bundesrepublik Deutschland,* 5th ed. (Neuwied: Hermann Luchterhand Verlag, 1980), 1212–13.

2 Leading commentaries on church-state relations under the Basic Law are Josef Listl, "Das Grundrecht der Religionsfreiheit in der Rechtsprechung des Bundesverfassungsgerichts," *Archiv des Öffentlichen Rechts* 92 (1967): 99–127; idem, "Das Staatskirchenrecht in der Rechtsprechung des Bundesverfassungsgerichts," *Archiv des Öffentlichen Rechts* 106 (1981): 218–83; Paul Mikat, "Staat, Kirchen und Religionsgemeinschaften," in *Handbuch des Verfassungsrechts,* pt. 2, ed. Ernst Benda, Werner Maihofer, and Hans-Jochen Vogel (Berlin: Walter de Gruyter, 1984), 1059–87; and Schmidt-Bleibtreu and Klein, supra note 1, 2:1349–1401. For a brief overview in English, see Klaus Obermayer, "State and Religion in the Federal Republic of Germany," *Journal of Church and State* 17 (1975): 97–111.

3 See John Golay, *The Founding of the Federal Republic of Germany* (Chicago: University of Chicago Press, 1958), 194–96.

4 Ibid., 196–98.

5 Koppel S. Pinson, *Modern Germany,* 2d ed. (New York: Macmillan, 1966), 165–67, 173–93.

6 Ekkehart Stein, *Staatsrecht,* 7th ed. (Tübingen: J. C. B. Mohr, 1980), 222.

7 Ingo von Münch, *Grundgesetz-Kommentar,* 3 vols., 4th ed. (Munich: C. H. Beck'sche Verlagsbuchhandlung, 1992), 1:303–343.

8 The wide berth granted to the value of free exercise seems greater in Germany than in the United States. The negative and positive character of this freedom, like that of free

speech, means that both governments and private enterprises must accommodate the religious practices of citizens and employees. German constitutional doctrine requires a higher measure of accommodation than does American doctrine. For example, Goldman v. Weinberger, 475 U.S. 503 (1986); and Estate of Thornton v. Caldor, Inc., 472 U.S. 703 (1985), would probably have been decided the other way, favoring religious exercise, in Germany. On the other hand, the German *School Prayer* case (no. 9.4) is in sharp contrast to the result in similar American cases. For commentary on American doctrine, see John Nowak et al., *Constitutional Law,* 3d ed. (St. Paul: West Publishing, 1986), 1067–79.

9   See Tobacco Atheist Case, 12 BVerfGE 1, 4 (1960); and Karl Doehring, *Staatsrecht,* 3d ed. (Frankfurt am Main: Alfred Metzner Verlag, 1984), 302–3.

10   12 BVerfGE 1, 4–5 (1960).

11   Ibid. This translation appears in Walter F. Murphy and Joseph Tanenhaus, *Comparative Constitutional Law* (New York: St. Martin's Press, 1977), 467.

12   35 BVerfGE 366, 375 (1973).

13   Ibid.

14   von Münch, supra note 7, at 1:335–37.

15   An exception to this generalization is when a serviceman seeks conscientious objector status after his induction into the armed services. In the Soldier's Conscientious Objector Case I, 28 BVerfGE 243 (1970), the court rejected a soldier's complaint that he had been invalidly placed in detention for refusing to carry arms while his application for conscientious objector status was pending. In this situation, said the First Senate, when the serviceman is an unrecognized conscientious objector, the claim on behalf of conscience must be balanced against competing legal values of constitutional rank and in the light of the "unity of the Constitution and the entire range of values protected under it." In short, the right of the serviceman was being weighed against the "necessity of the uninterrupted functioning of the armed forces" pending a final decision of the would-be objector's status. In another decision, however, handed down on the same day, the court invalidated a sentence of detention imposed prior to the soldier's recognition as a conscientious objector but carried out after he was so recognized (Soldier's Conscientious Objector Case II, 28 BVerfGE 264 [1970]). See also Soldier's Conscientious Objector Case III, 32 BVerfGE 40 (1971) (sustaining an order requiring a soldier to perform military duties pending his application for conscientious objector status).

16   Military Service Act of July 21, 1956, *BGBl* 1 (1956): 651.

17   See von Münch, supra note 7, at 1:774–77.

18   12 BVerfGE 45 (1960).

19   Ibid., 54.

20   Ibid., 55.

21   Von Münch, supra note 7, at 1:335–37.

22   Alternative Civilian Service Case I, 19 BVerfGE 135 (1965).

23   This conclusion resulted from two cases handed down, respectively, by the Second and First Senates. In Alternative Civilian Service Case II, 22 BVerfGE 178 (1967), the Second Senate — its jurisdiction extended to procedural issues involving basic rights — ruled that repeated convictions arising out of "the same act" would violate Article 103 (3) of the Basic Law ("no one may be punished for the same act more than once under general penal

legislation"). In Alternative Civilian Service Case III, 24 BVerfGE 178 (1968), the First Senate — its jurisdiction extended to substantive basic rights issues — reinforced the Second Senate's decision by ruling that no legitimate community interest in multiple punishment could be found to override freedom of conscience.

24   See tabular material in von Münch, supra note 7, at 1:346–47.

25.   Act of July 13, 1977, *BGBl* 1:1229.

26   *Die Zeit,* December 16, 1977, 4.

27   *Süddeutsche Zeitung,* December 6, 1977, 1.

28   Registration Injunction Case, 46 BVerfGE 337 (1977).

29   48 BVerfGE 127 (1978).

30   Ibid., 169.

31   Section 24 (2) of the Compulsory Civilian Service Act as amended on September 1983, *BGBl* 1:1221.

32   The Extended Alternative Service Case was brought by 195 members of the Bundestag and by four state governments (Bremen, Hamburg, Hesse, and North Rhine–Westphalia) controlled by the SPD.

33   69 BVerfGE 1 (1985).

34   See Engel v. Vitale, 370 U.S. 421 (1962); Abington School District v. Schempf, 374 U.S. 203 (1963); and Wallace v. Jaffree, 472 U.S. 38 (1985).

35   For a critical commentary on the *School Prayer* case, see Ernst-Wolfgang Böckenförde, "Zum Ende des Schulgebetsstreit: Stellungnahme zum Beschl. des BVerfGE v. 16.10.1979," *Deutsche Öffentliche Verwaltung* 33 (1980): 323–27. See also Ulrich Scheuner, "Nochmals: Zum Ende des Schulgebet," *Deutsche Öffentliche Verwaltung* 33 (1980): 513–15; and Christoph Link, "Die Schulgebetsentscheidung des Bundesverfassungsgerichts," *Juristenzeitung* 35 (1980): 564–66.

36   See Udo Steiner, "Der Grundrechtsschutz der Glaubens- und Gewissensfreiheit (Art. 41, 2 GG)," *Juristische Schulung* 22 (1982): 157–66; see also von Münch, supra note 7, at 1:226–27.

37   See Klaus G. Meyer-Teschendorf, *Staat und Kirche im Pluralistischen Gemeinwesen* (Tübingen: J. C. B. Mohr, 1979), 145–62; and Klaus Schlaich, *Neutralität als verfassungsrechtliches Prinzip* (Tübingen: J. C. B. Mohr, 1972), 26–39.

38   See C. Durham, "Religion and the Public Schools: Constitutional Analysis in Germany and the United States" (Paper presented at the First Annual Conference of the Western Association for German Studies, October 21, 1977), 14–23. The following discussion draws heavily from this marvelous and hitherto unpublished paper.

39   Ibid., 22–23.

40   Ibid., 14.

41   Ibid., 17–18.

42   See Ernst Christian Helmreich, *Religious Education in German Schools* (Cambridge, Mass.: Harvard University Press, 1959), 53–71, 132–50.

43   While Article 7 guarantees the right to establish private schools, it clearly accords priority to the public schools. The state may withhold its approval of private secondary schools if they are academically inferior to public schools or if they perpetuate the segregation of children on the basis of parental income. A private elementary school of a religious or ideological nature may be approved under the terms of Article 7 (5) only "if it serves a

special pedagogic interest" or when the state has failed to establish its own confessional or interdenominational schools. The *Hamburg Private School* case, decided on April 8, 1987, gave an enormous boost to private schools, in this case to a nonsectarian private school. The First Senate ruled that when a state permits a private school to operate on the request of the parents, it must guarantee the school's minimal existence (75 BVerfGE 40 [1987]).

44 *Frankfurter Rundschau,* July 21, 1988.

45 See Durham, supra note 38, at 39–67. This section of Durham's paper deals with the controversy surrounding the so-called Bremen clause — the provision of the Bremen Constitution providing for nonsectarian instruction in all public schools — and the equally controversial decision of the Hesse Constitutional Court holding unconstitutional a nonsectarian prayer recited in the public schools. Durham's critical analysis of these controversies includes comparative references to American constitutional case law.

46 Helmreich, supra note 42, at 254.

47 See "Christen fühlen sich irritiert und verletzt," *Münchner Neueste Nachrichten,* September 25, 1995, p. 33. See also the lead story on the controversy in *Der Spiegel,* August 14, 1995 (No. 33/14), 22–34.

48 *Frankfurter Allgemeine Zeitung,* September 26, 1995, p. 1.

49 *Frankfurter Allgemeine Zeitung,* August 18, 1995, p. 29.

50 *The Week in Germany,* September 8, 1995, p. 6.

51 "Wenn ein Gericht zuviel will," *Frankfurter Allgemeine Zeitung,* September 7, 1995, p. 1.

52 *Frankfurter Allgemeine Zeitung,* August 24, 1995, p. 3.

53 *Frankfurter Allgemeine Zeitung,* October 25, 1995, p. 9.

54 See Frederic Spotts, *The Churches and Politics in Germany* (Middletown, Conn.: Wesleyan University Press, 1973), 193–99.

55 Ibid., 198.

56 Church Construction Tax Case, 19 BVerfGE 206, 217–18 (1965).

57 See Church Construction Tax Case, 19 BVerfGE 206 (1965) (holding that the church tax applies only to natural persons); Mixed-Marriage Church Tax Case II, 19 BVerfGE 242 (1965) (invalidating a law that makes a spouse who is not a church member responsible for paying the tax of the spouse who belongs to the church); Bremen Church Tax Case, 19 BVerfGE 248 (1965) (invalidating a church tax that a salaried non–church member was required to pay on behalf of his nonsalaried spouse, who was a church member); Split Income Church Tax Case, 19 BVerfGE 268 (1965) (invalidating a law basing the church tax on half the income of both spouses in a marriage where only one spouse belongs to the church); Church Membership Case, 30 BVerfGE 415 (1971) (sustaining provisions of a treaty between Schleswig-Holstein and the Evangelical-Lutheran church defining church membership for purposes of taxation); Church Withdrawal Case, 44 BVerfGE 37 (1977) (invalidating court decisions extending the application of the church tax to the entire year even though the taxed wage earner had withdrawn from his church earlier in the year); and Lutheran Church Tax Office Case, 19 BVerfGE 288 (1965) (holding that a church tax measure is an act of public authority within the meaning of section 90 [1] of the FCCA). Other cases dealing with the legal character of a tax imposed by religious societies are the Bavarian Church Tax Case, 19 BVerfGE 282 (1965); and the Hamburg Church Tax Case, 19 BVerfGE 253 (1965).

58 Church Tax Construction Case, 19 BVerfGE 206, 216 (1965).

59 Ibid., 216–17.

60 See Otto Kimminick, *Deutsche Verfassungsgeschichte* (Frankfurt am Main: Athenäum Verlag, 1970), 141–64.

61 Meyer-Teschendorf, supra note 37, at 3–27.

62 See Josef Listl, *Konkordat und Kirchenverträge in der Bundesrepublik Deutschland* (Berlin: Duncker and Humboldt, 1987). Drawing on Listl's study, R. Taylor Cole reported that "the post–World War II period has witnessed an escalation of religious treaties." "Protestant church treaties," he noted, "differ from the Catholic Concordats in that they are negotiated between the state governments and the Protestant churches whereas the Concordats are negotiated between the state governments and the Holy See." See "Two Concordats of the Fascist Period: A Postmortem" (MS, undated).

63 Roman Herzog, a former president of the Federal Constitutional Court, put forth this view in "Die Kirchen in pluralistischen Staat" (MS, undated). These competing theories are discussed at length in Meyer-Teschendorf, supra note 37. An extensive bibliography on these competing views and on the church-state relationship generally appears at pp. 211–23.

64 42 BVerfGE 312, 333 (1976).

65 Ibid., 331.

66 The Constitutional Court has also ruled that the state must treat all religious bodies equally, but this does not rule out limited classifications based on the size of a religious body. Practical reasons, for example, may dictate that only religious bodies with a certain number of members may be represented on public boards such as the supervisory committees of radio and television stations. As a general rule, however, parity of treatment is as important a principle of religious freedom as tolerance and neutrality. See Blood Transfusion Case (no. 9.2), 32 BVerfGE 98, 106 (1971); and Interdenominational School Case, 41 BVerfGE 29, 49 (1975).

67 See, however, the *Bahá'í* case, 83 BVerfGE 341 (1991) in which the Constitutional Court reversed a judicial ruling denying the Baha'i religious community permission to register as an association under Section 41 of the Civil Code. The court ruled that Article 4 (1) and (2), in addition to securing freedom of faith and conscience, guarantees to members of a religious community bound together by a common creed to legally associate for religious purposes. The court distinguished between a "registered association" (*eingetragener Verein*) within the meaning of the civil code and an "incorporated association" (*rechtsfähiger Verein*) within the meaning of Article 137 (5) of the Weimar Constitution.

68 24 BVerfGE 236 (1968).

69 42 BVerfGE 312 (1976).

70 70 BVerfGE 138 (1985).

71 Ibid., 162.

72 Ibid., 163.

73 Ibid., 166–67.

74 In several related cases the court also invalidated judicial decisions involving the rights of labor in religious institutions. See, especially, Goch Hospital Case, 46 BVerfGE 73 (1977) (exempting religiously affiliated hospitals from general laws governing employee representation on industry work councils); Marion Hospital Case, 53 BVerfGE 366 (1980) (invalidating a state law regulating the governing procedures of religiously affiliated

hospitals); Bethel Case, 57 BVerfGE 220 (1981) (permitting religiously affiliated hospitals and rest homes to exclude union organizers from their premises); and Church Occupational Standards Case, 72 BVerfGE 278 (1986) (invalidating the application of the Federal Occupational Training Act to religious institutions).

75   6 BVerfGE 55, 72 (1957).

76   For a general discussion of constitutional cases related to marriage and the family, see von Münch, supra note 7, at 452–56.

77   See Child Adoption Case, 24 BVerfGE 119 (1968); and Orphan Benefit Case I, 28 BVerfGE 324 (1970).

78   31 BVerfGE 58, 68 (1971).

79   For a complete translation of the new family code provisions, see 1981 Supplement to the German Civil Code and the Introductory Act to the German Civil Code and the Marriage Law of the Federal Republic of Germany, trans. Simon L. Goren (Littleton, Colo.: Fred B. Rothman, 1982).

80   53 BVerfGE 224 (1980).

81   Ibid., sec. 1566 (2), p. 19.

82   Ibid., sec. 1568, p. 19.

83   55 BVerfGE 134 (1980).

84   In the light of the *Divorce Hardship* case, section 1586 of the German Civil Code was amended in 1986. The hardship provision has been retained save for the five-year clause. It now reads: "A marriage shall not be severed also when it has failed, if and as long as the maintenance of the marriage is a necessary exception for special reasons in the interest of minor children born of the marriage or when and as long as the divorce would result in [such] severe hardship to the party opposing the application owing to exceptional circumstances, that the maintenance of the marriage, also when the interest of the petitioner is taken into account, appears a necessary exception." See *The German Civil Code,* rev. ed., trans. Simon L. Goren (Littleton, Colo.: Fred B. Rothman, 1994), 267.

85   28 BVerfGE 324 (1970).

86   Orphan Benefit Case I, 29 BVerfGE 1 (1970); Orphan Benefit Case II, 29 BVerfGE 57 (1970); and Orphan Benefit Case III, 29 BVerfGE 71 (1970).

87   28 BVerfGE 324, 347 (1970).

88   See Child Support Case I, 22 BVerfGE 163 (1967); Child Support Case II, 43 BVerfGE 186 (1976); Child Tax Relief Case I, 45 BVerfGE 104 (1977); Child Tax Relief Case II, 47 BVerfGE 1 (1977); and Unemployment Assistance Case, 67 BVerfGE 186 (1984).

89   Common Marital Name Case, 84 BVerfGE 9 (1988).

90   Ibid., 20–25.

91   Child Custody II Case, 84 BVerfGE 168 (1991), overruling Child Custody I Case, 56 BVerfGE 363 (1981).

92   *The Week in Germany,* October 22, 1993, p. 3.

93   34 BVerfGE 165 (1972).

94   Ibid., p. 181.

95   Ibid., p. 183.

96   Ibid.

TABLE OF CASES

Principal cases (featured and discussed) are indicated by italic type

INDEX

PERMISSIONS

Permission for reprinting previously published materials is gratefully acknowledged. Sources are given according to case numbers assigned in this text.

3.1   From Walter F. Murphy and Joseph Tanenhaus, *Comparative Constitutional Law* (New York: St. Martin's Press, 1977). (Translated by Mrs. Renate Chestnut.)

3.2   From Walter F. Murphy and Joseph Tanenhaus, *Comparative Constitutional Law* (New York: St. Martin's Press, 1977). (Translated by Mrs. Renate Chestnut and Mr. Jonathan Young.)

3.3   From Walter F. Murphy and Joseph Tanenhaus, *Comparative Constitutional Law* (New York: St. Martin's Press, 1977). (Translated by Mrs. Renate Chestnut.)

3.4   From Walter F. Murphy and Joseph Tanenhaus, *Comparative Constitutional Law* (New York: St. Martin's Press, 1977). (Translated by Mrs. Renate Chestnut and Mr. Jonathan Young.)

3.10   Reproduced with permission from 33 *I.L.M.* 395–444 (1994). © The American Society of International Law. (Translated by Gerhard Wegen and Christopher Kuner.)

4.2   From Rudolf B. Schlesinger et al., *Comparative Law* (5th ed.). Reprinted with permission of the Foundation Press. Copyright 1988 by the Foundation Press.

4.8   From *International Law Reports 1952* (London: Butterworth, 1957). Reprinted with permission of the editor.

5.4   From Walter F. Murphy and Joseph Tanenhaus, *Comparative Constitutional Law* (New York: St. Martin's Press, 1977). (Translated by Mrs. Renate Chestnut.)

5.5   Reproduced with permission from 33 *I.L.M.* 395–444 (1994). © The American Society of International Law. (Translated by Gerhard Wegen and Christopher Kuner.)

5.9   From Walter F. Murphy and Joseph Tanenhaus, *Comparative Constitutional Law* (New York: St. Martin's Press, 1977). (Translated by Mrs. Renate Chestnut and Mr. Jonathan Young.)

5.10   From Theodore L. Becker, *Comparative Judicial Politics* (Chicago: Rand McNally, 1970). (Translated by Professor Donald P. Kommers.)

5.12   From Walter F. Murphy and Joseph Tanenhaus, *Comparative Constitutional Law* (New York: St. Martin's Press, 1977). (Translated by Mrs. Renate Chestnut.)

6.1   From Walter F. Murphy and Joseph Tanenhaus, *Comparative Constitutional Law* (New York: St. Martin's Press, 1977). (Translated by Mr. Fritz Kratochwil.)

6.2   From Walter F. Murphy and Joseph Tanenhaus, *Comparative Constitutional Law* (New York: St. Martin's Press, 1977). (Translated by Mrs. Renate Chestnut.)

7.2   From Walter F. Murphy and Joseph Tanenhaus, *Comparative Constitutional Law* (New York: St. Martin's Press, 1977). (Translated by Mrs. Renate Chestnut.)

7.6   From *Human Rights Law Journal,* vol. 5 (1984). (Translated by Professor Eibe Riedel.) Reprinted with permission of the editor.

7.10   From *John Marshall of Practice and Procedure,* vol. 9 (Spring 1976). (Translated by Robert E. Jonas and John D. Gorby.) Copyright by the John Marshall Law School. Reprinted with permission of the John Marshall Law School.

7.11   From *German Yearbook of International Law,* vol. 36 (1993). Headnotes reprinted with permission of the editor.

8.1   The version here is an adaptation of two different translations. The first is from Walter F. Murphy and Joseph Tanenhaus, *Comparative Constitutional Law* (St. Martin's Press, 1977). (Translated by Mrs. Renate Chestnut.) The other is from Herbert J. Liebesny, *Foreign Legal Systems: A Comparative Analysis* (George Washington University, National Law Center, Government Contracts Program, 1981).

8.5   From Federal Constitutional Court (Karlsrühe, Germany ([publication forthcoming]). Reprinted with permission of the administrative director.

8.10   From B. S. Markesinis, *A Comparative Introduction to the German Law of Torts.* Copyright 1986 by Oxford University Press. Reprinted with permission of Oxford University Press and author.

9.9   From Walter F. Murphy and Joseph Tanenhaus, *Comparative Constitutional Law* (New York: St. Martin's Press, 1977). (Translated by Mrs. Renate Chestnut.)

Donald P. Kommers is Joseph and Elizabeth Robbie Professor of Government and International Studies at the University of Notre Dame.

Library of Congress Cataloging-in-Publication Data
Kommers, Donald P.
The constitutional jurisprudence of the Federal Republic of Germany / Donald P. Kommers. — 2nd ed.
p.   cm.
Includes index.
ISBN 0-8223-1832-6 (cloth : alk. paper). — ISBN 0-8223-1838-5 (pbk. : alk. paper)
1. Germany — Constitutional law — Cases.   2. Judicial review — Germany — Cases.   I. Title.
KK4446.7.K66   1997
342.43 — dc20
[344.302]   96-32711 CIP